Quod scriptura, non iubet vetat

The Latin translates, "What is not commanded in scripture, is forbidden:'

On the Cover: Baptists rejoice to hold in common with other evangelicals the main principles of the orthodox Christian faith. However, there are points of difference and these differences are significant. In fact, because these differences arise out of God's revealed will, they are of vital importance. Hence, the barriers of separation between Baptists and others can hardly be considered a trifling matter. To suppose that Baptists are kept apart solely by their views on Baptism or the Lord's Supper is a regrettable misunderstanding. Baptists hold views which distinguish them from Catholics, Congregationalists, Episcopalians, Lutherans, Methodists, Pentecostals, and Presbyterians, and the differences are so great as not only to justify, but to demand, the separate denominational existence of Baptists. Some people think Baptists ought not teach and emphasize their differences but as E.J. Forrester stated in 1893, "Any denomination that has views which justify its separate existence, is bound to promulgate those views. If those views are of sufficient importance to justify a separate existence, they are important enough to create a duty for their promulgation ... the very same reasons which justify the separate existence of any denomination make it the duty of that denomination to teach the distinctive doctrines upon which its separate existence rests." If Baptists have a right to a separate denominational life, it is their duty to propagate their distinctive principles, without which their separate life cannot be justified or maintained.

Many among today's professing Baptists have an agenda to revise the Baptist distinctives and redefine what it means to be a Baptist. Others don't understand why it even matters. The books being reproduced in the *Baptist Distinctives Series* are republished in order that Baptists from the past may state, explain and defend the primary Baptist distinctives as they understood them. It is hoped that this Series will provide a more thorough historical perspective on what it means to be distinctively Baptist.

The Lord Jesus Christ asked, *"And why call ye me, Lord, Lord, and do not the things which I say?"* (Luke 6:46). The immediate context surrounding this question explains what it means to be a true disciple of Christ. Addressing the same issue, Christ's question is meant to show that a confession of discipleship to the Lord Jesus Christ is inconsistent and untrue if it is not accompanied with a corresponding submission to His authoritative commands. Christ's question teaches us that a true recognition of His authority as Lord inevitably includes a submission to the authority of His Word. Hence, with this question Christ has made it forever impossible to separate His authority as King from the authority of His Word. These two principles—the authority of Christ as King and the authority of His Word—are the two most fundamental Baptist distinctives. The first gives rise to the second and out of these two all the other Baptist distinctives emanate. As F.M. Iams wrote in 1894, "Loyalty to Christ as King, manifesting itself in a constant and unswerving obedience to His will as revealed in His written Word, is the real source of all the Baptist distinctives:' In the search for the *primary* Baptist distinctive many have settled on the Lordship of Christ as the most basic distinctive. Strangely, in doing this, some have attempted to separate Christ's Lordship from the authority of Scripture, as if you could embrace Christ's authority without submitting to what He commanded. However, while Christ's Lordship and Kingly authority can be isolated and considered essentially for discussion's sake, we see from Christ's own words in Luke 6:46 that His Lordship is really inseparable from His Word and, with regard to real Christian discipleship, there can be no practical submission to the one without a practical submission to the other.

In the symbol above the Kingly Crown and the Open Bible represent the inseparable truths of Christ's Kingly and Biblical authority. The Crown and Bible graphics are supplemented by three Bible verses (Ecclesiastes 8:4, Matthew 28:18-20, and Luke 6:46) that reiterate and reinforce the inextricable connection between the authority of Christ as King and the authority of His Word. The truths symbolized by these components are further emphasized by the Latin quotation - *quod scriptura, non iubet vetat*— *i.e.,* "What is not commanded in scripture, is forbidden:' This Latin quote has been considered historically as a summary statement of the regulative principle of Scripture. Together these various symbolic components converge to exhibit the two most foundational Baptist Distinctives out of which all the other Baptist Distinctives arise. Consequently, we have chosen this composite symbol as a logo to represent the primary truths set forth in the *Baptist Distinctives Series*.

THE

ECCLESIASTICAL POLITY

OF THE

NEW TESTAMENT

ALEXANDER CARSON, LL. D.
1776-1844

THE ECCLESIASTICAL POLITY

OF THE

NEW TESTAMENT,

BY

ALEXANDER CARSON, LL.D.,

MINISTER OF THE GOSPEL

With a Biographical Sketch of the Author by John Franklin Jones

DUBLIN:
WILLIAM CARSON, GRAFTON STREET
LONDON: HOULSTON AND STONEMAN.
EDINBURGH: WM. WHYTE AND CO.
MDCCCLVI.

he Baptist Standard Bearer, Inc.
NUMBER ONE IRON OAKS DRIVE • PARIS, ARKANSAS 72855

Thou hast given a *standard* to them that fear thee;
that it may be displayed because of the truth.
– *Psalm 60:4*

Reprinted 2006

by

THE BAPTIST STANDARD BEARER, INC.
No. 1 Iron Oaks Drive
Paris, Arkansas 72855
(479) 963-3831

THE WALDENSIAN EMBLEM
lux lucet in tenebris
"The Light Shineth in the Darkness"

ISBN# 1579788475

TABLE OF CONTENTS

	PAGE
BOOK ONE: Reasons for Separating from the General Synod of Ulster	vii
BOOK TWO: A Reply to Mr. Brown's Vindication of the Presbyterian form of Church Government, in which the Order of the Apostolical Churches is Defended	127
INDEX	555

REASONS FOR SEPARATING

FROM THE

GENERAL

SYNOD OF ULSTER.

CONTENTS.

	PAGE
Preface	xi

CHAP.
- I.—Reasons *a priori*, why it is probable that the Scriptures contain a Divine Model of Church Government 1
- II.—If there be a Model of Church Government in the New Testament, what is the Nature of that Form we are warranted to expect? . 9
- III.—On the Obligation of Apostolical Practice . . 21
- IV.—Presbytery Examined 29
- V.—Of the Office of Lay Elders 39
- VI.—Of Independency 50
- VII.—The Independency of the Apostolical Churches proved from the Apostolical Injunctions, and inferred from other circumstances in the Epistles 65
- VIII.—Objections Answered 72
- IX.—Reasons why some are apt to conclude, that there is no Church Model in Scripture . 80
- X.—Character of Church Members—or the necessity of Pure Communion 87
- XI.—Objections Answered 96
- XII.—Additional reasons for Separating from the General Synod 105
- XIII.—Objections Answered 119

PREFACE.

Every Christian is a member of two kingdoms perfectly distinct, but perfectly compatible in their interests. In each of these he has peculiar duties, in the discharge of which he is to pursue a very different conduct. As a subject of civil government, he is called to unreserved, unequivocal obedience, without waiting to inquire into its nature and quality, or even the legitimacy of the title of those in power. If he understands his Bible, he knows that "the powers that be, are ordained of God," and that he must "submit to every ordinance of man, not merely for wrath, but also for conscience sake." In Britain he will submit to monarchy; in America to a republic; and in France he will obey, without puzzling himself in determining whether Buonaparte be a legal governor, or a usurper. But it is not so in the kingdom of Christ. Here it is his duty in everything to judge for himself, and in no instance to be the disciple of man. He is commanded to examine, not blindly adopt the dogmas of his spiritual guides. He is nowhere required to conform and submit to that form of church government, under which he has been educated, or to which he may at any time have thought it his duty to attach himself. He is enjoined to "prove all things, and to hold fast *only* that which is good." He is

Christ's freedman, and should not suffer himself to become the servant of man, nor to be fettered by human systems.

Convinced that this is both the duty and privilege of every Christian, I have largely and leisurely examined the *original nature*, and *present state* of that church* in which I was educated, and in which I have for some years acted as a minister. I have examined, and am convinced, that both in *plan* and *administration*, it is contrary to the Word of God. It must appear to every man of candour, that I could have no interest in deciding as I have done. Every interest of a worldly nature was surely on the other side. The day I gave up my connection with the General Synod, I gave up all that the world esteems. I sacrificed not only my prospects in life, and my respectability in the world but every settled way of support. It is usual for men to desert a church under persecution; I have deserted one in the tide of her prosperity, or as some of her friends speak, in her "*meridian glory*." If people never begin to think anything amiss in their religion till they are persecuted for it, or till superior honours and advantages are held out to view, they have reason to suspect their judgments. But when wealth and respectability in society are in the gift of the church, when one of her members sits in judgment upon her, she is likely to get a fair trial. A man is not apt, upon slight grounds, to reason himself out of his living,

---

* I am obliged sometimes in this pamphlet to use the word church in this common acceptation, though not so used in any part of the New Testament.

his friends, and his reputation. It will not be out of whim he will exchange ease for labour, respect for calumny, present competency for the naked promise of God. Notwithstanding this, I am perfectly aware that the worst motives and designs will be attributed to me. I would indeed know little of human nature, and less of the Bible, if I did not expect the reproaches of the world. If they have called the Master of the house Beelzebub, much more those of his household. He himself experienced such treatment from the world, and he knows how to succour his children in like circumstances.

The divine right of the Presbyterian form of church government, it may be expected, will now become the *present truth* among all sects of Presbyterians in this country. Their inveterate rage against each other, will for a time be suspended, that they may unite against the common enemy. Every pulpit will resound with the cry of innovation; many an affecting representation will be given of the sufferings of our worthy forefathers, in erecting the *venerable fabric*. I would caution Christians not to suffer themselves to be imposed on by such senseless declamations. The appeal on both sides must be to the Scriptures; not a stone of the fabric can be lawfully rested on other ground. If classical Presbytery be in the New Testament, let its advocates come forward, and fairly refute my arguments. I have no object but truth, and whatever may be published against my pamphlet, in a Christian and candid manner, shall receive every attention. But let them not lose their temper, nor substitute railing for argument. Neither let them nibble round the surface of the subject, but let them enter into the essence of the debate. If any are convinced, let them beware of stifling convictions. Let them not suffer interest, prejudice, or the fear of reproach, to deter them from obeying *the least* of the commandments of Christ. "Whosoever shall be ashamed of me and my words in this sinful and adulterous generation, of him also shall the Son of man be ashamed when he cometh in the glory of his Father with the holy angels."—Mark viii. 38. "He that loveth father or mother more than me, is not worthy of me; and he that loveth son or daughter more than me, is not worthy of me. And he that taketh not his cross, and followeth after me, is not worthy of me. He that findeth his life shall lose it, and he that loseth his life for my sake, shall find it."—Matt. x. 37-39.

Though I am decidedly convinced of the complete independency of the apostolical churches, and of the duty of following them, I would not be understood as placing undue importance upon this point. Christians of every denomination I love, and I will never, I hope, withhold my hand, or my countenance from any who, after impartial investigation, conscientiously differ from me. I can from my heart say, "grace be with all those who love our Lord Jesus Christ, in sincerity and truth." Pity indeed, while there are so few friends of Jesus, that those should harbour hard thoughts of each other, for conscientious differences. But let it not be expected from this, that I shall "know any man according to the flesh," or avoid freely censuring whatever I judge unfounded in Scripture, out of compliment to any friend who may countenance it. This would be to " walk as men."

In endeavouring to overthrow the system of Presbyterianism, I have only assaulted the main pillars of the edifice ; if I have succeeded, the roof and all the rubbish will fall of course. The voluminous defences of Presbytery, of former days, I consider too stale to be particularly noticed. I wait till their advocates recognise them. But though every pin of that system could be proved to be divine, it would not affect my opinion of the duty of separating from the Synod. I would stand upon ground still tenable. I do not shrink from discussion. Truth will finally prevail.

CHAPTER I.

REASONS A PRIORI* WHY IT IS PROBABLE THAT THE SCRIPTURES CONTAIN A DIVINE MODEL OF CHURCH GOVERNMENT.

NOTHING can be more unfair than to determine *a priori*, with an air of demonstrative certainty, what must be revealed in Scripture; and then to open the book and compel it to favour the hypothesis. We are not arrogantly to prescribe to God what he must reveal; our conclusions upon what is proper to be revealed, must be ultimately determined by a candid inspection of the sacred volume itself. Controvertists upon the subject of church government have frequently abused this argument; and have, as it were, almost settled the dispute without opening the Bible. Their favourite system must be *there*, and they are determined to find it. In proportion to the poverty of Scripture materials, is there a wider scope for imagination; where Scripture fails them, *high probability* will amply compensate for the deficiency, and is even more convenient, as it will vary according to the necessities of the different writers.

But though this argument has been abused, we are not on that account entirely to abandon it. I apprehend that there is a legitimate use which it may have on many questions, highly serviceable, if restrained within its natural limits. Though we are not warranted to conclude with certainty, that there is a divine model of church government in the New Testament,

---

* By *a priori*, I mean those arguments that render it probable, that there is in the New Testament a Divine Model of Church Government, previous to the investigation of Scripture, and I use it here and elsewhere to prevent a circumlocution.

till we prove it from itself, yet there may be reasons to render the affirmative extremely probable; which, when considered, will animate us in our search, induce us to collect the scattered fragments, and prepare us to receive, with gratitude, even the scanty pattern which Scripture may afford. Suppose I live near a river on which there are many bleach-greens—after a flood I find a web—I am anxious to know to whom it belongs, for many have been lost. I instantly conclude that it will tell its owner itself—I open it, and examine the ends for the owner's name, but to my great surprise, though both are entire, I find no name. I recur to my argument *a priori*—I reason thus: Can it be possible that a linen-draper would be so careless as not to mark his cloth? This web is entire—therefore certainly it must have a mark, though I cannot discern it. Encouraged by this, I unfold the web, and glance hastily over it from end to end; but no mark can I find. Shall I give over? No: The principle upon which my expectation is founded, remains unshaken, therefore it must be owing to my unskilfulness that I am unsuccessful. I am not accustomed to the business, and therefore the mark has eluded me. I begin again— I search more leisurely; not a thread of the woof escapes my eye. As I advance I see some little strokes marked thus (\11)—this cannot, I say, be the mark; however I will keep it in view. I proceed again, and in a little I find some other of the same unintelligible specks (HH). Strange! what does this mean? These are not letters, say I, yet they are not accidental. I advance in hopes of some clearer discovery, but all I can obtain is something like the rest (ATI). The thought occurs to me to bring these together, and try what they will make when joined. At last, after trying and fitting them a thousand ways I make A H. Overjoyed, I exclaim, this is Mr. H—'s, my neighbour's web. Just so I reason, and so I act upon the subject under consideration. I see an evident necessity for Scriptural direction on this head. I perceive strong antecedent reasons to expect that the New Testament will contain the model of the apostolical churches for our direction. With these sentiments I open the Bible;

I read and read, collect and compare, and when I get the scattered fragments to make an harmonious whole, I am not doubtful of its divine origin.

1. Human manners are much affected by the difference of civil government. The genius of the constitution gives a turn to general manners and modes of thinking. Nations have their characteristic habits and customs which the philosopher can trace to this source. May not the same effects be expected from particular forms of church government? This influence may not be discernible in a comparison of two individual Christians, trained under different forms of church government, but will be sensible when sects are compared in the bulk. The government that is most spiritual will unavoidably communicate a tincture of its spirit to the mass of its subjects. Now, if the mode of the government of the church be in the smallest degree influential of manners, I cannot conceive that Christ would leave this to human discretion.

2. The different theories which have been adopted on this subject, have materially influenced the sentiments of their respective advocates, not only in the explanation of the passages of Scripture immediately concerned, but also of many in which they are not under the influence of a party spirit. All Scripture truths have a mutual connection, and it will often inevitably happen, that adopting a wrong theory upon one point, will lead us into other mistakes in the interpretation of Scripture, or hide from us the true key of analysis. To those who have attentively studied this controversy, it will appear evident that the elucidation of many places in Scripture is affected by it. Now, if a difference of opinion on this subject affect the explanation of other passages in Scripture, there is, besides its own importance, an additional reason why it is worthy the interposition of God.

3. The general sense of professing Christians in all ages, argues the necessity of Scriptural direction on this point. This argument is used with success in favour of revelation, and I see no reason why it should not have all its weight here. The great bulk of professing Christians have in all ages supposed, that they

have found in Scripture, at least the ground-work of their respective plans. When was the *divine right* given up? Not till the enlightened advocates of worldly churches saw that it could no longer be pleaded with advantage. When they found that the witness would not speak in their favour they endeavoured to keep him out of *court*, lest he should speak against them.

4. Either unanimity on this point is not a duty, or the Scriptures must afford us the means of effecting it. Now, the apostle frequently calls our attention to this as a duty in all things. True, indeed, perfect unanimity is not to be expected, but is this the fault of a defective revelation, or of our remaining corruptions and blindness. There can be nothing a duty which is not revealed. Our differences in the greatest *minutiæ* of religion are owing to ourselves, and not to a want of Scripture direction. Now I know of no way to effect unanimity, but by proposing self-evident truths, or the authority of God in revelation. That the mode of church government does not belong to the former, is sufficiently evident from experience; it must therefore belong to the latter. But unanimity upon this point is *consequentially* of more importance, than upon many others of more *intrinsic* importance. Upon many other points, if Christians have differences of opinion, they have it to themselves; upon this their difference affects each other. Either I must submit to be ruled by the opinion of my neighbour, by a church government which I think Christ did not appoint, or he must do so to me, or we must form different sects. Now upon many other questions perhaps more intrinsically important, each of us may hold our own opinions, and bear with each other in the same church. I cannot think then that God would leave us without Scriptural direction on this matter.

5. Will there ever be a day when all sects shall coalesce? I can see no reason to doubt of this. Without it, I cannot conceive that perfect harmony the Scriptures, with the general consent of professing Christians, give us reason to expect. Discrepancy on this point is too great to be consistent with the *increase*

of knowledge of the latter days. Whether is this to be effected by a new revelation, or by a more plentiful effusion of the Spirit upon Christians, and a greater attention to the *revealed will* of God? Is there any other way in which revelation can effect this union, but by giving us a model, or directions on this point? I think it not supposable, that the want of a model in Scripture would be a means of uniting all Christians. For if there be no model or direction in Scripture, unanimity or uniformity is not a duty. This would be saying, that the opinion that union is not a duty, would effect union. Never would there be a greater variety than when this notion should prevail. To effect union, on this supposition, it would appear to me to be necessary to enlarge the powers of the human mind, beyond what hath ever yet appeared in man. The sublimest geniuses on earth have their differences of opinion on every thing but self evident truths. But to effect union in this manner is derogatory both to revelation and the office of the Holy Spirit.

6. There cannot be that prompt, cheerful, and dutiful obedience to church rulers, if the model and laws of the church be not in Scripture. If church rulers have a discretionary power to enact laws, they may abuse that power, and therefore their decrees must be received with examination and caution. Thus there may be a difference of opinion with regard to their propriety; and, at all events, the conviction of the duty of obedience will be more slowly and circuitously obtained. This will gradually introduce either a spirit of disobedience, or of abject servility, among church members. They will be led either to slight the authority of church judicatories, or receive their dictates with a slavish submission. The truth of this remark is abundantly evidenced among those sects which more or less claim the right of acting according to circumstances; of enacting *laws of expediency and discretion.* The people are either the slaves and dupes of their church rulers, receiving the decrees of ecclesiastical assemblies, as the dictates of heaven; or they make light of, and despise their authority. Complete, unequivocal, cheerful, and conscientious obedience is to be found only

among those who dare not command without opening their commission, and appealing to the laws to which they enforce obedience. Here there is no room either for disobedience on the one hand, or slavish obedience on the other. Church members see clearly they are not obeying man but God.

7. Either all forms of church government are alike calculated to promote edification, or if one be better than another, that which is best will be so evident, that all Christians will readily agree in it, or the Scriptures must afford us sufficient means to discover it; otherwise they are deficient. I know not that there are any who will agree to the first, and it appears from fact that the second is not just. In the same times, in the same city, we find almost all the varieties of church government that have existed in times and countries the most remote. Now, if it be a matter of importance to adopt one form rather than another, and if the children of the same family, as well as the inhabitants of the same city, will differ in their opinions on this subject, it would appear to be a matter worthy of divine interference. If there be no divine model, I cannot see how God is not to blame for all the variety of sects occasioned by difference of sentiment on this subject. If we are left to our own judgment and prudence, there can be no sin in using them; and a variety of sects is the unavoidable consequence.

8. Whatever is left to human discretion in religion, is of such a nature that there is no room for the weakest Christian to err, nor the least foundation to dispute; nor would the smallest advantage have accrued to the church, by having those things determined, which are left undefined; but on the contrary such a determination would have been attended with inconveniencies: Such, for instance, are the times of meeting for public worship on the Lord's day, the order of the services, &c. Who ever complained that these things were not confined? Would it have been of any advantage to Christians, that Christ had appointed certain stated hours for public worship? Nay, would not this have been attended with many inconveniencies? But it is quite otherwise with the point in question. The deter-

mination of this would have been attended with no inconveniencies, but with many and important advantages. The leaving of it undetermined would give unavoidable occasion to dissention and schism.

9. Civil government and legislation require the highest exertion of human genius, and the greatest men who have written on the subject, are by no means agreed even in theory, what is the form best calculated to promote the happiness of mankind. In what respect is church government a less important or difficult matter than civil government? nay, I conceive the former to be the more difficult, by how much the government of the mind is more difficult than that of the body, and the more important as spiritual is greater than temporal happiness. Is it then supposable that Jesus would leave a matter of such importance to the discretion of man? Besides, Christ's disciples, upon whom this duty would devolve, are the unfittest imaginable for such a business. They are generally "the weak things of this world." True indeed, they all have spiritual wisdom, for "they are all taught of God;" but this requires political rather than spiritual wisdom. It is evident that every *human* form of church polity is, and must be, on the model of the most approved civil polities. A Christian then to be calculated for a legislator in the church must have the qualifications of a civil legislator. But the great body of Christians are destitute of these pre-requisites. They must then either yield to be led implicitly by the few learned and enlightened men among them, or be liable to the greatest mistakes.

10. I suppose there is not another question in religion about which so much human blood has been shed, or on account of which the earth has been filled with so much confusion, as this very question. Does not this argue the necessity of a divine model, that God may be vindicated, and the blame be wholly attachable to man?

11. If no divine model be given, it would have been impossible to prevent ambitious men from imposing on the simplicity of the multitude, and promoting schemes for their own aggrandizement, under the specious cover

of zeal for religion. Such men as Diotrephes would always assume the pre-eminence. Antichrist would on this supposition have some apology. Nay, in such a case some sort of Antichrist is unavoidable; and it is not very material whether he be one man, or several hundreds. I do think, then, that to leave the Christians of the first ages without excuse—that men may be clearly chargeable with the guilt of rearing and nurturing that monster, it was necessary that a divine model should have been given, from which the smallest deviation was sinful.

CHAPTER II.

IF THERE BE A MODE OF CHURCH GOVERNMENT IN THE NEW TESTAMENT, WHAT IS THE NATURE OF THAT FORM WE ARE WARRANTED TO EXPECT?

1. THAT form of church government which is practicable in all countries, ages and circumstances, is likelier to be the Scripture model than one which is not. Now there is no country, age, or circumstance, in which the Independent plan is not practicable; but to make either Presbytery or Prelacy practicable, there must be a number of congregations formed in a particular district. If there were but a single congregation in a kingdom, the Independent government would not be affected; if every individual of a nation were a Christian, it is equally adequate. In the former situation Presbytery could not exist; in the latter, if there were a sufficient number of pastors for every congregation, a general assembly would be altogether unwieldy. Independency is not fitter for one country than another; Presbytery and Prelacy are each peculiarly suited to one form of civil government rather than any other. The former was suited to the Republic of Geneva, the latter to the Roman Monarchy. Independency meddles not with the state, but in things civil, conscientiously obeys "the powers that be," *whatever be their form or quality.*

2. That form of church government that is capable of the least abuse, is the likeliest to be divine. Now unquestionably this is Independency. If a particular church on this plan degenerates, becomes erroneous, or indifferent, it has no power to injure others, or draw them into its errors. If all the Independent churches of a nation were to degenerate except one, that one cannot be compelled or overawed into their errors.

But it is quite contrary with Presbytery. When one congregation becomes dead or erroneous, it has an influence on all the rest; and when such become the more numerous, they have power to corrupt those that are more pure. On the other hand, in a period of general lukewarmness or apostacy, if any particular Independent church be impressed with the duty of reformation, there is nothing in their connection with other churches to clog or prevent them : but a congregation in such a situation among Presbyterians would find the whole weight of the connection hanging upon them, and that it would be absolutely impossible for them to succeed, without bringing the majority of the whole body to their mind, or by separation. I know indeed it is said, that Presbytery is better calculated to prevent error from creeping into congregations, by the power the majority claims over the minority. But how should one man, or one congregation, keep another from error ? By compulsion or persuasion ? I apprehend there is no lawful means for one church to keep another from error, but by remonstrance and exhortation. Nay, there is no other method, can be successful: if this fails, pains, penalties, imprisonments, confiscations, and death would be useless. Force may make hypocrites, but will never make a Christian. A law of synod may prevent a minister from preaching error, as to the five points, but can it enable him to preach "the truth as it is in Jesus?" Will it enable "the blind to lead the blind, without both falling into the ditch?" Where is the great difference between poisoning the sheep, and starving them? But let the history of synods vouch their utility and efficacy in restraining error, and preserving vital religion. They may, for a time, preserve orthodox, in *the letter*, but midnight darkness may reign with an orthodox creed. "The natural man cannot know the things of the Spirit, because they are spiritually discerned." Vital religion seems in a great measure extinguished, even among those sects who make the highest pretensions to orthodoxy. A violent wrathful spirit of party, and an ardent zeal for human forms and human creeds, seem pretty generally substituted for spirituality, and catholic

Christian love. Now, all the means of remonstrance, persuasion, exhortation, and entreaty are equally open to Independent churches, to preserve each other from backsliding and error. An Independent church may reform other churches, but can receive no injury from them: a Presbyterian congregation may be injured by its connection, if they are corrupt, but cannot reform them in any other way than what is practicable by an Independent church. I conclude then, that as Independency hath all the advantages without any of the disadvantages of Presbytery, as to their influence of connection, it is more likely to be the Scripture plan.

3. It is a maxim in philosophy as well as in divinity, that God does nothing in vain. According to this, if all the ends of government can be obtained in an Independent church, all foreign interference being useless, cannot be appointed of God. That a church under this form of government can subsist in vigour, is evident from experience; and that it is capable of exerting all necessary influence in preserving others from backsliding, we have also seen. What possible advantage can be gained by a numerous subordination of courts? If a light hat of fur be sufficient to preserve my head from the weather, why will I cover it with a mill-stone?

4. That form of church government which cannot preserve purity of doctrine without human expedients, is not so likely to be the Scripture model, as that which can attain and preserve the highest possible degree of vital religion, as well as purity of doctrine, without admitting, in any instance, the devices of the wisdom of man. Now it is generally acknowledged by Presbyterians themselves, that it is impossible to preserve uniformity of opinion among them, without a Formula or Confession,* of Faith, to be publicly recognized by

---

* The utility and lawfulness of human confessions and creeds, as standards of religion, does not lie immediately in my way at present, but as Christians in this country seem very generally in this instance "to be carnal" and walk as men "teaching and receiving for doctrines the commandments of men," I earnestly recommend to their serious perusal a late pamphlet by Mr. Ballantine of Elgin, entitled "Observations on Confessions of Faith

their members. Now, it must be evident to every unprejudiced person, that there is no formula in the Scriptures. That constitution, then, that requires one to maintain purity, is not likely to be of God. The same may be argued from the necessity they are under, to decide by majorities instead of unanimity; debarances, invitations, tokens of admission to the Lord's table, &c.

5. That form of church government that leads us most to the Scriptures, and requires in church-members the greatest acquaintance with them, is the most likely to be that of the New Testament. Now, without an intimate acquaintance with the Bible, Independents cannot advance a step in church affairs. I might speak from what I have witnessed of the knowledge of the Scriptures among Independents. I speak only of its necessity, arising from the constitution of their churches! With them it is absolutely necessary not only in church rulers, but private members. The Bible is their code of laws; they have no other confession or book of discipline. They can do nothing without it; it must be continually in their hand. The rulers rule only by the Word of God. But a man may be a Presbyterian all his life, either pastor or private member, with a very slender acquaintance with the Bible. The knowledge of forms and of ancient usuages, of ecclesiastical canons, and books of discipline, are the chief qualifications that are necessary for a Presbyterian judicatory.

6. That form of church government that needs most the presence of God and prayer, is the most likely to be the divine model. Now the Independent is the only plan in which there is, strictly speaking, room for the *manifest* interposition of God. There are instances in which prayer is their only resource. Their doing all things by unanimity, creates a peculiar necessity for prayer. If there be but one member of a different mind from the rest, it is the same as if there were the one half. In such a situation, the promised

of Human Composition," &c. Their attachment to these is the greater, as they have not been accustomed to hear their authority questioned by any, but those who are enemies to the doctrines which they contain.

presence of Jesus is their only refuge; prayer is their only remedy; and when the difficulty is thus removed, which perhaps will scarcely ever fail, if explanation, remonstrance, and intreaty be affectionately applied, all the praise will be seen to belong to God. On the other hand, a Presbyterian court can proceed as independent of God as a court of civil justice. True, indeed, it is usual to ask him to preside; but can they not proceed smoothly enough without him? Is there ever a situation in which they are not as competent to do business, and settle the most critical affair, as the Parliament of England? I cannot think, then, that an institution is of God's appointment, which does not *need* God's presence.

7. That form of church government which is most favourable to liberty of conscience, in which the individual experiences the least undue influence in determining his principles and conduct in religious matters, is the most likely to be the Scripture model. The Scriptures are the only rule of faith and practice, and every man is bound to judge of them, and determine their meaning for himself. He may use helps to understand them; but if he understands them differently from others, he is bound to act upon his own belief, rather than that of another. Now this liberty can be completely enjoyed as a right in no other than an Independent church. True, indeed, in some Presbyterian connections, individuals may enjoy all the liberty they desire; but does this flow from the nature of the constitution of classical Presbytery, or from the indulgence, or indifference of those connected with them? The very leading idea in Presbytery, that for which it is most prized by its greatest admirers, is this very power of restraining principle and conduct in matters of religion. If Presbytery is robbed of this power, what end does it serve? It is then nothing more than a selection of members from different congregations met for counsel and advice. But where is the Presbytery that acts solely upon this principle? If there be any, they are, as to constitution, Independents. There are indeed Presbyterian connections, in which individuals may be Socinians or Calvanists, but this is the result

of connivance in the general body, and not the genuine fruit of Presbytery. Whenever the body chooses to claim its right, a majority may compel an individual to embrace every shibboleth of their creed, and direct and circumscribe his labours as they please. But view genuine Presbytery among the stricter sects, and it will clearly appear that in all things there must be a complete uniformity. Forbearance is not known. I do not say that we are bound to hold religious intercourse with any individual, or body of men, that we judge destitute of the truth. But as long as we can look upon a man as a brother *born again* and walking in the commandments of God, we are bound to exercise forbearance towards him in other matters of comparatively less importance. But if there are some Presbyterian connections liberal as to principle, are they equally so as to religious conduct? Can any of their members enjoy the privilege of acting for himself, as well as of thinking? Is he not amenable to their bar, if he transgress any laws of theirs, although he judge them contrary to the laws of Christ? I conclude, then, that although from connivance, there may be more liberty of conscience in some Presbyterian connections than others, yet as a power of compulsion is inherent in the very nature of Presbytery, it is not likely to be the Scripture model.

8. Nothing is more universally felt in the human heart than ambition. Nothing our Lord found more difficult to repress in his immediate followers. That form of church government, then, which affords the fewest incitements to ambition, is likely to be the model which he would pitch upon. Here also, the Independent will stand foremost. It is not capable of an adulterous alliance with the world. Its spiritual nature has no charms to tempt the meritricious embraces of worldly men. Though Presbytery is not the most exceptionable in this view, yet it is not without objections. It has been courted by, and wedded to the world, and a hideous progeny has issued from the connection. It has fought for, and in its turn obtained temporal power and riches; and whilst it held the sword, it was more like to Mahomet of Mecca, than

Jesus of Nazareth. The forensic nature of their courts, also, is too much calculated to foster pride, by inducing men to aspire to be the leaders of parties, and make a figure in assemblies, collected from every part of a province or kingdom.

9. If there be any particular model of church government in the New Testament, it is probable that the enlightened advocates of it will rest the cause on the same foundation, however various may be their arguments. For if several intelligent men embrace the same model, and have the same means of information, they have every inducement to unanimity, and if uninterested, or unprejudiced, are likely to defend it on the same general ground. If they take different and opposite hypothesis to serve as a ground-work for their superstructure, they are not likely to have had a common ground in Scripture. Now the advocates of Presbytery take quite different grounds to rest it on. Some defend the whole machine as divine, to the smallest pin. Others pretend to see only the skeleton in Scripture, with a power to fill up the outlines. Others defend it as a lawful human system, upon the ground that we are bound to no particular mode of church government in Scripture. Some find the Presbyterian elder in Scripture, and some make him only a prudential human expedient. Some give him a seat in ecclesiastical assemblies in his own right; others in right of the people whom he represents. They are as divided also about the right of nomination of elders. Some give this right to the congregation, or seat-holders, whether servants of Christ or of Satan; others claim it for the old session. Now, I think the inference which any rational, disinterested, unprejudiced man would draw from this, is, that they have no common source from which they draw their ideas. If they had, certainly Presbytery would not be such a camelion. If they all saw the same picture in the Scriptures, surely they would not give so many contradictory accounts of it, when it was their interest to agree. If Presbytery had been in Scripture, of all its friends Dr. Campbell of Aberdeen, was the best able to defend it; yet Dr. Campbell gives up its divine right, and proves beyond

contradiction, that the apostolical churches were Independent. If ever Presbytery could be found in Scripture, the luminous and penetrating mind of Dr. Campbell, who lived and died at the head of a Scotch university, would certainly have traced it.

10. The end of church government, and church meetings of every kind, must be the edification and growth of the members, and the promotion of brotherly love. That form which is best calculated to promote these ends, is the most likely to have been instituted by Christ. Now, we might rest this upon matters of fact, in favour of the Independents; but we shall content ourselves by observing, that their peculiar advancement in experimental religion, deadness to the world, devotedness to Christ, zeal for His cause, and love towards the brethren, are much the result of the principles of their constitution, in which they are distinguished from other societies. Some of these are their separation from the world, into a spiritual communion, in which they can all look upon each other as Christians, upon good evidence—their frequent church meetings, and mutual public exhortations—the care and watchfulness that every member has over every other as his "brother's keeper," and not committing church power to a few—the opportunity of discovering every talent, and occupying even the smallest in its proper sphere—the close union of all the members rich and poor, each acting on the other as the different wheels of a watch set in motion by the main-spring. Their church order resembles the Macedonian phalanx, which so long as it kept its ranks, was invincible. There is here no possibility of playing the coward; each encourages, and in a manner compels the other to do his duty, as a good soldier of Christ. When individuals are under temptation to give ground, and begin to backslide, the whole body acts as a rere-rank, to encourage them to behave valiantly, to support them when overpowered, to give them an opportunity to rally when they are thrown into confusion, to prevent them from running from the field of battle, and to push them on again to the engagement. The great piety and zeal discovered in individuals of other sects, is no

objection to this. Such persons would have been still more eminent, had they enjoyed a purer communion. There may be healthy men in a very unhealthy climate. This, however, would not induce any man to say, that India is as healthful a climate as Ireland. Compare the nature of the church constitutions, and then compare the general body of the members of the one, with that of the other, and if you are unprejudiced, you will not be long in suspense. I forbear to draw a picture of the generality of Presbyterian connections: it is really too hideous to be reviewed. Besides, many of the evils among some of them, are not the necessary result of the Presbyterian constitution.

11. Christ's institutions father themselves. If a child had been lost, and after many years, several pretenders had come to the father, and there be not sufficient evidence from testimony to determine between them, would it not be very proper to look for a resemblance to the parents, and their other children, either in bodily appearance, temper, or genius? If such a striking resemblance is found in any of them, it will be instantly concluded that he *fathers himself.* In the same manner it is reasonable to expect a family likeness in all the ordinances and works of God. Let us then apply this rule in ascertaining the divine legitimacy of the form of church government. Christ has had such a child, but he has been exchanged at the nurse, and a vile impostor has been imposed upon the world, during all the dark ages of the reign of Antichrist. Since the reformation, various pretenders have laid claim to the honour of heavenly birth. It might be highly serviceable, in judging of their pretensions, to compare the features, mien, temper, and genius of each claimant, with those of the father and his other undoubted children. I shall content myself at present, by examining and tracing a few of the lineaments of two of them, Presbytery and Independency.

God's wisdom is foolishness to the world, and the wisdom of the world is foolishness with God. Whatever, then, be the divine form of church government, it is evident that it must not be one which would be suggested by human prudence or policy, that it may appear to be of God, analogous to his procedure in other instances, and having a necessity for his presence and guidance. It must be one which would appear defective and inadequate, in the estimation of the wisdom of this world, that God may have all the glory of upholding it himself. This is exactly the manner of the divine procedure in every other instance. The wisdom of the world expected Christ to have appeared in far different and opposite circumstances, and to have acted in a quite contrary manner, in erecting and establishing his kingdom; but the divine wisdom appears in this, that the almighty power of God is manifested in accomplishing what had evidently no other support. As the Gospel was first propagated by means the most unlikely to succeed, in themselves the most inadequate; to show that the unseen hand of God upheld and spread it, and that the divine procedure be consistent, it seems necessary that the government be seen solely to rest on *Immanuel's* shoulders. As this King was introduced and inaugurated, and his kingdom erected in a manner directly the reverse of human prudence and policy, so also is it probable will he govern it. To conduct the government of his kingdom upon any of the plans of human governments, by measures and assemblies formed upon a worldly model, would be inconsistent with the whole conduct and procedure of Jesus.

Now, if there be any justice in this reasoning, a very child may apply it to the point in hand—nay, let our enemies themselves be the judges. The very arguments by which they support Presbytery, the very objections which they make to Independency, fully prove to which of them this character belongs. Presbytery has every feature of a child of this world's wisdom. It is entirely a political institution, every part of it analogous to civil polity. In this view, it is really a vigorous republic, and so far as its power extends, it shows that it knows well how to exert it. Its decision, by majorities, instead of unanimity; representation in ecclesiastical assemblies; subordination of courts; and the right of appeal; forms and etiquette of business, &c., are all borrowed from the world. On the contrary, Independency, like Christ himself, has never approved itself to the wisdom of this world. Nay, the only arguments that can plausibly be urged against it, is its insufficiency for any other than *primitive times*. In no civil institution in the world, are the distinguishing features of Independency to be found. It could not govern a private family of unregenerate men. It has been called by those who did not understand its constitution, the *purest democracy*, but it is evident that it is rather a *Christocracy*. Christ alone governs. There is not a law or regulation left to the wisdom of man. What civil government ever existed, in which the unanimous consent of every member was necessary, in every instance? Human affairs could never be conducted in this manner, nor could a body of unconverted men be governed in a church in this way. Nothing but the unseen, almighty power of God could have protected and propagated the Gospel, in the circumstances of its appearance, opposed by all worldly powers; nothing but the presence and power of Jesus could make the simple machine of Independent church government, effect its end. I conclude, then, that if a likeness to God, and an analogy to his procedure in other instances, be any token of childship, Independency, and not Presbytery, is the lawful heir.

But let us pursue the comparison in some other instances, and we will see that Presbytery has not a feature of the family. In all the institutions of God there is a remarkable simplicity, but classical Presbytery is the most clumsy and complicated machine that could possibly be invented, and a tedious round-about way of settling differences, and transacting church business. Several hundred men, from the most distant parts of a province or kingdom, meeting annually, besides all their subordinate meetings, is a thing that bears no resemblance to the simplicity of other Gospel institutions. When united to those, it is like a sober, plain-dressed gentleman, with a huge military hat and feather; or like a small neat chapel with a towering steeple. But peep for a minute into their general synod or assembly. What pomp, what stateliness, what importance do they assume! See yon young orator artfully apologising for his youth, and this aged gentleman looking importance from his years of standing. Stop a little; here is rudeness; "*chair!*" "*chair!*" there will be a quarrel about a trifle; "but the apostles quarrelled at Jerusalem." Here now are several days spent, and what is done? Nothing about religion for its advantage; nothing but what could have been done to better purpose in any congregation.

I might trace the picture much further, but I shall only barely mention, that Presbytery is too expensive for a "kingdom not of this world." The other children of the family live on a trifle; if this is the heir, he is a rake.

CHAPTER III.

ON THE OBLIGATION OF APOSTOLICAL PRACTICE.

HAVING given some reasons to show the antecedent probability of a divine model of church government, with some observations with respect to the plan we are entitled to expect, before I proceed to examine the Scriptures respecting the claims of Presbytery and Independency, I shall endeavour, in this chapter, to establish the obligation of the practice of the apostolic churches. Not that this is more necessary to me than to the true Presbyterians, but because it is beginning to be fashionable with the members of worldly churches, when they are driven from the Scriptures, to take refuge in *the liberty of deviating from the example of the apostles.**

1. The combined weight of all the arguments *a priori*, fall into the scale of the obligation of the example of the apostolical churches. We cannot positively determine what the Bible contains, till we examine it; but if there be every reason antecedently to expect a divine form of church government, and if it is possible to trace the practice of the apostolical churches, is there not every reason to look upon this as the divine model, exhibited in the Scriptures as an universal pattern? The arguments *a priori*, I grant are inconclusive, if no form could be pointed out from the Scripture; but if it be possible to ascertain the constitution of the apostolical churches, I see no good

---

* Dr. Stillingfleet is the great patron of this hypothesis. In his *Irenicum* he endeavours to unite Presbyterians and Episcopalians, by proposing a scheme of a sort of Presbyterian-Episcopacy. But to effect this, it was necessary for him to rid himself of the obligation of taking the apostles of Jesus Christ for an example. I originally intended to have followed the Doctor through his performance, but I found I could not do so without exceeding all bounds.

reason why they should not have their full force. Like an 0 in figures, they draw all their value from their situation; standing alone they are worth nothing; united to the approved apostolical practice, I do not see how their worth can be depreciated or their force invalidated. If a divine plan of church government be extremely necessary, by what authority does any man reject the apostolical?

2. Not only the general sense of professing Christians is on the side of the obligation of apostolical example, but the very advocates of the contrary opinion evidently betray their chagrin, that it is not in their favour. How anxious are they to catch at every thing that looks like approving of their respective churches? What abundant pains do they take to detect every part of the system of their adversaries, that is not apostolical? Every sect goes as far as it can in company with the apostles; it is not till they cannot follow, that the apostles are acknowledged as insufficient guides. Did ever any man think of this hypothesis, till he found apostolical practice against him? Could any of the worldly churches produce uniform apostolical practice on their side, how would they triumph?

3. If the apostolical churches are not a model to us, then all those numerous Scriptures that are employed in describing them, or in giving them directions, are useless to us. Why is such lumber contained in the Word of God? All Scripture is said to be "given by inspiration," and "to be necessary;" but if we are not to imitate the apostolical churches, there are many passages in the New Testament that are now absolutely useless. Accordingly, it is very evident how uninteresting such portions of Scripture are to all that hold themselves at liberty to deviate from apostolical practice. Such persons have a much more barren and jejune revelation than others.

4. Either the apostles acted by divine direction, or by their own wisdom, in the constitution of churches. If the latter, they would undoubtedly have told us so, as they do in less important matters. But even on this supposition, I think the judgment of an apostle is entitled to more respect than to be rejected without the

most urgent necessity. I would really prefer the private opinion of Paul upon a matter of expediency, to that of a whole general council. But if, as there is every reason to believe, they acted by divine command, the form of church government they instituted, can never be changed but by the same authority. If any form is better than another, surely the apostolical is the best. It cannot then be a matter of indifference whether we follow the best, or adopt a worse. If the Holy Ghost had judged it expedient to adopt a different form in a different period, or in different circumstances, would we not have some intimation of it? Without a divine license we are not at liberty to alter or infringe in the smallest degree. We may as well assume the right of altering any other apostolical institution as that of church government.

5. There can be no danger in the closest imitation of the apostolical churches. Is any man sure that he does not displease God by refusing to imitate them? Between the certainty of pleasing, on the one side, and the possibility of offending on the other, the choice which a Christian should make, is evident.

6. No person who pleads the authority of apostolical example for the first day Sabbath, or any other purpose, can consistently reject it in this instance.

7. A plan in model and not in systematic description, is what we are entitled to expect. A direct and formal treatise on the subject, which some people look for, would be altogether anomalous in Scripture. After-ages are no where addressed but in the person, as it were, of the apostolical churches: we are not known but as members of them. Whatever is said to them, is said to us. Thus our Lord, promising his continual presence with his servants in preaching the Gospel, addresses them all in every age, in the person of the apostles then present, " Lo, I am with *you* always *to the end of the world.*" " Where two or three of *you* are met, there am I." The apostles also speaking of what was to happen in every after-age, address those to whom they write as concerned, and warn them of what was to happen to us and our successors to the end of the world. " We, which are alive and remain unto the coming of

the Lord, shall not prevent them which are asleep." Here the apostle addresses, in the person of the Church of the Thessalonians, which then was, those Christians which shall be on the earth at the time of the second coming of our Lord. I might quote innumerable examples, were it necessary. Now this being the case, that after-ages are addressed only in the person of apostolical churches, how absurd is it to expect a formal treatise on church government? Every necessary instruction must have been given in the forming of the churches. How preposterous would it be for an apostle, after he had formed a church, and left it, to write a treatise to that church, on the method of forming a church! All then that can be expected, is an incidental account of apostolical practice. The subject cannot be formally, but indirectly, and, as it were, unintentionally handled. Suppose, for instance, the apostle Paul had founded the churches of Edinburgh, and after his departure, had written a letter to them, to establish them in the faith; would any rational man expect a treatise on the constitution of a church, which he had already constituted? No, all we could expect, would be an allusion to what he had done. I say, then, according to the analogy of the manner of revelation, there is not room for any other information on church government, than an account of apostolical practice. Here, I think, Dr. Campbell fails of his usual acumen, or he would not have expected the subject treated in " another manner," upon the supposition, that we are absolutely bound to the constitution of apostolical churches. But some other observations on this subject, I will reserve to another place.

8. The tabernacle itself, was made according to model, and not from a verbal delineation, or treatise. "Moses was admonished of God, when he was about to make the tabernacle. For see (saith he), that thou make all things according to the *pattern* showed to thee in the Mount." Now we have also a pattern in the Mount, for our New Testament churches are exhibited to us in those of apostolical constitution. To this pattern, we are to look for every part of our constitution and discipline. Let every man take care that he make everything in a Gospel church, after the pattern of that exhibited to us in the

Scriptures. This is a divine model; to add to it, or take from it, will spoil the beauty, and diminish the strength of the building.

9. We are often called upon, to be followers of the apostles, without any exception or limitation. By what authority then do any except from this rule, the conduct of the apostles, in the formation of churches? From every general command, I think there can be no lawful exception, but what is impossible, sinful, or otherwise determined. If we are called upon without reserve, to follow the apostles, I think the injunction extends, not merely to their conduct as men, but particularly as our examples in all church affairs. If I justify a quarrelsome disposition, from the example of Paul and Barnabas, I am condemned by the Scriptures. But this quarrel was not recorded for nothing. It is for an example, to guard us against such a temper. If any one would contend for the duty of celibacy, from the example of Paul, his example, in this, is declared not to be binding. If any man would take it into his head to work miracles, like the apostles, this is impossible, without receiving the power of an apostle. Yet these, and such as these, are the mighty objections, alledged by Dr. Stillingfleet, against the obligation of apostolical example. But I ask, is the imitation of apostolical churches sinful, impossible, or otherwise determined, in any part of Scripture. If not, I demand a reason for excepting it from the general injunction.* With what reason, then, does Dr. Stillingfleet refuse, with triumph, to be bound by apostolical example, till we produce him an express command, for that particular instance? May we not, with the same reason, demand a positive

---

* Not only the conduct of the apostles in the churches, is exhibited as an example to us, but their very antecedent characters, as well as their after-trials, supports, joys, &c., are recorded for our encouragement, instruction, or example, to avoid or practice. The great design of the Almighty, in allowing the rebellion of Paul to proceed to such a height, is said, to be an example to us, that the most notorious sinners might not be afraid to come to Christ.—1 Tim. i. 16. Paul's declining to avail himself of his right to live by the Gospel, and his working with his own hands, are declared to be for an example to Christians to support themselves by industry.—2 Thess. iii. 9.

command, at the end of every apostolical example? Here is a general command; let it be shown, why this particular instance of the obligation of their example, in the constitution of apostolical churches, should be excepted. Besides, if the observation above be just, that we are known only as members of the apostolical churches, what room was there for a command to after-ages, as distinct from that in which they wrote? An express command to a church, to continue the form of government, which an apostle instituted, we would think superfluous. This is always supposed, without a positive declaration to the contrary. No, it lies not upon us to produce such a command, but on those who take upon them, to set aside the obligation of apostolical example; it is certainly incumbent, that they should produce their warrant. If God instituted the Independent plan, before any man can warrantably deviate from it, it behoves him to produce from Scripture a specific license.

10. But though the manner of divine revelation forbids us to expect a direct address to after-ages, upon the obligation of apostolical practice, yet we have what is equal to it. There are instances in which an older, completely organised apostolical church, is exhibited as a pattern to others, more imperfect. Now, if the apostolical churches are exhibited as a model to others, and if some are praised or blamed for their conformity to, or disagreement from them, it is very clear, that the apostles intended that all churches, in every age, should be upon the same model. 1 Thess. ii. 14—"For ye, brethren, became followers of the churches of God, which in Judea are in Christ Jesus." 1 Cor. vii. 17—"And so ordain I in all churches." 1 Cor. xiv. 33—"For God is not the author of confusion, but of peace, as in all churches of the saints." Here, the same order is intimated to exist in all churches. But how is God the God of order and peace in all the churches of saints, if he has not ordered every thing himself? If he has left men to choose their form of church government, and to make laws for themselves, could it be said, that he is not a God of confusion? The confusion that would exist on that supposition, would be bound-

less and endless. 1 Cor. xi. 16—"We have no such custom, neither the churches of God." Here, the other apostolical churches are exhibited, as a model to this. 1 Cor. xvi. 1—"Now, concerning the collection for the saints, as I have given order to the churches of Galatia, even so do ye." Here, the example of the churches of Galatia, is exhibited as a model to the Church of Corinth. Titus i. 5—"For this purpose, left I thee in Crete, that thou shouldest set in order the things that are wanting, and ordain elders in every city, *as I had appointed thee.*" Here, we see, that in setting in order the things that were wanting, even the evangelist Titus, was not left to his discretion, but was to act in every thing, *as Paul had appointed.* Titus had his instructions, as an officer from his general. Can we pretend to greater power?

11. Is it possible for a church to exist and flourish without observing any other laws, rules, or regulations, without any other offices, or modification of offices; without any other discipline, or sanction of discipline; without any other test of admission, or means of preserving purity; but what are to be collected from apostolical example, and the scattered information of Scripture? If this question can be answered in the affirmative, what apology can men plead for their innovations? The advocates for a liberty of deviating from the form of apostolical churches, lay the weight of their cause upon this argument: "No form of church government, could answer all ages, countries, and circumstances." What do men mean by this jargon? Do they mean, that no form would answer for a civil establishment, under every form of civil government? Do they mean, that none could be given to suit the various humours of carnal men? Yes, the true meaning of this objection, if they would put it into words, is, that no one form could be given to serve as a part of a political system, under different forms of civil government—that the simple apostolical model, suited only apostolical times, being incapable of governing that mixed multitude, of which all worldly churches consist—and that it was unsuitable to the dignity of an aspiring clergy. But these are the very credentials of its divine appointment. It

is eminently calculated to govern Christ's children, who, like the Spartan youth, have their minds moulded to their laws; but it will always be found to fail, when members are admitted, not of the character of the members of apostolical churches. Nay, one impure member, if not cut off, when detected, would stop the harmonious procedure of the whole machine, as effectually as a watch is stopped by the accidental admission of a hair. But, can a man be pleased with the prostitution of his wife? Can Christ be pleased, or his cause advanced, by the prostitution of his ordinances? Shall the spiritual kingdom of Christ, change its appearance, with the fluctuating opinions of the world; the varying laws of temporal kingdoms; or the caprices of carnal men?

CHAPTER IV.

PRESBYTERY EXAMINED.

HAVING, in the preceding chapters, stated some reasons to render a divine model of church government probable—having shown some characteristics of that which is likely to be the Scripture model—and endeavoured to establish the obligation of apostolical example—let us now proceed to inquire *what is actually the mind of the Scriptures upon this point?* Let Presbytery first come under review. One thing I would premise, as a caution to myself and all who treat this subject—*Let us never forget, when we are interpreting Scripture texts, that they are the words of the Holy Ghost.* He that forces them, to make them countenance, or avoid discountenancing his system, is guilty of an attempt to compel the Holy Ghost to speak a lie, and bear false witness. How guilty! how infamous is the wretch that employs, or compels another to perjure himself to serve his interest! But how much more criminal and infamous is the man who would put a forced interpretation on the language of the *Holy One!* I have heard a man say, that indeed it was very criminal to employ a person to *swear a lie;* but if at an assizes he should run short of an evidence, he would think no great harm of getting one *to swear the truth for him,* though he was not a witness of the truth of the matter. I am afraid there are too many Scripture critics who act upon this principle. They lay it down as a matter indisputable, that such a tenet is true, and expressed clearly in some passages of Scripture, and therefore they will set about to silence, or force other texts to compliance, by perversion. Let us then attend simply to the testimony of plain Scripture, in its plain acceptation. It is really the interest of the Christian, if he could allow himself to think so, to discover and embrace truth, though it should deprive him of the dearest earthly possession.

Another thing that must be attended to, by all who plead for the divine right of any particular form of church government, is, that nothing be admitted but what is clearly founded in the Scriptures, either in precept or example. Those that pretend a divine model, must produce it, without the help of conjecture, or probabilities, to complete it.

The great bulwark of Presbytery, according to its friends, is contained in the 15th chap. of the Acts of the Apostles. Let us therefore examine this portion of Scripture, by the rules of candid criticism, and see if in any thing, it gives its countenance to this mode of church government.* The matter of fact related, seems to be this: certain teachers had gone down to Antioch from Judea, who had inculcated the necessity of the observance of the Mosaic law. From verse 24, it appears, that if they were not actually sent out by the Church of Jerusalem, to preach the Gospel, they at least wished to have it understood, that they had apostolical authority. The Church of Jerusalem, in their letter, acknowledge that they went out from them; and do not deny their being sent by them; but affirm that they had no such doctrine in charge from them, as the circumcision of Gentile converts. Previous to this, Paul and Barnabas had returned thither from their first itinerancy. Of consequence, they opposed this doctrine; and after they had much fruitless discussion upon the subject, it was resolved by the brethren in Antioch, to send Paul and Barnabas, and certain others, to consult the apostles and Church of Jerusalem, from whom these teachers had come out. But let us read the chapter with calmness and attention, and we will see that it contains not one feature of modern Presbytery.

1. Where do we find here the Presbyterian subordination of courts? Was the matter first tried by the church session at Antioch? Was it next carried to a Presbytery?

---

* This subject is fully and ably discussed by Mr. Ewing of Glasgow, in "A Lecture on part of the 15th chapter of the Acts of the Apostles," which the reader would do well to consult.

Was this appeal from a Presbytery at Antioch? Who sent Paul and Barnabas to Jerusalem? It will puzzle the most metaphysical head to discover a session and a Presbytery, or either, at Antioch; yet, if it cannot be proved that this appeal came from a Presbytery of ministers and lay elders, at Antioch, the meeting at Jerusalem cannot be a synod.

2. If this be allowed to be a synod, it will cut off all superior and inferior courts. There cannot be a superior court, for this determined for the whole Christian world, and from it there could be no appeal. There cannot be subordinate Presbyteries and church sessions; for this appeal was not from any inferior court, but immediately from the brethren at Antioch. I know it is said, that the Presbytery of Antioch deputed Paul and Barnabas; but it is easier to say this than to prove it. The antecedent to the verb "determined," is not clearly expressed. The structure of the sentence, if the sense of the passage would admit, would allow Paul and Barnabas, or the false teachers themselves, or both together, to be the persons, who, "determined." But this will make nothing for Presbytery; nay, it would overthrow it. For if Paul and Barnabas, or these with the false teachers, or if the latter only, "determined" to depute the messengers, there is an end to Presbytery. It is no unusual thing, however, in reading the New Testament, to be obliged to look back a little for the antecedent to the verb, or to take it from the general sense of the passage. The most natural interpretation is, that the brethren deputed Paul and Barnabas; or that it was done conjointly by the brethren, the false teachers, and Paul and Barnabas. This is clearer, from the words, as they stand in the original, which are more literally translated: "They *appointed* Paul and Barnabas, and certain other of them, to *go up*," &c. The false teachers could not appoint Paul and Barnabas to go up to Jerusalem, nor is it likely they desired it, as they must have known that they received no such *charge* from that church. But, be this as it will, upon no supposition could they have been sent by a Presbytery, because no such thing is mentioned in the connection. Whatever be the antecedent to εταξαν,

it must be found among the persons spoken of in the preceding verses. It may as well be said that the magistrates of Antioch sent them, as the supposed Presbytery of that place. There is the same evidence for the one as the other. Besides, if the appeal had been from a Presbytery, would not the answer have been to the appellants? The letter of the Church of Jerusalem would not have been addressed to the brethren, which are of the Gentiles, but to the Presbytery of Antioch?

3. This assembly carried all things by complete unanimity; therefore can be no model to any assembly, in which a majority decides for the whole. Suppose it to have actually been a synod, no decree of a modern synod could plead its authority, which was not carried unanimously.

4. Suppose this to have been a synod, it only warrants their meeting, as a matter of dispute may arise among the churches. It would give no countenance to regular periodical meetings. But Presbyterian courts have their stated meetings, whether or not there be business of importance to justify their meeting.

5. The decision of the Church at Jerusalem was obligatory, not only in the Church of Antioch, which had appealed, but upon all churches in the world. In the letter, verse 23, Syria and Cilicia are expressly included. And in Paul's second journey, he and his companion gave the churches, in the cities through which they passed, the decrees ordained by the apostles and elders at Jerusalem. Will any man say, that there were representatives from these places, in the Jerusalem assembly? It cannot then be a model for a synod, where none are bound, but those represented. If synods will quote this for a precedent, they must no longer confine themselves, to make laws for their own connection, but decide in matters of religion, for the whole Christian world. But, as this assembly consisted solely of the members of one church, if it be a warrant for foreign interference of any kind, it will prove, that an individual church, consisting of its rulers, and brethren, should give law to all the churches of the universe.

6. By what authority is the meeting at Jerusalem

called a synod? Who were the members that composed it? Were they not the apostles, the elders, and brethren of the Church of Jerusalem *only ?* Was there a single representative, either minister or lay elder, from any other church upon earth? Those who accompanied Paul and Barnabas from Antioch, were not representatives, but messengers of that church, to report the matter of fact, and receive the decision. Accordingly, the letters are in the name, not of a representative council, but of the apostles, the elders, and brethren at Jerusalem, from whom the troublesome teachers went out. How absurd would be their language, upon the supposition that there were representatives in it, from the Church of Antioch, and others. " For as much as we have heard, that certain which went out *from us.*" Could the Antioch, and other representatives, put their signatures to this letter? Could they say that they went out *from them ?* They went out from the church at Jerusalem, and no one could say, " they went out *from us,*" but the church at Jerusalem. The language " went out *from us,*" plainly excludes from that assembly, all members from foreign churches.

7. As there were no representatives in this meeting, from any other church, so *all the members or brethren* of the church at Jerusalem, were admitted. What is there similar to this in Presbytery. So far from being admitted into general meetings, they have no share in the administration of the affairs of a single congregation. The minister and elders, are the sole judges, in all disputes. The people must make their mind known, by petition to church courts. Upon the supposition, that this was a representative assembly, consisting of members from the different churches of Judea, Samaria, Antioch, &c., by what authority did *the brethren* of the church at Jerusalem, take a share in the deliberations? What peculiar right had they over the brethren of all other churches, to a place in this assembly? Why did not the church at Jerusalem choose representatives, as well as the other churches? Or, if the Jerusalem brethren were to be admitted, why not all the members of all the churches, or at least, as many of them as might choose to attend?

D

What Presbyterian assembly is so constituted? This would destroy the balance of power. The admission of the brethren of the church at Jerusalem, plainly shows that it was not a representative assembly.

8. This was an appeal to inspired authority, which, in after ages, could be imitated only by appealing to the apostolical writings. The message was to the apostles, and to the elders, who were men endowed with the gifts of the Spirit. This was nothing else than our appeal to the Scriptures. The apostolical writings were not then in existence; the apostles themselves were in the room of the New Testament. There was no other possible way of deciding the dispute. The Scriptures that were then in being had nothing *express* upon the subject. But what question can now arise in any church, which the Scripture cannot determine. They contain a full and perfect rule of faith and practice. This question is settled for ever, and the decision is a part of Scripture. Never can the same, or a similar, again occur. Paul and Barnabas, it is true, were at Antioch; but they, in some sort, were esteemed a party, by the judaizing teachers. Besides this important question, the condition upon which the Gentiles were to be received into the church, behoved to be discussed and settled in the most public manner, that the Jews in every part of the world, might the more readily unite with them. Accordingly, it seems probable that this was the time, and this the occasion, that Paul went up to Jerusalem, by revelation—Gal. ii. 2.* The apostles might have decided the question themselves, but it behoved to be done in this manner, because it was a matter in which the Church of Jerusalem was concerned, as the false teachers had gone out from them, and because they wished, in this first church, to give a public specimen of transacting church business. This shows us, that matters of public concernment to a church, are not to be smuggled through a session, but conducted in the presence, and by the consent, of the whole brethren. Though, then, it affords not a precedent for one church to appeal to

---

* See Innes's Reasons, page 39.

another, yet this portion of Scripture will, to the end of the world, be useful to direct us in transacting church business.

9. The decision of the church at Jerusalem was the issue of the infallible interpretation of Scripture, and the voice of God in the previous conversion of the Gentiles. Peter argues, that if God had already given them conversion without circumcision, the matter must be already determined, as they were really already saved, when they were converted. If, then, circumcision, or the Mosaic law, had been necessary, they must have received it before conversion. He argues from their belief, that the Gentiles and themselves should be saved in the same manner, that is, wholly through the Lord Jesus Christ, which could not be the case, if they must be circumcised. James proves the same, by an inference from a passage of one of the prophets. Now, none can plead this as a precedent for any body of men to settle controverted matters for others, who cannot plead the gift of infallible interpretation of Scripture.

10. If the apostles presumed not to give their decision, without giving such reasons, upon which it was founded, how arrogant are those assemblies, who make their own opinion of expediency the law of every individual! Were such assemblies of God's own appointing, yet, if their proceedings are not directed by the Scriptures; if they cannot plead the sanction of the Scriptures for every decision, their acts would be invalid. Let synods apply this criterion to their decrees, and it will at once sweep away all their *prudential regulations, and human expedients*, and every act that cannot plead express Scripture. It will not be enough, that such a thing is the "*mind of this synod*," but that such a thing is the mind of Scripture, the voice of God.

11. No body of men can plead this as a precedent to determine in matters of religion for others, who cannot preface their decree with: "It seemed good unto us, and to the *Holy Ghost*." Without this, their decision is as invalid as an act of parliament without the sanction of the king.

12. Whatever be the divine model of church government, it is in no measure invested with a power of legislation. The question of a right to make laws according to circumstances, for the government of Christ's church, and the inquiry into the divine form of its government, are entirely distinct. Whether Episcopacy, Presbytery, or Independency be of God, to none of them can belong a right to enact new laws, any more than to promulgate new doctrines. The business of church rulers is not to make laws, but to execute the laws which they find enacted by Christ, in the New Testament. If an individual Independent church, were to take upon itself to enact laws, draw up a plan of rules and regulations for their government, and worship, I would have the same objections to it, that I have to Presbytery. To suppose a liberty to enact laws or regulations, according to the exigence of circumstances, is to arraign the competency of Christ, as the King of the church, and a declaration that he hath left the code of laws imperfect. Executive and legislative authority, even in civil affairs, are entirely distinct, and in the best governments, are lodged in different hands. The Parliament enacts laws, and the civil magistracy executes them. As well might the civil magistrates of a county meet to frame laws, in imitation of the Parliament, as church rulers plead the right of making laws, because the inspired apostles of God did so. Church rulers are to execute the laws which the apostles enacted. Every new law is an act of treason against Christ, and an attempt to rob him of the most valuable prerogative of his crown. How astonishing is it to hear men arguing so warmly, that Christ would not leave his church without a form of government, who suppose that he has left it without a sufficient code of laws! Surely it is as necessary to have divine laws for the government of Christ's church, as a divine plan of executing those laws. If the laws are human, what avails it that the plan of government be agreeable to the Scripture model? Were we then to allow that the plan of church government, by synods, &c., &c., was the true one, still their business would be very different from what it is. They would not

meet as legislators, but as jurors, to judge of the *application* of Christ's laws. Suppose, for instance, that a member of their communion was charged with being an extortioner, a reviler, a drunkard, &c., there is an express law of Christ, that he should become a subject of discipline. Now, their business would be, to judge the offender by the law of Christ, examine proofs, and determine whether or not the charge was fairly applicable. But it happens, that this rule is given to the brethren of an individual church, and not to a synod or Presbytery.

But the very idea of a right of legislation in the Church of Christ, supposes infallibility in the legislators. To suppose that Christ would give a commission to men, to make laws, and a command to his people to obey them, while at the same time, he would leave such men without infallible direction, is monstrously absurd. If synods are fallible, they may enact sinful laws, and enforce them in the awful name, and by the authority of the Lord Jesus Christ. If they are not infallible, why do they enforce their laws, as if they were infallible? Do they not enforce the smallest law they enact, with the same rigour they could do a law of God? Nay, it is very possible to break many of the laws of God with impunity, while a law of synod or Presbytery must be inviolable. If an individual approve not of any law, the only redress he has, is to separate. He has no liberty to act upon his own convictions. Their opinion of expediency must be his guide. Now, if they are not infallibly right, why do they not leave individuals to act according to their own convictions? Is not this, to " teach for doctrines the commandments of men?"

Upon the whole, in the 15th chap. of Acts, we have no precedent for any foreign interference among the churches of Christ. The distinguishing features in this assembly, are not to be found, nor ever can be found, in any assembly on earth. If it be asked, of what use is this relation to us, if it does not warrant us to decide differences in a similar way, I would answer, that whenever a text of Scripture is so explained, as to be rendered useless to after ages, I readily grant, that it certainly must be a forced explanation. But have we not here a precedent for appealing to the apostles, in all our controversies, as the Church of Antioch did? Have we not here a precedent of applying every doctrine, and *observance*, and *rite*, and *regulation* of churches to the Word of God? If the apostles drew their conclusions from this source, shall *human prudence*, and *expedience* direct church rulers? Every tittle must be brought "to the law and to the testimony, whoever speaks not agreeable to this, it is because there is no light in them." Have we not here, an admirable model for the transaction of all church business. The question could, indeed, only be determined by apostles; but as it was an affair in which the church at Jerusalem was concerned, and to give us a living model for transacting church business, the apostles consider the matter in conjunction with the whole church. What a beautiful picture does it give us of a church meeting! It is not a minister and session, nor the ministers and lay-elders of a district, but the apostles, elders, or pastors, and brethren. Whenever the pastors and brethren of a particular church come together now, they must have the apostles in their hands, by whose writings they are to conduct all their affairs.

CHAPTER V.

OF THE OFFICE OF LAY ELDERS.

HAVING, in the last chapter, examined the pretensions of Presbyterians, as founded on the relation contained in the 15th chap. of the Acts of the Apostles, I intend, in this, to inquire into the validity of the office of lay-elders. Presbyterians themselves are not agreed, either as to the foundation, extent, or prerogatives of this office; a circumstance that will go far, in the judgment of every unprejudiced inquirer, to prove that the office is not scriptural. As to the Scripture authority of lay-elders, some refer us to the office of deacon. "Though the name is not scriptural (say they), yet the office is." But here I would remark, that the names are not more different than the offices. A Scripture deacon is an officer in the Church of Christ, for managing its temporal concerns, and attending to the wants of the poor brethren. He has no concern in the ruling of the church, more than the rest of the brethren. A lay-elder is compounded of a New Testament deacon, the half of a New Testament elder or pastor, as he is a church ruler, and a part of the office of an apostle, as a legislator, to make laws for the church. In the superior courts, he is looked upon by some as a representative of the people; by others as the representative of his own order. In either view, his office is derived from our ideas of civil policy; for there is not the shadow of any such representation in the Word of God. It is absurd in the extreme, to found his office on that of the Scripture deacon, seeing it extends so much further. If he is the same as the deacon, let him do the deacon's office only. Besides, if he be the deacon, why has he been called elder? Has not the father the best right to give the name to the child? Is not the Spirit of him who instituted the office, the best judge of the most fitting name? Especially as the name was appropriated to another order in the church, why was *it* chosen? If men thought that they could give a more proper and decent name to this office, than the Spirit of God had done, which is not a very modest supposition, why did they take that which he had assigned to pastors? Has not the tendency of this been to mislead the English reader, and make him believe, that where he meets the word elder, in the New Testament, the Presbyterian elder was intended, and not the pastor. This has been one of the most successful artifices of priestcraft in all ages. But there are others who pretend to find both name and office in the New Testament, and produce as their authority, 1 Tim. v. 17—" Let the elders that rule well, be counted worthy of double honour, especially they who labour in word and doctrine." " Here (say they) is an evident distinction between ruling and teaching elders. There must be some elders to rule, and others to teach." To this I answer—

1. Allowing the Presbyterian explanation of this text, in its utmost latitude, what does it make? Granting that there should be a body of lay-elders to join with the preaching elders, in ruling a church, does this give any countenance to a church session as a body of legislators, to make laws, rules, and regulations for the congregation? Their being church rulers, does not constitute them church legislators. Upon this supposition, their business would be to carry the laws of Christ into effect, not to make laws. Neither would this give any countenance to a minister and session, exclusively judging of the application of discipline, and engrossing the whole power of the church into their own hands. Whether the elders of a particular church be all pastors, or some ruling, and others teaching elders, to neither would belong the sole right of judging when the laws of Christ were to be applied. If a brother was accused, the whole church would judge him according to the law of Christ; and if he is found guilty, the business of church rulers is to execute the law of Christ, which the church has judged

applicable; just as a judge pronounces the verdict found by the jury. But a church session is not only a parliament to make laws, but a jury to judge of the application of both their own and Christ's laws. The brethren are entirely excluded. They may lodge a complaint, or appear as a witness, but in judging of the guilt or innocence of the accused, they have no share. I do not stay here to show that this is contrary to the apostolical commands, in which the whole church is intrusted and charged with judging of the application of discipline. This I intend to show in another place. What I would observe here, is, that according to their own interpretation of this text, there is no foundation for the legislative or exclusive judicial authority of church sessions.

2. Allowing, from this text, an order of ruling elders, distinct from teaching elders, this gives no countenance to a body of what are called lay-elders; that is, men not invested with the pastoral office. Such ruling elders would be as really pastors, bishops, ministers, &c., as the preaching elders. The office of a preaching elder would not be superior to that of the ruling elder. The ruling elder would be a pastor of the church, invested with the pastoral character, in as full a manner as the preaching elder. The only legitimate conclusion that could be drawn from this interpretation, would be, that in every church there should be two orders of ministers, the one for ruling, and the other for preaching; and that neither of these had a right to interfere in the department of the other. The preaching elder was not to rule, any more than the ruling elder was to preach. The preaching elder, then, should not preside in the session, nay, he should have no seat in it, any more than the ruling elder should have in the pulpit. If the one is only to rule, the other is only to preach. If the one must not mount the pulpit, neither must the other sit in church-court. All then that can be fairly inferred from this interpretation, is, that in the pastoral office, there are two distinct departments, which should not interfere with each other; that those appointed to rule, should rule; and those appointed to preach, should preach; which, instead of

serving, would overthrow, from the foundation, the whole Presbyterian system. If, then, we should allow that there is in this text, an order of ruling elders, distinct from another order of preaching elders, still such ruling elders would be pastors or bishops, and nothing a-kin to Presbyterian elders. Nay, the ruling elders would be more eminently, if not exclusively, the bishops or overseers. Oversight surely belongs rather to the ruler, than the preacher.

3. Is it possible that two orders so different as that of ministers and lay-elders, should be called invariably in Scripture, by the same name? Is this like the perspicuity of the Bible? Is it probable, that when the New Testament writers employ so many words to denote the same office, as bishop, presbyter, shepherd, &c., they could not afford a distinct name for the office of lay-elder, if it was apostolical? Is this agreeable to the use of any language, upon any subject? Especially, is it agreeable to the genius of the philosophic language of Greece, where every shade of difference in idea, is marked by a different word, expressive of it? But the English reader of the most common understanding, must be convinced that it is impossible for the Greek word πρεσβυτερος, to denote two so widely different officers from the use of our own word elder. Though this is the exact translation of the Greek word, and in the estimation of Presbyterians, must include both minister and lay-elder, yet to avoid confusion, it has been appropriated by them to denote the latter only. What Presbyterian speaks promiscuously of ministers and lay-elders by the common name elders? Or who would understand him if he did? Yet such undefined, indeterminate language, they scruple not to put into the mouth of the Holy Ghost. If ever they use the word elder to denote the minister, they are obliged to prefix the word *lay* to it, when attributed to the Presbyterian elder, to prevent obscurity. Now, if we cannot talk in English of ministers and Presbyterian elders by the same name, is it possible that the Scriptures should be guilty of this obscurity?

4. Granting that this text does constitute two orders of elders, then there will be three orders of officers in

every church, and the Presbyterians want the third. They have not the deacon. "Yes (say they), our elder is the deacon." But upon what authority do they combine offices, which the apostles kept distinct. There is incontestibly an order of deacons; if there be two orders of elders, there should be three distinct orders in every church. No man hath authority to combine any two of them into one, any more than to make a new order over the rest. If it be said, that the office of the lay-elder and that of the deacon are the same, I have already shown that they are widely different. The office of a deacon is to take care of the poor; whereas, if there be a distinct order of ruling elders, their office must be to rule the church. Is there any evidence in Scripture, that these two offices were combined into one? The office of the deacon is in itself no more connected with ruling, than with preaching. To rule in the church, and to take charge of the poor, are offices distinct in themselves, and separated in the New Testament.

5. If there had been two orders of elders, so distinct as that of lay and preaching elders, is it possible that their offices and qualifications should be included in the same description? In describing the office of the elder, and his qualifications, no notice is taken of two orders, one as requiring a different kind of qualifications from the other. They are called upon, without exception, to feed the flock, take the oversight of it, &c.; and are all required to be διδακτικός, "fit to teach," which, as Dr. Campbell has observed, could hardly be the case, if some of them were to have no concern in teaching. This candid inquirer has given up this text, and thinks it is too trivial a circumstance, upon which to found so material a distinction. It is not said, that a preaching elder must have such and such qualifications, and do so and so, but *the elder*, which must include every distinction of elders. Besides, the words elder and bishop are perfectly interchangeable, constantly applied to the same officers, as all Presbyterians will allow. Now, if there be an order of lay-elders, there must be also an order of lay-bishops; that is, *men who have the pastoral office, yet are no pastors.*

6. Commentators seem generally agreed, and the 18th verse absolutely requires that τιμη, here translated "honour," signifies the *honourable maintenance of the ministers of the gospel*. The apostle proves that they are worthy of this τιμη, from the law of Moses, respecting the ox employed in treading out the corn, and from the words of our Lord, with respect to those engaged in preaching his Word. Now, the argument drawn from this, goes directly to show that all those elders, spoken of in the 17th verse, are worthy of honourable support. It does not indeed require that a church is, in every situation, to support all its labourers. Some may not need it; the church may be so poor that it cannot support more than one pastor. There is nothing to prevent it from using the labours of some who support themselves by lawful industry. But the text undoubtedly implies, that all elders are *worthy* of support, and if they need, and the church can give it, it is their right. Do Presbyterians think it their duty to support their elders, or will any one say, that they are worthy of it? If not, they cannot be the elders of which the apostle speaks. Besides, the 18th verse proves incontestibly, that all the elders spoken of in the 17th verse, have the same pastoral character, and are employed in the same work. They are all "treaders out of the corn," all "labourers worthy of reward." How do Presbyterian elders "tread out the corn?" In what manner do the most conscientious of them "labour so as to be worthy of reward?" These figures represent the elders as labouring constantly in the work of the Gospel, and having that for their employment, as the ox was daily employed in early days, and till the present time, in some countries, in "treading out the corn," and as a labourer is employed, not occasionally, but constantly in his labour. Should it be said, that the illustration in the 18th verse, is applicable only to the latter part of the 17th verse, I answer, that beside the necessity of referring it to the whole verse, the texts quoted by the apostle, would not be relevant in that view. They go to prove the propriety of support in general, and not a superiority of support.

7. Hitherto I have granted, that this text does create

two orders of elders; and even on that supposition, have shown that this constitutes two different orders of pastors in every church, not a separate order of what are called lay-elders. I will now endeavour to show, that the text neither proves nor admits a distinction of order among the elders spoken of. The opposition is not between ruling elders and preaching elders, but in the first part of the verse, between those who discharge the office well *in general*, and those who are particularly employed and distinguished for talents and labour in that difficult, important, and laborious branch of the office, the preaching continually to large public assemblies. In every apostolical church, that was perfectly organised, there was a plurality of elders or pastors, of different gifts. Some were distinguished as public speakers, others as church rulers, others for a talent of private exhortation, peculiarly fitted to converse with the saints, on the state of their souls, and to pour the balm of consolation into the wounded spirit. Now, each of these sustained the whole of the pastoral office or character, and might occasionally be employed in any part of it, while each was usually employed in that department of his office, for which his talents, and his temper, fitted him. The advantages which would thus accrue to the church, are obvious and admirable. It enjoyed this diversity of gifts, while at the same time, if any of the elders were absent, or should die, or that it could not procure, or support for some time, as many elders or pastors as were necessary, any one of them could officiate in the peculiar department of any other. Churches which have not this plurality of pastors, and diversity of gifts, are not aware of the disadvantage under which they labour. At the same time, some congregations which have a plurality of pastors, do not seem to know how to use them. They do not assign their pastors, each the peculiar province for which he is best qualified, but each statedly labours in every part of the office, alternately. This plurality of elders, is rather suited to the indolence of the labourer, than the edification of the church. This being the case, the reason of the injunction of the text is obvious and important. All such elders are worthy of "honourable maintenance;" those who are distinguished in their office, have a right to a double portion; especially those who are peculiarly and usually employed in preaching. This requires peculiar, and perhaps rarer talents; much more time, study, and expense to qualify them for the office; has much greater labour and fatigue; incurs more expense, by frequent excursions; exposes much more to public censure and odium; and requires much more intense application to furnish the mind, so as to be a workman that needeth not to be ashamed, rightly dividing the word of truth. To discharge this part of the office in a proper manner, requires a life solely devoted to it. Such is my view of this text; now to confirm it.

The word translated "rule," is by no means exclusively applicable to that department of the pastoral office called ruling. Προεστῶς is rather a military than a civil officer: rather a commander in the field than a president in an assembly. Προεδρος would be the most proper word for the latter. Accordingly, in the Athenian council of 500, the seven of the Prytanes chosen by lot to preside every week, were called προεδροι; and the president of the day was called επιστατης. This is a too peaceful and inactive office to give a name to Christ's officers. I know not that they are ever so called in the New Testament, though they early assumed this title. But προεστῶς is a word which fully expresses their arduous, dangerous, and honourable office. It signifies an officer who goes before his men, and stands in the front of the battle. He encourages them by his example and exhortations, and leads them into action. Officers have the command and the care of the army; train and discipline the soldiers; and keep them to their duty. They take care to supply them with provisions, and prepare them for battle, by military speeches. Such an officer is the elder in the Church of Christ. Like a military officer, he trains and disciplines his troops; supplies them with wholesome provisions; rules them by the laws of Christ; instructs them in the will of their king; and prepares them for battle, by his public preaching. I apprehend, then, that the word προεστωτες here, is not to be referred exclusively, to any one part of the pastoral office, but to the office in general. It means, the elders who discharge, in an eminent manner, the duty of an officer in the army of Christ, and preaching is as essential a part of this, as ruling. That προεστώς refers to the office in general, is farther evident, from 1 Thess. v. 12.—where the same persons who are said to labour among them, and to admonish them, are called also προϊσταμενους. Indeed, I am astonished that any person who has ever looked into the Greek Testament, should think that the προεστώτες were an order inferior to preachers. There is not a higher word to denote pastor, in all the Word of God. They are Christ's military officers. Accordingly, they are called also, Heb. xiii. 17.—ἡγουμενοι, or military leaders. Agreeably to this, we find, that when one of the elders began to be distinguished above his colleagues, he assumed these very appellations as the most honourable. He exclusively appropriated to himself, προεστώς, and ηγουμενος, as well as επισκωπος, or bishop. But especially, can there be any thing more unfit to the character of military officers, than an order of lay-elders?

My sense of the passage, may be illustrated by a simile. "Let the kings who rule well, be accounted worthy of double honour, especially those who distinguish themselves as the protectors of religious liberty." Here ruling well, refers to the whole kingly office, and the word "especially" distinguishes a particular department of the duty of a king. "Let virtuous and distinguished legislators, be esteemed worthy of double honour, especially those who labour for the abolition of the slave trade." Who would infer from this, that members of Parliament were each confined to a particular department. Each member has a right to speak and vote upon every subject, though his time and talents may be chiefly employed on his favourite object.

Besides, if I am not greatly mistaken, grammar requires that οἱ κοπιῶντες have προεστῶτες πρεςβύτεροι, and not merely πρεσβύτεροι, for its antecedent. The phraseology is οἱ καλῶς προεστῶτες πρεσβύτεροι, and not οἱ πρεσβύτεροι οἱ καλῶς προεστωτες. But common sense requires that the προεστῶτες πρεσβύτεροι, include the κοπιωντες εν λογω και διδασκαλια. If a general, after a victory, would write thus to the secretary at war, " the officers merit the highest praise, especially the general officers," he would write sense. But how ridiculous would it be to say, " the subaltern officers merit the highest praise, especially the general officers." In the first instance, the word "officers" includes the general officers; but in the second, the general officers are not included among the subaltern officers. Now, this is exactly what the Presbyterian interpretation of this text makes the apostles say, " Let ruling elders be counted worthy of honour, especially the preaching elders." Μαλιστα is properly used, when a part is distinguished out of the whole; or one out of a number. Compare this passage, with 2 Tim. iv. 13.—" Bring with you the cloak, and the books, especially the parchments." Here, the generic word books includes the parchments, as a particular sort of the books which he had desired him to bring. But how ridiculous would it have been to have said, " Bring the cloak, especially the parchments."

Thus have I examined the meaning of this much disputed portion of Scripture. I have first endeavoured to show, that granting Presbyterians their own interpretation of this text, and that it fully establishes an order of lay-elders, or an order of rulers in the church, who are not pastors, that even this did not give a church session any authority to judge in all matters for the church or congregation. Even in this case, the whole church should judge, and those officers carry the result into execution. Again, that granting the exclusive management of church affairs to the session, gave it no authority to legislate, as the whole church, or the united voice of all the churches upon earth, have no right to make the slightest alteration, amendment, or addition with respect to the laws of Christ's Church. Further, that granting a distinction of order in elders to be established from this verse, it would make two orders of pastors, and not a distinct order of lay-elders. And, lastly, that a distinction of order of any kind, is neither necessary, probable, nor possible, from this verse. It constitutes, indeed, a plurality of pastors, in every perfectly organised church, who, being of different gifts, should be usually employed in the department best suited to each; that there should be a gradation of support according to talents, zeal, and diligence; and that the highest is due to those who are distinguished *for labouring in word and doctrine.* This plurality of elders or pastors in a church, is called (1 Tim. iv. 14), the Presbytery or Eldership. The modern signification of the word Presbytery, as consisting of the ministers and representative lay-elders of the congregations of a whole district, is not known in Scripture, nor in all the first ages of Christianity.*

* Chrysostom supposed the Presbytery spoken of (1 Tim. iv. 14), to have been a synod of bishops. To what extravagance will men run, who give themselves up to a party, and take their opinions from their sect, and not from the Bible!

CHAPTER VI.

OF INDEPENDENCY.

I HAVE an objection against imposing names of *human invention* upon *the things of the Spirit*. When I use the words Independency and Independents, for that form of church government, instituted by the apostles, and those who now embrace it, I would be understood to do it, not of choice, but of necessity. The disciples of Christ are properly called *Christians, saints*, or *brethren*, and an assembly of these, for the purpose of enjoying the ordinances of Christ, according to his appointment, is called a *church*. Now, these are the words I would always wish to use to denote the same objects; but it has happened that some of them have been so abused and prostituted to other significations, that it is impossible to use these plain Scripture words without obscurity. There is now the Church of Rome, the Church of England, the Church of Scotland, the Church of Secession, &c., &c., &c. In speaking therefore of a church formed on the model of the apostolical churches, we are obliged to call it an *Independent* Church, to distinguish it from the others, which have usurped the name. Still, however, we use this, not as the name of Christ's Church, but of the particular mode of the government of an apostolical church, to mark its distinctive feature. The apostles had no occasion to use this, or any other word of the same nature, for the same purpose, because no different form of government had been erected. It is obvious, then, that this use of the word *Independency*, is very different from sacrament, eucharist, altar, clergy, and a multitude of other such names, which the wisdom of men has imposed upon the ordinances of God.

That the government of Christ's appointment, is what is called Independent, is obvious from the rule which he gave for the settling of private offences among his disciples. Matt. xviii. 15–18.—" Moreover, if thy brother shall trespass against thee, go and tell him his fault, between thee and him alone : if he shall hear thee, thou hast gained thy brother. But if he will not hear *thee, then* take with thee one or two more, that in the mouth of one or two witnesses, every word may be established. And if he shall neglect to hear them, tell *it* unto the church : but if he neglect to hear the church, let him be unto thee as an heathen man, and a publican." Here the last appeal is to the church. He does not say, if he does not hear the church, take him to the Presbytery, and if he does not hear the Presbytery, take him to the Synod, &c., but if he hear not the church, " let him be unto thee as an heathen man, and a publican." I know, indeed, that various subterfuges have been invented to evade the force of this plain Scripture. Every sect has attempted to find its own discipline in this passage, whilst individuals, to apologise for what they cannot justify, have attempted to darken its meaning so as to make it of no practical use. The multiplicity of interpretations, in the opinion of Dr. Stillingfleet, is an argument to prove that it is totally inexplicable ; in my opinion it proves only what is proved by the variety of sentiments on every other point in Scripture, the perversity, the selfishness, or the prejudice of professing Christians. What ! has the Lord Jesus given a precept, in a case of such importance, and of such frequent occurrence, which cannot be understood ? Did he wish to be, or could he not avoid being unintelligible ? Must the Holy One of Israel speak with the darkness and evasion of an heathen oracle ? If he did not mean to be understood, why did he speak ? If he meant to be understood, why did he not speak in intelligible language ? If we cannot find out who are the divinely appointed arbitrators of our differences, he might as well have said nothing on the subject. What an insult upon the Holy Ghost to represent his language to be so vague and indeterminate, that it cannot be understood ? Christ has said " tell it to the church ;" is there no way of coming at his meaning ? Has the word *church* no determinate meaning in the New Testament? But Dr. Stillingfleet is of opinion, that if the discipline Christ has appointed, be executed, it is not material by whom. Is it then the same thing, whether a law be enacted by the lawfully appointed legislators, or by any other body of self-constituted men? or that a criminal be tried by a lawful judge and jury, or by men who assume the right of judgment, without the countenance of lawful authority? If Christ has appointed any particular referees, it is as really a breach of his injunction to appoint any other, as it would be totally to neglect that instance of discipline. But is there any native necessary obscurity in the precept, arising from the promiscuous use of the word *church*, in the New Testament? If it is now in any measure obscure, it has been rendered so, not from the ambiguity of the Scripture use of the word, but from its prostituted application in modern acceptation, and the sophistry, and subtleties of interested, prejudiced, or bigoted men; we find no difficulty in the passage until we hear the forced explanations of it given by controvertists, and our mind begins to be distracted, and the subject obscured by the smoke of their unhallowed fires.

I lay it down, then, as an axiom, that Christ meant some *determinate thing* by the word *church*, and that there must be sufficient evidence in the New Testament to lead the humble, teachable inquirer into that meaning. Christ must have spoken intelligible language. Now, to investigate the Scripture-use of the word *church*.

In every language there are two different processes recognised, which affect the signification of words, appropriation and extension. The one confines them to a part of their original territories, the other extends them a little beyond their natural limits. This is not peculiar to the language of Scripture, but is practised in treating of all the arts and sciences, and the whole business of life. Thus the word angel literally signifies a messenger, and is not naturally confined to any description of messengers. But the Bible hath in a manner appropriated that word to denote an order of beings, whose employment is that of messengers of the Most

High, sent forth to minister to the heirs of salvation. And though it may occasionally, even in Scripture, claim its natural rights, being sometimes used for other messengers, yet it is the *appropriated name* of that order of beings called angels. The same may be said of the words *apostle, elder, bishop*, &c. Sometimes they are appropriated upon particular subjects or departments, while they enjoy the full extent of their signification upon others; and sometimes the same word is differently appropriated upon different subjects. Thus, while the words angel, apostle, &c., are usually confined to a particular province in Scripture, they have unbounded license in profane authors, of the same date; and thus when men use the word minister, conversing upon political subjects, it is immediately understood that they mean the first minister of state. But if they are conversing on religion, it is as readily understood to be *the minister of the congregation*. On the other hand, sometimes a word will come through time to exceed its natural boundaries, and be extended to include ideas not necessarily, nor naturally inherent in it. Thus χειροτονεω, literally signifies to vote by holding up the hand, and was used in the popular assemblies of Athens in contradistinction to the vote by scrutiny, which was denoted by ψηφιζω, from ψηφος, the pebble used by the voters. But in an advanced period of the history of this word, we find that it sometimes dropped the principal idea altogether, and was extended to denote election in any manner, and even the conferring of an office, not by election but individual nomination. Our language has recognised the same abusive principle, in the words man-midwife, head-pleurisy, &c. Now, to apply this reasoning to the point in dispute. We are to enquire what εκκλησια literally signifies; what it was originally applied to; what it came to be applied to in the process of its history; what is its use in other instances in Scripture; how it is used in profane authors of the same date; whether in the New Testament, it hath been appropriated, or extended; and if appropriated, to what? Proceeding thus, we shall find, that in the New Testament it is invariably used, either for an individual congregation, or the whole community of Christians.

Εκκλησια literally signifies an assembly *called out* from others, and is used among the Greeks, particularly the Athenians, for their popular assemblies summoned by their chief magistrate, and in which none but *citizens* had a right to sit. By inherent power it may be applied to any body of men *called out*, and *assembled in one place.* If ever it loses the ideas of *calling out*, and *assembling*, it loses its principal features, and its primitive use. I will not say, that by the operation of the abusive principle I have described, it might not have come to lose even both, after a length of time from its first introduction; but this I say, that I no where find it in profane writers, nor in the Scriptures speaking of civil affairs, to have lost either, but especially the latter. Nor will I be driven from my position by the use of this word in the 19th chap. of Acts. That assembly, however tumultuous, irregular, and unlawful it may have been, was a *meeting of the citizens called together* by the silversmiths. The craftsmen were *called together* (verse 25), by Demetrius, who, inflamed by his speech, burst out into intemperate acclamations to their goddess Diana. The rest of the citizens were roused and assembled by their noise, and adopting their zeal, though many of them knew not the cause, they rushed into the theatre—the very place of public deliberation. Though, then, it was an irregular, lawless assembly, it was nothing a-kin to an English mob, but rather like a parliament assembling, being summoned, not by the king, but by some incendiary among themselves. Still more strongly may it be affirmed, that it is no where used by profane writers to denote any body of men, but in their *assembled* capacity; they are called εκκλησια only as *assembled*.

Such being the origin and use of this word among the Greeks, to what may it be legitimately applied when used in sacred things? It may signify any *assembly called out* from the world, and *united in Christ.* Agreeably to this, whenever it is used in Scripture in a sacred sense, that is, as applicable to believers, we find that it is invariably appropriated to an individual assembly of Christians, meeting to enjoy the ordinances of Christ,* or the Christian community in general. Whenever the apostles made a number of converts in any place, they separated them from the congregation, by forming them into an εκκλησια, or church. And just as in the Athenian assemblies none but citizens could sit or vote, so none but the citizens of the new Jerusalem were allowed to join themselves to this company. As in the Parliament many may be present to hear, though none but senators speak or vote; so in a church of Christ, many are present to hear the Gospel of salvation, but none are admitted as members of the εκκλησια, but those who are first by that Gospel made citizens of heaven. But with equal propriety may this word be applied to all the Christians in heaven and earth, as assembled in Jesus. Nor does this application stretch it a whit beyond its natural and intrinsic meaning. It is as literally and as truly applied to the one as to the other. All the saints on earth, and all the saints in heaven, are assembled in him, as really as the branches of a vine are united in the trunk, the stones of a building upon the foundation, or the members of the body with the head. With the strictest truth all Christians may be said to be already "in heavenly places in Christ." This double application of the word is neither foreign nor forced, incorrect nor indistinct. When it is used indefinitely, it applies to the community of believers assembled in Christ; when it is used with respect to an individual church, which is its most general application, the context, or the nature of the circumstances, gives sufficient intimation. Let any one take the trouble to run over all the places where it is found in the New Testament, and I will be bold to say, he will not find a single text, which will not fairly explain on this hypothesis. The cases where it may occur in the civil or unappropriated sense, are not accompanied with the smallest difficulty, the context, or a note of appropriation as " Church of Christ,"

* Where this word is used, for the Christians of a family, it is rather a confirmation of this than an exception. Every Christian family, meeting morning and evening for worship, may be properly considered a little church.

&c., sufficiently marking the difference. Those who, from this circumstance, would argue the impossibility of ascertaining the meaning of the word church in Matt. xviii. 17., and elsewhere, will find the same difficulty in the words apostle, angel, and innumerable others. Indeed the admission of this principle, and I see it admitted, and acted upon, by some very ingenious men, would involve, in impenetrable darkness, the clearest point in theology. If it be maintained, that the meaning of a word so important, so frequently used in the epistles, could not be ascertained, why should not this be the case with others? Were such a principle established in criticism, I have no hesitation in saying, that there is not an ancient author could be understood; that there is not a passage so clear in any author, in any language, upon any subject, which could not be so perplexed by the ingenuity of a sophist, that the ablest critic could not unravel it. Critics would be ashamed to reason thus on a passage in Homer or Sophocles. Grant only to the inspired writers, what will be granted to all—that they had a meaning in their words, and wrote to be understood, and it will be our fault if we cannot understand them.

Having stated the literal meaning, the profane and sacred application of the word εκκλησια, let us next examine the claims of its modern* acceptations. It is quite a cameleon. It is as various in its meaning, as the necessities of each party require. Sometimes it is a church session; sometimes an individual church; sometimes a classical Presbytery; sometimes a synod; sometimes a general assembly; sometimes church rulers; sometimes all the churches of a province or kingdom. Truly, if the Scripture gives ground for all these, it is more dark and perplexing than was ever an answer of the Sybil. Is not the bare statement a refutation of the fact? and the supposition a calumny on the oracles of God? But the practice of Presbyterians themselves, is a complete refutation of this hypothesis. They do not speak promiscuously of all their assemblies

---

* I call them modern, because they are later than the New Testament.

by the name church, but have a distinct name for each, as the congregation, the session, the Presbytery, the Synod, &c. Now, if each order of these courts be a church, as well as each congregation, and the collective congregations, why do they not speak of them by the Scripture name? Why have they imposed upon them names of their own invention? Evidently because they would otherwise be unintelligible. If one of their writers on church discipline was to speak of all their assemblies by the name church, without additional marks of distinction, his readers would not understand him; yet this is the very inaccuracy they charge upon the writers of the New Testament. They suppose them to speak promiscuously of the greatest variety of subordinate courts, as well as assemblies of a different nature, by the same name, without any mark of distinction to guide the reader. Now, I think this is a very fair criterion; Scripture ordinances should be sufficiently intelligible by Scripture names, without the use of any other. I believe it will be found a very just conclusion, *that the institutions which have not a name in Scripture, have not an existence in Scripture.* Let Presbyterians, then, use nothing but the Scripture names, and their doctrine of subordinate courts will be jargon. By their unnatural extension of this word, they have taken it in modern use from that which alone deserves it—the individual assemblies of the saints. Let us suppose, then, that εκκλησια might have been legitimately appropriated to denote any one of these assemblies, this appropriation will take it from all the rest. If a session is a church, then a congregation cannot be a church; if either of these be a church, then a Presbytery cannot, without confusion, be usually so denominated; and if a Presbytery is a church, then it will take that name from all inferior and superior courts. Now, if these courts be Scriptural, let their advocates produce their distinct Scriptural names. No word can have two appropriate meanings upon the same subject; εκκλησια may be a civil assembly and appropriated also to a religious assembly; but in neither civil nor religious matters can it be appropriated as the distinctive name of two different assemblies, the one subordinate to the other. It may denote a particular assembly of saints, and the community of Christians assembled in Jesus; but without confusion, it cannot be used as the appropriated name of a particular and general assembly of the same sort. This is clear from the names of civil courts. Though some of these be such as to be literally applicable to all, yet they are not so appropriated. Thus sessions, assizes, &c. Thus also in the Church of England, though each of the orders are called clergymen, yet for this very reason it could not be the appropriated distinctive name of any one of them. There is curate, rector, bishop, &c. For the same reason, though *bishop* was the common name of all Presbyters originally, yet when it was appropriated to one of the number, it was taken from all the rest. If, then, the word church be generally applicable to such a variety of assemblies, each assembly must have a distinctive name besides; to produce which out of Scripture will be rather an arduous task. Besides, in speaking particularly of each of these assemblies, the common name could not be used, any more than the name clergyman would distinguish a bishop from a Presbyter. When our Lord says, then "tell it to the church;" if he intends Presbyterian ecclesiastical courts, to which does he refer? If to the session, then all higher appeals are cut off; for if the offending brother will not "hear the church, let him be as an heathen man and a publican;" if it means a general synod or assembly, then all inferior courts are cut off. But if *church* be also the Scripture name of an individual assembly of saints, consisting of pastors and church members, is not the obscurity still increased? Whether must the congregation or the session be appealed to?

I have hitherto combated this multifarious application of the word, upon the supposition that it was equally proper to any one of the things signified. But I have objections against the propriety of applying it either to church rulers, or the associated churches of a province or kingdom, both from the meaning of the word and its original application, as well as its use in Scripture. According to the intrinsic ideas contained in εκκλησια, the churches of a province or kingdom could not be so called, because they are never assembled. Now this would be *an assembly, never assembled.* Should it be said that they are present in their representatives, as the nation may be said to be present in the parliament (besides that, this is too figurative for a distinctive or appropriated name), then private individuals can no more be called members of the Church of Scotland, &c., than private subjects members of parliament. None are members of an assembly, but those actually possessing a right to sit in that assembly. A national or provincial church, in this view, consists of church rulers alone, or rather a selection of church rulers. Besides, church is used in Scripture, according to its literal signification, for an assembly of saints *actually* assembled; it would not therefore be used in such a loose sense in the first stages of its history. Words may come to lose their leading idea, but it is always by the operation of time, and change of circumstances. Add to this, that the Greeks did not use it for representative assemblies; but assemblies in which all the citizens had a right to be present. None were represented, but the members who composed the assembly. Children, females, and slaves were not represented. This last objection lies equally against church rulers being at any time exclusively called *the church.* Εκκλησια was a popular assembly, distinguished from συνκλησια, an assembly of nobles or senators. It seems very clear that this latter would be the most appropriate name for a court of church rulers: I freely acknowledge, that the literal ideas contained in the word εκκλησια might be applicable to a court of church rulers, but it would be upon a principle different from its usual application among the Athenians, as well as its other acknowledged applications in Scripture. A church of Christ is so called, because it consists of members called and separated from the world by the Gospel of Christ, and united in the enjoyment of his ordinances. But if a court of church rulers were so called, it would be, not because they were called out of the world, and united in the service of Christ, but called out from their brethren to legislate for, and govern them. Now, such a use of the word would be nothing a-kin to the other. They would not be the same word, though composed of the same letters. Between the particular and general use of the word church, the leading ideas are common; both are called out of the world by the Gospel, separated from it, and assembled in Christ. But between these and the word as signifying church rulers, there is no resemblance. To appropriate a word for a double purpose upon the same subject, by a process so different, is altogether unexampled. Neither is this agreeable to the principle that generally operates in language, to extend and diversify the signification of words. They are usually correctly and unambiguously applied at first; variety of signification grows by abuse and time, as a fact related by many individuals will be known in different countries, with a loss or addition of circumstances. Add to this, that in a new science or art, when an author is obliged to borrow and appropriate a word, he doth so generally agreeably to its natural import and approved use in the language from which it is taken. If, then, our Lord had taken εκκλησια to denote an individual assembly of saints, he would have taken συνκλησια for a court of church rulers, if he had instituted such a court.

But what saith the Scripture? This must finally decide the pretensions of these different claimants. Is there a single passage in which this word must be acknowledged to have any of those significations I combat? Does it occur in any place where it plainly refers to a court of church rulers, or to a number of churches under an associated government? Are not all the passages in which it is said to be so used as undecided as the present? Upon what principle, then, of fair criticism can it be argued? If they could produce any one occurrence of it, in which it must incontestibly be so understood, there might be some colour of ground so to understand it in others, though used with less perspicuity. But without an acknowledged foundation, they never can raise a superstructure. If the word church was in any one place explained to be a representative assembly, and an association of the churches of a kingdom, they might plead such a sense here with efficacy. But if it is never so explained, never can it be so interpreted here. On the other hand we can produce texts innumerable, where it signifies an individual assembly of saints, and in which our opponents must and do acknowledge that it hath such a signification. We can produce a number of passages in which a church of Christ is explained to consist of the saints of a particular church. By what authority, then, can they refuse it to have such a signification here? There is not the least intimation in any part of the New Testament of a representavive government. Nothing is said about a number of church rulers being selected as an ecclesiastical council over a number of individual churches; nor any such use of the word church, as including a number of individual churches. When the inspired writers speak of a single assembly of saints, they invariably call it a church; when they speak of a number of churches, or the churches of a province or district, they do not call them a church, but churches. Thus when Paul writes to the Corinthians, he addresses the "*Church* of God, which is at Corinth;" but when he writes to the Galatians, he addresses *the churches* of Galatia. Thus also when the Church of Jerusalem is spoken of, it is called *a church;* but when the aggregate of the individual churches of Judea and Samaria are spoken of, they are not called the Church of Judea, or the Church of Samaria, but the *churches* of Judea, and the *churches* of Samaria. Thus also *the Church* of Cenchrea, (Rom. xvi. 1), and the *churches* of Achaia; the *Church* of Ephesus, the *Church* of Smyrna, &c. But when they are spoken of in the aggregate, it is the seven *churches* of Asia, not the *Church* of Asia (Rev. i. 4, and ii. 1, &c). I know indeed that with respect to Jerusalem and Corinth, it is alleged that the saints in those cities must have been too numerous to have assembled in one place. But I need not take up my time in showing how or where they might assemble, or in ascertaining their numbers. They are not more numerous than I wish them to have been; and the

Scripture itself refutes the objection in both instances—Acts ii. 44, 1. Cor. v. 4, and xi. 18. In these passages they are expressly shown to have met in the same place.

But if there were really any ambiguity in Matt. xviii. 17., can there be a better way of ascertaining truth than by referring to the use of it in the writings of the New Testament of a later date, thus comparing spiritual things with spiritual? Can there be a better commentary on the Gospels than the Epistles? If any thing is not fully explained, but hinted at, by Christ, where will we go for farther information, but to the apostles, who were to finish the revelation he had begun, and fully illustrate, what may be said to lie in embryo in his words? Can any thing then be a clearer commentary on Matt. xviii. 17, if it needed any, than 1 Cor. vi. 1—where Paul speaks of another similar case of discipline? Can it be supposed that the apostle would institute one way of terminating disputes, and his master another? The apostles makes the *saints* of *an individual church* at Corinth, the arbiters of civil disputes. Would he have done so if his Lord had referred personal disputes to the cognizance of an ecclesiastical council? No man will say so.

The ingenious Dr. Campbell, who, in his lectures on church history, has treated this subject with demonstrative clearness, alleges the acceptation of the word among the Jews with signal success.* He shows that it was appropriated with them in the same manner either to the whole nation or Church of Israel, which was a type of the universal Church of Christ, or to those that met for worship in the same synagogue. Now, this being the then received acceptation in the time of our Lord, he would not have been understood, had he employed it in any other; and as he could not intend the whole commonwealth of Christians, it must be a congregation of Christians. But how unintelligibly do they represent Christ as speaking, who give so many acceptations to the word church? Suppose we insert

* See Dr. Campbell's Lectures on Church History, vol. 1, p. 320.

congregation instead of church, who would understand him to refer to ecclesiastical courts. Yet *congregation* is no more fixed by Presbyterians to their assemblies for public worship, than εκκλησια was to denote the members of a synagogue, or of an apostolical church. Neither is εκκλησια more applicable, nor indeed is it so applicable to the various Presbyterian assemblies, as *congregation*. A synod or general assembly might have been at first denominated congregation, as well as by the term by which they are now known. What Presbyterian now would say "tell it to the congregation," intending by that a church court. Yet this would not be more senseless than what they attribute to the Lord Jesus Christ.

Another argument Dr. Campbell brings, equally convincing, is derived from the practice of the churches in the first ages. "Another collateral and corroborative evidence," says he, "that by εκκλησια is here meant not a representative body, but the whole of a particular congregation, is the actual usage of the church for the first three hundred years. I had occasion formerly to remark, that as far down as Cyprian's time, which was the middle of the third century, when the power of the people was on the decline, it continued to be the practice, that nothing in matters of scandal and censure could be concluded, without the consent and approval of the congregation. And this, as it appears to have been pretty uniform, and to have subsisted from the beginning, is, in my opinion, the best commentary which we, at this distance, can obtain on the passage." See page 325, vol. 1.

I may add farther, that the circumstance of the word *church* being afterwards used to signify the house of worship, is a very clear corroborative argument to show that an individual worshipping assembly of Christians, and not a representative body of church rulers, or the churches of a particular district, was first so called. Though this be not Scriptural, yet it shows the primitive application of the word, when the house received the name of the assembly. Just as the Jewish houses of worship were called synagogues, from the assembling of the people therein. This shows what sort of assembly a church was. Had it been a meeting of church rulers, like a Synod, &c., none but the places of their assembling would have been called *churches*. This, in my opinion, is the most unexceptionable species of historic proof. It can never be biased, and is often the surest criterion of the truth of facts.

CHAPTER VII.

THE INDEPENDENCY OF THE APOSTOLICAL CHURCHES PROVED FROM THE APOSTOLICAL INJUNCTIONS, AND INFERRED FROM OTHER CIRCUMSTANCES IN THE EPISTLES.

NOT only is the independency of individual churches proved from the origin, and profane and sacred acceptation of the word by which they are denominated; but the laws and regulations given by the apostles for their direction, put the matter beyond doubt. The whole discipline of Christ's house is, without exception, committed to the individual church, consisting of the pastors and brethren of one congregation. Apostolical injunctions, which cannot be obeyed in any other than an Independent church, implies the necessity of Independency. Now of this sort, are all the rules, with respect to the administration of discipline. It is the whole church, and not a church session, that is to receive members. Rom. xiv. 1.—"Him that is weak in the faith, *receive ye.*"—"*Receive ye.*" Now, no Presbyterian congregation could comply with this injunction. The brethren have nothing to do with the receiving of members. This province is entirely usurped by the minister and lay-elders. The epistle to the Corinthians, is addressed to the Church of God at Corinth, which is explained, 1 Cor. i. 2, to consist, not of minister and lay-elders, but of "them that are sanctified in Christ Jesus, called to be saints." Now, the power of excommunication is expressly vested in the whole church (chap. v. 4), not in church rulers alone. If a Presbyterian congregation would presume to interfere with their rulers upon such a point, it would be actual rebellion. Nay, the whole congregation, minister, elders, and people could not put away from their communion the grossest adulterer, if the

F

superior ecclesiastical judicatories would think proper to skreen him. But the church at Corinth, is commanded to put away from *among themselves,* that wicked person (verse 13), and to purge out the old leaven (verse 7). To judge of the application of discipline, that is to examine and judge whether a crime be chargeable upon an accused member, is also stated (verse 12), to be the business of the whole church. " Do ye not judge them that are within ?" The whole church is to judge the accused person, though the church rulers are to execute the judgment. Now, a church which cannot admit an apostolical direction, cannot be apostolically constituted. Indeed, excommunication, though the highest act of church authority, is so peculiarly the business of the whole church, that the apostle does it not himself by an act of apostolical authority, but commits it to the saints themselves, that there might be an example and model to all future ages. Likewise, in Gal. v. 12, he does not say, " I cut off those that trouble you," but " I would that they were cut off." The restoration of fallen brethren upon repentance, is also the duty of the whole church, 2 Cor. ii. 6, 7, 8 ; Gal. vi. 1. Here, it is observable, that the excommunication was not the act of a select part of the church, but " was inflicted of many." We have also seen that the church was the final judge of personal and civil disputes among its members—Matt. xviii. 17 ; 1 Cor. vi. In these, and other instances, the instructions and commands given, necessarily suppose the constitution of the church to which they were directed, to have been Independent ; for to no other could they have been applied ; in no other could they have been executed.

It will not be deemed a sufficient answer to this, that the apostolical discipline may be executed in spirit and substance, though not by those apostolically appointed. The thing must not only be done, but done as it is commanded. The command must not only be obeyed in its primary object, but in the appointed manner, by the divinely appointed agents. Here we have not only the thing commanded to be done, but the persons commanded to do it. We may as well say, that we need not execute apostolical discipline, as that it may not be done by those apostolically appointed. The judges are here as clearly appointed, as the thing to be judged. To fulfil a law, we must not only do the thing the law directs, but in the manner directed by the law. The law ordains the murderer to die, but it does not warrant any but those legally appointed to judge, condemn, and execute him. The king summons his parliament; but the senators, intent upon their rural amusements, or the improvement of their estates, send their stewards. They meet; they enact laws; they send them to the king. Will he, will the constitution recognise such legislators? And will the Lord Christ recognise the proceedings of the unconstitutional judicatories, of what are called representative churches? Shall they be excused, who on account of business, amusement, or indolence have neglected their duty as church-members? They have no more authority to delegate the performance of this, than of any other duty which they owe to society, to their families, or to God. Would private Christians let any one persuade them, that they were to be present in heaven by representation only? It would be every whit as easy to prove the one as the other. In all the New Testament, there is not the shadow of a representation, in the Church of Christ.

To attend to the affairs of Christ's house, is the *privilege* of all church members. It argues ingratitude, contempt, and indifference, to transfer that right to others. But this is not only a privilege, but a duty, and each member is answerable for the personal discharge of it. Every individual member has the king's commission, and the king's command, to attend to the affairs of his kingdom, in concert with his brethren. If any neglect their duty, or pretend to depute others to represent them, they are guilty of disobedience to Christ, indifference to his laws, interest, and honour; and are traitors, as presuming to alter the constitution of his church. If any man, or body of men, assume the right by invasion, or accept it by delegation, they are usurpers, and act without, and contrary to the king's commands. But the very idea of a transference of duty, in religious matters, is absurd. None can think, judge, or act for another, with respect to spiritual things.

I have supposed the work to be done, and discipline to be duly administered. But I deny that this ever is, or can be the case in a perfect manner, when *they* do not the work who are divinely appointed. The imperfect state of discipline, in all Presbyterian churches, fully proves the assertion. Some of them, indeed, have a multiplicity of human rules, which they are very rigorous in putting into execution; but I know not any, that act fully up to the discipline of the churches of the New Testament.

Not only is discipline and all church power committed to the individual church, but every direction, command, and exhortation is suited to such alone. There are laws sufficient in the New Testament for the government and conducting of an Independent church, but not a single rule, or precept, or example for the government of a number of churches combined. All its rules and examples are applicable to individual congregations only. Independent churches have either precept or example for every case that can possibly occur. They are not obliged to proceed one step upon dubious ground. But it is evident that Presbyterians are obliged to vindicate their discipline, &c., by borrowing what is applied to individual churches. Thus the epistles to the church at Rome, to the church at Corinth, &c., &c., are epistles to individual churches, and speak uniformly either of individual duties, or reciprocal duties of church-members, and of the duties of the elders to the flock, and of the flock to the elders. But there is not a word as to the duties of elders as members of an ecclesiastical assembly, or of the duties of private Christians as members of an associated church. Now, if there was such a thing as an associated church under the same government, is it not strange we should have no rules with respect to it; that elders should have no directions as to their duties in these assemblies; and private Christians as to their relations to them? The individual flock is often called upon to obey their pastors or rulers, but never is either flock or shepherd commanded to obey a superior assembly. The apostles frequently and earnestly inculcate love among the church members, and warn them against schism and divisions. Not a word, however, do they say as to the duty of union among several churches under the same government, nor of the sin of one church separating from another. Is not this a plain proof that they were not externally joined? But men have got a convenient way of quoting Scripture now; for what is said (1 Cor. i. 10), against the members of the same individual church going into factions and parties, they apply to prove the sin of one church separating from another, or individuals separating from the church in which they were educated. We never hear the terrific word *schism* in any other sense in modern application. But it is evident that the schisms which the apostle here reprobates, are not the separation of a part even of an individual church, so as to form another; for this may be often done to advantage; it is the members of the same church running into factions and cabals, against which he speaks. Thus, in every other instance, they have to borrow what is spoken to individual churches, and apply it to associated churches. Either the Scriptures are lame, or such associations are unscriptural.

There are various other indirect hints in the epistles, which will occur to the reader who is accustomed *to mine* into the Word of God, and *weigh* each particle, as more precious than the gold of Ophir. Truth is ever consistent, and that opinion which does not gain strength from a progressive acquaintance with the Scripture, is not likely to be a Scripture truth. That hypothesis that forbids a minute attention to the most casual and indirect circumstance divinely recorded, cannot be well founded. An instance of what I mean, we have in 2 Cor. iii. 1. The apostle reasons that he had not, like others, need of recommendatory letters either to or *from the church* at Corinth. Now, the manner of the apostle's speaking here, would have been altogether improper, had the church at Corinth been under Presbyterian church government. He speaks of the recommendatory letters as necessary to some, but unnecessary to him, as coming from the *Church*, not the Presbytery. Had the apostle been a Presbyterian, he would have subjected himself and this church to severe censure, had he received credentials from it. This is the prerogative of the Presbytery or church rulers alone.* How would a modern church judicatory resent it, if a Probationer were to receive credentials from one of their congregations? The apostle himself could not be received into the General Synod, if he could not produce his credentials from his Presbytery. Nor could any minister or congregation *regularly* give him their pulpit.

The whole strain of the letters of the apostle Paul to the churches, shows them to have been Independent. He uniformly addresses, praises, or blames the church itself, and never a church session or ecclesiastical council of any sort. In chapters v. and xi. of 1 Cor. he blames the whole members, with respect to the incestuous person, and their irregularities in eating the Lord's Supper. Had they been under Presbyterian government, the *brethren* could not have been guilty, in keeping the fornicator, because they had no authority for putting him out. The session and superior courts would have been exclusively to blame; and would, undoubtedly, have received marked apostolical censure. If improper persons are admitted to communion among Presbyterians, what private member takes the guilt upon himself; but, if he disapproves of it, exclaims against the session. Upon the same persons should the abuses of the Lord's Supper have been principally chargeable.

In like manner, when our Lord writes to the seven churches of Asia, he praises or blames them individually. He never censures one, for the errors of another, though, with great severity, he reprimands each, for the errors of any part of itself. He charges the whole church as guilty, in keeping or retaining in communion an erroneous or profligate member; but he

---

* See also Acts xviii. 27. When Apollos was disposed to pass over into Achaia, he received recommendatory letters from the brethren, not a classical Presbytery.

never charges one church, with the errors of another. Now, if they had been under the Presbyterian form of church government, all the churches would have been chargeable with the faults and defects of each, as much as the whole individual church was chargeable with those of its members. Neither does he call upon the one to reform the other; but each to reform itself. Now, had the churches of Lesser Asia been Presbyterian, our Lord would have written to the Synod or Presbytery, and not to the individual churches to reform themselves. A Presbyterian congregation cannot reform itself. Christ, therefore, could not have been the author of Presbytery.

CHAPTER VIII.

OBJECTIONS ANSWERED.

Having investigated the claims of Presbytery and Independency upon Scripture evidence, it may be proper to take notice of some objections that I have heard urged against the scheme which I defend. Some of these are really so futile, that I am almost ashamed to bring them forward, to give them a formal refutation. But I have observed in conversation on this subject, that when the advocates of Presbytery are driven from the Scriptures, they sometimes shelter themselves under the supposed defects of Independency, or advantages of Presbytery. And it is really astonishing with what superficial reasoning, they will impose upon themselves. A few of such objections I will mention, and dispatch with the utmost brevity.

1. It is alleged that "there are too many sects already, and that we should rather endeavour to unite those that are already formed, than form another." I perfectly agree with the objector, that there are too many sects already, and that it is our duty to endeavour to unite Christians in all things. But how is this to be done? Is it by each party proposing to throw away a part of what they look upon to be truth, and embrace a little of what they consider wrong, that they may splice up a worldly union? Is it by the church rulers of different sects, meeting to compromise their differences, like a reference after a quarrel in a country fair? Is it by such language as this, "I will give up so much, give you up so much, and we will meet?" Is this a Scriptural way to unite sects? Is it not rather for each to appeal to the Bible, and meet on that common ground? Should not the language be, " we cannot all be right, let us then try our systems by the standard of truth, adopt whatever it recommends,

and reject whatever it condemns?" Truly it is a very modest way of reasoning, that there are so many sects already, that there is no room for introducing the model which Christ hath left us in the churches of the apostles! If once Christians could be brought to *feel* it their duty to *cease from man*, and renounce every standard but the Bible, they would not be long in uniting. Every union that is attempted, or effected upon other grounds, is not of God, but of the world.

2. It is suspected that "the encouragement that is given to call in question the opinions of our forefathers, and scrutinize them so severely by the Scriptures, will excite such a spirit of innovation, that it will lead to universal scepticism." Nay, some go so far as actually to fix the time when such inquirers must be advanced into atheists.

Truly it is a very astonishing thing that a habit of searching the Word of God, of relying implicitly upon it, and comparing all human opinions with that standard, must lead to scepticism. As well may it be said, that a habit of trusting God will lead us to distrust him. The Scriptures then are to blame for commending the Bereans for "searching the Scriptures daily whether these things were so." If our ancestors at the Reformation, had been afraid of these consequences, they never would have dared to call in question the ancient usages of their fathers, or to have condemned them by the Word of God. Never can any hurt arise from searching the Scriptures, and a habit of being regulated by them. "To the law and to the testimony, if they speak not agreeable to this Word, it is because there is no light in them."

I do not however mean to say, that there are no extremes on this side of the question; but I do say, that these do not consist in comparing every human opinion about divine things, with the Word of God; in rejecting every tittle of what is contrary to this standard; and adopting the merest minutiæ of what is pointed out. To run into extremes here, must be to go farther than the Scriptures. While we keep upon this ground, we cannot advance too far. But in searching the Scriptures upon this, as well as every other subject, there is great need of humility, and a consciousness of our own nothingness in the sight of God. If ever we begin the search with a desire to go beyond others, and have the honour to be more sharp sighted than those who preceded us, we shall certainly err. The natural pride of the human heart shows itself in various ways, and it is not strange that it should sometimes lead even good men into singularities. The Scriptures are plain, but it is only "the Spirit that can lead us into all truth." In searching the Scriptures for the mind of God, we should never neglect to ask, not formally, but earnestly and continually, the guidance of that heavenly conductor. O what prayer! what self-abasement! what a thirst for truth! what self-denial, are necessary in those who would advance in the knowledge of divine things! If we depend upon our own superior sagacity, if we prize not the smallest Scripture truth as more precious than rubies, and are not ready to give up the dearest earthly possessions and connections rather than part with it; if we have not simplicity of view, and a single eye to the glory of God, it will not be strange if we go astray in our search. But if we are made willing to receive truth at the greatest risk, and conscious of our weakness, incessantly and importunately to crave the direction of the Spirit, I do not think that the God of truth will suffer us to be led astray. Whilst, therefore, we, like the Bereans, search the Scriptures for ourselves, let us not be *heady* or *high-minded*, but humbly wait at the feet of Jesus, to learn wisdom from his lips.

3. It is alleged that "the Presbyterian form of government is better calculated to repress heresy, preserve purity of doctrine, and authoritatively settle all disputes that arise among their congregations." But I ask how have they this power? Is it by force or persuasion? If it is by the latter, then Independents enjoy it in its utmost latitude; if it is by the former, then the Gospel disclaims it; Christ abhors it. Is not this evidently inconsistent with the whole spirit and letter of the Gospel? These are carnal, not spiritual weapons. Is not this to put a hand to the ark, and a distrust of the power of the Great Head of the Church, who bears it

upon his own shoulders? What is the crime in the nations which God hath always punished with the greatest rigour? Is it not that of presuming to take upon themselves the defence and protection of his people the Jews? Those who injured his people, are indeed punished; but those who stepped in between him and them, to take their confidence off himself, are punished with the utmost severity. Egypt, that oppressed Israel, was punished; but the crime was, as it were, afterwards forgotten; but Egypt that became the staff of Israel is not pardoned till this very day. From the overthrow of Nectanebus by Ochus, 350 years before Christ, it never has had a king of its own. Degraded from among the nations, governed by foreigners, enslaved and oppressed, God hath exhibited it as a malefactor in the gibbet, for a warning to others. He is as jealous of the prerogative of supporting his Church, as a husband is of the confidence and affection of his wife, and views every foreign interference, as an attack upon his honour. Will men, then, never learn to trust God with his own cause, and use only the means that he hath appointed to preserve his truths? Will they never cease to provoke his jealousy, by associations to defend his church? Is there any fear that ever the gates of hell will shake it off Immanuel's shoulders? Alas! that ever Christians should have thought of substituting human bulwarks, for the continual presence of Jehovah, who is as a *wall of fire around his Zion!*

But the Presbyterian method of preserving orthodoxy, and settling disputes, is not only unscriptural, but is always without any real advantage. They may keep their members from preaching contrary to their standard, but can they enable " the blind to lead the blind, without both falling into the ditch." Force may make a hypocrite, but can never make a Christian. Interest may constrain a carnal man to profess the leading truths of the Gospel, but midnight darkness will reign in his congregation. Among many there is a continual cry of *soundness* and *orthodoxy*, who appear to every spiritual man to be destitute of the truth, as it is in Jesus, and to hold the truth in unrighteousness.

Even among the stricter sects of Presbyterians, I am constrained to say, that while some of them do not fail to show their zeal by lifting up a testimony against the corruptions of the General Synod, they appear to be *hunting* after the world with equal avidity. And I know where it is said, "If any man love the world, the love of the father is not in him."

4. It is alleged in behalf of Presbytery that "in the multitude of counsellors there is safety; that several congregations must have more wisdom than one; and that an assembly of learned men must be better qualified to transact church matters than an ignorant multitude."

This reasoning might have some effect, if there was any thing left to the wisdom of man. The generality of Christians, are the "weak things of this world," and of all men living they are the least qualified for the arduous duty of legislation. But thanks be to God, he hath left no such things to be done by any. Every necessary law and direction are given, and nothing more is necessary, than to judge of their application, to which the most ordinary capacity is equal, in the use of the appointed means, and under the promised guidance of the Spirit. Poor despised Christians would indeed be ill qualified to appear in what is impiously styled a court of Christ. But the meanest and most ignorant of them are equal to judge of every case of discipline, that can occur in Christ's house; for it is said that "they shall be all taught of God." And indeed I would expect a more just determination from such, than from the representatives of all the churches on earth. Christ's presence is with the one, as being according to his own appointment, while it is likely the other shall be left to their own wisdom.*

---

* Such objectors differ very widely from the Apostle Paul, who supposes that even the weakest saints are capable of judging not merely of the spiritual concerns of the church, but also of settling the civil disputes of the brethren. 1. Cor. vi. 4.—"If then ye have judgments of things pertaining to this life, set them to judge who are least esteemed in the church." We are not to suppose from this however, that a church is always to select "the least esteemed" for the arbitration of civil differ-

I have heard, that the most usual, and the most effectual way that certain persons have taken to prejudice the minds of the people of this country against Independents, is, by representing them as "disorderly;"—"without discipline;"—"breaking down the hedge;"—"not coming in by the door."

In the New Testament, Christ calls himself the door; if any one, then, come not in at this door, I

ences. In my opinion the spirit of the passage is this—differences among brethren should be settled by arbitration of the church. Some of the Corinthians had transgressed this rule, and shown, by their appealing to the civil law, that they supposed there were not any among their brethren fit for this office. The apostle takes fire at the supposition, that those who were to judge wicked men and angels as assessors with Christ in the great day, should be esteemed unfit to judge in such comparatively trivial matters; and to show them that he looked upon all Christians to be qualified for this business, he bids them choose from among themselves even those that were accounted the weakest. As if he had said, to show you that they are wise in whom the Spirit of God dwells, let the "least esteemed" brethren be singled out upon any emergency, and they will wisely determine the matter. Then he subjoins, "I speak this to your shame;" you have looked upon all your brethren as unwise or unjust; the Spirit of God declares them all, even the least esteemed of them to be qualified to settle your disputes. Are you not then ashamed of your opinion and conduct, with respect to your brethren, judging so unfavourably of them, and differing so much from the judgment of God? That the apostle looked upon all the saints as fit for such an office, is clear, not only from the words "least esteemed," but also from the arguments of illustration in the 2nd and 3rd verses.—The saints judging the world and fallen angels. All the saints small and great, shall have this honour; therefore, to make the argument conclusive, all the saints must be fit for the duty of arbitration. But that a church is not bound *always* to select the "least esteemed" for this purpose, is clear, not only from the spirit of the passage already explained, but from what follows in the 5th verse—"Is it so that there is not a wise man amongst you? No, not one that shall be able to judge between his brethren?" This question supposes, that the church was at liberty to choose the wisest among the brethren. If then, the "least esteemed," are qualified judges, they are inexcusable, who will not be amenable to the decision of the most esteemed in the church: Corollary: If the weakest brethren are qualified to decide in matters of property, without appealing to the superior learning, wisdom, or judicial knowledge of a Presbytery or Synod, nay, without even appealing to the civil law, much more are they qualified to judge of every thing, as to the discipline of Christ's house.

heartily consent that all pulpit doors be shut against him. God is said to have made a hedge about his vineyard. But it seems now, that not Christ, but the Presbytery is *the door*, and, that the hedge of God's laws and institutions is not sufficiently high and prickly to keep out wild beasts, but it must be new-made, or at least mended by synodical authority. I am afraid that the generality, even of Christians, in this country, are much mistaken in their notions of the discipline of Christ's house. It is not the punctual attention to a wide system of human rules and regulations, that deserves the name of discipline, but the faithful execution of all the laws, given by Christ in the New Testament. Those sects, who, in this country, are most highly applauded for discipline, have, indeed, a rigorous code of human laws, and are peculiarly strict in the observance of them; but this is not discipline, but ecclesiastical usurpation and tyranny. Christ's discipline is calculated to prevent the entrance of the carnal professor, or to discover him, if he has been admitted. But, such a person, if he has a decent behaviour, and a sound of orthodoxy, might pass his life in the most rigorous Presbyterian connections, without detection. He must, indeed, have a considerable portion of pharisaical righteousness, but he will be admitted and continued without the life and power of godliness. This is a bold charge; if any sect of Presbyterians think it unjust, let them repel it. Before they can do this, they must be able to declare, that there is not an individual in their connection, that they do not look upon as a member of Christ. If they cannot make this declaration, their discipline is defective. I can refer them to an Independent church, consisting of more than six hundred members, in which, each individual can make this declaration concerning his brethren. I am therefore constrained to charge such objectors either with the grossest ignorance, or wilful misrepresentation. A want of discipline is what I charge upon Presbyterians. This is among the chief objections I have to them. "By their traditions, they have made void the law of God." But let them produce one single rule of discipline, appointed by Christ, which Independents refuse to admit. If they can show them any thing in Scripture, which they have not hitherto observed, I am sure they will not act up to their principles, if they do not adopt it with gratitude. But if they must be called "disorderly," because they reject the interference of man, in the things of God, because they refuse obedience to any rules but those of Christ, they are not concerned to repel the charge.

6. When Presbyterians are driven from the Bible, they sometimes shelter themselves under the wings of learned and pious men. "Are you wiser or better than our ancestors, who have shed their blood for Presbytery? If ever the spirit of God was with any body of men, it was with the Westminster divines." With some, it is very common to point at the Reformation as perfect, and every declension in principle or practice in professors, is a declension, not from the Scriptures, but the *Reformation.* They must indeed be blind, who do not look upon the Reformation as the greatest national blessing any people ever experienced; but those who thus idolize the Reformers, are guilty of setting up another God in Israel. However much we have been benefited by their labours, however, eminent were their attainments, it is "to the law, and to the testimony," not to the Reformers, we are directed as the standard of truth. As to the Westminster assembly, I am neither concerned to accuse nor condemn them. Episcopacy, Presbytery, and Independency have each had some of the most pious men in the list of their defenders; the Christian then can have no safe guide but the Bible.

CHAPTER IX.

REASONS WHY SOME ARE APT TO CONCLUDE, THAT THERE IS NO CHURCH MODEL IN SCRIPTURE.

I HAVE now given my reasons, why it is probable that the Scriptures of the New Testament contain a model of church government, and have examined the pretensions of Presbytery and Independency. Before I dismiss the subject of church government, I think it not amiss, to point out a few reasons, why some ingenious and pious men have not been able to discover any definite plan of any kind. If disinterested enquirers differ materially upon any point, in the examination of which they draw from a common source, there is likely to be some circumstances in their situation which leads to the difference: something that tends to involve the subject of inquiry.

1. In my opinion, one thing that tends to prevent some from seeing a model of church government in the New Testament, is, their being accustomed to take their ideas of the government of a spiritual, from that of temporal kingdom. They are apt to expect a vigorous plan, a-kin to their ideas of the best constituted civil governments. Whatever they judge the best calculated to govern a kingdom of this world, they look upon to be the fittest for the kingdom of Christ. In examining the Scriptures, then, it is no wonder they pass and repass the apostolical model, without seeing it. This is too simple to be effectual. Like Naaman the Syrian, who thought he was mocked by the prophet, when he prescribed as his cure, to wash in the waters of Jordan, they do not think it worth their trouble, even to give it a trial. They must have a firm and coercive plan, calculated to sustain christianity, and avenge it of its adversaries, as civil

rights are by civil laws. In this view I grant that the apostolical government must disappear, when brought into contrast or competition with either Presbytery or Episcopacy. Presbytery is a vigorous republic; but as I said elsewhere, *this* is not calculated to govern a single carnal family. It would be totally inefficient in worldly policy. To those, then, who have these worldly ideas, of Christ's kingdom, Independency is like David going out with his sling and pebbles against Goliah.

2. Others are much influenced by the carnal institutions, and pompous and multifarious Jewish heirarchy and sanhedrim. They are apt to transfer their ideas of the government of the Jewish church, to that of the Christian. If they are too impartial and enlightened to pretend to see any thing of this nature in the New Testament, they are inclined to think, that for this reason, we are left to form a model of church government for ourselves, according to time and circumstances. They do not find what they expect, and they hastily conclude that nothing is to be found.

3. Many inquirers have been all their lives so accustomed to the pompous, multifarious, and complicated systems of Presbytery, and Episcopacy, that when they go to the New Testament, they are led to overlook the simple apostolical plan. Their minds are filled with these intricate and punctilious systems, and are so habituated to the voluminous canons, laws, rules, regulations, acts, &c., &c., &c., which are to be found in almost all modern churches, that the Scripture directions for church government, appear altogether defective, obscure, and inadequate. They look into the Scriptures —they can find neither the Church of England, nor the Church of Scotland, nor any of the numerous sects formed on the same model—they instantly conclude, that there is no form of government revealed, or at most, is only coarsely blocked, to be variously formed or shaped according to the different humours of succeeding ages.

4. Another reason why some are inclined to conclude that there is nothing delivered in Scripture sufficient for the government of a church, is, that many writers have represented the matter much more clear, full, and

G

express, than it is in reality. With some there is not a doctrine more clearly and fully revealed in Scripture. They can see their favourite system in almost every page. When we hear men arguing from the tabernacle of Moses, to the polity of the Christian church, and asserting that Christ's faithfulness engaged him to be as explicit, full, and particular in giving a model for the government of his church, as Moses was in erecting the tabernacle, and thus determining *a priori*, with the most arrogant confidence, what Christ must have done, instead of considering what he has actually done, we are apt to expect *the most stately fabric*. When we go to the Scriptures themselves, if we cannot see through the magnifying glasses of particular sects, and swallow their *high probabilities* for demonstration, we are ready to conclude that there is no definite model at all. They make us expect a giant; we see a man of nothing but the ordinary size; and from our disappointment, we are ready to look upon him as a very dwarf. When we are made to expect too much, we are apt to be chagrined with our disappointment; and from our previous high imagination, we think the object more insignificant than it really is. Dr. Pococke tells us he had formed such an idea of the celebrated cataracts of the Nile, from the exaggerated accounts of former travellers, that when he came in sight of them, so very much did they fall below his expectations, so far from thinking these to be the objects of his curiosity, he asked when he should reach them; and it was not without surprise, that he was told they were already in view. Such is the case with many when they go to look for church government in the Scriptures.

5. Another thing that tends to hide the Scripture model from some inquirers, is their expectation of a *systematic* plan, or a formal treatise on the subject. They look for a *jointed* scheme, as methodically detailed, as Presbytery is exhibited in the Westminster Confession. When they look into the New Testament for such a plan, there is nothing like it to be found; the half of the whole epistles would scarcely contain such a system. The conclusion, then, is, that no form of church government is revealed. I would ask such

inquirers, upon what do they found their expectation of a system, or formal treatise on church government? Is there in the whole range of revelation, anything like a system, upon any subject? Is there any doctrine, is there any precept in Scripture delivered systematically? Take, for instance, the doctrine of the atonement; we do not find all the texts that illustrate this doctrine, collected into a system, but scattered from the beginning to the end of revelation. In the same manner, doctrines and precepts are not kept distinct, but intentionally intermingled, as it were, to prevent daring men from separating them, and setting up the one in opposition to the other. Doctrines are there taught practically, and precepts as flowing from the doctrines. We have in the same reasoning, in the same period, doctrine and precept. Thus in Phil. ii. 5-11, we have the doctrine of Christ's equality with the Father, and the precept of humility, as flowing from this, in the same period.

Indeed the manner of the revelation of divine truth, seems everywhere calculated and intended to excite to industry and search, and overcome our natural love of ease. Nothing is got by the lazy and inattentive. While on the one hand the great truths of revelation are so plain, that a man may, as it were, "run and read," being found in every page, so that "the wayfaring man, though a fool, cannot err therein;" on the other, it is so wisely regulated to spur us to exertion, that to exhibit completely, in all its features and bearings, and effectually prove any one point, it is necessary to turn over and over, search every page, compare spiritual things with spiritual, and examine the same doctrine in the different connections and views in which it is found in Scripture. In one text a doctrine is taught, perhaps with all its essential parts, but with some of its features more marked and prominent than others, according to the purpose the Holy Spirit meant it to serve on that particular occasion. In another, the same truth is brought forward in a different point of view, to serve a different purpose, with the features that were less prominent in the other, now more marked and distinct. Like a painter who would exhibit the same scene in a multiplicity of views, alternately bringing forward and putting into the background the different objects which he wants to represent. In one representation we have a palace as the chief object of attention, and its owner and family walking at some distance, are seen indistinctly. In another, the owner, if a celebrated personage, is represented as the chief object, and the palace is put into the shade. In another, if the painter has an intention to show us principally, some surprising and romantic scenery, we will see the palace and the master both put into the back-ground. Now, that we may form a clear and distinct notion of the master, the palace, and the scenery, we must view all the three pictures alternately, though all are represented in every one of them. Just so it is in Scripture. Its truths are so scattered, and variously represented, upon such various occasions, for so many distinct purposes, that we cannot have a complete view of any one of them, without examining the whole Bible. They are so interwoven, and have such a connection and mutual dependence upon each other, that a knowledge of one truth cannot thoroughly be obtained without a pretty general acquaintance with all the rest.* How absurd is it, then, to expect a system or formal treatise on church government! If the greatest truths of Scripture are revealed in this manner, how unreasonable is it to expect a different method on this point! Yet it appears to me that an attentive observer will find that the reason why many conclude there is no form of church government laid down in Scripture, is, because they do not find *a system.*

6. Some are led to think that there is no complete model intended to be exhibited in the New Testament, because all we have on this subject is given indirectly, and as it were unintentionally, and not sufficiently and fully explained. I have already hinted at the reason why the subject could not be consistently handled in

---

* I am sure I have found the advantage of this mode of revelation in examining this subject. Had it been methodically laid down in one place, and been accompanied with no difficulties, I would have been deprived of much additional knowledge, which I obtained, on many points, in my search.

an express and copious manner. As we are nowhere known in Scripture, but in the person of the first churches, we could not expect a direct address on the subject of church government: what is said to them is said to us. And as it would be absurd to expect that an apostle, after *forming a church* in any place, would, in a subsequent letter, give them express directions for *the formation of a church*, seeing this was already done; all we can expect is an indirect, and as it were, an unintentional allusion to what was done, and a scattered picture of their church order. Instead, then, of being disappointed at this mode of communication, no other can we reasonably expect. Indirect hints, incidental observations, and a passing view of their practice, is all that the *manner* of revelation can admit. The knowledge of their church order must necessarily be obtained from passages where the apostles are professedly treating of something else. But this is not the only thing to be proved in this manner. The chief knowledge that we have upon many other points, is obtained exactly in this indirect and circuitous way. A distinction between ordinary and extraordinary officers is generally admitted; yet the exact boundaries of their office is nowhere professedly and directly treated. A standing ministry is generally granted, yet the chief proofs of this must be obtained from incidental, indirect, and as it were, unintentional hints, and the example of the apostolical churches. To prove the truth of the Scriptures themselves, or any of their doctrines, nothing more is necessary than sufficient evidence to convince the humble earnest inquirer. It is by no means necessary to silence the caviller, and divest the disobedient of every pretext. There is not a single doctrine of revelation, the investigation and proof of which, is not accompanied with difficulties. "There must be heresies, that they which are approved may be made manifest." If, then, there are difficulties, even with respect to truths necessary to salvation, is it strange that there should be more in matters of comparatively less importance?

But though the subject is not largely explained and directly inculcated, the scattered incidental hints we have, when united, will be found not at all deficient for the purposes of church government. They will be found so complete, that a church of Christ will not be obliged to advance a step but on sacred ground. If this be the case, I would ask, what more do people want? I acknowledge that this mode of conveying divine truth does not suit those who inquire under the influence of a worldly spirit. When this is the case, it will not be strange if the Scripture materials should appear extremely scanty, and obscure, or confused. He will be too ready to think himself justifiable to take the side of worldly interest, unless the glare of evidence be such that it is impossible to resist it. He must be driven to duty by the thunders of Sinai, and not constrained by the gentle voice of Christ, when he says, "He that loveth me, keepeth my commandments." But we should not ask, like Henry IV. of France, "Is there salvation in such a church?" but with the apostle, "Lord what would'st thou have me to do?" ready to perform the least, as well as the greatest, of his commandments. We should continually hang upon the lips of our Master, ready with the alacrity and alertness of an angel, to perform his pleasure, glad of discovering it, though it should rob us of our property, or even our life. Such inquirers, I apprehend, will, after leisurely investigation, have no need to complain of a want of Scripture materials on this subject.

CHAPTER X.

CHARACTER OF CHURCH MEMBERS—OR THE NECESSITY OF PURE COMMUNION.

I HAVE now stated my views of church government, which, after an impartial and leisurely search, I have been constrained to embrace. But I have other reasons for separating from the General Synod, which still more pungently touch my conscience. One of these is the continual necessity I would be under, of prostituting the ordinances of Christ, by promiscuous communion. I shall therefore devote this chapter to point out the character of the members of the apostolical churches, and prove the necessity of pure communion. If I succeed, it will be evident, that I cannot conscientiously remain in a connection in which I am obliged to transgress so important a law of Christ. Even were I still a friend to Presbyterian government, I could not hold communion with the General Synod, nor any other Presbyterian connection that I am acquainted with. In none of them that I know of, is there purity of communion. Many of them, indeed, have raised very high human hedges around the Lord's table, and have enjoined very rigid terms of communion; but in none of them, I believe, is *credible evidence of the new birth* the test of membership. The gate is indeed shut against the openly profane, but the *decent* worldling may pass. At the same time, the child of God is excluded, if he cannot digest all the peculiarities of the sect, and load his soul with a mass of human obligations. If I am mistaken with respect to any involved in this charge, I will be glad to retract my censure, upon convincing information. I do not write to compliment, neither do I write to expose, but to reform. This is a point which I know many Presbyterians will not dispute. They acknowledge its desirableness, but doubt in the present state of the church, as they speak, its practicability. Nay, all who exclude any, virtually acknowledge this principle. For if they exclude one sort of sinners, by what authority do they admit another? I beg, therefore, that Presbyterians of this description, will accompany me through this chapter. Though they are able to disprove all I have said on the subject of church government, yet if I can convince them, of the sinfulness of admitting to communion, any but the credible disciples of Christ, and to persuade them to act up to their convictions, I will not have lost my labour. I would be glad, indeed, to see any of the Presbyterian connections, even thus far reformed. I acknowledge, I have been guilty in this instance hitherto, and am persuaded, that nothing has contributed so much to render my labours so unfruitful, though I had not the same views of the subject which I have at present. I look upon promiscuous communion to resemble adultery —it must be viewed by a jealous God, with the utmost displeasure. What is the reason, while there are multiplied sects of flamingly orthodox Presbyterians, that darkness covers our land, and gross darkness the people? Is the fault in man or in God? "Behold the arm of the Lord is not shortened, that he cannot save, nor his ear heavy, that he cannot hear," &c.

When we look into the epistles for the character of the members of apostolical churches, we find that they were considered as members of the body of Christ, 1 Cor. i. 2. In writing to the church at Corinth the apostle denominates the members *sanctified in Christ Jesus, called to be saints.* Were I not already too voluminous, I would quote and illustrate the addresses and many other passages of the epistles to the churches, to show the character of the members of the apostolical churches; I must be contented with referring to them —Rom. i. 7; 2 Cor. i. 1; Eph. i. 1; Phil. i. 1; Col. i. 2; ii. 6; 1 Thes. i. 1; 2 Thes. i. 1; 1 Pet. i. 2; 2 Pet. i. 1; 1 Cor. vi. 11, 19, 20; x. 17; xii. 27; 2 Thes. ii. 13, 14; 1 Cor. x. 16, 17. These passages will clearly point out what is the character of those who ought to be recognized as church members. The church at Rome is commanded to receive him that is *weak in the faith*. Now, this supposes that they were in the habit of judging of those whom they admitted to membership, and that those who had *no faith* were not to be received. For if they deliberately received any without evidence of faith, there could be no propriety in commanding them to receive him that was *weak in faith*. " Give not that which is holy unto dogs," is as much a command of Christ, as "thou shalt not kill ;" and whatever be its primary meaning, it is a general precept, and will hold more eminently true in this instance than in any other I am acquainted with. 1. Cor. iii. 10-16, is more naturally interpreted of the admission of church members, than of doctrines. Both the preceding and succeeding connection fix it to this. Christians, not doctrines, are the lively stones in God's building, and God's husbandry. His temple is to be built of these materials. It is not any doctrine, with respect to Christ, that is said to be the foundation; but he is the foundation *himself*. New members might be added to apostolical churches, but new doctrines could not be lawfully promulgated. In this sense, the apostles not only laid the foundation, but finished the house. There are neither gold, silver, nor precious stones now remaining to be built upon the foundation of the apostolical doctrines. But the gold, silver, and precious stones, beautifully represent converted church members, who are not injured by the fire, and their different degrees of value.* All are valuable; but while some are silver, others are gold, and other precious stones. On the other hand, unconverted church members are like wood, hay, and stubble, which will be consumed whenever fire is applied. The fire of temptation and persecution will try every church, during which, unconverted members will show their combustible nature, and be consumed. At least the fire of the great judgment will try the house of what sort of materials it is built, and the builders will either have loss or gain, according to the result of the trial.

* This interpretation is strengthened from Isaiah liv. 11-13, in which church members are represented under similar figures.

"And he himself shall be saved, yet so as by fire," with the utmost difficulty, as a man escaping from the midst of the flames. He being a servant of Christ himself, shall certainly have an entrance, but not an *abundant* entrance into heaven. Yea, and very probably, when the church is trying, by means of the fire of temptation and persecution, although he may be preserved from falling, he will be "saved by fire." Heavy trials and afflictions may be laid upon him, and the Lord may chastise him sore, though he may not give him over to death. He may be sorely scorched in the fire of affliction, although he be not burnt up. If this be the true interpretation of the passage, which is adopted by some of the best commentators, and which I have always thought the most natural, from the first time I heard it suggested, there is an awful lesson in it to every church ruler, and to every church member, not to hazard the peace and comfort of their own souls here, nor the loss of a part of their reward hereafter, by building God's house with combustible materials; admitting unconverted sinners to membership. But the character of church members is clearly determined from Acts ii. 47. "And the Lord added to the church daily such as should be saved," which is literally translated thus: "The Lord added the *saved* daily to the church." It does not mean that the Lord added to the church universal by conversion, though that is previously supposed; but that he added such as were converted to the church at Jerusalem. As soon as sinners are converted, they are *saved*, and none but the *saved* were added to the church at Jerusalem. It was the *Lord added them*, because the terms of admission were not the *prudential regulations* of the church, but the Scripture evidence of their being *saved*. The church was only God's instrument. "The Lord saved them," and the church seeing this, received them.

When we consider the character of the generality who sit down at the Lord's table, and then read that awful asseveration (1 Cor. xi. 27), it is enough to make the hand to tremble, which distributes among them the emblems of the body and blood of Christ. Indeed, I am really astonished that my conscience could ever have borne it. Ah! the guilt of professing Christians, in this single instance. If every unworthy communicant is a murderer, yea a murderer of the Lord Christ, what must be the guilt of all sects of Presbyterians? Is it any wonder that the labours of faithful individuals among them, should be in a great measure unproductive. If the murder of a man like ourselves be a crime so heinous, in the estimation of God and man, how aggravated a crime is the murder of the Son of God? What countless thousands of stupid sinners are permitted rashly to embrue their hands in the blood of Christ? Dreadful sentence! "Whosoever shall eat this bread, and drink this cup of the Lord unworthily, shall be guilty of the body and blood of the Lord." Now, how much more aggravated is the guilt of the church that admits such members, and the pastor that administers this ordinance to them? I know, indeed, that they usually hold themselves excused, by faithfully warning them of their dangers, and thus laying their blood upon their own heads. This indeed was my own refuge. I wished to persuade myself, that if I was faithful to point out the characters of such as were unworthy, in a clear and explicit manner, and fervently warn them of their danger, that then I was innocent. But I now clearly see that this refuge is untenable, and have plainly told my people, that I would no more administer that ordinance among them, in the same promiscuous manner, than I would descend from the pulpit with a sword in my hand to destroy them. I have no standard but the Bible, and am ready to change any erroneous sentiment or conduct, as soon as I discover it. We are frequently mistaken for want of having made any matter the subject of particular consideration. But if any minister of a feeling conscience, can allow himself, in the promiscuous administration of this ordinance, after his attention has been called to the subject, and having made it a matter of prayer and investigation, I am really astonished. The apology of faithfully warning will not stand even in human judgment, far less in the awful day of God. If I put a sword into the hand of an angry madman, it will be no excuse for me that I have warned him not to kill the person against whom he is enraged. I might have known he would not have listened to my counsel. So, if I put the emblems of Christ's body and blood into the hands of impenitent sinners, I may warn and warn, they are mad, and will not take warning, but rush upon their ruin. Suppose there is a madman standing in an apothecary's shop, while the apothecary is mixing up a dose of poison in a liquor of which the madman is very fond—the madman asks for a drink of it—the apothecary tells him there is poison in it—and that it will surely kill him if he drink it—the madman insists to have it, alleging that there is no fear, and that he can drink it without any injury—the apothecary still asserts that it will kill him if he will drink it; but if he persists in desiring to have it, he will give it him, rather than disoblige him—the madman reaches for it—the apothecary gives it, taking the madman and those present, and God himself to witness, that he is clear of his blood, for he hath faithfully warned him—the madman drinks—and dies. Reader, were you one of the jury to try the apothecary, would you clear him? Will the Lord clear him in his judgment? And in what does the apothecary differ from the pastor, who puts the emblems of Christ's body and blood into the hands of impenitent sinners? In nothing but in the degree of their guilt. The latter is the more guilty, inasmuch as the shedding of the blood of Christ is a greater crime than the shedding of the blood of a mere man; and inasmuch as the murder of a soul is a greater crime, than the murder of the body. It is no excuse, that great as the crime of unworthy partaking of the Lord's supper is, it is nevertheless pardonable. This is altogether with God, whether he will grant pardon and repentance or not; and although the individual is afterwards pardoned, the pastor's crime is not thereby mitigated. I have applied it particularly to the pastor, but every church member is guilty, and will be accountable; for it is not to one or a few, but to the whole church, that Christ has committed the discipline of his house.

I believe that *debarring* or *fencing the tables*, and *giving of tokens*, like all other human expedients in religion, have been of the most serious injury.* It is a bungling expedient to supply the want of Scripture discipline, and an apostolically constituted church. If none but those who are credibly Christians, were admitted to church membership, what occasion would there be for tokens of admission, or debarring. They will take their seats around Christ's table, as naturally as children will seat themselves unasked around the table of their earthly father. Who dare debar any such? And who dare invite any other? The custom of debarring, under the appearance of excluding the unworthy, is, in reality, only a pretext for admitting worldly men, without seeming to share in their guilt. Church rulers dare not professedly admit unregenerate men, from fear of offending God, and they dare not candidly deny them admission, from fear of men. They have, therefore, found out a way to compromise the matter between God and the world, by *fencing the tables*. Thus, they avoid giving individual offence, and driving unregenerate men away from their society, and imagine themselves clear as to the crimes of prostituting the ordinance of Christ. I ask, was ever this means found effectual to preserve purity of communion? I am sure I have tried it in the most awful manner in my power, and I do not know that it was in any degree effectual. Often, very often the hardened unawakened sinner, will let all pass through his ear as the

---

* Every one who receives a token, has the solemn declaration of church rulers, that they consider them as real Christians. For if it is granted that none but real Christians have a right to this ordinance, of what is this a token, if not of their fitness, at least in the estimation of those from whom they receive it? Now, if church rulers give a token to any whom they do not upon good evidence consider to be Christians, they are guilty of the most awful deceiving of sinners that can be imagined. They lead them, with a blind upon their eyes, to the brink of a precipice, and tell them, as they are falling, that they are tumbling into perdition. I beseech those Christians, who are engaged in this murderous business, to stop and reflect; to weigh this with seriousness and prayer. I believe that there are many who give tokens with a trembling heart, and a smiting conscience. Let them beware lest conscience, by the repetition of guilt, become callous and seared. Their state is awful, if it has ceased to smite.

path of an arrow through the air, while the weak and timid Christian will take what is said as against himself, and be discouraged. Indeed, they know very little of the human heart, who think that an unawakened sinner will take such a warning. I have laboured several hours with individuals, without convincing them of their danger. Till the Lord open the eyes of their understanding, they will still have some refuge of lies. How then could it be expected to prevail with a multitude, in a few minutes speaking, before the administration of the supper? I demand that those who practice it, will produce me either precept or example, either expressed or implied, for debarring and tokens of admission at the Lord's supper. If this cannot be produced, I argue that that church, which cannot maintain apostolical purity, without human expedients, is not apostolically constituted. When I see a wall supported by a buttress, I judge it has not a good foundation. When I see a human invention employed to prop an ordinance of Christ, I form a similar judgment.

But not only is the necessity of pure communion proved from the character of the members of the apostolical churches, and direct Scripture precept—the very model of the apostolical churches could not be otherwise preserved. Christ's laws are not at all calculated to govern the devil's subjects. Spiritual laws will take no hold of carnal men. If there are unregenerate members admitted and retained, they will throw all into confusion. They will stop the equability of the church's motion, and whenever the fire of temptation begins to burn, the house will fall with a crash in the midst of the flames. If they are not excluded, a majority must instantly be substituted for unanimity; human laws and human sanctions must be substituted for those of the New Testament. From one step to another, they will arrive to a full grown antichrist, and the more heads he will have, the more monstrous will he be.

I may add, there are ordinances of Christ which cannot be attended to, if strict purity of communion is not preserved. 1 Cor. vii. 1. That civil disputes should be determined by the church, is an apostolical ordinance, for the neglect of which, the Corinthians are severely reproved. But this is an ordinance which no church can ever observe, if they admit unregenerate men to membership. Such persons will yield to the decision of the church, if it be in their favour; but if it be against them, they will show little respect to the determination. Neither does the apostle's reasoning hold good with respect to such as judge, for *they* will not "*judge the world.*" Something like this, may, in smaller matters, be attempted in a mixed communion, among a few individuals, generally poor, and not able to maintain law-suits, having little civil intercourse; but can never effectually take place in all cases, except purity of communion be strictly adhered to.

Mutual exhortation in church meetings,* is another apostolical ordinance, 1 Cor. xiv. 29; 1 Thes. v. 11. Let any Presbyterian congregation give this liberty to private individuals, and they will soon see the house in flames. The wood, the hay, and the stubble, would instantly take fire, and it would be altogether impossible to preserve any sort of order or decorum. This would shiver them, as a cedar in Lebanon is splintered by the lightning. None but the children of Christ could bear or improve such a privilege. Now, that church which cannot bear an apostolical institution, is not apostolically constituted.

* As hypocrites will occasionally find admittance into the churches of Christ, such ordinances as these, seem wisely calculated to detect them. That which appears to worldly churches the most exceptionable in these ordinances, is, in reality, their great perfection, and prove their heavenly birth. They afford an expeditious way to discover, and exclude carnal professors. They are useful also to discipline the true soldiers of Jesus; they grind off their asperities, accustom them to forbearance, exercise their patience, and improve all their graces.

CHAPTER XI.

OBJECTIONS ANSWERED.

Many who look upon purity of communion, as a desirable thing, and go a certain length in effecting it, do not aim at a strict separation, apprehending the attempt to be either fruitless or dangerous. Some go so far as to shield themselves under Scripture example: I was once of this number myself. I shall therefore employ this chapter in answering the objections usually alleged against any attempt to effect a pure church.

Objection 1.—It is said, "we cannot know men's hearts; if they are sober and decent in their external conduct, and acknowledge their belief of the orthodox doctrines, we can go no farther."

This objection, if there was anything in it, would go to show that Christ has given a command to the churches, which it would not be in their power to put into practice. If Christ has said, "give not that which is holy unto dogs," he supposes we are able to distinguish the persons whom he intends, otherwise his advice is unimportant. A physician cannot look into the inner part of the human body, to see what is the disease of his patient, yet he judges of this, by the symptoms and appearances he beholds. Just so are we to judge of the human heart. If the fountain be salt, so will the streams; if the streams are fresh, we may judge that the fountain has also been made fresh. Our Lord tells us that a tree is known by its fruits. If there is faith in the heart, there will be obedience in the life. If there be spiritual life, there will be some symptoms of it. The true penitent will bring forth fruits meet for repentance. The man who is born of the Spirit, will know the things of the Spirit, and will lead a spiritual life. If he be renewed in the image of him that created him, he will evidence this by his knowledge, righteousness, and holiness. If he loves Christ, he will keep his commandments. If his heart is with God, his person will not usually be found in the company of the wicked. If he loves him that begat, he will also love them that are begotten, and prefer their company and conversation to that of all others. In short, if there be a real change of heart, it will manifest itself in the life. In some instances, arising from particular circumstances, there may be difficulty; and if, after much prayer and necessary investigation, a church is deceived in any instance, it is not guilty. I dare say if the members of a church would take as much trouble in this, as they do in giving out their money upon interest, they would seldom be deceived. They are not apt, out of excessive charity, to hazard it with a man of a merely specious appearance, till they enquire minutely into his circumstances and character.

OBJECTION 2.—I have heard some allege, " that if they would go to such strictness, they could admit very few."

I perfectly agree with them in this sentiment; but this objection is not an alleviation, but a dreadful aggravation of the crime. Such pastors are building a Babel, not a temple of God. When their work will be tried by the fire of the great day, it will be burned up, and they shall sustain a dreadful loss; and be saved, admitting they are the disciples of Christ, with the utmost difficulty. But this is not the remedy, but the very cause of their fewness. If a church is once formed upon the apostolical model, and walking in the commandments and ordinances of the Gospel, it is impossible but they will increase. Though at first they should be no more than a dozen, the Lord will be adding daily to them, such *as are saved*. The presence of Christ shall be with them, and continuing in prayer, they shall be multiplied; for whatever two of them agree in asking, they shall receive. I am convinced, from experience, that this is the case. Since I ceased to prostitute the Lord's supper at home and abroad, my labours have been more visibly blessed, and I have had more evidence of a work of grace going on, than I had in the whole five years of my ministry; and I am convinced that if a Gospel church is formed amongst us, and ruled by the laws of Christ, we shall have still more promising prospects. But be this as it may, as to myself, I hope I would not again administer the Lord's supper in the same promiscuous way, for any earthly consideration.

OBJECTION 3.—It is said, that "this sort of strictness will drive sinners away from the Gospel altogether, and therefore will defeat its own end."

What a pity that Christ had not the benefit of the advice of these sage counsellors! he would not have given a command so contrary to his own intention. Such objectors may have an orthodox creed, but the objection arises out of presumption and unbelief. Not to mention that the rejection of unregenerate persons, is often overruled to their conversion, our business is to obey God, and leave events to himself. Have we a greater interest, or are we more heartily concerned in enlarging his church, than he is himself? He hath the hearts of all men in his hands, and he turneth them as rivers of waters. He can make the most violent enemies, the most devoted friends of his Gospel, whenever he pleases. If he says, "Saul, Saul, why persecutest thou me?" the answer will be, "Lord, what wilt thou have me to do?" Every human invention to enlarge and support the Church of Christ, will not only utterly prove abortive, but generally will have a tendency directly the reverse of what is proposed. The great encouragement given to the heathen to renounce their religion, buried Christianity in a heap of rubbish, in the time of Constantine. And in every age the admission of impure members, to make a party respectable from their numbers, has had the worst effects. While the life of those that are spiritual is almost extinguished, the unregenerate become secure and hardened. Nothing can tend more effectually to retard the progress of the Gospel, and keep the eyes of the multitude continually blinded, than to give them the Christian name and privileges, whilst they are still the servants of Satan. They think they are safe, and believe they are Christians, though not so good as some others. If their minister is so faithful as to lay open their character in public, and show them their danger, they will either shuffle it off upon their neighbour, or apologise to themselves for their own conduct. Those who are accustomed to examine the hopes of sinners, will find that admission to what they call Christian privileges, is a very prevalent ground of hope. If all the churches of Christ were to treat the world as heathens, till they are born again, it would be a likely means in the hand of the Spirit to rouse them to inquiry, and lead them to repentance. Even those who are in the habit of refusing admission to persons of a scandalous character, very frequently do it in an improper manner. They ground their refusal, not upon their want of conversion, but their irregularities, or their not submitting to rules. This tends to mislead the sinner, and keep him ignorant of his real state; whereas, if he were faithfully told that his non-admission was the consequence of his want of the *new birth*, and not of the straitened rules of a party, he would be more likely to receive it with benefit, and even less irritation. Often the minister will throw the blame upon the session, and they again upon their rules, from a cowardly disposition, lest they should give offence. Thus the person is led to believe that the fault lies more in the straitness of their rules, than in himself. The placing of his admission or rejection upon his discharge of certain external duties, has the same mischievous effect. He is led to look on this, not as an evidence of his state, but as forming his title to heaven. One thing I would ask at those who make this objection, let them answer it candidly to their own conscience. Whether are you more afraid that this would lessen the Church of Christ, or *the stipend?* Whether are you more afraid of injuring the cause of Christ, or the credit of *your party?*

OBJECTION 4.—It is pleaded in defence of promiscuous communion, "that Judas was admitted to the Lord's table." Judas was once a pillar upon which I thought I could safely rest my defence; but since I have more maturely and impartially considered the matter, I have entirely given that up. We are never in a likely way to obtain truth as long as we are searching for a justification of our own conduct, rather than the mind of the Spirit. I am afraid that there are many who examine this question in this temper. A drowning man will catch at any twig before he will sink. Thus many, overwhelmed by positive Scripture precept, perhaps producing some qualms of conscience, catch at Judas to keep them above water. They do not see anything to extricate themselves from their difficulty, and because, in their present situation, they cannot comply, they too easily impose upon themselves, as to the sin of setting the Word of God at variance with itself. There is certainly a difficulty in determining whether Judas was, or was not, present at the institution of the supper. It would appear to me, from the most impartial examination of the Gospels which record the relation, that he was not. We know Scripture cannot contradict itself; and when it seems to do so, that analysis must be admitted, which is most conformable to the general tenor of the whole. If, then, there are innumerable passages to prove the duty of pure communion, and if the presence of Judas at the supper be contrary to this, that passage which seems to say he was, must be understood so as to agree with that which positively, or even apparently says he was not. I think also that Luke's account can more easily be explained in consistency with John's, than John's in consistency with the order of the narration of Luke. The inversion of order in the narration of facts, is no singular occurrence in the Gospels; but John states the fact positively, circumstantially, and minutely. John xiii. 30—"He then having received *the sop*,* went *immediately* out." To make Luke agree with this, we have nothing to do but what must be done in many other cases, to suppose an inversion of order in the narration. But this I mention, rather to reconcile the evangelists, than to support my argument in the point under debate. I do not think, that in order to prove the duty of pure communion, there is any necessity to exclude Judas from the first supper. What was Judas? He was a polished

---

* This was in eating the passover.

hypocrite. What is a hypocrite? Not a man who pretends to be religious, signs an orthodox creed, and leads a heterodox life, but a man to all human appearance a real Christian, and for a time walking as one, though in heart and in the sight of God an impenitent sinner. Such was Judas. There was not a more plausible character among the apostles than this very man. None of his brethren suspected him more than themselves. Even when our Lord declared that one of them should betray him, their language was not " Lord is it Judas?" but, " Lord, is it I?" Now, such characters might be in any church without the smallest blame being attachable to either church rulers, or church members. If the church receives them as real Christians, it is guiltless, though they are like Judas. This, however, is no apology for those who admit carnal men, who discover no evidence of conversion, nay frequently of whom they have no hopes at all. It is argued, that though Judas was a hypocrite, yet that our Lord knew him to be such. A fact most unquestionable; but our Lord's omniscience is no rule of conduct for us, nor did he act according to it in many other cases. He had various and important reasons for choosing this hypocrite to the apostleship, and the same might he have had for allowing him to take his seat at his supper. Our Lord, by acting as the administrator of this ordinance, had no need to avail himself of his omniscience, by forbidding Judas to partake; because in this he could have been no example to us, as we had not the same means of detecting hypocrites. Besides, he might design to show us, that if such characters as Judas would afterwards get admission into any of his churches, they would be blameless. The guilt, in this matter, is not in receiving hypocrites, but in retaining them, after they discover their true character. Judas, the hypocrite, might be a church member, but Judas the betrayer, never was, nor could be. Granting everything, then, that the abettors of impure communion themselves can demand from the case of Judas, to what does it amount? that a hypocrite may be admitted to the Lord's table without sin in the church. Will any say that because Christ knew this man to be an hypocrite, that therefore we may admit persons whom *we* know to be hypocrites; if we know them to be hypocrites, then they are no longer hypocrites; for we cannot know this as Christ knew it, by looking into their hearts, but from their discovering this by their lives and conversation. The case of Judas cannot fairly be drawn any farther. Besides, if it be alleged to justify the admission of members who give evidence that they are not partakers of the grace of the Gospel, it will set Christ the master, and Paul the servant at variance. The latter positively commands them not so much as eat with one who is called a brother, when once he discovers an inconsistency between his character and profession—1 Cor. v. 11. Timothy is strictly charged to withdraw from those " who had a *form* of godliness, but denied the power thereof."

But can there be anything more truly ridiculous than for those who justify impure communion by the example of Judas, to spend whole hours in debarring and fencing? If our Lord did not debar Judas, and if this shows the propriety of admitting persons whom we know to be unworthy, the conclusion is, that it would be improper to forbid them. If the sober *worldling* is admitted, I ask by what authority is the drunkard, the swearer, the fornicator, &c., denied admission? Ah! brethren, you must be at a great loss for a foundation, when you are obliged to build upon Judas. It must be an ill-built house, in which Judas himself is the chief corner-stone.

OBJECTION 5.—The parable of the tares and the wheat, is usually one of the bulwarks of impure churches.* But this objection is founded on a misapplication of the parable. It supposes that the field is the church, whereas our Lord himself expressly explains it to mean

* For a full, clear, and satisfactory explanation of this parable, see "Mr. Innes' Reasons for separating from the Church of Scotland." I decline a full explanation of this, and some other things, as they are largely treated in that pamphlet, which I think should be in the hands of all who wish for information on the subject.

the *world*. The tares are considered as church members; whereas, this would make our Lord's injunction contrary to that of the apostle Paul, "Purge out the old leaven." "Do ye not judge them that are within." It was also the devil who sowed them, and not Christ's servants by mistake. Those, who from this, plead for promiscuous admission, acknowledge themselves to be, not the servants of Christ, but of Satan, employed in sowing the tare-seed in Christ's field, while his servants sleep. But without spending time in showing why it cannot have this interpretation, I will just briefly point out what I take to be its obvious and consistent meaning. The wheat represents the children of God; the tares the children of the wicked one; they both grow in the same field, the *world*. The servants of Christ are not to endeavour to root out the latter, lest in doing so, they would root out the wheat. The design of the parable, is to show the impropriety of persecution, from this reason, that if the wicked of one generation were cut off, thousands of the children of God, who are to spring from them, would thereby be prevented from coming into being. The lives of the wicked are now preserved, because they are the ancestors of multitudes, who shall turn to God in the latter days. This I take to be also the meaning of Matt. xxiv. 22—"For the *elect's sake*, those days shall be shortened." By *elect* here, we are, in my opinion, principally to understand the *unborn* elect. The Jews, who escaped at the siege of Jerusalem, were spared, because they were to be the fathers of all those Jews who shall turn to God in the restoration. God could have preserved the elect that were alive in the time of that siege, in various ways. But what other way could the prophecies of the restoration of the Jews, have been accomplished, than by preserving a number of that wicked generation, for the purpose of introducing his future people into existence? If all the Jews had been cut off then, what would have become of those countless thousands and millions of their descendents, that shall serve Christ in their return? The Jews, since their rejection of Christ, have been preserved, perhaps *chiefly* for the sake of their future offspring. This is clearly expressed in the prophecy of Isaiah lxv. 8. As the unripe bunch of grapes is preserved for the sake of the wine that it shall afterwards yield, so God preserves the Jewish nation for the sake of their future descendents, who are to serve him.

CHAPTER XII.

ADDITIONAL REASONS FOR SEPARATING FROM THE GENERAL SYNOD.

THOUGH I had no objection to the government of classical Presbytery, and could effect purity of communion in my own congregation, without experiencing any hindrance from foreign interference, still I could not with a good conscience remain a member of the General Synod. I have many reasons for this conviction; a few of them I will here state.

1. "How can a man mount a very high hill with a weighty burthen, having several hundreds pulling him back by the skirts? Is it not much better to climb up the precipice in company with others who are going the same way, to go arm in arm, the strong bearing the weak, so that if a foot slip, we may not be dashed to pieces by a fall?" The former was exactly my situation; the whole weight of my connection being as a clog upon me, retarding my progress, by their laws, example, and spirit. We have all too much inclination to indifference and negligence in our Lord's cause. There is no need of any external hindrance. "Can a man take fire into his bosom, and not be burned?" Who will say, that the very society of men indifferent to religion, is not a strong temptation to relax exertion in the cause of Christ? But especially, if they are not only indifferent but inimical to the spreading of the Gospel, the danger is increased. If the religion of the Bible be called enthusiasm and madness, there is a strong temptation to hide its peculiar features, and appear less zealous for its diffusion. "Two cannot walk together except they are agreed." What concord, then, can there be between them and me? They view me with jealousy, and I consider them traitors to my

Master.* My exertions for a revival of religion they think useless. Some suppose that I am actuated by a love of applause, while others, more friendly, think I am only mad. Now, in this situation, what mutual happiness can there be from the society of men so opposite in their views and conduct? We both contribute to make each other uncomfortable. I am sure I have never suffered more acute pain in my life, than in their assemblies. I avoided their meetings as much as I could, for I always entered them with horror and reluctance. But of late, I understand they have determined that I should not enjoy that liberty. Is it not, then, much better that I should act separately, for I am sure they are not more offensive to me, than I am to them? Shall I, for a morsel of bread, sacrifice my own happiness, and remain under continual restraint and temptation? "A man's life consisteth not in the abundance of the things he possesses." He must be a very inexperienced Christian indeed, who thinks that he does not need rather to be spurred than curbed in his course.

2. "I cannot be a member of the General Synod, without renouncing my Christian liberty, and submitting my conscience to be ruled and lorded over by man." I am not allowed to be directed by my own conscience in the service of my Master. I must act not on my own conviction of what is right and wrong, but according to the caprice of others; nay of those I esteem as decided enemies to the cause of the Lord Jesus. I might get drunk frequently; associate with the most profligate; spend the sabbath afternoons in gay parties; follow the world the whole week with my whole heart; preach against the peculiar doctrines of revelation; deny the very Lord and Saviour of men; attend the theatre, balls, and card parties; and still my

---

* When I involve the Synod in a general censure, I always intend a majority of the members, and not every individual, because a majority is the Synod, and can rule the minority as they please. I pretend not to determine what may be the number of faithful servants of Christ in that connection. For such, whatever be our difference of opinion, I have the most cordial affection.

brethren would extend their charity to me; except a formal charge would be brought against me by my own congregation, I might even pass unnoticed. Here human frailty, and freedom of inquiry would plead my excuse. But if I would dare to preach the Gospel out of my own bounds, or admit an evangelical minister of another denomination to occupy my pulpit, dreadful would be the thunder that would be hurled against me! Nothing less than public rebuke for the first, and suspension for the second commission of such *mortal sins*. "Whereas it appears, that our laws respecting the admission of men, not members of this body, or licentiates under its care, to officiate for us, are too generally expressed to be of any practical use: It is now enacted, that no man, not a member of this body, or a licentiate under its care (the Presbytery of Antrim, and southern association excepted), shall be permitted to officiate for us in our congregations, until he shall first submit his credentials to the Presbytery, in whose bounds he wishes to preach, and until he shall be approved of by the Presbytery; and any minister of this body, violating this law, shall, for the first offence, be publicly rebuked by his Presbytery, before his congregation, and for the second be suspended *ab officio, sine die*." If ever a child was known by its resemblance to the parent, this sure must be the daughter of the mother of harlots. This is her prominent feature; this is her very temper and genius. "O, ye Scribes and Pharisees, how long will ye make void the law of God by your traditions! In vain do you worship him, teaching for doctrines the commandments of men." Where is their authority for imposing such restraints upon the servants of the Lord? I cannot submit to this tyranny without calling men my master, contrary to the express command of Jesus. I am commanded " to stand fast in the liberty with which Christ has made me free." Though the apostle speaks this immediately of the Jewish yoke, yet, as no Scripture is of any private interpretation, it equally forbids any human imposition, in the things of God. When Christ has left us free, we are not to allow any man or body of men to bind us, or even to bind ourselves. Every human restraint in religion is usurpation and treason. A Christian, indeed, is sometimes to decline using his liberty, to avoid stumbling his weak brother, but he is not even in this case to come under bondage to him, still less is he to come under restraint to please those who are enemies to the *pure Gospel of salvation.*

I am truly concerned for the spiritual darkness of my native land. While the work of the Lord is flourishing in both parts of Britain, there is in this island as yet but little done. Ah! the thousands that are perishing for lack of knowledge! What profligacy of manners do we see everywhere abounding! I am convinced that there is no other remedy for the evil but the *unadulterated Gospel of Christ.* Shall I then submit to be cooped up in a corner, and restrained by human fetters from lending a hand to rescue my brethren from the pit of destruction? "Time is short;" the day of work is but a blink; I must soon give an account of my stewardship, and I know that however much I may incur the displeasure of men, however great may be my temporal loss, in the end I shall not repent the step I have taken. I know that God judgeth not as man judgeth. I know, indeed, it is said that I might employ all my time in my own congregation; but I answer, that I may do much abroad, and not do the less at home. I believe we will generally find, that those who do most abroad, likewise do most in their own congregation. It is my duty to feed the poor of my own neighbourhood rather than those at a distance; but it would be a hard matter, if I was so bound that I could not give a halfpenny to a starving beggar on my journey. Besides, the public preaching of the Gospel is that part of the office in which I take peculiar delight, and in which I am never weary. The hireling may work his hours, but he that loves Jesus, should, like him, "go about doing good;" like him it should be his very "meat and drink, to do the will of his heavenly Father."

3. "I do not find myself justified in recognizing as ministers, those whom I consider as destitute of the qualifications deemed essential by an apostle." A bishop must be blameless, the husband of one wife,

vigilant, sober, of good behaviour, given to hospitality, *apt (rather fit) to teach—not given to wine—no striker—* not *greedy of filthy lucre,* but patient—not a brawler, nor *covetous*—one that ruleth well his own house, having his children in subjection with all gravity. (For if a man know not how to rule his own house, how shall he take care of the church of God?) Not a *novice,* lest being lifted up with pride, he fall into the condemnation of the devil. Moreover, he must have *a good report of them which are without,* lest he fall into reproach and the snare of the devil"—1 Tim. iii. 2-7. "A bishop must not be self willed—*not soon angry—a lover of good men—just, holy, temperate—holding fast the faithful Word,* as he hath been taught, that he may be able, by sound doctrine, both to exhort and convince the gainsayers"—Titus i. 7-9. I forbear to make the application. Suffice it to say, that if these are essential qualifications in a pastor, I cannot recognise as brethren many of the members of the General Synod.

4. "A Calvanist and a Socinian or Arian, can with no propriety worship together." They do not address the same God. When they unite in prayer, they are like a friend to the Pretender, and another of King George, drinking *the king,* as a toast, when each intended his own favourite. They do not address the same being, though they use the same name. If I address the Father, Son, and Holy Ghost, as my God, he that denies the Godhead of the Son and Spirit, must look upon me as an idolater. In return, I look upon him as an atheist. "He that denieth the Son, the same hath not the Father; he that honoureth not the Son, honoureth not the Father that hath sent him." When he prayeth, he addresses not the Jehovah of the Scripture, but an idol of his own creation, as different from the true God, as Jupiter or Apollo.* His god

---

* The same thing will hold against making any unregenerate man the organ of prayer. When such men are set up to offer the prayers of an assembly, as they "know not God," so "they worship they know not what." They cannot pray with the Spirit, and consequently they cannot pray at all. Those who join them are partakers in their abominations.

is as really of his own making, as if he had hewn him out of wood or stone. He steals from the Scripture account of the true God, some of his properties, and those attributes that suit him best. When he robs him of his justice, and abusively extends his mercy, he can dispense with the sacrifice of Jesus; he has got a god to his mind; an idol of his own imagination. This god he loves, because this god does not hate sin; but the Jehovah of the Scriptures he hates, because he is the enemy of sin, and "hath revealed his wrath against all ungodliness and unrighteousness of men." In what then are we agreed? Not even in the God we worship: not in the way of salvation. How improper is it, then, for us to make each other the organ of prayer! How can we co-operate, seeing our principles are so entirely opposite? If each of us be conscientious, we must be at constant war. With as great propriety, might the French and English officers meet in a council of war, before an engagement, to concert the measures that each were to adopt, as people of such opposite sentiments to sit in the same Synod.

5. "By remaining in connection with the Synod, I contribute to deceive the public, as to the radical difference between my principles, and those maintained by many in the Synod." My example by continuing in that connection, might be the means of keeping some of the people of Christ under the ministry of those who corrupt the Gospel. It is natural for people to judge that there cannot be any momentous points in which we differ, or we would not continue to co-operate and acknowledge each other as brethren in Christ. This I know to be the case. The generality of private Christians in the General Synod, have no conception that we differ so materially. Suppose, then, I could remain a member of Synod, without injury to myself, yet I am guilty of deceiving others. If I think that any ministers of that body are wolves in sheep's clothing, not feeding, but devouring the flock, I am a partaker of their soul-murder, if I do not give the alarm, and warn the sheep to fly.

What is the use of the 8th chap. of 1 Cor. to us? Does it not teach us, that if in any particular instance, the use of our Christian liberty may prove an occasion of stumbling to weak brethren, we ought to forego it, rather than that they should be injured? If I sit in the idol's temple, eating the flesh of animals offered in sacrifice, though I eat it simply to satisfy my hunger, knowing that there is no divinity in the idol, and that the meat cannot be rendered in itself impure, by this improper use, yet my weak brother seeing me there, partaking with idolators, is led to think, that I am joining them in their worship, and by my example, is emboldened to eat it as a sacrifice to the idol.— "Through my knowledge, shall the weak brother perish, for whom Christ died?" Suppose, then, that my connection with the Synod was a matter not sinful in itself, yet by its consequences, it becomes sinful. Many may be encouraged by my example, to sit under a ministry, in which the Gospel is depraved, or hidden. If I should be the occasion of stumbling one of Christ's little ones, the loss I would sustain in the day of the Lord Jesus, would be infinitely greater than all I can lose by leaving the Synod. Awful will be our responsibility, and it is required, above all things, in a steward, that he be faithful. If this be not a lawful application of Scripture, I know of no use that this chapter can be at present.

6. "My connection with the Synod, is contrary to the law of love, and the duty I owe the members of it as men." If I believe, that "Except a man be born again, he cannot see the kingdom of God;" and if I believe that few of them evidence such a change; nay, if I know many of them to deny and ridicule this truth as enthusiasm, I would not be their friend, if in anything my conduct would lead them to believe, that I considered their situation to be less dangerous, than in reality I know it to be. Now, as long as I remain a member of Synod, and act with them as brethren in Christ, it is impossible for them to think that I am really in earnest, as to the importance of my views of the truths of the Gospel. Besides, there are many who would subscribe perhaps every doctrine of the Gospel, of whose state I have no better hopes. Such persons,

then, would have reason to complain of me in the judgment of the great day, that I acted an unfriendly part towards them; that while I considered them as "in the gall of bitterness and bond of iniquity," I acted with them as ministers of Christ; by which means they were led to conclude that I could have no very unfavourable opinion of them. I know I will be charged with a want of *charity of sentiment* when I express such an opinion of the Synod. Charity, however, is not a matter of opinion, but of feeling, and a man may have the purest love for another, while he is most strongly convinced of his guilt and danger. A juror may have every wish that the criminal may be acquitted, yet he may, by evidence, be obliged to join in the verdict "*guilty.*" Shall I go past my neighbour's house at night, seeing it on fire, and not awake him, lest I should disturb or grieve him? Shall I rather suffer him to be consumed in the flames, than alarm him? Yet this is the murderous charity for which many plead; that, while we have the clearest evidence that men are living without God, we should believe, or feign to believe, that they may be saved in their sins. In other words, we hope God is a liar—that he will not do as he has said. Dr. Johnson said that every man was to be held unlearned, till he proved the contrary. The observation is equally just when applied to religion. No man has a right to be esteemed a Christian, till his fruits prove it. What would we think of the man who would say, that in the judgment of charity, he looked upon all, or the greater part of men to be learned? The same should we think of the man who professes to believe, that men are Christians, who give no evidence of the fact. We have the word of unerring wisdom, declaring that all men are "by nature the children of wrath;" until we have evidence that they are born again, and adopted into the family of God, we are not warranted to look upon them as Christians. Eternal life is the worst I wish to any member of the Synod, or to any man on earth; but if I believe God, I must believe that all "who *know not God*, and *obey not the Gospel* of our Lord Jesus Christ, shall be punished with everlasting destruction from the presence of the Lord, and from the glory of his power.

7. "I cannot conscientiously join in licensing and ordaining those whom I know do not possess the prerequisite qualifications, pointed out in the Word of God." Paul states these minutely to Timothy and Titus. I do not think that it is right to give our countenance to any candidates, who do not answer to this description. The candidate for "the office of a bishop," must not be even a *novice*, or *new convert*, lest from his inexperience he should fall into temptation from the natural pride of the human heart.* But if it be improper to appoint *newly converted men* to the charge of a flock, how dreadful must be the sin of appointing the blind to lead the blind, and unregenerate men to feed the flock of Christ? Paul says to Timothy (1. Tim. v. 22), "Lay hands suddenly upon no man, neither be partaker of other men's sins: keep thyself pure." It appears, then, that those who give their sanction to unworthy men to preach the Gospel, are partakers of their sins. They share with them in the guilt of all the evil they commit in destroying the souls of men. He does not direct him to ordain no man without subscribing a human confession of faith. This could have been done in an instant; if this had been the test, there would have been no need of delay. The caution implies not only that Timothy should not ordain persons of a scandalous character, but even that persons who seemed to possess the requisite qualifications, should not be appointed to the pastoral office, till they had given sufficient evidences that they were what they seemed to be. All unregenerate men are the servants of Satan; and let them *subscribe* and *swear* what they will, Satan they will serve, "until they are turned from darkness unto light, and from the power of Satan unto God." How dreadful, then, is the crime of giving a

---

* Those who justify the appointment of unconverted men to preach the Gospel, and take charge of a church of Christ, from the example of Judas, would do well to consider the import of this portion of Scripture. If a man newly converted be unfit for the pastor's office, much more is he who is not converted at all.

public sanction to such men, as the servants of Christ! They will preach orthodoxy or heterodoxy as best suits their temporal interest, but though they have *the form* they have none of the power of godliness. They may preach a dead, dry system, but being blind, they cannot lead the blind; and having no spiritual organs to "discern the things of the Spirit, they cannot know them." I acknowledge the most conscientious may be deceived, but it is really awful to hear some good men pleading for the propriety of sending out unconverted men to preach the Gospel, because Judas was a hypocrite. It is no wonder, then, that some sects, with all their boasted orthodoxy, have little more of the life and power of godliness than those who do not make such high pretensions. Once acknowledge the principle that the servants of Satan, if they are orthodox and sober, are proper persons to feed the flock of Christ, and in a short time deadness and torpor will pervade the body. All the zeal of individuals will not be able to keep it alive. A profession of orthodoxy was not the test used by the apostles. "And when James, and Cephas, and John, who seemed to be pillars, *perceived the grace that was given unto me*, they gave to me and Barnabas the right hand of fellowship, that we should go unto the heathen, and they unto the circumcision"— Gal. ii. 9. The evidence of his qualifications was not the *subscription of a formula*, but *his appearing to have received the grace of God*. I cannot see how an unconverted orthodox minister is a less dangerous man than he who is most openly hostile to the doctrines of the Gospel. In my opinion, the former is the more dangerous of the two, as men are less aware of him. Paul, speaking of the deacons (1 Tim. iii. 10), says, "Let these also first be proved." This shows the great care that should be taken in choosing church officers. Their acknowledgment of the leading doctrines of the Gospel is not given as a test. Even persons that appear to possess the necessary qualifications, are not to be hastily appointed to office; *they must be proved.* " These also," that is, deacons as well as pastors. If this reasoning be just, it is applicable to all the denominations of Presbyterians, with which I am acquainted. But I am not obliged to rest any part of this argument upon the sinfulness of licensing and ordaining merely *unconverted men.* As a member of the General Synod, I may be forced to join in licensing and ordaining men whose *characters* and *doctrines* I condemn. I may be obliged to be the very organ of licensing and ordaining a man who preaches an opposite Gospel from what I believe to be true. What a monstrous inconsistency is here! If I believe the doctrines I preach, I must be convinced that I am sending out a murderer instead of a physician. Am I not guilty, then, of all the blood he spills? Surely I am partaker of this man's sins. Yes, I take shame and confusion of face to myself, that I have so long sanctioned my Master's enemies. I acknowledge myself to have hitherto been a partaker of the guilt of those who are the " enemies of the cross of Christ, whose God is their belly, whose glory is their shame, who mind earthly things."

8. "I have a positive and express command to separate from a corrupt church." 2 Cor. vi. 14–18— " Be ye not unequally yoked together with unbelievers, for what fellowship hath righteousness with unrighteousness? And what communion hath light with darkness? And what concord hath Christ with Belial? or what part hath he that believeth with an infidel? And what agreement hath the temple of God with idols? for ye are the temple of the living God; as God hath said, I will dwell in them and walk in *them ;* and I will be their God and they shall be my people. Wherefore come out from among them, and be ye separate, saith the Lord, and touch not the unclean *thing,* and I will receive you. And will be a Father unto you, and ye shall be my sons and daughters, saith the Lord Almighty." The Corinthians are here commanded to separate from their unbelieving and idolatrous neighbours; to abandon their worship, and form no intimate alliances of any kind with them. This command is given to me as well as to the Corinthians, for I am no otherwise addressed but as a member of the apostolical churches. All unconverted men are idolators, and unbelievers, and a connection with them

is even more dangerous in a country called Christian, than in a heathen country. The same reason also that forbids the marriage of believers with unbelievers, will equally forbid our connection in church communion with such. It is also exceedingly obvious, that though the command is particularly levelled against joining in the idolatrous worship of the heathens, it is expressed in a general manner, so as to include the view I now give of it, as literally, and with as strict precision, as the other. " Be ye not unequally yoked together with unbelievers." This will hold not only in this or that instance, but is universally applicable to the formation of any intimate union of believers with unbelievers, especially in church communion. Besides, there is not an argument here used to show the impropriety of this union, but what equally applies in this view. All believers are righteous, all unbelievers are unrighteous. All believers are light, all unbelievers are darkness. Christ dwells in all believers; Belial dwells in all unbelievers; he is the spirit that now worketh in the children of disobedience. Unbelievers of every description have different views, objects of pursuit, pleasures, and aversions, from believers. They have no common ground upon which they can found an intimate union. Every believer is a temple of God, which he inhabits through the spirit; idols of one kind or other inhabit the heart of every unbeliever. I would just further observe, that if some of those who have long successfully quoted this portion of Scripture to show the duty of separating from the General Synod, would look a little more narrowly into it, they might find that they should carry their separation to a greater length. I think it fairly condemns the admission of all carnal men to church communion. It is a union of believers with unbelievers, not merely of orthodox with heterodox, which is here forbidden. " Be ye not unequally yoked together with unbelievers."

A similar command have I in Rev. xviii. 4.—" Come out of her my people, that ye be not partakers of her sins, and that ye receive not of her plagues." This indeed is immediately spoken of the mother of harlots, but it will equally hold with respect to each of her daughters. If we are to leave one corrupt church, we are certainly to leave another. If our remaining in communion with the spiritual Babylon would make us partakers of her sins, and subject us to share her plagues, the same reasoning will prove that we are partakers of the sins of any corrupt church with which we are connected. If we must come out of the one to free us from her sins, the same thing will be necessary with respect to every other. As long as we countenance them we are sharers of their guilt, and liable to share their punishment.

Paul gives Timothy (2 Tim. iii. 1–5) a list of characters who would assume a profession of religion, without the power of it. From these, he positively commands him to "turn away." Now, if there be any such characters evidently in the General Synod, it is equally my duty to withdraw from them. This is another passage which the advocates of impure ministerial and Christian communion would do well to consider. These might be very orthodox men; they had a "form of godliness." They would have no objection to subscribe the Westminster Confession. Most of them appear also, not to have been openly immoral. They might have a very sanctified air in a church court. Yet from such, there is a peculiar necessity to withdraw; from such there is a peculiar danger. When men of such a character appear, and are acknowledged in a church of Christ, "the times are perilous." The devout worldling is more dangerous than the openly profane. Timothy is also commanded to withdraw from every teacher who would teach otherwise than the apostle had directed, " and consent not to wholesome words, even the words of our Lord Jesus Christ, and to the doctrine which is according to godliness," 1 Tim. vi. 3–5. Certainly, then, I am not justifiable in remaining in connection with the General Synod.

In writing to the Church of the Thessalonians, Paul gives them this charge: "Now I command you, brethren, in the name of our Lord Jesus Christ, that ye withdraw yourselves from every brother that walketh disorderly, and not after the tradition which he received of us." What Christ speaks to a church in general, is spoken to each individual, in particular. Though classical Presbytery were of God's appointing, yet, if there were but one disorderly member in the General Synod, and I could not get him removed, it would be my duty to withdraw; otherwise I am a partaker of his sins. As long as I am a member of that body, I am an accomplice with every irregular person in it, whether minister or private member.* We are positively commanded to "have no fellowship with the unfruitful works of darkness, but to reprove them"—Eph. v. 11. This precept we can never obey, while we hold professed communion with unbelievers. Nay, so far from holding communion with them in the ordinances of Christ, we are not even allowed to have a friendly intimacy with those that are called brethren, if their characters belie their profession. This would be a scandal to the religion of Christ, and would give occasion to the wicked to blaspheme. I cannot, then, be a member of the General Synod and an obedient servant of Christ.

* If there be any justice in this remark, it is a considerable argument against an associated church government. We would, in that case, be accountable for the conduct of those of whom we could not possibly have any knowledge.

CHAPTER XIII.

OBJECTIONS ANSWERED.

HAVING in the last chapter given some reasons for separating from a corrupt church, I will conclude this pamphlet by taking notice of a few objections that have been frequently urged upon me, to dissuade me from giving up my connection with the General Synod.

1. "It is said that a material error prevailed in the churches of Galatia, and that in writing to them, the apostle does not command one part of them to separate from the other, upon the supposition that the majority would not return to the truth—that in case the majority of the Corinthian church had taken part with the incestuous man, and refused to obey the apostolical injunction, Paul gives no command to the minority to separate from the majority—and that our Lord, in reproving the churches of Asia, does not command any separation of individuals, in case the greater part in any church might not return to their duty."

With respect to each of these instances, I answer, that there is not one of them parallel to my situation. These churches, with all their declensions and corruptions, were still churches of Christ, apostolically constituted, and the bulk of them real, though censurable saints. Consequently, when their errors would be laid before them, they would unite in correcting them. But the matter is widely different with respect to a church neither upon the apostolical model, nor constituted of members like those of the apostolical churches. As to the churches of Galatia, there was no room to give any such command. The apostle says (Gal. v. 10), "I have confidence in you, through the Lord Jesus, that you will be none otherwise minded." If he had such an opinion of them, and believed that they would comply with his injunctions, where would have been the propriety of giving a command of separation to the few, in case of the disobedience of the many? The error of the judaizing teachers, had indeed infected the body, so that the apostle found it necessary to express his doubt of them;* but he had confidence that they would return to the truth when he called them to it. Nay, he supposeth the whole matter to arise from a very few; " but he that troubleth you, shall bear his judgment, whosoever he be." "I would they were even cut off that trouble you." "A little leaven leaveneth the whole lump." Here he counts upon the allegiance of the great bulk of the members of the churches, and even intimates his wish, that the authors of this false doctrine should be cut off. In what, then, does this countenance the remaining in a corrupt church? Nay, it is directly against it. The apostle knew that the greatest part of them would return to the truth, therefore could not suppose it necessary to advise individuals to separate, upon the supposition that it would be otherwise. But the few that spread this doctrine, he advises to be cut off. This shows us what we should do with those who trouble a church with false doctrines. They are not, out of false lenity, to be suffered to remain and corrupt the body, but removed as morbid members.

This objection is entirely founded upon an improper conception of the nature of a church of Christ, judging of it as a wordly society, in which the majority is supposed to be the whole, and is enabled to direct all its proceedings. But it is not numbers, but the *obedient*, that constitute the church, whether they be the majority or minority. Had all the members in any one of the Galatian churches, except two or three, resolved to retain their error, in contempt of the apostolic authority, to these two or three obedient disciples, the apostle's direction was still given, "I would that they were cut off that trouble you." Obedience is the test of discipleship. Had the majority of any of these churches, refused to obey, the obedient few were bound to " cut off " the

---

* Even this doubting shows what he formerly took them to be, when organized as a church.

disobedient many. Those few, go where they would, were still the church.

Indeed if it be a duty to "cut off" one or a few disorderly and troublesome members, it will still be more so with respect to many. There is not one argument why three thousand should cut off three which will not prove that three should cut off three thousand, with an accession of strength proportioned to the increase of numbers. "If a little leaven leaveneth the whole lump," if not purged out there still is greater reason to dread, that the leavened mass will soon infect a few particles. If a whole church is in danger from one, two, or three; one, two, or three, must be in much greater danger from a corrupt body. What is the reason of cutting off one disorderly member? Is it not lest he bring a scandal upon the religion of Christ; be a stumbling block to weak Christians; infect the body; become an offence to unbelievers; and to reclaim the individual. Each of these reasons will derive additional strength when applied to numbers.

The same reasoning will hold good with respect to the Church of Corinth, and the churches of Asia. The apostle addressed the Corinthians as "saints sanctified in Christ Jesus;" and everywhere through his epistle considers them as true believers, though in many respects greatly to blame. How, then, could he suppose that they would not obey him? This would have been as if the king would send an order to the House of Commons to try one of their members for some improper language or conduct, at the same time applauding the members for their fidelity and zeal, and then add, "yet if a majority unite to screen the offender, let the faithful minority protest." How incongruous would such language be? Yet not more so than what such objectors would expect from the apostle. After all, I will suppose that the whole Church of Corinth had taken part with the incestuous person against the apostle, except one, two, or three, still it would have been the duty of such to have withdrawn from the disorderly society, which no more deserved the name of a church of Christ, than a congregation of Mussulmen. The few that obeyed the apostle were the church, and to them the command was given. 1 Cor. v. 4—"In the name of our Lord Jesus Christ, when ye are gathered together, and my Spirit, with the power of our Lord Jesus Christ, to deliver such an one," &c. The offender, and all who sided with him, were to be removed as disorderly brethren. The same may be said as to the case of the Asiatic churches. To the very worst of them Christ said, "As many as I love, I rebuke and chasten." They were much to blame, but with all their faults they were true churches of Christ. Nay, the very accusations Christ alleged against them, not only show the bulk of them to be saints, but prove the necessity of pure communion, and of cutting off impure members. He blames some of them for having the propagators of false doctrines among them. This shows that a church is to purge out the old leaven, and become a new lump. And if he blames them for having a few false teachers among them, how much more has he had occasion to blame me, for continuing so long with a corrupt body? With what propriety, then, can a Christian allege the state of these churches to justify his continuance in corrupt societies? With what face can any church allege this, to justify impure communion? If these apostolical churches had any improper member among them, they are not praised; they are not held excusable; they are severely reprimanded for it.

2. Another objection is, "that I give up an important station. I cowardly desert the field of battle, and in all probability deprive myself for ever of an opportunity of preaching the Gospel. Now Paul says, 'woe unto me, if I preach not the Gospel.' Christ says, 'the harvest is plenteous and the labourers few.' It must then be highly improper to leave a ripe harvest without labourers to reap it."

What is the amount of this objection? It is "do evil that good may come." If I have shown that such a connection is sinful, no supposed advantages resulting to religion from it should have the smallest weight, because they are nothing in reality. What good could I do in any situation on earth, without God's blessing upon my labours? And is it supposable that I am likely to have this blessing, when I refuse to obey him? Before my attention was turned to this subject, when my views were not so clear, God might have partially blessed my labours. But I could no longer look for a blessing, nor with a good conscience preach the Gospel at all, while conscious that I was not complying with his will. "I leave an important situation." What sort of language in the mouth of a Christian? If I had an opportunity of preaching the Gospel in every parish in the Island, could I of myself call one sinner to repentance? A station is only important as there may be the probability of doing good, and I can see no probability of this, as long as we live in the willful neglect, or the breach of the least part of the known will of God. Ah! friends, I am afraid if we search our hearts to the bottom, the real motive of remaining in corrupt churches, is rather the importance of it to our own temporal interest, than a concern lest the work of the Lord should stand undone. "Sirs, ye know that by this craft we have our gain." But "I am running as a coward, out of the field of battle." No, I am only repairing to the standard of my Captain, and deserting his enemies. I am only putting myself in a situation in which I can fight without restraint, and whether I am to be an officer or a private, must be left to my General, who employs every man in the situation that suits him best, and in which he can render the most effectual service. But "is it not a sin for me to put myself out of a condition to preach the Gospel?" Yes, if I would give up preaching the Gospel for the most splendid throne in Europe, I would be unworthy of opening my mouth to proclaim the glad tidings of salvation. If I would quit my station for the sake of a little more of the *unrighteous mammon*, I would be inexcusable. If I would quit preaching for fear of man, "woe would be upon me." But if I quit a station by the command of my General, I am not to blame.

But "the harvest is great and the labourers are few." True, very true; and what is the consequence? Is it that I must transgress the orders of Christ to reap the harvest? Is there no way of obeying one command, without breaking another? Put the objection into words, and it will run thus: "O Lord, thou hast a great harvest and few to reap it; I am an active young labourer, but I cannot serve thee unless thou allowest me to break one of thy commandments. It is but a little one; and it is much better for thee to give me this liberty, than to want my services, for thou canst not do well without me. Thou must either take me on these terms, or thou must lose thy grain?" Were I to reason and act thus, the Lord of the harvest could soon lay me aside, and let me see, he could have the work done without me. It is for us to do what is duty, and leave events to God. If he has any work to do, at present in Ireland, I am sure I am taking the way to do it. If he has work to do, who is he most likely to employ as his instruments? Will he let me stand idle in the market-place, and employ others to serve him, whose sole object is to serve themselves? If it be my supreme delight to win souls to Christ, I do not think I shall be disappointed. If it be in any measure my meat and drink to do his will, it is not likely he will refuse to give me employment. "And whatever we ask we receive of him, because we keep his commandments, and do these things that are pleasing in his sight." "He that loveth me, keepeth my commandments." "Follow me, and I will make you fishers of men." "Ye are my friends, if ye do whatsoever I command you." "And why call ye me Lord, Lord, and do not the things which I say."

3. No argument hath been more frequently used to reconcile me to the Synod, than "the duty I owe my family. 'He that provideth not for his own, especially for those of his own household, hath denied the faith, and is worse than an infidel.'" I acknowledge the obligation of this Scripture in its fullest extent. But am I obliged to neglect one duty by attending to another? I am to provide for my family; but will any say, I should rob and murder to support them? I am to provide, but it is things that are lawful. I am not to support them at the expense of a good conscience. If I cannot trust my family upon God, how will I trust him with my soul? He hath not only said, "He that provideth not," &c., but he hath also said, "Seek ye first the kingdom of God and his righteousness, and all these

things shall be added unto you." I must either renounce the 6th chap. of Matthew, or I must do duty, and trust myself and family to him who feedeth the fowls of the air, and clothes the lilies of the field. He that feedeth his enemies will not suffer his friends to starve. With what conscience could I press others to trust in Providence, when I distrusted him myself? When I read the history of Aristides, the Athenian, and many other pagan sages, who scorned riches for earthly fame, I am ashamed that the glories of heaven, and the love of Jesus should have a slighter impression upon me. Cyrus was fed upon brown bread and cresses, to fit him for a consummate general; and shall I think it a grievance to submit to that discipline, to enable me more successfully to fight the battles of my Lord. I must "endure hardness, as a good soldier of Jesus Christ." Perhaps there never was a general of distinction, who has not undergone more hardships, fatigues, wants, and dangers, to procure temporal glory, than I have any prospect of in my more honourable warfare. "Now they do it for a corruptible crown, but we for an incorruptible." A few years hence, and all my wants and sorrows shall be no more. I will be where "the wicked cease from troubling, and the weary are at rest." "They that are wise shall shine as the brightness of the firmament, and they that turn many unto righteousness as the stars for ever and ever."

> And must I part with all I have,
>   My dearest Lord for thee?
> It is but right, since thou hast done
>   Much more than this for me.
>
> Yes, let it go—one look from thee,
>   Will more than make amends
> For all the losses I sustain,
>   Of credit, riches, friends.
>
> Ten thousand worlds, ten thousand lives,
>   How worthless they appear,
> Compar'd with thee supremely good,
>   Divinely bright and fair!
>
> Saviour of souls! could I from thee
>   A single smile obtain,
> Though destitute of all things else,
>   I'd glory in my gain.

A REPLY

TO

MR. BROWN'S VINDICATION

OF THE

PRESBYTERIAN FORM

OF

CHURCH GOVERNMENT,

IN WHICH

THE ORDER OF THE APOSTOLICAL CHURCHES IS DEFENDED.

(FIRST PUBLISHED IN 1807).

PREFACE.

WHATEVER may be the judgment of the reader about the question, whether I "fully overthrow," I think all must allow that I "fairly meet the arguments" of my antagonist. I have not fastened on accidental oversights, nor filled my sheets with the refutation of his errors that were either not at all, or at least but remotely connected with the subject. I have not endeavoured to entangle the main principles in debate, nor have made up my book with tedious animadversions upon the weakest parts of his work. Every man must see that I have assailed him in the very places in which he thinks himself strongest, and have either not at all, or very slightly noticed whatever was not of vital importance in the question under discussion. His arguments I have not evaded, but have stated them in their strongest point of view; because I was convinced, that in their utmost force I could answer them. I was therefore under no temptation to misrepresent him, nor to answer one difficulty by proposing another. Before I relinquished my situation as a Presbyterian minister, I had so fully considered the question, that I was convinced as long as the New Testament was considered as the standard, the system of Presbytery could never be successfully vindicated; but had my antagonist produced a single particle of previously undiscovered truth, I was prepared to receive it. I will ever hold myself ready to add to, or subtract from my system, according to scriptural evidence. The moment that my views of church-order, or any part of them, cannot be supported by Scripture, I will not only be happy to see them rejected by the world, but whether the world will reject or receive them, I will reject them. In receiving the truths of God, and giving up errors, we are not to wait on the changing of the world.

The author of the work upon which I animadvert must be allowed to discover an uncommon, an almost unlimited acquaintance with the writers of all ages on both sides of the question. He has raked together the sentiments of almost every one who has written on the subject, and discovers a minute knowledge of the works of Independent writers, of whose very names I was ignorant. Yet with all this, I do not look upon him to be thoroughly acquainted with the subject, as founded in the Word of God. He treats it like a question to be decided by the authority of names. He seems to think that much can be said on the one side, and as much, or perhaps a little more, on the other; and that Presbytery has either a preponderance of evidence, or at least has equal pretensions with its rival to divine authority. Now, if the New Testament contains a divine model of church government, there cannot be one legitimate argument for another system. Owing to our remaining ignorance, and imperfect acquaintance with the Word of God, there may be difficulties opposed to the model which the Word of God contains, but to suppose anything like a comparison of well founded contrary evidence for two opposite systems, is an insult upon the Spirit of truth.

I have not made my antagonist responsible for any sentiments but his own, nor at any time have lost sight of *him*, in following the arguments of others who have written on his side of the question. Authorities I have not produced on my side, nor regarded them on his. As the Scriptures must decide the matter, to the Scriptures alone I have appealed. I have used the word *independent*, rather than *apostolical church*, that nothing like an unfair advantage might seem to be taken by the use of words. In writings not controversial, I do not like to see this word at all, as applied to characterise the churches of Christ, as it is both unscriptural and inadequate. So far from fully conveying a complete view of the distinguishing features of a church of Christ, it generally conveys a very false notion. On other occasions then, I would either use the word *church* alone, or *apostolical church*, to distinguish a church of Christ from other societies called churches; but in controversy, it might be thought to take for granted the thing to be proved, for these societies think themselves *churches* and *apostolical churches*. It is in this view only I ever acknowledge the word *Independent*, as applied to a church of Christ. Those who follow the Lord fully, ought to set themselves to reclaim the word *church* from the corrupt use of it in the world. Had it not been for the inventions of men, it would have needed no additional epithet to make it intelligible and distinctive.

Much of this work consists of critical analysis. The chief talent displayed in the work upon which I animadvert, is a certain evasive subtilty, and a dexterity in imposing the most arbitrary interpretations with an air of plausibility and confidence. As the question must be decided by the testimony of the passages which we interpret in an opposite sense, it became altogether necessary to examine the principles of interpretation employed by my antagonist, and fully ascertain their fallacy. I have therefore not only shown that his interpretations are not the obvious sense of the words, but have attempted to show that his principles of interpretation are utterly inadmissible upon every subject. For the justness and propriety of my interpretation of every text involved in the discussion, I appeal to the common sense of mankind, and to the common principles of language. I interpret the Word of God upon the same principles I would do any other book. There is not one principle of language held inviolable by my antagonist. Were his mode of interpretation admitted in courts of law, the true intent of every covenant might not only be evaded, but might be made to imply directly the reverse of its obvious meaning. Should the author then, upon whose work I animadvert, think proper to reply to my animadversions, this is the hinge upon which victory must turn. He explains one way, I explain another; the criterion of judgment between us then is, who explains most naturally? which of us explains agreeably to the usual principles of language? It were injurious to the character of revelation to suppose, that each of our opposite interpretations has any just foundation in sound criticism.

What I have written, I have written as under the eye of the Searcher of hearts. For every line I must render an account; and had I not more confidence from the review of the day of the Lord, than from the approbation of the world, I would never send my sheets to the public. I do not even wish that the world, in its present state, should approve of my performance. I have nothing to hope, I have nothing to fear. It is but a small matter to be judged of men, but I would not for a thousand worlds be found by the Judge of the world to have perverted his laws and ordinances, misrepresented his words, and taught his people to forsake his institutions. It may seem a light matter to many to give a turn to a passage of Scripture; to make it say something agreeable to our system, or evade a disagreeable consequence. To me it appears to manifest a most corrupt and base mind, and a most daring presumption against the Spirit of truth. Shall God deign to instruct us, and shall we dare to make him speak what we please? I have no notion that whoever of us is wrong, is innocently wrong. The book of God is intelligible, if we misunderstand it, we are inexcusable. With upright and unprejudiced minds, I cannot see how systems so opposite should be taken from the Word of God, after a thorough examination of the subject.

If for every idle word we shall give an account, how much more awful is the account we must render of our handling the Word of God! Let us then continue this correspondence, under the impression that we both shall soon appear before the tribunal of the eternal Judge.

LETTERS TO MR. BROWN.

LETTER I.

Sir,

I cannot begin my observations on your vindication of the Presbyterian system, by professing, as you do, in your first letter to Mr. Innes, " the utmost reluctance to address you on the subject of your late publication." I am satisfied that, on whichever side truth lies, the subject merits ample discussion, and that in the end, much good will result from having the arguments on each side of the question fully laid before the public. The works of darkness alone fear the light. It may indeed be peculiarly disagreeable for those, whose temporal interest would be materially affected by a change of opinions, to have their feelings and their consciences harrowed up, by being called to an examination of this subject; but the real disciples of Jesus should always be open to conviction, and willing to learn more fully the mind of their Lord. Though it is exceedingly popular to deplore " religious controversies," yet they must be very little acquainted with the apostolical writings, who do not know that they are almost altogether controversial. The Christian can never cease to oppose error, till error cease to exist. Had you bewailed the spirit in which controversy is frequently conducted, and which you have abundantly exemplified, there would have been good ground for lamentation. But surely, if we have any where a pattern of meekness in discussion, we have it from the pen of Mr. Innes. Though I can allow, that there is a comparative importance among divine truths;

yet I cannot admit, that anything revealed by the Spirit of the Lord Jesus is unimportant, and should not be brought into view, whatever may be the consequences. I am more than ever sensible, from your publication, of the great importance of the question under debate. I see, that to embrace an unscriptural system of church government, materially affects our understanding of Scripture in general. Multitudes of texts are thus either darkened or evaded. Indeed the spirit, propriety, and meaning, of a great part of the apostolical epistles, are entirely hidden.

You remark in your introduction, "That it is the *principles* only, and not the *practices* of Presbyterians, that are here defended. The advocate for Presbytery is certainly no more bound to vindicate the latter, in order to establish the former, than the advocate for Christianity is bound to prove that the conduct of Christians is blameless and praiseworthy, in order to show that Christianity is divine." As a Presbyterian, you are not indeed bound to defend all bodies of Presbyterians, more than a Christian is bound to defend all bodies called Christian, and every system which has been called Christianity. But, Sir, as an honest man, the very kind of Presbytery you defend, is the one you will adopt, and none other. A Burgher Seceder is not bound to defend the Presbytery of relief, nor the latter to defend the Church of Scotland; nor are you bound to defend either of the former. But each of you is certainly called upon to defend the system of Presbytery he has adopted, according to the manner of its administration among you. I will therefore look to you for a defence of Presbytery and its effects, as they exist in the Church of Scotland. Whenever you abandon the administration of Presbytery in that church, I will expect you, if you continue to hold it as a divine ordinance, to abandon your present connection, that you may enjoy it in its divine purity. As an Independent, I am not bound to defend any of the Independent churches, but that one of which I may be a member, or those which I approve by co-operation or fellowship, or which exactly agree with the model which I call divine. But certainly, if I am either a member or elder of any church, I am bound to defend it, not as it should be, but as it is. If Presbytery is a divine ordinance, and if it is not in the Church of Scotland what it is in the Scriptures, then you have not a divine form of government, and you are bound to separate, that you may enjoy your divine institution. A church might be called Independent, and in many features resemble an apostolical church, yet upon the whole be so far from the divine model, that I would think it duty to stand at as great a distance from it, as from the Church of Scotland. If the pastor, or the pastor with the deacons, or a few of the principal members, exclusively manage all church business; or if they decide by majorities like worldly courts, or are composed of saints and sinners promiscuously, or are "moved away from the hope of the Gospel," they may call themselves what they please, but they are not constituted upon the divine model. Such indeed, the advocates of the apostolical churches are not bound to defend. But when you write against them, you may properly require a defence of the independency they profess, with all its effects.

I should be glad to know how Christianity could be proved to be divine, if it uniformly had a bad tendency, or wanted energy, when received, uniformly to produce good fruits. The Christian is not indeed bound to show that all who bear that name are blameless and praiseworthy, in order to prove that Christianity is from God. But certainly no argument could prove it divine, if it had not happy effects upon those who understand and receive it. If when believed, it has not the effects which it is said to have, it cannot be true. A Roman Catholic is not bound to defend the Christianity of a Protestant, nor the latter that of the former. A Calvinist, or Armenian, or a Socinian, is not obliged to defend each others' system, when writing against infidels; but certainly it will be justly expected that each should defend his own. Our Lord himself was not afraid to rest the truth of his mission upon this very argument, "that they all may be one, as thou, Father, art in me, and I in thee; that they also may be one in us: *that the world may believe that thou hast sent me.* I in them, and thou in me, that they may be made perfect in one, and *that the world may know that thou hast sent me, and has loved them as thou hast loved me—* John xvii. 21-23. I will allow you then, Sir, to adopt any modification, or sect of Presbytery; but whatever denomination of Presbyterians you join, this one I shall expect you to defend. Nothing can be more ridiculous than to hold one sort of Presbytery in theory and another in practice. Sir, were you a member of a trading company, which enriched itself by fraudulent dealings, though in this you always opposed your partners; think you would the world take it as a sufficient apology were you to reason thus: "I request that it may be remarked, that it is the *principles* only, not the practices of trading companies that I defend. I do not justify this company. All I contend for is, that there may be such companies as will act honestly." But if you intend by this declaration, that principles and practice should be separated upon any subject, I apprehend you not only contradict the whole tenor of the Word of God, but the maxims of the soundest philosophy. Though the best system may be abused, and the worst system, in some instances, may not discover all its malignancy, it is still fair to try every system by the criterion of its tendency. This indeed should not be determined from a few solitary results, either good or bad, but from its general effects. If in the history of any among the various Presbyterian denominations, it is found that Presbytery has in general a good tendency, it would be idle in us to show that, in a few cases, it was abused. On the contrary, if we can show from the history of the Church of Scotland, that the Presbyterian form of church government has had a general tendency to promote corruption either in members, doctrines, or practice, or which is the same thing, has not had energy to prevent this, it is of no avail to display in the abstract the advantages of the constitution. That tree cannot be a good one which uniformly bears bad fruit, or no fruit. To suppose that the form of government instituted by Christ, is insufficient to attain the ends of government is in my apprehension to blaspheme him. Whenever then I write against a member of the Church of Scotland upon this subject,

I will take my ideas of Presbytery only from that church, and consider the corruptions which I find in it, as the native fruits of the system. He cannot deny me this, until he renounces his connection. The same shall be my conduct with respect to every denomination of Presbyterians. Their system and the fruits of it, I will ever consider in connection. This liberty I will also readily grant them in their turn. I will hold myself accountable for the corruptions of all the churches which I allow to be on the apostolical model. Now there is not an instance of abuse which you either prove or mention, belonging to Independent churches, which has not arisen from a departure from the apostolical model, in a greater or less degree. But I will undertake to prove that Presbytery even when fully acted upon, is insufficient to attain the great ends of government. It may be true, as you say, that Arminianism, or Socinianism, has crept into societies called Independent churches in England;* but such societies are not churches of Christ, for *they* consist of "saints, godly, faithful in Christ Jesus, an habitation of God through the spirit, united in the fellowship of the Gospel." I will consider myself bound equally with the Church of Scotland to oppose such societies, and even their mode of government, for it is far distant from that of the churches planted by the apostles.

"Let it be understood farther," (you remark, page 6. introduction), "That the arguments advanced will not be considered as overturned, though a number of mistakes should be pointed out in separate and detached observations, unless the body of the evidence be fairly met, and fully overthrown." This I fully admit; and as a proof of it, I will not trouble myself, nor fatigue my readers, by exposing your less important mistakes.

* That there may be Socinian churches in England calling themselves Independent is very probable. But it is a well known fact, that the great bulk of the Socinian churches are composed of the descendants of Presbyterians, and are maintained by the funds destined for the support of Presbyterian congregations. This is so notorious, that the late Dr. Priestley refused to allow application to be made for him to an Independent fund; while he cheerfully received from a Presbyterian fund.

Nor will I touch upon your more important errors, which have not an immediate relation to the point under dispute. But if I do not "fairly meet, and fully overthrow the body of your evidence," I shall consider myself as having done nothing. If I either shuffle, or evade the edge of your arguments, or endeavour to disentangle myself from one difficulty by proposing another, I shall consider myself as worse than an idler. If your reasoning were conclusive in the main, any attempt to skreen ourselves by exposing particular inaccuracies would manifest a conduct inconsistent with Christianity. Nothing but the authority of Jesus made me abandon the connection of Presbyterians; the same authority I hope shall always have the same influence on me. If then you are able to establish Presbytery from the Scriptures, I am ready to be your convert.

As I propose to trouble myself with nothing but your arguments, I will overlook your *personalities*, and employ the remainder of this letter in stating and replying to the general sentiment of your second letter to Mr. Innes.

In the beginning of the second letter you say, "The *first* point, I apprehend, in which you differ from Presbyterians, is *the nature* of that power which they grant to their rulers; and here, in words at least, the difference is important. Upon this topic Independents have often declaimed with the utmost keenness, and from this source they have derived their warmest invectives against the Establishment. Upon this topic, too, you considerably enlarge, and attempt to paint, in very shocking colours, the baneful consequences with which the authority of Presbytery is necessarily attended.

"Before however I attend to your arguments, I would briefly advert to a misrepresentation which has frequently been made by Independents, of the claims of Presbyterians with regard to the *nature and kind* of their authority. Often has it been said, that the power for which they contend amounts to nothing less than a *legislative* authority, and invests them with a right to enact at pleasure whatever laws they wish to establish in the Church of Christ. Than this, however, nothing undoubtedly can be more remote from their sentiments. They, as well as Independents, profess to admit that Jesus is the only head of his church; that those laws alone which *he* has revealed, bind the consciences and conduct of his subjects; and that the highest honour to which ecclesiastical *rulers* can now aspire, is to explain what the doctrine of the church is, with regard to the true meaning of the laws of Christ, and authoritatively to enforce among those of her communion the execution of *his* laws. In matters indeed of *inferior* moment, which regard simply the convenience, or external order and regularity of the church, and for which no explicit directions are given in the Scriptures, Presbyterians allow that Christ has intrusted a power with those who rule in his church, to appoint such regulations as may be requisite for the general ends of edification and utility. But this is no more than Independents themselves have uniformly claimed; while it is an incontestable fact, that, in every instance in which *legislative* power is disclaimed by Independents, it is *universally* and *explicitly* disclaimed by Presbyterians."

Here you expressly disclaim all legislative authority on the part of Presbyterians, and assert that they admit, " that those laws alone which Jesus has revealed, bind the consciences and conduct of his subjects." If this is really a matter of fact, as to any denomination of Presbyterians; if it is agreeable to the Presbyterian constitution, and acted upon as a principle by their assemblies, then with such we are so far agreed. But, Sir, this is contradicted by the general practice of all Presbyterian sects, and immediately contradicted by yourself. You add, " In matters indeed of *inferior* moment, which regard simply the convenience, and external order, and regularity of the church, and for which no explicit directions are given in the Scriptures, Presbyterians allow, that Christ has entrusted a power with those who rule in his church, to appoint such regulations as may be requisite for the general ends of edification and utility." Now, Sir, I ask you what do you mean by legislation? Do you mean the giving of new moral precepts, and positive institutions?

In this sense I admit, that Presbyterians do not *profess* to legislate. But legislation in a church of Christ comprehends, not merely these greater matters, but every act and regulation regarding the affairs of his people. Do the Scriptures anywhere limit the exertions of ministers of the Gospel within certain boundaries? What then do you call that authority by which Presbyterian assemblies forbid pastors to preach out of their own parish, without the consent of the minister in whose district they may wish to preach? Is this not an act of legislation? How can you pretend that you assume not a power of legislation? All you can say is, that you profess to carry that power only to a certain undefined extent. Now, to regulate a borough election, is as much an act of legislative authority, as that which regulates the succession to the throne, or ascertains the privileges of the different orders of the state. It is mere shuffling then, to repel the charge of legislation, by giving your laws another name; and to shelter them by the pretended inferiority of their object. A right of legislation is inherent in the Presbyterian constitution; it is acted upon by every body of Presbyterians in the world. The General Assembly of the Church of Scotland, in concurrence with the majority of Presbyterians, has always claimed and exerted such a legislative power. The General Synod of Ulster also, in conformity with this Presbyterian principle, has lately published " An Abstract of *Laws, Regulations,* and *Rules.*" In short, Sir, I call upon you to point out upon earth any body of Presbyterians, which does not exercise a legislative authority. The whole procedure of their courts is upon the model of assemblies of legislation. And though in their definitions of their authority they confine themselves to matters of inferior moment, in which there are no sufficient directions in Scripture, regarding external order, &c.; it is yet plain, that in practice they carry it to the most extravagant length. There is nothing they are not supposed equal to, when assembled. They not only explain the laws of Christ, but add where these are supposed defective. The majority is ever between individuals and the Scriptures. When they act upon their principles, there is no such thing as individual liberty. Expressly to claim an unlimited power of legislation, would be Antichrist without a mask. It is much safer to exercise it under a softer name. The clergy know well, that if in theory they are allowed to legislate in matters of inferior moment, &c., they are not likely to be restrained in practice. They will encroach by degrees; time will familiarize the world to their pretensions, and sanction their usurpation by antiquity. If in any age they are called to account for their conduct by individuals, "the world knows its own," the mass of mankind will believe as their forefathers believed, the prejudices of the multitude concurring with the interest of the *priesthood*, a little sophistry will reduce the most extravagant of their transactions to their modest definition, and at worst they can abandon practice as not worth defending, and entrench themselves within their *principles*. None will be louder than the clergy in maintaining that Christ is the only king and lawgiver of his church, as long as Christ will condescend to reign and give law through the clergy, and not through his Word. The honours and prerogatives of his government will not cease to be extolled and vindicated, as long as they have the exercise of them. All the dignities which they heap upon Christ, are reflected back upon themselves. The greater the prince, the more respectable the *ambassadors*. The clergy will claim honour for Christ, if Christ will consent to share it with the clergy. Like Oliver Cromwell, they will exercise every act of sovereign authority, under the modest name of Protectors of the Realm.

But, Sir, if, as you say, and as any man who understands the Scriptures will allow, "those laws alone which Christ has revealed, bind the consciences and conduct of his subjects," how are they bound to those laws of inferior moment, enacted by your assemblies? In the first instance, you say absolutely, that no laws but those revealed by Jesus, can bind the consciences of his subjects. You afterwards say, "that in matters of inferior moment, which regard simply the convenience, or external order and regularity of the church, and for which no explicit directions are given in the Scriptures, Presbyterians allow that Christ has intrusted a power with those who rule in his church, to appoint such regulations as may be requisite for the general ends of edification and utility." How can you reconcile these two assertions? The object and inferior moment of a law does not destroy its nature as a law.

But as to the regulation of those matters of inferior moment, &c., where do Presbyterians find this power intrusted to them by Christ? Where do they find this part of their constitution in the Word of God? Are any of the concerns of the kingdom of Christ of such *inferior moment*, as to be unworthy of *his* attention? Or have the clergy more skill in *prudential regulations*, than the Lawgiver of Zion? What do you mean by external order? or why should internal order be regulated by Christ and external order by the clergy? What are those things which respect the convenience, external order, and regularity of the church, for which no sufficient directions are given in the Scriptures?* If the Scriptures do not contain sufficient directions for everything regarding the individual or social conduct of the disciples, they are an insufficient rule. If Christ has not given sufficient laws for every exigency, I am bold to say that he is not an all-wise lawgiver. The best human code is in many respects defective, the best human laws are in many cases insufficient, because they are the offspring of the wisdom of man. But not so with the laws of the kingdom of Christ. His wisdom comprehends at the same time the greatest and the smallest matters: his prudence provided for every possible exigency; and his foresight embraced every future case. Is it possible then, Sir, that you can thus openly depreciate the Word of God, by denying its

---

* Why may not one of the pastors be exalted above his brethren, and turned into a diocesan bishop for the sake of external order? If Episcopal churches have raised some of the pastors above their proper rank and office; Presbyterian churches have degraded some of theirs into an inferior order. The crime is equal in both. If the right of regulating matters of external order, &c., is once admitted, an Antichrist of some kind must be the inevitable consequence.

sufficiency? Is it so dark, or so defective, that the clergy must come in to its assistance? For the government of the Church of Scotland, and every other Presbyterian and worldly church, the Scriptures are indeed insufficient. For the management of such machines we will find no directions, either explicit or implied. But for this very reason, they cannot have been instituted by Jesus. An Independent church has every necessary instruction, either in precept, example, or by fair inference, in the Word of God. If Christ has not provided for such assemblies as yours, it is because they are the offspring of men.

Did you think, Sir, to lead us from the argument by a dextrous piece of artifice that appears in this reasoning? You first absolutely and unequivocally deny the charge of legislation. Then to skreen the conduct of your courts you slightly mention, as a thing very trivial, a certain sort of authority which you claim, evidently wishing that it should first serve your purpose, and then slip away unnoticed. You must mention it, otherwise your cause must fall. But scarcely has the witness made his appearance till you hurry him off the table, lest he should be cross-examined. Instead of vindicating this sort of legislative authority which you claim, you just mention it, contenting yourself by saying that Presbyterians allow that Christ has given such authority. But shall we take this for proof? What is it to us that Presbyterians allow that Christ has given them this authority? this is the very thing to be proved. You should not have left this subject till you had shown us in what part of Scripture Christ has given Presbyterians an authority to make regulations respecting things of inferior moment, of external order and regularity, and that he has told them that his Word does not contain any explicit directions for these matters. The very thing you ought to prove, you evade, and have swelled your volume with much matter totally irrelevant. This has a double advantage. It will cause many to think that you have done some great thing; that in so large a book you must surely have overturned Mr. Innes, and all the Independents both ancient and modern; and at the same time it will hide the weakness of your cause, and lead many from the true merits of the point under debate. You prove at an unmeasurable length, and with a redundancy of reasoning, a thing that nobody denies, to wit, that rulers should rule with authority, and you wish to prove with a "Presbyterian's allow," the very thing disputed. As if this were granted, you pass with the utmost precipitancy to another point. You bring to my mind an artifice practised by Louvet in passing through a village in France, after he had been denounced during the tyranny of Robespierre. Conscious that his forged pass could not stand examination, and knowing that he could not proceed without showing it, he contrived to divert the attention of the officers by some good wine, and some good stories. Still as he was in the middle of his story, he would, as if recollecting himself, present his pass, but still as he presented it he withdrew it to finish his story. So from bottle to bottle, and from story to story, till they forgot to examine his pass, all swearing heartily when they left him, that it was as good a pass as ever was written, though they had not read a line of it. You understood well, Sir, that some sort of legislative authority you must claim; but as if conscious that it would not bear examination, you endeavour to lead us hastily away to something else.

It seems, however, that, if this kind of legislative authority is without foundation, Presbyterians are not singular in claiming and exercising it. If they are wrong, they are at least kept in countenance by Independents. "But this is no more than Independents themselves have uniformly claimed; while it is an incontestable fact, that, in every instance in which *legislative* power is disclaimed by Independents, it is *universally* and *explicitly* disclaimed by Presbyterians."

Now, Sir, allowing this to be a fact, it is a bad way of justifying the practice of one body by a corresponding impropriety in another. If, as you say, Independents uniformly claim this power as well as Presbyterians, the conduct of the one cannot justify that of the other. But, Sir, the assertion is unfounded. That some called Independents may have acted upon this principle, may be true. I am no more required to defend the practice of all called Independents, than you are that of all called Presbyterians. You cannot be ignorant, however, Sir, that the churches lately formed in Scotland *uniformly* disclaim, both in theory and practice, all legislative authority, in every instance, in every degree. If there are any who do not, I have no desire to vindicate them. Thus, you say in a note, " The Tabernacle churches in Scotland require their members to stand in singing." In this, Sir, you are mistaken. Most of the churches do indeed stand in singing: but it is not from decency or external order, left for them to determine by their laws, but because they have scriptural example for this. Now, Sir, although you should be successful in showing, that there is no Scripture example for this, what would you prove? Not that they acted from expediency, but that they were wrong in their views of those parts of Scripture upon which they found this posture in singing. If you were so ignorant of their principles as not to know this, you are unfit for the office you have undertaken. If you knowingly misrepresented the grounds of their conduct in this instance, it is inconsistent with Christian candour. Convince them that they have not scriptural authority for standing in singing—I answer for them, they will not insist on it. They will never reply, that they have the power of regulating things of inferior moment by their own discretion, nor vindicate either this, or any other practice, from the authority of the church.

If Christ has committed any such subordinate legislative authority to church rulers, then their laws, which are the result of it, become equally binding with any part of the Word of God. Consequently we have duties which are not contained in Scripture; and notwithstanding all the warnings Christ and his apostles have given us not to submit to the commandments of men, he has in fact established them, and made it equally duty to obey the laws of the clergy as his own. Here the Scriptures are no longer perfect; they are not a complete rule: we have only an imperfect revelation of the will of our King. But further, upon this supposition, the clergy must either be infallible, or Christ has bound his people to submit to regulations which may be improper. As the Scriptures are not supposed to contain these regulations, there is therefore no standard by which they may be tried. They must then be entirely arbitrary. If it is said that they have power to make such rules as are agreeable to Scripture; I answer, that as they are not in Scripture, they cannot be agreeable to Scripture. To do any thing agreeable to Scripture, is to do what the Scripture commands. If it is said that they have power to make any regulations that do not contradict Scripture; I answer, that if by this is meant express declarations of Scripture, then they may command whatever is not expressly forbidden. Thus for instance, they might for the sake of decency, order, and uniformity, command that all their disciples should be clothed alike, that men should wear long beards, &c., &c., &c., for these things are no where expressly forbidden. Upon this foundation the most stupendous Babylon might be raised. But everything not contained in Scripture is contrary to Scripture. For if the "law of God is perfect," every additional law supposes it imperfect. Besides, there is scarcely any human regulation in the things of God, that does not go to set aside some of the commandments of Jesus. Though they have "a show of wisdom," the traditions of men tend to make void the commandments of God. To make a law, for instance, as to the studies and qualifications of pastors, appears a very wise thing. Yet it must set aside the commandments of Paul upon that subject to Timothy and Titus. For if these were sufficient, why make any other? It equally affronts Jesus to require anything more, or to accept of anything short. The same observation will hold true of all other human regulations in the affairs of Christ's kingdom.

But pray, what do you mean when you say, "That the highest honour to which ecclesiastical rulers can now aspire, is to explain what *the doctrine of the church* is, with regard to the true meaning of the laws of Christ?" In which of all the numerous Presbyterian acceptations are we to understand the word church in this connection? Surely it cannot be the confession;

for you add, " and authoritatively to enforce among those of *her communion,*" to wit, the communion of this church. Yet it is the confession that is your avowed standard, which contains your doctrines and laws, and to maintain every part of which you are solemnly pledged. You cannot mean by it, those who made the confession, for it would be impossible for church rulers to enforce obedience upon all of *their* communion now. It cannot mean the present church rulers themselves, for this would be church rulers explaining the doctrine of church rulers. It cannot mean the whole body of the people, for this would be to set the body above the head, and to represent the clergy as explaining to this church its own doctrines. This may be called the *mysterious* acceptation of the word church. I do not by this, Sir, intend to vilify your talents for composition. I am convinced you could write intelligibly, if you had the truth on your side. But the genius of a writer is sometimes as necessary to darken, as at other times to elucidate his subject. As tyrannical kings do not wish to have their prerogatives clearly defined, lest they should be kept within their lawful limits, so any intelligible definition of the authority of the Presbyterian clergy, would tend to abolish their usurpation. When a writer then wishes to defend their prerogative, let him write with the most *solemn obscurity.* I am convinced that you must have found yourself a good deal puzzled here. There is every symptom of a mind labouring, without any accurate ideas, under its expressions; so that the claims of Presbyterians may be vindicated, while the nature of their authority may still remain involved in necessary obscurity. What a mixture of condescension and authority in this definition! The power of the church rulers is only to " explain laws," and to regulate things of " inferior moment," but *authoritatively* to enforce obedience. This must have an admirable effect in perplexing your readers; for while in one view the clergy are nothing, in another they are everything.

But whatever is the meaning of the word church here, you evidently assert, that it is the duty of ecclesiastical rulers to explain, not the laws of Christ themselves, but the doctrine of this mysterious church, with regard to the true meaning of the laws of Christ, and to enforce obedience according to this explanation. Now, I can see little difference between legislation in the highest sense of the word, and an unlimited authority to explain the laws of Christ, and to enforce obedience to this explanation, without regard to the conviction of the individual who is to obey. Authority and obedience are commensurate, for they are correlatives. There can be no divine authority on the one hand, where there is not duty of obedience on the other. Now, if Christ has given the Presbyterian church rulers an unlimited authority to explain his laws, and to enforce them according to this explanation, without respect to the conviction of those governed, it must be the duty of the latter to obey them without reserve. If they are the divinely appointed, absolute expositors of the laws of Christ, *their* explanations are then the laws of Christ. The elders of a church of Christ have indeed authority to enforce the laws of Christ, but it is only in the presence, and with the consent of the church. They have no authority in their office distinct from the authority of the law they enforce. Therefore it is to the law, as they themselves understand it, and not to " the authoritative determination" of church rulers, that the flock of Christ should submit. The laws of Christ when understood, will have sufficient weight with any spiritual man, without deriving any additional obligation from the authority of office.

If it is replied, that those who cannot conscientiously comply with the decisions of their church rulers may separate, I answer, that the habit of deciding every matter, not in the presence of those who are to submit to the decisions, and without their consent, will accustom them to blind obedience, and thus have a pernicious tendency, even where the decisions may be just. There is a proneness in men to attach an undue weight to the opinions of the clergy, and to receive for doctrines the commandments of their teachers. Everything then that tends to cherish this evil should be avoided. Besides, they must have a very imperfect acquaintance with human nature, who do not know that men will submit to many things when they have not a power of reversing them, which they would have prevented, had they been admitted to a share in the deliberations and judgment.* How many bugbears have the clergy to keep the people in awe of them, and deter them from separation! The mysterious word church! the awful word schism! What a wretch must he be, who will rend the bowels of his mother, and forsake the hallowed walls in which his forefathers sung the praises of God! These and such like motives weigh with the bulk of mankind, more than the most forcible reasoning. Thus they submit to one encroachment after another, till they become completely familiarised with clerical despotism. Thus we find, that in every age, all the crimes, and all the tyranny of the clergy, do not prevent the bulk of mankind from adhering to them. And what is still more dreadful, even many of God's children will thus be detained in Babylon.

But the clergy have a still more forcible way of convincing any of their discontented clerical brethren. A good living is more powerful than all the logic of Aristotle or Lord Bacon. This will tame the wildest among the wild; or at least so far domesticate him, that he will remain in the stall without any other fetter. You indeed seem to grant the right of separation when the conscience cannot submit, with regard to things of inferior moment. But if we are to judge from the spirit in which you attack a member who left you very quietly, and took his leave very politely, it is not difficult to conjecture what sort of arguments you and your brethren would employ to convince, had you but the power.†

---

* We have the most incontestible proof of this remark, in the conduct of the congregations of the General Synod of Ulster. By far the majority of almost every congregation of the Synod were strenuously averse to the measure of the classification of royal bounty, and I am confident would have prevented it had it been left to them. Yet every congregation among them has submitted to it.

† The standards you defend, and to every part of which you are sworn, do not allow of separation. They allow the sword as the last argument to convince the judgment of the weak. So far from permitting her members quietly to depart, her avowed principles will not give toleration to any other sect.

Notwithstanding all the apparent modesty of this definition of the authority of Presbyterian church rulers, it is yet so darkly, and vaguely worded, as to support all the extravagant proceedings of your ecclesiastical courts. An unlimited power of explaining and enforcing the laws of Christ, and an authority to make laws respecting things of inferior moment, will sanction the most unlimited exertion of the clerical prerogative. Upon these two points, the whole machinery of the great Antichrist might safely turn. When any matter cannot be called " an explanation of a law of Christ," the clergy have nothing to do but call it a matter of inferior moment. Nothing is more dangerous than admitting any claim of authority which is not precise and defined. There is no saying how much ecclesiastical rulers may, on particular occasions, choose to include under the head of " matters which regard simply the convenience, or external order and regularity of the church ;" and that they must be the judges, is evident from Mr. B.'s words. Nor is his other limitations more perspicuous, " for which no explicit directions are given in the Scriptures." Every one knows, that Christians of all denominations find nothing *explicit in the Scriptures* which differs from their own practice ; so that here we have an avowed claim of legislative power on every subject which the rulers may choose to consider of inferior importance."—*Missionary Magazine*, Vol. xi., p. 248.

Now, Sir, if this is the case, the difference between Independents and Presbyterians respecting the nature of that power which the latter give to their rulers is not only important in words but in reality. It matters not that the Westminster divines and you, call this power merely " ministerial and subordinate." *Subordinate* and *ministerial* are not words opposite to *legislative* authority. Presbyterians claim and exert the right of legislation. It does not mend the matter to tell us, that they do so *ministerially* and *subordinately*.

Those who yet in reality, as well as in profession, adhere to the standards of the Church of Scotland, it is well known, lament toleration, and confess it as a national sin.

The Roman Pontiff issues his decrees only *ministerially*. He pretends to be nothing more than Christ's Vicar. The highest Presbyterian assemblies can pretend to nothing less. The point in which they differ, is not the power of legislation, but the degree of that power. While the mother claims unbounded authority, the daughter is contented with a limited and subordinate share of hereditary prerogative. Infallibility, though not equally avowed, is equally necessary to both. Indeed every system which supposes that the Word of God is not a complete rule, needs infallibility and acts upon that principle. Of all worldly churches the Church of Rome is the most consistent. If she acts as infallible, she openly avows infallibility. All others act as if they were infallible, yet disclaim infallibility. They are however rising in their demands, and if the mother were dead, it is hard to say, that some of the children might not openly avow the same pretensions.

You proceed, "But admitting that the power with which rulers are invested is not legislative, but simply of the kind which has been now stated, what is the *degree* of it which they are warranted to exercise? Are they entitled, as Independents affirm, merely to deliver their decisions to those whom they govern as *matters of opinion?* or have they a right to announce them, as Presbyterians maintain, as *authoritative determinations*, and require their cheerful and universal obedience? In the former of these schemes you profess your belief, and reprobate the latter, as subservient merely to promote the purposes of tyranny and oppression," p. 13.

Here, Sir, you make a very uncandid statement of our sentiments. You suppose that we claim the same *kind* of authority with yourselves, and that the only difference between us, is about the *degree* of it. We disclaim a legislative power of every degree, the least equally with the greatest. Upon this supposition, you ask, "Are they entitled, as Independents affirm, merely to deliver their decisions to those whom they govern, as *matters of opinion?* or have they a right to announce them, as Presbyterians maintain, as *authoritative determinations*, and require their cheerful and universal obedience?" If I am to answer these two questions, I will give a negative to both. Church rulers are neither to deliver *their decisions as matters of opinion,* nor as *authoritative determinations.* Church rulers have no right to make decisions at all among themselves. They call the attention of the brethren to the laws of Christ that are applicable to the subjects before them, but deliver to the church no previous decision for their consideration. When a church ruler insists upon obedience to a law of Christ, there is all the authority of the Lord Jesus Christ in that law, to produce the most cheerful and universal obedience, without acquiring any additional importance or force, from his pastoral or ministerial authority. If it is not a law of Christ, and if the individual does not see it himself to be a law of Christ, the authority of office is nothing. In the execution even of the laws of Christ, Presbyterians hide his authority, by holding forth their own. The most important command of the Lord Jesus, when it passes through the courts of these official gentlemen, is much more obligatory. It will have little weight except it comes from the lips of the reverend ambassadors; and is delivered with *ministerial authority.*

You say, that of the former of these, Mr. Innes professes his belief. Pray, Sir, where does Mr. Innes make this profession? I do not recollect any such passage. Mr. Innes indeed says in a passage you afterwards quote, "Whatever is done by those who are appointed to rule, is carried on in the presence of the general body, and with their consent." But this is quite another thing from church rulers previously and separately deciding a point, and then proposing their decision, to be adopted or rejected by the church.

But what do you mean by an authority to make decisions which may be adopted or rejected by those for whom they are made. The very idea is absurd. If there is authority to make decisions, there must be also a duty of obedience. In some arbitrations indeed in civil things the parties may either agree to, or reject the decision of the arbitrators. But in such cases we never talk of *the authority* of the arbitrators. In no case is there authority, or any degree of authority, in those who make a decision, in which there is not a corresponding degree of duty of obedience in those for whom the decision is made. If church rulers have authority to make laws, those who are governed are bound to obey them. Whatever is the degree or extent of authority in the one, the same is the degree and extent of the duty of obedience in the other. The one can have no right to make any decision which the other is not bound to obey. If it were otherwise, it would suppose that God gave an authority to one to command that, which he gave authority to the other to disobey. If then this is the case, church rulers have no authority distinct from the laws of Christ which they enforce. Ministerial authority can be nothing but the authority of the laws of which they are the executors. Again, as to the question with respect to the degree of authority of explaining, and enforcing the laws of Christ, and of making others of inferior moment, &c., you reply that they are *authoritative determinations* ; the degree of this authority must be absolute : consequently the obedience of those who are governed must also be absolute.

But allowing that it were a part of the office of Independent church rulers to make decisions, to be submitted to the church to be accepted or rejected, for what possible purpose did you range this in the class of *the authority* of church rulers? There is no authority in the matter. This is no more than one man proposing his opinion to another. The difference here is not in degree but in kind : not in one being a lower authority than the other ; but in one being a matter of authority, the other a matter of opinion or advice. But in order to sanction Presbyterian legislation, you must suppose that Independents have such a practice, and this practice you must bring under such a denomination as to kind, that the dispute may be only about the degree. This gives you afterwards an opportunity of exercising your wit in showing the absurdity of governing by opinion or advice.

Sir, you uniformly in your book appear to be incapable of distinguishing between a right to make a law, a right to judge of the application of that law, and a right to execute that law, when judged to be applicable to any particular case. The first belongs to Jesus alone—the second, to the whole church—the third to the rulers of that church. Had you attended to this, you would have been preserved from many blunders which appear in your work. Thus you say, p. 15, that "Independency in its number of rulers, resembles and equals the lowest form of political democracy;" and p. 19, "that it constitutes every member of the church, man, woman, or child (for such sometimes, from early piety, are received to that privilege), a ruler in the church."

Now, Sir, I must tell you, that this shows you to be very imperfectly acquainted with the constitution of the churches against which you write. Every member is indeed bound to judge in all matters that come before the church; none, however, are rulers but the elders. Is there no difference between judging of the application of a law, and executing that law? Church members then, are not church rulers, those only excepted who are appointed to the office of the elder.*

The indefinite use of words is a source of much obscurity in reasoning. Your conclusions, in the following passage, are drawn from an undefined, ambiguous, use of the word authority. Authority is so dear to Presbyterians that it is no wonder they labour hard to sanction it in themselves by the example of others. "I would observe, moreover, that you yourself have admitted a case (and it has frequently occurred) in which, even in an Independent church, authoritative power must be exercised by your rulers. 'Suppose,' you say (p. 50), 'a case of discipline to occur in an Independent church, in which a difference of opinion obtained, how far a charge was distinctly proved. The church must act in one way or another. If the party be excluded against whom the charge is brought, those who think him not guilty, will take offence at the measure. If, on the other hand, he be continued

---

* We must always remember that the legislative authority exclusively belongs to Christ, and is already exercised in his Word. The church is an absolute monarchy, though the subjects are a willing people.

in communion without reproof, those who think him guilty, will be equally offended.' A decision notwithstanding must necessarily be made, and the minority you admit must either submit to the majority, or withdraw from their communion. Now, in this instance, I would ask you, if an authoritative power be not used by *the majority* of this Independent church without regard to the will of the minority, as much as by any class of Presbyterian rulers? and if they do not act as decidedly, without any regard to the convictions of their brethren? Besides, I would inquire, whether this must not be the case in Independent, as well as Presbyterian churches, *in every instance* (and they cannot be few) in which a question is carried and acted upon by a *majority* against a minority? Is not *the opinion* of the latter uniformly disregarded? Is not the will of the former executed *as a law*? Can *any* religious society *exist* without it? Does not this unquestionably involve *of necessity*, as much authority as the decision of any Presbyterian court? And is not the minority obliged as readily to submit to this authoritative determination, if it be an inferior point—or if it be a fundamental article, as universally to separate from their former brethren, if they are so disposed as in Presbyterian churches?

"When a majority, in a word, of any of your churches determines against a minority, that a brother who has happened to offend before all, should be *rebuked* before all, that he may be taught by it to be ashamed, I should be glad to know, if it is only a *simple advice* which is delivered? And when such a majority decides against a minority, that a brother is to be *excommunicated*, and their decision is fulfilled, I should be happy to be informed, if it is only a *simple opinion* which is stated? This, I believe, you will hardly maintain; and consequently, since in these and all other instances, where the will of a majority is carried and acted upon against a minority, from the very nature of things, authority is exercised, I hold it to be unfair and contradictory in Independents to declaim against Presbyterians, when they claim for *their rulers*, the *same portion* of authority which is necessarily assumed by the majority of *the members* in each of their congregations; and without which, whatever *persuasion* might be employed, and whatever *advices* might be delivered, not one of their societies can be conceived to exist"—pp. 26, 27.

That every society of men must have authority to exclude from it all persons acting contrary to its fundamental rules, is a truth which will not be disputed. No society could otherwise exist. But in this, a church of Christ differs from every society upon earth, as well as from all the churches of this world. In all other societies, there are laws of human institution; but in a church of Christ, there are no laws but those enacted by Christ himself. Now, when we talk of the authority of a church of Christ, and that of a Presbyterian church, it is exceedingly improper to speak of their authority as the same. The authority of a church of Christ, extends only to judging of the application of the laws of Christ, and the execution of these laws: the authority of the rulers of a Presbyterian church, extends to explain and authoritatively to enforce their own explanation of the laws of Christ, without the consent, often contrary to the conviction and conscience of the individual; and to enact whatever new laws they may choose to call of inferior moment; and to control the conduct of individuals at pleasure. The authority reprobated by Mr. Innes, is not the same claimed and exercised by Independents. "What is the meaning," says Mr. Innes, " of the authority vested in a Presbytery, of that power by which they can command any one under their jurisdiction to act according to their will? Does not the very existence of this authority imply the necessity of it?" The authority here censured, is not that of your rulers executing the laws of Christ, nor even of judging of their application, but that authority by which they enact rules to regulate congregations, and the conduct of individuals. Such authority every Presbyterian denomination uniformly exercises. Such authority, Jesus never gave to any body of uninspired men upon the earth. The authority claimed and exercised by a church of Christ, is to try the conduct of individuals by the laws delivered in the New Testament. For this they have the sanction of their royal Lawgiver, " Do ye not judge them that are within ?" The question between us then, Sir, is not whether church rulers have any authority, nor about the comparative *portion* of similar authority; but, what is the *nature* and *extent* of church power : not whether Independents exercise as much authority when they decide upon and execute a case of discipline, as Presbyterian rulers do upon a similar case; but whether the authority of a church, let its form of government be what it may, is confined to judging of the application of the laws of Christ, and to the execution of them, and whether this is to be done in the presence and with the consent of those governed, or whether it reaches to the making of human regulations, and governing congregations and individuals by other rules in addition to those of Christ, and whether church business is to be conducted without the concurrence of the general body. Upon the supposition that Presbyterians have a right to enact regulations of their own, we should not condemn them for asserting their authority to put them in execution ; but we deny that they have any such authority.

Now, Sir, in any of the cases you have supposed to occur in an Independent church, let the decision go as it will, the authority claimed by either one party or the other, is quite different from the undefined authority of Presbyterian assemblies, which not only judge of the laws of Christ, but make laws of their own, and execute them at their pleasure. Besides, there are neither majorities nor minorities in a church of Christ. You are always dreaming of your Kirk-Sessions, Presbyteries, Synods, and Assemblies. Though upon a case occurring, in which forbearance ought not to be exercised, the one part of a church must exclude, or separate from the other, it is never by majorities they should proceed. I do not by this mean, that by perverseness and obstinacy a member may at any time obstruct the application of the laws of Christ. In such a case, he himself would properly become a subject of discipline. Still, however, it is true, he must be either satisfied or excluded. Complete confidence must ever prevail. With one dissenting voice, the church could not proceed. If ever there arise such a difference as to cause a separation, it is not the majority that makes the church, but those of them who are obedient to the laws of Christ. If there were only three against three thousand, these three are the Church of Christ, and have a right to cut off the three thousand, if disobedient to the laws of Christ. The separation of an individual, or of a few individuals from a corrupt church, is the very same thing with the general body of a church cutting off one, or a few corrupt individuals. "From *such* turn away," and "turn away *such*," amount to the same thing, and either one or other becomes duty, according to the circumstances. The majority of the Church of Scotland, is indeed still the Church of Scotland, and it is right that it should be so, for it is a worldly society, governed and regulated upon worldly principles. But it is not so with a church of Christ. A society that deserves that name, must not only be called a church, but must walk in all the commandments and ordinances of the Lord. So soon as they refuse to obey the laws of the kingdom, they justly forfeit the name and character. There can, therefore, be no ground for the complaints and apologies of certain pious individuals in worldly churches: "What can they do? they are but a few, without respectability or influence. They cannot prevail against the general body." They can do just what they could do if they were the majority. They can, after laying the truth before their brethren, turn from them if they will not obey it. They might indeed make but a ridiculous spectacle to the world, but they would be glorious in the eyes of the King of Zion, and of all his loyal subjects. Yet I am not at all astonished that you always speak of the majority of any of our assemblies as being the church. It is certainly very difficult for one who, like you, has formed his ideas of the kingdom of the Lord Jesus, from the kingdoms of this world, to conceive how a few individuals, perhaps the most contemptible in the eyes of worldly men, should be honoured with the presence and blessing of Christ, in preference to the most respectable majority. As in worldly societies, a majority is equivalent to the whole, it is not at all wonderful, that the same idea should be transferred to a church of Christ, by all who are unacquainted with the nature of his kingdom.

Judging of the offences of individuals also, is quite another thing in a church of Christ, from the same thing in a court of law, or a Presbyterian judicatory. In every assembly of carnal men, a leaning towards kindred, friendship, interest or popularity, may be expected. This will envelope the clearest case. Friendship on the one hand, and enmity on the other, will protract every discussion. But in a church of Christ, there is nothing of this nature to entangle the inquiry. If they are Christians, they are all brethren in the closest bonds, and the King, whose laws are to be obeyed, is the nearest relation to each of them. They cannot then be swayed, either by private affection or resentment, to obstruct the operation of the laws of the kingdom. The judges have no relation so near as the Lawgiver, no interest so dear as the honour and prosperity of his kingdom. In judging of a charge, church members neither know husband nor wife, son nor daughter, father nor mother. Jesus has every relation in himself. Besides, they well know, that they cannot manifest their love to their dearest relations in a more effectual manner, than by having the laws of Christ executed with respect to them. This is the very appointed means to recover them from the snare of the devil. The laws of Christ are all love, even to those upon whom they are executed. But worldly men, judging of the laws of Christ by the laws of men, which look rather to the prevention of similar crimes by the example of punishment, than to the correction of the individual, are ever for skreening their friend from the laws of Christ. Christians, however, know that the laws of Christ embrace both these points, and in a very particular manner the latter. With such judges then, it is not likely that there shall often arise a great difference of opinion as to the guilt or innocence of a person accused. The only danger will be in admitting carnal men to membership.* Then indeed the house will soon be in flames. Only those who are the children of Jesus can have a proper regard for the honour of his laws; only those who are spiritual are fit to judge. But they must indeed be little acquainted with Presbyterian judicatories, who do not know, that the bulk of the members bring with them their private attachments, and their private enmities. Some are unreasonably persecuted, while others are unjustly cleared. By the subtilty of argumentation, the plainest case is involved in such mystery, that it becomes sometimes at last difficult even for an unprejudiced person to know on which side lies truth. The eloquence of the orators on each side of the question, is generally exerted for their party, not to investigate and elucidate the subject under discussion; as in the pleadings at the bar, all their exertions are to clear or criminate, according to the side they have taken. A man will be either an atheist or an orthodox believer, not according to his sentiments, either written or declared, but according to the strength of his party.

When you say then, Sir, page 30, " If authority, moreover, as exercised by Presbyterians, as you (Mr. Innes) evidently insinuate, is not consistent with liberty of conscience, I demand how it is consistent with it, when exercised by the majority of an Independent congregation over the minority ?" I answer, the authority claimed and exercised by Independents and Presbyterians is not the same: that which is claimed and exercised by Independents is, to judge of, and execute the laws of Christ; Presbyterians, on the other hand, assume a discretionary power, to enact laws of

* There may be partialities in a church of Christ from remaining corruption in the members, and the less there is of the power of religion, the more this will increase, and some confusion may be the consequence; but this will lead those who truly fear God, to search and try their ways, as well as to admonish each other against the evil which they have witnessed. But the laws of Christ are so simple, that there is little danger of a long continuance of division from this cause. When it occasions much trouble, it generally proceeds from ungodly men who have crept in unawares, and will tend to make them manifest.

expediency and external order, even avowedly. With the former, the whole church, rulers and ruled, are judges, and the laws are carried into effect by universal consent. With the latter, church rulers alone judge, and execute the laws of Christ according to their own explanation, and their own laws, not only without, but often against the consent of those who are called to obey.* Now, is it the same thing to say, "Here is a law of Christ, and you must obey it," and to say "Here is a law of the church rulers, and you must obey it?" Is it the same thing to say, Christ has said, "Do this in remembrance of me," or "Put from among yourselves this wicked person," and you must obey him; and to say, "The Presbytery has forbidden you to preach in any place without leave, except in your own parish; and you must obey them!"

Upon the admitting of the members to judge of the application of the laws of Christ, as well as the rulers, you have the following observations, page 29. "It is in fact constituting those who should be *ruled* the *rulers*, while the decisions of those who are dignified with that name, are entirely subject to their determination. Their opinions, it is evident, where this system is adopted, can only be passed into laws,† when it pleases the majority of those who are to *obey them;* and when it does not please them, they are completely rejected. All the power, therefore, which is vested in the rulers, according to this plan, is merely nominal."

Now, Sir, you fall into your old mistake, that all who judge in a church are church rulers. That man

---

* It is well known, that members of the Church of Scotland, are often forced to do things against their consciences; and sometimes, it would appear, for the very reason that it is against their consciences. Some will not even scruple to advise to sacrifice scruples of conscience to the peace of the church.

† The idea of legislation is so deeply rooted in the minds of Presbyterians, that they cannot get rid of it, even when they would wish to be thought to disclaim it. Passing laws is a thing so common in their courts, that they speak usually the language of parliament. Though in words you deny the power of legislation, you evidently appear, here and elsewhere, to suppose, that no society can exist without it. Why else do you speak of Independents passing "the opinions" of church rulers "into laws?"

must be very ignorant, who needs to be told, that judging and ruling are two different things. You have been labouring a considerable time to show, that the difference between us upon the point of authority was little more than in words; yet, according to our plan, it seems, all the power which is vested in the rulers is merely nominal. Strange! very strange! Our rulers are extremely tyrannical and even absolute, yet in the midst of all their tyranny, they have nothing but the mere name of power!!

What do you mean, Sir, when you say, "Their opinions (viz., of rulers) can only be passed into laws, when it pleases the majority of those who are to obey them?" Do you insinuate, that there are any opinions, either of rulers or ruled, passed into laws among our churches? If you do, you are either very ill-informed, or you misrepresent those upon whom you animadvert. The power claimed by the whole church is, not to make laws, but to judge of their application. The power claimed by rulers is not to propose that their *opinions* should be passed into laws, but to carry into execution the laws of Christ, when judged applicable by the church.

Your observations about governing by authority, as distinguished from governing by persuasion and advice, are mere trifling. Mr. Innes never denies that church rulers rule by authority, nor gives the smallest ground for you to suppose, that when, with the consent of the church, they execute the laws of Christ, they give only an advice. He very properly distinguishes between the manner in which the rulers of a church of Christ call the attention of the church to any of his laws, and that by which Presbyterian rulers enforce theirs. The former never proceed to enforce even a law of Christ, without explanation and persuasion. According to the constitution of a Presbyterian church, this is not necessary, nor, so far as I know, ever practised. They pass their laws, and peremptorily enjoin and enforce obedience. When Independent church rulers call for the obedience of the church, it is never to a law of their own (I speak of consistent Independents), but to the laws of Christ, to which they ever point. When they call the attention of the members to a law of Christ, there is no room for hesitation or disobedience. As soon as they see that it is a law of Christ, they will implicitly obey, knowing that they are not obeying men, but God.

You say, that Presbyterian judicatories may explain their decrees, and give any necessary information and satisfaction to their people. But I ask you, is this necessary? Is it a part of their constitution? A master may explain to his servant, if he please, the reasons why he requires such a piece of work to be done; but he may also, if he please, require him to perform it without any explanation. I ask you further, is it a usual practice with Presbyterian rulers not to execute their laws, till they are assured of the conviction of those who obey them? I can give you manifold examples of the contrary. Obedience is often enjoined and accepted, when it is known to be contrary to conscience, and consequently abomination to God. In the face of so many stubborn facts, especially as long as you are a member of the Church of Scotland, I cannot give you credit for your declaration: "The authority then for which I argue, I wish it to be remembered, is not intended to supersede, but to promote inquiry." How can the defender of that church that requires at least equally absolute obedience to its own laws as to the laws of Christ, wish to promote inquiry into the propriety of those laws?* Convinced, or not convinced, they must obey, or be excommunicated. Many will

* On a certain occasion not long ago, a minister of the Church of Scotland made a very able speech on the subject of debate, in which he referred less to the *laws of his church*, and more to the Scriptures, than is common on such occasions. One of the principal leaders afterwards observed, that it was not sufficient to argue from the Scriptures alone; for after a man had, by entering the Church of Scotland, declared his approbation of her standards, he ought to argue from them upon any question which came before her judicatories. If he considered her doctrines as contrary to Scripture, he ought to renounce his connection at once. Here is a specimen of the freedom of inquiry, which, according to a very competent judge, the constitution of the Church of Scotland promotes amongst her members. Let it be observed, that both the persons alluded to are of the orthodox party, in which, it is presumed, Mr. B. wishes to be included.

think it the safest way not to inquire, lest they should be convinced on the wrong side, as some avoid reading the Confession, that they may, as they think, have less guilt in subscribing it. If your laws could be obeyed or not obeyed, according to the conviction of the individual, there would be room for inquiry. But when it is said, " Here is a law, and you must obey it, or be no longer of the church," you take away every stimulus to the investigation of its propriety.

You observe also, page 31, " That whatever is delivered by any class of rulers, whether sacred or civil, must be much more regarded when clothed with authority." Whatever is commanded by rulers, must certainly be commanded with authority. But the analogy does not hold between sacred and civil authority. If church rulers command obedience to a law of Christ, there is sufficient authority in the command. It has no need of being pompously uttered, or clothed with ministerial authority. If it is not a law of Christ, but a regulation of men, there is all the authority of the Lord Jesus forbidding obedience. But in civil things, obedience can never be suspended upon the opinion of those who are to obey. The magistrate's command is *clothed with authority,* because he has power to enforce obedience, whether it is right or wrong; but, as in sacred things nothing ought to be obeyed but the laws of Christ, nothing else can be clothed with authority. It must be confessed however, that this authority of office, distinct from and beyond the laws of Christ, is very necessary to procure *regard* to the commandments of men. And the certainty that a man will be excommunicated, and, if a minister, deprived of his benefice, upon disobedience, certainly present the most " commanding incitements to examine, and the most powerful enforcements and obligations to obey the truth," that is, to obey the clergy.*

---

* What should we think of the general who, in the field of battle, would declare to his soldiers, before the engagement, that he would give his commands only as "incitements to examine into the prudence and propriety of his measures: that if his orders did not seem to them to be the most judicious, they might every man follow his own plan?"

What do you mean by your four pages of learned quotations, proving that church rulers rule with authority? Do any of the churches against whom you write deny this? You are fighting a phantom of your own brain. It is impossible to rule without authority; authority is necessary to the very existence of ruling. We do not deny—we affirm, that church rulers rule with authority; and that the church should submit to those who are over them in the Lord. But, Sir, our dispute with you is about the nature and extent of that authority. Independents differ from Presbyterians, not in their rulers having no authority, but in having no authority to make laws of their own, in their having no authority to execute discipline without the consent of the church. Independents profess both to obey, and very highly to esteem their rulers for their work's sake; but their obedience to them is only due when their authority is legally exerted, when they call the attention of the church to the laws of Christ. Does not the king of England rule with authority, although he has no power of himself to make laws, nor to explain laws, but to execute the laws of the land? Do not the elders of an Independent church rule with authority, although they have no power to make laws, nor exclusively to judge of the application of laws, but to carry into execution the laws of Christ?

But, Sir, do you not mean to insinuate by these quotations, that the authority of church rulers is greater than what is allowed by Independents? This consequence I deny. The nature and extent of the authority cannot be determined from the words employed to denote it, but from the prescribed limits of the office. King George is a ruler, the Grand Signior is a ruler; but their rule has very different limits. The one rules by law, the other according to his will. If you did not intend to ascertain the nature, extent, and degree of the authority of church rulers, from this investigation of the names of their office, your labour is lost. If you did, you fail in your object; for it would be easy to prove, that the authority varied in each of the different examples, according to the nature of the relation or office with respect to which it is used: while in some of them, it is the lowest degree of rule; in others it amounts to absolute despotism. Sir, some people carry their books in their head, as porters do on their shoulders; their reasoning is rather incumbered than confirmed by their learning.

LETTER II.

Sir,

In entering on the consideration of your third letter, I cannot repress my feelings at the reasoning you employ, nor do I think that I should. I must say, that you appear to be either greatly deficient in information as to the principles of your adversaries, or that you want candour to combat them fairly.

It seems to me altogether unnecessary to give a particular answer to every part of that letter. What do you propose to investigate in it? Is it whether all or a few should rule in a church of Christ? There is no need for discussion on the subject; it is self-evident. The elders alone are the rulers in a church. All your quotations and deductions to prove this are nugatory. We hold ourselves as much bound as you to prove this, if there were any so weak as to deny it. But do you mean to prove by it, that each of the members of a church should not judge in everything which concerns that church? Here we are at issue with you. The difference between us here, is both real and momentous.

Judging and ruling are things distinct in themselves, and are separately exercised, even by the best civil governments. While then we hold, that every member of a church of Christ is appointed by the Great Head, a judge of the application of his laws, there are no rulers in our churches but the elders alone. Their rule is not nominal, but real; and not the less so, because they cannot carry the laws of Christ into execution till they are judged applicable by the church, nor because they have no right to make and execute decrees of their own.

The only part of this letter which requires to be particularly noticed, is your first argument, and a word or two will dispatch it. You there endeavour to prove, that the greater part of the members of a church are unfit to judge in such matters as come before them, as being illiterate and mentally weak.

I freely allow you, that the great body of almost every church of Christ are very unfit for being civil legislators or judges. I know they would make but a poor figure in the General Assembly. I do not suppose that most of them could have said much upon the metaphysical questions relating to cause and effect, lately agitated in the case of Mr. Leslie. But, Sir, in a church of Christ there are no laws to make, and none of those intricate and perplexed questions, handled in Presbyterian courts, ever come before them. All they have to do, is to judge of the application of the laws of Christ, and for this all Christians have spiritual wisdom. From the least to the greatest of them, they are all taught of God. "The law of the Lord is perfect, *making wise the simple.*" If church members did not understand the laws of Christ, they would be as unfit to obey them, as to judge when they were applicable. Indeed, Sir, there are many acquainted with almost no book but the Bible, who discover much more knowledge of the nature of the kingdom of Christ, and even more sound sense, than others who can quote a farrago of authors, and who never look into the Scriptures, but through the medium of their works.

You say, Sir, and I perfectly agree with you, that " to suppose that Jesus, the King of Zion, has warranted those whom he has not qualified to exercise this authority, is worse than contradictory." Jesus indeed qualifies his servants for every situation for which he designs them; but, for this very reason, I am sure he never has appointed the General Assembly. The most distinguished legislators are as unfit to judge in the house of God, if they are not Christians, as the meanest Christian cottager is to speak in the House of Commons. The two kingdoms are not only distinct, but opposite in their nature, and require quite different qualifications in the members. For this very reason, I am convinced that the great body of your church rulers, though they are *dignified with the name,* and though their mandates are *clothed with authority,* have never been appointed by the Lord Jesus Christ, as they have not the qualifications mentioned by Paul to Timothy and Titus, as requisite for that office. For this very reason, I am persuaded that by far the majority of the clergy of the Church of Scotland, though they arrogantly style themselves the ambassadors of Jesus Christ, and thunder out their anathemas, in his name, against those who will not submit to their usurped dominion, are yet unfit to be members of a church of Christ, as it has often been allowed by some of their orthodox brethren, that they do not know the Gospel. Upon this point then we are apparently agreed. If church members are not fit for their duty, I will freely grant that their membership has never been recognised by the Lord Jesus.

But your opinion, or mine, as to the right and qualifications of judging in the Church of God, is nothing to the purpose. What saith the Scripture ? Your opinion, on that point, is not more contradictory to that of Independents, than to that of Jesus and his apostles. I will not enter upon this point fully at present, as I have to meet you in another part of the subject upon this matter. The sixth chapter of First Corinthians is sufficient to settle the dispute. The saints are there supposed not only to judge of the personal, but also of the civil disputes of the brethren.* I ask you, Sir, as Paul does the Corinthians, " Do you not know that the saints shall judge the world? and if the world shall be judged by them, are they unworthy to judge the smallest matters ?" It requires no great mental culture to judge of every matter that comes

---

* The apostle indeed does not erect the church into a civil tribunal, but recommends that civil disputes between brethren should be left to the arbitration of some other of their brethren. They were never to go to law with each other, as if there were none of their brethren in the church sufficiently wise and prudent to judge of, and settle their differences. They might choose the wisest among them for this purpose. To show that no church will want persons sufficiently qualified, he indignantly asks, " Is it so, that there is not a wise man among you ? No, not one that shall be able to judge between his brethren ?" Nay, he supposes that even the least esteemed were qualified to make an equitable decision.

before a church of Christ. Common sense is sufficient to judge of the proof of a brother's offence, whether it be drunkenness, swearing, covetousness, &c., or the breach of any positive law; and a spiritual understanding will enable them to discover whether he is to be deemed a hypocrite, or has been overtaken in a fault.

Your fourth letter contains another argument, drawn from the circumstance of the keys being given to Peter. You state several hypotheses, which have been adopted by the different denominations who wish to find their system of church government sanctioned by this passage. Roman Catholics suppose that they were given to Peter, as the representative of Christ, and from him to their popes. The Church of England, you say, see their bishops coming in succession to Peter. *You* plead for Presbyterian church rulers, while Independents, you say, look upon Peter, in this instance, as representing all believers. Indeed, Sir, I agree neither with the one nor with the other. In my opinion, you are all equally astray. I dare say, a hundred hypotheses might be suggested, and supported with ingenious conjectures. Whenever men go upon fanciful ground, there is no end to absurdity. I do not doubt but the Emperor of France might plead his right of succession, with as good reasons as any of you have alleged. There is not the smallest degree of darkness in the passage itself, and I do not think that any Protestant party would ever have thought of founding church authority upon it, but from a desire of wresting it from the pope. The greater part of the difficulties of Scripture are not in the Scriptures themselves, but in accommodating them to a particular system.

The keys of a house are the instruments of opening a house. The keys of heaven, then, are the instrument by which that kingdom is opened to sinners; that instrument is the Gospel, for "we are born again of the incorruptible seed of the Word." Jesus gave Peter these keys, because he gave him power and infallible qualifications to preach the Gospel to sinners, by which they were to be introduced into the kingdom of heaven. Peter represented neither one nor another; neither Pope, Prelate, Presbyter, nor church member.

He received the power to himself. There is not the smallest ground to suppose any representation; nor could it have arisen from any other source than the ambition of the clergy, who could not be contented with any dignity inferior to that of successors to the apostles, and ambassadors of Christ. "I give unto *thee*," is the address, without ever hinting at his representing either colleagues or successors. The very same power indeed that he gave to Peter, he gave to all the apostles; but he gave it to themselves in the commission which they received from him, and not by being represented in Peter. The keys are not an emblem of church power, but of apostolical power. This language amounts to neither more nor less than the import of the commission, which all the apostles received from Jesus before his ascension; the power of infallibly preaching the doctrines of the Gospel, and of declaring to what characters the kingdom of heaven is open, and to whom it is shut. All who believe in the Lord Jesus Christ are admitted into this kingdom, all who do not are excluded; while the characters of believers and unbelievers are infallibly drawn, so that those who are approved by the apostles are approved by Jesus; those condemned by them will be condemned by him. This is evidently the meaning of John xx. 23—"Whosoever sins ye remit, they are remitted unto them; and whosoever sins ye retain, they are retained." While the apostles declare that all who repent and believe shall be saved, and draw the characters of the saved, they also declare that all whoremongers, adulterers, drunkards, &c., shall not inherit the kingdom of God. The apostles remit and retain sins by the gospel which they preached.

Now, Sir, no such authority is vested in any man or body of men at present upon the earth. Whoever preaches the Gospel, and thereby brings sinners to salvation; whoever declares the doctrines of the apostles, as to those who shall be saved and condemned, may indeed, in one sense, be said to open and to shut the kingdom of heaven. But the keys are not his; they still hang upon the shoulders of the apostles, and are to be found only in the Scriptures. Accordingly we find, that whenever another key is used for this purpose, or any fancied improvement made upon the keys, it never answers the purpose. The doctrines and declarations of the apostles at this day, open and shut the kingdom of heaven as much as when they were upon earth. Nay, they will sit upon twelve thrones in the day of judgment! By their doctrines shall all who have heard the Gospel be judged, and admitted or excluded accordingly.

It is very remarkable that our Lord (Matt. xxviii. 19, 20), not only gives, but confines the commission of preaching the Gospel to the apostles. He says " *Go ye,*" without taking the smallest notice of any others who should afterwards be engaged in the same work. He commands them (Mark xvii. 15), to "*go into all the world,*" or *to disciple all nations,* as if they were to have visited every nation of the earth, and to have spoken to every creature; whereas, a great part of the world was not discovered till many ages after their death. He says, "Lo, I am with *you,*" as if there never were any others to be engaged in the same work. "Lo, I am with you *alway, even to the end of the world,*" as if they were to live for ever. The reason is obvious. Our Lord foreseeing, intended to cut off the arrogant pretensions of the clergy. The commission of infallibly preaching the Gospel, is given and confined to the apostles. To them alone his presence and his blessings are promised. When others go to preach the Gospel, it must be the apostolic Gospel; otherwise they are uncommissioned. Whoever then takes the apostles with him, has Christ's licence to preach. Let him introduce them to the world, and they will speak for themselves. Properly speaking, it is the apostles only that preach: those who declare the Gospel now, only call the attention of sinners to hear the apostles. *They* go into all the world, and disciple all nations, because they are wherever their Gospel is. If a sinner is converted at the poles, it is by the preaching of the apostles. Christ will be with them, and with them alone; therefore they need expect no success who do not travel in company with the apostles. He will be with them to the end of the world, because, though dead themselves, they will not cease preaching wherever their Gospel goes. All the sinners that shall ever henceforth be brought into the kingdom of heaven, shall* " believe through the apostle's word." Yet there have been as many disputes about the question, Who has a right to preach the Gospel? as about the more important one, What is the Gospel? Our Lord cuts off all succession. The apostles alone have a right, in the chief sense of the words, to preach the Gospel. Any man who knows their Gospel, has a right to make others acquainted with it.

If the passage (Matt. xviii. 18), be supposed to refer to the apostles, as from the similarity of the language, and some circumstances in the connection, is by many thought most probable, it contains the same absolute commission. But from the connection in which it is introduced, I am rather inclined to think that it relates to the ratification of the sentence of the church, mentioned verse 17, as far as they have acted agreeably to the doctrines and laws of the apostles. And perhaps it is for this very purpose that our Lord changes the address in the 17th and 18th verses, to show that it is only as far as the church coincides with the apostles, that he will recognise and ratify their decisions. The observation upon Matthew xxviii. 19, will tend to solve this difficulty. As it is still the apostles who preach; so it is still the apostles who excommunicate, and re-admit the excommunicated upon repentance. " To whom ye forgive anything, I forgive also." It was the apostle Paul, properly speaking, that put away and restored the incestuous person, for the church was only the instrument of executing the apostolical law. So likewise upon every other case of discipline. The retaining and remitting of sins, mentioned John xx. 23, appears to me to be equivalent to the commission Matthew xxviii. 19, while the binding and loosing mentioned in this place refers solely to the laws of discipline; the former referring to those that are without, the latter to those that are within: the one declaring how sinners shall be

---

* Therefore also when Christ prays for all his disciples to the end of the world, he includes all that were not at that time converted, under the character of persons, who should believe through the apostles' word—John xvii. 20.

saved; the other how those who have given evidence of believing the Gospel, and in consequence have been admitted into the church, shall be treated when they offend against the laws of the kingdom. In which ever manner this passage is explained, it must overthrow the pretensions of Presbyterians. If it solely refers to *the church*, then we claim it; for after all your subtleties, we do not despair of rescuing that word out of your hands. If it immediately refers to the apostles, it is to their power of discipline, and from the connection in which it is introduced, the church, verse 17, are appointed the judges of it. Did our cause need the aid of sophistry, it would have been easy to have said many *plausible things* to show that the keys were lodged with the body of believers. But it is not to darken, it is to elucidate Scripture I write; neither to overthrow nor to establish the theories of men, but to vindicate the Word of God. I have therefore, Sir, thought it better to give the true meaning of these passages, as I understand them, than to follow you through the various hypotheses you have stated and tediously canvassed. There would be no end to conjectures. I might prefer one, you might prefer another; and every denomination upon earth might propose one to suit themselves, and defend it with *plausible* arguments. The passage that relates the giving of the keys, when properly understood, will support no party. Long have the different denominations of the world agreed to banish the apostles, and have quarrelled for their titles, honours, and prerogatives. Instead of putting in a claim, I would wish to restore them to their lawful owners. The apostles, "though dead, yet speak," and bear the keys of the kingdom.*

* If the giving of the keys to Peter conveys a right to the Presbyterian clergy to admit and exclude members, independently of the church, then how can you reason in your observations on 1 Cor. v., that the church members may be said to do it by their rulers. If our Lord gave this exclusive prerogative to church rulers, then it cannot be said that in using it they act as the church's representatives. It is not the business of the church, but of the rulers. The rulers then act for themselves, and not in the name and as the representatives of the body. The church members then in 1 Cor. v. could not in any

But allow to any of the denominations that claim this text that it gives the keys to their church rulers, what will it prove? Not that they have a right to make laws, nor exclusively to judge of the application of laws, but merely to execute them. It would prove that pastors were rulers, not that rulers were legislators. It would prove that they were to carry the laws of Christ into execution, not that they were to execute them at their pleasure without the concurrence of the church. A door-keeper in any public place, or the beadle of a meeting-house, or even the highest steward under the crown, has a right to open to none but according to instructions. There is no inconsistency between allowing the church rulers to be the instruments of admission and exclusion, without any power of acting independently of the judgment and consent of the church members.

Again, if Peter, as a presbyter, represented presbyters, does not this exclude Presbyterian lay elders from all share of church power? Peter, as a presbyter, could only represent the clerical presbyters; unless we suppose that he was *both a layman and a clergyman!!* Farther, if Peter received the keys as an apostle, he could not, as such, have been the representative of presbyters; and if he received them as a presbyter, they did not belong to him as an apostle. Consequently the apostles, as such, were excluded from the exercise of the keys, and the authority of presbyters is paramount to that of apostles.* If he received them as an apostle, they did not belong even to himself as a presbyter, nor could he convey them to such. Now Peter was a presbyter in no other way than either as that office is included in the apostolic, or as he actually discharged that office in any particular place. If he was an elder in the latter sense, then at the time he received the keys he was not an elder; and consequently could not receive them as such. If he was

sense be commanded to do that which it was not their duty in any sense to do.

* This indeed agrees very well with your obliging the apostle Paul to come to Jerusalem, to get instructions from a fallible and uninspired council.

an elder in the former sense, then it could not be as an elder he received them, for he was only an elder as he was an apostle.

It is sufficient to show you that this passage, with respect to the keys, can be fairly explained in consistency with our views. I will attempt to do more. I think I can show that the phrase, *kingdom of heaven*, never signifies what is called the visible church. Consequently that "the keys of the kingdom of heaven" do not mean the power of admitting to, or excluding from the privileges of church communion. If this shall appear, there will no longer be occasion to dispute about the possession of these keys, nor fatigue ourselves by ascertaining whether they should be lodged with the Conclave at Rome, or with the General Assembly at Edinburgh. Every kingdom consists of its king and his subjects. *The kingdom of heaven*, or the *kingdom of God* consists of Christ and his people. Part of these are on earth, and part in heaven; but these do not make two kingdoms, but different parts of the same kingdom in different stages. The one is sometimes distinguished by the name of the kingdom of grace, the other by that of the kingdom of glory. The Scriptures however do no where make this distinction, and there is this evil in it, that it leads people to think that they are not the same kingdom in different situations, but two kingdoms entirely distinct; and creates obscurity by multiplying the meanings of the word.

The kingdom of heaven includes all the saints in heaven, and all the saints on earth; and whenever it is used without any restricting circumstances, it is always to be so understood. Sometimes, however, it refers to one part of the kingdom, and sometimes to the other; sometimes to that part of it which is above, and sometimes to that part of it which is on earth, just as the word church does when it denotes the general body of the redeemed. Now, of this kingdom no one is ever a member on earth more than in heaven, but a real saint. The most accomplished hypocrite that ever deceived any of the churches of Christ was never a member of this kingdom, because he was not a subject of its King.

He might appear to have been such, and from this entitled to be treated by Christ's subjects as such, as long as he maintained this appearance. In that kingdom, however, he never had a place. But in the present church on earth there may be hypocrites; consequently the kingdom of heaven never signifies what is called the visible church. The word no where occurs, in which it cannot be explained on this principle. The phrase, *kingdom of heaven*, is indeed interpreted by commentators very variously, and represented as exceedingly indeterminate in its application. To me it appears as uniform in its acceptation, as any other word or phrase in Scripture. It is altogether as precise in the idea attached to it, as the phrase, *kingdom of Great Britain*. The application of it by John the Baptist, and by our Lord in his parables, is thought to be of the most difficult interpretation. "Repent, for the kingdom of heaven is at hand," *i.e.*, the Messiah is about to appear and set up his kingdom, and none can enter into it but by repentance. The coming of Christ to erect his kingdom, was also a good argument to call them to repentance. He was to be exalted as a Prince and as a Saviour, to give repentance unto Israel and remission of sins. The times of the former ignorance God overlooked, but now he commanded men everywhere to repent, and intended to bless the command to multitudes in every place where it should be proclaimed. Our Lord, in the parable of the tares, Matt. xiii. 24, says, "The kingdom of heaven is likened unto a man that sowed good seed in his field; but while men slept, his enemy came and sowed tares." Here it is said, "This must be the visible church, as the invisible kingdom does not contain any tares." But the kingdom here spoken of is not said to contain the tares. The tares and the wheat are indeed said to be sown in the same field, *the world*, but the good seed only are "the children of the kingdom." The tares are "the children of the wicked one." Though they are mixed in the world, and in the same families, the kingdoms to which they respectively belong are not mixed. The tares are not said to have been sown *in the kingdom*. What is the point of resemblance designed to be exhibited? It is this: the subjects of the kingdom of heaven are placed in the same civil society with the subjects of the kingdom of Satan. The righteous and the wicked, though entirely separated as to the kingdoms to which they belong, are nevertheless externally mixed upon earth; and the design of this parable is to teach the disciples of Christ, that they are never to attempt to extirpate the seed of Satan. The parables of the mustard-seed and of the leaven, represent the small beginning, the gradual progress, and the glorious enlargement of this kingdom. Again, *the kingdom of heaven* is said to be like a treasure hid in a field, because Jesus (its King) is the most inestimable treasure to those who find him, and he is to be found only in the Word. For the same reason, *the kingdom of heaven* is likened to a merchant seeking goodly pearls. Many persons, in quest of other things which they account most valuable, find Jesus; and when they do so, give up all for him to be a subject in his kingdom. *The kingdom of heaven* is like to a net. Why? Because the Gospel of that kingdom being preached to the world at large, will bring many to a profession, who shall be cast away in the great day. These, however, never were members of that kingdom. The great mistake in explaining this phrase in these parables, seems to be from supposing the likeness to be universal, or that it is between what constitutes the kingdom spoken of, and every point of the resembling objects. It is sufficient that it holds as to any part of the objects compared, or as to any of their properties, circumstances, &c. The Emperor of France might be likened to Cromwell, or Julius Cæsar, not because of any resemblance in their persons, but because he resembles them in fortune, arms, or successful enterprizes. In short, there is not one instance in which this phrase occurs, where it can be shown that it refers to any visible assembly of men on earth. Many of the subjects of it are upon the earth, but they are not all visibly united. On the contrary, there is not an instance in which the phrase occurs, which may not be explained upon the principles of interpretation here adopted.

If this then is well founded criticism, *the keys of the kingdom of heaven* cannot mean church power, nor the power of admitting and excluding church members. If *the kingdom of heaven* is Christ's real and invisible kingdom, composed solely of the members of his body, the administration of this kingdom he commits not to another. The Gospel is the key that opens this kingdom to those that believe, and shuts it against all who remain in unbelief. But were I even to allow that the *kingdom of heaven* might signify what is called the *visible church*, yet, if it is so taken here, all that is meant to be given to Peter, is no more than the power of discipline, or of admitting and excluding from the visible church. The expression would be synonomous with, " I give unto thee the keys of the visible church." I give you power to admit and to exclude. If it is said that it may also include the power of infallibly preaching the Gospel, to open the real kingdom of heaven, then if Peter represented the Presbyterian church rulers, they must also claim this part of the apostolic commission, seeing there appears no limitation in the words. Besides, upon this supposition, if Peter received this commission as a presbyter, the office of infallibly preaching the Gospel belongs to elders, not to apostles; and the apostolic office is inferior to the eldership. And what is worse for your system, if Peter represented Presbyterian church rulers, and received this commission as their representative, then the lay elders, as church rulers, have as extensive a right to preach as the clerical. Moreover, to include this, would be to suppose two different significations of the phrase, *kingdom of heaven*, which it certainly cannot have in the same place. However, it might at one time signify the real kingdom of heaven, and at another the visible church; yet it cannot in the same place signify both. It must be confined to the one or to the other. The keys of the kingdom of heaven, are the instrument by which that kingdom is opened. This kingdom consists of Christ and his subjects, and this instrument is the Gospel.

LETTER III.

Sir,

In your fifth letter, you profess to treat of the evidence in favour of your side of the question, from the right of admitting members, and of ordaining office-bearers. As to the first, your proofs are altogether inapplicable. Elders are not the successors of the apostles, and cannot claim an authority like theirs. An ordinary magistrate in Ireland might as well attempt to extend the limits of his jurisdiction, by appealing to the power of the Lord Lieutenant. If we wish to know the limits of the office of elders, we must examine it as delineated, and practically exhibited in the New Testament. When a superior office includes inferior under it, which inferior offices are separately administered by distinct officers, we cannot tell from *any particular exertion of power* in the superior officer, whether it *solely* belongs to his superior office, or is a part of such inferior offices as are enjoyed by him in common with others. This must be determined by showing the limits of these inferior offices, either as described, or exemplified by instances of sufficient authority. We are never warranted to consider an official action of a superior officer, as resulting from an inferior office, included in his superior, until we can show that such inferior office has power corresponding to such an action. For instance, when we read that the Archbishop of Canterbury, or the bishop of London, baptized an infant of the Royal Family, we could not determine from this relation whether, according to the constitution of the Church of England, the right of baptism *solely* belonged to the episcopal office, or was enjoyed by bishops of that communion, in common with the inferior clergy. Of this however we may be certain, that baptism belongs to the episcopal office; whether or not it belongs to it *ex-*

clusively, must be determined from other proof. For this purpose, we must examine the extent and prerogatives of the inferior offices of that church, from her constitution and from her practice. From this quarter we shall find, that the right of baptism, according to the constitution of the Church of England, belongs to the inferior clergy in common with the superior. But if neither the constitution nor the example of that church proved the right of the inferior clergy to baptize, we should be warranted in concluding, that it belonged *solely* to the bishops. Again, if we should read that the bishop of Derby *ordained* such a person to the clerical office, or that he is going through his diocese, *confirming* the youth, how should we ascertain whether, according to the constitution of the Church of England, *ordination* and *confirmation* were *exclusively* performed by bishops, or that it belonged to them, not as bishops, but as clergymen? That the administration of these was a part of the episcopal office, we could, from the relation itself, have no doubt; and that it belonged to it exclusively, we must also conclude, unless we learn from the constitution or practice of the church that *ordination* and *confirmation* were administered also by Presbyters. We must then examine the duties and prerogatives of the subordinate offices of the Church of England, and from this we shall find that they do not extend to the administration of these ordinances. Now, I apprehend that these illustrations are altogether in point. The apostolic office included all subordinate offices, and was paramount to any other office in the church. In the execution of this office, therefore, they may do many things which do not *exclusively* belong to the apostleship. But how are we to know these things? How are we to distinguish between the things which they did *solely* as apostles, and the things done by them, which might also have been performed by others? Not certainly from the bare relation that such things were performed by them, but from a scriptural examination of all inferior offices, to see to what height these actually reached. When we read that an apostle did such a thing with respect to church matters, we may be sure that such a thing was included in the apostolic office; but whether it was confined to it or not, we must learn from another quarter. The apostles were extraordinary officers. Their office, as such, included all inferior. They were also church members in any church where they resided. In consequence of this, many things they did, which none other had a right to do; many things they did, which ordinary officers might do; and many things they did, which all church members might do. But whether any particular action was performed by them in the capacity of the first, the second, or the third, cannot be known from the bare relation of the fact, but from either subjoined testimony, or from the account of the several duties and privileges of an apostle, of an ordinary church ruler, and of a church member. When we examine the two latter, if we do not find that it is included in any of them, it must be attributed to the first. We are never warranted to say on any particular occasion that may suit our purpose, that such an exertion of power belonged to the second, unless we can prove from other circumstances, that the power of the second was equal to it; nor that it belonged exclusively to the second, if it come within the sphere of the duties and privileges of the third. Now, instead of investigating the different duties of apostles, of elders, and of church members, upon these principles, you artfully make your Presbyterian church rulers step into the place of the apostles, and whatever you can find done by apostles, and other extraordinary ministers, you think yourself sufficiently warranted to claim for your favourites. "The apostles were church rulers; therefore, whatever was done by apostles, may be done by Presbyterian church rulers now." Might not I as well say, "The apostles were church members; therefore whatever the apostles did, church members may also do?" And another say, "The apostles were men; therefore whatever the apostles did, all men may do?" The apostles, you say, introduced members into the churches without the consent of the members; therefore Presbyterian church rulers may do the same. A Welsh curate may as well say, "The Archbishop of Canterbury has authoritative inspection over all the churches in England, why may not I have the same?"

The lowest order of the English clergy may as well vindicate their claims to the right of *ordination* and *confirmation*, by the example of their bishops.

Now, Sir, if the preceding observations are well founded, this gigantic argument, derived from the precedent of apostles and extraordinary officers, will fall to the ground. The power of the apostles included every other power. The whole government of the churches was vested in them. Whatever they did with respect to the affairs of the churches, they did with the same unlimited power with Jesus himself; for they were in Christ's stead. They were his accredited ambassadors. It will not serve you then to allege, that the three thousand converted on the day of Pentecost, could not have been examined by the whole church in one day. So soon as the apostles were satisfied with their profession, the brethren would gladly receive them. Besides, Sir, they could be as easily examined by the whole church as by one member; for if they were examined by one, in the presence of the church, it is the same as if every member individually had examined each of them. You might not only have said that there was not time for each of the members to examine each of the three thousand, and publicly to give his opinion, but that there was not time for such an examination, even by the apostles. We are certain, however, that these persons gave evidence of believing the Gospel. Besides, Sir, from the example of Barnabas introducing Paul (Acts ix. 27), we see that it is not necessary that every individual should converse with the member proposed. It is enough that a brother, in whose judgment we have confidence, introduces him as a believer. You say indeed that Barnabas was a Christian minister. Do you intend by this that he was a church ruler? Was Barnabas an elder of that church? If not, did his itinerating as a preacher of the Gospel give him authority in that church? Did he bring him in by the authority of office? Was it not by the attestation of facts—that Paul had seen the Lord—that the Lord had spoken to him—and that he had, as a confirmation of this, preached boldly at Damascus?" Could not any brother, acquainted with these facts have introduced Paul as well as Barnabas? Had Barnabas even been a church ruler, could his authority have constrained the apostles to submit? Whatever he was then, Sir, maketh no matter. He did this, not as bearing any office, but from the knowledge of facts. This instance will for ever warrant the churches to receive members upon the recommendation of a brother. But they must be always brought to the apostles before they be received. The churches must be satisfied that those they admit are approved by the apostles.

But it is exceedingly plain from this narrative, that even when the apostles were present in the churches, members were introduced with the full approbation of the brethren. When Paul came to Jerusalem, "he assayed to join himself to the disciples; but they were all afraid of him, not believing that he was a disciple." There can be nothing plainer to any man, that hath no system to support by a contrary supposition, than that those who were afraid of him would not receive him. The whole body, rulers and ruled, apostles, elders and brethren, are evidently included. All the disciples were afraid of him; therefore he was not received. But one of the brethren, acquainted with the truth of the matter, introduced him to the apostles, not to the elders, and he was in consequence received. When the apostles were fully satisfied, no brother would have any objection. Nothing can be more forced than your paraphrase of these words, " that so general a fear of him was entertained by the church, he could not be received by those whose prerogative it was to admit him." This is not *the simple statement.* This meaning is forced out of it in a very *complex* manner. Besides, if in consequence of the disciples not being persuaded he was a believer he could not be received, then the brethren have a vote. They have a power of preventing any member to be admitted, which amounts to the very thing for which we contend. Add to this, that if Paul's application for admission had not been publicly notified to the church, all the disciples could not have been afraid of him. When it is said that he attempted to join the disciples, but that they were afraid of him, it is necessarily implied that the application was made to the whole body. Had the church been Presbyterian, application would have been made to the session alone. The brethren would have known nothing of the matter till after he was admitted, and perhaps many of them not even then, for a considerable time. In a very large church, unless the candidate is publicly proposed, his admission or rejection might not for a length of time be known to many of the members. When then it is said, that before Paul's admission, all the disciples were afraid of him, I hold it an incontrovertible fact that he was publicly proposed. And when, in consequence of this, he was not received, I hold it also incontrovertible, that the rejecting of him was the deed of the whole body. Public application was made for admission; the whole church was afraid of him; therefore they did not receive him, till it was ascertained by one of their number that he had believed the Gospel. You tell us indeed in a note, p. 75, "that were it judged expedient,*

* Can it then be judged expedient to dispense with apostolical example? Were this the extent of the example, by what authority dare you pretend to set aside its obligation? When you say, "Were it judged expedient," you plainly suppose the propriety of it not being judged expedient. Here then, "by your traditions you confessedly set aside the commandments of God." What you allow to have been the practice of this apostolical church, you suppose it to be *expedient* to dispense with. You even claim a greater authority than the apostles exercised; for what the apostles thought it expedient to do, with the concurrence of the whole church, you think it expedient to do without this concurrence. This is not only supposed in your language, but is confirmed by the universal practice of the Church of Scotland. Besides, it is not even *the theory* of Presbytery professed in your standards which you are here defending. It is altogether an ideal Presbytery. If it is a better one than that professed by the Church of Scotland, then the latter cannot be divine; for there cannot be supposed to be anything better than what is divine. What sore straining you have to adjust the different interests of the theory of the Church of Scotland with her universal practice! and what endeavours to hide, or at least to draw the attention of your readers from the disconformities of the latter with the former! Then, when even the professed theory of the Church of Scotland fails, you strike out a new theory; but you are evidently much cramped by the old one. You could give your imagination much more play, were you not restrained by the fear of censuring the standards, which you profess to defend. There is no man, however, who will not, by reflecting a moment, evidently see

even upon the Presbyterian system, when any person applies for the privilege of membership, it could be announced to the congregation, and any member who could substantiate any objections to his admission, as in the case of election to the office of elders, be invited to state them to the minister or session." "It could be announced to the congregation." I ask you, is this done by the Church of Scotland? I ask you, is this a necessary part of the constitution? I ask you if *you* think this to be a part of that *divine system* you defend? If you really think this to be a part of your divine model, why do you not practice it? If you do not think so, why do you mention it? Is it not as an unworthy subterfuge, to avoid the edge of our arguments? You hold this to be compatible with your constitution, evidently for the sole purpose of bringing your paper Presbytery a little nearer to a Gospel church. But if it is not a part of your constitution, it is of no value that it is compatible with it. It is not enough that such a thing might be done in a Presbyterian church. These questions will follow, Is such a thing done by the generality of Presbyterian congregations? Are they even bound to it by their constitution? If not, what security have we that ever it will be complied with? But allowing that the constitution required this, and that it was acted upon, of what use is it, when, after all the remonstrances of the congregation, the church rulers may, even according to their constitution, receive any member? The congregation could only act here as informers; and after all their objections, the obnoxious person may still be admitted. Nay, suppose the whole session and the whole congregation agree to exclude, or not to admit any individual, they may be forced to comply, by a superior jurisdiction.

that in every amendment of Presbytery which you suggest, you either condemn that professed by the Church of Scotland as not being, in such defective cases, agreeable to the divine model, or that the divine model may be improved, or that it is not in every part worthy of scrupulous imitation. Indeed, from the many improvements, additions, and compatibilities which you suggest, you plainly show that you suppose, either that the divine model is not complete, or that it is not in everything binding.

The rejection of Paul could not have been by the church rulers, in consequence of any new information as to his character received from the disciples. He was rejected because, from his former character, they were all afraid of him. Now this character of Paul was known by the apostles and church rulers previously. If then he was rejected on account of circumstances which were previously as well known to the church rulers, as to the body of the church, it could not have been in consequence of any additional information given to the former. But how absurd is it for a church, or tne defender of a church, which embraces the body of a nation, to speak of not admitting improper persons! Once give a liberty to any individual member among you, who knows the Gospel, to make just exceptions to the characters of your church members, and exclude all he points out, you will soon have empty houses. How absurd is it for you to speak of submitting to the judgment of the congregation the admission of members, while you remain in, and defend a church which does not allow the congregations to choose even their pastors; nay, which will, with a body of armed men, ordain ministers over congregations against their consent! The church you defend in theory, and the church of which you are a member, are not only not the same, but entirely opposite. If the church you defend is upon the divine model, the Church of Scotland is upon a human model. You add, " And it is well known to be consistent with our Presbyterian constitution, that the first time a person receives a token of admission to the supper, it may be delivered to him in the presence of the whole congregation." Is this a part of your divine model? Does the Church of Scotland comply with it? If not, why do you not forsake the Church of Scotland, to adopt your divine model? Ah, Sir, what pitiful resources are men reduced to, when they employ their pen to force the Scriptures to sanction a worldly system! The Church of Scotland differs so very materially from the church you defend, that it is with difficulty I can believe that you are seriously convinced that there is any divine model. You say, " that it is consistent with the Presbyterian constitution, that the first time a person receives a token for admission to the supper, it may be delivered to him in the presence of the whole congregation." If this is necessary and agreeable to Scripture, why does not the Presbyterian constitution demand it? If it is not necessary, why does it admit of it?

You observe in a note, p. 73, " Since writing the above, I have looked into Pardovan, book 2, title 4, section 4, and find that, by the constitution of Presbyterian churches, no minister, though he may examine, can admit any person to the privilege of membership, till the whole of his session, as well as himself, are satisfied both as to his knowledge and piety."

Why had you to look into Pardovan for the constitution of a Presbyterian church! Is not this a tacit acknowledgment that it is not in the Scriptures? Had your constitution been contained in the Word of God, could you not as well have appealed to every part of the model there exhibited, and, upon the principle of only defending the theory, have condemned all Presbyterians who did not act up to the model? You find from Pardovan, that the Presbyterian constitution is such; show me that constitution in the Bible. Where do you in that sacred volume find the above instructions? Nay, the argument you have used from the conduct of the apostles, will overthrow this constitution of Pardovan. For if church rulers were represented by the apostles, the session, as composed of laymen, must be excluded from church power. You must show me then, not only from Pardovan, but from the New Testament, how a session of lay elders can come in succession to the apostles. If the apostles represented church rulers, the minister, or ministers only, of a congregation have a right to admit or exclude members. How is it also, I ask, that the Presbyterian congregation requires perfect unanimity upon this point, when the highest matters in their supreme assemblies are settled by majorities. A single vote on this side or on that side, would retain or reject the most important article of the creed. Is it then Presbyterian to require perfect unanimity in the lowest court? I ask also, Where is it determined in the Scriptures, whether the minister *alone* may examine him, or the session also? For I take your expression, " though he may examine," to imply that he may exclusively examine. If it does not signify this, it is absurd; for no one would suppose that he may not equally with the lay session examine any candidate. I ask again, if the minister has the sole right of examination, how it is, in all cases that may occur, possible for each member of the session to be satisfied, when he has it not in his power to put a question himself?

But farther; if this is really a part of the divine Presbyterian constitution, then all Presbyterian churches which do not comply with it are so far not on the divine model. If there are members admitted without the full consent of the whole session, they are trampling upon a part of a divine constitution. It must then be duty for all who think so to separate from such, if they will not submit to the divine model. Now, as I am not sure of the practice of the Church of Scotland in this instance, I will ask you what it is? I will tell you that the practice of the General Synod of Ulster is quite the reverse of this. So far as I know, the young communicants are admitted by the minister alone. I am convinced however, that this is not the case with the stricter Presbyterians. The use I will make of this here is, that all churches which do not admit every member with the full consent of the whole session, are off the divine model, if you have given a fair representation of it.

Again, if every member of session must be satisfied both as to the *knowledge* and *piety* of the candidate, I will draw one of two conclusions as to every body of Presbyterians; either that such sessions are incapable judges of *knowledge* and *piety* in candidates, or that they are not convinced of the knowledge and piety of all they admit. I know of none that is pure, I know of none that professes to be such. Which ever of these conclusions is the just one, I will infer that there is then not in existence a Presbyterian church upon the divine model you defend. Indeed, Sir, it is something worse than effrontery for a member of an established church, that embraces the body of a whole nation, to pretend that all who are admitted to the privilege of membership give *satisfactory evidence of their knowledge and piety;* or who, thinking the divine model to be such, will attempt to vindicate a church that acts upon principles so opposite. In reality you do not vindicate, you indirectly overthrow the Church of Scotland. If the divine model is such as you describe and defend, the Church of Scotland is a mere pretender.

You descant also upon the superior advantages of Presbytery as to the exclusion of corrupt members. "If, through mistake," you remark, "an improper person be occasionally admitted,* the members are permitted to communicate what they know of the applicant to the pastor; and if, after remonstrance, he be continued in communion, the lowest individual in the congregation is allowed to call these pastors to an account, with the whole of their session, before a superior court; and if that court should decide amiss, to summon even it, with these pastors and elders, to a still higher tribunal; and even that, to a higher, till the obnoxious member be at last excluded." What a beautiful chain! Is it possible that there could ever be an unjust decision, even in the lowest Presbyterian court, seeing there is such an admirable provision of subordinate courts! You might have lengthened the chain by a vast number of links, until you come to the grand council, which is to govern the whole world, according to your divine scheme. But after all, you have not said what was to be the case, if the highest court was to confirm the act of the lowest. You have supposed that the obnoxious member was at last excluded; what if he were to be retained? Mr. Ewing has given you an instance of this. It is enough to say, that this subordination of courts is not in the Scriptures; and therefore, though it may have a show of wisdom to the satisfying of the carnal mind, full of the pompous ideas of this world, we are sure it is not only useless, but injurious. None can be such good judges of the conduct of a member as

* "*Occasionally admitted.*" Let those who know the Church of Scotland, pause a moment, and reflect upon this. What may we not expect from a writer who can defend that church after this manner?

his brethren, who are in immediate and constant communion with him. And if they can determine the matter themselves, why should they employ others? But especially as to the courts of the Church of Scotland, where is the security that a Christian will meet with impartiality in their decisions. In the first instance, as the bulk of them are carnal men, they are spiritually blind, and therefore incapable judges of the affairs of Christ's kingdom. If you and I disputed about the colour of any object, where would be the use of submitting our difference to the decision of blind men? And what would it serve to have one arbitration after another, until we had the judgment of all the blind men in the world? In the second place, all carnal men are enemies to the King of Sion, and consequently to his laws. It may be expected then, that such worldly men will side with the world against Christ, his laws, and disciples. Thus we always find, that in every worldly church, when a conscientious individual wishes to have the laws of Christ respected and executed, he is always not only opposed, but hated and calumniated. In the opposition to the laws of Christ, none will be so violent as the clergy. Their constant ministering in sacred things, gives them a greater degree of disgust against them, than we will find in other carnal men. Besides, the contrast between their own conduct, and the purity of the religion and laws of Christ, is so striking, that they cannot bear to have it brought under their contemplation. It is easy then to see the reason why, in your courts, those who wish to maintain any purity always miscarry. Christians in your connection are objects of greater aversion to the carnal clergy, than even to the rest of the world. None are so unmerciful to the *wild* as the *moderate* brethren. How then could it be expected that an individual, offended with the admission of a corrupt member, could succeed in his application to have him excluded? The world has the superior interest in the Church of Scotland; and while this is the case, all attempts towards pure communion must be abortive. When a magistrate hates the king, and hates the laws, it is not likely that he will be very zealous in having them respected. He will allow of every quibble to evade the true spirit of the laws.

"Among Independents, however," you observe, "with all their boasted liberty and purity of principle, this is impossible: for if an unworthy applicant be received as a member by a majority of any of their churches, there is no superior court, on earth at least, before whom a conscientious minority can arraign them, and procure the expulsion of that member from their society; however unfit, he must continue in fellowship, while no alternative is left to them, but immediate separation, or patient submission amidst obvious corruption." Did you really think, Sir, that a majority of any of our churches are in the habit of introducing members, contrary to the opinion of a minority? If this is the case, I am really astonished that you should bring so black a charge, without acquainting yourself with the truth of the fact. A majority bring in a member against the opinion of a minority! Those against whom you write would not do so against the conscience of a single brother. There is not a single member admitted, but with the full consent of the whole church. Our churches know nothing of the words majority and minority. If any church called Independent acts upon such principles, I abandon its defence. It is nothing a-kin to those planted by the apostles. What shall I say if you knew this, and have represented the matter as you have done?

If a hypocrite thrust himself into any of our churches unawares, as *may frequently* be the case, so soon as he is detected, every child of God would instantly unite in excluding him, as bees join in expelling the drone, or in removing a dead bee from their hive. Yet the natural conclusion any one who should give you credit would draw from your statement is, that a majority admits and retains even corrupt members, contrary to the convictions of a conscientious minority.

But you say, Sir, that they must either separate, or submit patiently *amidst obvious corruption.* Here you seem to make the admission of a single improper member being a very great grievance and *corruption*, as it is in reality. Can I believe that you are in earnest?

Are not these crocodile tears? Tell me, Sir, if your conscience is so tender upon this point, how do you remain in the Church of Scotland? Is there not a single improper member to your knowledge in that connection? Tell me, is there one of your congregations in all Scotland, in which there are not many; in most, perhaps the greater part of the members? Nay, are there not some even in your own congregation, admitted to privileges, who, even according to your own loose notions of Christianity, are not Christians. Ah! Sir, you affect to make a mighty matter, even of the possibility of an improper member being continued in an Independent church; yet you remain in a situation in which the grossest corruption cannot be avoided. For if you and your whole session would agree to admit none but those who should give sufficient evidence of believing the Gospel, you may be compelled to admit the most obnoxious at the discretion of the superior courts. Let any minister of the General Assembly make the experiment to accomplish purity of communion, and he will see whether it shall not interpose its maternal authority.

You say some things about the baptism of Paul and the Ethiopian eunuch, to which I shall not take the trouble to advert; for though no adults should be baptized, but those who have a right to be admitted to every other ordinance, yet baptism does not constitute church membership. It is the privilege of individuals as believers, not as church members. There is no church authority involved in the question. When an individual goes out to preach the Gospel, there is certainly no reason that he should consult a church before he administers the ordinance of baptism to believers, for that ordinance does not exclusively belong to a church, as such, nor does the admission to baptism give a formal right of membership. It is enough that the church be consulted, when the individuals apply for admission. Then indeed their right to be satisfied is indispensable. Paul was baptized at Damascus, yet he was not without difficulty admitted afterwards to membership in the church at Jerusalem. The Ethiopian eunuch was not a church member, even after he was baptized, though he certainly had a right to be such, had there been a church in the place to which he was going. The person also who baptized him was not an elder; for though it were even allowed that Philip was at this time an evangelist, yet as such he was a different officer.

In your dissertation on ordination, I see something right, much wrong, and still more to no purpose at all. You say, "That it is committed to the latter (elders) alone, appears to be the general opinion of your churches; for ministers alone, so far as I know, ordain your pastors." About what then, Sir, are you contending? If this is our opinion and practice as well as yours, why are you at so much trouble to prove it? Are you at all this pains to convince us that we are right? But do you wish to prove from this, that, according to our principles, they ought not to ordain? Now Sir, whatever be the nature, properties, and circumstances of ordination, it is altogether executive, and as long as the churches have the right to elect their officers, it is quite consonant with my views of a church of Christ, that elders ordain them. Your error here is that which runs through your whole work; that of not distinguishing between judging and determining any matter in a church, and executing such determinations. Take this away from you, and your reasoning falls like a baseless fabric. As to the point in hand, I care not what you make of ordination. It can make nothing for or against any system. Though then I find many things unscriptural in your notions of ordination, I will not be led off my road. Your view of John xx. 21, 23, I have already considered. Your reasoning from what Paul says to Timothy and Titus, is built upon the common fallacy of confounding the office of an elder with that of an evangelist. That every case of discipline is entirely committed to the whole church, though always to be executed by the elders, I shall elsewhere endeavour to prove.

LETTER IV.

Sir,

I come now with pleasure to review your sentiments of Matt. xviii. 17, in which you attempt to evade the force of Mr. Innes' most clear and cogent reasoning. Upon the primary and appropriated meaning of the word εκκλησια, I do not find myself called on to write anything here, as there is nothing in your book that at at all affects what I have said on that point in my "Reasons for Separating from the Synod of Ulster," to which I refer you. I will confine myself here to an examination of your objections to our views of this passage.

In answer to Mr. Innes, you reply, p. 38, "that it seems by no means just to affirm, that the *church* in Scripture means either the church universal, or a particular congregation." Now, Sir, how do you attempt to prove this? I must be allowed to say, that whether you are right or wrong, you proceed neither like a critic, nor a man desirous of investigating truth. Instead of tracing the word to its original, and showing what it may signify from its intrinsic meaning, or what it actually does signify from an enumeration of the various passages in which it occurs in the New Testament, you tell your antagonist that Presbyterians understand it sometimes in a sense different from what he had stated. If, as you pretend, the word church has any other meaning than what Mr. Innes has assigned to it, why do you not prove it? Why do you not quote the places where it *must* have another sense. It is not sufficient to show, as you have attempted, that it *may* have another application, even were you successful in your efforts. Mr. Innes has pointed out places where it *must* be understood as he contends; and every other passage can be fairly explained on that hypothesis.

To overthrow him, you must refer to places where your antagonists will be obliged to allow that it has the signification for which you contend. What is the reason that Roman Catholics cannot prove that the pope is not intended by the term church here? The very same that forbids the Presbyterian interpretation; because, in no instance can they produce a passage in which the word is incontestibly so used. Both the Roman Catholic and the Presbyterian interpretation of this celebrated passage stand upon the same sandy foundation. Both are built upon an arbitrary supposition. The former may be defended by as *plausible* arguments as the latter. When we say, that it signifies a company of saints joined in church-fellowship, we can prove from numerous passages that it hath this meaning; in which even our opponents cannot differ from us. We use it in its literal, plain, and usual acceptation. I challenge you, Sir, and all the world, to produce one such passage in all the New Testament, where it must incontestibly be understood according to your interpretation. If you succeed, I will surrender to you this part of the argument. To fix an interpretation on the word *church*, in this place, which it has not incontestibly in others, is altogether unphilosophical. The most daring critic in the world would not take such a liberty with a verse of Homer.

You tell us that Presbyterians think that the Church of Jerusalem had a number of congregations, and complain of Mr. Innes' candour in not disproving this. You think that he begs the question. But, Sir, Mr. Innes was not bound to disprove every conceit of Presbyterians. He determines the meaning of the word with strict precision, by an enumeration of the passages in which it is used. If from this he has established his point, his reasoning is not invalidated by any objections but such as are founded upon the occurrence of the word clearly in another signification, or such as cannot possibly be explained upon his system. Objections arising merely from supposed difficulties can have no weight.

Now, what is your proof that the Church of Jerusalem was divided into a number of separate congregations?

Is this anywhere related? Are the saints of that city anywhere represented as meeting in separate places for the enjoyment of public ordinances? Are they in any part of the inspired records represented as separated into distinct bodies? No, no, no; you do not, you cannot allege this. Quite the contrary is often said, and everywhere supposed. What then is your proof? O! *the great number of disciples. No house in Jerusalem could hold them; therefore a church signifies a number of separate congregations.* What I have further to say upon this point, I will defer till I come to consider your letter, in which you attempt formally to prove your position. I will only say now, that I care not how many you make them. If I can prove that the word is universally upon other occasions used for a single congregation of saints meeting for worship, when it is not used for the whole kingdom of Christ; and that in no case can you prove the contrary by an example which is clear and undisputed, I am not obliged to show you how or where they might meet, or how they must have been dispersed. If I can show from the meaning and use of the word, that such is its application, and never otherwise, I am not obliged to measure houses, nor the extent of the voice of the first preachers. If I can show that there was only one church in Jerusalem, though the whole nation had been converted in that city, the necessary conclusion is, that no more of the disciples remained there constantly than could meet in one place. If objections from supposed difficulties were allowed to invalidate the truth of facts, there is not a point in ancient history which could be indisputably proved. The truth even of our Lord's resurrection would not stand clear, nor that of revelation itself.

Equally nugatory are your observations on the occurrence of this word (Acts viii. 1), where you say that the word seems only to imply the church rulers. This interpretation is perfectly arbitrary. It is not necessary here, nor is it supported by any other passage in which the word is unquestionably used in such a sense. Why then should it signify only the church rulers? I know of no reason, except it should be out of complaisance to the Presbyterian system. It is to no purpose that you show that it *may* have this signification here. Before this can be esteemed an exception to the general use of the word, and a valid objection to Mr. Innes' reasoning, you are obliged to show that it *must* have such a meaning. All your probabilities we can overthrow by a single touch. When we establish our meaning of the word from other clear instances, all we have to do to overthrow your conjectures, is to show that every passage in the Scriptures can be explained in consistence with our system, and that supposed difficulties may have possible solutions.

Let us hear your reasons for this interpretation of Acts viii. 1. As to the church rulers being most exposed to persecution, and the reasons you allege for the apostles not departing with the rest, notwithstanding their greater notoriety, though it would be easy to expose this, I will not follow you into the fairy regions of conjecture. Anything like argument I will answer. I will only trample on may-be's and might-be's. Your argument, derived from the circumstance that those of the dispersed, who are afterwards particularly mentioned in the history, were ministers, even allowing it to be a fact, would amount to nothing. It does not follow, that all the rest were so too. But if it were a thing worth an argument, it might be affirmed, that there is not the smallest reason to suppose that some of those mentioned were as yet anything but deacons. Does it follow, because Philip is afterwards called an evangelist, that he was then so. Besides, I will allow you that they were all evangelists, and even on that supposition will undertake to prove, that they are not comprehended in your definition of the word church, as signifying church rulers, from their being the representatives of that church. As evangelists, they were not rulers in any church, as being the representatives of that church, but as having authority paramount to the whole church, in setting in order things that were wanting, according to the apostolical directions. They could not then be called the *church*, because they were the representatives of that church. This conclusion would not be effected by the supposition that evangelists are ordinary officers, whose business it is to itinerate and plant churches according to the apostolic model. This would not make them stationary rulers in any church. This would not be an officer in a formed church, but an officer for forming churches. Upon neither view then of the office of an evangelist, could these persons mentioned have been included in *the church*, according to your definition of it. But all preachers of the Gospel you reckon among your church rulers. If they cannot be called pastors or elders, they may come under the description of *Christian ministers* ; whereas both then and now, there were many who preached, and do preach the Gospel, who are not church rulers. Are your probationers church rulers ? If not, according to your definition, they are not included in the word *church*.

Your argument from the use of the word *church* in the third verse, is not only irrelevant, but overthrows completely your conjecture. You make the word church in the first verse signify the pastors ; in the third, you make it denote the brethren. Now, Sir, would you take the liberty to explain a verse of the Sybil in this manner? If the Holy Ghost had used words in this loose manner, to signify the most opposite classes of people in the very same assembly, employing it indiscriminately almost in the same breath, without anything in the connection to inform us of his intention, would it be possible to arrive at any certain conclusions from the Scriptures ? Had the pastors only of that church been dispersed, could he not have told us so ? Would it not have been as easy for him to have said, " The *pastors* of the church at Jerusalem were all scattered abroad ;" as to have said, " The *church* at Jerusalem were all scattered ?" Did he mean to lead us astray ? Or did he wish to enhance the importance of the clergy, by leaving room for the exercise of their ingenuity in explaining rhetorical figures ? Surely he could not, upon this supposition, have been the instructor of the simple. The common people will undoubtedly expect, when they go to the Bible, that the Spirit of God will speak plainly what he means, and when he tells them, that " the Church of Jerusalem was dispersed," they will never dream that after all the church was not dispersed, but only its rulers. From the different specimens we have of your method of interpretation, one would be tempted to suspect that you had embraced that sentiment of Origen, "The Scriptures are of little use to those who understand them as they are written."

You ask, if the whole of the church mentioned in verse 1 was scattered, how is another church spoken of in verse 3? I answer, if the word in the two places be supposed to refer to different persons, it must mean those immediately afterwards converted by the apostles; for they certainly did not remain in Jerusalem to be idle. There is also no absolute necessity to suppose, that every individual was dispersed. In common language, a body of people may be said to be scattered, when the bulk of them are so. But the word in both places evidently refers not only to the same kind of church, but also to the same individual church. In the first verse, the fact is told generally; in the second, the burial of Stephen is recorded, not as happening after the dispersion, for this would be contrary to reason and fact. The first thing the disciples would do, after the death of Stephen, would be to bury him. The devout men then are not different from those scattered abroad. In the third verse, a particular fact is recorded, not only as illustrative of the first verse, but as a specimen of the spirit and conduct of Saul, who was afterwards to make such a figure in the cause of Christ, in preaching the faith which he then attempted to destroy. The church of which Saul made havoc, was the very one said generally in the first verse to be scattered. The first verse gives a general account of the persecution, the third gives a specimen of it. Instead then of proving that there were two churches of two different orders of people, the one ministers, the other individual members, the third verse shows the violence of the persecution, and proves that the word church, in the first verse, refers to the members as well as to the church rulers. The havoc that Saul made of the church, was not after the first dispersion, but during the persecution which occasioned the dispersion. This is put beyond all question by the fourth verse: "Therefore they that were scattered abroad went everywhere preaching the Word." Why is the fourth verse introduced by a *therefore ?* What connection has it with the verse preceding? The fourth verse comes as a consequence from the third. " They that were scattered went everywhere." Why ? Because so dreadful was the persecution, of which a specimen is given in the third verse, that it was utterly impossible for them to return with safety.

"Here then," you say, " is one instance in which it would seem, that by the church we are certainly to understand its office-bearers, as distinguished from its members." How far, Sir, you have made this good, I leave to those who shall read these observations to determine. But granting you your own interpretation for a moment, what would you make of it? It would indeed be a proof that the word church was more vague in its application than we allow, but would not prove anything to your purpose. It serves you not a whit. The church in Matt. xviii. 17 you explain to be church rulers, composed of pastors, and lay elders making a session. The church here, according to your own explanation, refers only to ministers. Now, Sir, were you even to be indulged in this fancy, it would overthrow your own system. "Tell it to the church," would not be tell it to the session, or church rulers, as composed of *lay* and *clerical*, but "tell it to the clergy ;" and if there was only one minister, "tell it to him." Your reasoning, if it proves anything, would establish Popery. You add, "And this application of the term, appears no less defensible upon the principle of substituting a part for the whole, than the application of it to the members, exclusively of the ministers, in Acts xv. 22, agreeably to the view which you have given of that passage."

Upon this I would remark, 1st, That though the word church in Acts xv. 22 refers to the members in contra-distinction to the rulers, as being already mentioned, yet that the rulers are not excluded, as being no part of the church; they are excluded, because already mentioned. When I say, that the conduct of Lord Nelson excited the admiration of the parliament, with the whole nation, I do not mean to hint that the parliament is no part of the nation. 2ndly, That the members may be called a church, in contra-distinction to their rulers, is very plain, because they exist before their rulers, and even are a church without them; neither of which can be said of the latter. 3rdly, There is this natural reason why the members may be called the church, in contra-distinction to their rulers, and that the rulers can never be so called in contra-distinction to the members, because the one is a matter of fact, the other is only a conjecture; because the former are so distinguished in the New Testament, the latter never are. Besides, if it is a fact that the members are sometimes called the church, in contra-distinction to their rulers, this very reason would prevent the latter from being so called, otherwise there would be inextricable ambiguity. 4th, When a part is put for the whole, it is always the greater part. If a mob should disperse the General Assembly, except the king's representative, his suite, and the moderator, it might still be said that the General Assembly was dispersed. But if none were dispersed but the commissioner, his attendants and moderator, it could not be said that the General Assembly was dispersed.

But further, if the word church, in Acts viii. 1 denotes the rulers only of that church, by a part being put for the whole, this is a figure, and upon the figurative use of the word nothing can be built. To allow that the rulers can only be called the church, as a part put down for the whole, acknowledges that the primary meaning of the word includes the whole members. Now, if church here figuratively signifies the rulers, as a part for the whole, this application of it can never be adduced elsewhere to prove the meaning of that word; for the very supposition that it is figurative, allows that it is not usually so taken.

Again, if it denotes (Acts viii. 1) the rulers, as a part for the whole, then it is a different figure from that by which you suppose it to denote the same thing in Matt. xviii. 17. Church rulers there are supposed to be called the church, as the representatives of the church. Now this not only makes the word figurative in both instances, but supposes a different figure employed to make the word denote the same thing. Besides, although you make it signify church rulers in both places, yet they are not in both of the same class. In Matthew, it is the ministers and lay elders; in Acts, it is the ministers alone. Nor is it in both a church of the same description. In the one, it is a *session*, composed of the minister and lay elders of a single congregation; in the other, it is a church composed of the ministers of a city. What bungling criticism! In every place where you allege the word to have a different sense from that which we invariably give it, you must acknowledge it to be figurative and forced; and these figures to be essentially different from one another. In attempting to overthrow the independency of churches, you overthrow the most simple and acknowledged principles of language.

Had a church any such thing as representatives to legislate for them, those might indeed figuratively be called the church, because in their assembled capacity the whole church would be supposed to be met in them. But it is not so with respect to the dispersion of these representatives, for, as dispersed, they do not represent the church. A nation, by a figure, may be said to be assembled in its representatives; but all the figures described from Aristotle to Dr. Blair, could not make a nation be scattered in its representatives. Besides, Sir, if, as you say, the word church (Acts viii. 1) signifies the rulers as a part for the whole, how is it said that they were *all* scattered? That the word church does not here denote a small part of the church, is clear from this, that not *all* of a part, but *all* of the whole, except the apostles, were dispersed. Then, Sir, you must rack your brain for another figure; this one is too short. Whatever the word church signifies, the whole of it, and not a part of it, is said to have been dispersed, the apostles excepted. The persecution was against the church at Jerusalem. Were there no others belonging to it but ministers? If there were, they were all scattered abroad. But the very exception made as to the apostles, shows clearly that the recorder of this fact intended to be precise, and not general. Had only the church rulers been scattered, the members would have been excepted as well as the apostles.*

So much then, at present, for the meaning of the word church in Acts viii. 1. You next proceed to show us what are the opinions of the most celebrated ancient Independents, with respect to Matt. xviii. 17. But, Sir, as we call no man father upon earth, you might have spared yourself the trouble. If I am fairly to meet and fully to overthrow such passages as this, it will be only by walking over them. Presbyterians are so much in the habit of being ruled by the authority of names, that it is difficult for them not to suppose the same propensity in others.

That the word church in Matt. xviii. 18 refers to the elders of the church, you apprehend is probable, from the allusion that is made to the Jewish ecclesiastical courts. But how do you prove that there is an allusion to the procedure of these courts? "Because," say you, "the word εκκλησια was applied to the synagogue, and that the discipline of the synagogue was committed to the rulers." That the word εκκλησια was employed to denote the whole nation, and also each synagogue of the Jews, I readily admit, and the knowledge of it will undoubtedly help to illustrate the meaning of this place. But that the word εκκλησια was appropriated to the Jewish judicatories, I altogether deny. On the contrary, the chief council was not by appropriation called εκκλησια but συνεδριον; and the rulers of a synagogue not εκκλησια, but πρεσβυτεριον. The application of the word εκκλησια among the Jews, not only gives no countenance to this conjecture, but absolutely forbids it.

---

* If the plain Christian is at a loss to comprehend the strain of the reasoning here, let him go to his Bible. There is no difficulty in the passage itself. My reasoning is not necessary for any one who wishes simply to know the fact. The weakest Christian can be at no loss to discover the meaning of the word church in Acts viii. 1; Matt. xviii. 18. To prove it, can only be necessary to silence the subtleties of false learning. There is no danger of any one mistaking the true meaning of these passages, but those who have got so much learning as is sufficient to *light* them astray.

ON PRESBYTERY. 205

The passage quoted from Josephus, is the clearest refutation of your opinion of the meaning of the word εκκλησια. Συνειδων δε την μεταβολην Ιησους τον μεν δημον εκελευεν αναχωρειν, προσμειναι δε την βουλην ηξιωσε, p. 98. It is very evident from this, that not the rulers alone, but the whole of a synagogue, was an εκκλησια; for when he speaks of the individual members and the rulers, as distinguished from each other, he calls the one δημος, and the other βουλη. It could not serve your purpose, unless he had called the rulers εκκλησια in contra-distinction to δημος, the people.

Εκκλησια being applied to the whole nation of the Jews, as the Church of God, and to each particular assembly of them, this very circumstance would prevent that word from being appropriated to their courts, although it might in a literal sense be even equally applicable. This would produce confusion which the most barbarous language never admits. Accordingly we find that their courts received other names. The use of the word εκκλησια among the Jews was exactly similar, as Dr. Campbell proves, to the use of that word in the New Testament, denoting either the whole nation, or a particular congregation. Now, as it signified the whole of the members of a particular congregation or synagogue, if our Lord used the word as the Jews did, as it is most probable he would, he must intend here the whole of the members of a Christian εκκλησια. "Tell it to the church," then, according to the exact use of that word among the Jews, would be, "Tell it to the congregation of the saints." There is no allusion here to a Jewish court; the word is borrowed from a Jewish worshipping assembly. It is of no manner of use then upon this subject, to acquaint us with the procedure of the Jewish courts in cases of discipline. Our Lord neither mentions nor alludes to them. If the Jews had a council of elders in every synagogue, exclusively to judge of offences, then a person directed to make a complaint to them, would not be instructed to tell it to the synagogue, but to the council of that synagogue. If it be said, that the council of that synagogue might be called the synagogue, I answer that it could be in a figurative sense only, and a figure that would not, in a case of specific direction, be likely to be used. The kirk session is such a council for a Presbyterian congregation. What Presbyterian writer would direct the injured party to tell his complaint to the congregation, when he intended to direct them to the session? I say then, that this would have been an unnatural phraseology had it been directed to a Jew. Εκκλησια was a Jewish worshipping assembly, not a Jewish court. It is then idle to show that εκκλησια denoted a Jewish synagogue. Before it could serve you, it must be proved that it was the appropriated word for the council of that synagogue. But this it not only is not, but could not be, for the very reason that it was used for the whole synagogue. The congregation and the kirk session might as well, among Presbyterians, have the same appropriated name. There is here then a complication of fallacies. First, in supposing εκκλησια a Jewish court, or that a Jew would have used εκκλησια to denote the rulers of that εκκλησια in distinction from the assembly, which would have been figurative and indeterminate. 2nd, That though such a figure might have been occasionally used, our Lord would found a specific direction upon the use of a word highly figurative. This would be the same as to suppose, that because an English writer might say, "The nation has given a public sanction to the ministry of Mr. Pitt," meaning the vote of approbation passed by the parliament, therefore a foreign kingdom, instituting an assembly like our parliament, might call it *nation*. If the rulers of a synagogue could only be called εκκλησια as acting for the synagogue, it no more signifies church rulers, than nation does parliament. It was not the name of the rulers of a Jewish synagogue, nor could it be transferred, as such, by allusion to the rulers of a Christian congregation. 3rd, That as our Lord borrowed the name of his worshipping assemblies from those of the Jews, therefore he must establish the same modes of government and discipline. Under the French monarchy, there were courts which had the name of parliaments; but were these assemblies of the same nature, or similarly constituted with the parliament of Great Britain and Ireland? Yet the one nation undoubtedly borrowed this word from the other. Your disquisition then upon the Jewish sanhedrim, however useful it might be in itself, is altogether irrelevant. You might as well have indulged yourself in a dissertation on the origin and constitution of the Cortes of Spain. Upon this question, no matter whether that assembly was of divine or human appointment, or took its origin from an earlier or later date. The constitution of the Jewish and Christian churches is entirely different. If in any respects there is a similarity, it is not in consequence of any part of the former remaining as binding, but from the appointment of our Lord Jesus Christ. The former had a carnal and worldly polity; the latter is a kingdom not of this world, which not only does not require, but does not admit the same government. The laws and ordinances of the one are carnal, of the other are spiritual. It is in vain to investigate who were the persons that judged of offences among the Jews. Our Lord does not give a hint here that the mode of trying offences in his churches should be the same as among them. On the contrary, he bids them tell it to the εκκλησια, and that εκκλησια even according to the use of the word among the Jews, is the members of the synagogue in general, not the rulers of it alone.

You say in a note, that this "passage is not here advanced as an argument for Presbytery." For what purpose then do you advance it? If it proves not the similarity of discipline among Jews and Christians, it proves nothing. You cannot destroy our inference from this text, upon any other terms than by establishing something else. Nay, if your reasoning were just, it would decide the controversy. If you could prove that εκκλησια signified the rulers of a synagogue, that in this passage our Lord alludes to the procedure of discipline among the Jews, and that the rulers of the synagogue exclusively judged of offences, you would not only produce an argument in favour of Presbytery, but you would at once incontrovertibly establish your point. The plain and express meaning of our Lord when he says, "Tell it to the church," would be, "Tell it to the church rulers." I cannot then account for your uncommon modesty in any other way than by supposing you to be conscious of the insufficiency of your argument. Had you had confidence that it was well-founded, you might have sat at your ease on the top of your fortress, and smiled at our puny efforts to dislodge you. But it appears plainly that you know your reasoning upon this point to be fallacious, and that you do not design to prove that Presbytery is established by this passage, but to obscure it so that we cannot effectually use it. You would willingly consent, that both parties should give up their pretensions to this portion of Scripture. Your drift appears evidently to show, that upon this passage the one party can say as much as the other; and that therefore we should both lay it aside, or divide it. Like the woman before Solomon, you would butcher this text, because you know that it is not your own. We will not consent to this. We know that Jesus spoke intelligibly, for he designed to be understood. To determine what he meant, we will not demand any unnatural suppositions or far-fetched allusions. We will take the word εκκλησια in its proper and usual acceptation.

You endeavour, by a second argument, to prove that the word church (Matt. xviii. 18) denotes not the whole members, but the rulers alone, because a body may be said to do that which is done for it by its representatives.

How does this consist with your first argument? If εκκλησια denoted the rulers of a synagogue, if these exclusively judged of discipline, and if our Lord intended the Jewish courts to be a model for his churches, then in a strict and proper sense the rulers of a congregation would be denoted by εκκλησια in this passage. But according to this second argument, they are the church, as its representatives, in a figurative sense only. Your first argument goes to prove, that the proper sense of εκκλησια is a council of church rulers, your second goes upon the supposition that the strict and proper sense of εκκλησια is a whole congregation, and only figuratively transferred to their representatives. Now, just in proportion as the evidence of the one of these arguments appears strong will the other be invalidated.

Every degree of accession of strength that you can derive to the one, must be taken from the other. If the one is true, the other must necessarily be false. When two weak forces act in conjunction, they produce an effect which neither alone could produce; but if they oppose each other, they tend to destroy each other, and the stronger will have an effect only in proportion to the superiority of its force over the weaker. These two arguments then of yours, whatever weight they may have, or be thought to have, act not with a combined but an opposed force. Neither of them can act against us till it has destroyed its companion.

Were there such a thing clearly pointed out in Scripture as representatives of a congregation, who acted in the name and by the authority of the whole, no man will deny that such an assembly of representatives might occasionally be called in a figurative way, in cases where precision was not necessary, upon subjects sufficiently known to those addressed, by the name of those whom they represent. But upon this I remark, that before this figurative interpretation can be applied to this passage, it must fully be proved that there is such a body of representatives, appointed to act for the congregation. A passage is always to be understood literally, except it be necessary to the meaning, to understand it otherwise. Where a word is used figuratively, other circumstances will fully prove that it is so, and that it cannot be otherwise. A figure is never used by any good writer in cases where it could create the smallest degree of obscurity or uncertainty as to the meaning. The ordinary use of words is the primary one, the figurative is rare. Unless then it cannot possibly be explained in the literal and obvious sense, you have no warrant from sound criticism to understand it figuratively. If men may use the liberty of turning into figures every portion of Scripture that is obnoxious to their system, there is no truth they may not evade, there is no fancy they may not establish. Upon this principle you might prove that the churches should eat the Lord's supper by their representatives, and indeed obey every injunction of the Lord Jesus in the same way.

I observe again, that though a word may with elegance be used figuratively, in general description, or in allusion to things well known, yet it never can properly be so used in giving specific directions upon a subject of which those addressed are supposed to have no previous knowledge. I might say, "The nation has rewarded her brave officers who conquered for her at Trafalgar," because the parliament has done it. But here I speak a language that is not subject to mistake; all that hear it know that the nation does all such things by their representatives. But the case before us is different from this. Jesus is giving a specific direction not merely as to the treatment of an offender, but as to the procedure in matters of offence, and as to the persons who are proper to try the offender. He is *most particular* in every other part of the direction. He prescribes not in general terms, but with the most minute specification. First, the offended brother is to go himself alone to the offender, without acquainting any other with the offence, that so if the offender can be brought to repentance, other brethren may not receive an unfavourable impression of him, nor be wounded by his offence. If this will not succeed, the offended is directed to take with him, not a multitude of the brethren, but one or two only, that still, upon repentance, the offence may not be made public. If this also fails, then the offended is to tell the matter to *the church*. Now is it supposable, that after being so minute and precise in the former parts of the direction, he should all at once end in the most obscure manner by an indeterminate figure? In these circumstances, to use the word church figuratively would be a source of inextricable confusion. If in giving directions as to the final judges of our disputes, he speaks of them figuratively, he speaks unintelligibly. Why should he be so precise in the beginning of his description of the process, and so vague in the end? Nay, if the preceding steps were necessary to be most plainly and directly determined, much more the ultimate resource of the injured. It is much more necessary to know exactly how and by whom our disputes shall be *finally* settled, than to know what steps we are to take to prevent us from having recourse to the last appeal. Add to this, he is not describing the process of a court already established, but speaking of the affair of a new kingdom. He is giving a model with which those to whom he spoke were unacquainted, not describing or alluding to a model already known and in use. Precision is much more necessary when a writer is describing the constitution of a court which he proposes as a model, and with which none are supposed to be acquainted but himself, than when he is speaking of a court with which those whom he addresses have long been familiarized.

I remark farther, that such a figure as you suppose can only be legitimately employed when the one are the representatives of the other, and act for them in their name and by their authority, so that the action performed by the one may be said to be the action of the other. If the party which acts, acts for itself, in its own right and authority, so that the action is not vicarious, there is no propriety in such a figure. The king may be said to do what his ambassador does in his name; the nation may be said to do what the parliament does as its representatives, because here the one acts for the other, and have a right to act solely upon the principle that they stand in room of the other. On the other hand, under those governments in which the supreme legislative assemblies are not considered as the representatives of the people, it cannot properly be said that the people do what they do, because they do not legislate vicariously. Now church rulers, as such, are not the representatives of the church in which they rule. Rulers do not represent the ruled. A shepherd does not represent his flock. The rulers of a church enforce the laws of Christ upon that church, not in the name and by the authority of the church, but in the name and by the authority of the Lord Jesus Christ. The eldership of a church must be obeyed, not because they represent and are competent to the whole body, but because by their office they are the appointed executors of the laws of Christ. When an elder calls the attention of the church to a law of Christ, he does not insist on obedience because he represents and is competent to the whole body, but because it is a law of Christ, and it is his duty, as a church ruler, to see that it is obeyed. Until you can prove then that the rulers of a church are the representatives those over whom they rule, you cannot suppose such a figurative mode of speech to be employed by our Lord. If our Lord had appointed the eldership of each church exclusively to judge of offences, then the eldership, in this instance, would not be the representatives of the church acting in its name, but a council acting in their own right, independent of the church. The church, in such circumstances, would not be considered as judging, nor had they any right to judge. The decisions of such a council would in no sense be the decisions of the church, but the decisions of the eldership.

Again, although we should even suppose that the eldership of a church are the representatives of that church, yet the figure here supposed could not be properly used in any case in which those addressed might understand the represented themselves, instead of the representatives. Thus, though an historian might say, "The British nation enacted a law," &c., because it is sufficiently obvious that it could only have been through their representatives, yet he could not with propriety and distinctness say, "The nation bestowed the highest encomiums on the conduct of such a general," meaning the vote of the parliament, because this would not sufficiently distinguish the approbation of the parliament from that of the nation itself. The nation can bestow encomiums by itself as well as by its representatives, and as it is most natural to understand all language literally, the former would be the most likely to occur to the mind of the reader. Now in the present case, if our Lord used this figure, it would have been utterly impossible for those whom he addressed, to have with any certainty discovered his meaning. After having the offence laid before one or two brethren, and, in their judgment, proved against the offender, the injured person is directed to lay the matter before the church. How is he then to know that it is not the church itself, but in its representatives? It is very possible to lay the matter before the whole church, when it should be assembled; nay, there is nothing more natural, than to acquaint the whole society with the conduct of an offending brother. It is also in such circumstances, as I already observed, most natural to understand language in its literal import. What then should have hindered the disciples at that time so to understand it? Nay, would it have been rational to have understood their Lord otherwise? If then our Lord used such a figure in such circumstances, his language was not only indistinct, but unavoidably subject to mistake in its most obvious import.

From these considerations, then it is utterly improbable that the word church is to be understood in any other than the literal sense in this place. I demand a reason why it is to be taken figuratively in this instance. That reason must be peremptory necessity, otherwise it cannot be admitted. Nothing less than a clear and positive proof that the church is itself excluded from judging between brethren; that the elders judge exclusively; and that they do so as the representatives of that church. It can never be proved from the circumstance of the elders alone being rulers, from their right of ordination, from the keys given to the apostles, from the apostles adding members to the churches, without consulting the brethren, which are the *illustrious evidences* you have produced for the high prerogatives of church rulers. These are the pillars upon which you rest the whole fabric. These are your *clear and express* proofs, to quadrate with which, you must turn the remainder of the New Testament into figures.

To say that because a word *may* be taken figuratively, therefore it is lawful for us to have recourse to this mode of explication, whenever it may serve our purpose, is very bad reasoning. Because a word is occasionally used in some circumstances in a figurative sense, therefore such a figure may be supposed here, is not argument, nor is it the language of those who are in search of truth, but of those who are determined to force the Scriptures to sanction the traditions of men. Nothing but absolute necessity, arising from other more clear and express testimony of Scripture, would engage a candid interpreter, whose real object was to know the mind of God, to remove a difficulty in this manner. The speaker of the House of Commons, addressing the king, might say, 'The nation has granted your Majesty a liberal supply, from the confidence they have in you, that it will be frugally employed for the service of the public.' But what would you think of the judgment of the man, who reading from a paragraph in a newspaper, 'Let the nation rouse from its lethargy, and firmly withstand the despot of France,' should thus criticise the passage: 'The word nation here signifies the parliament alone. Nothing more is meant by this language, than that it is the duty of the House of Commons to rouse from their lethargy, and firmly oppose the pretensions of France. I can prove it; at least, that the meaning of the writer may be this.' The speaker, addressing his Majesty upon the supplies granted him by parliament, used the word in this sense, 'The nation has granted your majesty a liberal supply.' There is therefore no possibility of determining whether the word nation in this passage of the newspaper intends the whole nation, or their representatives only. It is therefore *equally fair, and much more consistent, to understand by the term nation, the representatives of the nation, than the nation itself.* Would not any one pronounce this perfect trifling? yet not more trifling and ridiculous than the criticisms of those who would here make a representative church. The same rules of criticism which, when employed upon a common newspaper, would render a man ridiculous to every workshop in the kingdom, comes with acceptance and admiration from the cells of erudition, when employed to darken the Word of God! there is no such trifling with language upon any other subject. A regard to common sense, and the common principles of language, are laid aside in the interpretation of Scripture alone. If the quibbling logicians can succeed in perplexing the question, their cause is supposed to stand unshaken by the most vigorous assault of their antagonists. There is nothing so absurd that a sophist may not make out, when guided by such mistaken rules of criticism. A critical attention to the meaning of words, and the structure and phraseologies of language, may undoubtedly be useful in investigating questions in theology; but the greatest use of it is, not so much to find out truth, as to remove the rubbish that has been heaped upon the Scriptures by the learned reveries of commentators. An ounce of common sense is worth a pound of learning. A man may be able to quote from a great number of languages, and make his pages groan under the names of ancient and modern divines, yet not himself be a critic. The principles of universal grammar, the procedure of the mind in the various application of words, and the analogies of language, with the different processes that usually affect its signification, is more to be attended to in the explication of Scripture, than the weight of venerable names, or even the opinion of the most respectable lexicographers. Let a man go into a library with the plainest text he can find, let him examine the interpretation of it by the different commentators, and he will find it to be darkened by erudition. How many meanings! How many conjectures!

To prove then that by a figurative expression a body of people may be said to do that which others do for them, is nothing to the purpose, unless it be also shown, that from express example, or more precise precept in some other parts of the Scriptures, such a figure must undoubtedly be supposed here. As all the other arguments you have alleged to this purpose are, to say the least, as vague and indeterminate, there is not the shadow of foundation to plead such a figure in this instance. Independent of all the proofs I have exhibited against the probability, nay, possibility, of the use of this figure in the connected circumstances, there is not even room for the allegation, until you establish your point by incontrovertible evidence. Had you established your system from other plain passages, then I would freely allow you to remove some difficulties in this manner, because Scripture can in no case contradict Scripture. But as long as the literal meaning of $\epsilon\kappa\lambda\eta\sigma\iota\alpha$ is what we understand by it, you can never lawfully have recourse to figures to evade the literal meaning, until you can show, that to understand it literally would contradict other more plain passages of Scripture. The utmost you can demand for a figure, is a possibility in case of absolute necessity.

Were we even to allow you here to have recourse to this figure, all it could serve you at its utmost amount, would be to evade this single passage. It could be of no use to you in determining the meaning of the word church in other instances where it occurs; for a figure never changes the meaning of words. It is absolute nonsense to say that, because a word may be used figuratively, where another word might be more naturally expected, therefore this word assumes the signification of that for which it is figuratively employed. When a word is used figuratively, it does not by any means alter its meaning, even in that instance of figurative acceptation. The whole beauty of the figure lies in not giving the word a signification different from its literal one. When Moses says (Num. xxxv. 24), "The congregation shall judge," &c., (at present allowing your interpretation of this passage to be just) meaning the congregation judging by its elders, the word congregation does not alter its signification. It signifies the very same thing here that it does in the most literal occurrence. The difference lies in the figure. No man from this would say, that the word congregation sometimes signifies elders. Those terms are never convertible. It cannot be said that congregation signifies elders, nor elders congregation. *Congregation* still signifies what is literally denoted by that word, although it does not literally, but figuratively judge, not by itself, but by its representatives. No new meaning is by any means given to the word *congregation* by such a figurative application.

But how are we to know that there is a figure in the words of Moses? Not certainly from the words themselves, but from more specific direction on this head, as you allege, by Moses himself. Were this truly the case, it would warrant what, without much more precise direction, would be utterly unwarrantable, the understanding of the expression in Num. xxxv. 24, figuratively. In this case, both the custom of the nation, and explicit explanation of the same precept by the same writer authorize this. Sir, produce me this authority for your figure, and I will grant it; never otherwise.

In the same manner, to recur to the former example by which I illustrated this figure, when the speaker says, 'The nation has granted your Majesty a liberal supply,' &c., he expresses not only an intelligible fact, but he does it in an elegant manner. The word nation used figuratively, gives vivacity and strength to his language, which the word parliament would not have had, and figures are used only for that purpose. They are not admissible into plain preceptive discourse. Besides the figure here serves a higher purpose; it recalls the sovereign's attention to that great truth, that the whole nation is supposed to be present in their representatives, and that it is really the whole nation that affords the supply. It is a literal truth that the nation granted the supply, although they did not grant it *literally* by themselves, but by their representatives. Properly speaking, the figure is not in the substitution of nation for parliament, but in the manner that the nation acts, not personally, but by its representatives. No one would ever suppose from this, that the word nation sometimes signifies the parliament. The figure supposes that it does not signify this; and it is because it does not signify it that it is used. It is not for want of an adequate word to represent the legislative assembly, nor is it merely as a synonymous word, but to give interest to the discourse, and convey some ideas that would not have been brought into view by the word parliament or House of Commons. What would you think of the writer of a dictionary, who upon this authority should assign parliament as one of the meanings of the word nation? I argue then that the word church not only does not here, but never can signify church rulers. Although upon the principles I have mentioned, a church might be said to do that which others do for them, in their name, and in their place, this never alters the meaning or application of the word in any manner. It would still signify the same body, although that body should act not personally, but by their representatives.

If this reasoning is just, it will serve to lay open a fallacy with which you introduce the argument under consideration, and which pervades a great part of your book; namely, that because a body may be said to act by their representatives, therefore the name of that body comes to denote the representatives as one of its significations. If you can prove the figure in any one place, you suppose yourself justified in assigning the figurative use of it as the real meaning of the word whenever it may serve your purpose. You say, "It seems equally fair, and much more consistent, to *understand by the term church*, the elders of the congregation, than the congregation itself." Now, Sir, not only is it not equally fair to understand a word in a figurative, as in the literal acceptation, but the using a word figuratively never conveys to it the meaning of the word for which it is figuratively used. Even allowing our Lord's expression to have been figurative, the term church never alters its signification, nor becomes an adequate word to represent the rulers of a church. Still the church would be one thing, and the eldership of that church would be another, which could not be denominated by the same name. As long as the body existed, its name could not be given to its representatives.

I have hitherto granted that the example, Num. xxxv. 24, upon which you found this argument was in point. Taking Moses as the expositor of his own words, this does not by any means appear decisive. On the contrary, there is nothing can be deduced from Deut. xix. 11, 12, or xvi. 18, which at all excludes the whole congregation from judging in this matter, even personally. In Numb. xxxv. 24, he says, "The congregation shall judge between the slayer and the revenger of blood." There is nothing in Deut. xix. 11, 12, that contradicts this in the literal sense. "But if any man hate his neighbur, and lie in wait for him, and rise up against him, and smite him mortally that he die, and fleeth into one of those cities, then the elders of his city shall send, and fetch him thence, and deliver him into the hands of the avenger of blood, that he may die." Though the elders are here appointed to be the executive officers in this matter, yet it is not said that they shall, exclusively of the congregation, judge of the slayer. Though judgment is supposed, yet it is not here ascribed either to the congregation or elders; far less does this passage describe the process of judgment, and confine the phraseology in Numb. xxxv. 24. As judgment then is here supposed, but the manner of it not determined, the legitimate mode of explication is to have recourse to Numb. xxxv. 24, to cast light upon this matter. Nothing but the limitation of this matter to the elders, and the most positive exclusion of the congregation itself, could warrant us to impose this restriction on the words of Moses in Numbers. Even had it been said, that 'the elders, after judging him, shall deliver,' &c., it would not have excluded the congregation from all participation in the trial of the offender. In a passage not designed to describe the process of trial, the principal persons engaged in the judgment, and the only persons executively engaged in it, might be said to judge him, though it might be with the approbation and express consent of the whole assembly. According to our laws, it might be said, that 'the magistrates apprehended the murderer, and, after trial the judges delivered him to the executioners,' although we know that there must have been twelve of the peers of the criminal to judge of the evidence of his guilt, and find a verdict against him, before the judges could decide his fate.

Nor does Deut. xvi. 18, exclude the personal interference of the congregation either in this affair or any other. "Judges and officers shalt thou make thee in all thy gates. They shall judge the people with just judgment." Might not the same thing be said of our judges, though a jury is joined with them in the trial of criminals? The elders might be the only official judges, yet the whole congregation might judge of the evidence of the criminal's guilt.

Your interpretation of Joshua xx. 4, 5, is equally unsatisfactory. "And when he that doth flee unto one of those cities shall stand at the entering of the gate of the city, and shall declare his cause in the ears of the elders of that city, they shall take him into the city unto them, and give him a place, that he may dwell among them. And if the avenger of blood pursue after him, then they shall not deliver the slayer into his hand; because he smote his neighbour unwittingly, and hated him not before-time. And he shall dwell in that city, until he stand before the congregation for judgment." It is not said in the former part of this precept, as you have chosen to understand it, that the elders of the city to which he fled decided upon his case. Nay, he was not to be judged by either one or other in the city to which he fled. When he came to the gates of the city of refuge, he was to declare his cause in the ears of the elders who waited for this purpose in the gates. Upon this declaration, not upon the evidence of his innocence, were they to receive him. Nay, from Deut. xix. 11, we find that the murderer was received as well as the accidental man-slayer, but that he was not to be continued under that shelter, but to be delivered to the elders of his city when they should send for him. In this very passage also it is supposed, that the elders of the city of refuge were not to be the judges of his guilt or innocence, for he was to dwell in that city, until he stood before his own congregation for judgment. Indeed, how was it possible that the elders of the city of refuge should be able to judge of the guilt or innocence of a man running up to their gates, who could give no proof of his innocence but his own declaration? There can be nothing more plain than, from the conclusion of this passage, "Until he stand before the congregation," that the congregation was personally concerned in the trial of the man-slayer, although the elders were undoubtedly the official judges. You produce nothing from Josephus, nor Philo, nor any of the Jewish writers, to contradict this; nor, if you did, can I allow that the authority of all the rabbies of Israel is sufficient to overthrow the plain sense of the words of Moses. Nay, though it should be proved that the elders were the sole judges upon every other matter, this language of Moses would necessarily make the case of the man-slayer an exception.

Were we even to indulge you for a moment with the supposition that the word church is to be taken figuratively here, and that it judges of offences only by its rulers, still this passage would cut the sinews of classical Presbytery. I am still disposed to stand upon this ground, notwithstanding what you have advanced, p. 105, to subvert it. You say our argument amounts to this, " that because a thing is not mentioned in one passage of Scripture that treats of a particular subject, it is not to be found in another that relates to the same subject." If this were indeed the spirit of our argument, I would grant at once that it is altogether fallacious. We know well that the various parts of this machine are not to be found in Scripture in any one place ; that they must be carefully collected and adjusted in their proper places. We cannot expect in one passage more than that passage professedly treats of in precept, or might be expected from example. This much, however, we may certainly look for. Although in a general reference, allusion, or description, we cannot look for anything detailed in all its parts, yet when the speaker or writer is evidently detailing a particular case, and giving the most minute directions as to the steps to be employed before final decision, we are warranted to expect full information. Such exactly is the case as to the grand law contained in Matthew xviii. 17. Every step of the process is minutely specified. The last in the series is the exclusion of the offender by *this church*. Now, if there was any appeal from this sentence, if it could be reviewed and reversed by a higher court, is it not unaccountable that he should not at the same time inform us of it?

If in the laws of a university we were to read one to this effect, " When any student is injured by another, let the injured speak privately to the person who has injured him ; if he refuses to give satisfaction, let him take one or two fellow-students, and speak to the offender before them, that they may judge between them. If he refuses to listen to their remonstrances, let the injured person complain to the faculty. If they cannot bring him to make proper acknowledgments and satisfaction, let him be expelled." Would we not here immediately conclude that the faculty was the highest court, and that there is no other to which the student expelled may appeal from the sentence pronounced? Is it not evident, that if ever he is to be re-admitted, it must be by having his sentence reversed by the same authority?

But, Sir, natural as this expectation is, our argument is not drawn merely from the silence of this passage about courts of review. We not only mantan that no mention is here made of them, but that they are virtually and effectually excluded. In this passage, our Lord not only does not direct to them, but he says what implies that they are no where else instituted, by committing the power of excommunication to this church, whatever it may be. Now, Sir, I will contend it with you, that this is more than silence. This church is supposed to exercise the highest authority, without having its proceedings subject to any review upon earth; with this engagement of the King of Sion, that whatever they bind on earth shall be bound in heaven, and whatever they loose on earth should be loosed in heaven. Every decision agreeable to the revealed will of Jesus, every instance of the application of his laws, and as to the execution of discipline, according to the apostolical instructions, shall be ratified in heaven by the Head of the church. Is it not here said, that this church has power to bind, and that it also has power to loose? This must certainly include not merely the clearing of the offending brother by the church, who was found guilty by the brethren who conversed with him, but also more especially the restoration of the offender after repentance. Whatever is loosed must have previously been tied. This offender must have been proved previously guilty of the offence, and now upon repentance is acquitted. This must extend not only to repentence before the church excludes him, but also to repentance after he hath been cut off. The same body that is here said to bind, is also said to loose. If this church has power to exclude unworthy members, it is also natural that it should have the power of re-admitting them, upon sufficient evidence of their repentance. It is not said that this church had power to bind, but that if they bound partially or erroneously, a higher court could loose. The binding and the loosing are ascribed to the same body.

But our Lord cuts off any possibility of their decision being reversed by a superior court, by his positive promise to ratify the sentence. Now if their sentence, as soon as it is passed, is confirmed in heaven, how absurd would it be to suppose that that sentence could be reviewed and reversed upon earth by men! Nay, so positively does our Lord affirm his ratification of their sentence, that he does not even expressly except the case of an unjust determination. This indeed is necessarily implied, but to have made such an express exception here, would have insinuated that there might be true churches which should be composed of members who might be inadequate or partial judges, neither of which should be supposed; for if they are either, they are not a church of Christ at all. As the plainest understanding is capable of judging between brethren as to offences, and as a church ought to be composed of spiritual men alone, Jesus does not provide for instances in which, from partiality, they will favour any party. This may be the case in a body called a church; but whenever it is so, they forfeit every title to the character of a church of Christ. The only redress which the injured could receive from them, must be by their repentance. If this does not appear, he is commanded no longer to consider them as a church, but to turn away from them.

Our Lord does not affront his churches by enacting regulations which imply, that either out of ignorance or partiality, they will pervert his laws. Now I demand, if the sentence of this *church* is ratified by Jesus, who has a right to review or reverse it? We argue then, Sir, that not only such courts are not mentioned, though there is every reason to suppose that they should had they been instituted, but that the possibility of their existence is here necessarily excluded. This church, whatever it is, has the power of excommunication, of binding and loosing, with the promise of ratification to their sentence by the Head of the church. Besides, we shall afterwards show, that courts of review are not only not mentioned here, but that they are mentioned, or exemplified in no other passage of Scripture. Even allowing Acts xv., to establish courts of reference, it by no means could be strained to justify courts of review. There is a mighty difference between settling a disputed matter, and reversing a sentence already passed into execution.

But let us hear your reasons why Presbyterian courts of review are not here expressly mentioned. " Besides, even granting that courts of review are not specified, a very good reason seems to be suggested from the passage itself, why they should not at least be *directly* mentioned. It is obvious that an appeal could only have been made to a superior court, if *the brother who was offended* had not received justice from the court to which he at first applied; for it is *he alone* who is represented as bringing the matter before an ecclesiastical assembly for their determinaion. Such a case however is not here supposed; for it is expressly stated, that the *first* court to which he applied gave a decision in his favour. But if the *first* court, as has been said, is here supposed to have given a decision in his favour; and if the *offending brother* is never said to have thought himself aggrieved by the decision which this court passed against him; and, as is insinuated, was even totally unsolicitous, and completely regardless, of bringing it before an ecclesiastical court at all; what propriety would there have been of introducing the possibility of an appeal to a higher court ?"—p. 105.

You say that such an appeal could only have been supposable, if the first court had not done justice to the offended brother. But according to this reasoning, as the one or two brethren determined in his favour, they should have carried the matter no farther. When the offender refused to hear these brethren, he should then have become as a heathen man and a publican, without any reference to the church. What is the reason that the matter was brought before the church, seeing the matter was already determined in favour of the offended brother? Plainly because the one or two brethren had no right to exclude a member from a body of which they were only a part. As he was received by the consent of the whole, he must also be excluded by their decision. Now, undoubtedly the same reason that made it necessary to bring this matter before the church before the offender should be cut off, will also make it necessary to bring it before the whole body, or at least those who are adequate to the whole body, before he can be excluded from that body. If a congregation is only a part of a great whole, neither itself personally, nor in its representatives, can it cut off a member from the general body. This must be done by the body itself, or those who are adequate to it. Now, Sir, if this church had not been the highest court, it would not have been commanded to execute the highest act of authority that can ever possibly be executed in a church of Christ. Had there been such a thing as a universal church, composed of particular congregations, this alone would have exercised the right of excommunication. No one could be cut off from it but by itself, either personally or by representation. One member of this great body could not have been privileged with the power of cutting off another.

Nor will the circumstance that the offended brother is supposed to have justice done him, warrant the omission. Why is it supposed that he has justice done him? Why is not the reverse of this case supposed? If the first court might have given sentence against him, and if there was a superior court to which he might appeal, this case also should have been supposed and provided for. But the reason why the former case alone is supposed, is clear from what I have already said, and from the consideration that there was no higher court of appeal, even in case of unrighteous sentence. The existence of a court of review would have required the supposition of a case in which sentence was unjustly pronounced.

But why was there no provision made for the supposed offender, in case he had been unjustly excluded or censured? If there was any court superior to this, this case also would have been supposed and provided for. It will not meet the difficulty to allege that these two cases are not supposed. We must have a reason why they are not supposed. If either of the parties might have been injuriously treated by the church, and if there was any court on earth paramount to that

Q

church, they would certainly have been directed to this. If it is alleged that Christ did not suppose an unfair decision in this first Presbyterian court, for the same reasons that I supposed the same thing as to that of a church, because the judges are competent and faithful, this will cut off, not establish courts of review. For if the first court be both competent and upright, there can be no need for a higher to review its decisions; and if there be no need for it, there is no such thing, for Jesus has no useless wheels in the government of his churches, any more than useless agents in nature.

Having now endeavoured to dispel the cloud in which you have attempted to involve this illustrious law of the kingdom, I will conclude my remarks on this part of your book by observing, First—That the very supposition which you make to evade the true meaning of this text, implies that the primary and usual acceptation of this word, is that for which we contend. If, as you argue, church rulers are here called church, because they represent the church, it shows that the name belongs to the whole body in its most simple sense, and not to any part of them. The rulers could not figuratively be called church from those they represent, unless that was the proper name of those represented. The only argument then which could serve your purpose here, overthrows your system every where else. For you allow that church rulers are called church, not properly, literally, or in their own right, but figuratively, in right of those whom they represent, as the parliament might be called the nation. Here then, out of your own mouth we have it, that our interpretation is the primary one, and that the word every where literally is to be understood as we understand it. Now, if the whole body of the believers of a congregation are properly called a church, and church rulers only so called in their right, improperly, and in a secondary sense, this word ought never to be supposed to assume such a figurative meaning, when the literal and natural meaning is not contrary to express Scripture.

Secondly—As this is the literal signification, so in its usual acceptation it can have no other meaning.

This will be seen hereafter, when I examine the different passages in which this word occurs in the New Testament.

Thirdly—The distinctive application of the word churches, applied to a plurality of such assemblies, shows that the word, when used in the singular number, refers only to one congregation, and to the whole of that congregation, except where it is taken as synonymous with the kingdom, or whole body of Christ. This argument is urged most clearly by Mr. Innes. You mention it, but you never attempt to answer it, by assigning other reasons.

When the Scriptures speak of the saints of a city, they are uniformly called the church in such a place; but when they speak of the saints of a province or district, they as uniformly call them *the churches of that country*. Thus, the church at Jerusalem, and the churches in Judea; the church at Corinth, the church in Cenchrea, but the churches *of* Achaia, the churches *of* Galatia, the churches *of* Samaria; the Church of Ephesus, the Church of Smyrna, &c., but the seven churches of Asia. This plainly shows that the word church, in the singular number, was appropriated to an assembly of saints.

Fourthly—As from these reasons, the word church appears clearly to have been appropriated to an assembly of saints, so in Matt. xviii. 18, it is evidently used in its appropriated sense. "Tell it to *the church*"— *the church*. Whatever then is the meaning of *church* here, it is used in its appropriate signification, and as this is a company of saints, so it must be here understood.

Fifthly—The matter is put beyond all controversy by a similar precept given by Paul, with respect to the civil disputes of the brethren—1 Cor. vi. 1. Here the saints, not the church rulers alone, are said to be the judges. Yea, the very weakest of them are said to be qualified for this business. Paul would not erect a tribunal different from that of his master.

LETTER V.

Sir,

In reviewing your seventh letter, in explication of the fifth chapter of first Corinthians, I am utterly at a loss to know what hold to get of the writer who is capable of taking such daring liberties, as are here used, with the Word of God. The chapter is too plain to need explication as to any person really desirous of knowing the true meaning of the Spirit upon this point, and I greatly fear, that the mind which admits such perversion of divine truth, is far beyond the reach of argument. I do not expect that any who will not be convinced by reading the chapter itself, would yield their assent if one should rise from the dead to expound it. To attempt to make it plainer, would, in my opinion, be an insult to the meanest understanding. For the sake, however, of those not conversant in the subtleties of evasive criticism, I will endeavour briefly to unfold the fallacy of your principles of interpretation.

The apostle's disapprobation of the conduct of the Church of Corinth, with respect to the incestuous person, you explain as occasioned by their not mourning on account of the corruption of a Christian brother, to the end that their rulers being stirred up to a sense of their duty, *as a consequence of their sorrow*, the offender might be thus removed. Ah, Sir, can I believe that your own conscience is entirely satisfied with this evasion? Had this been all that the apostle intended, is this likely to have been the language in which he would have conveyed his meaning? Were government displeased with the conduct of a magistrate who neglected to execute the laws against offenders, is it likely, Sir, that they would write to the district in which that magistrate resided, to censure them for his negligence. Especially, would they rebuke them, because they had not mourned, that, as a consequence of this, the magistrate might have been stirred up to a sense of his duty? What has the people to do with the neglect of the magistrate? Would not the supreme power have instantly deprived him of his office, or have written to himself, censuring him for his unfaithfulness? Does any one think of blaming the people, when the laws of the land are not executed? Does any one think of blaming the whole nation, when an obnoxious bill is passed by the parliament? Suppose the General Assembly of your church should discover an unusual concern for the maintenance of discipline, and should hear that there is in one of their congregations such a person as is here described, admitted to communion, would they write to the congregation at large, or to the kirk session? Would they blame in any measure the private members of the congregation? Would not the admonition be directed to the church rulers? Especially, would it ever come into their thoughts to blame the people, because they had not by their sorrow stirred up the session to do its duty, without attaching the smallest blame to those upon whom alone it should fall? Allowing that the Corinthian church had such a session, and that the whole of the fault of the individual members was in not stirring up the rulers to their duty, still this would have been a very inferior crime compared with that of the rulers; and if the inferior fault of the former was censured with such marked disapprobation, much more severe, doubtless, would have been the expression of displeasure against the conduct of the former. Is it possible that those chiefly in fault should be suffered to pass without notice, while those, whose only fault was not mourning for the others neglect, should be so keenly admonished? Let any impartial reader consider this, and judge whether your hypothesis be rational.

But supposing that the only fault of the Corinthians was in not stirring up their rulers to do their duty, was there no other way of effecting this but by the publicity of their grief? Have the people no other way of exciting their rulers to faithfulness but by their tears and sighs? Even Presbyterian forms do not render this necessary. Would they not have been blamed rather for not speaking with their rulers upon this subject, than for not mourning in their presence? It must indeed be a shocking despotism that leaves the ruled no other way of expressing their sentiments to their rulers than by their mourning? You yourself zealously clear Presbytery of this charge, yet you are not ashamed to charge it to the account of the churches planted by the apostles. This is not the resource that you point out to your congregations if they are aggrieved by the conduct of their rulers. "If, through mistake," you observe, "an improper person be occasionally admitted, the members are permitted to communicate what they know of the applicant to the pastors; and if, after remonstrance, he be continued in communion, the lowest individual in the congregation is allowed to call these pastors to an account, with the whole of their session, before a superior court; and if that court should decide amiss, to summon even it, with these pastors and elders, to a still higher tribunal; and even that to a higher, till the obnoxious person be at last removed."—p. 73. If then the people in a Presbyterian congregation are in any sense to be blamed for the neglect of discipline, it must be because they do not first remonstrate with their rulers, and then, if they are not attended to, complain to the higher judicatories. Now, if the Corinthians had been Presbyterians, the apostle's method would have been to write to the Session, Presbytery, or Synod, to reform that abuse. Had he blamed the members in any measure, it would have been because they neglected to remonstrate with the session, and because they did not complain to a superior court. According to the Presbyterian constitution, if a member is displeased with an act of discipline, or cannot have an act of discipline put into execution, his way is to appeal to the Presbytery. Had the Corinthian church been formed on the Presbyterian model, the neglect of this certainly would have been the crime charged upon the individual members as to this matter.*

* When the pastoral duties are inculcated, the pastors are exclusively and distinctly addressed, and mentioned—2 Pet. v. 1, &c.

But, Sir, take away the literal meaning of this chapter, and other similar portions of Scripture, and there is no way left to prove that the individual members of a church have either the right of remonstrating with their rulers upon their measures and decisions, or of appealing from them to a higher court. I ask you, how do you prove from Scripture that the ruled have a right to remonstrate with the rulers, or to appeal from their decisions? Have you either precept or example for this part of the Presbyterian constitution? If the members of a church have not all a right to judge of the application of discipline, and if the passages of Scripture that represent them to have this right must all be taken figuratively to denote their rulers alone, I know of no authority from Scripture to say that they have either the right of remonstrance, or appeal, or indeed any right at all. If both our Lord, when he speaks of the persons who have a right to judge of offences, by the word church, and the apostles, when they speak of the same thing, literally addressing the whole members, must be understood in a figurative sense, applicable only to the rulers, where shall we find that church members should even dare to remonstrate against the decisions of their rulers, let them be never so unreasonable? I apprehend, that if you take away the true spirit and literal meaning of these passages, you will not leave anything but absolute submission on the part of the members. Either these passages are to be understood literally, and establish the right of the whole church to judge of the application of discipline; or, if they are to be understood figuratively, as alone applicable to the rulers, they leave no foundation for any kind of interference or concern about church affairs on the part of the people. These passages, if they are to be understood figuratively of the rulers, certainly will not also serve to prove that the ruled should have any modification of right in the same matter. Acts xv., however it is strained, will not prove the right of appeal on the part of the people from the decisions of their rulers, for this is not an appeal of the ruled from the decisions of the rulers, nor indeed an appeal of any kind. I should be glad to know then upon what foundation you rest the right of the people to remonstrate or appeal.

But, Sir, your argument here is built upon a fallacy, which, when rendered palpable, will cause your reasoning to fall to the ground. Your interpretation supposes that the apostle here solely addresses the individual members of the Church of Corinth as distinct from their rulers, and blames them for not discharging a duty incumbent on them solely as individual members. The apostle's language however is not solely addressed either to rulers or ruled, but to both together as one body. It is not the individual members only, as you wish to have it supposed, who are here blamed for not mourning that the incestuous person might be taken away from among them. The epistle is written to the whole church at Corinth, and out of that church surely you never can except the rulers, especially as you are so fond of making them, often exclusively, the church itself. All the members, rulers and ruled, are blamed for not mourning. It is not said that the individual members are blameable, because they did not mourn on account of this affair, and thereby stir up their rulers to do their duty; and that the rulers are blameable, because that they did not put the incestuous man out of the church; but the whole church, without exception, is blamed for not mourning, that he might be taken away. Here then your criticism fails. The ruled are not blamed for not mourning, that thus they might bring the rulers to a sense of duty, but both are blamed for not being properly affected by this instance of corruption, that they might be brought fully to know and to perform their duty as a church in this point. It is very plain that if a church does not mourn, and feel as the greatest grievance an instance of corruption in any of the brethren, they will never heartily unite in executing the laws of Christ against the offender; on the other hand, if a church is really brought to grieve for a brother's fall, to tremble for his condemnation, to feel for the interests of the Redeemer's kingdom, and to be jealous of his honour, they will not a moment wink at a brother's corruption; and when they come to consider his offence, there will be but one mind among them all. If they are not deeply affected with sorrow on account of the reproach that such conduct will bring upon the cause of Christ, they will not be likely to discover much zeal in excluding him from their communion. It is not without reason then that the apostle takes notice of their want of humiliation and sorrow on account of the corruption of their church. Without this, the laws of Christ could not have been executed. According as they felt upon this point, would be their conduct.

Besides, it appears from the connection between this and verse third, that they probably did not fully know how to proceed with him. They had not yet received any particular information on this point; the direction recorded here does not appear to have been previously known. Their crime was then particularly in neglecting to be more fully informed upon this point, by consulting the apostles, and by fasting and prayer. Had they instantly humbled themselves, and looked for direction in the matter from the Father of lights, it is likely that he would have been removed much sooner. The Spirit of the Lord would have directed the apostle sooner to have given the precept, contained in the following verses.

You proceed, "Nor will the command of Paul to the Corinthians, 'to deliver up the incestuous person to Satan, when they were gathered together, and to put away from among themselves that wicked person, with his declaration that they had a power to judge them who were within,' suffice to prove that the members at large exercised a similar power with those who were their rulers in administering the government of that Christian church. That they are *susceptible* of this interpretation, if viewed in themselves, and without attending to other passages of Scripture, I readily grant —but not more so than those passages which assert that Christ is the propitiation for the sins not only of the Jews, but of *the whole world*, and that he gave himself a ransom for *all*, if considered merely in themselves, are susceptible of an explication which excludes the doctrine of *particular*, and establishes the Arminian doctrine of *universal* redemption."—p. 108.

And are you indeed so exceedingly candid as to allow that these words, when viewed in themselves, are capable of our interpretation? Pray, Sir, could words more expressly contain the doctrine for which we contend? Could it possibly have been made more explicit? What circumstance does the language want to make it precise? Suppose, for a moment, that the apostle had really intended what we think he did, tell me what he could have said more pointed, more express, and less susceptible of a different meaning? What should he have added to render the passage incapable of being misunderstood?

But as you think that the passage is equally susceptible of a Presbyterian interpretation, let us submit for a moment to the irksome task of examining your reasons. It is much more easy to clear up a real difficulty, than to vindicate the clearest texts from absurd interpretations. The latter are only alleged by those who are either unable or indisposed to weigh the force of argument. What then are your arguments for understanding these commands in a Presbyterian sense? Argument did I say! Argument you have none. You think you have found another difficulty upon another subject which will puzzle us as much as this chapter does you. You say, that Christ's being said to be a propitiation for the sins of the whole world, and to give himself a ransom for all, with such like expressions, are equally susceptible of an Arminian interpretation, as the passages in dispute are of the sense given them by Independents. Here, Sir, I remark,

1. That it is unfair to remove one difficulty by proposing another upon another subject. If we cannot fairly and clearly prove our doctrines, and consistently explain the passages alleged against them by Arminians, we must yield. If there were no other way of explaining the texts alleged to support Arminianism, than by having recourse to such evasions as you employ, I would surrender the point in debate. You might as well answer the Arminians, by alleging that the Presbyterian interpretation was as foreign from the words of this chapter, as the Calvinistic interpretation is from the passages they quote to support Arminianism. Even

allowing your argument to be in point, as it is built upon the certainty of the Calvinistic system, it could have no weight with any but Calvinists, and therefore must go for nothing, perhaps with a great majority of the Church of Scotland, though it should pass with us. Instead then of proving the Presbyterian interpretation of this chapter, by the Calvinistic interpretation of the texts alleged by Arminians, you must prove both by sound criticism, and the acknowledged and usual principles of language.

2. That it is not fair to mention a few solitary phrases, that may apparently stand in opposition to the general view of the Scriptures, as equal to the plain meaning not only of this whole chapter, but even to the strain of the whole epistles. But,

3. It is not a fact that these expressions are equally susceptible of an Arminian interpretation, as this chapter is of an Independent one. The literal, the direct, the obvious, the consistent meaning, not of one phrase, or of one verse, but of the whole chapter, is that for which we contend. With respect to the other, the meaning is not only restricted by the whole tenor of Scripture, but in the sense in which the words are understood by Calvinists, they are used not in a refined and unusual acceptation, but according to the common practice of all languages. We do not explain these passages used by Arminians upon principles incomprehensible to the unlettered mind, but upon principles acted upon by the most illiterate peasants. In the latter case, I am not able to see a difficulty, with respect to any who are willing to be instructed by the Word of God. It is not the difficulty nor the ambiguity of the language that leads people to misunderstand the phrases you allude to, but the pride of the human heart, and its opposition to the sovereignty of God. The phrases themselves are used in no sense different from common practice, the general regulator of language upon all subjects. There is not a fish-woman in the streets capable of misunderstanding such language. It is daily practiced by all ranks, learned and unlearned. In answering the Arminian then, I would have recourse to no evasions as you have in answering us, nor to

abstruse and metaphysical subtleties; I would appeal to the common practice of language to confirm my views of the contested passages. You seem to think, that in these passages, while the inspired writers speak one thing, they are to be understood as meaning another. I understand them to speak directly and plainly what they mean. You seem to think that there is no way of determining or limiting their meaning, but by those other passages which they seem to contradict. I am persuaded that they must be understood in a limited sense, not merely from the general voice of Scripture, which indeed is the primary argument, but also that such limitation is clearly justified from the scope of the passages in which those phrases are found, together with their circumstances and connection.

4. That if there was any real difficulty in such phrases as you quote, many clear and specific declarations necessarily limit their meaning. As to the meaning of the chapter under consideration, the whole tenor of the New Testament, with every other direct precept and example upon the same subject, establishes the plain and literal meaning. It is altogether clear, direct and precise in itself. There is not one direct passage of Scripture that can reasonably be alleged to give it another sense.

5. That were we to suppose that there is a real difficulty in each of these cases, the difficulties are not of the same kind. What connection or resemblance could you find between the case of a direction addressed to a body of people, instructing them how to perform a certain duty in an affair that concerned the whole, and the limited use of the words *all* and *world?* These are not the words that are used in this chapter. Why then do you run away from the subject, by supposing a difficulty upon another subject, a difficulty not the same with what you suppose here? We argue, that because the whole church, without exception, are here addressed, and commanded to assemble and perform this duty, therefore they ought themselves to do it. What can you allege against this? Why, that the phrases, "Christ gave himself a ransom for all," and "is a propitiation for the sins of the whole world," are, when considered

in themselves, capable of an Arminian interpretation. Is this anything to the purpose? Do the words *all* and *world* here only signify some of those who are spoken of? By no means, but are applicable to every soul referred to by the writer. They do not indeed include all the individuals of the world, but the writers were not either addressing or speaking of all the individuals of the world. When the inspired writers use these words in general, they are speaking either of the different nations of the world, and not the individuals of the world, or of all God's children, not of all the children of men. When the apostle says, "He that spared not his own Son, but freely gave him up to death for us *all*," shall I say that *all* here means only *some;** that it is taken only in a part of its extension? Nay; but I will say that *all* here includes every individual of whom the apostle speaks. But he speaks of the elect, not of the human race; therefore it is for all them alone that he is said to die. Now, allowing that the strength of our argument lay in the use of the word *all*, it would still be valid until you could show that the apostle was not here addressing *all* the church, but *all* of something else. It is contrary to all sense, as well as to the rules of criticism, to say that *all* sometimes only signifies *some*. But it is sound sense and sound criticism to say, that when the Scriptures use this word, speaking of the extent of the efficacy of Christ's death, they do not refer it to, or include in it, all the individuals of the human race. In this chapter, however, the church is addressed without exception; the members therefore, without exception,

---

* It is very usual, in opposing Arminians, to say that *all* and *world* are sometimes taken only in a part of their extension, *i.e.*, that they signify only *some of all*, and *some of the world*. This I think is false criticism. *All* ever extends to all the individuals addressed or spoken of by the writer, though not to all the individuals of the human race. When *all* is applied to three, it is equally taken in the whole of its extension as when applied to three thousand. When Christ is said to be the propitiation for the sins of the *whole world*, *world* does not refer to the individuals of the world, but the nations of the world. It includes then all referred to. Upon this fallacy of Mr. Brown's, the above argument is founded.

must be understood to be commanded to observe this injunction.

Your argument then is inapplicable, because it supposes a mode of address not here used, and because, while it supposes that all the members of the church are addressed in the command, it is the duty of some only to perform it, which is contrary even to the examples you allege. To make your argument in point, it would be necessary to prove that although in appearance all are addressed, in reality only some are addressed. If the apostle speaks to them all, the command is to them all. As the words, *all*, and *all the world*, include all the individuals addressed or referred to, so all those addressed in this command, are even according to that explication, to perform the command. If the Calvinistic explanation of these phrases be alleged at all, it must be to show that the apostle, although he appears to address the church, yet in reality he addresses the rulers only. If it could prove anything, it would be, not that all are addressed, but some only, *i.e.*, the elders are to perform the command; but that the church is not at all addressed, though the words are capable of that interpretation, but the elders alone. Do you think that when the inspired writers speak of Christ's being " a propitiation for the whole world," and of giving himself " a ransom for all," that the words are directly applicable to every individual, but only to be understood of some? But indeed the manner in which you propose this argument, sufficiently shows that you did not well understand your own meaning. You do not attempt to show how these examples should bear upon the point in hand. You do not illustrate the one by the other, or even point out how you wished this passage to be interpreted. You tell us that it is capable of a Presbyterian interpretation, and then, as your only proof, you refer us to what you suppose an equal difficulty that hangs on the Calvinistic system. Is this like reasoning? You come out against your antagonist like a Goliah, but sculk behind every subterfuge to avoid fairly meeting him. I demand then, Sir, that you will show how you wish this argument to bear upon the point in hand.

But proceed with your analysis: "Can such expressions however as those which are here used be equally explained upon the supposition of Presbyterians, that it is the rulers of the church, and not the members at large, who are intended? Yes; for as was remarked, nothing is more common than to represent a thing as done by a body at large, while it is done only by those in that body to whom it is competent."—p. 109.

Here, Sir, you again have recourse to your convenient figure. It is indeed to you a most useful device, for whenever you are like to sink, it serves to keep you above water. When a specific direction was given to the saints, called by their appropriated name, in their united capacity, by the help of this figure, you make *the church* act by its representatives; now, when they are addressed not only as a body called *a church*, but with the explication of the meaning of this word, or of the materials that compose it, " to them that are sanctified in Christ Jesus called to be saints," and themselves directed in their assembled capacity to perform this apostolical command, you will make the same figure serve your purpose. What doctrine of Scripture could not be evaded by such lax interpretation? Does your antagonist in all his book demand any such unnatural suppositions? When the apostle says, "Let no corrupt communication proceed out of your mouth, but that which is good to the use of edifying, that it may minister grace unto the hearers," by the help of this figure, how easy would it be to get rid of this precept! "Nothing is more common than to speak of a thing as done by a body at large, while it is done only by those in that body to whom it is competent. The people speak by their ministers. The latter are here admonished against uttering corrupt doctrine, and exhorted to speak sound doctrine for the edification of the hearers. Individual members are not here tied down to that Puritannical preciseness, for which some sour religionists contend. The precept only relates to ministers." Again, when they are commanded, " Not to forsake the assembling of themselves together," all that is meant hereby relates to the meetings of the clergy. A body meets in its representatives. Indeed, there is no extravagance that might not be proved in this manner.

Your example from Rev. xvii. 18, which you think similar, is not to the point. It is not only the obscure language of prophecy, but it is not the citizens, but the city that is said to reign over the kings of the earth. Rome reigned over the world, because her kings did so. What possible resemblance could you find between these two cases?

The people of Great Britain governing their colonies, is an expression highly figurative, and everything I said upon this subject in the last letter is applicable here. There is a mighty difference between the language of an orator alluding to a well-known fact, and an apostle giving a specific direction, as to a proceeding to which they had not been accustomed; a similar they could never previously have witnessed. The florid language of oratory would not be, and indeed is not employed to instruct them, but the most minute and circumstantial directions as to the whole affair. There is here nothing that could have the smallest tendency to tempt any sober critic to impose a figurative meaning upon this plain letter.

In the passage you quote from Deut. xiii. 6, you are incorrect in saying that the precepts, though addressed to the people, are to be observed by the judges. There is not one of these precepts to be obeyed for them by their rulers. To the same persons that all the preceding precepts are addressed, is addressed this also, "Thou shalt surely kill him," and this they were to perform in their own persons as well as any other. Although they were to kill him legally, yet it does not mean that they were to kill him by the judges, but to kill him by bearing witness against him, and by having *their hand first upon him.* This surely was not performing their duty by the judges. Even among us, it is usually and properly said, that it is not the judge, but the witness, who hangs the criminal.

You are also mistaken in saying that the Jews in general are often reproved by their prophets for the crimes of their rulers. This would be contrary to common sense and common justice, and therefore could not be the language of the just and holy God. The people cannot be to blame for that which they cannot help, and have no hand in doing. If their rulers make laws for them, they do not sin for them. Would any one think of censuring a servant for the crimes of his master?

The passages you refer to in Jeremiah v. 28, vi. 5, &c., do not confirm your idea. The words of the prophet are indefinite, as prophetic writing very usually is, yet they are not universal; nor do they blame the whole nation for the crimes of their rulers. "They judge not the cause;" who judge not the cause? Why, the judges of the land, those employed in giving judgment. There is here nothing like a universal censure upon the ruled for the injustice of their rulers. A traveller might as well be hanged for being robbed by a highwayman.

It is also a mistake to say, that Deut. xvi. 19, is addressed to every Israelite. They were commanded in verse 18, to appoint judges and officers, whose duty it would be to judge the people with just judgment. The 19th verse is not an address to every Israelite, but an immediate address to those who should be appointed to judge. It would be absurd to tell a man not to take a bribe, or pervert judgment, who was never to judge at all. The language is addressed only to the judges. Suppose a patron should present a profligate and infidel clergyman to a Scotch parish, would any one think of blaming the parishioners for electing this man? They would indeed be to blame, if they should submit to his ministry; but for his election they were not blameable nor accountable.

But these figures are not only inapplicable to the present case, but if the passage in dispute must be explained in a figurative manner, it contradicts your first argument. Could you establish your point by *all* and *the whole world*, the supposition in these figures is overthrown by this. When several circumstantial arguments are combined, though each of them is weak in itself, yet being united in a common centre, they make a strong one; but when they are built upon opposite grounds, they are all rendered suspicious. What should we say of one who wished, when tried for a crime, to prove an *alibi* by two witnesses, the former of whom swore that he saw him in Dublin on the same day that the other saw him in Edinburgh? Now this is exactly the case with the examples in your analysis, to force the Presbyterian interpretation upon this passage. If the Calvinistic explication of the phrases we have so often quoted can at all be brought to bear upon this passage, it must be by supposing, that though the apostle uses language that seems to be addressed to the whole church, yet in reality he is speaking to the rulers alone; that the church itself is not at all mentioned or addressed, but all the expressions that seem apparently to mention them, must be understood only to include the rulers. Though the apostle seems to write to the whole church, as sanctified in Christ Jesus, and called to be saints, yet that by all this we are to mean nothing more than the rulers of the church; the epistle does not speak a word to the whole body, but is entirely in reality directed to the church officers, though apparently directed to the church. If it is not upon these principles that your unillustrated argument from *all* and *world* must be applied, I am unable to comprehend its meaning. On the other hand, these figures all suppose that the church itself, yes, *that very church which includes every individual member*, is addressed and commanded to observe this injunction, but that it is to do it not personally, but by its representatives. The former supposes the language to be really applicable to none but those who obey the command, *i.e.*, the rulers; that the church itself is never mentioned in reality; that when he says, "It is reported commonly that there is fornication among *you*," *you* means not the church, but the church rulers; when he says, "*Ye are puffed up,*" it was not the church he blames for being puffed up, but its rulers. Yea, it must be the rulers only who are blamed for not mourning; whereas, as you have supposed, that the individual members only are here censured. In like manner, every part of the address must be confined to the rulers, for they are the same persons he addresses from the beginning to the end of the chapter. It will then be only the elders who are commanded to be "gathered together to deliver him to Satan," which is also contrary to another part of your interpretation. The latter argument supposes the whole church to be addressed and commanded, though they are only figuratively to execute the command.

We have a very curious specimen of reasoning when you endeavour to silence that expression, "When ye are gathered together." I never read anything more like what we should expect to issue from a school of the Jesuits. "Thus even though it were granted that the incestuous person was to be delivered over to Satan when the whole of the members were met together, it will not follow that every one of them in a judicial capacity was so to deliver him up, but only the rulers; for it has been contended even by many Presbyterians, with Cyprian of old, that whatever is done, should be done in the presence of all the members of the church for their satisfaction." And dare you refuse to grant what the apostle so expressly enjoins? Dare you set aside such a clear, precise and circumstantial precept? Were even the mere presence of the people all that the apostle commands, as you would wish to have it thought, you cannot reverse his sentence. It must be binding for ever. Why then this chicane? Why this unwillingness to grant what you cannot pretend to deny? Does not the apostle expressly say, even according to your own interpretation, that this affair is to be performed "when ye are gathered together," although it should be supposed that it was only to be done in their presence? Dare you say that he does not enjoin this to be done in their public assembly? Why then are you so reluctant to confess it? Why do you say, "though it were granted?" Does not this imply that you might dispute it, if you thought proper? I ask you then again, does the apostle enjoin this affair to be transacted in their public assembly? Why have you not directly and unequivocally granted this? Because it condemns your church proceedings. You do not observe this apostolical precept, even in the sense in which you explain it.

But you endeavour to cover the practice of Presbyterian

courts, by telling us in a note, that the apostles, elders, and brethren of Jerusalem did not repair to Antioch, to discuss the matter in the hearing of the Christians there. But allowing this example to be in point, does it prove that the apostle does not here command that the incestuous person should be given over to Satan, "when they were gathered together?" Granting that the cases are similar, though the example is not conformable to the precept, it cannot prove that the precept is not given in these words. Nor can it prove according to your own views of Acts xv., that the precept is not binding. How do you set aside this precept, according to your own interpretation of Acts xv.? By the example of what you call an uninspired Synod or Council. The command of an apostle of God annulled by the example of an uninspired Council! This is greater extravagance than was ever exemplified in the thickest darkness of the middle ages. Though men in those days exalted the acts of Councils to a level with the Scriptures, yet they never alleged the authority of the one to set aside the other. Might not the example of the General Assembly of the Church of Scotland be with equal validity alleged as a reason to set aside any apostolical command? You might as well quote an old act of Assembly for the same purpose, as Acts xv., upon your view of it.

But the cases are not parallel. The example recorded in Acts xv., is not contrary to the injunction here given. As far as the object of the two assemblies was similar, the example is a confirmation of the precept. It does not annul, but corroborates it. As the affair of Acts xv., was a piece of church business that concerned the hurch of Jerusalem, it was discussed not only in the hearing, but with the approbation, co-operation, and concurrence of the whole Church of Jerusalem. As it determined a matter for Antioch, and for the whole Christian world, the decision was infallible; the people of Antioch had no more necessity to be personally present, than all the Christians on earth. I contend then, Sir, not only that the example recorded Acts xv., was agreeable to this as far as the example came under the precept, but that this precept forbids your interpretation of Acts xv., and that even to explain Acts xv., agreeable to your own theory, it cannot set the precept aside. Allowing that all that is intended by the gathering together of the church, is their being present when discipline is executed, to the end of the world it can never be reversed. You might as well set aside the sixth commandment, or the whole moral law. You might as well set aside the declarations, "He that believes shall be saved—without holiness no man shall see the Lord." These all stand upon the same authority.

But, Sir, even supposing that this was all that was to be made of this precept, there is another difficulty respecting your opinion as to the Church of Corinth. You somewhere, I think, express your confidence that it contained more congregations than one. Granting you this for a moment, then, according to your own interpretation, no act of Presbytery is valid, unless all the members of all the congregations in the Presbytery are present. Now, it will be full as easy to accommodate them with a house when met for worship, as when met for discipline. But though in the note you endeavour to cover the practice of your courts, and to protect them in the breach of this apostolical command, even according to your own interpretation by the example recorded Acts xv.; yet, in order to get rid of this passage with as good a grace as possible, and to give no advantage from the practice of Presbyterians, you say that many Presbyterians contend, with Cyprian at their head (it is the first time I have heard of that proud prelate heading Presbyterians), "that whatever is done, should be done in the presence of all the members of the church for their edification." Presbyterians who are of this mind should practice it; and you, Sir, should either refute them, or follow their example. If such Presbyterians are right, the Church of Scotland is wrong; and if the former are wrong, you are equally bound to prove their practice without a just foundation in Scripture, as you are in the case of Independents. The circumstance of some Presbyterians being of this mind, and observing this injunction, will not sanction but condemn other Presbyterians who despise it.

"But is it a necessary consequence," you subjoin, "that because discipline was to be exercised in the presence of all the members, each of them was to exercise it? Though the court of civil justice, in a particular town, may be held by the magistrates in the presence of the inhabitants, who are invited perhaps to attend, does it follow that every inhabitant, though not officially a judge, is allowed either to speak or vote upon the decisions which are passed, before they are adopted?"—p. 113.

This, Sir, is a most disengenuous representation of the apostle's words. Your statement insinuates that there is nothing more said with respect to the church, than that it should be present when discipline should be exercised; and that the command to exercise discipline was given to the rulers. But there are not two descriptions of persons addressed. The same persons who are commanded to assemble, are commanded to "put away the incestuous person from among *themselves*." Had it been said that the rulers were to judge of and execute discipline in the presence of the church, it would not indeed have been a necessary consequence, that each of the members of the church were to have a share in the discussion. But, Sir, the command is given not to the rulers, but to the church at large, and to prevent a few from engrossing this business to themselves, like a Presbyterian session, they are expressly commanded to do it themselves, and in their public assembly. It is not possible for language to contain a more exact, and punctual, and explicit direction, the thing to be done, the persons appointed to do it, the manner of their proceeding, are all specifically marked. The very possibility of acting by deputation is cut off. The very persons who are commanded to do this, are the persons commanded to assemble, and to do it in their assembled capacity. The very persons who are commanded to be gathered together, are commanded to "deliver to Satan." If they are not all to be joined in delivering to Satan, neither are they all to be gathered together. If they are to deliver to Satan by their representatives, so likewise are they to be assembled in their representatives. It may as well be argued that they are not commanded to be assembled, as that those assembled are not to perform this injunction. Indeed, if this could reasonably be disputed, I would despair for ever of coming at any certainty as to the meaning of the Bible upon any point, or of any other book. More bare-faced perversion never was employed upon a papal bull, to avoid the thunder of the Vatican, by the Dominicans, Jansenists, or Jesuits, than you have employed to evade this apostolical command. With all the charity I can muster, I am not able to persuade myself, that this mode of analysis has entirely satisfied your own judgment. I think you must have been exceedingly perplexed upon this part of your subject. I can easily see you at your ease in displaying the advantages of Presbytery, drawn from abstract principles, and a comparison with the kingdoms of this world; because there is here something really agreeable to carnal wisdom. I can readily perceive how men are imposed upon here. When men reason at a distance from Scripture, they can go on with freedom in supporting a corrupt system. But the matter is different when they come to silence the testimony of Scripture evidence. If all reverence for the Word of the dreadful God is not extinguished, a critic must find himself exceedingly cramped when he attempts to make him speak according to an unscriptural system. I beseech you then, Sir, to recollect that this letter was written to the Church of Corinth, by the Spirit of Jesus. If it be an awful thing for a man to rise against his neighbour, and attribute to him sentiments that he never avowed, how dreadful must it be in the day of God, to be found to have represented the Holy Ghost as saying what he never intended! I beseech you, Sir, examine your motives for writing your defence of Presbytery. Do not suffer yourself to be flattered by the smiles of a national church, nor allow your judgment to be warped by the prospect of its honours and preferments. Be not intoxicated with the praises of men. Remember, that though it is very agreeable to human nature to be hailed as the champion of a prosperous church, their ambition is much better founded and directed, who are waiting for the sentence, " Well done, good and faithful servant." I beseech you, Sir, to re-examine this chapter by the rules of sober criticism, and do not allow yourself to be hurried away by the heat of argument, the desire of victory, or the love of the 'praise of men,' to wrest it from its evident purport.

What resources could you possibly imagine you had found in the proceedings of civil courts, to uphold your falling cause? Though the multitude be present, yet as they have nothing to do, their presence is never required. The judge and jury can transact business not only equally well, but much more conveniently, when there is no crowd. Was it ever known that the sheriff summoned the inhabitants of a whole county to be present at the trial of a criminal? But to make the example similar, the multitude must not only be summoned to be present, but they must also be commanded, when assembled, to try the criminal, and condemn him when found guilty; meaning all this time that no one was to have any concern in the matter but the judges and jury.

"Admitting also," you say, "that all the Corinthians were to put away from themselves this wicked person, it cannot be inferred that every member was to do so, either virtually or nominally, as an ecclesiastical judge, but, as has been already evinced, only the elders; while at the same time it was his duty, by every proper testimony of respectful acquiescence in the sentence of the latter, and by abstaining even from all unnecessary intercourse with the offender in common life, in his private capacity, to confirm their deed."—p. 115–117.

Shall we never have done with this figure? Must it pervade the whole Scriptures upon this single point? Is this the only subject upon which the inspired writers did not speak plainly? Really, if the apostle uses as many figures in every chapter, and upon every subject, as he does upon this, he will be very hard to be understood. But Sir, there is no figure in this; there is nothing here but plain preceptive language. "Put away from *among yourselves* that wicked person." Pray, Sir, could the apostle have used more express language? Allow for a moment that he wished to say what we think he did say, what could he have said more precise and particular than this to enjoin it? Did not the apostle write to a company of plain people, for the use of the most illiterate, to the end of the world, who would never imagine that he would say one thing and mean another? Allowing you however this figure again, you are much mistaken in saying, that it could not be inferred from what you admit, that all the Corinthians put the incestuous person away virtually, as ecclesiastical judges. Whatever another does for you in your name, is *virtually* done by yourself. Without this supposition, there is no foundation for the figure. If they were commanded to do this, and yet did it not, either *virtually* or *nominally*, pray, in what sense did they do it? Even this figure supposes that the action still was theirs, and that the judges did it only in their right.

But, Sir, you take the precept, "Put away from among yourselves that wicked person," in a double sense, including a command for the rulers to perform that piece of discipline, and a command for the individual members respectfully to acquiesce in this sentence, &c. If it means the one, surely it cannot mean the other. This would be to make the precept both figurative and literal. If, by a figure, they are commanded to do what their rulers are to do for them, then they cannot in the same words be literally commanded to acquiesce in the sentence of their rulers. You make them do one thing figuratively, and another literally. They must *judge by their representatives*, but they must *submit personally* to their decisions.

"And though it should be admitted, moreover," you continue, "that the sentence, as we are told (2 Cor. ii. 6), was inflicted by many, it will not follow that it was passed by many, or all of them, for there is an essential distinction, in every government, between the making and the infliction of a sentence. The former might be performed only by a few who were rulers, while the latter might be executed by all the members of the church, who were bound to concur with the elders, by inflicting the sentence; and who were all, as we have said, under an obligation to refuse to have fellowship with him, that he might be ashamed, and that others might fear."—p. 117.

"Though it should be admitted!" What do you mean by such language? What makes you so reluctant to admit unequivocally what you yet have not the hardiness to deny? Why do you concede these things that are so evident, in terms that allow you to retract your concession at pleasure? Is this like a candid enquirer after truth? It is of no consequence to my argument; but I cannot approve of the disposition that leads to this over-cautious mode of disputation. I do not expect an antagonist to surrender any post that is tenable, and it is often very proper to admit, for argument's sake, what need not be admitted, and should not be admitted in reality; yet what cannot be disputed, should never be surrendered in terms that imply that there was sufficient ground to retain it. Your concessions appear to me as ridiculous as the conduct of a petty village representing it as a matter of choice that they opened their gates to a vast army.

Do you suppose that the *making* of the sentence is inferior to the execution of it? The contrary of this is the fact. There is indeed in every government an essential difference between these. The legislative government makes laws, and the executive enforces their observance. But it happens that the office of the latter, not of the former, corresponds to that of church rulers. The jury finds the verdict, the judge pronounces it. Perhaps, however, you take your illustration from the office of the common hangman, who, after sentence is pronounced, inflicts the punishment on the criminal. Some sort of power corresponding to this honourable office, you would be willing to give to the illiterate crowd. But there is in the infliction of an ecclesiastical sentence, *i.e.*, the sentence of a church of Christ, nothing that corresponds to the infliction of a penal sentence of the civil law. Nor even are the ghostly fathers themselves now armed with the civil sword. There is no corporal punishment to be inflicted after the fallen brother is excluded from the church. I ask you how this sentence was to be inflicted? Was it not by giving over the wicked person in their assembly, unto Satan? What was the sentence, but the command to exclude him? How was this sentence inflicted, but by complying with the command contained in 1 Cor. v. 4, 5? How could it then be inflicted by the many, if the many did not themselves personally perform the command? Not only is the whole church commanded to deliver the incestuous person to Satan in 1 Cor. v. 4, 5; they are also said in 2 Cor. ii. 6 to have performed this personally, and not by representatives. It is "the sentence inflicted by many." Now, when this sentence is said to be inflicted by many, it cannot be understood in any other sense, than that it was the act and deed of the many of the whole church.

But, Sir, open your Greek Testament, and read the passage, 2 Cor. ii. 6. There you will find no word corresponding to *inflicted*. The words are, ἡ επιτιμια αυτη ἡ υπο των πλειονων, literally, *this punishment—the punishment of* or *by the many*, in every respect the act and deed of the whole church; not decreed by the rulers, and inflicted by the people; nor decreed by the people, and inflicted by the rulers; but in every view the punishment of the many, ruled and rulers. How could it be the punishment of the many, unless it were the deed of the many? The pronouncing of the sentence belonged to the church rulers. In vain, Sir, you try to diminish the weight of this passage; it will prove a mill-stone for ever around the neck of the cause you espouse.

But go on, Sir, with your analysis. "Is it said, in short, that as *all* the Corinthians are commanded to forgive their offending brother (2 Cor. ii. 7–10), they must *all* have been rulers? It is replied, that this consequence appears by no means to follow; but that all that can be deduced from it is this, that as they had all been offended by him in their various stations, so they were all to forgive him upon tokens of his repentance, and express their forgiveness in a manner which was suited to their situation in the church. Those who were rulers, and were offended by him in that capacity, were commanded as such to forgive him, and restore him again to the privileges of their society; and those who were members, and had been offended by him as such, on account of the dishonour which he had done to God, were called as such to express their forgiveness, and restore him once more to the comforts and advantages of private fellowship."—p. 117, 118.

To the question you propose in the beginning of this paragraph, I answer as you do, that it by no means follows, that because they are all to forgive the incestuous person, therefore they must all be rulers. This certainly does not follow; for though he is to be received back, as he was put away, by the unanimous voice of the whole church, yet in this they act not as rulers, but as church members. Even as to the societies of this world, there are many so constituted, that each member of the society has a right to be satisfied with others who are proposed for admission. Yet it is never supposed from this, that every member is an officer in the society.

But why did you not try your favourite figure upon this word? Could you not have said, "Can this be explained upon the Presbyterian system? Yes; for nothing is more common than for a body to be said to do that which others do for them. All that is meant here is, that they are to forgive him by their rulers."

Let us examine what you have made of it. You say, that "all that can be deduced from it is, that as they were all in their respective stations offended by him, so they were all in their situations in the church to forgive him, rulers as rulers, and private members as such," &c.

Here I observe, that though there are different stations in a church, yet this offence committed against them, did not respect them in those stations. This person did not commit one offence against a ruler, and a different offence against an individual member. The offence was the same with respect to all. They were all offended, not as officers and individuals, but as Christians and church members. A church ruler is offended by a public sin in a brother, not in a way different from any other member. Your criticism then is a mere refinement. It is a distinction without a difference, invented for the sole purpose of getting rid of the testimony of Scripture. It is not possible that any man who has the smallest reverence for the Word of God, could seriously think that such subtleties are necessary to explain its meaning. The whole church was commanded, in the first epistle, to put away the offender. The whole church is, in the second, commanded to forgive him. What can the writer mean, but that the restoration of him is the act of the body at large?

Your interpretation gives the words also a double meaning, and makes them convey a twofold precept. You make forgiveness as to the rulers, mean formal and official re-admission, according to their exclusive prerogative; as to the members, you make it signify only mental forgiveness, not in an official manner, nor by any public expression. Here then, in the same word, we have a command given to a body, which has not the same meaning as to all addressed, but is in reality two commands quite different; directed to two different classes of people, although they are addressed as one. If this was the case, the apostle must have been exceedingly parsimonious of his words. He is more laconic than the Lacedemonians themselves. Forgiveness must be taken in a sense, as to one part of those addressed, which it cannot have as to the other, nay, in which it would be presumption in the latter to understand it. The forgiveness which is inculcated upon the one part, it would be sin in the other to attempt to exercise, although these two different kinds of forgiveness are inculcated in the same words, addressed to one body, without any distinction. My good Sir, do you recollect that it is the Bible you are thus attempting to disfigure? Really the rhetoric of old Strepsiades, in the Nubes of Aristophanes, to evade the demands of his creditors, is scarcely more ridiculous. Some words you reduce to a very small part of their proper power; to others, you give a double power whenever it suits your purpose.

The apostle however did not mean to speak in such a dark and doubtful manner, as to give the disciples of Socrates any just occasion to pervert his words. He speaks what he means, fully and unequivocally, without intending at one time less, and at another more, than what his words naturally import. The whole church is commanded to forgive him in the same way. They are not addressed as rulers and ruled, considered in the distinct classes, but as one undivided body, which, though composed of different orders, are in this to act together. The way in which they were all as a body to forgive him (2 Cor. ii. 8), was to "confirm their love to him," or, as the original word implies, publicly to ratify their love to him by a re-admission. They did not cease to love him, even when he continued to sin; but when he repented, they were publicly to show him their love as a brother, by constitutionally receiving him back into communion. Κυρωσαι signifies to confirm, to ratify authoritatively by a public deed. How could the whole body be commanded κυρωσαι εις αυτον αγαπην, unless it was by the consent of the whole body that he was to be re-admitted? This language would be absurd, if addressed to a Presbyterian congregation. But the ninth verse puts the matter beyond controversy. "For to this end also did I write, that I might know the proof of you, whether ye be obedient in all things." Did the apostle write to the Corinthians, for this very end, that he might know the proof of them, whether they would be obedient in all things? Was this injunction to be the very test of their discipleship? What proof could they have given of their obedience to this command, if they had not the power of obeying it themselves, and of refusing to obey it? The church could have given no proof of its obedience or of disobedience, if the whole matter rested exclusively with its rulers. He might as well have written to the servants of a nobleman to put away a fellow-servant, with a view to have a proof of their obedience, while the whole power of keeping or dismissing the servant was vested in the master. Could the servants in such a case give any proof of obedience or disobedience? Would they not answer, 'To put away a fellow-servant does not belong to us. This is the privilege of the master alone. You must apply to himself.' The whole church was commanded to put away from among themselves the wicked person. This command was given to them for this very purpose, that the apostle might have a proof of their obedience. Therefore, they must have had the power of obeying or disobeying the injunction.

"Your glorying is not good," saith the apostle; "know you not that a little leaven leaveneth the whole lump?" But what although they did know this, if they had no power to remedy it? Where was the use or propriety of this remonstrance, if the persons addressed had no more authority to remedy it, than the Church of Scotland has to remedy the disorders of the Church of Rome? Does not the apostle speak here in the language of high indignation, which, when impressed with his rebukes they felt in their turn against themselves, plainly criminating those addressed, and implying that they had power to correct the evil, or purge out the leaven? Accordingly he adds, "Purge out the old leaven, that ye may be a new lump as ye are unleavened." Here a command is given to them in the most decisive terms, which they are supposed to have full power to perform. It is not, 'Stir up your rulers to purge out the old leaven, and if they do not comply, complain to the higher courts; but addressing the whole church, both rulers and ruled, he commands them to "purge out the old leaven." The whole church is blamed; the whole church then must have possessed the requisite authority to obey. There is not in the New Testament a chapter more plain than the fifth of first Corinthians. The utmost license of interpretation that ever has been used by Socinians, Quakers, or Roman Catholics, has not exceeded what you have employed to make it quadrate with the views of Presbyterians. It is not a solitary expression that you distort, it is not single words only that you turn into figures. It is figuration with you from beginning to end; nay, often both figurative and literal. In one place you suppose the apostle to speak exclusively to the individual members, in another to speak exclusively to the rulers, in another figuratively to the individual members, giving a command that they were to obey by their representatives, in another he speaks figuratively and literally in the same words, in another a command is to be understood in a double meaning; the apostle all the while addressing, without variation, the same persons. The church members only should have mourned; the church rulers only should have excluded the incestuous person: the former may be literally assembled, but they can only figuratively perform what they are commanded, when assembled; the latter are to decide: the former must acquiesce in the decision, while these two peculiar duties, separately incumbent upon these two orders, are conveyed in the same words. What a hodge-podge! But all your subtlety, and all your figures, will fail to darken these precepts. Though every Christian may not be able to unravel your sophistry, the most unlettered will see that your criticism is unnatural and forced. After reading your seventh letter, let them take up the New Testament, and again read the chapter, and I have no fear but all the mist you may have raised before their eyes, will be dispelled by the bright rays of the Sun of righteousness. If the Word of God were really so dark as you represent it; if it were really necessary to have recourse to such rules of criticism to understand it, as you employ to explain the most obvious precepts, it is darker than an oracle of Delphi. We should then need an infallible interpreter. The common people need never open the Bible. They may despair of being able to judge of the meaning of the plainest passage in Scripture. Yea, they could not be certain of the personal obligation of the ten commandments. Why might they not obey the moral law by their representatives? If such clear passages of Scripture may lawfully be explained by a meaning so distant from their obvious import, what may not be imposed upon those passages that are really dark? Upon this mode of interpretation, it would not be possible to refute any system that ever has been foisted upon the Word of God. The Originists, the Mystics, &c., might keep their ground in defiance of criticism. Yea, I would despair of being able to bring down the pillar saints from their aerial habitations.*

* The apostle commanded the epistles to the Colossians, Thessalonians, &c., to be read to the brethren: but of what use would it be to them to have these read to them, if they

But, Sir, the directions respecting the expulsion and re-admission of the incestuous person, are not the only places you must turn into figures. You must also metamorphose the whole epistles. There is not a case of discipline, nor a direction as to the management of church affairs in all the New Testament, which are not delivered to the churches. There is not a single instance in which church rulers are represented as exclusively possessing this authority. Rom. xiv.—" Him that is weak in the faith, receive ye." The admission of members then is the business of the whole church. Is this also a figure? Where are we to look for the plain passages? The same thing is also plainly taught in Acts ix. 26, notwithstanding all your labour to evade it. Paul attempted to join the church at Jerusalem; what prevented him? The disciples were all afraid of him, and did not believe that he was a disciple. This is the only reason that is alleged for his rejection. Had the Church of Jerusalem been a Presbyterian congregation, Paul would have been admitted or rejected without consulting the disciples; nay, without their knowledge. He might have been a member of that church for many years, without the privity of any but such as had previously known him. Should it be said that his application was publicly notified, to give the brethren an opportunity of communicating what they knew of him to the rulers; I answer, even this supposition will overthrow the practice of the Church of Scotland, and so far you must confess yourselves to overlook the model that yourselves call divine. I answer farther, that this could not have been the reason of his rejection, because the disciples could give no additional information as to Paul. They knew nothing of him more than their rulers. They all knew what he once was, a persecutor; and therefore they were all afraid now that his conversion was not real. When it is intimated then that he was rejected in consequence of the fears of the

must be understood by such rules of interpretation as these? He should have sent with his epistles some huge folio commentary. If 1 Cor. v. must be understood in your sense, he might as well have presented the Corinthians with a volume of the intricate philosophy of the Stagirite.

s

disciples, it cannot be interpreted that the church rulers rejected him for the additional knowledge they received respecting him from the disciples, because the rulers knew as much themselves. Since then the fear of the disciples is the only reason to which his rejection is attributed, the rejection of him is thus virtually ascribed to the disciples. Had the disciples acted only as informers, the rulers would not be represented as rejecting Paul on account of the fears of the disciples, but on account of their own fears of him. A jury does not condemn a criminal on account of the opinions of the witnesses, but on account of their evidence, and the degree of weight they place in that evidence. It is then upon their own convictions from the evidence they act. It is not said that the jury condemned the criminal, because the witnesses declared *they thought* he was guilty, but because the jury itself, from the depositions of the witnesses, were convinced of his guilt. When the fear of the disciples is alleged as the cause of his rejection, it cannot be understood then, that this was the cause why the rulers rejected him, but the cause why they rejected him themselves. Even according to your own interpretation of this passage, the disciples had a negative. No person then should be received in a church, of whom the body of the disciples have any doubt.

Acts xviii. 27.—Apollos received his letters of recommendation, you see, from the brethren, not the Session or Presbytery. Paul also supposes, that such letters which were necessary for others, but unnecessary in his case, should come from the same source.—2 Cor. iii. 1. The public certificate, as we may call it, or the approbation of the character of a person who had been discharging the duty of a messenger of the church, is also directed to the whole body, not to the rulers only.— Phil. ii. 29, 30.

It is of the Church of Colosse also whom the apostle commands to receive Mark. Col. iv. 10.—" Touching whom, ye received commandments; if he come unto you, receive him." From the circumstance of Paul's dispute with Barnabas, on account of Mark's conduct, and from the command contained in the latter part of this quotation, the commandments that he here mentions as formerly given to the Colossians touching Mark, must undoubtedly mean, that they were commanded not to receive him. When Mark acted in such a manner as to lose the confidence of the apostle, this church was commanded not to receive him; when he was brought to repentance, the apostle forgave him, and reversed his command to the Colossians. Both the former command and the present is directed, not to the church rulers, as it would had they been Presbyterians, but to the whole church.

But, Sir, to put the matter beyond all dispute, there is a direction as to discipline in Gal. vi. 1, which your figure cannot possibly twist. "Brethren, if a man be overtaken in a fault, ye which are spiritual restore such an one in the spirit of meekness, considering thyself, lest thou also be tempted." *Ye which are spiritual;* here they are commanded to restore a brother who should fall into sin by surprise. There is a difference to be made between the case of such a person, and one who sins by premeditation, as a hypocrite. But who is fit to make this distinction? If ever there should be a case in which the pastors alone ought to judge, this surely is the case. But are the rulers alone commanded to judge? No, but the whole church; and their qualification is specified. "Ye who are *spiritual.*" Spiritual men alone are capable of judging in this matter. The carnal man is not acquainted with the wiles of Satan, the deceitfulness of the human heart, &c. Such a precept would in vain be given to a General Assembly, though all the judges of the land were present. But the plainest congregation of saints have the requisite qualifications. 'Ye who are spiritual, restore such an one.' Are the church rulers the only spiritual people in the church? This precept is given to the whole church, as composed of spiritual men, who were capable of making this distinction. Sir, try your figure upon this.

Let any one examine the epistles upon this subject, in the same manner as Archdeacon Paley proves the authenticity of the epistles of Paul, and he will meet such a multitude of these indirect, incidental proofs, as will abundantly corroborate this argument.

But not only are the members in conjunction with the rulers entrusted with the discipline of the church, as it respects the brethren; even the pastors themselves are to be judged by them, and admonished if negligent or faulty. Col. iv. 17.—" And say to Archippus, Take heed to the ministry which thou hast received in the Lord, that thou fulfil it." How would a Presbyterian minister take this? His dignity would be highly insulted, if the individual members of his congregation should sit in judgment upon his conduct, and admonish him to diligence. Paul then was not a Presbyterian, nor was this a Presbyterian congregation to which he wrote, or he would have committed the admonition of Archippus to his Presbytery.

In fine, of all the directions as to discipline, of all the censures as to the neglect of it, in all the New Testament, there is not one given to the rulers, as distinct from the brethren. Would it not then be the most unaccountable thing, if the rulers alone have a right to judge of discipline, that in all the commands given upon that point, they should never be named? That all the censures as to the neglect of discipline, and abuses which church rulers alone, upon this supposition, could reform, should fall upon those, who were neither guilty in the matter, nor had a power of remedying? That those who alone should in this case have borne the blame, are neither reprimanded nor mentioned?

LETTER VI.

Sir,

As your book is rather a set of miscellaneous remarks than a regular treatise, I am obliged to pass by your eighth letter, till I meet it in its proper place, where you finally give your views of Acts xv. I proceed to the consideration of the doctrine of the lay-elder, handled in your ninth, tenth, and eleventh letters. Here I do not think it necessary to pull down by piecemeal the frail edifice you have reared. If I pick out the key-stones, the arch, with all its supports, will tumble of itself. A tedious refutation of arguments that are *palpably* nugatory or irrelevant, would rather be to insult the understanding of my readers, than useful to assist them in their researches. You would have spared yourself and your readers some trouble, had you omitted your frequent and copious extracts from the ancient Independents. To what purpose do you place in your van the celebrated names of Goodwin, Watts and Owen? You might as well have substituted in their room, Rutherford, Dixon and Guthrie. To arguments, not to names, do we attach any respect. I am afraid you are so much accustomed to be guided in these matters by authority, that you imagine that no party can be without their leaders. I must tell you then, Sir, that we have no patriarchs with us. We agree with the ancient Independents just as far as we judge them to agree with the Bible, and so far we will also agree with Presbyterians and every other sect. If any doctor on any side states or defends your opinion better than you can do yourself, you are welcome to borrow his arguments, or use his language. But no writings, the Bible excepted, can we allow you to quote as authorities.

Your first argument for lay-elders, taken from the

plurality of elders in every church, has no substance. Though there are to be more elders than one in every church where they can be obtained, does it follow that some of these must be what Presbyterians are pleased to call lay-elders? Yes, you say, because it could not maintain them all.* And is this the distinction between preaching and lay-elders, that the one are supported by the church, and the other support themselves? Every pastor not supported by the church is then a layman. Few of the clergy will forfeit their title by this crime. Not to mention that all elders are said, 1 Tim. v. 18, (the chief passage from which you attempt to prove this office) to be worthy of maintenance, of whatever kind they may be, and that this difficulty will meet the one system as well as the other, is it necessary that every labourer should be supported, whether he needs it or not? or that all should be supported in the style of parish ministers, suitable to the dignity of a civil establishment? Is it necessary that a man, when he becomes a pastor, should live more splendidly than formerly? That all labourers have a right to a comfortable support, is clear both from reason and express Scripture. But it is equally clear from both, that where a church is poor, those who have the qualifications should labour as they have opportunity, while they support themselves, as they were formerly accustomed, by their own industry. The elders of Ephesus were commanded to work with their own hands, not only to support themselves, but to minister to the wants of others. It is also very clear, that it is an unscriptural idea, that all the pastors of the same church who need support, are entitled to an equal sup-

---

* You argue here, that of the plurality of elders found in every apostolical church, the greater part must have been lay-elders, because otherwise they could not be supported: yet to avoid the argument against lay-elders, from the circumstance that they are all represented as entitled to support (1 Tim. v. 17), you elsewhere declare, that you see no reason why these lay-elders should not be supported. How does this consist with your present argument? It is totally impossible to be consistent in forcing a false system upon the Bible. The genius of Leibtnitz or Newton could not, in like circumstances, avoid incongruities.

port. 1 Tim. v. 18, leaves us at no loss as to our duty on this point. While it is exceedingly desirable that some, at least one, should be solely devoted to the service of the church, others may properly spend much of their time in their worldly business. An acquaintance with the original languages of the Scriptures, with history, &c., is very necessary to be possessed by the church in at least one of its pastors; but though this is desirable, even as to every Christian, it is by no means indispensable as to some of the pastors. They may be very useful labourers in many respects without this accomplishment. Those therefore who must devote all their time to such acquisitions, must undoubtedly require a much greater support than others who can devote the greater part of their time to worldly business. The previous habits of living, with many other circumstances, must also be considered; so that while one will need much, another may need nothing but a small remuneration for the loss of time.

Besides, Sir, I do not think with you, that there are few churches able to support three pastors. If Christians were less conformed to the world, should they save what others spend unnecessarily, they could support several labourers in a church, and be as rich at the year's end as their neighbours. The expense of costly entertainments, for show, not for hospitality, would be sufficient to make a considerable augmentation to the funds of a church, if applied to that purpose. Christians do not so much want the ability, though they are generally in the lower ranks of life; but in some places they appear criminally ignorant of the extent of their duty on this point, and many seem emulous to support a rank like the men of the world. These, I think, are the reasons, generally speaking, why churches cannot support a sufficient number of pastors. But this appears a very strange argument in the mouth of a defender of a national church. Could not the same authority that secures the manse and stipend to one minister in every parish, equally provide for thirty or a hundred?

You have a curious observation upon the number necessary, upon the supposition that there should be more than one. "At any rate," you say, "it is certain that it can never properly be less than *three*, for if there were only two, and if they should happen to differ upon any point of discipline, or any case of government, no decision could be made."—p. 150. You can never divest yourself of that Presbyterian idea of majorities, minorities, and decision by vote. Sir, the elders of an apostolical church have no private decisions, and upon no business in the church is there ever a balancing of votes.

Your second argument shall not detain me a moment. The extent of the oversight of elders proves nothing as to the question, whether all the elders should be of the same order, or whether a part of them should be what are called lay-elders. It proves indeed the necessity of a plurality, numerous in proportion to this extent, but it does not imply that one or two of them only should be pastors. You might as well argue, that because the city of Edinburgh is too extensive for the inspection of one magistrate, therefore, instead of creating a number of magistrates of equal rank, the first magistrate should be assisted in his office by the town beadles.

Your long quotation, p. 152–156, to show the duty of these lay-elders, I lay upon the same shelf with my Apocrypha. Sir, be so good as to point out to me the duties of a lay-elder from the New Testament. Where this fails, I will not acknowledge the writings of Dr. Owen for canonical Scripture. Surely, Sir, this is a tacit confession that the office is not in Scripture, when to describe its duties, you must leave the Bible, and have recourse to Dr. Owen.

Your third argument will be as easily dispatched. This is the necessity of an order of lay-elders to curb the ambition of the clergy. Christ has left his churches in possession of a very good restraint upon their rulers, for the latter can carry no measures without the consent of the former. Had church members always been faithful to Christ, in personally discharging their duty as to church affairs, Antichrist could never have arisen. But by neglecting this, and deputing others to act for them, the Man of Sin has entered and grown to maturity. "The ministers of religion," you observe, p. 156, "however amiable and venerable their character, are subject to the frailties and imperfections of humanity, and that a desire of an undue and extravagant authority has too often been one of these imperfections, is a truth which will scarcely be denied." No, indeed, Sir, we are not disposed to deny this. A peep into the General Assembly, or any of its subordinate courts, would convince the most obstinate infidel. The high notions which you have conceived of this office, and the lordly language in which you speak of the *authoritative decisions* of church courts, sufficiently intimate that you are not beyond the reach of temptation from this common propensity of human nature. But the way to prevent or repress clerical ambition, is for every church to observe all the commandments and ordinances of the Lord, not to employ for this end the maxims of worldly prudence.

But is it possible that pastoral ambition shall be more effectually restrained by joining a few with him in the exercise of church power, than by associating with him in every transaction the whole body of believers? Is it not more likely that a few will give way to schemes of clerical aggrandizement than the whole church? You could not but foresee this answer, and therefore you attempt to evade it. You think that the clergy would have more influence upon the bulk of a congregation of ignorant people, than upon a few of the most enlightened. Sir, have not those enlightened few, as church members, the means of restraining the ambition of their pastors, equally as if the whole power of doing so was vested in them alone? When there are no majorities appointed to decide differences, a pastor would in vain carry with him the ignorant. But, Sir, if a church is composed of proper materials, much as they may esteem their pastors, they esteem Jesus much more, and prefer his authority to influence of any kind. You think you are in a promiscuous Presbyterian congregation, I suppose.

Nor is your observation, that pastoral ambition is more likely to prevail over the bulk of a congregation, than over the enlightened few, founded in an accurate observation of human conduct. We know that a man can have more influence over those nearly of an equal rank, or even of a superior rank, but inferior as to office, than over those at a great distance below him. By his attentions and condescension, he may flatter the former, who are easily convinced that they are his equals, because they are not far from him, or in some respects above him; but the latter can never be deceived, nor deceive themselves in this manner. They are at too great a distance from him, ever to imagine that he esteems them as his equals. This is not only agreeable to human nature, but might be confirmed by many examples. I might refer to every man's experience, whether or not those who are esteemed the better sort of people, or the enlightened few, are not more frequently of the minister's party, than the bulk of the congregation. This was remarkably verified in the affair of the classification of the ministers of the General Synod in Ireland. Generally speaking, the only persons who contributed their assistance to advance clerical dignity, at the expense of their constitution, were those who would be thought the enlightened few. Those that you look upon to be a mere rabble, would have curbed clerical ambition had it been in their power.

Your fourth argument, though it does not lead to the conclusion which you draw from it, has yet a foundation in truth, and should carefully be attended to by the churches. "There are many to be found in the church, who, though not fitted to be teaching elders, are eminently qualified to be rulers. Most men have it not in their power to attain that learning, and that facility of expression, which are requisite for the former, while many of them have acquired that experience and sagacity which may fit them for the useful discharge of the latter. Shall the church then, because they are not qualified to be numbered among her instructors, be totally deprived of the benefit of their endowments?"— p. 159. Though there is no distinction of office in eldership, there are distinct provinces in it, and some are fitted more eminently for one part of it, and some for another. The churches not only may, but ought to choose pastors with a variety of talents; that each excelling in one department of the office, the saints may, with the more accelerated progress, grow up in all things into Christ. One, from a deep acquaintance with the Scriptures, and the languages in which they were written, may usually be employed in expounding; another, who is perhaps acquainted with no language but that which is usually spoken, may have a greater facility of speaking, and a more happy manner of arresting the attention of the careless, may be usually employed in preaching the Gospel; another may want talents for public speaking, yet be eminently qualified for conversation with the newly awakened, the weak, the tempted and the sick; qualifications in which the others may be as much defective, as he is as to those which they possess; another, from a particular strength and presence of mind, joined with prudence, patience, gentleness, firmness, experience, knowledge of the world, and a thorough acquaintance with the laws of Christ, may be peculiarly qualified to preside in the church, and to be usually engaged in what is called ruling. If a church had so many elders usually employed in these different departments, each of them would be a pastor, and no one of them could with more propriety than another be called *her instructor*. Why should one of these bear the name of pastor, to the exclusion of the rest? Especially, why should the *ruler* forfeit his name and office? If any in a more eminent manner than his associates is entitled to the name of bishop or overseer, he is the one.

When a church can obtain a plurality of pastors, they ought undoubtedly to employ them in different departments of the office. If they are all engaged alternately in the same things, they are thereby prevented from excelling in the discharge of the duties of any one branch, in such a degree as might be expected, were their whole attention usually directed to a single point. Even artists, in every branch of manufacture, are found to carry their art to a much greater perfection, by dividing the work. This argument then undoubtedly shows the propriety of the elders dividing the work of the eldership, but not of dividing the eldership itself.

"It is surprising, in short, that the commission of

the government to a few of the members who do not teach, but merely rule together with the pastors, should be so displeasing both to Episcopalians and Independents, since something similar exists among themselves."—p. 160. And again, p. 162, you say, "It is intrusted nominally by the latter to all the members together with the pastors, but is exercised in *reality* only by a *few* of those who influence the rest." I have only to remark upon this passage, that your assertion as to Independents is false. Though it is not necessary nor proper, that every member should speak upon every question, yet, as each has a right to communicate his views with a weight equal to their truth and importance, there must be a complete difference between an Independent church and a Presbyterian congregation. Government is indeed committed to a few, *i.e.*, the elders, not these with a few of the select brethren. The judging of discipline is committed neither nominally nor in reality to a few. Cases are submitted to the whole church; but is it necessary, in order to show their privilege, that every man should speak? It is sufficient, that if a brother has anything worthy of communication, he has it in his power; and that nothing can be carried but with unanimity. There exists in no church that is worthy of defence, any influence, but that of truth. Individuals have no farther influence than as they exhibit this.

You come next to give us what you call arguments from Scripture for the office of the lay-elder, and in the tenth letter call our attention to Rom. xii. 6; 1 Cor. xii. 28. It is a very easy thing for the advocates of any system of church government professed among Christians, to exercise their ingenuity, and say many *plausible things* in endeavouring to accommodate these texts. But I apprehend that no sober critic, of any denomination, will attempt to establish anything from these passages, either as to the plan of government, or different offices, ordinary and extraordinary, till he has discovered the mind of God upon these subjects, from other more plain declarations of his Word. When these points have been satisfactorily settled in a man's own mind, he may bring with advantage his previous discoveries to illustrate what seems more obscure. Indeed, it is necessarily supposed that those addressed in these quotations were already acquainted with the ordinary and extraordinary offices, both as to number and limits. They were not designed to instruct them in what they did not know upon this subject, but taking it for granted that they knew these offices, and had them among themselves, in Rom. xii. 6, they are instructed how to employ their gifts, whether officers or individual members; and in 1 Cor. xii. 28, appealing to what they knew of the different offices, &c., they are exhorted to corresponding duties. What then was so plain to them, that their knowledge of it is taken for granted, because they had the objects before their eyes, hath become dark to us by the ceasing of extraordinary officers, and the changes that have been made by human wisdom and ambition in those offices that are ordinary. Hence the obscurity of these texts to us. Hence, to understand them, we must previously examine and determine this matter from other testimonies of Scripture. When you and I have examined which are the ordinary, and which the extraordinary offices, by enquiring which are found in every apostolical church, &c., we may then lawfully employ the result of our investigations, for the explanation of the present passages. No man of candour would say that a man newly converted to Christianity, without any previous acquaintance with the Bible, could determine the government, and officers appointed by Christ, from the passages under consideration. In reality, no man was ever led to embrace any form of church government from these texts, in the first instance; though all parties are sufficiently peremptory that they establish their respective systems. They adopt their principles on this subject from other sources, and then explain these texts suitable to their pre-conceived views.

In the explanation of any writing, be the subject what it may, it is usual to illustrate places that are dark, by places more clear and explicit. This custom approves itself to common sense, and is not an arbitrary rule, or confined to the interpretation of the Scriprures. You, Sir, contrary to all critics, proceed upon principles directly opposite. The most clear, and precise, and literal precepts in the apostolical epistles, you represent as unintelligible in their obvious and primary sense, and to explain them, you have recourse to the supposition that they are figurative; while those passages that are really dark or prophetical, are represented as entirely clear, and the most striking evidence of the truth of your system. Like those animals that see best in the night, you can penetrate the most obscure texts of Scripture with the utmost facility, and bring them, when explained, to elucidate those passages which to others have no difficulty, but which to you have no meaning until it is fixed by this ingenious process. When things are simple and obvious, you can see nothing but confusion. Where every rational critic finds difficulty, and expresses his opinion with diffidence, you are quite decisive. The language of prophecy is to you as plain as the alphabet, while the precepts of Jesus and his apostles are as dark, and uncertain, and full of figures, as an answer of the Sybil. When our Lord gives the keys to Peter, you are as confident that the figure implies the church power vested in the sacred hands of the Presbyterian clergy, as the Pope is that he has the keys of infallibility at Rome. But when our Lord gives a specific, and simple, and minute precept to a church as to offences, there is no possibility of ascertaining what he means. The figurative interpretation of the keys, must impose its supposed meaning upon the literal precept. You do not determine the meaning of figurative language, by that which is literal and plain; but that which is literal and plain, you determine by that which is dark and figurative. When the apostle alludes to offices, gifts, &c., which were personally witnessed or enjoyed by those to whom he wrote, but which have now ceased or been perverted, you can recognise in his language every feature of your system; but when the same apostle gives a command to perform, and instructions how to perform a case of discipline, all is figure and confusion. As the lay-elder cannot be found in any of those places which directly treat of the office of the elder, and describe his duties and his qualifications, he must be forced from passages which circumstances have rendered obscure.

In this general observation, I am sure there is no unprejudiced reader of your book but will agree with me; and I make it, not so much to serve any purpose in this place, as to show from the complexion of your reasoning that you stand upon bad ground. No good cause needs such unfair resources. Much less attention to the subject than you appear evidently to have given, would have enabled you to defend a good cause with triumphant and indisputable evidence. Really, I am often astonished that you are not ashamed to employ such shifting.

As to the great variety of opinions upon these texts, which you have stated and canvassed, the absurd conjectures of one party, and the absurd replies of another, I do not find myself called upon to take a side. I not only grant, but contend, and this independent of both these passages, that there is a distinction of departments in the pastoral office; that while all elders are pastors, some ought to be usually employed in one department, and some in another, according as they are gifted. This is the voice both of common sense and of the clearest Scripture. If any of the ancient or modern Independents do not see this, I am not their advocate. Had you attended to Mr. Haldane's 'View of Social Worship,' which you profess to review, you would have seen this opinion stated and defended. I must charge you, then, with wasting your time, and that of your readers, with a very long discussion, the greater part of which is, in the present controversy, totally out of place. The point which you should have contended with us, is not whether the gifts of teaching and of ruling are different, whether some possess a talent for the one who do not possess in a great degree a talent for the other, and that they should be employed accordingly; but whether teaching and ruling are distinct offices, the affirmative of which is not proved by requiring distinct talents; and whether, supposing it proved that they are distinct offices, exercised by distinct officers, the ruling officer is not a pastor as well as the teaching one. Had you kept to these points simply, you would have saved yourself the trouble of raking together all the wise and foolish things that have ever been said upon the texts under your examination.

Now, Sir, the opinion stated thus is ready for discussion. We contend that teaching and ruling are different branches of the pastoral office; that this plainly appears from many Scriptures, but that this is the utmost that can be made either of the passages under dispute or any other. We hold that these different branches of the office require different talents, usually found in different individuals, and that consequently, every church should, if possible, have a Presbytery or plurality of elders. We contend however that all elders are pastors, invested with the full character, and may discharge any part of the office when requisite. If you think that these passages, or any other, prove anything farther, or establish two different orders of elders, we are ready to dispute it with you. That all elders are pastors, I will afterwards show; all I mean to say here is, that the circumstance of teaching and ruling being mentioned distinctly, by no means shows that there are two offices, more than exhorting and teaching, and teaching and preaching, by being mentioned separately, are shown to belong to different offices. They are indeed distinct things, but belong to the same office. Writing, reading, arithmetic, &c., are different things, and in the best conducted schools have separate teachers, because few men equally excel in all, but in other schools they are all taught by the same person. When every branch has a separate teacher, the teachers will become more eminent in their respective departments, and the scholars will make a more rapid progress. But this by no means proves, that when there is but one teacher, he is not to initiate his pupils in all these branches, although he may excel only in one.

If this be questioned, it will be easy to prove it at length. But to assert that there must be different offices, because some have talents for the one without having talents for the other, would not serve Presbyterians. For if the offices are distinct, then the preaching elder cannot be a ruling elder also, without having two offices, which the wisdom of Christ could not allow.

He would not confer a plurality of offices upon one order of his servants, as princes do upon their favourites. If from being two offices, the elder that rules cannot preach, then it will follow, for the same reason, that the elder who preaches cannot rule. If they are two offices, they must stand unconnected. Again, if the ruling elder may not preach, because he has not that talent in a peculiar and eminent degree, the same thing will forbid the preaching elder to rule, because he has not a peculiar talent for ruling. It will as readily happen that one will have a talent for speaking, who will not have a talent for ruling, as that one will have a talent for ruling, without a talent for public speaking. Indeed, it perhaps seldom happens that the same man is peculiarly gifted for both. If, then, this circumstance must divide the offices, the limits must not be passed on either side.

But granting all that you can demand from these passages, allowing that there are distinct offices, and that the ruling elder should never preach, still he is a pastor, a bishop, an overseer, a leader, &c., and fully as much so as the other. Ruling is not an inferior, but the highest office, either in church or state. Perhaps you make the lay-elders to the minister, what beadles are to a magistrate. This, then, is the second point upon this subject which we should discuss. Upon the supposition that they are distinct officers, is the ruling elder a pastor?

After these general observations, I do not judge it necessary formally to refute your interpretation of these texts, even where I judge you wrong, because it would not bear upon the point in hand. I think it proper, however, to point out some things in your remarks upon them, which are calculated to mislead your readers as to the intention of the apostle, and the spirit and scope of his reasoning.

You say, p. 159, "Does not Paul, when demonstrating that there are to be various offices in the Church of Christ (Rom. xii. 6; 1 Cor. xii. 28), urge in proof of it, that he has bestowed upon its members a variety of gifts, which qualify them for these offices." There is here a fallacy in supposing that it is the apostle's design to demonstrate, that there is a variety of offices in a Church of Christ, as striking as that of the offices of the members of the human body. Were this the case, every brother and sister in the church would be an officer. So far from intending to demonstrate that there is to be such a striking variety (it would, indeed, be a very striking number !) his design is not to prove this variety at all. This variety, whatever it amounted to, was already appointed, and well known to the churches, and therefore the apostle had no need either to demonstrate it, or to call them to believe it. The apostle taking for granted that they knew this variety, brings it to bear upon another point, and to urge them to the duties that correspond to this, or resulted from it.

Every member of the human body has a distinct office, so has every member of a church his peculiar position, talent and function, according as the great Head has gifted him. But here the comparison between the offices of the members of the human body, and of the members of the spiritual body, refers not to the variety of offices Christ has instituted, but to the variety of the gifts and duties of the different members. You play upon the word *office*, making it, when applied to church members, an *office of government;* and represent the contrast as drawn between the offices of government in a church, and the different functions of the members of the human body. When we speak of the *offices* of the different members of the human body, we do not mean offices of government, but distinct functions or employments. As to the office of government in the human body, when we speak of this, it is attributed to the head or mind alone. What is intended to be conveyed by this illustration, is the resemblance of the different gifts, talents, and functions of the members of the spiritual body to those of the natural body. The resemblance is not between the offices of government in these two bodies, or between their governors, but between their members, rulers and ruled, and the different functions of these. The apostle does not mean to say that there is an office of government in the spiritual body, corresponding to every member of the human body ; for this would be a palpable absurdity, and would make every member of the church an officer. His design is to illustrate the duties of the members of a church from the different functions of the members of the human body. According to your interpretation, the officers of a church alone make the body of Christ. The apostle, however, is not merely speaking with respect to the rulers, but with respect to the whole members.—Rom. xii. 3, 5.

You also err in supposing, that for every gift there must be a distinct office. For the exercise of every gift there must, indeed, be scope, but those who have the same office may have different gifts, and many gifts may be both possessed and exercised in a church without any office at all. The apostle teaches, in one of the passages illustrated above, that as the members of the human body have not all the same employment, but each something peculiar to itself, so in the spiritual body each member has his peculiar talent, which he is to cultivate and employ for the good of the whole, without envying the gifts or talents of others. Yet to neither, as members, belongs any office of government or authority. Though then a gift for ruling certainly implies that there is an office in which that gift may be exercised, yet it by no means proves that ruling is a distinct office itself, and not a branch of the pastoral office.

In answer to your long letter upon 1 Tim. v. 17, I consider myself as having nothing to do, but to refer you to the fifth chapter of my Reasons for Separating from the General Synod of Ulster, as the view there given of that passage, is in no part of your vindication either refuted or stated. That there are distinct departments in the pastoral office, which require different gifts, and which should be usually occupied by the elders of a church according to their gifts, is clear from these words. I have no desire to skreen the practice of any Independent churches who do not comply with this apostolical institution, and who, to correspond with this practice, may at any time have endeavoured to explain the passage under consideration, as if no such distinction were implied. As I have no interest to support but that of truth, I can have no temptation to swerve to the one side or to the other. As it is the happiness of our churches not to be obliged to walk in human trammels, and to have no bonds to keep us from following light when it appears, when any part of our principles or practice is discovered to be contrary to the Word of God, we are under no temptation to have recourse to evasive arguments, unnatural figures, far-fetched suppositions, &c., to make darkness appear to be light. When we see a thing to be wrong, we can change it. But in worldly churches, as there is no remedy for the disorder, all the art of the physician lies in his skill in persuading the patient and the world, that the disease is only fanciful, or at most is not mortal.

That this passage establishes a distinction between the duties of this office, we maintain; but that ruling and teaching are separate offices, is neither said nor supposed. Nay, the very contrary of this may incontrovertibly be proved from it. So far from exhibiting the ruling elder as an officer distinct from the preaching elder, the latter is included in the first part of the verse as plainly as language can convey an idea. The obvious import of the words is this: "The elders who discharge the duty of a προεϛως well, are worthy of a double support, especially those of them who are employed in that part of the duty of the προεϛως, the labouring in word and doctrine." The οι κοπιωντες εν λογω, &c., are of necessity comprehended in the προεϛωτες. The language would otherwise be absurd. I have not even the trouble to search for examples. You have put the weapons in my hand to cut down your own argument. Every instance which you quote, in which the word μαλιϛα is used, supports me. Thus, verse 8, of this chapter: "If any man provide not for his own, and *especially* for those of his own house," &c. Here "those of his own house," are included in the general words, *his own*, in the preceding part of the sentence. Those of his own house are particularized out of those who are *his own* in a more general sense. Thus too, chap. iv. ver. 10—"Who is the preserver of all men, *especially* of them that believe." Here those who believe are comprehended in the general expression *all men*. Those who believe are particularized out of the *all men* who are preserved. 2 Tim. iv. 15—"Bring the books, *especially* the parchments." The parchments are included in the general word books, and are particularized out of them. Gal. vi. 10—" Let us do good to *all men*, but *especially* unto the household of faith." Here the household of faith is included in *all men*, and particularized out of them, not contrasted with them as different from them. Phil. iv. 22—" All the saints salute you, *chiefly* they that are of Cesar's household." Here the saints of Cesar's family are included in *all the saints;* they are not contrasted with, but particularized out of the others. Tit. i. 10—" For there are many unruly and vain talkers, and deceivers, *especially* they of the circumcision." The vain talkers and deceivers of the circumcision are included in the general proposition, " For there are many unruly and vain talkers and deceivers." They of the circumcision are particularized as eminently culpable. 2 Pet. ii. 9, 10—" The Lord knoweth how to deliver the godly out of temptations, and to reserve the unjust unto the day of judgment, to be punished: but *chiefly* them that walk after the flesh," &c. Here wicked people of a certain description are particularized among the unjust. The Lord shall punish all the wicked, but *especially* such persons. Acts xx. 38—" Sorrowing most of all, *especially* for the words which he spake, that they should see his face no more." Many things excited their sorrow; among the rest, and above all others, this circumstance, that they should see his face no more. The seeing of his face no more, is included among the other causes of their sorrow, in the general statement, but afterwards exhibited above all the rest. In short, in every example where it occurs, or in any language where it can legitimately occur, the word μαλιτα, and those in other languages by which it is translated, are used when one thing is particularized out of a number, or a part out of the whole. The preceding part of the sentence always includes the succeeding, though the succeeding is always distinguished. I contend then that according to the legitimate use of words, the οι κοπιωντες, &c., are included in the προεςωτες πρεσβυτεροι. The προεςωτες πρεσβυτεροι cannot be that order of elders which Presbyterians call ruling elders, or any separate order, because they contain the οι κοπιωντες, &c. This would involve the absurdity that the preaching elders were a part of the lay-elders. The προεϛωτες πρεσβυτεροι must be a general name of the whole office of the pastor, including those who are called οι κοπιωντες, &c. The οι κοπιωντες εν λογω και διδασκαλια, are προεςωτες πρεσβυτεροι, though it is implied that they labour in a certain part of the office, and that there must be others who labour in other parts of the same office. Προεϛωτες here cannot however refer to those only who labour in those other parts of the office, because different departments are here supposed to be included in it, and among the rest, "those who labour in word and doctrine."

We must then, Sir, have something more than the *peremptory* language of Owen, Whitaker, Whitby, &c. We look for good reasoning and sound criticism. It is idle in you to rear up the exploded theories of the old Independents, that you may make a useless parade of learning, in attacking and combating views which we do not hold. In answering Mr. Innes, you might as well have assaulted the philosophy of Decartes or Gassendi, as the views of the Independents of the seventeenth century. But προεϛως, so far from being appropriated to denote an order of lay-elders inferior to preaching elders, more limited in their rights, and in their sphere of action, is the very highest word employed to denote the pastoral office. If there is any difference, it is a word superior even to επισκοπος. Indeed, you yourself appear to know how to appreciate its value when it serves your purpose to exalt the prerogatives of church rulers. Both προεϛως and επισκοπος are given as names to this office from the idea of superintendence, which is the most prominent in the pastoral office; yet they both refer to the whole office. In 1 Thess. v. 12, not only are all their pastors called προιϛαμενοι, but the προιϛαμενοι are said to labour among them, and to admonish them. Had this term been appropriated to any one order, that order would not be an inferior, but the highest in a church. If the lay-elders are the προεϛωτες, they alone should be the presidents in all assemblies, and in all things enjoy the highest authority.

But that προεϛωτες πρεσβυτεροι neither denotes nor includes an order of lay-elders, *i.e.*, men who are no pastors, is clear from this circumstance, that they are all said to be worthy of support. If the πρεσβυτεροι, who are καλως προεϛωτες are worthy of a *double* portion, it implies that they are all to have some portion. But lay-elders do no service in the church sufficient to entitle them to maintenance, nor have they ever, so far as I know, been considered as deserving of it. Besides, if it is an objection to the opinion that the plurality of elders in every church are pastors, because they could not be supported although only three in number, how will Presbyterians contrive to support a dozen of lay-elders, in addition to their ministers? You say indeed, that you see no reason why they should not be supported; but this answer can never be sustained, until you see it a duty to comply with the injunction. Here is a positive command as to all elders being worthy of support; none can plead that any of these elders were lay-elders, who are not in the habit of observing this command. If you really felt the force of the precept, you would obey it. When you grant this, and do not observe it, it plainly appears that you grant it, not from conviction of the propriety and obligation of this duty, but to get rid of the present difficulty. No body of Presbyterians, so far as I know, are in the habit of respecting this injunction, by supporting their lay-elders. Nor is there anything in their sphere of duty, that takes their attention so much off their worldly business, as to deserve remuneration. The deacons have an office which requires more time to be devoted to its faithful discharge, yet the apostles no where assert their right of maintenance. I know of no expenses necessarily incurred by lay-elders, except now and then by a Presbyterial dinner, and an annual journey to JERUSALEM, a meeting of Synod or Assembly. But to defray this expense is not remuneration for services, is not τιμη, or honourable maintenance. Besides, it must come but very seldom to the lot of each elder.

I shall now state some additional reasons why there cannot be in Scripture two distinct orders of elders having separate offices.

1. If there were in Scripture two offices so widely different as those of ministers and lay-elders, they would not be denominated by the same appropriated name. If preaching and ruling were two distinct offices, they would have distinct and separate names. They would not be uniformly spoken of promiscuously under the denomination *elder*. Presbyterians, to avoid this absurdity, have appropriated the word almost exclusively to lay-elders, and they cannot use the word elder alone, without great obscurity in any other signification. When they are obliged to speak of ministers under the name of elders, they must prefix the word *lay* to the ruling elder. I appeal to you, if the idea which the word, when it has not this prefix, always conveys, be not that of elders who do not preach. Nay, I will prove it from your own language, p. 74, "And if that court should decide amiss, to summon even it, with its pastors and *elders*." Here pastors and elders are set in opposition to each other, as if the lay-elder was alone the elder, and the pastor entirely excluded from this name.

2. Were there such an office as that of the lay-elder, the distinct qualifications of the candidate, and his duties and deportment in the office would have been pointed out. The apostle Paul, so minute in his directions as to the qualifications of bishops and deacons, would not have left this department to be described by Dr. Owen. When Paul enumerates the different stated offices in a church, and describes the qualifications of those who should fill them, he mentions only the bishop and deacon. The lay-elder is not to be found.

3. The words elder and bishop are perfectly synonymous in Scripture, and always used promiscuously to denote the same officers. If the word bishop is exclusively applicable to pastors, so is the word elder. The elders of the Church of Ephesus were all bishops—Acts xx. 17–28. All elders are called bishops by Paul to Titus, chap. i. 5–7. Peter considers all the elders as bishops.—1 Pet. v. 2.

4. That the elders were all bishops, is clear from Phil. i. 1, " with the bishops and deacons." Here, if all the elders are not bishops, those who are not

are overlooked. But it is not possible that the apostle would particularly salute the deacons, an inferior order, and superciliously omit mentioning the lay-elders.

5. If it be said, that the deacons are the lay-elders, I answer, the office of the deacon is described and exemplified in Scripture, and it includes in it nothing like the office of the lay-elder. There is nothing of rule in any sense attached to this office.

6. As there are only two offices described in Scripture, or exhibited in the practice of the apostolical churches, as from Phil. i. 1, it evidently appears that there were only two offices, those of bishop and deacon, so it appears that the eldership cannot be split into two offices.

7. Gal. vi. 6.—If all elders are not here included, and if this precept is not as extensive as that in 1 Tim. v. 17, then Paul requires more from the churches in 1 Tim. v. 17, than from the Galatians. While he here declares that all the elders are worthy of support, if the precept, Gal. vi. 6, only refers to the preaching elder, then those who labour in the other department are neglected, even where the apostle treats of the support of labourers. But Paul taught the same things in all the churches; yea, in 1 Tim. v. 17, he speaks of elders everywhere: therefore elders who are usually employed in ruling, must in Gal. vi. 6, be included as teachers. "Let him that is taught in the word, communicate to him that teacheth in all good things." As then all elders are worthy of support, as the apostle would not here inculcate it in favour of one party, and at the same time neglect the other to whom it was also due, we must then conclude that all the elders are here included in the words, "him that teacheth."

8. The elders at Ephesus are all commanded to feed the flock.—Acts xx. 28. This shows that none of them were what are called lay-elders. To this I do not deem it a sufficient answer, that lay-elders may instruct privately. So may individual brethren. But this is a thing which they not only may, but must do. It is no part of the lay-elders office to instruct the flock. But they are here commanded, in virtue of their office,

to feed. Now official feeding is of the same nature, whether it be public or private. There is no difference between officially feeding in public, and officially feeding in private, but the talents that fit for each. The one is as much the business of the pastor as the other. If it is said that the lay-elder officially feeds in private, then so far as he does this officially he is a pastor, and not less so than if he did it in public. The difference between public and private official teaching, lies not in belonging to different offices, but to different talents. Besides, if the lay-elder thus feeds officially, then he is no longer merely a ruling-elder. What becomes in this case of the distinction between him that ruleth only but doth not teach, and him that laboureth in word and doctrine? Does not the lay-elder upon this supposition labour in word and doctrine? You here destroy the distinction that you formerly endeavoured to establish. Add to this, that the idea of private official teaching, belonging to the office of the lay-elder, is merely an arbitrary hypothesis to serve a turn. You do not appear to say this from a conviction that the lay-elders should be usually engaged in private official teaching, but to suggest the possibility of it as a salvo to your system, to rid yourself of this troublesome passage. If this is really a part of the duty of lay-elders, how is it that they never think of discharging it? How is it that it is never expected from them? If this is a part of the divine model, then in this at least the Church of Scotland is not conformable to it. It is really a shame for you to handle the Word of God in this manner; to suggest distinctions, and grant certain modifications of duties, which are evidently intended only to serve a turn at the time, and which you have no serious notion of reducing to practice. If then private official teaching is a part of the duty of the lay-elder, why do not Presbyterians comply with it? But if this be the case, let them drop the distinction between him that preaches as well as rules, and him that rules only; for it will hold no longer. If this is the case, let them no longer call this officer a layman; for he is a pastor, although it may be in an inferior sense. But before they begin, let them show us this distinction declared in the Word of God. The apostle makes no such distinction. He enforces the duty in the same words upon all. Why then suppose that some of these elders were to obey it in one way and some in another? This is quite chimerical. The distinction is only the child of your own brain. We might prove anything, if common sense would allow us to have recourse to such distinctions, without any warrant from Scripture.

Nor will I take it for a sufficient answer, that ποιμαινω signifies to rule as well as to feed. It signifies both, and therefore with the utmost propriety is used to denote the duties of these different departments in the pastoral office. It signifies literally to *shepherdize* a flock, or to discharge every duty that a shepherd owes to his flock. Now this implies everything that a pastor owes to a church; ruling, and instructing, and comforting, and healing, and reproving, &c. All the elders of Ephesus then are commanded to do the office of a shepherd to the flock over which the Holy Ghost had made them overseers, *i.e.*, bishops. All the elders are then shepherds, *i.e.*, pastors; for a pastor is just a feeder or a shepherd.

Nor is it to the purpose to say, that 'general declarations admit of particular exceptions.' Do you mean by this to say that, though the elders, without exception, are here commanded to feed, &c., it might notwithstanding be the duty of some not to feed? I do not know by what sort of reasoning you could make this good. The examples you quote to prove this, are not apposite. It is not a fact that it is said (Deut. xxxiii. 8–10), respecting the whole tribe of Levi, that they should burn incense. All that is said is, that this should be done by men out of the tribe of Levi. Moses is not showing that this is the duty of the Levites in general, but that those appointed to do this belonged to the tribe of Levi; or in other words, the privilege of burning incense, &c., belonged to the tribe of Levi, and not to any other of the tribes. The design here is to mark the privilege of the tribe of Levi, contrasted with the other tribes. The right indeed was peculiar to the tribe of Levi, but was not common to the

Levites. Nor is such a thing either said or implied, either in one way or another. Though he speaks indefinitely of Levi, and then adds, they shall do it, the language by no means imports that this was the general duty of the individuals of the tribe. In 2 Chron. xxix. 4-11, the priests and the Levites are both addressed. Is it strange then that some things should be said as applicable to the one, that could not apply to the other? To make this example similar to that in Acts xx. 28, the apostle must have addressed, and we must be told that he did so, both ministers and lay-elders. In the passage of Chronicles, we are informed in the 4th verse that "he brought in the *priests and the Levites*—and said unto them." When addressing both these, can we be surprised that he spake some things that would not apply to both? After all, had the Levites only been addressed, without particularizing the priests, it is still a literal truth that God did choose the Levites to burn incense. He chose that tribe in preference to the others, and it is not insinuated here that this was the business of all the tribe. There is also a remarkable difference between an address, alluding to a well known fact, and a precept instructing as to a present and future duty. Besides, in both these passages, there is something said applicable to all the Levites, which will justify their being mentioned in general. But upon your supposition, the lay-elders are not addressed at all in Acts xx. 28. The illustration then is not at all in point. Do you think that the apostle would be guilty of the unpardonable absurdity of addressing a set of men by name in the beginning of his speech, yet say nothing that is directed or applicable to them? If there were any lay-elders among them, would he not have given them a charge also?

10. Peter also, addressing the elders, never hints at two orders, but gives them all the same instructions; which could not have been the case, had their offices been distinct. Besides, the expression which he uses, "for filthy lucre's sake," shows that all the elders alluded to received a support. If they did not, there would have been no temptation to take the office for the sake of filthy lucre, nor any need of this warning. They are also all

supposed by him to be bishops and shepherds. If then they are bishops, and shepherds, and rulers, are they not pastors? What is a pastor but a shepherd? Presbyterians in vindicating their lay-elder, must give him everything belonging to the pastoral office, but the name, titles, and dignities. Indeed, were I to admit all you contend for, that they ought never publicly to preach, yet they are pastors, even from what you yourself concede.

11. As the elder is the same with the bishop, and as all bishops are required to be διδακτικος, *fit to teach*, (1 Tim. iii. 2), so all elders must be teachers. They would not be indispensibly required to be fit to teach, if they were not to be employed in teaching. It cannot be sustained as a sufficient answer to this, that the lay-elder may teach privately.* What I said to obviate your allegations upon Acts xx. 28, will equally apply here. Private official teaching is still the office of the pastor. Besides, where is this distinction found? And if it is found, then it can no longer be said that the lay-elder does not labour in word and doctrine. But it is not said that one class of these elders must be διδακτικος in one way, and another class in another way. They are all required to be διδακτικος in the same way. You seem to think that the fitness to teach consists in a facility in conveying the ideas of the speaker. But the fitness to teach, which the apostle here requires in a bishop or elder, is independent of this. A man might have this facility, yet not be διδακτικος and a man might *want* it and yet be quite *fit to teach*. Fitness to teach consists in the knowledge of what is to be taught; a full and thorough acquaintance with the doctrines and laws of Christ. This is indispensable in

---

* So far from any of the elders being *private* teachers only, without a liberty of public speaking, even individual members might and did publicly teach.—1 Cor. xiv.; Rom. xv. 14; Col. iii. 16, &c. It is the privilege of every member to address his brethren, if he hath anything worthy of communication. The publicity or privacy of teaching then, cannot be a distinction of office in the eldership. The distinction between the teaching of individual members, and that of elders, is not in the publicity and privacy of it, but in being official in the one, and not so in the other; the former *may*, the latter *must* teach.

every teacher, whether public or private, and equally so in the one as in the other. It is this fitness then that the apostle insists on in an elder, and not merely a talent for public speaking. As then the same fitness in this respect is necessary in private teaching as in public, the elder that teaches privately, call him a lay-elder if you will, must be as perfectly acquainted with the doctrines and laws of Christ as the preaching elder. This distinction then, useful as it may seem at first view for a salvo, will not avail you. Your private teaching elder must be as well instructed as your public teaching elder. And indeed, even in the capacity of a ruler, the same thing is requisite. No man can rule without a knowledge of those doctrines, laws, and ordinances which he is to enforce, and by which he is to rule. A king is not fit for his office, if he is not well acquainted with the laws of the realm. But in a church ruler, this is still more indispensable, because he must not only know the laws, doctrines and institutions of Christ, to know when they are violated, when they are observed according to their Scriptural meaning, and when to apply them; but also, because it is not sufficient for himself to be acquainted with these, before he can enforce them, he must be able to persuade those that are ruled, that they are Scriptural doctrines, ordinances, laws, &c. He must rule not only according to the laws of Christ, but according to the views of these laws entertained by those who are to obey them. He must then, before he can be able to rule, be fit to teach, and to convince the believers of the truth of the doctrines he presses, the divine origin of the ordinances he calls them to observe, and the laws which he enforces. Your lay-elder then, both as a ruler, and as a private teacher, must be acquainted with divine truth equally with your preaching elder. But as to this distinction between private and public teaching, where is the exact line of separation? Where do the limits of the one end, and the other begin? What constitutes the difference? Does it consist in the time? Must the private teacher teach only on week days? If this constitutes the difference, then all the preaching of the public teachers through the week is only private teaching. Does it consist in the place? May the public teacher alone teach in the house of worship? Then whenever you preach out of the house dedicated to public worship, you are only a private teacher. Does it consist in speaking from a pulpit with a greater degree of dignity, and the power of commanding men to believe the Gospel, &c., with the authority of the ministerial office, as being peculiar to the public teacher? How much more is a sinner rendered guilty, by refusing to believe the Gospel when called to it by a *reverend* ambassador, than when only called by a lay-elder? Does it consist in the numbers addressed? Upon this supposition, how many may a lay-elder constitutionally address? In which ever of these things, or in whatever other thing this distinction may consist, it is exceedingly important that it be accurately defined. If it be the duty of the lay-elder to teach privately, and a sin for him to teach publicly, have pity upon your humble associates, and determine the boundaries of their office with philosophical precision.

But what, my dear Sir, is the imperious necessity that drives you to such distinctions, evasions, &c.? Is it to reconcile these passages with a more clear and decisive testimony of Scripture? No; but to prop a rotten system, that has not even the appearance of sanction from one direct testimony.

LETTER VII.

Sir,

Cyrus, in the famous battle fought against Crœsus, to deceive the enemy as to his numbers, caused the ammunition and baggage waggons to be drawn up in a line before his *corps de reserve*, and extended his wings that he might not be surrounded. In reviewing your letters, I have been frequently reminded of this piece of generalship. The size of your volume, and the number of your arguments, are upon first view calculated to excite alarm in the assailant; but when we come to engage in close fight, and have once penetrated your thin centre, we find most of your supposed force to be mere baggage carts. Many of your arguments, nay, some whole letters, are quite distant from the point. The whole of your twelfth letter is of this description. I will not then waste my time, nor blunt the edge of my arguments, by cutting down such bloodless antagonists. When I come to a baggage cart, I will pass it to see if there is anything worthy of opposition on the other side. The extracts which you make from Cotton, and Owen, and Goodwin, and Hooker, &c., show indeed that these good men had, like the Puritans in general, very imperfect and erroneous views of a church of Christ. I have no concern to vindicate them from being tinged with a portion of the spirit of antichrist. It is not men or parties I defend, but the institutions of Jesus. As far as these worthy persons understood and followed the truth more fully than others of the same day, I proportionally respect them. But when you quote their opinions as authorities, they weigh no more with me than the sentiments of Peter the Hermit. We acknowledge no ancestors but the churches planted by the apostles, none other do we defend.

As to courts of review and associations of ministers, my views are entirely similar to those stated in the "Missionary Magazine" for October 1804, p. 448, to which you allude. Nor do you produce anything against that paper worth a moment's consideration. "Before this reasoning," you say, "can be considered as valid, it must be proved that *infallibility* has been the attainment of every Independent congregation," &c., p. 192. What a noble dilemma! How shall we escape from between its horns? Either we must profess ourselves to be infallible, or say that it is better to be in an error than to receive information from others. But indeed, Sir, its horns are only painted. It is quite harmless. You might as well say that because every head of a family will not submit to have his conduct in family-government subjected to the review of a council of neighbours, or that all the individuals who do not form themselves into societies for the purpose of directing each other in the duties of civil life, must profess themselves to be infallible. I can see none of those exceedingly difficult matters which you pretend to see, as likely to come before a church, that meddles with nothing but its appointed duties. Let each church confine itself to its proper business, as delineated in the New Testament, walking in love, in the fear of God, and in the comfort of the Holy Spirit, there will then be no danger of the occurrence of any insuperable difficulty. If ever they go off the King's high-way, they may indeed expect to be swallowed up in the bogs of expediency on the right and the left hand. This ground they must leave entirely to Presbyterians, and others, who have the wisdom of superior courts to draw them out when they sink. As to a church of Christ, when it attends only to the laws and institutions of his appointment, being composed of spiritual men, there will always be some among the brethren who will be able to judge of the conformity or non-conformity of individuals to their spirit and meaning. But, Sir, we do not hold ourselves above listening to advice. There is surely a mighty difference between erecting an institution for advice, and being willing to listen to advice when any are so kind as to give it. Indeed, we would not refuse to take advice from our greatest enemies. If the General Assembly could show us anything in Scripture which we have not yet attended to, we will, upon conviction, adopt it with promptitude. I do believe that the churches lately formed, owe much of their superior conformity to Scripture, compared with that of the ancient Independents, to the very objections of their opposers. Their attention has been called to many things formerly neglected or not understood, perhaps chiefly by those who argued against the obligation of the practice of the apostolical churches. In their zeal to overthrow this, they endeavoured to search into the whole practice of the first churches, that from the neglect of some, on the part of their adversaries, they might overthrow the obligation of others.

That congregations should not be Independent, you argue, in your thirteenth letter, from the scriptural representations of what you call the visible church. Your views of Presbytery are so opposite upon paper to what is universally practised, that I shall quote your words, p. 209. " When it is affirmed by Presbyterians, that every particular congregation ought not to be independent of a Presbytery or Synod, it is not intended that its rulers, or office-bearers, are to be dependent upon them for the exercise of their power after they are invested with it, or that they may be deprived of it by them at pleasure, in that society which they govern. All that is designed is simply that they are subject, in any case of error, or any instance of mal-administration, to the authoritative review of the ministers and elders of a number of congregations met as a Presbytery; and perhaps it would be better, as the judicious Hoornbeek has observed, to express their relation to such a court by the terms *subjection* or *subordination*, than by the word *dependence*, which is occasionally used by some ancient Presbyterians."

If this is the kind of Presbytery you defend, this is what you should adopt. This is nothing a-kin to the Church of Scotland, or any other Presbyterian denomination of which I have ever heard. In these, individual office-bearers both receive their commission from the superior courts, and are completely and constantly dependent upon them for the exercise of it. They may deprive them of it at pleasure. Not only are they subject to their review, in case of misconduct, but bound by their regulations, and circumscribed in their exertions, even in cases that affect their consciences. An individual may suffer the highest censures for discharging what he may think indispensable duty, and if he continues faithful to his conscience, may be deprived of his office. In defending the Church of Scotland, it is vain to say, "All that is designed, is simply that they are subject, in case of error, or any instance of mal-administration, to the ministers and elders of a number of congregations met at a Presbytery." Is it not the Presbytery alone who has the right to judge of what is error, and what is mal-administration? May they not, do they not often class under these heads the doctrines of the Gospel, and the observance of some of the precepts of Jesus? It is in their own power what to call error and mal-administration. If a minister were to preach in his neighbour's parish, without his consent, would not this be mal-administration? It is mere white-wash to represent their subjection to superior courts only in case of error or mal-administration, as long as they may brand the most sacred doctrines and duties with these names. How absurd is it to say, with Hoornbeek, whose language you quote in a note, that, according to the Presbyterian form of government, a particular congregation is possessed of all essential church power in itself, and receives it not from synods or superior councils, seeing no congregation can of itself exercise discipline! Their particular office-bearers cannot exercise discipline till they receive a commission from the superior court, which they recal when they think fit. Church power then can neither, according to this system, originate in a particular congregation, nor independently be continued and exercised in it. If every particular congregation has all essential church power within itself, why do they receive this from another source? Upon the Presbyterian system, how absurd is it to say, with Hoornbeek, that a single congregation situated in a part of the world, where it could not be associated with others, is a complete church, not at all mutilated? If it is in this state a complete church not at all mutilated, when it concresces with others, they must be a monster. But if superior courts be essential, and all church power derived from them, no individual congregation can in any circumstances be called with propriety a complete church. How can it be complete wanting that which is essential to its well-being? How can that which is only a part of a great whole be called complete, in the same sense as the whole? How can a body be complete without the head? These colourings then of the Presbyterian pencil will never deceive any who have seen the original picture, or have any judgment in the art of painting. In vain you attempt to hide, or throw into the back ground, the hideous deformities of your system. It only serves to show that it is not fit to be exhibited as it is in reality. Yours is Presbytery in theory; was there ever such a Presbytery in practice? In fact, you here not only abandon the defence of the Church of Scotland, which you profess to vindicate, but you indirectly condemn her as unscriptural. If you have fairly exhibited the features of Scripture Presbytery, the Church of Scotland must give up all pretensions to divine origin. Instead of vindicating her, you imagine a Presbytery of your own, and give it excellencies which never existed in any Presbyterian church. But I stay not longer in pointing out the essential difference between the form of Presbytery you have painted, and that church which you defend, for even this sort of Presbytery I condemn; even this goddess of your imagination, adorned with all the excellencies your fancy can bestow upon her, I will not worship. Both courts of review, and associations for advice, are equally unfounded in the Word of God. As to a visible universal church, it exists no where but in the ideas of polemical writers, and the absurd distinctions of scholastic divinity. There is nothing like it in the Scriptures, as to either name or thing. The first passage you quote (Romans xi. 17), is not at all to the purpose. It has no relation to the universality of union among Christians, nor even to their union with one another, in any sense, either limited or extended. The apostle is neither treating of the visibility nor invisibility of believers in a church state; but of the cutting off of the Jews from Abraham, and the grafting of the Gentile believers in their place. In explaining figures, attention must always be paid to the single point intended to be illustrated by them, which must be collected from the scope of the passage. Further than this, a figure is never supposed to bear resemblance to the object of its illustration. The scope of this passage then is simply this, that the natural children of Abraham had been cut off from their relation to the God of Abraham, on account of their rejecting the Messiah; and that the Gentiles had been taken in, as the children of Abraham, by faith. The latter were a wild olive, but by faith they had been grafted into the good olive, Abraham being considered as the root or father of the faithful. The Jews were cut off as a nation, not merely from external privileges, as your illustration of the figure supposes, but from all the blessings of the Abrahamic covenant. The Gentile believers were admitted, not merely to external fellowship of the church, but to partake of the root and fatness of the olive, *i.e.*, to share the blessings of Abraham. By unbelief, the Jews not only lost all the spiritual privileges which, as the natural descendents of Abraham, they had enjoyed, but they were cut off from being heirs with Abraham of the true Canaan. Their being said to be cut off from those things which they never actually enjoyed, no more militates against the doctrine of perseverance, than its being said that some made shipwreck of the faith, or its being supposed that some branches may be cut off from Jesus.—1 Tim. i. 19, 20; John xv. People may be said to lose that which they appeared to have enjoyed. But in the case before us, there is no need of this mode of analysis. The Jews, as a nation, did enjoy spiritual blessings from their connection with Abraham, but these, as a nation, they forfeited by their rejection of the Messiah.

This passage then is designed to exhibit no view of Christians in a church capacity, not even their invisible union. The union of Christ and his people is indeed beautifully exhibited (John xv.), under the figure of a vine and its branches. The chief and prominent idea intended to be conveyed, is the union of all believers with Christ, having their life, nourishment and fruitfulness from him, as the branches have from the trunk of the vine. From this consideration, our Lord presses upon them the necessity of constantly abiding in the faith, in order to spiritual health, and fruitfulness in good works. They are not to live upon themselves, their frames, their feelings, their past experience, their evidences, &c. He warns them, that the moment they let the truth slip out of their minds, they will become barren and unfruitful, like a branch broken off from the vine. This is the only kind of union that is designed to be exhibited in this passage. It is true indeed that the branches have a union with one another, but this is not the truth exhibited by the speaker. Besides, this union of the branches is only in consequence of a vital union with the trunk, not by mere juxta-position. A branch that is not vitally connected with the trunk, cannot have a connection with the other branches. This figure could not then be at all employed to signify visible external union. Some may indeed appear for a time to have been branches, who will be afterwards found to have had no real union with the trunk, and will be certainly removed even from what they appeared to have, but such persons may or may not have been members of any visible church. They may have appeared for a time to have been branches of Christ, without having had an opportunity of connecting themselves with any visible church. Besides, all believers, although they should from circumstances have lived and died without being members of any church upon earth, have a real and vital union with this vine, and an invisible union with all the branches. Add to this, that the Christians of all denominations are thus united. It cannot mean then any visible external union in church-fellowship.

It is astonishing that any man of common sense should understand 1 Cor. xii., of a visible church. It is Christ the head, and all saints in heaven and in earth his members, who compose this church. Are they not said, "by one Spirit to be baptized into one body?" This is what is not true of a visible universal church upon earth, either in reality, or appearance, or even profession. But though it should be true in the latter sense, it would not justify this application of the language. Though a man may be said to be what he gives evidence at the time of being, yet he can never properly be said to be what he himself only professes to be. Then all the knaves in the world are *very honest men.* That the apostle is here speaking of a visible universal church upon earth, is an idea that could never suggest itself to any one who had not been accustomed to look at the Bible through the glasses of the schoolmen, who by their subtle distinctions endeavour to stretch the Scriptures to equalize with their chimerical systems. Where did the idea of a universal, visible church originate? Is it anything but the figment of imagination? Has it any existence in any part of the Word of God, that you will press it upon this chapter? If it can be taken out of the Scriptures, it must be by the rule of the *hidden sense* of Origen. But if these, and such like passages, speak only of the visible church, then of that real church, consisting of Christ and his living members, of their union with him and with one another, &c., we have nothing said. So much said about a thing called a visible church, consisting in all ages, almost from the apostle's days, mostly of those lying in the wicked one, and not a word of the true city of God! Are all the glorious things spoken of this city of God to be applied to such a motley mass? As well might the rude attack of a mob be a proper representation of the charge of the Macedonian phalanx.

As to what you say about this church, spoken of in 1 Cor. xii., being represented as *alone* possessing miraculous gifts, such a thing is not said. It is indeed said that the church possessed these miraculous gifts, but it is not said that none but members of this church possessed such gifts.

You argue, that the church spoken of 1 Cor. xii., cannot be the invisible church, because it is set forth as furnished with a variety of offices, which could not be said of the former, as a part of it is in heaven. Indeed, Sir, in speaking of the kingdom of Christ, I neither use the words visible nor invisible, because the contrast that this distinction supposes between two supposed churches, is altogether fanciful. When the word church in Scripture, in its religious sense, does not denote a congregation of saints, it refers to the whole body or kingdom of Christ, part of which is in heaven and part on earth. In a more enlarged sense than a single congregation, there is no body that can be called a *visible church*, for in their church state they can be visible in no other way; therefore the epithet *invisible*, attached to the whole body of Christ, is altogether unnecessary, for it supposes another church that is properly called the *visible church*. Accordingly we find, that the sacred writers do not find these epithets necessary in using the word church. They are under no apprehensions of obscurity from the double use of the word, because no such double use was attached to it by them. This is a discovery, the honour of which belongs to after-ages. Indeed, I would ask nothing but the necessity of attaching these epithets to the word church, to distinguish its different meanings according to scholastic interpretation, to prove that the word itself had in Scripture no such acceptation. The abettors of worldly systems cannot now speak of the church as referring to the true saints in heaven and earth, without prefixing the epithet *invisible*, because they have extended the word itself to what they call the *visible church*. Now if, to prevent obscurity, such distinguishing epithets must be added constantly by those who embrace these views, is it not certain that the inspired writers would also have used these epithets for the same reason? Is it less necessary in an apostle to be precise, that his words may not be misunderstood, than for theologians? Is it peculiar alone to the inspired writers to speak nonsense? As then the distinction of *visible* and *invisible* is now indispensable to prevent obscurity, we may, by every rule of candid criticism, conclude that the ideas represented by these words have no existence in the writings of the apostles. The Church of God—of Christ, &c., are names perfectly synonymous with the phrase *kingdom of heaven*. The saints above and those below, do not constitute two churches, but one church or family, consisting of different parts.—Eph. iii. 15. In speaking then of this church, what is said sometimes refers to the one part of it, sometimes to another, and sometimes to the whole, according to the connection, and the nature of what is said. This criterion will easily direct us in the application of what is said respecting the church. As the whole members make one body, so what is said of one division of the members, or one single member, might be said of the whole. The man who hurts my finger, hurts my body; the physician who relieves me from a headache or gout, has relieved my body. The church then is furnished with different offices, because the members of it upon earth are so. As the members above and below make only one church, one body, the church may literally and properly be said to have these offices in it. Your fallacy proceeds from the supposition, that the saints in heaven are one body, and those below are another. A man of fortune may be said to have provided tutors *for his family*, although the greater number of his children are out of their pupilage. God then hath set in the church first apostles, secondly prophets, &c., because that part of his family, yet in their minority, possess these. The word *church*, according to no acceptation of it, either sacred or profane, could be applied to all the Christians upon earth, whether professing or real. If a single state should be called so, it is united in itself, collected into one district, and separated from other nations. The Jewish nation is termed a church, not only because they were assembled in the wilderness, but because they were gathered together in the land of Canaan, and principally because the whole nation was a representation of the whole Church of Christ. But upon no principle can all the professing Christians on earth be called a church, for in no sense are they ever assembled together, neither in themselves nor by their representatives, neither literally nor figuratively. But believers of all denominations, and of all countries, have a real union, and are truly and properly at all times assembled in Jesus Christ. In him, those on earth are assembled with those above. Therefore the apostle writes (Heb. xii. 22, 23), "But ye are come to Mount Zion, and unto the city of the living God, the heavenly Jerusalem, and to an innumerable company of angels; to the general assembly and church of the first-born, who are written in heaven, and to God the judge of all, and to the spirits of just men made perfect." Here the saints whom he addressed are said already to have joined the general assembly and church of the first-born. In Jesus, those in heaven and those on earth are assembled, as one church, one city, one Zion.

But if the twelfth chapter of first Cor. relates to the visible church, and if to this visible church belongs these offices, &c., of whom is this visible church composed? Where is it? If it be visible, let us see it. As the different denominations taken together cannot make a church, because they are in no sense assembled, nor even united by a common profession of the same principles, it follows, that of all the denominations in the world, one only is the *visible church.* What then is this church? Is it the Church of Rome? She says so herself, but you will not believe her. Is it the Eastern church? Is it the Lutheran church? Is it the Armenian church? Is it the church of the Morophysites? Is it the Church of England? Is it the Church of Scotland? Is it any of all those who have sprung from these? Now, to which ever of these the character belongs, it will exclude all the rest from being considered as churches. Nay, all who are not connected with it, will necessarily be excluded from every thing spoken of in this chapter, and other passages, concerning this church. As these offices spoken of are said to be set in this church, they cannot belong to any other. This church then will unchurch all other churches both of their visibility and reality, yea, and even of the blessings peculiar to the members of it, and eternal life among the rest.

Farther, if the apostle is here speaking of the visible church, this church can contain no more than are assembled in it. Now, allowing even the assembling by representation, this visible church must be confined not only to one denomination, but to one association of that denomination. It cannot embrace the Church of

Scotland and the General Synod of Ulster, for they are never assembled even in their representatives. The Burgher Seceders of Scotland and of Ireland cannot both put in their claim. But the absurdities to which this arbitrary interpretation would lead, are endless. And as there is no ground for it in the passage, so there is no occasion that it should be forced on it to cover a system.

As to the thirteenth chapter of Matthew, I hope I have already shown, that neither there nor any where else can the phrase, 'kingdom of heaven,' signify what is called the visible church. Where did you learn, Sir, that the kingdom there spoken of is said to resemble a field in which there were tares as well as wheat? The points of resemblance are not between the kingdom and the field, but between the kingdom and the wheat, and the wicked and the tares; and the drift of the parable of the tares, is to show the common situation of these opposites. Accordingly, if our Lord was any judge of his own meaning, he says that the field is not the kingdom, but the world, the commons, as it were, upon which these two classes meet. The good seed are the *children of the kingdom*; the tares are not the children of the kingdom, but *the children of the wicked one.*

But, Sir, were all the congregations in the world united under a common government, the unity described in the above passages of Scripture, would not be exhibited by this circumstance. The union of Christians in the same particular church, is not pointed out by their being under the same government and governors. This is represented by their union in ordinances, especially in the Lord's supper.—1 Cor. x. 17. The oneness of the body is represented by their participation of the one bread. The circumstance of being under a common government is not even taken into the account. Besides, though all the congregations of the world were Independent, there not only may, but if they are Christians, and act as such, there certainly will be among them the strictest union, both external and internal. This may not appear to the carnal eye, but it is not on that account the less real. Like the apostolical churches, they would mutually receive each other in the arms of Christian love, because Christ has received them, and forward the business of brethren personally strangers to them, even in temporal matters. A church at the north pole would receive a brother, upon his letters of introduction from his church, in the opposite extremity of the earth. Is there no union among the children of the same father, though they are scattered in different kingdoms? Must they, in order to show their union to the world, enter into an association to assist and defend each other? Would not such an association, instead of showing the world their real union, and brotherly affection, convince it that they wanted the true bond of union. If there existed real brotherly love, there would be no occasion for any formal external bond. It is not the existence of love, but the want of it,* that causes such associations among professing Christians. If they had real union, there could be no need for visible external bonds.

Your dream of a universal visible church, comprehending all the professing Christians of all the nations of the earth under one government, I lay aside with the reveries of Mathias and Buccold, the enthusiasts of Munster. What idea would an intelligent man of the world entertain of a scheme, even for a universal political government? Such a scheme for the government of the people of Christ, ought to have proceeded from the pen of the wildest enthusiast. You dare not directly suggest the expediency of such a universal government, even for the nations of this world, lest you should be understood to sanction the pretensions of some bold innovator, in endeavouring to climb to the summit of universal power. You content yourself by saying, that all the nations of the earth *virtually* constitute one great political government, to which every individual nation is subject. But here, Sir, your illustration is not in point; first, because that this balance

---

* See the National Covenant, and Solemn League and Covenant, with the Acts of Assembly and Parliament, ordaining the subscription of them. See also the Acts of Assembly and Parliament respecting the Westminster Assembly of Divines.

of power among the nations of the earth, is only for mutual security against the encroachments of one another. However opposite the views and principles of government of the different nations, they all unite to prevent any one among them from getting such an ascendency as to endanger the liberty and the security of all. They are not supposed, in virtue of this, to unite to regulate or review any of the affairs of any of the nations that are merely internal, and have no influence upon the interest of the whole. In this there can be no resemblance, because there can be no external danger apprehended by any one church from another. Church association is for internal government, not for curbing the ambition of each other. In this point, the churches of Christ can have no likeness to the kingdoms of this world, whose associations are for mutual defence against external danger. Secondly, if the analogy were good, it would suppose, not the union of all Christians under one government, but an association, either *ostensible* or *virtual*, of all the different denominations, to prevent any individual among them from obtaining such an ascendency as to endanger the liberty of the rest.* It must be a political union, and have influence only by carnal weapons. Before then your analogy will serve you, were we even to grant you that our Lord was mistaken when he said, "My kingdom is not of this world," you must roundly assert that it would be for the benefit of the human race that all the nations of the earth should be under one government, and though you might perhaps teach this doctrine at present with safety in France, I doubt if it would be so palatable in Britain.

But if it is so monstrous in politics, how much more monstrous is it when applied to the kingdom of Christ. If all the nations of the earth were under one government, if such a thing could even be imagined, it must be the most complete despotism that can be conceived; and if all the professing Christians upon earth, were to be under one government, it must be the most absolute despotism also. Had God intended such a universal

* The spiritual balance of power! What a ludicrous idea!!

church upon earth, an infallible head would undoubtedly have been appointed. I am convinced that the idea of an infallible head must have sprung out of the idea of a universal visible church. They are corresponding parts of the same wild hypothesis. Nor is it possible to conceive how such a machine could be guided, without an unerring spring to keep its wheels in perpetual and regular motion. This infallibility would be as safely lodged with one man as with a number. If there ever should be such a church, the supreme government must certainly be vested in a few comparatively; and if they be invested with authority, without resort or appeal any where else, they must indeed be infallible.

Suppose there should be in this chief council in the latter days, no less than one million of representatives, but we cannot at most suppose more than what could transact business together, still this would be no proportion to the numbers whom they represent. It would not be perhaps one out of every provincial Synod. Congregations then would be entirely governed by a foreign power. Even national assemblies would be of no account. Europe itself would perhaps be insufficient to turn the scale in a vote. But I am almost ashamed of noticing such whimsies. They are unworthy of a moments thought. Upon the forehead of this scheme I see written in large characters, MYSTERY, BABYLON THE GREAT!

You say, p. 215. " As far as the truth is disseminated and embraced, it appears required by *the authority*, or at least by *the representations* of Scripture, that all who are united in religious principle, should connect themselves under the same government, and form one great and general church." What do you mean by the distinction between the *authority* and the *representations* of Scripture? Do you really think that if the views you have given of the Scripture passage in question are the true representations of Scripture, there is any doubt about the authority of such representations? But Sir, I see the reason; you are professedly the defender of the abstract theory of Presbytery, but you are also a member of the Church of Scotland. It is not easy for any writer to adjust matters so, that he can defend the one without directly censuring the other. You are really in an awkward situation, and it requires great dexterity in manœuvring between them. Hence that mixture of boldness and caution in your book. In fact, the theory you defend is almost in every point different from the Church of Scotland. Here, if these supposed Scripture representations should be absolutely pronounced binding, the conduct of the General Assembly must be highly reprimanded. They are making no efforts to unite, with those of the same sentiments in other countries, under one government. They are totally unconnected even with their brethren in Ireland, who boast of being descended from the kirk. Nay, I am bold to say, that if your reasoning is good, it would overturn the Church of Scotland. If the Presbyterians of all the kingdoms of the world ought to be under one common government, then the Church of Scotland, as far as it is connected with the state, may be altered, or entirely changed. This superior court might alter parts of its constitution that are even fixed by act of parliament, and consequently interfere with civil affairs as well as ecclesiastical. I can see then the reason why you soften your language, and endeavour to make these passages strongly prove Presbytery, and at the same time bear lightly upon the constitution and practice of the Church of Scotland. But you cannot defend a universal church upon any principles that will not rob the Church of Scotland of her independence. I am persuaded that many of the clergy would be unwilling to part with this privilege. Nor, if they were all willing, is it likely that the government of the country would permit such an essential change, a change that would deprive government of every political advantage arising from a civil ecclesiastical establishment. Nor do I think that this scheme would ever have entered even your head, had it not been to defend your theoretical Presbytery. You could not have made use of these portions of Scripture with any colour of plausibility, had you not avowed the necessity of a universal church. You saw plainly that your reasoning led to this conclusion, and it was with a better grace you acknowledged it, than that it should be forced on you by your antagonist. But you trifle in such a manner with the Scriptures, as often tempts me to doubt that you are ignorant of something still more important than the nature of a church of Christ. Your own views of it seem to make little impression upon you. The Scriptures make such representations, yet a doubt is admitted whether or not these representations have authority. But if they have no authority in the one case, neither have they in the other. If they represent all congregations as under one government, yet do not imply an authoritative obligation of imitation to the whole extent, neither do they to any extent. If there can be any excuse for the Church of Scotland, the General Synod of Ulster, the Church of Geneva, the Presbyterian churches of America, &c., not uniting themselves under one government, the same might be pleaded with respect to the congregations that compose the Church of Scotland, &c., upon the supposition that they should dissolve their union. All the churches or associations of Presbyterians are independent; the only difference as to the external disunion between them, and churches individually independent, is in the extent of their independence. Allowing your own interpretation of these passages, they condemn all Presbyterian associations as well as Independents. The unity of this supposed body is equally broken in the one case as in the other. Nay, it is more so with you than with us. If the poorest member from one of our churches were to visit another, with proper letters of recommendation, he would be received without hesitation. But I believe a Doctor of Divinity from the General Synod of Ulster, might live in Edinburgh for two months, without an opportunity of preaching in any of the parish churches; and, if presented to a Scotch Kirk, would be declared inadmissible. This is a specimen of your boasted union.

But it is altogether absurd to suppose that our Lord would institute a form of government which it would never yet have been possible to put in practice. The wars that have at all times existed, would completely have prevented the meeting of delegates from the contending countries. How would it be possible, for instance, at this time, for the representatives of France and of Great Britain to meet in the same council? Must the existence of anything necessary to the well-being of the churches of Christ, depend upon the will of princes, the fate of empires, or any external circumstances? Besides, if their actually existed such a universal church, no case of discipline could be finally decided, if there were any to object, until it would go before the representatives of this church. To determine every dispute between individuals, if either party wishes successively to appeal from one court to another, there must be a meeting of representatives from all quarters of the globe. Christianity has nothing to do with such a clumsy machine, nor would any sober Presbyterian ever wish to see it in motion. That one which has been so universal, is much more simple and ingenious; yet the world is beginning to tire of it.

Towards the end of this letter, you ask a question, p. 222. "How, moreover, even upon the principle of this objection, can a particular congregation be a representation of the universal visible church, if that church is not united under one government?" Who says that a particular church is an emblem of the universal visible church? It is indeed an emblem of the whole Church of Christ, but not of the aggregate of Christian congregations. Much better you had studied the Scriptures themselves a little closer, in their native dress, than to have filled your head with the fanciful opinions of musty authors.

In your fourteenth letter, you endeavour to confirm the doctrine contained in your last, by several other arguments. The first is p. 222. "That if every congregation is made so independent of every other, that corruptions and improprieties may be admitted in them, without being accountable to any superior court on earth, much greater opportunity must exist for the introduction of error and tyranny than on the Presbyterian system." There is here a show of fleshly wisdom, but to silence you, it might be sufficient to reply, that God hath not so ordained. We are willing, however, to examine and contrast the tendency of the two

x

systems in all their bearings. To show, *a priori*, that such a thing is necessary in a church of Christ, is indeed to go far to establish it. But this reasoning, *a priori*, must not proceed upon worldly principles, but from an analogy to the other institutions and facts of Scripture. In this you are through your whole work entirely deficient. Your arguments which are not pretended to be founded on express Scripture, are all taken either from the kingdoms of this world, or the circumstances of other societies. You have no appeal to the sister institutions of the divine author, the procedure of God in other instances, or the general spirit and design of the Christian religion. Your principles would serve very properly to estimate the value of the Mahometan constitution, but are not only totally inapplicable, but directly opposite to the nature of the kingdom of Christ, which is not of this world. When our Lord said that his kingdom was not of this world, he certainly did not mean to say that it was not situated in this world, the contrary of which he teaches us in the parable of the tares. He must mean, that it is entirely different from the kingdoms of this world, in its nature, its subjects, its laws, its institutions, its mode of government, its support, &c.

But, having premised this, we are willing to enter with you most fully into an estimate of the respective merits of these two systems. There is no manner of doubt that the form of government instituted by Jesus, is that which has the greatest advantages with the fewest disadvantages. We shall bring the matter to a short issue.

To prevent the spreading of corruption, I ask what advantages hath Presbytery which Independency hath not? You will say, the power of your courts over congregations, and of the superior courts over the inferior. If a minister, or congregation, or whole Presbytery were to become corrupt, you could recover them. I ask you how would you recover them ? By persuasion and conviction? We have this equally in our power. By excommunication and depriving of temporal emoluments? As to the former, what is it but a simple separation from the communion of the church? We have what is fully equal to it. If any Independent church becomes corrupt either in its doctrine or its members, we withdraw our countenance from it. With such we hold no communion.* This, Sir, is certainly virtual excommunication. Where there is no visible association, there can be no room for any visible separation from a part of that association. In such a case, the duty is to have no " fellowship with the unfruitful works of darkness." As to the latter, a power to influence by temporal motives is not a benefit, but the most serious disadvantage. Every incitement that a church possesses, the truth excepted, to allure men into its communion, or to retain them in it, is an essential evil. There are few people so conscientious, especially of those churches who are thus confessedly corrupt, who will not rather dissemble and temporize, than part with a good parish. When we look into church history, and review the various instances in which individuals of the clergy have been called to account for their erroneous opinions by the superior courts, we find comparatively few who have not either renounced their opinions verbally, or modified their language in such a manner as to agree with the orthodox system in appearance, while in reality they have held their sentiments. Indeed, if men are changed merely by authority, and mere authority is all you can be allowed more than is common to us, he cannot be an honest man; and there is no gain to the church by the seeming recantation of his errors, but that of hypocrisy. For a particular proof of this observation, I refer you to certain transactions, not very many years ago, in the General Assembly, respecting one gentleman in the

---

* This, Sir, is the most effectual excommunication, both as to its tendency to reclaim those who go astray, and to prevent our being corrupted by them. With all the boasted advantages of Presbytery to repress corruption, you, as an individual, could not in your connection withdraw from the communion of the vilest character. You have communion with all the reprobates belonging to the Church of Scotland, as well as with all the most worthy members, and without separating from the church, you cannot avoid it. As soon as we lose confidence in one another, we are under no obligation to continue external fellowship.

Synod of Galloway, and another in the Synod of Glasgow and Ayr. Do not all the ministers of the Church of Scotland solemnly declare the Westminster Confession of Faith to be their faith? Do they all believe it? If a minister or congregation is not reclaimed by admonition, and withdrawing of the countenance of other pure churches, all the inventions of men would fail to reclaim them. Authority might make them dissemble, and silence them, but they would still be as black as the Ethiopian. Presbyterian discipline is indeed well calculated, as Mr. Innes remarks, to make them hypocrites; but if a straying brother is not reclaimed by advice and remonstrance, the bastile and guillotine would be ineffectual. "A man convinced against his will, is of the same opinion still." The awful fruits of such human restraints are evident in the perjury, insincerity, and hypocrisy which they introduce wherever they are practised. There is nothing more usual than for men to solemnly pledge themselves at ordination to support one system of articles, and through all their life set themselves to overthrow them.

But you think that you sufficiently answer this in the following passage, p. 223. "Do you say that congregations may admonish one another when they fall into error, and endeavour to reclaim them? You allow, however, that unless there be a power of punishing, as well as of admonishing an offending member, the evils which he may introduce can neither be prevented nor removed. On what principle then can you refuse a similar power to be necessary for the prevention or suppression of offences committed by a whole congregation?" Yes, Sir, we allow that unless there is a power of putting away a corrupt member, he is likely to injure or to destroy the whole body. Did I labour under a mortification in one of my members, I would have it cut off, lest the rest of the body should be affected. But if you laboured under the like disease, however I might advise you to cut off your limb, there would be no occasion for me to force you to this, for the disorder could not be communicated to me. Here then, Sir, lies your fallacy; and the question which you so triumphantly propose as unanswerable, has not the smallest difficulty in its solution. A church puts away a corrupt member, because corruption spreads and eats like a gangrene; but there is not the same danger where there is not the same connection. If such a member were continued in a church, he would spread his corruption; but if there be a corrupt member in another church, or a whole corrupt church, all we have to do, is to keep him or them out from us, and not to go in among them. Corruption in individuals or churches with us, cannot necessarily extend beyond the limits of each church. A little leaven leavens a very large mass of dough; but a very large portion of leaven cannot leaven that which has no communication with it. The leaven will extend to all the dough in the same trough; but it will not extend to that in another trough, except there be some conductor. If then you could prove that the churches should all be united in one universal church, I allow that this universal church ought to have the power of excommunication, because such a union is a conductor for the leaven to pass from one congregation to another. But where there is no such union, it is enough for us to keep ourselves from mixing with those who are leavened. If a person infected with a plague should come into my house, I should have him removed; but if the plague is in his house, all I have to do is to avoid going into his house, and not to allow him to come into mine. Now, Sir, I contend that Independency can exert every legitimate influence to prevent corruption in the churches, as well as classical Presbytery. Let us now enquire as to the tendency to propagate corruption. Here you quote a specimen of incontrovertible reasoning from Mr. Innes. It is as demonstratively conclusive as any proposition in Euclid. How do you endeavour to overturn it? Not by meeting, but avoiding it. Instead of showing that Presbytery, when corrupt, is not the most formidable engine to spread corruption, you dexterously carry away your reader's attention from the consideration of that point, to another totally distinct, viz., the supposed advantages of Presbytery, and defects of Independency, in preventing corruption, both considered as pure.

Upon this subject, you dare not look your antagonist in the face. Presbytery is the god of the plains, but not the God of the hills. You employ every art of a wily general to draw us off this ground, as not a proper criterion of the merits of the question, that you may engage us in a situation which is more suitable for loose skirmishing. What a dexterous manœuvre have we in the following statement! p. 228. " The question, however, in the present discussion, certainly is, not what system, when perverted from its original end, is calculated to produce the *least evil;* but what system, when conducted according to its design, is calculated to produce the greatest good?" Who granted you this? When contrasting the comparative excellence of two systems, must we not consider their possible disadvantages upon misapplication, as well as their advantages, when used aright? In considering the tendencies of any institution, it is equally fair to estimate their disadvantages as their advantages. That which has all the advantages with none of the disadvantages of others, is likely to be the plan of government that Christ would adopt. If every influence consistent with the nature of Christ's kingdom, to prevent corruption, can be exerted on the principles of Independency, would it have been consistent with his wisdom to institute a form of government, which would be calculated to do more injury, when corrupted? This becomes demonstrative, when it is considered that Jesus knew what corruptions were to take place among his real, as well as professing followers. Allowing Independency to have been the plan instituted by Jesus, all the blame of introducing Antichrist must lie with men, for as long as the churches remained independent, it could never rise higher than one congregation. Will any other plan so fully justify Jesus and condemn men in this instance? Granting that the churches had been independent, let them be supposed as corrupt as they can be imagined, that monster could never have been reared;*

---

* Is it not remarkable that the apostle, after warning the Thessalonians of the rise of Antichrist, gives them no other rules to prevent his rise among others, nor his power over themselves, but to stand firm in what they then professed, and

and whenever light should have appeared, there would have been no external obstacle to prevent its reception. But if Christ instituted a universal visible associated church, whenever the churches became corrupt, they unavoidably were subject to an Antichrist of one sort or other. A universal church of any form, having its heads corrupted, whether one or a thousand, must have been the most powerful obstacle to prevent reformation. Independency then has all the advantages of Presbytery to prevent corruption, both considered as pure, without any of its tendencies to spread corruption, both considered as depraved; it must then be from heaven. Nor is this, Sir, as you say, arguing from the abuse of a thing, against the use of it. Some government is necessary; that therefore which has the greatest advantages, and is capable of the least abuse is the preferable, both politically and ecclesiastically.

You observe, p. 231. "The great object of inquiry in our examination of different forms of government, sacred or civil, should undoubtedly be, which of them, when acted upon *according to its ends*, is best fitted to prevent *the entrance* of corruption among societies, as well as individuals; not which of them is most calculated when *misapplied from that end*, and conducted by men whose principles and practice appear to us to be wrong, to be productive of *the greatest evil*." This, Sir, is fallacious reasoning, both in civil and ecclesiastical matters. In choosing any government, attention is to be paid to its possible abuse, as well as to its actual advantages. As all human things will be corrupted, and divine things in human hands, this is as necessary a consideration as the other. Every wise politician takes this into the account; and it is confessedly none

---

to hold fast *the traditions* which they had been taught both by word and letter? The παραδοσεις, or traditions which have a divine origin, are principally the ordinances and institutions of Christ's churches—1 Cor. xi. 2; 2 Thes. iii. 6. On the other hand, the παραδοσεις, or traditions of men, chiefly intend the ordinances and institutions of human invention—Matt. xv. 2, 3, 6; Gal. 1. 14; Col. ii. 8. Had all the churches then held fast only what they received from the apostles, Antichrist could not have risen.

of the least momentous advantages of the British constitution, that from its peculiar temperament, it is capable of fewer abuses than any other. Every writer on the subject hath observed this. Nay, to reason upon your principle, absolute monarchy would be preferable both in church and state. There cannot be a question but an absolute monarchy is the simplest and the most beneficial form of government in every country, if we could always be assured that the plan *would be acted upon according to its end.* If there could be any certainty of a perpetual succession of monarchs sufficiently wise and sufficiently virtuous, every clog upon their will would be not only useless, but a calamity to their people. Who is it that does not know, that the peculiar temperament, and nice equipoise of the different parts of the British constitution, is principally, if not solely, with a view to the possible abuse of the different kinds of government of which it is composed? This observation is so obvious, that I am astonished that any man who has ever thought for a moment upon the subject of which he treats, should hazard such crude assertions. The principles upon which you here defend Presbytery would, with tenfold strength, support the throne of the universal Pontiff. If that system could assuredly be acted upon to its professed end, *i.e.,* if the head of it were really infallible, it would doubtless be one of the simplest and best forms of government upon earth. How absurd is it then to say as you do! p. 229, " By adopting this principle, you invalidate the authority of the most important institutions, and set aside many in which you yourself believe. On this ground, for instance, as a standing ministry, when prostituted to the purposes of error and worldliness, is much more fitted to disseminate corruption, and prevent reform than private instruction is, it should be laid aside; and we ought to believe, with a certain sect of levellers, that ministers of the Gospel are no longer necessary, but every Christian himself should teach his neighbour, and every Christian his brother, to know the Lord. On the same ground also, since civil government, when administered by rulers that are unfaithful, is no less fitted, by its subordination of courts, to propagate most extensively *every species of corruption,* and to present an unsurmountable obstacle to reform, it ought to be laid aside; and all the nations of men, correcting those errors into which, by your reasoning, they have in every age fallen, should at once abolish their civil courts of review, break down their kingdoms into a countless multitude of little principalities, and make each of them entirely independent of the rest." Sir, this reasoning is not worthy of a boy coming out of the nursery. Mr. Innes does not reason against the institution of church government, which these illustrations suppose, because any form of it may be corrupted; but granting that it is necessary, he rightly contends, that as all forms cannot be equally good, that is most likely to be the Scripture plan, which has the fewest disadvantages when corrupted, along with equal advantages with any other, to prevent corruption. He does not argue, that because church government may be abused, therefore it ought to be abolished. Nor does he argue that Presbytery may be abused and that Independency cannot be abused; but allowing them both to be abused, as they often will, he inquires which of them, in this state, can do the most mischief. This, Sir, is a lawful inquiry respecting any institution, sacred or civil, human or divine. To apply Mr. Innes' principles of reasoning to this, is not to say that, because it may be abused to spread error more extensively, therefore every kind of ministry should be abolished; but that, as all forms of ministry may be abused, that form which is capable of the fewest abuses, is most likely to be divine. In every country, some kind of civil government is necessary, but all kinds are liable to abuse. Does it then follow, upon Mr. Innes' mode of reasoning, that all forms of government should be abolished? No; but that that plan of civil government least capable of extensive abuse, should be preferred to any other. Nay, and this will hold, even were we to suppose that other forms when rightly used (as absolute monarchy, for instance), have more actual advantages. If you are disposed to dispute the matter with us, let us have something better than mere froth and declamation. Let us have solid arguments.

Although the analogy between the kingdoms of this world, and that of our Lord Jesus Christ, will not hold in any distinguishing features, yet I must observe, that your views of the advantages of extensive civil governments in this and your last letter, are contrary to the soundest policy. Though petty states are not desirable, the great defect of them is, not that they must be deficient in the means of promoting the welfare of their citizens, but in the necessity of their being dependent on, or of becoming a prey to, their more powerful neighbours. Internal policy may certainly be best administered in small states. In widely extended governments, the grievances of the provinces are long in reaching the ear of supreme power, and their redress is both partial and circuitous. Small states are to be avoided then only on account of external violence. The just and most happy bounds of every government appears to be determined, not from its own extent, considered in itself, but from its comparative extent and strength, considered in one point of view with its neighbours. If it is so extensive, and possessed of such resources as will render it truly independent, and fearless of foreign violence, it is as extensive as its happiness requires. Here, Sir, the analogy between civil and sacred things entirely fails. This evil can never be experienced nor dreaded by the latter. In the former, a great nation is necessary for defence against foreign invasion. In every other respect, small states have the advantage. There can be no need of extended forms of church government for external defence, for her weapons are not carnal.

But even in civil things, so far from your Romantic scheme of a universal empire being desirable, governments very extensive are not approved of by the ablest politicians, for many other reasons besides their defects as to the just and regular administration of internal policy. The chimera of a universal government would meet, I imagine, with little else but ridicule among philosophers.

Let us hear an observation, by Mr. Hume, upon the different effects of extended and confined civil governments, with respect to literature, which may also be applied to the subject before us. The observation he deduces is different, but the principles are the same. This writer, whose penetration and talent of investigation none will question, states it as a general maxim, " that nothing is more favourable to the rise of politeness and learning, than a number of neighbouring and independent states, connected together by commerce and policy." The chief advantage of which is, " the stop which such limited territories give both to power and to authority." On the contrary, that extended civil governments are prejudicial to learning. This he proves by the example of the states of Greece, and the copy of these, the states and kingdoms of modern Europe, contrasted with the Roman Christian spiritual monarchy and the empire of China. " Not only power but authority influences opinions, and the more extended the government, the more sensible will be the operation of these causes. During the reign of Rome Christian, the Peripatetic philosophy alone was admitted into the schools; after men were freed from this yoke, Europe attained to its former situation. The Cartesian philosophy of France was overthrown by the opposition of the other nations of Europe. The severest scrutiny of Newton's theory was by foreigners." Now, the whole of the reasoning on the second observation of the 14th Essay, Vol. I., which seems as just as it is ingenious, is equally applicable to the forms of church government. In proportion as it is extended, will it tend the sooner and more effectually to enslave the people. Not only the power of superior courts, but the authority of names will give currency to errors throughout every part of the association. Independent churches are neither awed by each other, nor influenced by the authority of names; habitually acknowledging and acting upon this principle, that there is nothing that commands respect but the Word of God. On the other hand, when an error or a corruption springs up among the leading men of associated churches, it spreads like a pestilence. It soon becomes a fashion. It is generally a sufficient evidence of the truth of any doctrine, that it is the opinion of the *ancient rabbins*.

Your next argument is from the practice of ordination. Upon this subject we need not be tedious, let ordination be what it will. For if the kind of ordination you talk of be absolutely necessary to the validity of the pastoral office, then, Sir, there is not an ordained minister in all the Protestant churches. Their ordination is originally derived from the Pope, or from laymen. The first Protestant ministers were either laymen or excommunicated priests. As to ordination, the truth seems to be this; office-bearers are to be set apart to that office by prayer, fasting, and imposition of the hands of the Presbytery of that church. If it is a newly formed church, in which there is no Presbytery, the Scriptures no where make that necessary which is impossible. In planting churches, the evangelists "set in order things that were wanting, and ordained elders in every city." But there is no instance in Scripture of the elders of one church setting apart the elders of another. Nor can the elders of a number of churches, with any propriety, plead the right of succession to the office of the evangelist. If this argument can be used at all, it will go to prove that the office of an evangelist is a standing office in the church, which is not necessary for me, on the present occasion, either to affirm or deny. Of one thing we may however be assured, that God would not make the validity of an office depend upon any external rite, which it might often be very inconvenient, sometimes impracticable to obtain. If an individual church member were cast accidentally upon a heathen island, and by his labours many were converted, could these persons never become a church, could they never have a minister, because there were no ministers to put hands upon him? Such was the situation of the Reformers, such may be the situation of many churches. Be this as it may, there is not an example of the elders of one church ordaining the elders of another, in all the Word of God. This is sufficient for my purpose at present, and I will not waste time with useless digressions.

But ordination is nowhere in Scripture represented as conveying an office. The officer is by that rite solemnly set apart to the discharge of the duties of his office, and recommended to the grace of the great Head of the church. When this is done by the elders of another church, it never implies that they give him a right to discharge that office in that church. The choice of the church, in consequence of their judging that he possesses the Scriptural qualifications, gives him that right. This is only the manner of setting him apart to that work. In circumstances where it is practicable, it is proper; when otherwise, it is not necessary.

Your next argument is, page 235. "In the 4th place, if the pastors of a particular congregation become heretical or immoral, and persist in these evils, in another point of light, even upon Independent principles, a court of review appears necessary to judge them. The members of the congregation, according to the acknowledged tenets of all Independents are not entitled in the first instance to judge, but are merely allowed to acquiesce and consent to the proposals of their office-bearers."

Where did you learn that a court of review was necessary in this instance, according to Independent principles? Who told you that the people are not to judge in the first instance, but only to acquiesce in and consent to the proposals of the office-bearers? Suppose a church had only one pastor, yet it is not complete in that situation, that church may not only judge of him, but exclude him, if they find him unworthy of executing that office any longer. In judging of him, no doubt they will depute one of the brethren to preside for the time, as in the case they had no pastor at all. A church may not only do this, but any other act of discipline, if they have not other pastors. But I need not waste time on the subject, when an express direction on the point is given in Colossians iv. 17.—" Say to Archippus, take heed to the ministry which thou hast received in the Lord, that thou fulfil it."

Your last argument in this letter is p. 236. " And, 5thly, if every particular congregation, however small, is, in every case, to be the final judge in every point of government, this plan seems to be less fitted to secure an enlightened and candid administration than that of Presbytery."

In answer to all this, I think it sufficient to reply in general, that as a church of Christ is composed of spiritual men, there will always be among them some who are able to judge of anything that respects that church—1 Cor. vi.; Gal. vi. 1., and as they are all brethren in Christ, and members one of another, if they act as such there can be no partiality. If they are worthy of their name and place, they cannot favour one to the disadvantage of another. Therefore, seeing they are supposed capable of judging aright, and disposed to exercise justice according to their judgment, no Christian brother need fear their decision. On the contrary, suppose that they are carnal men who are united under this form of church government, if they give a wrong or a partial judgment, the sooner the injured can separate himself from them the better. What would it signify to him to complain to a superior court upon such men? Could a superior court make that church Christians? And could such an individual, if a Christian, unite with them again, after all the penances that a superior court could oblige them to undergo, till he should see them changed men? Should it have any tendency to reconcile him to them, that he had got the judgment reversed, or that they had been punished for injuring him? What would it serve were they obliged to make a pilgrimage to Jerusalem? Again, suppose that the church is composed of Christians, but that, through want of information on the point, they have passed an injurious sentence, as soon as they see this, they will be ready to make reparation, without being compelled by a superior court. But if they cannot both be brought to understand one another, their union in the same church is far from being desirable. The external power that keeps them together is holding a handful of sand, which, if left to itself, would scatter. A superior court may 'film the sore, but corruption will spread within.' As to the enlightened and candid administration of justice by Presbyterian church courts, if this were my business at present, it would be easy to give abundant specimens.

In p. 239, you ask a question which a word will answer. "Besides, if any of the members of a particular congregation exhibit a charge against the rest of that congregation, and there be no superior court, who are the arbiters that are to determine between them?" If a part of the church has injured an individual, the church will judge between them. If an individual be injured by the whole church, if the church will not make reparation upon his remonstrance, they forfeit their title to their name. He is no longer to acknowledge them for a church. Would it be of any advantage that a superior court should make them confess a fault of which they did not really repent? Or could the injured person remain with them upon such terms? Presbyterian discipline would here hide an evil which it would be of advantage to discover. It binds together what ought to be separated.

LETTER VIII.

Sir,

I COME now to answer your fifteenth letter, in which you endeavour to prove that there must have been a number of congregations in Jerusalem, from the vast number of disciples in that city. You set out, by paving the way for courts of review among Christians, from the example of the ecclesiastical courts of the Jews. Upon this point I am not concerned to follow you. You may as well describe the constitution of England or France. The Jewish Church was a worldly kingdom, with carnal ordinances and a worldly polity. Nothing else could have answered the end. The nation was the church, and as the most of them were carnal men, they were not fit subjects for any government, but one on the principles of other states. But the kingdom of Christ is not of this world. Its constitution is entirely spiritual. The civil and sacred code of the Jews was in one body, the rulers of the nation were the rulers of the church. The principles then of the constitution of their church with their forms of procedure, must bear an analogy to those of the kingdoms of this world. Christ's churches have nothing to do with the regulation of political matters, nor the government and laws of the different nations in which they live. The end of their association is purely spiritual. Doubtless, it was ignorance of this distinction that led so many enthusiasts after the Reformation to endeavour to establish a pure political kingdom, under the sanction of our Lord Jesus Christ. They saw evidently that the churches of Christ were described as composed of saints, but confounding his kingdom with the kingdoms of this world, they were led to attempt the chimerical project of establishing a political kingdom of saints.

But I cannot pass an observation which you make

upon Matt. xxiii. 1, 2, 3, in which you say that our Lord commands his disciples to obey these courts. Obedience to the Scribes and Pharisees is not here inculcated as they were members of any council, but as they sat in Moses' seat, *i.e.*, read and expounded the law and the prophets. To sit in Moses' seat was not to be members of an ecclesiastical council, but to declare the laws of Moses. Their obedience then was only to Moses; by no means either to the doctrines or ritual inventions of men, or any human impositions. They are not here commanded to obey the decisions of these Scribes and Pharisees considered as an ecclesiastical court, but as they individually sat in Moses' seat, and read the law to the people.

You say indeed that our Lord " reprobated those human inventions that were contrary to the precept or spirit of the law." But our Lord makes no such reservation in his censures of human inventions. Upon all such, of every kind and degree, he expresses the most unqualified disapprobation. " In vain do ye worship me, teaching for doctrines the commandments of men." " Every plant which my heavenly Father hath not planted, must be plucked up." " Why do ye also make void the law of God, by your traditions?" Every human invention is of this description, and human inventions were as much forbidden under the Jewish as under the Christian dispensation. The various washings introduced by the elders were in themselves as suitable emblems of purification, as those instituted by God himself. Why then did not our Lord condemn his disciples, upon the remonstrance of the Pharisees, for eating meat with unwashen hands? Because they had not the divine sanction. The difference between such rites, and those instituted by God, did not consist in the greater spirituality, or even emblematical fitness of the latter than of the former, but in the one being of divine the other of human origin. Even under the carnal Jewish dispensation, the church rulers had not the power of regulating things simply of an external nature, nor of adding the slightest amendment. Now, if under that carnal dispensation and worldly policy, in which the wisdom of man might have place, it was nevertheless entirely excluded, is it supposable that, under the Christian dispensation and spiritual kingdom, Christ would give scope for the ingenuity of men? In pleading for the right of legislation as to matters of external order, Presbyterians claim more than was enjoyed by the high priest of the Jews, and the whole Jewish hierarchy. In what consisted the superior excellency of the rites of God's appointment over the washing before meat, and other inventions of the elders? In what was the latter contrary to *the precept or spirit of the law* of God? Is it in any other way than as every other human invention is? This rite contradicts no precept, nor is it contrary to the spirit of the law in any other way than as it, like every human invention in religion, supposes God's law imperfect, and arraigns his legislative competency. Why then, Sir, do you misrepresent the words of our Lord Jesus, and insinuate that, in those passages in which he condemns all human interference in the things of God in the most decisive and unqualified language, he only censures a certain class of such inventions? Will you dare to sanction such will-worship by the approbation, connivance, or silence of the Lord Jesus? But the reason of this unfair gloss upon our Lord's language is very plain. Our Lord must not condemn, in an unqualified manner, the inventions of the Jewish rulers, because he would thereby condemn the principles of Presbyterians. If he would not allow of any human regulations among the Jews, there could be no pretext for the most daring arrogance demanding any such privilege now. The claims of the ancient and modern rabbins are so entwisted, that it is impossible to condemn the one without, at the same time, condemning the other. "Master, thus saying thou reproachest us also."

You say your argument acquires additional force in supposing that such courts are of human invention. "Must not corresponding courts in the Christian Church be equally worthy of our approbation and submission for the very same reasons, even though it could not be established, that they were explicitly enjoined in Scripture?" I thank you; Sir, I thank you for this discovery of your real sentiments upon this subject. The divine right of Presbytery must be supported, if possible; because it would shock the old staunch Presbyterians to put it on a human foundation. Hence Scripture must be silenced, mangled, distorted, evaded, according to exigency. But conscious, after all, that this crazy fabric would not be able to withstand the storm of a vigorous opposition, when it falls, there is an inner retreat, another refuge to shelter the cause. Though God shall forsake it, it will not on that account be left destitute and naked; the supposed divine sanction of human courts among the Jews will take it up, and give it protection. Such and such arguments prove that God is the author of Presbytery; but if God should disown it, it is no great matter: it can do tolerably well without him. Is this like the language of a man thoroughly persuaded of the divine origin of that system which he defends? Is this like the reasoning of an author fully persuaded that he was using his pen in the cause of divine truth? Is it like the spirit of a writer, whose only intention is to vindicate the institutions of God? Is there any symptom of a mind candidly in search of truth, and wishing to know the mind of the Spirit of God. If it is possible to see the soul of a writer in his unguarded moments; if there is anything to be gathered from the spirit of a book, this may be gathered from yours—that you are unwilling to rest Presbytery solely on a divine institution; that you are not convinced that you have a full and perfect model, and therefore, while you struggle hard to defend the divine right, you are at the same time anxious to provide a shelter in case of a defeat. The evident spirit of your performance shows, that you are determined to defend Presbytery at all events. If it is divine, so much the better; but if it is not divine, it is notwithstanding defensible. You say in your Introduction, p. 7, " He (the writer) has no wish that Presbytery should be retained any farther than it can be supported by Scripture, and the moment that it is proved that it cannot be so supported, he will be happy to see that it is rejected by the world." But how can I understand in what possible manner this consists with the passage under review? Will this mode of defending

Presbytery allow me to think that you are in earnest in your assertion? How can it be so, seeing here you attempt to vindicate Presbytery, upon the supposition that its courts of review were merely of human invention? Now, if such courts in the Christian Church be worthy of our approbation and submission, even although it could not be proved that they were explicitly enjoined in Scripture, how can you consistently with this declaration, declare that if they cannot be supported by Scripture, you would wish to see them abolished? If these two passages can be reconciled, it must be by such rules of criticism as you have employed upon the fifth chapter of first Corinthians.

But how does the argument acquire additional force from the supposition of the Jewish courts being of human origin? If the Christian Church courts correspond to the Jewish, and if the former are to be proved from the latter, is not the argument stronger upon the supposition of their divine, than of their human institution? Can a human institution, supposed to be sanctioned by Christ, give a firmer foundation to courts that correspond to this institution, than a divine institution would do? No; but here is the point in which it has superior force. You are aware that the proving of the Jewish courts to be divine, will not prove corresponding Christian courts to be divine also, any more than every other part of the Jewish dispensation must have corresponding parts under the Christian. Then our Lord's sanction to Jewish courts of divine origin, would be of no force, unless it could be proved that Christian courts were of divine origin; and, in this case, they would not need the sanction here supposed to be given them. But if the Jewish courts were of human origin; and if as such, our Lord approved of them; then the inference is, that it may also be supposed that he will now be equally complaisant to the pretensions of Presbyterians, and sanction their courts, although they should be found to be only the inventions of men. Here then is the manner in which this illustrious argument comes to have this superior force. It can have superior force upon no other supposition, than that Christian courts are of human invention. Now, this is a very odd kind of reasoning in a writer who contends so pompously for the *jus divinum*. I cannot think that it would ever come into the head of an author to attempt to derive superior strength to an argument, from a supposition that overthrows the very cause for which he contends, unless he were reduced to a sad pinch. For what are you contending through your whole performance? For what purpose do you attempt to refute Mr. Innes, and every other writer who defends the divine right of the Independent form of church government? Is it not to establish the divine right of Presbytery? And is it possible that you can keep your ground, and give up the very subject of debate? It is not like granting a single argument to your adversaries, nor a whole class of arguments. In this supposition, you give up the very thing for which you are professedly contending? What! grant courts of review to be of human origin, and yet defend their *jus divinum !* It is not possible for the same author consistently to be the author of both these hypotheses. One Presbyterian may defend Presbytery as a human institution, and another defend it as divine. But the same man ought not upon any supposition to do both. If Presbytery is really defensible as a human institution, why is not this the footing upon which you have grounded your defence, as the most learned and illustrious of your brethren have done? If this is really your opinion, if Christ would approve of our submission and obedience to these courts of human invention equally as if he had instituted them himself, you need not have been at so much trouble in torturing the Scriptures to countenance such courts. You should at once have justified them as a human device, which, from their wisdom, could not fail to be sanctioned by Christ. But Presbyterians would find a difficulty even upon this supposition, which you do not seem to have noticed. If courts of human invention may be sanctioned by Christ, one kind of them may be sanctioned as well as another.* Upon this supposition, I leave

* Upon this supposition, the Church of Scotland is highly censurable, for giving at different times such opposition to the government, in attempting to regulate her external polity.

you to struggle with all the other churches of this world. Upon this footing, I will not defend Independency. I know that, when brought into view with the blooming children of this world's wisdom, this would appear like an orphan. Besides, if she is not of heavenly birth, I will let her perish in her blood. I call upon every believer of the truth to examine the spirit of this passage, and to consider whether the writer is not determined to defend Presbytery, or at least that he is not inclined to renounce it, upon the strongest evidence of its being only a child of this world's wisdom. If this is not his meaning, there is no sense in language. As long as he is in this temper, I despair of making him a convert.

But such courts you assert were also in use in many of the cities in which the Gospel was first preached. You could easily prove this by an induction of facts with respect to Ephesus, Corinth, and Rome, but you are contented to show that this was the case with respect to Jerusalem. And indeed, had you succeeded, I would acknowledge that it was sufficient to prove the general point. But how do you prove this? Is it by any positive authority from the Word of God? Is it from any direct testimony? Is it from the circumstance of the disciples of that place being called *churches*, or from their being represented as assembling for worship and ordinances in different places? No such thing; your proof is altogether negative. Negative proof will never establish anything opposed by positive credible evidence. All I have to do, is to prove the matter of fact. Your negative arguments, were they like mountains, would weigh lighter than vanity. Upon this point then, I shall look upon my business to be to establish the matter of fact from positive evidence. I

Upon the supposition that the churches of England and Scotland are both of human origin, the former is by much the preferable. Supposing both plans to be acted upon *agreeable to their end*, the former is by much the simpler and the more effectual; supposing them to be abused, it is much easier to please one tyrant than several hundreds. Mr. Innes passes a compliment upon the comparative excellence of the Scotch national establishment, which, in my opinion, it does not deserve.

shall, in that event, bid defiance to all your probabilities and conjectures. All I have to do, is to show that your objections are not insuperable. It will not be necessary to prove that such and such things were actually the case; it will be enough to show you that *they may have been the case.* Difficulties, if not absolutely insuperable, are never supposed to invalidate a well-authenticated fact. In establishing the matter of fact from plain, and positive, and decisive evidence, the proof doubtless, is to be expected on my part. Here, if I rest anything upon probabilities, or possibilities, *i.e.,* if I argue that the Christians of Jerusalem constituted one church, because such a thing is probable or possible from such and such reasons, my fabric is so far baseless. In that case, I would reason like a child; for a positive fact cannot with security be rested on what is probable or possible. If the evidence is only probable or possible, there is still room to suppose the contrary, and the matter of fact is not proved, but rendered probably or possibly true. In this part of the subject, I must make the attack, and if I cannot force you from your trenches, I will not claim the victory. If you can sustain the charge, my cause as to this matter of fact is lost. I say, that as to the proof of this matter of fact my cause would be lost, if you are able to prove that my arguments do not establish it. But even in this case you do not gain a victory, unless you are able not only to defend yourself in your trenches, but to charge me in turn, and drive me off the field. Suppose I were unable positively to prove that the Christians of Jerusalem were only one church, it would not follow of necessary consequence that they were more. It might have been the case, and yet no sufficient documents left to prove it. If you could do no more then than sustain my charge, it would in that case be a drawn battle upon this point. It will not serve you to show that we cannot prove the Christians of Jerusalem to have constituted only one church, unless you can show that they positively constituted more than one. You would only in that case deprive us of this argument. Before this could serve your system essentially, you must positively show that there were in

Jerusalem a plurality of churches. If I cannot positively prove that there was only one church in Jerusalem, I cannot use this argument; if you cannot positively prove that there were more, you cannot bring it as an objection to my system. In that case, we must both lay this argument aside. Though then, if I wish to make use of this argument, I must positively prove the matter of fact, yet to defend my system it is only necessary to show, that it cannot be positively proved that there were in Jerusalem more than one church. So much I thought necessary as to the manner of conducting this part of the debate, for you very artfully endeavour to throw the whole weight of the positive proof on your adversary, and content yourself by starting objections. The things that your system positively requires to be fully established by direct evidence, you suppose it necessary for your antagonist positively to disprove. Now the system of your adversary only requires him to show that such things cannot positively be proved. In answering your letters then on this subject, I shall think it sufficient to receive your charge, to stand on the defensive, and show that your objections may be answered. If your objections are not such, that upon no possible supposition will they quadrate with my hypothesis, they are nugatory. What I shall be obliged to do, is to show that such and such difficulties are capable of such and such solutions. Whatever I do farther, I shall consider as entirely gratuitous. There is not a matter of fact recorded in ancient history, that might not be overthrown or invalidated upon the principles of your reasoning. Christianity itself could not stand the test of such a species of objections. Had you, from the meaning of the word church, by which the saints of Jerusalem are called, established your point, or from actual testimony as to their assembling, &c., you might lawfully corroborate your reasoning by the circumstance of the vast numbers of Christians in Jerusalem. But in the face of direct testimony, you build a system upon certain supposed difficulties, without a single positive proof. This, Sir, upon all subjects is inadmissible.

But let us come to the point. Let us inquire what

is the actual testimony of the Acts of the Apostles upon this matter. The first thing is undoubtedly to look out for positive evidence. What saith the whole tenor of the history in the Acts of the Apostles? If there were only one, or if there were more congregations in Jerusalem, it may be lawfully expected that the history which gives an account of the saints in that city, will undoubtedly inform us. This it does, both from the name by which they are called, and from the actual representations of their assembling and acting as one body.

1. As to the name by which the saints of Jerusalem are called, this is *church*, never *churches*. Now what is the meaning of the word *church*? Its primary meaning and usual acceptation cannot be denied to be what we contend for. The very supposition of Presbyterians allow that this is its common and proper acceptation. Even according to their theory, it could not be figuratively put for church rulers, unless it literally denoted the people whom they are supposed to represent. If then the literal, proper and usual acceptation of this word is a congregation of saints, this is the sense in which it is always to be understood, without peremptory necessity, and in such cases only as the circumstances and connection will easily show that it is not to be understood literally. A figurative sense can never be imposed upon any word, except the literal would be absurd, or contradictory to positive and notorious fact.

Farther, I contend that this is not only its literal and usual acceptation, and that it should never be understood differently, except in the circumstances stated above, but also that it never can be appropriated to a number of congregations united, either literally or figuratively. Not literally, for there would not be one *assembly*, but different *assemblies*; not *church*, but *churches*, for they are never assembled together. Not figuratively from the circumstance of being assembled in their representatives, for although a figurative expression might be used in florid composition, it is not allowable, but would be highly unsuitable in plain narration. But in no composition, from the florid style of Hervey to the unornamented style of Swift, can the figurative use of a word be given as an appropriated name. As I showed before, a figure never changes the meaning of a word, and when a word is so used, it retains its own proper meaning, and from this circumstance is derived the beauty of the figure. Although such a figure might be occasionally used, yet upon every ordinary occasion, its acceptation must be literal. The phrase 'the church at Jerusalem,' could never be appropriated to the plurality of congregations in that city, even although it might occasionally, in circumstances already stated, be so used. Could it be possible with perspicuity, to use the word nation as the appropriated name of the Parliament? Yet, on some occasions in oratory, it might figuratively be so used. If it should be given by appropriation to the representatives, it must be taken from the represented.

But I contend still farther, even *such a figure* could not be occasionally used. An assembly may figuratively get the name of those for whom they act, but they can get no name in their right which those for whom they act do not themselves enjoy. The *Parliament* may be figuratively called by the name of the *nation*, but not by any name which is enjoyed by that nation in common with others. When the Parliament does anything, it may figuratively be said Great Britain does it; but it would be absurd to say that Europe does it, because the people of Great Britain do not exclusively enjoy that name. If there were any such thing as a representative church, a kirk-session might figuratively be so called, because those whom they represent enjoy that name. But as a number of churches are not literally *a church*, and cannot be so called, as they are not an assembly, so the assembled representatives of such churches cannot be called a church, even figuratively, because their constituents do not enjoy that name. The figurative use of a word must be founded on the literal. It appears then that neither a Presbytery, nor any superior court could, even figuratively, be called *a church*, because, even allowing the system of representation, the represented are not so called. Such assemblies are not churches in the figurative sense of the word.

Again, if it is contended that such assemblies are a church from the civil or unappropriated sense of the word—not to remark at present upon the absurdity of giving, in sacred things, the civil unappropriated sense of a word which has been appropriated to certain religious assemblies of a certain description, let it be observed, that upon the first appropriation of a word in a religious use, respect must undoubtedly be had to the profane acceptation of it, from which it is borrowed; but after it hath thus been appropriated, it is absurd to apply it to sacred things in its civil sense. Besides, even in the civil acceptation of this word, it was not any assembly, but usually applied to assemblies of a certain kind. It is not equivalent to οχλος or πληθος, or even those other words which denoted regularly organized assemblies. Εκκλησια was as much appropriated in the civil, as it is in the sacred use. But not to dwell at present upon these things, I observe, that if such assemblies are called a church, from the circumstance that that word, in its civil acceptation, was applicable to any assembly, and not from the members of such assemblies being the representatives of the people, who are literally called a church, then such assemblies, being literally so called, can give no countenance to the body whom they represent, to be called a church. This destroys what it means to prove. It takes away the name of church from the united body of Christians in Jerusalem, and gives it literally to the assembly of their rulers. So far from proving this circumstance, it would absolutely disprove the supposed application of this word to a plurality of congregations in Jerusalem. I contend then, in the most positive language, that if there had been different congregations in that city, they could not have been called a church, either literally or figuratively. Not literally, for they are never assembled personally, their rulers not figuratively from them, because they do not literally enjoy that name, and therefore cannot give it to their representatives figuratively; nor figuratively from the assembly of their rulers being literally called a church, because these are not even an εκκλησια in the civil sense of the word, and because, though they were, the representatives, from being a church as any assembly, could not give that name to those whom they represent, who are never assembled. Though the Parliament might be called the nation, the nation could never be called the Parliament. The Parliament acts for the nation, but not the nation for the Parliament.

Again, if there were different congregations in Jerusalem, the word church was the literal and appropriated name of each of them; to distinguish each of them, there must have been some particular appellation, such as the church meeting in such a street. No one of them could have been called the church at Jerusalem, any more than one of the churches of Edinburgh could be called the Church of Edinburgh. But we know that at first there could have been in Jerusalem but one congregation. This was then called "the church at Jerusalem." Had there ever been a division, the phraseology would have been changed, and each church would have got a distinctive name, or prefix to its name, from its place of meeting or some other characteristic circumstances. How would it be possible to speak intelligibly of any of the Presbyterian congregations of Edinburgh, by the phrase, 'the congregation of Edinburgh.' When the Gospel was first planted in Edinburgh, there would be but one congregation; this would then be called 'the congregation of Edinburgh.' But as soon as the members increased so as to cause a division, 'the congregation of Edinburgh' must be changed for 'the congregations of Edingurgh.' And when any one of them is spoken of, it must receive an additional epithet to distinguish it. We shall hear no more then of 'the congregation of Edinburgh;' but speaking of the whole together, 'the congregations of Edinburgh,' and of each of them separately, 'the congregation that meets in the High Church,' &c. In speaking of the saints in Jerusalem, however, this is never hinted. When they are spoken of at the latest period, the phraseology is the same as at their origin; when its numbers were greatest, they were called by the same name by which they were known when at the smallest.

Again, as the word church was the appropriated name

of each congregation, had there been a number of such congregations under one Presbytery, the aggregate body could not have been called a church for this very reason. Even allowing that the word church could have been at first literally applied to the whole body of Christians in Jerusalem, as composed of different congregations, yet the circumstance of the word church being appropriated to a single congregation, would have prevented its being applied to the other. What Presbyterian would apply the word congregation both to a worshipping assembly, and to the aggregate of the worshipping assemblies in a Presbytery or Synod? This would be appropriating the word upon the same subject in two different senses, a circumstance never known in any language, either in things sacred or civil, either by the learned or the vulgar. Even when a word is allowedly common to two different things, it is not the distinctive name of any one of them; and the moment a common name becomes appropriated to one of the common objects, that moment it ceases to be common. Thus, as to the former, the word congregation is common to all the congregations of Presbyterians, but it is the distinctive name of none of them; as to the latter, *congregation* is equally applicable in a literal sense to the General Assembly as to a single congregation, yet because it has been appropriated to the latter as distinguished from the former, it can never be applied to the former. Thus also with the word elder. What an absurdity then would it be to call each worshipping assembly a church, and the whole also, at same time, nothing but a church? Presbyterian courts might all as well get the same name. Still greater absurdity is it to suppose that the word church could signify every congregation and the rulers of every congregation; each congregation in particular, and the whole of the congregations of a Presbytery; the congregations of a Presbytery, and the rulers of the congregations of a Presbytery; the congregations of a Presbytery, and the congregations of a Synod, General Assembly, &c.; the rulers of the congregations of a Presbytery, and the rulers of the congregations of a Synod, &c. In short, Presbyterians make the same use of the word church that the Welchman, in the story, does of the word *zom'at, i.e.,* somewhat. Every object with which he was unacquainted, he called a *zom'at.* So with them the word church is applicable to any assembly, nay, the very distinctive name of all their assemblies for worship, and courts of discipline, from the congregation and session, to the universal church and its representatives. It is a perfect *zom'at.* But the absurdity they charge upon the Scriptures, they avoid themselves in the appropriated names of their assemblies of all descriptions. Congregation, though an exact translation of εκκλησια, they use only as we do church, which practically disproves their own theory. They never think of denominating every court by the name congregation, although they charge such an absurdity upon the Holy Spirit. Indeed, there is nothing covers the nakedness of this hypothesis, but the circumstance of εκκλησια being a word in a dead language. If any man would attempt to write a book, applying any word upon this principle, he would not only be unintelligible, but ridiculous. When men go to explain words in a dead language, without having considered the general principles and processes of all languages, there is no shape into which they may not turn them. Their meanings will be as various, as unsettled, as the possible combinations of the letters of the alphabet. Every word is figurative or literal, must be stretched above its meaning, or squeezed below it, must signify this or that, just as it suits their purpose,

Again, if the word church was in the apostolical days used to signify a number of congregations, how comes it to pass, that when the congregations of a district or nation are spoken of, they are not called a church, but churches. If the congregations of Jerusalem are called a church, why are not all the congregations of Judea called a church? Why are not the different congregations of Galatia, Samaria, Asia, Achaia, &c., called a church. Are they not called churches, never church? This is the most positive proof that the word never was applied to more congregations than one.

Again, produce me one passage where it is clearly and incontestibly applied to more than one congregation, except when it is equivalent to the whole saints in heaven and earth. If you cannot, upon what principles of criticism can you demand such a meaning for it here? In disputing upon any subject, before we can prove that such a word has such a signification in such a place, we must produce instances in which it cannot reasonably be denied to have such an application. Without this, nothing could ever be proved. You cannot even pretend to one positive proof, either in the sacred or civil use of the word. All your strength lies in supposed difficulties. If the Roman Pontiff says that the word church properly belongs to himself, how would you disprove it, but by calling upon him to show any one passage, where it had plainly such a meaning, or a similar meaning upon another subject? He may as well be called church, from being the sole representative of the church, as any body of Presbyterian rulers, as being representatives. The difference in point of number is nothing.

Having shown that the disciples at Jerusalem were called a church, and that different congregations could not in any sense be so denominated, let us now examine what is the farther testimony of the Acts of the Apostles upon this point. Are the Christians at Jerusalem anywhere represented as subdivided into different congregations, each with rulers and ordinances separate from the rest? To determine this, it is not sufficient to inquire into the numbers said to be converted there; but to establish the fact on either side, by actual testimonies and positive evidence. Now, if my reasoning against the propriety of the application of the name church to a plurality of churches holds good, I consider the fact is already proved, and that nothing can invalidate this, but the most positive assertions or plain representations to the contrary. If the meaning and application of the word church is such, and only such, and if it is applied to the saints in Jerusalem, what shall hinder it to be understood so? Nothing could even apologize for our looking out for another meaning, but the most decisive proofs that the matter of fact was not so as this seemed to represent it. Here then, Sir, I am entrenched; and it is no way incumbent on me to bring any actual testimony from positive declarations to corroborate the fact. The proof of the contrary lies wholly on you. It might very readily have happened, that a church might have been mentioned, without any documents on either side, farther than the name. When a Presbyterian speaks of the congregation of such a town, I am at no loss to know that there is but one worshipping assembly of his denomination in that town. Nothing but his expressly telling me the contrary, would cause me a moment to doubt of this; and, in that case, I would tell him that his language was very improper, and altogether calculated to mislead. Here then I sit on the top of my strong-hold, without the least apprehension from your assault. Not a stone of it can be shaken, but by positive testimony. I am not obliged to show you by any other testimony, that there was but one church at Jerusalem. The only reason we have to prove that the saints of that place constituted one church, is because the word church is applied to them. Were it not for this, it would not invalidate our system, if there had been one hundred churches there. All we have to do then, is positively to prove the meaning and legitimate application of this word. The field is then ours, and we cannot be driven from it, but by your proving that there *actually were*, not that there *probably were* more churches than one in that city. If we can sustain your assault, and show that you cannot positively prove the contrary, our victory is undisputed.

But though our argument only requires us to defend our trenches, we are willing to come forth and take the field with you, because that there is not only no evidence to prove against us, but the strongest, the most direct evidence in our favour. Our cause requires no farther actual proof, yet we can produce an irrefragable chain of testimonies. The question then is this; are the saints at Jerusalem always represented as one body assembled for the enjoyment of ordinances, or are they considered as separated into different congregations with distinct office-bearers? No one will hesitate a moment for an answer, who has no interest in darkening the subject. There is not a single passage in the whole history that gives the smallest foundation to the supposition, that they were separated into distinct churches. Let us run over a few of the evidences, Acts ii. 41, 42. Here they are considered as one congregation, and as having continual fellowship in the ordinances of Christ. That they ate the Lord's supper together, is expressly mentioned. In verse 44 the believers are all said to be together. They are also said to continue with one accord in the temple, which proves that they must have met as one body. Besides, at this time they were called a church, or rather *the church*, at that place; ver. 47, "The Lord added the saved to the church." They are represented as one body which was increasing by daily additions, and this one body was the church at Jerusalem, *the church*. At the time they are described (Acts i. 15), they were undoubtedly one body; when they come to be divided, we must be informed of the change. In Acts iv. 32, they are one company, and verses 31, 32, they were assembled in praying and hearing the Word. There is yet but one church; they were assembled; they were of one heart and one soul, and had all things in common. In verses 33, 34, the apostles preached to them all, and great grace was upon them all. None *among them* lacked. Can it be more expressly declared, that they were one body usually meeting for every purpose of worship, &c. They had one common collection, not a collection in each of several congregations. The apostles are always considered as labouring among the same body, not in different congregations, as otherwise would have been the case. The apostles are always considered as labouring jointly in this assembly. Had there been different congregations, they could not have been together, but each in a different congregation. Acts v. 12. Here they are represented as being *all* with one accord in Solomon's porch. Acts vi. 1–6. What is here spoken, is supposed to be spoken before the whole multitude of the disciples, and approved of by them. "The saying pleased the whole multitude." They are represented as one body also, choosing officers. The office of a deacon belongs to a congregation, and he has no authority in other congregations. These seven deacons are jointly chosen by the whole multitude, and not separately by different individual congregations. They are also jointly appointed to the charge of the poor Christians of all Jerusalem. Had there been different congregations, there would have been deacons appointed for each. The whole multitude are not only supposed to be together, but as jointly choosing officers belonging to a single congregation. Had there been more congregations than one, the deacon would not be an officer of a particular church, but a general officer in a Presbytery, or whole connection of congregations. According to this, there should only be a certain number of officers in every Presbytery, to take care of all the poor of that whole Presbytery. The deacon's office would then be more extensive in its range than that of the pastor's. But the deacon's office not only belongs to the congregation, but it is absolutely necessary that in every congregation, there should be such officers to provide for the poor. These seven deacons were chosen for the joint, not the separate discharge of their duty. Had there been different congregations, the whole multitude would not have chosen so many in common, but each congregation so many for itself. It would have been much better to have had a collection in each, and officers to distribute in each, that the wants of individuals being better known in their particular congregations, they might the more easily be supplied. Does not the practice of Presbyterians prove this? Have they not men appointed to take care of the poor in each congregation, not so many for a Presbytery? Does the money collected in each congregation go into a general purse to be distributed through the whole Presbytery?

Acts xxi. 18, 22. Here, at this advanced period, the multitude could come together. Acts xv. 4, 12, 22. Here the whole church are expressly said to meet and transact business. "Let any one judge what is the plain and obvious import of these passages. Do they not all express or imply that the believers at Jerusalem were one undivided body, assembling in one place for the the worship of God? By whatever rule of interpretation this is denied, the most important facts and doctrines of the Gospel may be set aside."—*Social Worship*, p. 157. 1st edit.

Now, Sir, from the name by which they are called, and from the unvaried tenor of their history in the Acts of the Apostles, it appears most evidently, that the disciples at Jerusalem formed only one congregation. Is there a single passage in all the history, in which they are said or supposed, either expressly or by implication, to have been divided into distinct congregations? If there were really a difficulty as to their numbers, a difficulty can never destroy a fact, far less be the foundation of an opposite system, as you attempt to make it. When I have shown from the plain meaning of the word church, and the plain declarations of Scripture, that they all met in one place, you cannot invalidate the fact, or make it the least suspicious by anything but an insuperable objection.

Your objection, however, at its utmost amount, is not insuperable;* and I defy you to show them *positively* at any one time, to have exceeded five thousand. Suppose it is said that they were on such a day five thousand, and that on the very next five thousand were

* We are informed by Dr. M'Laine, in a note to his Translation of Mosheim, that there were present at the council of Placentia (A.D. 1095), 200 bishops, 4,000 ecclesiastics, and 300,000 laymen. Why might not an objector, upon the principle of the impossibility of the Christians at Jerusalem meeting in one place, here boldly contradict this fact? 'There was no such meeting, because there was no house could hold so many; nor could any speaker make himself audible to them all at the same time.' Yet doubtless it was for the purpose of hearing the deliberations, that each person was present. But how each speaker made himself audible, we are not informed. This however cannot invalidate the fact. Could not persons appointed, and stationed at certain distances, have reported the substance of what was said by each speaker to those in the remotest parts of the assembly. Allowing the Christians then to have been ten times as many as your estimate even supposes, it could not invalidate a fact authenticated by such a multitude of the clearest testimonies. Not however that I think the disciples of Jerusalem ever at any one period amounted to more than could stand within the compass of the human voice. Indeed, various circumstances lead us to believe they were not near so many, even as this would accommodate.

converted, I am not necessarily obliged to give you credit for ten thousand. There is a *possibility* that most of the first five thousand might have died or emigrated. I do not say it is probable, but all I have to do is to show that it is possible. For when a fact is established by positive proof, negative allegations may be answered by a bare *possibility*. We know that the Scripture cannot convey an untrue representation, and therefore everything that seems to contradict its positive declarations must be only in the want of proper information as to such things. Things that appear difficult to us at this distance of time, had no difficulties to those acquainted with the times and circumstances to which the facts relate. A thousand things may be unknown to us that would, if known, remove these difficulties. Although then I hold myself bound to give every attainable satisfaction upon this point to a person seriously in search of truth, yet, in answering a writer who is evidently determined to make the plainest Scriptures bend to his system, I think it enough to silence him. Sufficient reasons have been given by different writers to account for the accommodation of vast multitudes in Jerusalem. For my part, I care not if there was not a single street in Jerusalem sufficient to hold them, as long as I have such positive testimony. Wherever they might meet, and however numerous they might have been, the canopy of heaven was large enough to cover them.

But though I would not fear to admit your extravagant estimation of their numbers, without the smallest diminution, I will submit for a few minutes to examine your items, that we may have a specimen of the accuracy of your rule of calculation.

As to those converted on the day of Pentecost, you say, p. 246, "Nor were these three thousand souls Jews, who had come up to the city of Jerusalem, merely to wait upon the feast, and who immediately returned to their native countries, as Independents have asserted." Sir, Independents do not assert that they positively *must have been* all such. They argue that it is probable, or at least possible, that many of them *may have been* such. This is all that is necessary on their part. This will serve to remove a difficulty from an established fact. It lies with you *positively* to prove that they were not such Jews; otherwise your objection has no force. The reasons which you allege are, 1. 'The Jews that dwelt without the land of Canaan were not bound to appearance at the festivals there.' It is not necessary that they *must* have all been bound to come; it is enough to show that it was their privilege, and a privilege which such a people as the Jews could not fail to embrace upon every convenient opportunity. 'Nor, 2, was it possible that they should do so, if they had been commanded, unless they did nothing almost the whole year but go up to Jerusalem and home again,'* &c. Nor is it necessary that all of them should come from the most distant countries. It will serve our purpose sufficiently well, if those who chose might come from the neighbouring countries. 3. 'What had the dispersed Jews to do with the feast of harvest, when their harvest, in many of the places where they dwelt, was not yet begun?' No matter as to the harvest of the Jews in other parts of the world: let them live where they would, they had an interest in this as a feast of their country, appointed of their God. The Jewish feasts were typical, and, as such, all Jews wherever they lived, had the same concern in them. 4. 'If their distance from Jerusalem made them to choose to come up but to some one of the feasts, and omit the rest, why to Pentecost, which was the least solemn of the three?' &c. Those who could might come occasionally to any of them, as they had opportunity. Your fifth reason is a good one, and although many might have come on account of the feast of Pentecost, many more might have come on account of the universal expectation of the appearance of the Messiah, and have dwelt in Jerusalem. These, however, it is probable, or at least possible, might return upon their conversion, for the purpose of carrying to others the glad tidings.

You add, p. 247. "Besides we are told in Acts ii. 5,

---

* I think the meetings of your universal church will keep the inhabitants of the world pretty busy.

that these Jews who are said in the 41st verse to have been added to the church, had dwelt for a considerable time at Jerusalem, and were then residing there. Such, according to the authority of Mintert, is the term κατοικεω, there employed in the original to signify their residence: "for it properly denotes in the Greek writers, a certain *fixed* and *durable dwelling*, and is opposed to παροικεω which signifies to sojourn or dwell in a place for a time only." This reasoning is not good; because it is not founded on just criticism. Your distinction between κατοικεω and παροικεω is not agreeable either to their intrinsic import, or the practice of the language. There is indeed a very great difference between these words, but neither you nor Mintert, upon whose authority you hazard this criticism, seem to understand that difference. The former word is not opposed to the latter; the one as signifying a durable dwelling, and the other to dwell in a place for a short time only. The idea of the duration of time, either long or short, is in neither of the words. They may, and are both applied to denote residence in a place for a period either longer or shorter. The length of time is never known from the words themselves, but from other circumstances. Κατοικεω can be opposed to παροικεω in no other way than as the former signifies to dwell in a place in general, without reference to that place or country, whether we are aboriginal natives, or strangers; the latter signifies to dwell as a stranger, and may be applied to a man's whole life, or any given period, as well as a single day. It is compounded of the preposition παρα, signifying *by*, *at*, or *near to*, and οικεω *to dwell*. By an opposite process, the word παροικια was used to signify the place of sojourning as a stranger, as it is used in the Scriptures; and by ecclesiastical writers for a contiguity of houses, from which we have the word *parish*. The process in the latter is obvious. In the former it is this, when we say a thing is *near to* another, it implies that it is separate from that object, let the distance be ever so small. Hence arises the idea of distance in the word παρα. It is upon the same principle we speak when we say that a man is *by* or *beside himself*. As οικεω signifies to dwell at home, παροικεω signifies to dwell at some distance from home. This is the prominent idea in the word, and this feature it never loses, whenever it is used in the Septuagint or New Testament. It refers not in any measure to the length of the time of sojourning, but signifies that the person spoken of is a stranger in the land where he dwells. The Jews were παροικοι all the time they were in Egypt. Christians are always considered as παροικοι, while on earth, as not being in their own country. This distinction in the use of these words is everywhere preserved. Though those who are said παροικειν may also be said κατοικειν, when the idea of being strangers is not intended to be brought forward into view, yet παροικειν is never used in a general sense like the other. Though undoubtedly the word οικεω was intended to be modified by the addition of κατα, yet it was by no means to adopt it to signify a longer time of dwelling. They are often used promiscuously. The idea of *direction*, or *direction of place*, is literally contained in κατα. Κατοικειν εν Ιεροσολυμοις is literally *to dwell in the direction of Jerusalem*—the place of lying of their habitations was in Jerusalem. Every example of the occurrence of the word which you quote justifies my criticism. It is mere idleness then to run over your concordance to show that the word often signifies a very long term. To serve your purpose, you must show that it never can be used to a short duration. I care not though you could produce ever such "a countless multitude of instances in the Septuagint in which κατοικεω signifies a very long period." Were Adam yet alive, and had he lived till this day in one house, it might indeed be applied to him, but it might also be applied to the settlers in Botany Bay. Were you to hear a man saying that Mr. ——— lives in High-street, could you tell whether that man had lived there all his life, or only removed thither the day before? But upon your principles of reasoning, you might reason thus: "It is said that Methusalem *lived* 969 years; besides, I can produce a countless multitude of instances in which the word *live* is applied to a very long period. Certain it is then, that Mr. ——— must have resided in High-street, at least a very long time."

You proceed, p. 249. "Nor will it suffice to disprove this, to tell us, that some of them are represented by Peter (Acts ii. 9), as dwelling in Mesopotamia and other places which are there mentioned, and consequently they could not be statedly residing at Jerusalem. This only describes the places where they had dwelt before they came to Jerusalem, and from which, of course, they received their appellation; but it will not demonstrate, in opposition to the fifth verse, and the most general acceptation of the verb κατοικεω, that they were not statedly dwelling, at that period, in that city."

When I would prove from Acts ii. 9, that those persons were only residing for a time in Jerusalem, I would do this without reference to the meaning of the word κατοικεω altogether. My argument would be this: These persons now in Jerusalem are said, in the present tense, to be inhabitants of Mesopotamia, &c. I would argue that this cannot signify, as you explain it, that these were merely the countries from which they came, but that these were still the countries to which they belonged. The words are rendered literally thus, "and they that inhabit Mesopotamia," &c. Here it is not said merely that these people were formerly inhabitants of these countries, but that they were still the inhabitants of such places, though they were sojourning for a time at Jerusalem. Those students who reside in Glasgow or Edinburgh, during their academical education, are even, during that time, considered as the inhabitants of the various countries to which they belong. When I introduce a person to a friend in Edinburgh, saying, 'This gentleman *lives* in Ireland,' it will be immediately understood, that though he may have been for some time in Scotland, he has not fixed his residence there. Should I say, 'This is a gentleman who *lived* in Ireland,' my friend will instantly conclude, that wherever he may have fixed his residence, he has removed from Ireland.

Upon the whole, from the representation here given it appears, that most of those strangers intended to return to their own country. Many probable reasons might be given to show this. The disciples are the salt of the earth, and the good seed; it is likely then that God would sprinkle them over the earth, to communicate the savour of his name, and sow them in a wide field, that they might have the greater increase. At all events, they would return to their own countries when persecution arose. At a time when those who were the native inhabitants of Jerusalem were obliged to fly, the strangers could have had no possible inducement to stay. But all that is incumbent on us, is to show that this might have been the case. The solution of the supposed difficulty is good, so long as the supposition is not positively contradicted by Scripture testimony.

As to the five thousand mentioned (Acts iv. 4), it lies upon you positively to prove that this was not the sum total of all the disciples. If such a thing is possible, it is enough for us. But that this is actually the fact, I think is most probable, although it could not injure us upon any supposition. It is not said that the number of those who believed on that occasion was about five thousand, but that "many who heard them at that time believed; and the number of the men *became* about five thousand." Had the narrator intended to relate the exact number that day converted, there was no reason for him to tell it both generally and particularly. Besides, it is not ειμι, the verb, that denotes simple existence, that is here used; but γινομαι, which denotes a commencing existence. Not the number *was*, but the number *became* or *began to be* about five thousand. On that occasion, many of the hearers believed, which so increased their number, that they now amounted to about five thousand.

As to the use of ανηρ, I acknowledge the distinction between this and ανθρωπος. The distinction is always observed when speaking of one sex, in opposition to, or in contrast with the other. Whenever there is anything in the narration, that could present to the mind the distinction of sex, this distinction, in the use of these two words, is demanded by accuracy. But when no circumstance of sex is intended to be brought into view, ανηρ is frequently used as generally as ανθρωπος. See Luke xi. 31, 32; Matt. vii. 24, 26; Acts v. 36;

James i. 20; Rom. iv. 8, &c. It is quite enough for us then that it can be so used; we have not to show that it must of necessity have such a signification here. To serve your purpose, it must be shown that the word never can be so used. Besides, there is this reason that it should here include both men and women; for as to the disciples of our Lord Jesus Christ, there is neither male nor female. What purpose would it serve to give us an account of the male disciples only? Why should the females be of so little estimation as not to be included? Was it a matter of great importance to inform us of the number of the male disciples, but a matter of no importance whether any females believed the Gospel? This would be contrary to the practice of the evangelists, who take full as much notice of the females as of the males. As to the miracle of feeding the multitude recorded in the Gospels, there is a sufficient reason for mentioning the women and children separate from the men, because they were but few in proportion. Men-children are also distinguished from the men for the same reasons. There might be also a view to the superior quantity of food necessary for men, to show the true extent of the miracle. But in reckoning the disciples of our Lord Jesus Christ, there can no good reason be given, why the females should not be as particularly noticed as the males. Five thousand then is the highest calculation you can demand with certainty; and I defy you to prove positively, that at any one time afterwards, they are said to exceed this number. All the after additions cannot be an equal increase of the number, because there is a possibility many ways of the former number being greatly lessened. Before you can bring the circumstance of the number of the disciples at Jerusalem as an objection to their constituting one church, you must prove that it was such that they could not possibly meet together either in the house or in the fields.

We come now to consider your observations on the dispersion, which took place upon the death of Stephen. Here also we stand on the defensive. If such a thing as a general dispersion were possible, your objection as to the supposed numbers, is not of force. Although you should succeed in proving, that a general dispersion could not be necessarily inferred from this account, you can never prove that the words will not bear this meaning; nay, that the most obvious import of the words does not require it. But your argument falls to the ground, unless you can show that the words will not admit a general dispersion.

It is not necessary that I should say more on this subject, than barely to show that it cannot be determined from this narrative, that the dispersion which it relates *was not general*. But I will undertake to prove to the satisfaction of any unprejudiced judge, that, from the account here given, *it must have been general*.

With respect to Mr. Robertson's observation upon the word ημερα, it will be found to be a distinction unsanctioned by the Greek language. Both this, and *day*, the corresponding word in English, frequently mean time indefinitely. The difference in the use of the phrases εν εκεινη τη ημερα and εν εκειναις ταις ημεραις, is not that the latter includes a longer portion of indefinite time, but that it points out more indefinitely the date of the commencement of that period. Had Luke here used the phrase εν εκειναις ταις ημεραις, or κατ' εκεινον τον καιρον, the period of the continuation of the persecution would not thereby be proved to have been longer, but the commencement of it would have had a more indefinite date assigned to it. From the phrase here used, we have the date of the commencement of the persecution precisely determined. It began exactly at the death of Stephen, not about it. The truth is, the phrase used does not determine in any respect, nor was it designed to determine, the period of the continuation of the persecution, but merely the date of its commencement. The narrator has no design to inform us, nor could he by any of these phrases have informed us of the time this persecution lasted. Translate it as literally as possible, it makes nothing against our sense of the narrative. "Upon that day there arose a great persecution, against (or upon) the church which was at Jerusalem." The duration of the persecution might, as far as the word ημερα is concerned, have been one hour or fifty years. The length of that period must be determined from other circumstances. Now γινομαι is the verb which is used to modify *the existence.* It is not simply said there *was,* but there *began to be,* &c. If then it is said that a persecution began on such a day, it is a very plain intimation that it did not cease on that day.

Your second argument is, that it was not all the church that was scattered, but only the ministers. This however, plainly contradicts the inspired penman; for he expressly says, that they were all scattered abroad except the apostles. Now, the excepting of the apostles plainly shows, that the narrator meant to be precise. I have already shown, that the word church could not be employed to denote the representatives of a particular congregation, even had the constitution been Presbyterian, in any other than a figurative sense, and that it could not be applied either literally or figuratively to the rulers of many congregations, for in no sense are they a church. You must overthrow that reasoning, or the matter is settled. Upon the passage in question, however, I will make a few additional remarks. The word church, it cannot be denied, even by Presbyterians, primarily and properly signifies a congregation of saints. It cannot be applied in its figurative meaning, but upon this supposition. Now it is said here, in the language of plain narrative, "There arose at that time a great persecution *upon the church, the church which was at Jerusalem.*" Here the word church is evidently used in its literal and appropriated signification. The narrator mentions *the* church, as if it were a well known thing of which he wrote. He particularizes it—*the church at Jerusalem.*

But the church at Jerusalem cannot mean the ministers alone of that city, seeing these could not be called so even figuratively, but as they represented the church. Now, though the church rulers, met in council, might figuratively be called by the name of their constituents, yet they could not, even figuratively, get that name in bearing persecution; for in this, they do not represent the church. It was no part of their official duty, which they performed in name of that body. I contend then, that, even granting the system of representation, and the propriety of figurative language upon such an occasion, church cannot be here used for church rulers by the boldest figure imaginable.

But, according to you, it must not be the church rulers of a congregation, but of several congregations, who are meant. This signification it could not have upon any terms. Besides, the Presbyterian interpretation of this passage supposes, that it was the ministers alone who were dispersed, not the lay-elders. Now, the ministers, without the lay-elders, could not, even by Presbyterians, be called the church. The lay-elders are representatives as well as the ministers. Nay, the ministers cannot be representatives of the laity at all, for on that supposition they would act in a double capacity. They would both represent the laity and themselves. At all events, if church rulers are called the church because they represent the church, by what rule of criticism do you exclude the lay-elders? Again, according to you, the church at Jerusalem consisted of different congregations. Now, if all the congregations of Jerusalem were called a church, or *the Church of Jerusalem*, when the persecution is said to be against that church, it must mean all those congregations. Allowing it possible to be figuratively given to their rulers, a figure cannot be supposed where the literal meaning will answer. The circumstances and connection must necessarily demand such a figure, before it is lawful to have recourse to it. Besides, the expression, *the church which is at Jerusalem*, plainly supposes that there was nothing in that city which among Christians bore that name, but one determinate assembly. Had this been the appropriated name for all the congregations united, it could not have been appropriated to any one of them. I defy you to produce in language any such ambiguity. Were all the Christians of Jerusalem the church at Jerusalem? Could what is said here be literally applicable to the whole? Is this a thing in which they could have been personally concerned? If it must be answered in the affirmative, would it be proper in the inspired penman to relate a thing in language literally applicable to the whole church, relating a fact which might have happened to the whole, while at the same time he only means it of a very small part of that church? But this is not only a fact which might have happened to the church itself, but it is one which could not happen to them in the person of others.

But the matter is put beyond controversy by the word παντες *all.* "At that time there was a great persecution against the church which was at Jerusalem, and those who composed it were *all* scattered abroad," &c. Whatever constituted the church at Jerusalem, is here said to be all scattered, the apostles excepted. The ministers could not be the whole of the church. Suppose even that they were not said to have been scattered, but to have been assembled to transact business for their constituents, it could not be said they were all the church. Although it might be said in high rhetorical language, 'Great Britain met to consider such a question,' meaning that the Parliament met, it could not be said that all, or all the individuals of Great Britain met. But there can be nothing more completely absurd than to suppose any figure in the simplicity of narrative. What would any man think of the historian who should write thus, 'Oliver Cromwell dispersed Great Britain, or all Great Britain?' meaning that he dispersed the Parliament. What then I ask was the church at Jerusalem? Did the ministers alone compose this church? This is all that the Roman Pontiff professes to demand. But if the whole body of Christians in that city constituted the church, of the body in general it is affirmed, that they were scattered.

With respect to the occurrence of the word in the third verse, I deduce from it the very contrary conclusion from what you have done. I have already shown that this conduct of Saul was not subsequent, but antecedent to the dispersion. But whether it was the one or the other, the word church, according to every rule of interpretation, must have the same meaning in the third, that it hath in the first verse. The historian is evidently speaking of the same object, at least the same kind of object. It is not possible that the inspired writer should be guilty of such absurdity as to use the same word in two such different senses, in the same narrative, in the compass of three verses. He tells us in the first verse, that there was a great persecution against *the church*. He tells us in the third, that Paul made havoc *of the church*. Could he intend two sorts of churches? Though it should not have been the same individuals, surely it must have been the same kind of church. If a Presbyterian were to use the words, 'There was a great persecution against the congregation,' would any one understand him to mean that the persecution was only against the minister, or ministers. If he would add, 'such a one made great havoc of the congregation,' would any one understand he spoke of two different kinds of congregations? Though it were allowed that the church which Paul persecuted was composed of different individuals from that spoken of in the first verse, it must still be of the same kind. It must mean those converted by the apostle's subsequent labours. Besides, why should it be thought that there was no persecution against any but the ministers, when Saul is said to have dragged to prison men and even women. Surely the latter were not church officers.

Your third observation is, "That the word $διεσπαρη\sigma αν$ does not imply that they were dispersed in consequence of very violent persecution, but only in allusion to the command of Christ, 'when they persecute you in this city, flee ye to the next,' that $διασκ orπιζω$ would have denoted a more violent persecution." This, Sir, I look upon to be unsound criticism. The violence of the persecution is not to be gathered from the word used to denote the dispersion, whether it was the one or the other. This must be determined by what is really testified, and from the effects attributed to it. Neither the one nor the other of these words necessarily imply a dispersion by violence, and both may equally be applied to a dispersion effected by the most violent means. Whether a dispersion is forced or voluntary, must be known by the cause to which it is attributed.

This must be the case with every word that signifies to scatter, in every language. When I say, after the rising of a session of college, 'that the students are now widely dispersed through many countries,' it will be easy to see that I do not mean that they were dispersed by violence. I do not attribute their dispersion to a violent cause; nay, the cause is so obvious I do not assign it at all. But when we read in the Newspapers, 'The Russians were defeated in the battle of Austerlitz, and are dispersed in all directions,' would any man, with one scruple of common sense, understand the writer to mean that their dispersion was voluntary? The dispersion of an army, stated in connection with a battle, necessarily attributes the dispersion to a defeat. As to the point in hand, we are left at no loss about the cause of their dispersion. "There was *a great persecution* against the church which was at Jerusalem, and they were all scattered abroad." Is not the dispersion expressly attributed to the persecution? The critic who would look out for another cause of the dispersion, if I could not make some allowance for the blindness of prejudice, and the eagerness to support a falling church, I would really consider as labouring under some mental debility.

As to Mr. Robertson's distinction between the meaning and the use of $\diaspeiro$ and $\diaskorpizo$, it is not founded either in the composition or application of these two words. There is not the smallest degree of inherent violence in the one more than in the other. The latter is used often, and among others in the following places, where there is no violence supposed—Matt. xxv. 24; Luke xv. 13; xvi. 1. It is quite childish in Mr. Robertson to show, that $\diaspeiro$ is often used when no great degree of violence has been used. It might be used with equal propriety to express the sowing of seed in a field, and the dispersion of the French nobles at the revolution. Nor would the use of the word $\diaskorpizo$ be a whit more determinate. But it must also be remarked, that though the word $\diaspeiro$ does not always denote a dispersion by persecution or violent means, yet it always includes in it the idea that the scattering spoken of has been effected by some degree of force. It is not necessary indeed that this should be external force; it may be inclination or interest. The dispersion of seed to which this primarily alludes, does not imply violence, but it implies that the seed which has been placed on the field in a separated state, has been forced to occupy that situation by some impelling cause. The degree and kind of force employed is known only by other circumstances. Thus even when I say, 'The bees are dispersed or sown over the heath,' or, 'The cattle are dispersed over the plain,' though I do not mean to attribute this to a violent cause, it yet implies that there has been some cause, some motive that has impelled them to take this situation. The appetite that prompts them to seek for provision, is this impelling cause, and though it is not external, the form of the expression requires this analysis. They are dispersed. What is the dispersing cause? Their appetites.

Mr. Robertson's supposition as to the use of the passive for the middle voice here, is still more grossly unnatural. " It may be further observed," says he, "that in all languages a verb in a passive form may sometimes have a neuter, or, as the Greeks say, a middle signification." It is indeed true, that in all languages a passive verb may be used in circumstances where the middle would have served the purpose, or, in other words, where the agent and the sufferer, or the thing acted upon, are the same; yet this by no means destroys the passive nature of the verb even in that use of it, nor warrants us to say that the passive voice in that instance is the same as the middle voice. This sort of bungling criticism would confound the principles of language, and overwhelm every subject to which it might be applied in inextricable darkness. If one voice is exactly of the same meaning as another, and may at any time be used for it, what purpose do they serve? Why does language recognise them? If they are not a proper means of distinction, why is language loaded with any but one? No man who understands the genius of language would think of confounding the use of the voices. Although, in certain circumstances, one may come to have the effect of another, or to be used where another might be expected, each has still its own province, and it is only by understanding that province that the process can be traced, by which it comes seemingly out of its own territories. When a young man goes out in the morning, with his dog and gun, if he returns after a little, saying, 'I am wounded,' the family will immediately understand that he means that he has wounded himself. There is no other cause assigned, and the circumstances of his being engaged in fowling, will lead to the conclusion that the agent and the sufferer are the same. He is understood in the same sense as if he had said, 'I have wounded myself.' But shall we say that the passive voice here assumes the signification of the middle, and that 'I am wounded,' is just the same as 'I have wounded myself?' No, verily; the passive voice has here all its essential features, and there is still an agent and a sufferer, though they are the same person. Nor are these expressions, though any of them might be used upon this occasion, exactly of the same import. When he says, 'I am wounded,' he means to call the attention of the hearers to the fact that he is wounded, without any reference to the cause of the wound. When he says, 'I have wounded myself,' he means to inform us, not only that he is wounded, but to prevent us from thinking that another was the cause of it. Again, suppose two persons go out to fight a duel, and after a few minutes a messenger reports, 'Mr. —— is wounded,' we instantly conclude that he has been wounded by his antagonist. The connection of the circumstances forces this conclusion on us without hesitation. Though the cause is not attributed, it is because it is too obvious to be stated. We would laugh at the pedant, who should exercise his critical talents upon a newspaper account of a duel as is here done with respect to the dispersion recorded in Acts. Whenever the passive voice is used in circumstances where there is no adequate external cause alleged expressly, or implied, or taken for granted as sufficiently known, it is then lawful to suppose that the sufferer is the same with the agent; yet even in this situation, the properties of the passive voice are not destroyed, nor its use confounded with that of the middle. But in every circumstance, without exception, in which an adequate external cause is alleged, or from the connection supposed, to this must the cause be attributed. If there were not some regulating principle of this kind, it would be impossible to come at the meaning of any passage. The voices would then not contribute to the precision of language, but to its indistinctness and confusion. There has nothing contributed more to embarrass subjects of religious controversy, than the principles of criticism that the generality of Bible commentators have adopted. They have so much learning as is sufficient to lead them into difficulties that would never occur to the unlearned reader; yet they seem to have so little understood the genius and principles of language, and its uniform analogies, that they are guided by the most arbitrary rules of interpretation. One word stands for another, one voice for another, &c., just as it suits their purpose. The Scriptures are dragooned, by their figures, to countenance the most absurd fancies. Would any man follow out the principle of this observation of Mr. R. he might defy the precision of every writer to communicate their sentiments with any degree of certainty and perspicuity. The wildest conceits of the most extravagant sects might not only evade the censure, but claim the protection of Scripture. Paul says, "Thrice *was I* beaten with rods." Here, says the bold flagellant, is a sanction for the wholesome discipline of the whip. It is true Paul says, thrice *was I* beaten, but "it may be observed, that in all languages a verb in a passive form may sometimes have a neuter, or, as the Greeks speak, a middle signification." Here then, '*I was beaten*,' signifies, '*I beat myself*.' Now, it is evident, if the great apostle Paul inflicted this severe discipline upon himself, it is equally necessary for us. Hence it is evident that the substance of true religion consists in flagellation. 'Lord Nelson *was slain* in the battle of Trafalgar.' But a cautious critic replies, 'Take care how you nnderstand the writer. This by no means necessarily signifies that Lord Nelson was killed in consequence of the fire of his enemy. As the passive verb sometimes assumes a middle signification, it may also be understood to mean, that Lord Nelson *killed himself*.' Is this ridiculous? Not more so than the supposition, that the dispersion spoken of in Acts viii. 1, was not caused by the persecution. 'There was a great battle—the Russians are dispersed.' 'But we must not conclude from this, that the defeat was the cause of this dispersion. It might be quite voluntary. They might have only gone home to recruit themselves for another campaign.' Is this ridiculous? Equally so is your interpretation. The dispersion of the Russians is only stated in connection with the battle, and if we are to understand that the dispersion was caused by a victorious enemy, upon what principle of interpretation is it pretended, that the dispersion of the Christians from Jerusalem was not caused by the persecution stated in connection with it? "There was a great persecution, and they were all dispersed." Is there any supposable cause but the persecution?

The application of the principles already explained, will enable any one to solve your examples from the Septuagint. Λαος διεσπαρη does not literally signify that the people *scattered themselves*, but that *they were scattered*. The command of Pharaoh that they should get no straw, obliged them to be dispersed in gathering stubble. Pharaoh's commands dispersed them. The same analysis will apply to your other examples, and any instances that can possibly be alleged.

Would it ever enter the mind of any sober writer to suppose, that the persecution was only a signal to depart; or that they dispersed rather in obedience to the command of Jesus, than from the violence of the persecution? This very command of our Lord was designed to be put in execution only when persecution should be so violent that they could not stand it. It was never understood that to obey it, the disciples were obliged to leave a city upon the smallest opposition or persecution. Had this been the case, the Gospel never could have taken root in any place, for they were not long without opposition when they entered into a city.*
If this was the meaning of our Lord's command, the apostles paid no regard to it; for they always re-

---

* Were this the spirit of the precept, Christians would be as unsettled in their habitations as the *Erimites*. They would not lodge, perhaps, during their lives, two nights in one house, or in one city.

mained as long as they possibly could; till persecution arose to the most dangerous height. Often they did not go before they were stoned and scourged. The spirit of the precept is, that the disciples of Jesus should rather fly than fight. When they cannot remain in any place with the safety of their lives, they are at liberty to fly somewhere else; not to form any combinations to defend themselves, like the men of the world. How unnatural is every feature in this analysis How unlike the reasoning of a man who has entered into the genius of the Christian religion! Every line of the picture is distorted.

But that the persecution was the cause of the dispersion, is absolutely said—Acts xi. 19. "They that were scattered abroad *by* or *from* the persecution that arose about Stephen." Not only are they said to be dispersed, but to be dispersed by a cause assigned, and that cause is the persecution. Three times the passive form of the verb is used, speaking of this dispersion—Acts viii. 1, 4; xi. 19. Must it, in any occurrence, be understood in a middle sense? But the preposition $\alpha\pi o$ completely assigns the persecution as the cause of the dispersion. 'They were dispersed—cause of their dispersion, the persecution.' Would any honest interpreter ever look for another cause, when the Holy Spirit here ascribes one both sufficient and obvious. Add to this, that if it be supposed that they dispersed themselves voluntarily, it is not at all likely that the pastors, more especially all the pastors, and these alone, should desert the flock. Can any man assign a reason why all pastors in Jerusalem should, without any violence offered to them, leave the flock over which the Holy Ghost had made them overseers, for the purpose of preaching elsewhere? Besides, this persecution is expressly called a great persecution. Why then should it not be thought to have caused the disciples to fly? But how curiously is this accounted for by Mr. R. as quoted by you in a note. "This persecution, moreover, might be styled a great persecution, which for a time deprived the saints at Jerusalem of so many faithful pastors," p. 256. Yes; but it was not a great persecution against the pastors, but a great persecution against *the church*.

But this is self-contradiction. He argued before, that the persecution was not the cause of the dispersion, but a signal to disperse. Here he allows that it was a great persecution, because it deprived the saints at Jerusalem of so many faithful pastors. Now, had it been only a signal to depart, it could not have been the acknowledged cause of the dispersion. If I have a friend in a distant country, whom I appoint to meet me at a certain place, the signal for our setting out being the first grand engagement between the French and the Prussians, my family could not say that it was a great battle, because it deprived them for a long time of my society. This was only the signal, not the cause of my leaving home. But the truth will frequently come out upon the cross-examination of the witness. It is very difficult to be consistent in attempting to impose such a series of ridiculous solutions on the Scriptures. Never was there a more complete contradiction between two accounts of a transaction, than that of the Acts of the Apostles, and Mr. Robertson's. One of them is certainly false. There is scarcely a common line between the original, and the pretended picture. I have however reaped this one advantage from it: I have seen how far the desire of supporting an established system will contribute to choke the plainest dictates of common sense, when they stand opposed to its pretensions. I have seen that men are capable of endeavouring to force the Word of God to countenance the wildest fancies; but it is a mournful picture of human nature.

Upon the whole, it appears that, according to the literal, and natural, and necessary signification of the words, not the ministers alone, but the general body of disciples at Jerusalem, were dispersed on this occasion. On your part, you cannot pretend that your interpretation is as obvious from the words, or that it is as literal as ours. You have, as usual, to turn the account into figures, search for causes of the dispersion, not assigned or suggested in the narrative, while that which is assigned is refused; to suppose the same word variously used to the most opposite objects, in the same connection, and substitute perpetually one voice for another, &c. With us, everything is natural; with you, everything is forced. A very child could not be at a loss to know the meaning of the passage according to our interpretation; according to yours, the subtle genius of a Peripatetic Philosopher could scarcely follow your distinctions. Now, for what purpose have you and your friends invented all these extravagant suppositions? Is it to vindicate the character of the Scriptures, and prove them consistent with themselves? No; it is not to solve a difficulty, but to create one. The disciples at Jerusalem are called one church. All these suppositions must be made, not to remove an objection as to the propriety of this denomination, but to raise an objection to it. As I already observed, I was no way obliged by my cause to follow you through these discussions. I might have contented myself by showing that this might have been a general dispersion. Were I to give you credit for all you have attempted to do, to wit, to show that this persecution might not have been general, it would not do you the smallest service; as long as the fact of a general dispersion is possible, so long it will be a valid solution. But you have not a refuge to shelter you. You may be driven from every hiding-place. Every shelter you can avail yourself of, is merely a perversion of Scripture.

If then it is proved from the meaning of the word *church*, and the representations given in the Acts of the Apostles, that there was but one congregation of saints at Jerusalem; and if the most natural interpretation of the words of this narrative will obviate your objection from their numbers, would any candid critic refuse to allow the narrative to be understood in its most obvious sense, and acknowledge this as a sufficient removal of the difficulty? It would sufficiently serve our purpose to show that this might possibly have been a general dispersion. But this is not only a possible, it is the plain meaning of the account. To the serious inquirer, no degree of obscurity hangs over the narrative; and as for those who love darkness rather than light, they will never be without a pretext.

The next passage you produce is Acts xxi. 20. Ποσαι μυριαδες, how many myriads! Upon this I remark, in the first place, that whether μυριας be definite or indefinite, it maketh no matter. The Jews here referred to, do not seem to be the Jews of Jerusalem alone, but of the whole nation, as distinguished from the believing Jews among the Gentiles. The proportion of these that might be supposed to be in Jerusalem, it is idle to attempt to estimate, especially for the purpose of founding an argument on the result. Overturn a well authenticated fact by probable calculations! Nothing but a positive account could serve your purpose. All that is incumbent upon us, is to show that it cannot necessarily be inferred that they all belonged to Jerusalem. In the second place, even allowing that those referred to were all at that moment in the city, I adopt and defend the language of Mr. Ewing, quoted by you, p. 259—you by no means invalidate his argument by anything you allege. You say, that "no argument can be adduced from the *number* of those who went up with Paul at this time to Jerusalem, to show that they were travelling thither to observe that solemnity." It is sufficient that this is the most probable errand. It serves us that it may have been the case. As to the numbers being too few for such an occasion, and the foreign Jews not being commanded to attend, the latter of these objections obviates the former. It was their privilege, therefore they came when convenient. It was not their indispensable duty, therefore from the most distant countries, they did not come in great numbers. A few from every direction, would make a great sum total. But had only numbers of the believing Jews of Judea been present, it would have fully justified the expression contained in Acts xxi. 20.

You say, that it has been questioned by the Westminster Assembly, whether Paul arrived at Jerusalem before the day of Pentecost. Their questioning it signifies nothing. We are expressly informed of his design to be there on that occasion, and of his haste on that account. There is every reason to suppose that he would not be disappointed. Can you prove, however, the contrary? Nothing less will serve you. In the third place, whether the believing Jews of Jerusalem alone, or of all Judea, or of all the world, are referred to, the word μυριας is equally with μυριοι used indefinitely. It is evident, even from the occasion and the intention of the speaker, that this word is not designed to intimate the precise amount of the numbers referred to. The design is, not to acquaint Paul with the exact number of believing Jews either in one place or another, but simply from consideration of the great numbers, to show the necessity of the conduct afterwards recommended. He adds, " The multitude will come together."

It is not said that there are such a number of μυριαδες, but ποσαι, how many? appealing to the knowledge of Paul himself. As we would say in English, ' consider, brother, how many, or what multitudes,' &c. Your observation upon the difference between μυριοι and μυριας is not well founded. What should make the one of these definite and the other indefinite? The only difference between them is, that the one is the substantive, and the other the adjective. They are both used sometimes definitely, and sometimes indefinitely, just as we use such a round number for a great number, whether it is more or less. Μυριοι is used Matt. xviii. 24, as μυριας Acts xix. 19. Yea, in each of the places which you quote, Acts xix. 19, excepted, μυριας is indefinite. Your observation, that if it is indefinite, it is used in these places for nothing less than its intrinsic amount, proves nothing. The very circumstance of its being an indefinite word of number, will make it go as far beyond the mark, or fall on this side of it. When Mr. Ewing contends that it is indefinite, and may be applied to any great number, when the speaker does not mean to convey exact information, he will as readily grant that it may be extended to a number ten thousand times its original amount. As an indefinite word of number, it may be, and is applied to the whole hosts of heaven, and all the redeemed on earth. But understand it as you will, you will find that it is applied in the plural number (Luke xii. 1), to the multitudes attending the preaching of Jesus. But how many soever the numbers of the disciples of Jerusalem at this time might have been, we are sure that they could meet, because, it is actually said on this occasion, that "the multitudes must needs come together."

You say, such large numbers could not be accommodated with a house. Why should not an area or court serve the purpose? What multitudes meet on certain occasions in the woods of America, and continue whole days, and even weeks on the place. Rate them at even the extravagant number of 30,000, still they might have met. If I were asked how they could enjoy ordinances, my answer is ready. If they really amounted to so many, they must have met, for they are called a church, the multitude is spoken of as coming together, and they are everywhere in the Acts represented as meeting in one assembly. But why should we suppose that they were so numerous that they could not meet in a house, seeing *the many myriads* here referred to, are not necessarily applicable to the Christians of Jerusalem?* And why should they be supposed to meet without, seeing the temple could contain such vast multitudes? You desire us to prove that they had the liberty of using the temple. We know that they enjoyed the temple till the death of Stephen, and it does not lie upon us to prove that they still had it, but upon you positively to prove that they had it not. But, for my part, as long as a field will hold them, I do not think it necessary to join you in measuring Solomon's porch, or the temple, or any other building in Jerusalem.

You think it very strange in Mr. Ewing, that he will not allow the Christians in Jerusalem to have amounted at any one period to the vast numbers alleged by Presbyterians, in order to defend Christianity against infidels. Indeed, Sir, Christianity needs no such rotten

---

* There can be nothing more obvious than that Acts xxi. 20, refers to the Jewish Christians of all Judea. The conduct enforced upon the apostle from the consideration of the numbers of believing Jews, would be equally prudent and necessary on account of the believing Jews throughout all Judea, as well as those of Jerusalem. The Jews in every part of that country, would soon be informed of Paul's conduct on this occasion. I am then not at all concerned about the satisfactoriness of any other solution. I support the other suppositions, merely to show that your criticism fails in every item of the series.

props as exaggeration. If this were a criterion of a divine religion, Christianity would not have the highest pretensions. While we rejoice most heartily in the success of the Gospel in Jerusalem, we do not think it proper to contradict the Scriptures, either to humour Presbyterians, or to silence infidels. And we are just as much concerned for the success of the Gospel in every other place. I am afraid that there are some who are anxious to heighten the numbers of Christians in Jerusalem, rather to support an hypothesis, than to increase the kingdom of the Redeemer. The Gospel has now been preached upwards of seventeen hundred years; perhaps there are not in the world seventeen cities (are there seven?), the Christians in which could not stand within the compass of the human voice. Besides, it must seldom happen that nearly all the members are present at one meeting.

LETTER IX.

Sir,

Your sixteenth letter continues the subject of the preceding. That there must have been a plurality of congregations in Jerusalem, you think is evident, "from the number of ministers who, for a very considerable time, were continually employed in labouring in that city." As the fact could establish nothing were it proved, for the same number of members would need nearly the same number of labourers, whether in one congregation or many; but especially, as it rests on Apocryphal authority, I do not consider it my duty to waste my time with the hypothesis. That there were very many labourers in that city, I have no doubt; that the seventy disciples at first sent out by our Lord were continually resident in Jerusalem, is neither recorded, nor is at all probable. For I think with you, that "it cannot be believed that so many labourers would have statedly resided at Jerusalem, while the rest of the world was so destitute of religious instruction." Besides, this was not the purpose for which they were chosen, but to carry the glad news through the cities and villages of Judea. What was the number of teachers in Jerusalem, we have no sufficient documents to prove.

You say, that the same thing is evident from the diversity of languages of the Christians at Jerusalem. To refute this, I need only say that, if the strangers mentioned were any time resident in that city, though they might not be able themselves to speak the common language with fluency, they would sufficiently understand it when spoken. Accordingly, on the day of Pentecost (Acts ii.), Peter addresses the whole multitude in the same language. You answer by anticipation, that "before this be of force, it must be demonstrated that Peter spake to them *at once* in the *same language.*" The demonstration of the contrary lies upon you. This, as I have shown, is agreeable to universal experience, with respect to strangers resident on business in large commercial towns. This also is the plain and obvious import of the narrative, and the only thing that would present itself naturally to the mind of the reader. That they were all addressed at the same time in the same words, is as clear as language can convey a meaning. Verse 14—" But Peter standing up with the eleven, lift up his voice, and said unto them, ye men of Judea, and *all ye that dwell at Jerusalem,* be this known unto you, and hearken to my words." Here it is evident, that the whole multitude were addressed *at once* in *the same language.* As to the supposition, that Peter "might have spoken to each of them in order, in their respective languages, as is evident the apostles did, verses 5, 6," there is not room for it in the narrative; verse 14, is too precise to admit it. Whereas, in the other case, we have certain intimation that every man heard them speak in his own language. This then must necessarily have been either from different speakers at the same time, in different parts of the house, or at different times. But in the 14th verse, Peter addresses the whole multitude in the same language. But you forget yourself; if the apostles addressed the different nations at different times, in fifteen or twenty languages, all in one assembly, could not the same thing take place in all the other meetings of the saints? Though it were even granted that Peter did not address these different nations all at the same time and in the same language, yet he spoke to each of them in the presence of all, which is all that is necessary for our purpose. From verses 5, 6, this must certainly have been the case, at the time the multitude came together. Indeed it is extremely reasonable to suppose, that as there were continually strangers coming from other countries, they would generally interpret, at least if the language spoken at Jerusalem was not commonly understood by foreigners. Such a direction is given to the church at Corinth. When one should speak in an unknown tongue, those who did not understand it, were not to separate themselves and form a new church, or even to leave the assembly during the time; another was to interpret. We know that this is actually the case with some of the travelling preachers in the Methodist connection in Ireland. They speak in Irish, and interpret in English, or *vice versa.* While this is so obvious, I do not think it necessary to fatigue my readers with more upon the subject.

You come next to consider some of the passages which represent the disciples at Jerusalem as meeting in one place. Upon Acts ii. 41–47, you observe, " Though it were granted that the church at this time, when it was comparatively small, met in one assembly, it would not follow that it could meet in one place, when it was much larger." Indeed, Sir, it does not need the penetration of Sir Isaac Newton to discover, that when a church becomes so numerous that they cannot meet in one place, they would like the bees divide, and form a second church. But when this should be the case, they would be no longer the same church, no longer the church at Jerusalem, but the churches at Jerusalem. We should then, from that period forward, have heard no more of their meeting for worship, &c., in one place, but have had the history and transactions of each. But it is not more clearly stated here that they met in one place, than it is when their numbers were the greatest. Why then do you come down so far as to make this supposition in this case more than in others? Not because it is more clearly stated that they met in one place at this period, but because you think you could make a shift at this time without the division.

But if this will not serve your purpose, you have another resource at hand. You are determined by all means to carry your point. You will silence the plainest evidence the Spirit of God can give. Like the cuttle-fish, when you are in danger of becoming a prey to your antagonist, you will render the water muddy that you may escape him. I could not have thought it possible that any critic could have been so disingenuous, as to use the sophistry, perversion and evasion contained in the following reasoning. " Besides, all that is mentioned in this passage is, that, from the love which subsisted among these primitive converts, they were frequently together, and cultivated eagerly each other's society. But to this it was not necessary that they should statedly meet in one great assembly. And though we are told moreover, in this and other places, that they assembled in the temple, it cannot be proved from this fact, that they convened in one congregation even to hear the word, for, as was before observed, the temple contained a variety of places, each of which could conveniently accommodate a congregation."—p. 273.

Leaving out of view the reverence that is due to the words of the Holy Spirit, a candid critic would be ashamed to offer such violence to the text of Aristotle. Indeed I cannot say more plainly that I believe them to have met in one place, than this Scripture assures me that they did. I despair of convincing the writer who is capable of defending his hypothesis in such a manner. Let the Christian of the most ordinary talents read the passage with a teachable spirit, and I have no doubt of the result. I can easily see how a Christian, through weakness, prejudice, or neglect of examination, may be attached to the Presbyterian system of church-government. But to wrest the words of God in a manner palpably contrary to their intention ———
———! As long as a writer uses argument, he should be refuted; but when, through a whole treatise, in defence of every part of a whole system, there is one perversion of Scripture after another, it is very difficult, if not improper, to repress indignation.

You hint in a note that the Greek words, $\epsilon\pi\iota\ \tau o\ a\nu\tau o$, might be otherwise translated than by *together*. Though you are not the only critic who has said so, it is altogether without any just foundation, either in the analysis of the elliptical expression, or in the practice of the language. There is not an instance, so far as I know, in all the New Testament or Septuagint, in which it has another meaning. See Matt. xxii. 34; Acts i. 15; Acts iii. 1; 1 Cor. vii. 5; xiv. 23. Nor is there one instance you quote upon the authority of Lightfoot, in which it has not the same meaning. Jeremiah, vi. 12, represents their houses, fields, and wives, as *together* passing to strangers. In 2 Sam. ii. 13, if *together* be only referred to David's servants, it represents them as sitting together on one bank of the pool. But I see no reason why it should not mean the meeting together of both parties, for they were really together when so near each other as to be able to converse. Psal. xxxiv. 3, is an exhortation to people joined together in one worshipping assembly, to praise God. Psal. xlix. 2, represents the rich and poor as *together* addressed by the Psalmist. He is addressing the whole world upon a subject equally interesting to the rich and to the poor. Psal. ii. 2, represents the Jewish rulers as *met together* in consultation against our Lord Jesus Christ. But I am at a loss to know what you mean by this supposed possible alteration. How do you think should it be translated? If you are really convinced that the translation is faulty, why do you not propose what appears to you to be a more just translation? This, however, you do not attempt. You content yourself by referring to different meanings of the phrase according to Lightfoot, without discovering a preference to any one of them that is different from the common one. You must be conscious, that any other way of translating the passage would be here perfectly ridiculous, and therefore you have done no more than to state other possible ways of understanding it, leaving your reader to choose any one but the common one. I say, but the common one, for if you wished your reader to adopt this, there was no occasion for hinting at others. Your scope seems to be, that, as the phrase is supposed to be capable of different meanings, the common one can be less certainly relied on. Like the disguised papal emissaries, your object is gained when you have succeeded in rendering the meaning of Scripture uncertain. There will be then room for the Presbyterian acceptation, as the others make way for papal infallibility. But I cannot understand what you mean by "an assembly in different places." An assembly may be separated by a wall, or by a river, &c., yet being met together for common business, they are not in different places in any sense that could serve you. If people are met in different apartments in the same house for worship, &c., they are not one assembly, when each company is separately engaged. They are then many assemblies. On the other hand, if they are unitedly engaged, our hypothesis would not suffer, though they should occupy as many apartments as there are cells in a honey-comb.

As to the possibility of their meeting in different congregations in the temple, I think you must have found yourself greatly galled when you had recourse to this expedient. If the apartments of the temple were so large, that each of them could ' conveniently accommodate a congregation,' much more would the great courts in which such multitudes of Jews met for united worship, contain the most numerous assembly. But nothing can be more unnatural than the supposition, that they met in separate assemblies for distinct worship. When it is said that "they continued daily with one mind in the temple," the very design of the Spirit of God in giving the account, is evidently to show their meeting together, and union in one place. Nothing could justify a contrary interpretation, had it not been directly afterwards said, that they met in different congregations for distinct worship and discipline, in different apartments of the temple. As to the circumstance of the different congregations of the High Church of Glasgow, it could not be said of them, that ' they continue every Sabbath, with one mind, in the High Church.' What would be the meaning of ὁμοθυμαδὸς in such a case? How could they be said to be in such a place *in one mind*, when they are in different apartments, having no more connection with each other than with the congregations in the Hebrides. The congregations of the High Church are never said to meet together, nor are they ever represented as one assembly. It might as well be said of the inhabitants of the different floors of the highest house in Edinburgh, that 'they all live in one house, in one mind.' Now, according to your mode of interpretation, a traveller returning to his country from visiting Glasgow or Edinburgh, might assure his countrymen, that ' it was a very common thing for several hundred individuals to live in the same house with the greatest harmony.' Would it not be concluded by those who were unacquainted with these places, that they were actually in the same family? He would really be a lying traveller; and although, when detected, he might use your sophistry, and reply, that though he had said that they lived in one house, he did not say that they lived together as the same family, I doubt if sound morality would excuse him. When people are said to live in the same house, it is understood that they live as one family, unless the contrary is intimated. The very language then which would be pronounced a falsehood among men, you without scruple put into the mouth of the Holy Ghost. When the disciples are said to continue in the temple *in one mind*, it supposes that they have an intercourse, and such an intercourse as among the men of the world would lead to *different minds* and to disputes. Such language could mean nothing when applied to the different congregations of the High Church, except perhaps that they manifest such a Christian spirit that they do not abuse each other, like the mob at a contested country election, nor jostle each other as they pass and repass at the great door. But in this case, it would not be, ' they continue in the High Church,' but ' they go in and out of the High Church in one mind.'

You add, page 273, "Still, however, Mr. Ewing contends that his assertion is confirmed by Acts v. 12, 13, where it is said, that ' by the hands of the apostles were many signs and wonders wrought among the people ; (and they were all with one accord in Solomon's porch : and of the rest durst no man join himself unto them : but the people magnified them).' But before any argument from this can be conclusive, he must prove that by *the all* who were in Solomon's porch, are intended, not the apostles alone as distinguished from the people, but the whole body of Christian converts. That it was the apostles alone, is probable from the connection of the passage. The same fear which fell upon the multitude in general, and which for a time kept them at a distance from the apostles, is asserted in the 11th verse, to have fallen equally upon the whole church, and, we may naturally suppose, would produce upon them a similar effect. But if the rest of the church, as well as the multitude, durst not for a time join themselves to the apostles, is it not obvious, that it must have been the apostles alone who are said to have been all in Solomon's porch?"

That by the *all* who are here said to be in Solomon's porch, is intended the whole body of the disciples, no reader would think of questioning, if it did not stand in the way of his hypothesis. Let the plain Christian read over the passage, and he will find no difficulty to make him pause for a moment; and the plainest and most obvious meaning of Scripture is always the true meaning, except it contradicts reason, or the general tenor of revelation. The Scriptures were designed for the use of persons of the plainest understanding; therefore, though there may be grammatical incorrectness sufficient to offend the delicacy of a fastidious critic, it is never such but the scope of the passage will explain itself. In such cases as this, the half-learned critic is in most danger of going astray. While *he* is hunting after curious solutions, the plain Christian easily finds the true one, from the general spirit and substance of the passage.

That the word *all* here refers to the disciples in general, as well as to the apostles, is obvious from several reasons.

1. For what purpose would the disciples be alone in Solomon's porch? It is no answer to this that Peter and John are said to go up to the temple together, without any other company. They might go thither for the purpose of joining in the temple worship; and though they went up alone, they were not in the temple alone. They had many to hear the Gospel. But in Solomon's porch they could not be, for the sake of the Jewish worship, nor, if they were alone, for the purpose of preaching either to the disciples or to the people. Had it been a private meeting, like others recorded, it would have been in a private room. When a dozen of friends wish to enjoy each others company for a few hours, they are not likely to meet at the market-cross. Public meetings only need be held in public buildings, or places of public concourse. Their meeting in

Solomon's porch clearly proves that it was a public meeting, open not only to the disciples, but to all who chose to attend.

2. Had there been none present but the apostles, I do not think that the word παντες, *all*, would have been added; not but that three may be as properly all as three thousand; but because there is no business related as having been transacted, to make the circumstance of *all* the apostles being present a matter worthy of notice. When it is said, Acts i. 14, "These all continued with one accord," &c., they are represented as living together in that apartment, not merely meeting together for an hour or two in a place of public resort. The apostles are here represented as residing with many others. These circumstances make it necessary emphatically to call our attention to the consideration that the persons alluded to lived together. *They all* lived together. But I cannot see the purpose of telling us that the apostles were *all* in Solomon's porch, when they are not said to be engaged in anything to justify this emphasis. On the other hand, it is a matter of importance to inform us, that all the disciples were together, because, among other ends, it settles this dispute.

3. Had the apostles been alone, I do not see the propriety of their being said to be in that place, ομοθυμαδον, *of one mind*, when there is nothing recorded which could have given rise to disagreement. They are not represented as met for any public business. It is not said, that in conference they *were of one mind*, but that they were all in one place *with one mind*. Now, had this been their place of residence, the word ομοθυμαδον would have a proper meaning, though none but the apostles had been together. But if it were only a place where they were alone for a short time, without being said to have been engaged in any public or intricate business, what could provoke them to have been of many minds? Such a thing would not be worthy of a particular emphasis. But it is a matter of much importance, and well worthy of being recorded by the Holy Spirit, that a multitude of disciples, some of whom might formerly have been pests to society, and

have lived in revelling and drunkenness, or in hostile sects and sentiments, were all *in one place*, and *of one mind*. It shows us plainly, that when there is not unanimity, there is so far a want of conformity to the churches planted by the apostles. Harmony in such a multitude would indeed be a wonderful thing among the people of the world. It requires all the authority of the magistrates, sometimes with the aid of military force, to keep order in worldly assemblies for public business. I think something like this has happened at settlements of ministers among you; nay, even in the General Assembly—*vide* Debates in Mr. Leslie's business.

When the apostles are represented, Acts i. 14, as ομοθυμαδον, it is in company with the other disciples, and not in a meeting of a few hours, but in a place of usual residence, where disturbance and jealousies would be most likely to arise among worldly men.

You observe, that the same fear which kept the multitude from joining the apostles, came also upon the church, and would be likely to have had the same effects upon them. Why do you think so, Sir? There is nothing less probable. An awful sense of the omniscience and justice of God, did indeed, as it always ought to do, fill the minds of believers. But this was by no means of the same kind with the fear of the wicked, nor would it have at all the same effects. You know, Sir, there is everywhere in Scripture a distinction between the fear of God as influencing Christians, and the fear of wicked men, justly dreading his vengeance. The former leads to watchfulness against offending God; the latter leads to hatred and desperation. The latter is a just anticipation of hell; the former is a word denoting the whole of religion. When children see an instance of their father's displeasure against an offence of a servant, they should be filled with an increasing sense of his just severity, and be induced to avoid more strictly every occasion of offending him. But this is quite different from the fear of wicked servants, when they see one of their fellows punished, if they are still determined to act improperly. Their fear does not make them abhor the crime, but the master. This is exactly the fear of the wicked. They see God's displeasure at sin. They know they deserve it, but they are determined to persist; therefore they are still more filled with fear and abhorrence of God. This fear then that came upon the church, instead of driving the believers from the society of the apostles, would bind them closer to them. They would the more fear to offend God, but not to approach his servants. This sort of fear of man would be more suitable to the superstition of the dark ages, than to the enlightened devotion of Christians in the times and presence of the apostles. But,

4. It is not said that either the crowd or the disciples were afraid to enter the porch with the apostles. The contrary is clear with respect to both. The part of the narrative in which this parenthetical circumstance is contained, gives an account of many signs and wonders performed by the hands of the apostles *among the people.* Now, Sir, could this have been the case, if the apostles had been alone in Solomon's porch? Not only then must the disciples have been present, but many others also. When it is said, " *and of the rest* durst no man join himself to them," it does not mean *the rest of the church,* but of unbelievers; and when it is said, " They durst not *join themselves* to them," it does not mean that they were afraid to come into their presence, but that they were afraid to profess faith with a view to obtain membership. The apostles did nothing upon the multitude, either now or at any other time, to make the people afraid of coming near to them. But by this instance of their power exerted against hypocrisy and falsehood in two of the church-members, wicked men were kept from afterwards desiring admittance to church membership. This is still an awful lesson to hypocrites, who, for sinister ends, desire communion with any of the churches of Christ. When a church does its duty, it is likely that it will not long be polluted with hypocrites. God can easily bring it about that hypocrisy can be detected.

If the word κολλασθαι does not absolutely require, it unquestionably justifies this interpretation. I know not that it is ever used for joining a crowd as a spectator.

It signifies the most intimate union. See it in several instances of its occurrence in the New Testament. Luke x. 11; xv. 15; Rom. xii. 9; 1 Cor. vi. 16; Acts xvii. 34. It literally signifies to glue, and in each of the above instances denotes the closest union. Joining a crowd for a little, as a mere spectator, could not with propriety be pointed out by this word.

As to your *corps de reserve*, " that though they all should have met in Solomon's porch, they might have met in separate apartments," it is liable to the objections stated with respect to the same thing in the temple. It will fly the first shock. It also gives fresh courage to the assailant, for he must see that the resources of the enemy are totally exhausted. How could they be *with one accord* in Solomon's porch, if they were not in one assembly? Every circumstance of the narrative shows that they formed but one assembly. The apostles were together; the money of Ananias and Sapphira was laid at their feet, ver. 2. Now, if there had been different assemblies, the apostles would not have been all in one of these only. The disciples are all represented as assembled with the apostles. Ananias and Sapphira came into their presence, and great fear is said to have come on all them that *heard* the things spoken by Peter. At this time then the disciples not only were in the porch, but in the hearing of the apostles; and not only the disciples, but others also: verse 11 — " And great fear came upon all the church, and *upon as many as heard these things.*" Many others then, as well as the church, were present. Here then there is only one assembly, and in that assembly, many besides the believers. During this meeting, the apostles were employed in working many signs and wonders among the people: so that when the place was so crowded, that there was no way of access for others, they laid the sick in the streets, &c. Now, it is not after these things, but during them, that they are all said to be with one accord in Solomon's porch. This is not given as a fact in subsequent continuation, but an intercalated fact, for the purpose of informing the reader of the place where this assembly was met, with the other circumstances mentioned in the parenthesis. There is then not the shadow of reason for supposing that the apostles were alone. The intercalated relation does not inform us of the assembly leaving the presence of the apostles, but of the place where they were assembled with the apostles, and the effect of the punishment of the crime of Ananias and Sapphira upon the multitude. The whole series of transactions here recorded, is represented as happening in one assembly, not going on at the same time in different assemblies. Besides, the transactions here recorded respect the miracles and speeches of the apostles among those who were present. The disciples are not exhibited as in the act of immediate public worship, but as witnessing these miracles, &c. Now what could separate them into different assemblies in the same house? Such a separation, had it been possible, would have prevented all but one company from witnessing these things recorded. And if this porch could contain them all, and if it was only intersected with rows of pillars, why should they not all form one assembly? What absurdity! In your last letter, Solomon's porch was not capable of containing the multitude of the disciples in one congregation. Now, it can contain the same multitude in a great number of different congregations, without any one being annoyed by the speaker in each of the others, though it was only intersected by rows of pillars!! O fie, fie, fie!!! When you reason, I will answer; when you trifle, you are worthy only of ridicule. Truth could never reduce its advocate to such contradictory and absurd suppositions. Nothing can be more clear than that the body of the disciples of Jerusalem were both in the temple and in Solomon's porch, in the same assembly. But, independent of all the evidence from the history, what could possibly be their object for meeting in the temple and in the porch, in different assemblies, having no communion or intercourse in their public worship, and administration of discipline? If they were met in different apartments of the temple, and in separate companies in the porch, as different congregations in a city, without having any more connection than with the congregations in other parts of Judea, would it not have been much more convenient, and have exposed them much less to persecution, to have met in private houses? What should induce them to meet in different assemblies in the same house, when they could have met with much greater advantage in different streets and in different houses? If all the parish churches of the city of Glasgow were to be destroyed by an accident, is it likely that the different congregations should meet in the Tontine, suppose it were so spacious as to contain them, in separate assemblies? Would it not be more likely that they would meet in the different public halls in the city? What should impel them all to meet under the same roof, to disturb each other with their separate worship? It must indeed be a ludicrous spectacle to behold fifteen or twenty congregations, with as many preachers, all under the same piazza, upon the same floor, without any separation but the pillars that support the edifice, and even this certainly not between each congregation!!! What will not men say to avoid the testimony of the Scriptures against themselves? What clumsy abutments will they raise, rather than suffer their *venerable fabric* to fall? "The merchants of these things which were made rich by her, shall stand afar off for the fear of her torment, weeping and wailing; and saying, Alas! alas! that great city that was clothed in fine linen, and purple, and scarlet, and decked with gold, and precious stones, and pearls. For in one hour, so great riches is come to nought."

The next passage that comes under your review is Acts vi., which gives an account of the election of deacons. It is said, verse 2—" Then the twelve called the multitude of the disciples unto them." I call upon every unprejudiced reader to declare who are the persons here spoken of? Is not the language of the Holy Spirit as plain and precise, as it possibly could be? How could he have told in plainer and more unequivocal words, that the apostles called unto them the multitude of the disciples? What is the circumstance he should have added to prevent his meaning from being misunderstood? Can any man be found so hardy as to put this upon the rack, and by inquisitorial tortures, force it to contradict itself?

You say, "But it might be only the heads of them who *in reality* were summoned." If the inspired historian tells us that *the multitude of the disciples* were summoned; and if, *in reality*, only the heads of them were summoned, then the Spirit of God tells us what is not *in reality* a truth. Your assertion is directly contradictory to that of the Spirit of truth. Whether it is better to believe God, or to believe you, let the disciples of Jesus judge. Nothing can be plainer than that the body of the disciples were called into the presence of the apostles. "The twelve called the disciples, yea, the multitude of the disciples, unto them." As if it were not sufficiently precise to say, 'They called the disciples,' and as if anticipating the sophistry of such daring critics, the narrator declares in the most emphatical manner, in the most diffuse style, "*Then the twelve called the multitude of the disciples unto them.*" Why then should we suppose that they called only the heads of them? Nothing can be more afronting to the Word of God than such a mode of interpretation. If the Holy Ghost speaks in such language, always saying one thing *in words*, and meaning another *in reality*, he cannot surely intend to instruct, but to bewilder the reader. Is it not strange that the person, who perhaps would be shocked with another for denying the authenticity of the Scriptures, scruples not to affix a meaning to every passage that stands in the way of his hypothesis, contrary to its words and most evident intention? I think it is even more audacious to admit that God hath spoken, yet make what we please of what he has said, than to deny that he hath spoken at all. If the passage under dispute would admit of your interpretation, I am bold to say that there is not a doctrine of revelation that could be certainly proved. It might be argued with equal plausibility that Christ did not die, but a phantom was affixed to the cross.

The circumstance of Moses speaking his song in the ears of all the congregation, which you bring as a justification of your own interpretation, is not at all to the point. Where did you learn that Moses, though he declares that he spoke it in the ears of all the congregation, in reality spoke it only in the ears of the elders?

This interpretation is as arbitrary and as unnatural as the other. The most likely interpretation is, that he spoke it in the midst of the camp, with all Israel around; and though they could not all hear him, yet he might very properly, especially in the language of the Old Testament, be said to have spoken it in the ears of all the congregation, because he spoke it in the presence of all, equally directed it to all as equally applicable to all. If any did not hear it from his own lips, it was on account of their distance; those that could not hear his voice from the extremity of the camp could learn it from their neighbours. It was also to be put into the hands of all, as equally and immediately suitable to all. When we are told that he spoke the words of his song in the ears of all the congregation, why should we suppose that he does not in reality mean what he says? Before this illustration could be suitable to your purpose, it must be said, ' that Moses called all the congregation of Israel unto him, and repeated in their hearing the words of this song.' It must afterwards be said, ' that Moses did not call the congregation of Israel unto him, nor pronounce his song in their presence; that he called only the heads of the congregation into his presence, and pronounced the song in *their* hearing only.' Such an absurdity and contradiction, however, we will nowhere find in the Word of God.

But if it was only the heads of them the apostles called into their presence, then it is only the heads of a congregation that should choose the deacons; for the very persons who came into the presence of the apostles, are commanded to choose these officers. Nay, upon your hypothesis, it must be only the heads of a Presbytery, for you suppose that there were here many congregations. If you could make this good, no doubt you would be entitled to the solemn thanks of the General Assembly, which, though it may allow this right in the people as to the choosing of lay-elders, does not recognise it as to the choosing of ministers. The same persons who are addressed, are commanded to " look out among themselves seven men of honest report," &c. If your interpretation is good, there is not then the shadow of privilege left to congregations. This however is completely contradicted immediately afterwards, verse 5, "And the saying pleased the whole multitude, and they chose Stephen," &c. It is not said that the saying pleased the elders only, but that it pleased the *whole multitude;* and it is added, they chose Stephen, &c. *They those*—the multitude chose. The saying pleased the whole multitude, and the whole multitude chose Stephen, &c. Now, when it is said that the apostles called the multitude of the disciples unto them, and are represented as speaking to the persons summoned, commanding them to choose these officers; and when again it is added, that the saying pleased the whole multitude, and that *they* chose Stephen, &c., it is demonstratively evident, that it was the disciples themselves in a body, and not their heads, that were summoned to attend the apostles. It is really vexatious to be obliged to prove with minute and critical discussion, things that must be evident from the narrative to the understanding of a child. A captious person might, with equal propriety, call upon us to prove that the sun is the source of light and heat.

You continue, p. 275, "Let it be admitted, however, that the multitude of believers at large were called, it is not said, either that all of the apostles, or all of the disciples were in one place, and from anything that is here mentioned, they might convene in a number of separate assemblies."

Yes, Sir, it is said as plain as possible, that the apostles were together, and that the multitude came together unto them. The apostles are represented as acting in one body, οι δυδεκα, *the twelve*. The disciples are represented as one, το πληθος. The twelve are said to call the multitude unto them, not every one of them a different part of the multitude in a different place. The twelve are not only here, but everywhere represented as being and acting together in this church. Had each apostle called into a separate assembly a part of this multitude, it could not be said that the twelve called *the multitude* unto them. The το πληθος considers the numbers that compose it as one body. What would you expect the narrator to have added, had it been his intention to inform us, that the multitude met the apostles together? If it were said, 'the Session called the congregation unto them,' would it be at all doubtful whether the Session acted together, and that the congregation as a body met them? Would any one ever suppose from this account, that each of the members of the Session called into a separate apartment a distinct company?

Your example is not in point: " Were we to be told, for instance, that the ministers of Glasgow called the multitude of the members, and asked them to elect a General Session, would it not immediately occur to us from what we know of the congregations of Glasgow, that the members would not all meet in one place, but in their different churches, and with their respective office-bearers."

1. No such thing ever could be told, for the congregations in Glasgow are not a το πληθος, except they were considered as one body. But considered as one body, it could not be said that the ministers called that body unto them. Each of them only called a part of it. In their different congregations they might be πληθη, but they could not in that disjointed view be called το πληθος. Πληθος is used to denote numbers only in their assembled capacity. I know not that ever men or things are called το πληθος which are not assembled, or at least considered as an undivided body or group, in the point of view in which they are represented. See Mark iii. 7, 8; Luke i. 10; ii. 13; v. 6; Acts xxviii. 3; James v. 20; 1 Pet. iv. 8.

2. It could not be said that the ministers (or rather ministry, representing the ministers of the city as one body, as οι δοδεκα does the apostles) called the multitude unto them; for if this were said, it would imply both that the ministers were in one place, and that the people assembed in a body with them. From what some people might know of the manner of proceeding in such cases, they might not believe this to be a correct statement; but certainly this is the conclusion every one would draw, who was not acquainted with these matters, and if so, it must be an improper account. When a historian uses language which most obviously leads those unacquainted with the facts he relates to wrong views of his meaning, he is unfit for

his office. You suppose here a form of expression which no accurate historian could use, in transmitting facts to posterity. Were an historian to record the fact to which you allude, he would express it in some such form as the following: 'the ministers of Glasgow desired their respective congregations to assemble and choose,' &c.

3. It could not be said that the whole multitude chose Stephen, &c.; for this supposes that each officer was elected by the whole body; whereas, including this General Session, each congregation elected only one part. Here the whole multitude are represented as one body, jointly electing each of the seven officers. It is not said that one congregation chose one, and another chose another, and so on, but "the whole multitude chose Stephen," &c. This General Session of Glasgow would be said to have been elected thus: 'the congregation of St. Andrew's chose Mr. ———; the congregation of St. Enoch's chose Mr. ———; the congregation of the Ram's Horn chose Mr. ———,' &c. It would not be said that the whole multitude chose Mr. ——— and Mr. ———, &c.

4. The fifth verse represents the saying as uttered and received in one place only, and that it was pleasing *in the presence of the whole multitude.* The apostles are represented as addressing, not separately but conjointly, the whole of this πληθος at the same time: "Then the twelve called the multitude of the disciples unto them, and said, It is not reason that we should leave the word and serve tables." There can be nothing more plain than that this was addressed to one body only. It is added, "Wherefore, brethren, look ye out among you *seven* men," &c. Now, if this language was addressed, not to one body, but to many congregations, it was a command to each of them to choose seven deacons; but we find that the command to choose seven was given to the whole multitude, and that seven was the number that was chosen by the whole multitude. When the apostles then deliver the command to the whole multitude to choose *seven*, and when seven were all that were actually chosen, I hold it as demonstratively evident, that they did not meet

in different assemblies. As the whole multitude chose only seven in all, it is not possible that this language could have been separately addressed to them in several congregations. To make your example analogous to this, each of the ministers of Glasgow must desire his congregation to choose a whole General Session.

5. If the twelve met the disciples in different companies, if each apostle had been engaged, there must have been twelve congregations. If there were fewer than twelve, then in some of the assemblies there would be more of the apostles than in others. If there were more congregations than twelve, then there would be none of the twelve to meet them. But according to your hypothesis, there were at least fifteen or twenty congregations. How could twelve apostles speak at the same time in fifteen or twenty congregations?

6. Had each of them chosen one, there must have been seven congregations; otherwise some of them would have chosen more than others. If there were more than seven, all but that number must have chosen none. Besides, if there were only seven congregations, and the number of disciples to have been thirty thousand, not having the use of the temple, but meeting in private rooms as you contend; then these thirty thousand could no more be accommodated in seven private rooms, with all that might attend in each of the assemblies, than they could be accommodated in one room. But if there were an hundred ministers in Jerusalem, as you suppose, according to the general ideas of Presbyterians, there must have been nearly a hundred congregations, the number of collegiate charges among them being exceedingly few, even where they have large houses and extensive districts for an audience. Now, if one minister is sufficient for a Scotch parish, one would surely be sufficient for as many as could meet in a private room in Jerusalem.

7. If there were not seven congregations, some of them must have contained more of the deacons than others. If there were more than seven, all but this number had none. Seven deacons for a hundred ministers! Seven deacons for, according to your account, fifteen or twenty congregations!

8. If they were chosen as a general board for the whole Christian poor of Jerusalem, even in this case it would have been necessary that one or more of them should have been resident in each congregation, to know the necessities of the poor. A general board for a number of congregations, is not as effectual as a particular one in each.

9. If this was a general board for a number of congregations in an association, then the deaconship belongs not to separate congregations. It is no precedent for each congregation to have an order of officers to take care of the poor. If the institution was at first a general board for a Presbytery, then it is improper in Presbyterians to commit this to the lay-elders of each congregation. The collection and management of the money for the poor of each Presbytery, should be committed to the care of a joint order of deacons, belonging not to any single congregation, but equally related to the whole. If this is the case, the office of the deacon is more extensive in its sphere than that of the pastor. He is then not an officer of a church, but of a Presbytery.

I may add also, that the occasion of the institution of the order of deacons was not because the congregations were multiplied, or that the church divided, but because of the increase of the disciples. The murmuring also of the Grecians against the Hebrews, shows that they were all in one congregation. Had they not been supplied out of one common stock, there would have been no ground for one party murmuring against another. The poor of one Presbyterian congregation will never think of murmuring about the division of the poor's money in another congregation.

You add, p. 275—bottom, "It is said further, that all the deacons were brought to the apostles, and ordained by them in one place. There is a material difference however between election and ordination, and though the latter might be performed in one assembly, the former might be done by the members of the church in their different congregations."

But the difference between election and ordination is not here the subject of dispute. We are enquiring about a matter of fact, if the disciples met in one assembly. Now this is equally proved if they met in one assembly at ordination, as if they had met in one for election. Now, if these deacons had been officers in different congregations, they would have been separately ordained in these different congregations. Besides, Sir, the strength of the argument lies not in their being merely ordained in one place by the apostles, but in their being presented before the apostles by the whole multitude that elected them. "Whom *they set* before the apostles." The very persons who elected them *set them before* the apostles. This then shows what we are here contending for, that the whole multitude of the disciples could, and did usually meet in one place. It is also plain from the narrative, that the election and the ordination took place at the same time, the latter in immediate succession to the former, in the very same assembly. There is no intimation of the smallest delay, or change of the scene of action. But why do you allow that they were ordained in one place? Is it because this is more clearly related than that they were elected in one place? I cannot think so; the latter is even more circumstantially and fully recorded. You think that it is not necessary to your system to put this latter passage upon the rack; otherwise, I have no doubt it would have undergone similar tortures. It would be as easy to make it prevaricate as the former. Indeed, Sir, I cannot persuade myself that any one could so far impose upon his own understanding, as really and seriously to have any doubts whether the plain and obvious meaning of this whole narrative is not that the disciples met in one assembly. I have no fear that any subtleties will ever succeed in making it dark, as to any persons who are inquiring in earnest; but I would seriously caution you against accustoming yourself to take such liberties with the Word of God. It must really have the most pernicious effects upon the mind, not only as to the explanation of Scripture upon this subject, but in general as to every other. It must induce a general want of reverence for the plain dictates of revelation, and accustom you to explain everything, not according to the most obvious import of the words, but according to your interests, passions or prejudices. If such plain scriptural narratives cannot positively be understood with precision, what may not be made out of the more difficult parts? If the Spirit of God is not intelligible in the plain import of his words, even when he speaks of earthly things, or records facts that any other historian could record, how shall we understand him when he instructs us in heavenly things? How shall he communicate to us those things "which eye hath not seen, nor ear heard, nor have entered into the heart of man to conceive," which notwithstanding he has revealed to his apostles, and by them in those very Scriptures revealed to us? If the passages under dispute might be understood, according to any lawful rules of criticism, in the sense which you affix to them, I have no hesitation in saying that the historian, so far from being worthy of recording the apostolical transactions for the instruction of after generations, was unfit to keep a register of the births and deaths of a country parish.

"And in those days, when the number of the disciples was multiplied, there arose a murmuring of the Grecians against the Hebrews, because their widows were neglected in the daily ministration. Then the twelve called the multitude of the disciples unto them, and said, It is not reason that we should leave the Word of God, and serve tables. Wherefore, brethren, look ye out among you seven men of honest report, full of the Holy Ghost, and wisdom, whom we may appoint over this business. But we will give ourselves continually to prayer, and to the ministry of the Word. And the saying pleased the whole multitude: and they chose Stephen, a man full of faith and of the Holy Ghost, and Philip, and Prochorus, and Nicanor, and Timon, and Parmenas, and Nicolas a proselyte of Antioch, whom they set before the apostles: and when they had prayed, they laid their hands on them."

Read this again, my dear Sir, and try if it is possible for you to find any real difficulty. I ask you, as you shall answer in the day of God, did you really think that you gave the fair sense of this narrative? or did you not merely suggest the things you have stated, as possible ways of evading the obvious import of the words? It is really a serious thing for us, Sir, to explain the Word of God, which he hath given for the instruction of his children. It is not like boys in a disputing club, arguing for victory, and saying every thing that can be thought of to perplex their antagonists, envelope the subject, and evade truth. Our minds should be filled with horror at the thought of suggesting anything merely for the sake of escaping from the edge of the sword of the Spirit. Possible evasions, and *plausible* things are at hand upon every point of revelation. There is no doctrine so clearly taught, but many possible and plausible evasions may be found by those who are disposed to look for them; and there is no Scripture that might not be as plausibly evaded, as the united assembling of the disciples of Jerusalem is by your arguments. Remember, that the victory is not to be decided by the voice of this world. We must come before another tribunal. Short and inglorious will be his triumph, who triumphs at the expense of truth.

That the disciples of Jerusalem constituted one assembly, is as clear as language can express it, from Acts xv. Accordingly I am not much surprised at your efforts to darken this evidence. Your criticism is indeed the rarest I have ever seen upon any subject. Words, with you, can signify nothing, anything, or everything, according as it will suit your purpose. Appropriated words will assume their most general sense, and in an instant sink down to the lowest degree of particular application. Words appropriated to one thing, you can easily appropriate to another, and enlarge and confine their extension at your pleasure.

"Is it contended once more," you say, p. 276, "that the church at Jerusalem was a single congregation, because the members are represented (Acts xv.), as all assembled at the decision on the reference from the Church of Antioch? It is replied, that the whole of the members are not said to have convened with the apostles on that occasion; but all that is mentioned is simply this, that such of the disciples as could attend, and were so disposed, were allowed to be hearers of that interesting discussion."

Pray, Sir, what part of the chapter is it upon which you found this assertion? Where is it simply mentioned, that such of the disciples as chose were admitted merely to hear this discussion? But before I reply to this, I shall consider the interpretation which you propose, of the words, *brethren*, and *church*, and *multitude*. "Nay, it might perhaps be alleged," you continue, "with considerable plausibility, that it is not evident from the sacred history, that any of the private members of the church were present. The term *brethren*, we know, by which it is supposed by Independents that they are here distinguished, is frequently given to ministers as such, and to them alone. It is the name by which the ministers of the Church of Ephesus are characterised by Paul (Acts xx. 32), whom he had before denominated (verses 17 and 28), elders and overseers—by which he describes other ministers (Phil. i. 14), whom he speaks of in that passage as preaching the word—and which he often bestows upon the evangelists, Titus and Timothy, and others—(2 Cor. ii. 13; viii. 18. 23; 1 Thess. iii. 2, &c.). Should it be asserted then, that by the brethren here specified, besides the apostles and elders, may be intended the evangelists and prophets in the city of Jerusalem, as well as any other ministers who might be then in that place, it might be difficult to disprove it."—p. 276.

No, indeed, Sir; there is not the smallest difficulty in disproving this conceit. It is a much more difficult matter to avoid expressing contempt for the author who could suggest such a wild fancy. It is a misfortune to be engaged with an antagonist who is capable of availing himself of such resources, and of employing such wretched evasions. The terms *brother* and *brethren*, though frequently applied in Scripture in the signification which they bear in the world, to express the natural relation of the children of the same parents, yet are appropriated to denote those who are related to each other in Christ, as born again of his Spirit, through the instrumentality of the incorruptible seed of the Word, whenever they are applied to believers, or addressed from one believer to others. All mankind are brethren, and are frequently so called in Scripture, but Christians are so in a relation that surpasses any other among men; therefore they are emphatically and appropriately *brethren*. This is the very name which our Lord himself gives his disciples. This is the only title, in a religious sense, he will allow them. In Matt. xxiii., addressing all his disciples, as appears from verse 1, he says in verse 8, "Be not ye called Rabbi; for one is your Master, even Christ, *and all ye are brethren.*" Accordingly we find all the disciples everywhere addressed by this appellation conferred on them by their Lord:—Acts i. 16; vi. 3; xvii. 6; xxii. 13; xxviii. 14-17; 1 Cor. v. 11; vi. 5, 6, 8; vii. 15; viii. 11; xv. 6; Gal. ii. 4; Phil. i. 12; iii. 1; iv. 1, 8; Col. i. 2; 1 Thess. i. 4; ii. 1, 9, 14, 17; iii. 7; iv. 1, 6, 13; v. 1, 4, 12, 14, 25; 2 Thess. i. 3; ii. 1, 13, 15; iii. 1, 6, 13, 15; 1 Tim. v. 1; Heb. iii. 1; xiii. 22; James i. 2, 9, 19; ii. 1, 5, 15; iii. 1, 10; v. 10, 12, 19; 1 Pet. iii. 8; v. 12; 1 John ii. 7, 9, 10, 11; iii. 14, 15, 16, 17; iv. 20; v. 16; 3 John 3, 5, 10.

Yea, this is the very word by which Jesus expresses his relation to his people—Matt. xxv. 40, 45; xxviii. 10; Luke viii. 21; Rom. viii. 29; Heb. ii. 11, 12, 17. Jesus is not ashamed to call the meanest of his flock by this endearing appellation, though the lordly ambition of the clergy would confine it to themselves.

Brotherly love is the love which is to be exercised between these *brethren*. If *brethren* in the New Testament denoted the ministers of the Gospel, then *brotherly love* would be the mutual and reciprocal love of these ministers to each other. But we find that *brotherly love* is the love of all saints to each other—Rom. xii. 10; 1 Thess. iv. 9; Heb. xiii. 1; 2 Pet. i. 7.

Αδελφοτης, or the *brotherhood*, is the aggregate body of these brethren. If ministers were *the brethren*, then the brotherhood would be the aggregate body of ministers. But the brotherhood is the aggregate body of the saints—1 Pet. ii. 17; v. 9.

Brethren was also the appellation by which the Jews addressed, or spoke of each other. The whole nation were brethren. The term was not confined to their rulers.—Acts xxii. 1, 5; xxiii. 5, 6; xxviii. 21.

But above all, the οι αδελφοι, *the brethren*, is ever appropriated to the body of believers. Whenever the New Testament writers speak of *the brethren*, it is as fully understood that they mean the believers, as when they speak of *the disciples*. The terms, *the disciples, believers, saints*, &c., are not more strictly appropriated to the servants of Jesus, than *the brethren*. It is not more clearly understood whom they mean when they speak of *the twelve*, nor is it now more clearly understood what the Moravians mean when they speak of *the brethren*, nor what the Quakers mean when they speak of *the friends*.—Acts xvi. 2, 40; xvii. 10, 14; xviii. 18, 27; xxi. 7, 17; xxviii. 15; Rom. xvi. 14; 1 Cor. viii. 12; xvi. 11, 12, 20; Gal. i. 2; Eph. vi. 23; Phil. iv. 21; Col. iv. 15; 1 Thess. iv. 10; v. 26, 27; 1 Tim. iv. 6; John xxi. 23; Acts ix. 30; xi. 1, 29; xii. 17; 1 Pet. i. 22; 1 John iii. 14, 16; 3 John 3, 5, 10, with many others. Indeed, throughout the Acts of the Apostles, and the Epistles, the disciples are as usually and as indiscriminately called *brethren*, as they are called saints; and *the brethren* is their appropriated appellation.

To what purpose is it then, Sir, that you allege those passages where the elders or evangelists are called brethren? These were brethren indeed, but in no other sense than the meanest of the flock. By what authority do you say that the term brethren is given (Acts xx. 32; Phil. i. 4, &c.) to ministers, *as such?* They are not called brethren as ministers, but as Christians, as must appear to every one who will examine the different places where the word occurs. You might as well argue from the king's addressing the House of Commons by the term, *gentlemen*, that there is not another gentleman in England, but the members of that house. Church officers can no more be called exclusively *brethren*, than they can exclusively be called *disciples, saints, Christians*. These words are perfectly interchangeable. I defy you to show, that in the New Testament this term was ever appropriated to ministers.

Yea more, I say it could not have been appropriated to them: 1. Because, as pastors, they are not more peculiarly brethren than the other members, according to the religious use of that word. 2. Because the word was appropriated to the disciples in general, and therefore could not have, in the same book, upon the same subject, with respect to the same body, a more limited appropriation. The term *brethren*, as the term *church*, includes the pastors, when the latter are not spoken of in contradistinction; but the pastors are neither *the brethren*, nor *the church*. Nay, more, when the rulers are contradistinguished from the body of the disciples, and separately named, the terms brethren and church, as in this very chapter, are the words used to denote the general body that remains. The same thing takes place, when the rulers of any body are contradistinguished from the body with which they are connected. Thus we might say, such a thing 'met the approbation both of the Parliament and of the nation.' The clergy have reversed this process, and have taken from the individual members the appellation *church;* and you would now follow up the usurpation, and endeavour to take from them the appellation brethren; nay, you seem determined not even to leave them the ugly word *multitude*. Instead of these appellations by which the Holy Spirit has distinguished the body of believers, the family pride of Antichrist, almost among all sects, has affixed to them the contemptible appellation of *laymen*.

But who are *the brethren* mentioned in the first verse of this very chapter? "And certain men which came down from Jerusalem taught *the brethren*, and said, Except ye be circumcised after the manner of Moses, ye cannot be saved." Was it only upon the ministers of Antioch that the Jewish teachers inculcated the necessity of circumcision in order to salvation? Who are *the brethren* in the very next line of this same 23rd verse? "The apostles, and elders, and *brethren*, send greeting unto *the brethren*," &c. *The brethren* of one place send to *the brethren* of another. Is it possible that the word *brethren* in this address should not have in both instances the same meaning? In both instances, it is evidently used as the appropriated appellation of the bodies to whom it is applied. Is it then possible that in the same sentence a word should have not only two meanings, but two appropriated meanings? Would language be at all intelligible upon this supposition? If the Quakers of Great Britain and Ireland were to write to the Quakers in America, and address their letter in the following terms, '*The friends* in Great Britain to *the friends* in America,' would any one ever suppose, that there was any doubt whether the term *friends* in the former instance had the same extension as in the latter? Now, the terms *the friends* are not more peculiarly and descriptively appropriated to the body of the Quakers, than the terms *the brethren* were appropriated to the body of the disciples. But upon your principles of interpretation we might reason thus: 'Many examples might be adduced, in which one of the rulers of the Quakers, addressing others of the same class, calls them *friends*; therefore, if we were to say that the terms *the friends* in the first occurrence of it in this address, signify *solely the rulers of the Quakers*, and not the general body, it might be difficult to disprove it.' Common sense however would instantly reply, 'True, one of the heads among the Quakers might address another of the same class by the term *friends*, but he does so, not as an official character. He would use the same address to the meanest of the society. But the heads of the Quakers could not be called exclusively and appropriately, *the friends*, because this is the appropriated appellation of the whole body.' Upon the same principles, a foreigner newly arrived in London, and hearing one of the members of the House of Commons addressing another by the title Mr. ——, would conclude that every other person whom he might hear addressed in the same manner, was a member of Parliament. A little acquaintance, however, with the manners of the country, would convince him that this was not the distinguishing title of a member of Parliament, but was common to him with the meanest man in England.

Farther, according to you, the word brethren is appropriated to all ministers, whether apostles, elders, prophets, or evangelists. Your references are intended to prove this. But here it must have a more limited appropriation, *i.e.*, to prophets, evangelists, and foreign ministers, in contradistinction to apostles and elders. *The apostles, the elders,* and *the brethren*, are three different orders; it lies upon you then to prove, not that *the brethren* was appropriated to all the orders of ministers, but to those alone, to whom you here apply these terms. *The brethren* must here mean an order contradistinguished from the two before mentioned. Now, as an order contradistinguished from two other ministerial orders, why are prophets, evangelists, and foreign ministers called *the brethren*. Why were the prophets, evangelists, and foreign ministers, called *the brethren* rather than the elders? Why was it not said, *the apostles, the prophets,* and *the brethren ?* As prophets, evangelists, and foreign ministers, the appellation *brethren* does not characterise them. You must be able to show that these different orders are called *the brethren,* in contradistinction to apostles and elders. This they never are in Scripture, nor could they be. For it must be upon one of these two principles: either that the appellation *brethren* is their peculiar descriptive appellation, and not common to them with the apostles and elders? or, that this appellation being common, is used to denote prophets, evangelists, &c., in contradistinction to apostles and elders, the former as constituting the general body of ministers, and the latter as distinguished out of the general body, from their superior power, or their superior consequence. The former is not the case by your own reasoning. The latter is not the case, because the general body of ministers are elders, not evangelists and prophets. Nor are elders of superior distinction to prophets and evangelists, nor deserve more specific mention. Clergy is a general word, applicable to all the orders of the Church of England. The expression, 'The English clergy are a learned body,' includes all orders from the archbishop to the curate. But when the higher orders are specifically mentioned, and the word *clergy* afterwards used, the latter will apply to all those not included in the former, as in contradistinction from them. Thus, 'The

English *bishops* and *clergy*, since the time of Archbishop Laud, lean towards Arminianism.' Here, though the *bishops* are *clergy*, yet they are distinguished out of them, as an order over the rest. But clergy here contradistinguishes *the body* from *the rulers*. In the same manner, *congregation* is a word which, when it stands alone, includes the minister and session of a Presbyterian congregation. But when the rulers are to be contradistinguished from the body in general, we say 'session and congregation;' and when the different orders of rulers are to be distinguished also from one another, we say, 'Minister, session, and congregation.' But here again those called in contradistinction *the congregation*, are the general body; and those called in contradistinction *the Session*, are the general body of rulers, out of which the minister is distinguished. Now, I apprehend from these illustrations I have done your argument all the justice you can demand, and stated it as fairly as you could wish. Were I then to allow you that the appropriate appellation, *the brethren*, was peculiar to ministers, yet it could not be applied to any order or orders in contradistinction to others, but as those to whom it was thus applied constituted the general body. Upon this supposition, it would undoubtedly have been given, not to the prophets, but to the elders. The address would have been, 'The apostles, the prophets, the evangelists and *the brethren*,' *i.e.*, the body of ministers in general.

Again, if elders are supposed to be a higher order than that of prophets and evangelists, and if, as you say, the prophets and evangelists were also elders, they are already mentioned by their higher office. They are included in the elders already mentioned. Why should they be mentioned again? This would be like saying, 'the bishops, and clergy, and curates,' as if curates were not clergy. If they were not ordinary church officers, nor acted here, as you affirm even of the apostles, as inspired, what right had they to a seat in this assembly, according to the ideas of Presbyterians? If prophets and evangelists are each an order higher than that of elder, or equal to it, why are they not as specifically mentioned? Why should they be grouped under the terms *the brethren?* This supposes not only that the general body of those called brethren are prophets and evangelists, but that they are of much inferior consequence, as a general body is to those who are over them.

Again, if these brethren, or any of them, were foreign ministers, as you suggest, and if they were not elders, what right had they to sit in this assembly, if it was a Presbyterian General Council. If they were elders, are they not already mentioned? This would be saying, ' the apostles, and elders, and elders.' Do you mean to insinuate that the foreign ministers were not elders, or being such, that they were of an inferior order to those of the city of Jerusalem? This is like the working of the mystery of iniquity, which very early began to make a distinction between the city and country bishops, calling the latter *chorespiscopi*. The terms *the brethren* here, cannot include any that were elders, because the elders are distinctly mentioned; nay, are mentioned in contradistinction from these brethren. If the foreign ministers are here called *the brethren*, in contradistinction from the city ministers, who are in contradistinction from the former called elders, then no ministers should be called *elders* but those who live in the city, where the General Council meets. The clergy of Edinburgh are the only elders of the Church of Scotland; the rest form a common mass, called in contradistinction from these elders or city clergy, *the brethren.* But upon what principles could the terms *the brethren*, be given as the contradistinguishing appellation of prophets, evangelists, and foreign ministers? But where do you find these foreign ministers? From what circumstances are you led to believe that there were such at this meeting? Upon what authority do you argue from this as a point granted? What are the documents you can produce to prove this? Can anything be more palpably absurd, than to go about to prove that such a phrase might denote foreign ministers, until you prove that such were actually present? Could any interpretation be more arbitrary than this? You might as rationally suppose that they were angels or devils, as foreign ministers, when it cannot be proved that there was any such in that assembly. Indeed, Sir, it is hard to see how you yourself can believe this absurdity, from the efforts you make to prove that those termed *the brethren* did nothing but *acquiesce* in the decision of the apostles and elders. Had you been thoroughly satisfied that this was a stable foundation, you never would have so strenuously endeavoured to prove a hypothesis that completely overturns it. Whoever reads your eighth letter with impartiality, will be convinced, that the man who there takes every means to lower *the brethren*, cannot at the same time be persuaded that they were prophets, evangelists and foreign ministers. Had they been such, they would have had the same official concern in the deliberations and decisions at this meeting, as the elders of Jerusalem, even according to the Presbyterian model. Nay, had they not, it would destroy that model. The man who was thoroughly persuaded that they were such, would have turned the whole force of his genius to show that those termed *the brethren*, had the same share in the deliberations and decisions, as the elders of Jerusalem. Every argument that goes to show that they had not the same authority, lends its force to overturn the Presbyterian system. Another might take up your own arguments, and from your own confession prove to you that foreign ministers had not a right to a seat in the General Assembly; that they might be admitted to hear, and to express their submissive acquiescence; but that they ought by no means to speak, deliberate, or vote with the ministers of Edinburgh. How could you, in consistency with what you have said, refuse to grant him this? It is not possible for the same man consistently to vindicate the different hypotheses you have adopted. Every argument that goes to serve the one, in proportion as it does so, or may be thought to do so, it injures the other. I am afraid your friends have been too kind to you; that they have loaded you with their opinions; and that you wish to strengthen the cause by supporting a variety of theories, with all the address you can command. Now, whatever effect this might have coming from different men, it undoubtedly does not serve you to vindicate them all. It would be both safer for the candour of your own character, and more effectual to your cause to adopt one thing, and defend it *solely*. At least, you should never attempt to defend theories that oppose each other. Your theories are so opposite, that when you proceed to the second, you are as much called upon to refute the former as I am. You are like a man raising abutments to an old house that has a bad foundation; who, from his great anxiety to keep it up, raises so many, and so weighty, as to crush in the building. You say, p. 122, "The truth therefore seems to be, according to the sentiments of some Presbyterians, that though the members at Jerusalem expressed their *acquiescence* in the decision of the apostles and elders (a circumstance which could not fail to have uncommon weight upon the minds of the believing Jews at Antioch, as they must previously have been no less attached than themselves to the distinguishing peculiarities of the law of Moses), they by no means appear to have judged authoritatively, or even voted in the matter." Now, if this is good reasoning when applied to *the brethren*, considered as individual members, it is also good reasoning when applied to them, considered as foreign ministers. If, upon the one supposition, they by no means appear to have even voted in the matter, how will it appear that they did so upon the other? Whether this is your own opinion or not, you here support it as strenuously as possible, and endeavour to render it plausible by every shadow of argument you can find. But how does this consist with the other hypothesis, that makes these persons, termed *the brethren*, to be foreign ministers, upon which supposition they must have had equal authority, and an equal vote with any of the elders of Jerusalem? You say also in p. 276, "But all that is mentioned is simply this, that such of the disciples as could attend, and were so disposed, were allowed to be hearers of that interesting discussion. What this number was, is not specified." Now, if this is simply stated, how is it consistent with this simple statement, that, after all, these brethren were not the individual disciples, but really ministers, who not only were present, but must have enjoyed a full share in the deliberations? Must the simple statement of the narrative immediately assume another shape when *the brethren* are supposed to be clergymen? It must simply say one thing if the brethren were individual members; but it must simply say the contrary, when they are considered as ministers. If *the brethren* were the body of the church members, the narrative must simply say that only some of them were present, and that those who were present did nothing but hear the discussion; if *the brethren* were the other ministers, the narrative must as positively say that they both were present, and deliberated and voted. There is really such inconsistency and contradiction in these sentiments, that it is difficult to allow them to be the children of the same parent. You affect a mighty triumph, when you think you have discovered a diversity of sentiment between Independents, though, were it a thing worth dispute, it would be easy to show that it is unfounded. I will be much surprised if you can show the consistency of these different hypotheses. Though it is not necessary that different authors should be consistent with each other, it is surely necessary that an author should be consistent with himself.

It must indeed be a very strange thing if the narrative gives a foundation for two so opposite theories upon this subject as these. The one makes *the brethren* to be the disciples; the other, the prophets, evangelists, and foreign ministers. The one makes only a part of the brethren to be present; the other, the whole. The one makes *the brethren* only hear; the other makes them speak, vote and decide. Can the same narrative support each of these hypotheses? Can the same author consistently support them? Indeed there is something in the complexion of your language in support of the hypothesis, that *the brethren* were ministers, which strongly intimates, that it is rather a desperate resource than a fixed and sober opinion. You say, "It might perhaps be alleged with considerable plausibility," &c. "Should it be asserted then, that by the brethren here specified, besides the apostles and elders, may be intended the prophets and evangelists in the city of Jerusalem, as well as any other ministers who might be then in that place, it might be difficult to disprove it." Is this like the language of one fully convinced that he was giving the true and direct meaning of the sacred page? And is it consistent with that reverence we ought to have for the Word of God, and the teachable spirit with which we ought to receive its dictates in their genuine meaning, to speak of "alleging plausible things," and of starting theories that might not be easily disproved? I will ask you then this question—Have you supported this theory from a conviction that it is the true spirit of the passage, or have you taken it merely as a refuge in case you should be beaten out of your other fortress? Are you not rather trying what plausible things may be said to support this theory, than fully persuaded that it is the mind of the Spirit? It is a very dangerous thing to sport with the Word of God. By it he speaks to his children. It is highly insulting to his majesty, and unbecoming the character of a Christian, to say plausible things, and start novelties, merely to avoid the true meaning. In my mind, your reasoning upon this point is so far from being *plausible*, that it is rather the wildest extravagance. But had you even succeeded in saying a number of plausible things to support a fanciful theory, and in proposing difficulties that might not be easily removed, you would still be very far from gaining your point. Plausible things have been spoken against the Scriptures themselves, and difficulties have been started of tenfold more difficult solution than any you here allege against the plain meaning of this narrative. Nor is it for the credit of an author to rack his brain in saying plausible things, rather than acknowledge the simple account of the transaction here recorded. How many plausible things might you say even against the divinity of our Lord Jesus Christ! How many plausible things might you say against the corruption of human nature! And though you are not disposed to say plausible things against these doctrines, what can you, upon your own principles, say against those who do? Do you not here set them the example? And if plausible things be said against the plain meaning of the words of this narrative, why may not plausible things be said against the plain import of any other passage of Scripture? Nay, if you say plausible things against the obvious meaning of this account, what security have we that you would not say plausible things against any other doctrine of Scripture, if the defence of the Church of Scotland needed this.

But they are not only called *the brethren*, but the assembly is said to have been *a multitude*, ver. 12. You must then say some more of your *plausible* things, to show the possibility that your council might be called a multitude. And nothing is easier than this; for " the Jewish Sanhedrim, who were rulers only, are called το πληθος (Acts xxiii. 7), and which was probably not more numerous than this *Christian Council*." Indeed, Sir, a multitude of any class or kind of people is *a multitude*. If all the kings on earth were assembled, they would make a multitude of *kings*. A General Assembly might be called a multitude. And though *the multitude*, with the words that correspond to it in other languages, when used as an appropriated appellation, which may be known by having no reference to any other assembly pointed out in the connection, denotes *the many* in opposition to *the few*, or the ruled in contradistinction to their rulers, I freely acknowledge that it refers here to this particular assembly, and not to the body of the disciples in contradistinction from their office-bearers. *The multitude*, when the contrary is not ascertained from the connection, refers to the body of the disciples in general, but in this place, it evidently refers to the general body of this assembly. "All the multitude," is plainly all the assembly. But πληθος, to what body soever it is applied, must be a multitude, and a multitude can never be a small number. If you wish to prove or suggest this, common sense will revolt. The Jewish Sanhedrim was a numerous assembly, and at this time it must have been numerously attended, or it could not have been called το πληθος. That it was probably not more numerous than this meeting, upon the supposition that the individual Christians of Jerusalem formed no part of it, is a gratuitous assertion, for which not a shadow of proof is, or can be produced. Your conjectures, and plausibilities, and probabilities, go for nothing in argument. If you exclude the church members, you have none you can count upon to make up this multitude but the apostles, and the elders or ministers of one church. Upon no rational calculation of their numbers could they be called a multitude. If you wish to convince any rational man that the church officers of that meeting were a multitude, you must produce your proof. None but the most simple can be influenced in their decision by your intemperate guesses. I call upon you then to produce your numbers to complete this multitude. I have mine at hand—the whole Christians of the city of Jerusalem. Nay, more, not only have you no proof of any office-bearers being present, but those of Jerusalem alone, but there is proof that none other could have been there. There was no summoning of foreign ministers; and even those who might accidentally be in Jerusalem, could not, upon Presbyterian principles, have enjoyed a seat in the assembly. They were not representatives themselves, nor had their congregations an opportunity of sending lay elders to keep up the balance of power. Nor could this assembly be a lawful General Assembly, had not all in connection with it, or bound by its decrees, been summoned to attend by their representatives. Now, not only is there no account of this summoning, but there could not have been such a summoning, consistent with the complexion of the narrative. In verse 6, the apostles and elders are said to have come together, in language that leaves us no room to suppose that there were others expected from a distance.

$Oχλος$ is not $πληθος$, and therefore I have here nothing to do with your observation on the application of it (Acts i. 15). I may observe, however, that though these two words may, and often are applied to the same numbers, and that though the former may be applied to as great a number as the latter, they are not at all perfectly synonymous. The one might very often be expunged, and the other inserted in its place, without any difference in the sense; yet there are occasions when this could not be the case. The former might most literally be translated a *crowd*, the latter a multitude; the former denotes numbers considered as *crowded, confused,* or *disturbed,* and is often connected with tumult; the latter denotes numbers considered as numerous. This will appear even from the use of the words, to any one who will take the trouble to run up and compare the different places where these words occur. Though, as I observed, they will often find them interchangeable, they will often find the contrary. See Luke v. 15, 19; vi. 19; Acts xxiv. 18; Luke viii. 4, 45; ix. 12, 16; Luke viii. 37; xxiii. 1, 27; Acts vi. 5; v. 14; iv. 32; xxv. 24, &c. The same thing evidently appears from their derivatives and cognates. Πληθυνω signifies *to fill,* οχλεω *to disturb.* It is evident then that an assembly might be an οχλυς that could not be called a πληθος, and the same numbers might in one situation be an οχλος, and in another not. The literal translation of the passage to which you refer is, 'there was a crowd of names (or persons) together, about an hundred and twenty.' The historian intends to call our attention to the number that were *together*.

Indeed, it would be altogether vain to attempt to ascertain the exact number that may be called a πληθος, for this in different circumstances, will be exceedingly various. But in no circumstances could it be applicable to the number of church officers whom you can prove to have been at this time in Jerusalem. This is quite enough for me. Instead of an hundred and twenty, you cannot positively show that they amounted to even twenty. However, what cannot be ascertained by exact calculation, does not cause the smallest difficulty, in practice. The most vulgar mind is at no loss as to the idea it should form of the indefinite numbers included in πληθος, or *multitude.* This criterion, as well as the word, will abundantly prove that there must have been truly a multitude present in this assembly, This is strongly marked in the complexion of the verse. " *The multitude—all* the multitude—all the multitude *kept silence.*" Every feature shows that there was a great assembly.

Let us now come to εκκλησια, which you once more put upon the rack. You have already had it a single congregation, a number of congregations, a kirk-session, the clergy of Jerusalem as distinguished from those church rulers that are termed lay-elders. Here you must have it an assembly, *i.e.*, any assembly in the civil or unappropriated acceptation.

To this I reply, 1, that, leaving out of the question at present its most proper and legitimate civil application, in the New Testament it hath been appropriated to the meetings of the saints for worship, &c., and when employed to denote religious Christian assemblies, it is never otherwise used. I call upon you to point an instance, where it applies to any of the assemblies of Christians, in which it is not used in that appropriated acceptation. The very circumstance of its being appropriated in religion to a particular kind of assembly, will prevent its being used in an unappropriated sense upon the same subject. The tumultuous assembly at Ephesus (Acts xix. 39, 41), might be called an εκκλησια in the civil sense of the word, not only because it was a popular assembly, but also because the historian was there speaking of civil, not of religious assemblies. He wrote of that as if a profane historian had written.

To appropriate a word in any branch of science, or in an art, and to use it promiscuously in an unappropriated sense, upon the same subject, would be altogether absurd, and lead to inextricable confusion. Indeed, a word comes to be appropriated in one sense, or to one particular object, or class of objects, though it could intrinsically, with equal justice, be applied to many others, just to avoid confusion, or circumlocution. Every congregation among Presbyterians might as well have been called an assembly as *congregation;* yet each of these words is now absolutely confined to one only of each of these objects. *The congregation* is the congregation of a particular parish; *the assembly* is the General Assembly. *Congregation* might literally be applied to the Parliament, and Parliament (from parler *to speak*, a meeting for public debate or discussion) might literally be applied to the General Assembly; but they are each appropriated, without exception, upon a different department to particular assemblies only. If, in speaking about religious matters, a person says, he is a member of *the congregation*, we readily understand that he speaks of the religious assembly that bears that name, in that particular neighbourhood. In some places, the house of worship is called the meeting-house, and those who meet are called *the meeting*, and they are spoken of by those names without any confusion or danger of misunderstanding; yet these words might be literally applied to the market-house, and the people assembled in the market. When a man in the north of Ireland says he is going *to meeting*, we know he does not mean the market. But that word becomes more limited in its appropriation, from the circumstance of the assemblies of different denominations, and it could no more be applied to the meeting of some religious assemblies, than it could be to the market. When a man says, '*I am going to meeting*,' we not only understand him to mean a religious meeting, but that such meeting is a dissenting congregation. In the same manner, the terms *the church*, when used indefinitely by a member of either of the established churches of Great Britain, are readily understood to be the Established Church. Thus also a churchman in England is a member of the Established Church. There is not a more settled and universal principle in language.

The same word may indeed be appropriated, without any confusion, upon different subjects, or as to different denominations upon the same subject. Thus *the church*, when used by a Presbyterian in Scotland, will readily be understood to refer to the Established Church; when an Independent speaks of *the church*, except when he is conversing of the Established Church, in which case he may use the word in its vulgar and improper acceptation, it is always known that he speaks of one particular congregation, that one, to wit, to which he belongs, or which is the subject of conversation. But even here, if the parties addressed are not aware of the sentiments of the speaker or writer, there is danger of his meaning being mistaken. Hence the necessity that we are under, in rescuing some Scripture words from improper application, to use them in their scriptural sense, with some additional mark, to show that we do not take them in their misapplied acceptation. Thus, when we speak of the Scripture *presbytery*, we are in some part of our treatise or conversation obliged to intimate that it is the eldership, or plurality, of elders of a particular congregation. Without this, many might suppose that we used the word according to its vulgar erroneous appropriation. In the same manner with respect to the words bishop, elder, &c. As to appropriations upon different subjects, they do not cause such obscurity. Thus there is no confusion in calling the place of meeting for a civil court, and the place of meeting for the rulers of a Presbyterian congregation, by the name *session-house*. But two courts, both of them civil, or both of them religious, could not have the same name. Even as to the word session-house, if there is both a civil and religious house of this name in any town, the one will generally absorb the name from the other, and the one of lesser importance must have some additional mark of distinction. This is a principle of criticism which the most ignorant, as well as the most learned, constantly acknowledge in their application of words in their native tongue. But strange! no sooner do the critics look into a book written in a dead language, than the words signify anything that can be found in the original ideas, or most extensive unappropriated use. It is a great misfortune to be able to turn over the leaves of a lexicon, without understanding the principles upon which the application of words in all languages proceed. With persons of this description, in every connection, and upon every subject, words may be taken in any of all the numerous significations that can be found affixed to them in a lexicon. The circumstance of appropriation that operates so universally in all languages, hath no respect paid to it. This error hath some apology in those whose limited acquaintance with the writers in such dead languages disqualifies them for ascertaining the actual practice, and obliges them to make their observations from second hand; but it is totally inexcusable in those who pretend to strengthen or prove their cause by an appeal to the original. From this very source arises the absurdity of the application of words, by those who may be called dictionary speakers.

They use the words, not from their observation and knowledge of the practice of the English language, but from the significations they find attached to them in their dictionary. Hence the ridiculous figure that some people of a vulgar education make, when they attempt to speak fine. Now this custom, so disgusting in our own language, is quite analogous to the principles of criticism which you here employ to explain εκκλησια and the absurdity of it is only concealed by the circumstance of its being applied to a dead language. Εκκλησια signifies an assembly, any assembly, an assembly of rulers. I can get it in such a signification, therefore it may be so understood here.

Upon the principles of interpretation which I am here reprobating, let us take up an old newspaper, written during the French republic. We read, 'The *Convention* condemned Louis XVI. to suffer death.' The most vulgar man in Great Britain would find no difficulty here. No discussion would be necessary to find out the meaning of *convention*. But a captious critic upon your principles might answer: 'Gentlemen, take care of forming a rash judgment upon this matter. It is by no means certain, that the word *convention* here refers to the national legislative assembly of France. Many strong reasons might be given to show the improbability of this; and though the word *convention* is sometimes given to that particular assembly, yet certain it is that the word is frequently applied to other assemblies. It signifies a *coming together;* any body of people coming together may be called *a convention*. This therefore may have been any other party of men in the nation.' Now, would this be like reasoning? Yet *convention* was not more strictly appropriated to the national legislative assembly of France, than εκκλησια was to a religious Christian congregation. I might illustrate the same thing from the words, congress, synod, synagogue, seceders, Dissenters, Protestants, the Revolution, the Reformation, the speaker, the minister, with innumerable others. Indeed, to allow your mode of interpretation, or rather of evasion, to be justifiable, would render the clearest propositions the most unintelligible.

The word εκκλησια, I contend, then, has an appropriated meaning, when applied in its religious use, and is never, never can be, otherwise applied upon that subject. Speaking of civil things, it may have its civil acceptation; but speaking of religious meetings of Christians, it always must be taken according to its appropriation. And this difference between its civil and religious use is not peculiar to this word; but common to it with angel, apostle, elder, bishop, deacon, &c. Nor is this difference between the civil and religious appropriation of words peculiar to religion, but is common to it with the different departments of civil things. There are different appropriations of the same word in distinct subjects as to civil things. Yet there are always common ideas upon which they are founded, and when the process has been retraced to the origin, they will be generally found to be warranted by the root. In places where the chief magistrate of a town is called governor, when a person speaking of civil things uses the term, 'The governor,' every one will perceive to whom he alludes. When a student under a preceptor speaks of *the governor*, conversing with respect to his education, it is as certainly known that he intends his tutor. In the same manner, when a countryman in Ireland speaks of *the rector*, we know without hesitation that he means the established parish minister. When a student in a university or academy speaks of *the rector*, it is as clear that he intends the master of the academy, or the superintendent of the university, who bears that name. But according to your principles of reasoning, he might mean any ruler or governor. Just so with respect to the civil and religious appropriations of εκκλησια. When I read in the orations of Demosthenes anything spoken of η εκκλησια upon the affairs of Athens, I know that he means the great assembly of the people. When the sacred writers of the New Testament use it for a religious assembly, I know that it refers to a congregation of saints.

Again, εκκλησια must be taken in the 22nd verse to denote the same kind of assembly that it signifies in verses 3 and 4. Now, in the two latter instances, you do not pretend to deny, and some sects of Presbyterians are forward to affirm, that it refers to the body of the

Christians. *The messengers from Antioch had the expenses of the journey defrayed by the* εκκλησια. Here then the people may be honoured with the name *church*. Perhaps this might be a good rule to adopt in the interpretation of this word in the various places where it occurs. Whenever the church is to have any power or profit, let it mean the clergy; whenever anything is to be given by it, let it be the people.

In the fourth verse, the messengers from Antioch are said to have been received of *the church, and of the apostles and elders*. Here, if the disciples are not the church, what is it? They are here called *the church*, even in contradistinction to the apostles and elders. From this it is evident, 1st, That if the brethren are called the church, in contradistinction from their rulers, that name can never be given to the rulers in contradistinction from them. If, to contradistinguish the people of Great Britain from their legislators, we say, 'The Parliament and nation,' the latter word can never be given to the legislators to contradistinguish them from the people. This would make the distinguishing name of the one, the distinguishing name of the other; which, instead of contradistinguishing, would induce insuperable confusion. We might as well say, that the word *laity*, which Antichrist has invented to contradistinguish the body of the beast from its head, which he calls *clergy*, may be reciprocated; nay, that *laity* may sometimes not only be given to the clergy without the people, but in contradistinction to them, and that the people might be called clergy to distinguish them from the clergy. If the word church then is the contradistinguishing name of the brethren, it can never be given to their rulers, as such. 2nd, If they were received of *the church* as well as of the apostles and elders, this could not have been a Presbyterian congregation, for in this the congregation would have had nothing to do with the reception of strangers. Nor can it here even be alleged that they acted by their rulers, for their rulers are also mentioned as acting for themselves. 3rd, Whether or not *the church* here is the same with *the church* in verse 22, yet it is here represented as being and acting together. The church received the messengers from

Antioch. They did it themselves. This then at all events decides the matter under debate; to wit, whether the disciples of Jerusalem met as one body.

Here then the word church must undoubtedly signify a single congregation; and not only so, but the brethren in contradistinction from the apostles and elders. You yourself do not pretend to deny that it refers in verses 3, and 4, to the body of the disciples. But you say that in these verses, "it may include also the common members at Jerusalem." Why do you say *it may?* —it must. Why do you say it may *include* common members? It must not only include such, but exclusively refer to such in the 4th verse; for the apostles and elders are expressly contradistinguished from them. Now, leaving out every other consideration, is it at all credible that the same name would in the same connection be given to two religious assemblies of different kinds, in the very same religion; the one an assembly of Christians for worship, or even, if you will, the aggregate of the individual Christians of different congregations, and the other to an assembly of church officers in the unappropriated sense of the word? Would it be possible that *church* should characterise both of these? or that it should be applied to both of these without confusion? Suppose an individual of your congregation to appeal from a decision of the Session against him. Suppose the Presbytery to decide in his favour; in consequence of which, we are told that 'the minister, the session, and the congregation, were displeased with the conduct of the Presbytery:' Suppose again that, in consequence of this displeasure, the Session should meet to consider of an appeal to the Synod, and that they agreed upon it: In this case, would it be proper, or at all intelligible, to record or report this transaction in these words, 'The congregation met to consider the conduct of the Presbytery, and unanimously agreed to appeal to the Synod?' Who, in reading this, would not take the word congregation in the same sense as in the former instance? Would it ever come into any one's mind who should read this account, to suppose, that in the former of these examples, the word congregation was taken in its appropriated acceptation, but that in the latter it is taken in an unappropriated sense, to denote any assembly? Yet this Session is as literally a congregation, as this supposed council is an εκκλησια. A critic, upon your principles, might allege, that although the word congregation usually denoted a particular assembly, yet, as it literally signifies any assembly, it may properly be so applied to a kirk-session. In all your evasions, I ask nothing more to convince, even the most illiterate, of your absurd principles of explanation, than that he shall transfer them to his own language.

You say in a note, p. 278, "In verse 22, it certainly can only denote the whole of that assembly, or εκκλησια who were referred to." Do you mean by this that it denotes only the whole of the assembly referred to by the word εκκλησια, or the whole of that assembly, of what kind soever it might be? If this is your meaning, no man will dispute it. This is an identical proposition, which, however true, conveys no information. It is just saying that εκκλησια signifies εκκλησια—that *the whole assembly* can mean nothing more than *the whole assembly*. The whole εκκλησια can indeed denote only the whole of the εκκλησια or assembly spoken of; but that εκκλησια must be the same kind of εκκλησια that is spoken of in verse 4, and in every other place where it is appropriated to religious meetings of Christians. But do you mean, by the above question, that εκκλησια in the 22nd verse denotes those only who are expressly mentioned in the reference from Antioch; to wit, the apostles and elders? This would both make nonsense of the narrative, and after all would be inconclusive. First, it would make nonsense of the narrative. If it means only the whole of the apostles and elders, the language of the inspired writer would be to this amount, 'Then pleased it the apostles and elders, with the whole apostles and elders;' a form of expression which would be abundantly edifying! Secondly, it would also be inconclusive reasoning, as well as nonsense. It would not follow, of necessary consequence, because the apostles and elders were alone referred to, that the apostles might not join the brethren with them also in writing this letter. This would be saying, that if a person refers his cause to the decision of the king, the king may not join with him his privy council. Not to mention that the letter related to more than the decision of a question, even to a matter of fact, in which the brethren of Jerusalem were as much concerned as the apostles and elders. The apostles, though inspired, might do so, to exhibit a model for transacting church business. But if, as you say, they were here uninspired, the joining of the brethren with them would be a real accession of strength to their opinion; for upon this supposition, not only the apostles alone, but the apostles and elders, and the whole church, might be wrong in their decision. I do not say this, as if it were at all supposable that the apostles were uninspired, but to show that, in consistency with this, your *glorious discovery*, you cannot plead with any plausibility against the possibility, nor even against the necessity of the whole brethren being joined with the apostles and elders.

You add in the same note, " The same remark too will hold as to the different acceptations of the term *brethren*, in verse 22; and certainly it will be allowed, that when satisfactory reasons seem evidently to require it, different meanings may be attached to a word in the same chapter, and even in the same verse." If by *satisfactory reasons* you mean anything more than that such suppositions are absolutely necessary to defend the Presbyterian system, I am at a loss to know what these are. From sound criticism, and the scope of the narrative, I cannot perceive reasons of any kind. Does the evident sense, scope, and consistency of the whole relation require this supposition? No such thing —quite the reverse. The whole spirit and strain of the chapter, the simple and obvious meaning of the language, the consistency of the different parts, the common sense of the reader, all require that both *the church* and *the brethren* should have the same meaning throughout. The only *reason* then I am able to see for this absurd suppostion, is, that without it the Presbyterian system must fall. This however, I doubt not, will be quite satisfactory to a great multitude of your readers, and so long as this is the case, you may, with impunity, trample upon the rules of grammar and the dictates of common sense. In such a situation, Tetzel would be more than a match for Luther.

As to the assertion itself, that in some cases words may be taken in different senses, I observe that this is the case only with general and indefinite words, and those comparatively a few. It never is the case in a single instance, as to appropriated names or appellations. With respect to the former, there is still something in the immediate connection or circumstances, that will make the meaning plain and precise. We are never obliged to recur to a system to explain them. Nay, more, of all others, the sentences in which such words are used, are the plainest, and it is on this very account that they are used, without a more minute specification or circumlocution to make them sufficiently distinct. No determining or illustrative epithet is added, because the meaning is so clear that the application of these general words can admit of no doubt or delay. Let us suppose an example, for it is of no use to deal in general assertions, without supporting them with particular illustrations: 'People in every part of the *world* generally acknowledge a future state of rewards and punishments; yet, strange! the greater part of the world live as if there was no hereafter.' Here, in the first instance where it occurs, the word *world* signifies the earth, and in the second its inhabitants. But here a child will not hesitate one moment about the meaning. There is no necessity to recur to extraneous proofs to fix the acceptation. The sentence itself affords abundant means for this purpose. Yea, so glaring is the evidence, so instantaneous the conviction, that the mind decides as quickly after the ear receives the report, as the flash follows the explosion. *The world lives*—who will reflect a moment whether it is the earth or its inhabitants that live? But respecting names and appropriated appellations, if they are not precise in themselves, the obscurity is irremediable. When names are common, they cease to distinguish. There must then be something added to limit and determine them; thus *senior* and *junior*, the place of abode, the denomination, &c. When a proper name becomes an appellative, or when the name of an individual becomes the name of those of the same order with the individual, it ceases to be the distinguishing proper name. Thus the emperors after Cæsar were called by that name, and it ceased to distinguish him from them, during their time. He must be otherwise particularized, as Julius Cæsar, &c. When a family or tribal name becomes as it were a proper individual name, on account of the distinction of an individual of the family or tribe, it ceases to be common. Thus, by Cicero, we understand always Marcus Tullius Cicero. When we read anything of Bonaparte in the newspaper, we are sure that it refers to that one of the family, who is the head of the French government. Now, were it not that all men reason on these principles in general, though upon particular points their interest or their prejudice may make them reason otherwise, every paragraph of the newspaper would be either absolutely unintelligible, or intelligible only after long and formal discussion, and that only by probability.

The same exactly must be the case with appellatives and appropriated words of every kind. If they do not always bear the same meaning upon the same subject, it would be impossible in many situations to come with certainty at their meaning. Upon this supposition, you might speak of your assemblies for worship, your Sessions, your Presbyteries, your Synods, your General Assemblies, &c., all by the name congregation. Let it be publicly announced in your place of worship, that on such a day there will be a meeting of the congregation, it will not be understood of Session, or Presbytery, or Synod, or Assembly, but of the members of your congregation. Is it the province of the Spirit of Christ alone to speak indeterminately? *Church*, when not in contradistinction to its rulers, includes all, rulers and ruled; *brethren*, in the same circumstances, does the same. But never can they be applied to the rulers in contradistinction from the ruled. And the terms, *the brethren*, and *the church*, are the appropriated names of the whole body of the disciples. Were it allowable one time to give them to the rulers, and another to the ruled, it would render them in every place ambiguous. There could then be no certain rule to determine which of these meanings we were to affix to them in each of the instances where they occur. Some cases might occur in which it would be impossible to determine; in all, the decision must be circuitous, and not immediate; whereas these appropriations are designed to prevent obscurity, and give direct information. When the inspired writers use the terms, *the church, the brethren*, in an appropriated manner, *i.e.*, when there is nothing in the connection to give them a particular determination, if they do not refer to a body well known under these appellations, they had better have been silent. What is the use of words, but to communicate ideas? and if writers do not use their terms and phrases in an intelligible and precisely ascertainable sense, they communicate no information. If, for instance, the terms *the brethren* were sometimes appropriated to the disciples in general, and sometimes to church rulers, it would be utterly impossible to determine with certainty their application in such sentences as these: "Salute the brethren"—"The brethren were of one heart"—"The brethren support their afflictions with patience," &c. Whatever is the meaning of this appropriation, it must be altogether as precise as an individual name. It must as clearly and as exclusively point out those to whom it refers, as George III., or *the king*, does the present monarch of Great Britain and Ireland. In the above examples, what is spoken with respect to the brethren, is equally applicable to them, whether ministers or individual members; now, if the terms are sometimes appropriated to the one, and sometimes to the other, how are we to know which of them are here meant?

Your general assertion then has a just foundation as to words of the description above illustrated, but is totally inapplicable to names, appellations, and appropriated phrases. The principle is of particular, not of general application. Instead of investigating the principles upon which words may be used in the manner your argument requires, to determine whether it is peculiar to some kind of words, or common to all, and whether the words under dispute are of the number of those to which it is peculiar, should it be found to be peculiar: instead of this, you have found that some words may be so used, and from this rashly conclude that it may be so with all. Indeed, through the whole of your book, you treat words as if there were no certain regulating principles in language. You seem to consider that they may not only be used according to the discretion of the writer in the most arbitrary manner, but also that they may be explained according to the inclination or caprice of the interpreter. You here however discover consummate dexterity in hiding the weakness of your reasoning, and in carrying your reader away from this point, as if it must be universally granted. After putting the most extravagant, and inconsistent, and forced explanation upon the words under examination; after understanding them in different senses, not only in the same connection but in the same sentence, you gravely tell us that this will certainly be allowed. This indeed is an excellent mode of reasoning. To prove the most extravagant things, there is nothing to do but take it for granted, and confirm it by a general unexemplified assertion. Even this you tell us in a note, as if your reasoning no way depended upon it, as a matter of so little importance as not to be worthy of being incorporated in the body of the treatise. No reasonable man, forsooth, could question the propriety of the manner of interpretation; and the general assertion in the note is only necessary for the information of those who have not the perspicuity to discern that propriety. Such general unillustrated assertions have an admirable effect in deceiving the careless reader. He will never think of suspecting the truth of an assertion that is uttered with confidence, and supposes its propriety so clear and undisputed, as to preclude the necessity of particular proof. Thus, while you are insufferably tedious in proving what nobody denies, you prove the most monstrous propositions by taking the consent of your adversary for granted, or by a general assertion. Your antagonist is not only obliged to refute you, but to find out particular illustrations for your general unexemplified assertions, and to show how far, in some cases, they may be true, as well as to show that in the present they are false.

But were we even to allow, that the same terms might, upon the same subject, have a different appropriation, and that there was nothing to determine this, but circuitous reasoning from the nature of what is said, and its suitableness to those of whom it is said, with other indirect arguments, and that the highest proof on either side could only amount to probability; still I would combat the application of your principles in the present case. There is every feature of family likeness between *the churches* and between *the brethren* spoken of in the different parts of this narrative. There is every probability from the connection. By connection, I do not mean merely the proximity of situation of the words. I mean more especially the probability the narrative affords, that they are the same or similar objects of which the historian speaks in the whole account by those terms. These are such, that I would have no apprehension from leaving the determination of the matter to the common sense of the most illiterate reader. In the first verse, the historian informs us, that certain men from Jerusalem taught *the brethren* the necessity of the observance of the law of Moses. In the third verse he informs us, that Paul and Barnabas, on their way to Jerusalem about the above question, declared the conversion of the Gentiles as they passed through Phenice and Samaria, which news caused great joy to *the brethren*. In the 22nd verse, he tells us that Judas and Silas, chief men among *the brethren*, were chosen to accompany Paul and Barnabas to Antioch. In the 23rd verse, we are told that letters were written to Antioch with this address, "The apostles, and elders, and *brethren*, send greeting unto *the brethren*," &c. Now, I appeal to the common sense of both peasant and philosopher, will propriety warrant the writer to have used, or the reader to understand, this appropriated appellation differently in these examples? Does it require any argumentation to make good this position to the conviction of any one who will only condescend to use his understanding with impartiality.

But this will still be more evident from the different places of this narrative, in which the terms *the church* occurs, as the word in each instance is evidently referable to the same, or a similar object; and not only so, but referable to the same, or a similar object with *the brethren*. In verse 3, we are informed, that on their journey to Jerusalem, they were supported by *the church*, i.e., the Church of Antioch, which you do not pretend to deny includes the body of the members. Now, as in the first verse, the body of the disciples at Antioch are called *the brethren*, and as the same body is here called *the church*, it is demonstratively evident that both *the brethren* and *the church* refer to the same object, and are different appropriated appellations for the same body. In verse 4, we are told that the messengers, when they arrived at Jerusalem, were received of *the church* which must be the body of the disciples, as the apostles and elders are specifically mentioned. In verse 22, we are informed that it pleased the apostles and elders, with *the whole church*, to send, &c. Here the apostles, elders, and church, are also specifically mentioned, as well as in verse 4. Is it not then evident, that the apostles, and elders, and church, are the same in the one verse as in the other? Is it not as demonstratively certain that it is the same church, as that it is the same apostles and elders? If you take the liberty to suppose that it is a different church that is referred to in verse 4, from that which is referred to in verse 22, by what arguments will you refute me, if I suppose that they are not the same apostles and the same elders in both places? If you say that in verse 4, the church is taken in its appropriated meaning, but that in verse 22, it is taken in its unappropriated civil acceptation for any assembly, by what reasons will you refuse to grant me, were I so extravagant as to demand it, that in verse 4, it is the apostles and elders who are appropriately so called, of whom the historian speaks, but that in verse 22, it is any other persons who may be called messengers and *seniors;* that it might be the messengers of Antioch, and the old men of Jerusalem? But if both these verses refer to the same classes, and in the former the church means the body of the disciples, the same must it likewise signify in the latter.

Farther, in verse 22, we are informed that the apostles, and elders, with the whole church, chose messengers to go to Antioch, and wrote a joint letter. In verse 23, we are informed that these letters were written in the name of the apostles, and elders, and *brethren*. Therefore the brethren in the 23rd, must mean the same class with the whole church in the 22nd verse. *The brethren* then, and *the church*, are both applied to the same object. If it is proved that *the brethren* refers to the body of the disciples, it is also proved that *the church* refers to the same. In each of verses 4, 22, and 23, the apostles and elders are mentioned conjointly with another class, which class in the two former instances gets the same name, in the latter, a name proved to be appropriated to the same in other parts of the same narrative. There is not then only proof that in these verses the body of the disciples are spoken of as the third class, equal to the proof that the same apostles and elders are spoken of, but superior proof. Not only are they called by the same name in verses 4 and 22, as well as the apostles and elders; but the same class is spoken of in the 23rd verse by another name, equally appropriated to the body of the disciples. If this proof is not completely satisfactory, I am at a loss to know what would be esteemed such.

But there is not only such a redundancy of evidence, from the multitudes of examples in which these terms are shown to be appropriated, and that a single incontestible instance of a contrary appropriation cannot be adduced; from the whole complexion of the present connection in which they are used, and their mutual reference in all the places in which they occur to the same object; and from the necessity that our adversaries are under, in all the other places of the connection, to confess that they refer to the body of the disciples: there is also a sort of phraseology in the address of the letter, that evidently obliges us in propriety, to suppose *the brethren* who write, to be the *same kind of brethren* with those to whom they wrote. " *The brethren* at Jerusalem to *the brethren* at Antioch," &c.

You say, indeed, that a word may not only have a different meaning in the same connection, but also in the same verse, *i.e.*, if it answers your purpose here, the very same sentence. Not taking into account at present what I have said to show what class of words might be so used, and that an appropriated appellation was none of them, I question if your assertion is true even as to the general words of which I gave an example. We might indeed find multiplied examples of this in the heavy divinity of the seventeenth century; but I doubt if it be altogether consistent with perspicuity, which is the most essential requisite in all kinds of compositions. We might indeed, expressing ourselves in aphorisms, exhibit the following series: 'The world is round.—The wisdom of this world is foolishness with God.—The world is exceedingly wicked. Love not the world.' But in most cases, to use the same word in different senses in the same sentence, would create obscurity. "Another source of obscurity," says Dr. Campbell,* " is when the same word is in the same sentence used in different senses." Now, if in any situation the different acceptation of the same word could cause obscurity, and is therefore unlawful, this is the situation. *The brethren* of one place write to *the brethren* of another. If the word has not the same meaning in both instances, the composition is faulty in the highest degree. It is a mode of address, of which I can neither find nor make an example in which the terms have not the same signification. 'The Seceders of Scotland, to the Seceders of Ireland, send greeting. The church at A. to the church at B.,' &c. I call upon you to produce me, from any good writer, a similarly worded address, in which the repeated word has not the same sense with what it has in the first part of the sentence. You cannot claim even to be heard till you do this.

To show that the expression, 'with the whole church,' does not signify the body of the disciples, you observe (p. 277) that the meaning may be, "that the decision was perfectly unanimous, or that what was

---

* Philosophy of Rhetoric, Vol. II., p. 17.

proposed obtained the complete concurrence of the apostles and elders and other ministers, who were members of this assembly." Here is a very dexterous piece of management to deceive the inadvertent reader. As those who leave out the second commandment are obliged to split the tenth, to keep up the number; so, in order to make up the three classes enumerated, you make a distinction between the country clergy and the prophets and evangelists, on the one side, and the clergy of Jerusalem on the other. The latter you call elders, and the former ministers. The prophets and evangelists, you say, were elders; if so, they are included in the second class: if they were not elders, what business had they, according to your principles, in this assembly? Besides, if they were there as prophets and evangelists, the terms used do not distinguish them. The country clergy must also have been elders, and therefore are also included in the second class. The expression, with the *whole church*, must refer only to those who are not comprehended in those classes previously mentioned, *i.e.*, who were neither apostles nor elders. Now, according to Presbyterians, none but such had a right to sit in it. The apostles and elders are then the whole assembly. The phraseology would be similar to this: 'The minister and elders, with the whole Session.' And the address of the letter, 'The apostles, and elders, and brethren,' would be as if we should say of a Presbyterian Synod, 'The ministers, and clergy, and elders.' Besides, such foreign ministers as you suppose to be present, you do not consider as regularly summoned or advertised for the purpose of joining in this grand council, but to have been at Jerusalem merely accidentally. Is this consistent with the regularity of a Presbyterian Synod? Why were not all the elders of all the world summoned? Even if such had been accidentally there, they could not have been representatives. Add to this, if there were ministers there from distant places, and no lay-elders, what comes of the Presbyterian model?

You add, "Besides, that it is so to be interpreted here seems evident from this, that as the reference was made only to the apostles and stated pastors at Jerusalem, as well as the prophets and evangelists, who were also elders, it appears necessary, upon every principle of fair explication, to understand by the whole of the rest of the assembly, or εκκλησια (ver. 22) besides the apostles and ordinary elders who delivered this decision, the other ministers alone, since to ministers alone the affair was submitted." To what does this *perspicuous* sentence amount? The apostles and elders alone are mentioned as being referred to. The assembly then who considered the matter must contain no other. The conclusiveness of the reasoning I have already discussed; and as to the phraseology, "The apostles and elders at Jerusalem," it equally excludes the prophets and evangelists, if they were not elders; and if they were, they are already mentioned among the elders. Foreign ministers, or elders, are also equally excluded from the words, "elders at Jerusalem," as the individual members. If, then, none could constitute a part of this assembly, but those who are named in the words, "The apostles and elders at Jerusalem," all the elders on earth besides are excluded. If the apostles and elders at Jerusalem alone were appealed to, why should any foreign ministers judge in the matter, more than individual members? If the one are excluded, because they are not named among those to whom it is said the reference was made, so also are the other. According to this, the apostles and elders at Jerusalem alone constituted the whole assembly, and the phraseology would be, 'The apostles and elders, with the whole of the apostles and elders.' By varying and jumbling the words by a sort of legerdemain, you involve the matter in a little necessary obscurity, so as to impose upon the understanding of the reader, who may think it safer for him to have a skilful interpreter to judge for him, than to judge for himself.

But what do you mean by, "Since to ministers alone the affair was submitted?" Have you forgot you are a Presbyterian? This might come from other worldly churches with propriety, but it is passing strange in the mouth of the advocate of the divine right of Presbytery. What becomes of that order called lay-elders? Had they nothing to do in this

General Council, the grand model for the universal visible church? If this is a truth, you have given with your own hand the death-blow to the Presbyterian model.

You observe farther, "And it deserves to be remarked, that the only individuals of the brethren, or as it is expressed (verse 22) *the rest* of the assembly (this, Sir, is not expressed), who are here mentioned, and are said to have been leading men among them (ἡγούμενοι), are Judas and Silas, who are affirmed in verse 32, to have been prophets." Indeed, Sir, they must have greater perspicacity than I possess, who can see how this deserves particular notice. As I have frequently remarked, the terms *the brethren*, even according to your own application of them, do not characterise or distinguish the prophets: would belong to them only in common with apostles and elders, and with them, under this appellation, you yourself join the foreign ministers. This observation then, which, if I understand it, seems to be intended to prove that the prophets were the brethren, would in this view contradict your former hypotheses, as well as tend to prove, if it had any strength, that the apostles and elders were excluded from this appellation. But the reasoning is extremely puerile, if I understand the spirit of the passage. 'Judas and Silas were prophets: Judas and Silas were chief men among *the brethren;* therefore *the brethren* were prophets.' Take a parallel example: 'Mr. Brown is a minister of the Church of Scotland: Mr. Brown is a chief man among the advocates for Presbytery; therefore the advocates for Presbytery are all ministers of the Church of Scotland.' Judas and Silas, as *prophets*, were not necessarily church officers. The gift of prophecy, like the gift of tongues, of healing, of miracles, of exhortation, &c., was enjoyed by many of the individual brethren, and even by females. But had they also been said to have been elders as well as prophets, it would have made no matter. An elder is included among the brethren, when they are not contradistinguished; but every brother is not an elder. It seems, however, pretty obvious from the phraseology, as well as from other circumstances, that Judas and Silas, though prophets, were not elders. It is not likely that a church should send away its pastors as messengers, while they had a multitude of others equally suitable. And did the historian mean to tell us, by the word ἡγουμενοι, that they were rulers, it is not likely that he would have used a periphrasis. Instead of "leading men among the brethren," he would have used the appropriated word ἡγεμονες, *leaders*. But truly I do not care, as to the point under debate, what you make of this. I do not understand why you have particularized ἡγουμενοι, unless it was to show that they were rulers. Grant it then for a moment. *The brethren* you understand to be the prophets, &c. This then will make Judas and Silas rulers among the prophets and other clergy. They must then have been diocesan bishops, or some such superintending officers.

But not only is it evident from the foregoing arguments, that *the church* signifies the body of the disciples; the form of the expression, "the apostles and elders, with the whole church," shows that the two former classes, which are particularized, constituted but a comparatively small portion of this assembly. It is quite the same with, 'The minister, and elders, with the whole congregation,' speaking of some unanimous resolution of a Presbyterian particular assembly. 'The king, and the Parliament, with the whole nation.' Or, speaking of a Freemason society, 'The master, and wardens, with the whole lodge.' 'Mr. and Mrs. ———, with their whole family.' 'Our ambassador and his lady, with his whole suite, arrived at Dover.' Such a form of expression is nowhere used, but when those who are grouped in the concluding class are either of inferior importance, or of superior numbers; generally both. Such as, 'The king and queen, with the whole royal family.' Those mentioned in the preceding class or classes, are specified on account of the distinction of their rank, or office, or character, &c. Were we to grant that there were at Jerusalem ministers from every congregation in the world, and that all the prophets and evangelists were elders also, it is not possible that the class of their enumeration should be this general group, or any class different from the elders of

Jerusalem. They would be included in the second class. If the prophets and evangelists had been distinguished at all from the other elders, it would have been as prophets and evangelists. The phraseology would then have been such as this: 'The apostles, and prophets, and evangelists, and elders, with the whole church.' If the prophets and evangelists were elders also, they would even have been more worthy of a particular mention than ordinary elders. I am not able even to devise an example in which such a mode of enumerating an assembly does not suppose that those included in the general class are the body of the assembly. 'Resolved, by the rector, and church wardens, with the whole vestry of the parish of ———.' If you can think of one of another kind, produce it.

Lastly, if you claim the liberty, in the most arbitrary manner, to make εκκλησια in this place any assembly in an unappropriated sense, why may not every other do the same in every other place where the word occurs, if it may happen to suit their theory or inclination? If you impose this sense on the word here, by what mode of reasoning will you show the impropriety of the same application of it by Dr. Stillingfleet, Matt. xviii. 18? "Tell it to the church," he explains, 'Tell it to the select assembly,' *i.e.*, to any number of persons the parties may think proper to choose for referees. But the fashion of the times change. It was the Doctor's great aim to unite all the various denominations into one; to wit, the Church of England. To effect this, his chief aim was to show, that there was no precise, full, and perpetually obligatory model. He therefore, like the generality of mediators, compromised matters, and endeavoured to lay a foundation for union by removing the divine foundation. It was his business then to force this unappropriated meaning upon *church*, in Matt. xviii. 18. But your design is to prop the venerable fabric, cemented by the blood of your ancestors, as the only divine model of church government. Matt. xviii. 18, must then be a kirk session with you, as it was a select assembly with Dr. Stillingfleet, and Acts xv. 22, must be, not a church, but any assembly. If such liberties were allowable to be taken with language, we might evade the most obvious precept of Holy Writ.

Upon the whole, you have no right to demand attention to your theory with respect to the *church* (verse 22) and *the brethren* (verse 23) till you prove, not only that such foreign ministers were at that time in Jerusalem, but that they came for the express purpose of sitting in this assembly. You cannot prove that there was a single representative from any congregation in the world. What reason then, Sir, have you to suppose that the οι αδελφοι were such, with prophets and evangelists; and that these, with the apostles and elders, constituted this assembly? Shall wild suppositions pass upon us for arguments? Since it is neither said that they were there, nor should be there, upon what principles do you suppose that they were actually there? Is there any other passage in Scripture which shows that representatives did, or ought to have come from other congregations? Prove this as a foundation, or you cannot lay a stone in the building. The disciples are called *the church* often, they are called *the brethren* often, they are called πληθος, or *the multitude*, often—they were in Jerusalem. Why then should it be supposed that these words, usually appropriated to them, should, in this instance, be unaccountably applied in another sense, even to the exclusion of them? Whatever these words may, or may not signify, it cannot be such ministers in this passage, because none such were present. But had they been present, there is no reason can be given why they should be denominated *the brethren*, in opposition to the elders of Jerusalem, were these terms even appropriated to ministers. But such an appropriated application they never possessed.

Now, Sir, I will dispute the matter with you, upon all the words in question—*church, multitude, brethren.* All apply usually to the disciples in general. To support your theory, it is necessary that you succeed in your explanation of *each* of these words. If I succeed even as to one of them, I baffle all you say, because all the terms are applied to the same objects. The same persons who are called church in verse 22, are called *the brethren*, verse 23; and if it cannot be proved that there were present any church-rulers but the apostles and elders of Jerusalem, the disciples must have made the multitude. How far I have succeeded as to each of these points, I leave to the unprejudiced Christian to determine. It will need no great penetration to discover which theory strains the words most. I take them in their natural, and usual, and appropriated sense. You cannot take one of them as they usually occur. Nay, your favourite word *church* you were obliged to part with, as the peculiar possession of the clergy, and to receive it as a fief from its profane acceptation. You have to force different meanings on the same words in the same connection—nay, in the same sentence. *Church* must now be this and now that, changing its appearance with the versatility of Proteus. *Multitude* must here be a few church rulers, and *brethren* prophets, evangelists, and foreign clergy!!! Now is it not a most unaccountable thing, if that can be the true system, which must defend itself by the distortion of every word by which the assembly is denoted? Is it not strange, if the inspired historian intended to say what you make him say, that he did not use more unequivocal language, and apply terms which would have conveyed his meaning in their usual sense? Was he at such a loss for words? Was the spirit who directed him unable to make a judicious choice, that these three must be used in such a forced and unnatural signification?

You proceed (p. 278) "The grand argument advanced by Mr. Ewing, in common with his predecessors, is founded upon Acts xxi. 22. 'After all, however,' (says he (p. 32) speaking of the many ten thousands of Jews who were pointed out to Paul as professing the Gospel) 'no inference is drawn from the many myriads of believers, that it would be impossible for them to meet in one place. We have an inference of a very different kind. What is it therefore? The multitude (not the pastors and a few delegates from the rest, but the multitude) must needs come together.' But before this reasoning can be admitted to be conclusive, it must be proved by Mr. Ewing, that at that period there was a universal concourse of the Christian Jews from *every quarter* to Jerusalem at the feast of Pentecost, and that it was possible for the multitude who would then convene to assemble in one place."

Mr. Ewing has neither to prove the one nor the other. *The multitude* are here said to be about to come together; therefore he has neither to count their numbers, nor provide a place for them. It is equal to him whether they should meet within doors or without; whether the multitude consisted of the Christians of Jerusalem alone, or of numbers from other places along with these. The fact however is evidently this; the many thousands, or myriads, to whom the elders call the apostle's attention, are the Christians of Judea, in opposition to the Jewish Christians among the Gentiles; and the multitude whom they represent as likely to come together, is the disciples of Jerusalem. As if they had said, ' Consider what vast numbers of believing Jews there are in Judea; these are all zealous of the law, and they will hear such things of thee as shall offend them, for they will soon be informed of your conduct; nay, more, the church in this city, as soon as they hear of your arrival, must come together to hear an account from you of your success,' &c. But whatever may be thought of the reference of the many thousands, it bears not upon this point. Though you should even find it a valid argument as to the number of the disciples at Jerusalem, yet it can never tend to show that the multitude did not come together. Nay, as Mr. Ewing argues, granting you that these many thousands referred entirely to the disciples of Jerusalem, they must all have been in the habit of meeting, for *the multitude* must needs come together. Is it not a silly evasion, to say that the multitude could not come together, unless that Mr. Ewing proves that it was composed of vast numbers from other places as well as the disciples at Jerusalem, and that this vast multitude could then meet in one place? What obliges him to prove that they might meet in one place, when it is said that *they must needs meet?* What obliges him to prove that there were many present from other places, when the possibility of their meeting is, according to your own hypothesis, more supposable without this? It must be a very curious thing, if, to prove a fact, we are obliged to prove something that our adversaries think is calculated to invalidate that fact, before it can be established. If you think such a supposition of any service to you, the proof lies upon yourself; we have no need of it.

But you say (p. 280) "The truth seems to be, that James does not refer to any regular meeting of the church which was to take place, but to a tumultuous concourse, such as actually ensued as soon as it was announced that Paul was at Jerusalem." To this I reply: Upon the supposition that this multitude was a tumultuous concourse of unbelieving Jews, the reason that is just assigned for this conduct recommended to the apostle, would be altogether irrelevant. That reason is founded upon the offence that would be taken at Paul's conduct, not by the unbelieving, but by the believing Jews. If the speaker referred to a mob in the 22nd verse, what connection has the foregoing arguments with the conduct, to enforce which they are given? But from the conduct recommended, and from the connected account in the 25th verse, it is abundantly evident that this conduct was recommended to Paul to avoid offending the believing Jews, for the same reason that the Gentiles were commanded, in Acts xv., to abstain from things strangled, and from blood, and from things offered to idols. Again, if the motive for the conduct recommended, was to prevent displeasing the unbelieving Jews, it was, we see, without effect—nay, the very occasion that brought on the tumult to which you allude. Lastly (for I need not waste time upon a thing so palpably evident), It is not said there will be a concourse, tumult, mob, riot, or any such thing; but 'it is altogether necessary that the το πληθος, *the multitude*, come together, for they will hear that you are come.' It is not stated merely as a probable event, but as a thing altogether necessary and proper for *the multitude* to meet. It was requisite that there should be a meeting of the disciples to receive the apostle, and to hear his report. It is intimated that the meeting could not be avoided, because they would hear that he was come. Besides, there does not appear to have been any such tumult till "the seven days were almost ended." But the meeting in verse 22, is connected with the first hearing of his arrival.

Add to this, that πληθος, would not have been the word chosen to denote such a tumult, but θορυβος or some word of like import. See verse 34; Matt. xxvi. 5; xxvii. 24; Acts xx. 1, &c. But it is not only πληθος but το πληθος that is here used, *i.e.*, not a multitude, or any multitude, but *the multitude* must needs come together. The word is here plainly taken in an appropriated acceptation, referring to a multitude which the hearers then, and the readers now, are in no danger of mistaking. *The multitude* is here synonymous with *the brethren, the church.* See also Acts vi. 2, 5.

With respect to what you say upon the supposition that there were a plurality of congregations in Jerusalem, I think it unnecessary to make any observations. The fact is not proved, and therefore cannot be a foundation for farther discussion.

Having taken up a considerable portion of these sheets with a critical examination of the word *church*, for the benefit of those who cannot enter into discussions of this nature, I shall, as concisely as possible, exhibit under one view the various passages in which it occurs in the New Testament, as far as I can collect them. This is at once the most certain and the most simple method of ascertaining the meaning of words. That explanation of any word, appellation or phrase, which is the most literal, the most obvious, and the most generally applicable, is undoubtedly the true explanation. If we can show that every passage, in which the word church is used to denote a Christian religious assembly, will naturally explain according to the signification which we affix to it, while at the same time it preserves one uniform meaning, it can admit of no doubt in the mind of every unprejudiced person, that such must be its true signification. On the other hand, if, according to the Presbyterian interpretation, many passages where the word occurs must be forced, or receive a figurative meaning, while the word must receive a variety of widely different senses, it is the most decisive proof that such cannot be the meaning attached to it by the Spirit. I propose but one meaning to the word εκκλησια, in every instance in which it is applied to any of the assemblies of Christ's disciples upon earth. When it is taken as synonymous with the phrase, *kingdom of heaven*, it refers not to any visible earthly assembly; and from this, as well as the circumstances of the connection, there is not the smallest danger of mistaking the one for the other. Besides, these two applications proceed upon perfectly similar principles, and the latter is as literal as the former. The objects are also not only kindred in their nature, but the latter is the great antitype of the former. All believers on earth, though absent at present from the church in heaven, are members of that church, just as the members of a particular church are considered as a church when in their respective habitations. The brother who, for a length of time, is detained from meeting with the church, is still a member of the church. In the same manner are all saints on earth members of the church above. As soon as they believe the Gospel, " they are come to the general assembly and church of the first-born."

Now, if the passages in which the word occurs will bear me out in this view of the subject, does the man stand upon ground equally firm, who must give it such a diversity of meanings, in many of which there are not common principles; who must force or figurize every passage, in which he takes it in a sense different from me; and who must understand it differently in the very same connection? I most earnestly call the attention of my readers, both learned and unlearned, to this consideration. I could rest the whole cause upon it, and it requires nothing but common sense to weigh the argument. Let us then run up the different passages in which this word is found in a religious sense in the New Testament, examining them by the criterion stated above.

Matt. xvi. 18—" Upon this rock I will build my church." This is the church universal. All the saints in heaven and earth are built upon the rock Christ Jesus, according to the confession of Peter. There is no danger of confounding this with any particular congregation, for Christ speaks as having but one church in the same sense, and the declaration is applicable to all believers. See Eph. ii. 20, 21.

Matt. xviii. 18—" Tell it to the church." There is no danger here of confounding a particular congregation with the church universal, for to that church it would not be possible to make a complaint. There was no other external visible assembly upon earth called church, but a particular congregation, and when they are commanded to tell it to *the* church, it determines it to that particular church of which they might be members. How simple then, and perspicuous does this view of the passage appear, when contrasted with the Presbyterian acceptations of it? In the former, there is no possibility of mistake; in the latter, there is no possibility of determining with certainty. If the word has so many meanings as Presbyterians affix to it, by what rule shall it be incontestibly proved which of them we are to apply to it here? Whether is it, Tell it to the congregation, or tell it to the Session? tell it to the Presbytery, as consisting of pastoral and lay-elders, the representatives of their respective congregations, or tell it the ministers of a Presbytery, as contradistinguished from the lay-elders? tell it to the national church, or the church universal? tell it to a religious assembly, or to any assembly the parties may think proper to depute? according to Presbyterians, the word has all these acceptations, and many others. All these are assemblies upon earth; and that the complaint ought to be made to it in particular, each of these could afford some plausible pretensions, were there only advocates for each as strenuous as you are for one. As the word is taken by Presbyterians in all these senses, there is danger of mistaking that particular assembly intended here by our Lord. If they should even happen to be right, it must be by guess, rather than rational evidence.

Acts ii. 47—" The Lord added the saved to the church." Here, according to our view, there is no obscurity. *The saved* are added *to the church*. This must be the Church of Jerusalem, because their being added to this church is represented as subsequent to their being saved, but to the church universal they are added the moment they believe. Their being saved, and their being added to the church universal, are the same thing. But how unintelligible is it upon the Presbyterian system! To give only a few of the many possible interpretations upon this plan: According to Presbyterians, the word *church* sometimes denotes the saints above as contradistinguished from those below. How then can it be certainly known but the meaning is, that the persons referred to were added to the church above by death? Why may not the church be taken for the Session, and the passage be explained to signify that the persons spoken of were made ministers or lay-elders? You might from this argue, that those who were real believers were chosen to fill the offices, which implies that a mere profession of religion, with a sufficient quantity of external decorum, was sufficient to be an individual member. But perhaps even this would not favour the Church of Scotland. Why may it not even be taken in its unappropriated signification, to signify the worshipping assembly as any assembly, and the meaning be, that God so ordered matters that those who were to be saved, attended the place of worship? I cannot see upon what principles you could oppose an innovating Presbyterian who should adopt any of these interpretations. If there should arise any new modeller of the Presbyterian system, your own weapons might be successfully turned against yourself.

Acts v. 11—"And great fear came upon all the church." A single congregation is the only consistent interpretation this will bear; to wit, the church in which this was performed. But upon the lax principles of interpretation adopted by Presbyterians, there is no certain rule for discovering what sort of church is intended. Is it one of many congregations in Jerusalem? Is it the whole of the congregations of Jerusalem considered as a Presbytery? Is it the churches of the nation? Is it the churches of any particular division of the world? Is it the universal visible church? Is it the universal militant invisible church? Is it the session of the congregation in which this affair happened? Is it the clergy of all the congregations of Jerusalem? Is it any assembly, to wit, the promiscuous meeting that was then present, or perhaps the sanhedrim, &c.?

Acts viii. 1—" And at that time there was a great

persecution against the church which was at Jerusalem." We have already at length considered the reasons for understanding the word here in its proper and usual sense. But admitting the Presbyterian latitude of signification attached to this word, could any man say definitely what it must mean here? It is as lawful to defend any or all of the other meanings, as the one you have chosen to affix to it. Could it be proved that it was not a general council assembled at Jerusalem? Why might not any assembly, of any description, as well here as in Acts xv. 22?

Acts viii. 3.—" As for Saul, he made havock of the church, entering into every house, and haling men and women, committed them to prison." This text you give up to denote the body of the disciples of Jerusalem; but there is nothing to prevent you from claiming it here, more than in any other place, were you not obliged upon that supposition to share the clerical prerogatives with females.

Acts ix. 31—" Then had the churches rest throughout all Judea, and Galilee, and Samaria," &c. Here I would be glad to know how this can be interpreted upon any other principle than that *church* in the singular number was solely appropriated to a single congregation, when applied to an assembly of Christ's disciples. It is not the Church of Judea, the Church of Galilee, and the Church of Samaria, but the churches of Judea, &c. Nay, more, had these been Presbyterians, all under the same government, the phraseology would not have been even the Church of Judea, and the Church of Galilee, and the Church of Samaria, but all these would have been in one church, and even then but a small part of a church. The phraseology would have been something like this, 'The church had rest throughout Judea, Galilee, and Samaria,' *i.e.*, the part of the church that lies in these countries. Presbyterians may in theory argue that each of their assemblies, classical as well as worshipping, is a church; but in reality they give the appellation church only to the general body under the same government, or to those who are supposed to represent them. They never speak of *the Church of Edinburgh, the Church of Glasgow.* They never speak of their Presbyteries as churches, or of their Synods as churches, though without scruple they will make the inspired writers speak of the Church of Jerusalem as a Presbytery. As you explain the persecution in the eighth chapter of Acts, as dispersing the clergy solely, perhaps this passage means that the clergy in those countries were now freed from persecution. If it was the clergy alone who were disturbed, it could be the clergy alone who got rest.

Acts xi. 22—"Then tidings of these things came unto the ears of the church which was in Jerusalem, and they sent forth Barnabas," &c. Here, what shall hinder the word to be understood in its literal and obvious import? *Yet the church sends forth Barnabas.*

Acts ii. 26—" And it came to pass that a whole year they assembled themselves with the church." Can you deny that the church here spoken of is a congregation of saints? Or that the whole disciples of Antioch constituted one church or congregation only? The writer evidently refers to the stated meetings of a particular body, so well known under the appropriated name, *the church*, that he supposes farther specification to be unnecessary. Is it not then most evident, that when the same writer speaks of *the church*, he must mean a similar body? I contend that, either he does so, or he does not write intelligibly.

Acts xii. 1—" Now, about that time, Herod the king stretched forth his hand to vex certain of the church." Can anything be plainer than that the historian speaks of the disciples of Jerusalem? And that they constituted but one congregation, is known from their being called church, not churches.

Acts xii. 5—" Peter therefore was kept in prison; but prayer was made without ceasing of the church unto God for him." Does not *the church* here signify the body of the disciples of Jerusalem? Not churches, but church.

Acts xiii. 1—" Now there were in the church that was at Antioch," &c. Of what did the Church of Antioch consist? Of church officers only, or of a number of believers in an organized society? That there was but one church in Antioch, is clear from the disciples being spoken of in their organized capacity as one church, not churches. Besides, in Acts xi. 26, they are all said to assemble in one church.

Acts xiv. 23—"And when they had ordained them elders in every church." Here the disciples of Lystra, the disciples of Iconium, and the disciples of Antioch in Pisidia, are each considered as a separate body called a church. The expression is illustrated by another which refers to the same thing in Titus i. 5. Titus was left in Crete, among other things, "to ordain elders in every city." "In every church," and "in every city," are expressions here supposed equivalent. There was one, and but one church, as yet, in every city in which there were disciples.

Acts xiv. 27—"And when they were come and had gathered the church together." Here it is positively declared that the Church of Antioch was one congregation only; for the disciples are not only called *the church*, not *the churches*, but this church is said to be gathered together. The Church of Antioch is also said to be gathered together by the brethren sent down from the church at Jerusalem. Acts xv. 30—"And when they had gathered *the multitude* together." This shows not only that the disciples at Antioch formed one church, but that *the multitude* and *the church* are equivalent appropriated names given to the disciples; which fully proves what I advanced upon Acts xxi. 22. Besides, the gathering together of the church at Antioch on the return of Paul and Barnabas, and the latter rehearsing all that God had done by them for the information of the former, is just analogous with what is recorded in Acts xxi. 22. In the one case, the church did come together to hear what Paul and Barnabas had done; and in the other, it is asserted that it was "altogether necessary that the multitude should come together." It is then evident that *the multitude* in Acts xxi. 22, is the same with *the church* in Acts xiv. 27.

Acts xv. 3—"And being brought on their way by the church;" to wit, the Church of Antioch, represented in Acts xiv. 27, as assembled all in one place. Here the church must incontestibly mean the disciples, because the apostles and elders are mentioned and contradistinguished from the church. That the disciples of Jerusalem constituted one assembly only, is evident in this place, besides the usual arguments, from their being said to receive the messengers from Antioch. It cannot be alleged that they received them representatively, for the rulers are also said to have received them.

Acts xv. 22—" Then pleased it the apostles and elders, with the whole church." What should prevent the word church here, from having its primary, appropriated, and usual meaning?

Acts xv. 41—" And he went through Syria and Cilicia confirming the churches." Here, when he speaks of the disciples of a country or province, he speaks of them not as a church, but as churches. When he spoke of the disciples of Antioch, he called them *the church that was at Antioch;* but when he speaks of the disciples of Syria, in which lay the city of Antioch, he calls them *churches.* Is it not then palpably evident to any impartial upright mind, that *the church* was appropriated to the body of the disciples in one assembly? As the inspired writer, speaking of a number of congregations, uniformly call them *churches,* what farther proof do we need that there was only one congregation in every place where the disciples are called *church?* Why does he not say the churches of Antioch, as well as the churches of Syria, if there were more congregations than one in the former?

Acts xvi. 5—" And so were the churches (not the church) established in the faith." The churches in this verse, is an expression equivalent to the cities in the preceding verse. They went through the cities, delivering to them, *i.e.,* to the churches in them, &c. The church in a city, but the churches in the cities.

Acts xviii. 22—" And when he had landed at Cesarea, and gone up and saluted the church." How could he salute the church, if it was not one assembly? or could there have been more than one congregation as yet in Cesarea? *The church* is here an appropriated appellation of a body as well known under that name, as the supreme civil governor of Rome was known by the terms, *the emperor.* If it was not so appropriated and used in this sense, how could it be understood what he meant by it here?

In Acts xix. the word occurs in its civil sense for a popular assembly.

Acts xx. 17—" And from Miletus he sent for the elders of the church." It is not *the churches,* but *the church* at Ephesus. Besides, from this we learn, not only that *the church* here necessarily denotes the disciples in contradistinction from their rulers, but that the elders can never be called the church on this very account. The word church is here the name that contradistinguishes the body of the disciples from their rulers, and the word elders is the name that contradistinguishes the rulers from the church. It is absolutely impossible then that ever these two words should be interchangeable. If they are contradistinguishing names of two parties in a body, the one the name of the body in general, the other the name of the rulers of that body, how absurd would it be to suppose that the distinguishing name of the body should become the distinguishing name of the rulers? It might as well be alleged that the contradistinguishing words king and people, or ministers and people might be interchanged, and that *the people* in a civil sense might denote the king, as distinguished from his subjects, and that *the people* in a religious sense might denote the clergy, in opposition to their flocks. The elders are here called not *the church,* but *the elders of the church.* If the word church could properly and as intelligibly have denoted the church rulers, why is it not said that he sent for *the church,* meaning the church rulers? Was there any need to be more precise here than in Matt. xviii. 17, &c. Would there have been greater danger of misunderstanding this application of the word in this, than in other instances? Would his real intention have been less easily discovered from the connection and circumstances in this passage than in the others? By no means; but much the contrary. The connection and address of Paul to the elders would absolutely have shown in what sense the word was to be understood, for he speaks to none but the elders. All to whom he addresses himself are considered as bishops, having oversight of the flock. Here then, if in any place, we would have church used for church rulers, because from the circumstances, it could not have been misunderstood. Since then the inspired historian, when speaking of church rulers, both in cases where the body of the disciples are also brought into view, and in others as the present, where the latter are not named as having any share in the transaction; since the historian speaks of the rulers, not by the name church, but as distinguished from the church, I hold it to be irresistibly evident, that the word church can never be substituted for church rulers, or elders; and that consequently, when he speaks of the church, he refers to the body of the disciples. When he says that Paul sent for *the elders of the church*, it plainly supposes that *church* and the *elders* were two different classes, and that the latter were the officers of the former. I then demand a substantial reason why Christ did not say (Matt. xviii. 17), 'Tell it to the *elders of the church*,' if it had been the elders of the church whom he intended. Had Paul sent a message to Ephesus, desiring the attendance of *the church*, tell me with the candour of an upright enquirer after truth, do you think he would have been understood to mean the elders? Would not the whole church have resorted to him at Miletus? If so, with what consistency do you suppose the Lord Jesus Christ to use such enigmatical language in Matt. xviii. 17? When he says, 'Tell it to the church,' would it be understood that he intended only the elders of the church? If, on every occasion, when the inspired writers evidently speak of church rulers, they give them their own distinguishing name, why should it be supposed that they would at any time use the word which distinguishes the body of the disciples from their rulers, as denoting their rulers? Suppose again, that the word church sometimes denoted the church rulers, and sometimes the brethren in general, and that Paul's message had been addressed to the church at Ephesus, without farther specification, would he have been understood? Would the message have been intelligibly precise? How would they have known whether he meant the pastors or the disciples in general? Yet this is the very absurdity you charge upon our Lord Jesus, in his direction above referred to; and on the writer of the Acts of the Apostles, chap. viii. 1; xv. 4, 22, &c. Were men in common life to speak upon such principles, language would not be intelligible.

Acts xx. 28—"Feed the Church of God," *i.e.*, as in the preceding part of the verse, "the flock over which the Holy Ghost had made them overseers;" the single church committed to their joint oversight.

Rom. xvi. 1—"—a servant of the church, which is at Cenchrea." Could this have been more than a single congregation? And is it supposable that the same phraseology has not always the same meaning? Why should the expression, "the church which is at Cenchrea," signify one congregation of saints, and the church which is at Jerusalem, or the church which is at Antioch, signify either a number of congregations, or the clergy of a number of congregations, &c.? Whatever *the church* is at one place, *the same* must it be at every other place.

Rom. xvi. 4—"All the churches of the Gentiles." Not the Gentile Church. This phraseology clearly evinces, that neither the Christian commonwealth, nor any combination of particular congregations, were yet considered as *a church*. Such expressions as, 'the Eastern Church,' 'the Western Church,' 'the Church,' considered as referring to all professing Christians, 'the Church of Scotland,' 'the Reformed Church,' 'the Lutheran Church,' &c., took their rise, not from the New Testament, but from the working of the mystery of iniquity.

Rom. xvi. 5—"The church which is in their house." Could this have been more than a single assembly?

Rom. xvi. 16—"The churches of Christ salute you," to wit, the churches in the neighbourhood where he then resided. These he calls, not the Church of Achaia, but the churches.

Rom. xvi. 23—"Gaius, mine host, and of *the whole church*," *i.e.*, the Church of Corinth.

1 Cor. i. 2; 2 Cor. i. 1—"Unto the Church of God which is at Corinth." What this church was, is

explained " to them that are sanctified, called to be saints." That they constituted but one assembly, is clearly seen among other reasons from their being actually said to meet usually.—1 Cor. xi. 17, 18, 20, 22; xiv. 23.

1 Cor. iv. 17—" As I teach in every church." Church is here supposed to be the appropriated denomination of every particular congregation.

1 Cor. vi. 4—" Least esteemed in the church." The congregation of the saints.

1 Cor. vii. 17—" So ordain I in all the churches:" *i.e.*, I not only give these regulations to the church at Corinth, but I ordain the same to be observed in all the churches of the world. Every particular congregation is considered a church, and the aggregate of them are not a church, but churches. The apostle does not say, ' So ordain I in every part of the church,' but in all the churches. These churches also are all to be formed on the same model, and receive the same regulations.

1 Cor. x. 32—" Give none offence, neither to the Jews, nor to the Gentiles, nor to the Church of God," *i.e.*, the church at Corinth.

1 Cor. xi. 16—" Neither the churches of God." The aggregate of congregations are invariably called churches.

1 Cor. xi. 18—" When ye come together in the church." Could it be more evidently stated that they usually met as one assembly?

1 Cor. xi. 22—" Despise ye the Church of God," *i.e.*, the assembly of God's children at Corinth.

1 Cor. xii. 28—" God hath set some in the church." The church universal, in the part of which that is upon earth God hath instituted these offices.

1 Cor. xiv. 4, 5, 12, 19—" He that prophesieth, edifieth the church—that the church may receive edifying—to the edifying of the church—yet in the church I had rather speak," &c. Do these passages need a commentary? He could not speak in an assembly that was not present.

1 Cor. xiv. 23—" If therefore the whole church be come together." Could language more plainly assert that the Church of Corinth was one assembly?

1 Cor. xiv. 28—" If there be no interpreter, let him keep silence in the church." Does not this imply that the church was one assembly?

1 Cor xiv. 33—" As in all the churches of the saints." Here again we have the regular distinction between the use of the singular and plural number of this word. God was the author of peace and order, not only in this, but in every other church of his saints.

1 Cor. xiv. 34—" Let your women keep silence in the churches," *i.e.*, the different meetings of the church. The appropriated name of the body characterizes them as actually met. Strictly speaking then, they are a church, or act as a church, only when met. The different meetings of the body are, in this point of view, so many churches. Yet this and all other words, appropriated to any body from particular circumstances, come to be given to such bodies in all circumstances, or at least when the distinguishing circumstances which gave rise to the name, are not held up to view. Thus, that body called the Parliament, though thus designated from their public discussion of matters that regard the national welfare, are called by this name when they are sleeping as well as when they are speaking. And thus, 'There was a church-meeting to-day,' is a more usual phraseology than 'There was a church to-day;' though undoubtedly the latter is the more strictly proper. The apostle then forbids women to speak in the meetings of the church, or more literally in the churches. Now this must have been an assembly of the members at large, for in assemblies of church rulers women had no place, and therefore it would have been absurd to command them not to speak in them. This was an assembly of which women were members, but not public speakers. Besides, that church is here a single assembly, is clear from the circumstances of forbidding women to speak in it, which supposes that there were others that might speak in it. It must then have been single congregations to which he refers, for in the church, considered as the aggregate of many congregations; there could be no speaking, as it is not an assembled church. That *the church* here refers to the different meetings of

the same body, is not only evident from the above analysis, but from the connection of the whole chapter, in which the body addressed are supposed in several places to be but one church. In verse 23, he says, " If therefore the whole church be come together." In this it is supposed that the body addressed usually assembled in one church. They could not in the same letter be considered as constituting a number of churches. The phraseology is exactly similar to the following that might be used by a Presbyterian : 'We have good congregations in the evening, but very thin ones in the morning.'

1 Cor. xiv. 35—" For it is a shame for women to speak in the church." Here again church must be a single and popular assembly. But according to the Presbyterian latitude of application assigned to the word church, I do not see how it could be decisively proved that women ought not to speak in the church, considered as a congregation. Those who should choose to support the contrary, might allege that the word church here means the assemblies of church rulers alone; that females were not allowed to speak in church courts, but that they might speak in the public congregation. Would not this be every whit as plausible as the Presbyterian interpretation of Matt. xviii. 17 ; Acts viii. 1, &c.

1 Cor. xv. 9 ; Gal. i. 13 ; Phil. iii. 6—" I persecuted the church of God." This is the church as synonymous with the kingdom of heaven, rather than the particular church at Jerusalem, although it does not appear that Paul had actually persecuted any besides. But he persecuted the church universal, because he persecuted that part of it which was exposed to him. It is one whole. He that persecutes one individual of it, persecutes the whole; yea, the persecution of the least esteemed of Christ's members, is a persecution of himself. " Saul, Saul, why persecutest thou me ?" If the nail of a finger is parted, the whole body is pained. He that wounds another in the foot, wounds *the man.*

1 Cor. xvi. 1—" As I have given order to the churches of Galatia," not the Church of Galatia.

1 Cor. xvi. 19—" The churches of Asia salute you ;"

not the Church of Asia. In every instance in which a number of congregations are expressly spoken of, they are called not church, but churches. Every single congregation of Christians is called a church. Is it then at all warrantable, without any example or authority from the meaning of the word, in the face of a multitude of examples to the contrary, to force the word church by an arbitrary interpretation to denote a number of churches? I call upon you to produce a single example in which a number of congregations, evidently mentioned or referred to, are called *church*. I call upon you to show me upon what principles of grammar it could be so used. If you can do neither, I am confident that I will have all the learning in Scotland on my side. I am confident that there is not a man in the Church of Scotland, of an established literary character, would hazard his reputation, by vindicating the propriety of giving a signification to a word which it neither intrinsically possessed, nor of which a single well-authenticated example could be found. I shall also be very much mistaken, if there shall be found a single man among those of acknowledged literary eminence in the Church of Scotland, who would undertake to defend the hypothesis, that there is in the New Testament a complete and unalterable model for church government. Why else was the defence of the divine right of the Presbyterian form of church government entrusted to you and Mr. Smith alone? Shall the National Church of Scotland be repeatedly attacked, and shall the learning of Scotland refuse its aid to defend her? Is there more learning in any part of the world than in Scotland? Why did not the Universities pour forth their learning, and overwhelm the adversaries of the Church? Shall that Church which possessed a man who could silence a Hume, be now left destitute of the defence of her most eminent doctors, if its divine right were really defensible? No; if the Church of Scotland were founded upon divine authority, it possesses men who would irresistibly prove it. Her refractory sons would soon be obliged to return to their allegiance, or skulk from the field of battle. But it is a fact too well known to be particularly corroborated, that all the learning of both the British religious establishments, opposes a complete and unchangeable model of any kind. Conscious that there is nothing like a model in Scripture for these stupendous fabrics, they rightly judge it safer and easier to defend their particular systems, by supposing much left to the governors of the nation, to the wisdom of the church rulers, and the changes of times and circumstances. This method, though equally false, is fraught with much less absurdity, and has less mischievous effects upon the interpretation of Scripture, than the other. Thus, we find many of them giving a tolerably fair account of the first churches, because their system does not require the testimony of Scripture to be disguised or perverted. They can admit that such and such was the case then, because times and circumstances are now greatly changed. This is the true reason, I apprehend, why none of the first-rate talents have appeared in this contest. To vindicate the Church of Scotland as a good human system, would, in the estimation of the bulk of the good people of Scotland, be nearly as bad as to oppose it. The divine right must then be abandoned to such as can believe it. The former, no doubt, will look on, applauding in public, and laughing in private. Like those statesmen who disbelieve Christianity, but see its advantages upon society; though they do not believe the divine right themselves, they will be very well satisfied that others should believe it.

1 Cor. xvi. 19—"Aquila and Priscilla, with the church that is in their house." A single assembly without doubt.

2 Cor. viii. 1—"The churches of Macedonia," not the Church of Macedonia. The distinction is without exception.

2 Cor. viii. 18—"Whose praise is in all the churches," not in every part of the church, or in the church.

2 Cor. viii. 23—"Messengers of the churches." These messengers, chosen by the Macedonian churches to carry their contribution to the poor saints at Jerusalem, are not called the messengers of the church, but

of the churches. Here, if any where, the different congregations of Macedonia would have been called a church, for they are now represented as united in a common message and gift. Why then is it not the messengers of the Macedonian Church?

2 Cor. viii. 24—"Before the churches." The same Macedonian churches, who by their messengers would hear of the conduct of the Corinthians.

2 Cor. xi. 8—"I robbed other churches." The Christians at Corinth are here, as a church, contrasted with other churches.

2 Cor. xi. 23—"The care of all the churches;" not the care of the church. Is not this distinctive phraseology completely decisive?

2 Cor. xii. 13—"Inferior to other churches." The Church of Corinth is here contrasted with, and supposed equal to every other church. The apostle would only compare kind with kind.

Gal. i. 2—"Unto the churches of Galatia;" no where are they called the Church of Galatia. If there were several congregations in Jerusalem, Antioch, Corinth, &c., why does he not address them in the same manner as he does this, as churches, not church? Why does not the writer of the Acts of the Apostles observe the same distinction?

Gal. i. 22—"And was unknown by face unto the churches of Judea." Why does he not say, the Church of Judea? Why does he use the word church, when speaking of the disciples of Jerusalem, and churches when he speaks of the disciples of Judea?

Eph. i. 22; iii. 10, 21; v. 23, 24, 25, 27, 29, 32; Col. i. 18, 24; Heb. ii. 12; xii. 23. Church universal; no danger of mistaking the application.

That the church at Ephesus was one single congregation, and complete in itself, is clear from chap. ii. 22. "In whom ye also are *built together*, for an habitation of God, through the Spirit." They were all in one building, and, without any others joined with them, composed a complete house or habitation for the Spirit of God to dwell in.

Col. iv. 15—"Nymphas, and the church which is

in his house." This must certainly have been but one congregation.

Phil. iv. 15—"No church but ye only." The Philippians, as a single congregation, are contrasted with other churches of the same kind.

Col. iv. 16—"Cause that it be read also in the church of the Laodiceans;" *i.e.*, in the church of the Laodiceans, as well as in your church. Church must here be one assembly, for in another sense the epistle could not be read in the church.

1 Thess. i. 1; 2 Thess. i. 1—"Unto the church of the Thessalonians." Had there been more than one, they would have been called churches.

1 Thess. ii. 14—"Followers of the churches of God which are in Judea." Here again we have the distinction between the use of church and churches. Remember that the saints in Jerusalem are always called the church at Jerusalem; while those of the whole nation are called the churches of Judea.

2 Thess. i. 4—"Glory in you in the churches of God." Every congregation of the saints is here considered as a church, in each of which, as Paul was labouring among them, he spake with approbation and exultation of the church of the Thessalonians.

1 Tim. iii. 5—"How shall he take care of the church of God?" to wit, the church in which he should be a bishop.

1 Tim. iii. 15—"In the house of God, which is the church of God." Every individual church is a complete representation of the body of Christ. They are one body as they eat of the one bread. They are a house or complete building for the habitation of God— Eph. ii. 22. When Timothy was labouring in any of these churches, he was labouring in the house of God. Each of these churches, like a pillar, held the truth out to public view. They are like a city set upon a hill; like lights shining in a dark place. Their union in the ordinances of Christ, preaches the Gospel to the world.

1 Tim. v. 16—"Let not the church be charged;" *i.e.*, the church to which these poor widows belonged. As he is speaking of the duty of maintaining poor widows, it is not likely that the clergy will claim it here.

Philem. 2—" To the church in thy house;" only one congregation surely.

James v. 14—" Let him send for the elders of the church." Without doubt, the elders of the particular church of which he should be a member.

3 John 6—" Thy charity before the church;" the congregation of which he was a member.

Ver. 9—" I wrote unto the church;" that particular church. He wrote to the church itself, not to the elders alone, with respect to the brethren to whom he alludes. But the mystery of iniquity had already begun to work in this church, and through the influence of Diotrephes they were not received. It was then, by criminal negligence on the one hand, and usurpation on the other, that the members of the churches came at last to be mere ciphers in the church.

Ver. 10—" Casteth them out of the church." By this usurped authority, Diotrephes lorded it over the rest of the brethren, and cast such out of the church as disobeyed his mandates. Here then it is evident excommunication belongs to a single congregation. Had it not been the privilege of the church, Diotrephes could not have usurped it. He could not have succeeded, until he had got the same ascendency in the superior courts, had this church been a Presbyterian congregation. Here then is a church just in the state which you represent an Independent church to be in. The evils of this situation, you would correct by a superior court. If you were consistent, you would blame the constitution of this church. Now, the same excuse that you made for our Lord's silence with respect to an appeal to superior assemblies, will not serve you here. Here is an injurious sentence passed and executed; yet the apostle speaks nothing of an appeal to a higher assembly. Had there been any such thing as a superior court, the apostle would certainly have directed the aggrieved to apply to it, to review the unjust sentence procured in this church by the influence of Diotrephes. Neither does he write to a Presbytery or Synod to punish Diotrephes, but declares he would remember him if he came.

Rev. i. 4, 11, 20; ii. 7, 11, 17, 23, 29; iii. 6, 13, 22;

xxii. 16—"The seven churches which are in Asia;" not the Church of Asia. When spoken of unitedly, they are churches; when separately spoken of, each of them is called *church*.

Rev. ii. 1, 8, 12, 18; iii. 1, 7, 14—Each of them also is addressed as complete in itself, and unconnected with the others. Each is praised or blamed individually. Each of them is required to rectify its own disorders.

Now, Sir, I call upon you to run over these passages, and show us how you understand the word church in each of them. They will all, without force or figure, explain according to our hypothesis, which is so simple as to give but one meaning in every instance in which it applies to any visible assembly of Christ's disciples. With you, the word must assume the most discordant variety of meanings, without sanction from its primary import, its usual acceptation, a single positive example, or any of the common analogies of language. It is now literal, and now figurative; now appropriated, and now unappropriated; now appropriated to one thing, and now to another; without any fixed rule to regulate us in this perplexity, without any clew to lead us into the labyrinth. Besides, you employ figures which I have attempted to show are utterly absurd. You must overthrow this, or your cause is overthrown.

LETTER X.

Sir,

Having considered your arguments for a plurality of churches in Jerusalem, and your objections to the presence of the individual members in the meeting recorded in Acts xv.; I shall now return to review your eighth letter. Before we proceed, on either side, to draw consequences from the transaction here related, it is absolutely necessary that we accurately determine what were the component parts of the assembly. This is the reason I have been so diffuse in proving, that there was in Jerusalem one Christian church only. If I have succeeded in this, I shall have little trouble in what remains.

" Let it be supposed for a moment," you say (p. 118), " that the brethren here mentioned, were not *the other* ministers who were then at Jerusalem besides the apostles and elders: If it be asserted that these members, *in any form*, voted and judged in the case referred to, while it seems to establish in one view, it completely subverts in another, the scheme for which it is urged. You argue against Presbyterians when they attempt to demonstrate from this passage, that one congregation, with its rulers, may be subject to the rulers of a number of congregations met as a Presbytery, and tell them that this case was *extraordinary*." Yes, Sir; the circumstance of this case being extraordinary, and infallibly decided by the apostles, will indeed equally prove, that neither the elders of one congregation alone, nor these with the whole congregation, can decide for any other congregation. But we contend, that if this history gives the elders of one congregation a right to judge for another, it will equally give the members of one congregation a right to the same. The infallible determination of this question entirely precludes this transaction from being considered at all as a model for uninspired assemblies to make decrees. But as to the determination with respect to the matter of fact; to wit, whether the church had sent out the judaizing teachers with directions to inculcate the obligation of the Mosaic law, the whole church was equally concerned, and equally qualified to declare, as they do in their letter, "to whom we gave no such commandment." In this it is evidently a model, recorded for our imitation. This then is a sufficient answer to your next argument. "But if the argument which is advanced by Presbyterians from this passage for a court of review, above the ministers or elders of a particular congregation, composed of the ministers of a number of congregations, seems to you inconclusive, because this assembly was inspired, and delivered an extraordinary inspired decision, must it not be equally inconclusive when urged by Independents for the right of the people to judge and vote in their religious assemblies?" Yes, Sir; it is equally conclusive against the members of one congregation judging and voting in the affairs of another, as against the elders of one congregation, judging in the affairs of another congregation. It shows, that neither elders nor individual members of one congregation, should judge for another congregation; but it shows, that whenever the elders are admitted to judge, the individual members are also admitted. The horns of this dilemma, then, are exceedingly harmless. There is nothing proved, but that individual members have no better right to judge for others, than elders have; which is a very unimportant proposition. As to the matter of fact above stated, the model is still proper.

"If the ministers and elders of different congregations now, who correspond to the elders associated with the apostles, are not to judge as a *Presbytery* in matters which relate to *another* congregation, because, though they determined along with them in the appeal from Antioch, the whole of them were guided by a miraculous energy, on what principle can it be proved that *the people* now are to judge and vote, because *the people* at Jerusalem judged and voted under the guidance of **this** extraordinary infallible energy?" There is here an uncandid statement. The judging and voting of the ministers and elders are supposed to refer to other congregations, and that of church members to the concerns of their own church alone; while you make it equally improper for individual members to judge in their own affairs, as for the former to judge in the affairs of other congregations. Had you reasoned fairly, the conclusion from the infallible determination of this question would have been, that it is equally improper for one Independent church to judge for another, as for a classical Presbytery to judge for the congregations connected with them: or that it is equally improper for individual members to judge for others, as it is for ministers and elders to judge for others. This indeed is an undeniable truth, but of all truths the most unimportant; for I suppose there are not in the world any who would question it. Will this hold, however, as to the affairs of the church itself, which require no inspiration, such as the fact so often referred to? Besides, if inspired apostles joined the brethren with them, in a matter which they might have determined without them, by what pretext will uninspired ministers and elders exclude the individual members from their deliberations? If they were admitted to join in a decision with inspired men, what should forbid them to join in the decision of every matter with their uninspired rulers. If their approbation and consent was in any measure, or in any view, either necessary or useful in this matter, which was determined by the apostles of Jesus, will not the same be much more necessary and useful when matters are decided by fallible men? There is no reason that can be alleged for admitting the brethren to a participation in this decision, that will not have ten-fold strength, as to the decisions of fallible men. Even upon the supposition that this was a fallible council, the supposition would not tend to exclude the members from a share in the decision of church business, but to increase the evidence of its necessity. As inspired men, each of the apostles was indeed of himself qualified to decide the matter; but if they are considered as uninspired men, they had need, not only of the brethren of Jerusalem, but of all the churches in the world; and even after all, the decision should not command obedience. If this was an ordinary and fallible decision, designed as a precedent, it establishes the right of the individual members, as well as of the rulers of one church, to judge and determine for another. If it was an infallible decision of the question about circumcision, as well as of the matter of fact with respect to the instructions given to the teachers that went down to Antioch, the circumstance of the brethren being joined with the apostles and elders, will for ever prove, that in every decision of the church, the brethren ought to be joined with the elders. The infallibility of this decision will indeed cut off all pretensions, both of elders and brethren, to decide for other churches; but it will incontestibly prove, that in all cases in which the elders are admitted to judge, the consent of the brethren is necessary; and that the laws of Christ must be executed among them with the approbation of the whole church. Whether this decision was inspired or uninspired, the rights of the brethren are unaffected.

"The argument, besides, adduced by you and Mr. Ewing, in common with Mr. Glas, for the right of the members to judge at present in the affairs of the church, from what is here said of the brethren at Jerusalem, if it prove anything, proves undoubtedly *too much*. It demonstrates not merely their right to judge and vote in matters which relate to their *own*, but in those which concern even another congregation. But does not this contradict a first principle of Independency, that neither the members nor the rulers of *one* congregation have a right to interfere, even according to your own acknowledgement (p. 30), and according to the favourite position of Glas which he so keenly defends, with any *other* congregation under heaven?" Indeed, Sir, if this history could be alleged to prove any superior courts, it would certainly establish the right of a single church, in its officers and brethren. Those who extend it as a model for references and appeals, must certainly allow it to go that length. But this absurdity is not attached to our views, but to those of Presbyterians. It is very easy to see how it may prove enough for our purpose, without proving too much.

As I have said more than once, the brethren and elders of the Church of Jerusalem were of right joined in this decision, so far as it regarded the affairs of that church. As the teachers who went down to Antioch inculcating the necessity of circumcision, received no such doctrine from the church at Jerusalem, it was quite proper that the church should signify this to the brethren at Antioch. Now this may very lawfully prove the right of church members to a participation with their elders in the business of their own church, without proving either that elders or brethren, should judge for other churches. As to the obligation of circumcision, none but inspired persons could infallibly determine it; yet the apostles chose to join the whole brethren with them in this, as well as the elders; and if the elders were not inspired, they were both equally unfit to decide, though with the clearest conviction they might join in the infallible decision of the apostles. Now, if in the decision of a question which none could infallibly determine but inspired persons, the apostles thought it proper to have the approbation and explicit consent of the whole brethren, as well as of the elders, it will follow, that in every instance in which the elders decide, the brethren must join in the decision. If they were admitted to join the apostles, will any arguments forbid them to join the uninspired ministers? Now, Sir, in both these ways the argument will prove enough, without too much. After all, I am not much concerned to prove from this passage the right of members to judge in their own affairs. This is established by so many other passages, as to take away every temptation to force it on this place. I urge this rather to illustrate the history, than to support my theory, which stands impregnably firm without it. But it is very evident, that the great intention of the Spirit in recording this whole affair, is not only in this public manner to annul the Mosaic dispensation, but to give us a model for the transaction of church business.

"Besides, would not the subordination to which this argument leads, a subordination of a particular congregation, not merely, as Presbyterians maintain, to the ministers and lay-elders, the wisest and most enlightened of a number of congregations, but to the members indiscriminately of a sister congregation, be much more intolerable, even upon your own principles, than that for which the former contend?" Indeed, Sir, of two things evidently absurd, it is of very little importance to determine which is the more absurd. I will allow you, without any disturbance, to take which of these opinions you please. But I will contend, that whether it be tolerable or intolerable, absurd or proper, if this history affords a model for any courts of reference, appeal, or review, it establishes incontestibly the right of one church, in its members and officers. Now, make you what you please of it.

It follows also, you say, not only that the brethren of one congregation may judge for those of another, but even while the latter are not present. You add, "But does not this contradict another Independent principle?" Rather you should have said; does not this contradict the Scriptures (1 Cor. v. 4), and therefore cannot be deducible from this passage? The contradiction is not between two principles of Independents, but between the principles of Presbyterians and the Word of God. Independent churches judge for others, neither in their presence nor out of it. Nor does the argument derived from this history prove that they ought to do so.

"Or is it said, that the assembly at Jerusalem was not inspired, and that the reference made to them was simply for *opinion* and *advice?* On this supposition, no *judicial power* at all was exercised, no act of *government* was performed by *any of them:* and consequently, though it were admitted that the brethren at Jerusalem were allowed, along with the apostles and elders, *to state their opinion* upon the controverted points, no argument can be adduced from it for the right of the brethren at present to *govern* and *vote* in the church. *Governing* the church and *exercising discipline* are certainly very different from a *mere statement of opinion* upon a controverted point, which either might be received or rejected. And if the apostles, and elders, and members, in the case before us, merely gave an advice, and stated an opinion (as is done by the occasional association of your ministers, while, as you declare, p. 31, 32, &c., it is not binding upon any of your congregations), it will never follow that because the brethren were permitted to do this, they are authorised to govern or exercise discipline."—pp. 121, 122.

I believe indeed, that the ancient Independent writers have poured forth abundance of nonsense about meetings for council and advice. Some of them have supposed, that though this narrative does not afford a model for meetings of ministers to make authoritative decrees for the churches, yet that it sanctions such meetings for the purpose of giving council and advice to the churches. Their error I treat with the same freedom that I do yours. I look upon this theory to be much more absurd even than the Presbyterian. For it is not possible to explain the passage in such a manner as to establish the divine right of assemblies for advice. This meeting gave not advice, but decrees; did not submit opinions to be canvassed, but doctrines to be believed, and precepts to be observed. If it is at all a model for any foreign interference, it establishes absolute authority on the one hand, and passive and unlimited obedience on the other. I cannot see anything that could tempt inquiring Christians to adopt this theory, except they have not been thoroughly purged from Presbyterian prejudices, or a desire not to appear all at once to go to so great a distance from the churches of this world. Perhaps a mixture of these motives have operated with them. They are a little shocked themselves, and perhaps afraid that others will be more so, with the idea of being so unlike to other societies called churches, in every distinguishing feature. On the contrary, I am of opinion, that we ought not to wish to hide from the churches of the world, how much we differ from them. We ought to be solicitous rather to show them, that in every distinguishing feature the kingdom of Christ differs from the kingdoms of this world. We ought not to keep the worshippers of the beast in countenance, by making an image of the beast. There is no reason to fear alarming the prejudices of the world, or of Christians. If the cause is the Lord's, we may safely rest it upon his shoulders. If men will receive instructions from the Word of God as to the nature of Christ's kingdom, it is well. But if any man will be obstinately and perversely ignorant, let him be ignorant. It is our duty to hold forth the Word of life, in every part of it; it is in the Lord's hand who shall receive it. He has no need of our wisdom to help forward his plans.

But if such meetings are not instituted from this passage *jure divino*, they cannot plead it to sanction their innocency. If they are not the offspring of the wisdom of God, they must be the offspring of the wisdom of man; and the Lord will no more countenance one human religious institution than he will another. To say that such assemblies are useful, yet not instituted, is to arraign the wisdom of Jesus, as a legislator, and to deny the competency of his institutions. If they are not divinely appointed, they cannot be useful, they cannot be innocent. I am bold to predict, that wherever they are tried, either an increasing acquaintance with the Word of God, and a deeper knowledge of the nature of Christ's kingdom, will lay them aside, or they will degenerate into an engine of Satan. In the very first instance, they must tend to damp inquiry in the churches, and gradually habituate them to allow others to have the trouble of thinking for them. It is also a needless waste of time and of money; without attaining even the legitimate advantage of an interchange of opinions. It must be well known, that more than half-a-dozen cannot maintain conversation; the rest must be mute, or, if they must all speak, time will be greatly consumed. Besides, the formalities of a club or association must render conversation vapid and formal. If we wish the benefit of an interchange of sentiments, let us individually correspond, or rather as often as possible let us visit each other's churches, and let us receive one another in the Lord. This will have incalculable advantages, and for this we will have the sanction of the apostolical churches. I look upon all such religious associations to be both unlawful, and exceedingly injurious. The increase of knowledge in the churches is not to be effected by their pastors meeting to plan, reason, confer, propose and solve difficulties, &c.; but by their labouring among them abundantly. The doctrines, precepts, and institutions of the New Testament are not enveloped in such mystery, as to require the wise men of the world to assemble to draw them from their obscurity. As to the association to which you allude, I believe it does not now exist. I am persuaded that you will find, that most of those who composed it, are at this time entirely opposed to it.

"Again, supposing that this assembly at Jerusalem was neither an extraordinary assembly, nor a meeting convened merely for delivering an advice, but, as will afterwards at least be attempted to be proved, an authoritative, though an uninspired ecclesiastical court, I do not see how any argument can be drawn from it for the right of the members to judge in the church. If so, it would follow, as has been already said, that, like the brethren at Jerusalem, the brethren now could exercise even an authoritative power; that they would be entitled likewise, like those at Jerusalem, to govern not only their own, but even other congregations; and that they would be warranted also authoritatively to govern these congregations, even when they were not present, and could not consent to their decisions; all of which suppositions are manifestly inconsistent with the declared principles of Independents."—p. 122.

Yes, Sir; if this was an ordinary uninspired authoritative decision, it would prove that church members, as well as church rulers, may make laws, prescribe doctrines to be received, and precepts to be observed, with respect to other churches, even when the latter are not present to give their consent. Therefore, to avoid this absurdity, it must be supposed to have been an extraordinary and infallible decision. But it is not more absurd that church members of one church should decide for those of another, than that church rulers should do so. Your reasoning in this place is exceedingly inconclusive. To what does this extract amount? Why to this, that such a thing cannot be the case, because it would imply what is contrary to the principles of the Independents. The principles of the Independents are in these points taken for axioms. They have not always the same weight with you; but in this instance they must not be questioned, because that it answers your purpose to take them for granted. But you here abstract the principles of Independents from the grounds on which they are founded. Independents do indeed deny that church members have those powers to which you refer. They suppose that this passage gives no foundation for such an opinion. But what determines them in this opinion? The conviction that this decision was extraordinary and infallible. Once take away that supposition, and they cannot but admit, that church members have a right to judge even for other churches, and that not in their presence. Upon the supposition that this was an uninspired assembly, these consequences will follow, in opposition both to Independents and Presbyterians. It is indeed lawful to argue from the acknowledged principles of our opponents; and though the reasoning should not be conclusive as to others, if it is fairly deducible from their principles, it must be allowed valid by them until they alter such principles. But in such cases, we must not separate between their principles, and the reasons upon which they are rested. In this place, you reason from the principles of Independents, taken them to be true, while at the same time your argument is rested upon a supposition that takes away the reasons of their truth. Independents believe that the brethren have no such prerogatives, because this decision was inspired. You take the truth of the first for granted, while your theory denies the latter. This reasoning then has no force either in itself, or against Independents. Make the supposition good which you have taken for granted, and I will take all the consequences to which it would lead. I will argue both against Independents and Presbyterians, the extensive authority of some single church, in its elders and brethren. And indeed, as to uninspired assemblies, I see no greater absurdity in church members judging for other churches, than in church rulers doing the same. They are both supremely absurd, and contradictory to other passages of Scripture; therefore cannot be the legitimate meaning of this narrative. The theory then that admits, or cannot prevent such consequences, is a false one; consequently this decision must be an inspired one.

"The truth therefore seems to be, according to the sentiments of some Presbyterians, that though the members at Jerusalem expressed their acquiescence in the decision of the apostles and elders (a circumstance which could not fail to have uncommon weight upon the minds of the believing Jews at Antioch, as they must previously have been no less attached than themselves to the distinguishing peculiarities of the law of Moses), they by no means appear to have judged authoritatively, or even voted in the matter."—page 122.

Indeed, Sir, there was no voting either of apostles, or elders, or brethren. The apostles decided the matter; and the whole church, elders and brethren, heartily joined in the decision. The obligation of the decrees arose from the infallibility of the determination. But the letter was a joint one, and the decision expressed as a joint one. It is not said in the letter, that the brethren informed the brethren at Antioch that they acquiesced in the decision, but the apostles, elders, and brethren, unitedly speak through every part of the address. "It seemed good unto us, being assembled with one accord." Similar is the strain of the whole letter. The brethren are as particularly associated with the apostles as the elders. The brethren, as well as the elders, were assembled with one accord with the apostles, and are represented as fully as they are, to have joined in all that was transacted. As to the authority of the judgment of elders and brethren, if they were both uninspired, it was in both the same. There was no authority in the opinion of any who were not inspired. But as to a distinction between the weight of the judgment of the elders, and of the brethren, or the manner in which they concurred in this decision, there is not the smallest hint in the narrative or letter. The acquiescence of the whole assembly to the truth stated by the apostles, is expressed in the same manner. But view the matter in any light you please, exhaust your invention in finding out distinctions; still the brethren were present, and had their names subjoined to those of the apostles and elders in these decrees. In whatever then this transaction is designed to be a model, it must include the brethren. Allowing your own statement to be altogether just, it must overthrow your ecclesiastical constitution, as in one view or other it makes the acquiescence of the brethren to be a part of the divine model. If the names of the brethren were necessary to give weight to apostolical decrees, much more so to those of uninspired men. If this is the model, why do you not embrace it? Why do you not separate from the Church of Scotland, that you may enjoy it? Why should this part of the model be void of obligation, more than any other part of it? Why are the people among you cut off from that which even this interpretation allows to be their privilege? This model then is on the one hand defective, and on the other redundant. You have not only to supply it with Presbyterian wheels and springs, but also, in making room for them, to cut away some of those which it originally possessed. Indeed, the improvements of the machine are so many and important, that the new model is very well entitled to a patent. But if this was an uninspired assembly, as you profess to believe, and if the truth of the matter seems to be, that those here called *the brethren*, were no farther concerned in the decision than they are here represented, how does this tally with the supposition that *the brethren* were really themselves ministers? Does not this go to prove that in a Synod or General Council, the clergy of the city in which the meeting is held, have alone a right to make every decision, and that all the privilege of the other ministers consists in dutifully acquiescing in the determination of the former? Certainly, whatever weight is in the above extract must go to prove this, if these brethren shall be found, agreeable to your theory, to have been ministers from foreign places, with evangelists and prophets.

"It was to the apostles and elders alone," you say, "and not to the members, that the church at Antioch referred their cause." Certainly none were fit to determine the matter, but those who could infallibly know the mind of God; but though it were a fact, that the elders at Jerusalem were not inspired, it was proper to join them with the apostles, as being the rulers of the church from which the judaizing teachers came. As the message not only referred to the decision of a disputed question, but to the ascertaining of a fact with respect to the church at Jerusalem, the rulers of that church were properly advertised of this. It was their business to lay the matter before the church. Had the apostles been all dead, and the extraordinary gifts of the Spirit enjoyed by none in Jerusalem, it would have been proper to have written to the elders of that church for satisfaction upon this point. The improper conduct of brethren, when at a distance from their own church, should certainly be noticed by other churches, and reported. This report is very properly addressed to the elders, as the executive officers of the church. But a reference to the church at Jerusalem, either in its rulers or brethren, as to the settling of any point of doctrine, never would have been made, except there had been inspired authority there. But if it was to the apostles and elders at Jerusalem alone that the church of Antioch referred its cause, how does this agree with the notion that this was a General Council? How does this dispose of your foreign ministers? If *the brethren* here mentioned in the address of the letter, could have no share in the decision of this question, though those who determined it were equally uninspired with themselves, because they are not mentioned specifically as referred to (Acts xv. 2), how do these same brethren come to have a vote and authoritative judgment, the moment they are supposed to have been ministers? If, as church members, they are excluded, because not mentioned in the reference, how are they admitted as foreign ministers, though not mentioned? for this argument excludes the brethren, not as individual members, but as not being mentioned (Acts xv. 2). If there were no more joined in this decision than those mentioned, (Acts xv. 2), then it cuts off the brethren, whether they were ministers or individual members. It cuts off all foreigners; none are concerned in the matter, but the apostles and elders at Jerusalem.

You continue, "But if the members at Jerusalem,

who were greatly more numerous than the apostles and elders, sat in the court, and if the decision could have been carried only, according to the constitution of the Christian Church, if agreeable to a majority of them, then since, on account of their number, it must have been known at Antioch that it was they alone principally who were to fix the determination, the reference should have been made principally to them."—pp. 122, 123.

Upon the supposition that this was a reference to an uninspired court, this might have some weight; but as the matter was to be decided by inspiration, it has none in any point of view. It was not by the votes of a majority of uninspired men that the brethren of Antioch were to be determined as to their duty, but by, "It seemeth good to the Holy Ghost." I do not know in what part of Scripture you have got the idea of a majority being necessary in the decision of every question, according to the constitution of the Christian Church. Is it from precept, or example, or inference, you have derived this piece of information? Complete unanimity is necessary in all the proceedings of a church of Christ. Presbyterians surely have borrowed this idea from worldly societies, from which they have got the other distinguishing parts of their constitution. But I may retort, if this was an uninspired assembly, so numerous that it is called a multitude, and if the decision was to have been made by a plurality of voices, then the elders, being but a small part of the assembly, might have been almost overlooked, or at least the reference ought to have been principally made to those who were not apostles. There is no foundation for your allegation, upon the supposition that the apostles were inspired, but certainly if they were uninspired, and a majority of votes to decide the question, the apostles might as well have been at Gartmore as at Jerusalem.

"It is the apostles and elders too alone," you say, "who are said to have come together to consider the matter." Sir, it is as expressly said in one place that the whole church came together, as it is in another, that the apostles and elders came together. Is it any strange thing, that the principal persons only are at first generally mentioned as coming together? Indeed, if nothing more had been added, we would have no right to suppose that there were any others present. But it is afterwards as clearly shown that the whole church was assembled, as that the apostles and elders were assembled. All who are mentioned as joining in the letter, are expressly said to "be assembled with one accord." Now, it was the apostles, and elders, and brethren, who joined in this letter; therefore the apostles, and elders, and brethren, were assembled with one accord in deciding with regard to the contents of this letter. But if none but the apostles and elders came together, what comes of your foreign ministers? If the brethren, as church members, are here excluded, because not said in the same verse to have come together with the apostles and elders, how are they admitted as ministers when not mentioned (Acts xv. 6)?

"During the deliberation, moreover," you say, "it was only the apostles and elders, and not the brethren, who are said to have spoken, and the decrees are called the decrees of the apostles and elders, not the decrees of the apostles, and elders, and brethren." The apostles alone are specified as having spoken. There is no more room to suppose that an uninspired elder spoke, than that an uninspired brother spoke. In determining the mind of the Spirit, none had a right to give judgment who were not inspired, though they might all join in this, when the mind of God was infallibly made known. That the individual members were equally concerned with the apostles in determining the mind of God upon this question, we do not affirm, because the determination was infallible. But there is no more reason to believe that uninspired elders had a greater share in it, than uninspired brethren. Strictly speaking, the decision was made by Peter and James, or by James alone, and unanimously adopted by the whole assembly. That the decision is called (Acts xvi. 4), the decrees of the apostles and elders, determines nothing, seeing not only as to the decrees, but in the whole of the letter, the brethren are joined with them. Though then, for the sake of brevity, they are called the decrees of the apostles and elders, yet they might also have been called the decrees of the apostles, and elders, and brethren. For though the decrees were given by James alone, yet it pleased the apostles to join the brethren with themselves in giving them. If Mr. Carey should write a letter in the name of all his fellow missionaries, to which, in testimony that it was their joint letter, they should all subscribe their names; in speaking of this letter, we might call it, for the sake of brevity, Mr. Carey's letter; or, if we wished to convey particular information as to those concerned in writing it, we might call it the letter of Mr. Carey and his fellow-labourers. Yet the letter is not so much the letter of the others as of Mr. Carey, for he is supposed to have composed it. A bill might also be called, Mr. Fox's India bill, although a number had been at the framing of it. In such cases, when particular information is not intended to be conveyed, the principal and most conspicuous persons alone are mentioned.

But what suppose they should have been the decrees of the apostles and elders alone? What suppose the brethren had neither been admitted to join in the decision, nor had been even present? This can be no precedent for the elders of different churches making decrees, nor for the elders of one church to make decrees without the apostles being with them. The decrees of the elders would not be valid without the names of the apostles standing in front, as well as those of the brethren subjoined. Whether then the elders were inspired or uninspired, this, upon no consideration, can be a precedent for any but the elders of one church, and to them only, when they can get the apostles to come down from heaven to sit at their head. For whatever reason the elders were joined to the apostles, the former cannot act upon this model without the latter. Even were we to grant, for argument's sake, that these elders were pastors of different flocks in Jerusalem, it would afford a precedent only for the elders of one city deciding for those who had no elders or representatives present, and in this case also the presence of the apostles is required.

"It is also said," you continue, " that it pleased the whole church, as well as the apostles and elders (ver. 22), to send chosen men with their determination to Antioch. Admitting, however, that by the whole church or assembly (εκκλησια) is not intended the rest of the office-bearers who composed this meeting besides the apostles and elders, it deserves to be remarked, says the ingenious Mr. Muir, that what is here stated respecting the members, if it be the members who are meant, did not take place till the deliberation was finished, and the sentence was passed, which, as we have now seen, was performed entirely by the apostles and elders."—p. 124.

Indeed, Sir, it makes very little matter at what time the whole church joined the decision, seeing that it is evident that they really did so. Allowing this statement to be altogether correct, it only affects the etiquette of the court. If, in the decision transmitted to Antioch, the names of the whole church were subjoined to those of the apostles and elders, I do not see how the discovery of this *exceedingly ingenious* gentleman can effectually relieve you. It might be some consolation indeed to the pride of the clergy, that the brethren would not be allowed to signify their assent to any proposition, till their very reverend fathers had first given their judgment. But if it is necessary that their decrees should have the sanction of the whole church, *i.e.*, in Presbyterian language, the whole people, their present constitution derives no countenance from this model. I do not then think it worth while to spend time in ascertaining the etiquette of this assembly. It is entirely sufficient for my purpose, that even the apostles of God thought proper to join the whole Church of Jerusalem with them in their decision. At what stage of the business this was done maketh no matter. I am persuaded, indeed, that the matter was decided before the church expressed its consent; but it was decided no more by the uninspired elders, than by the uninspired brethren. You here represent the matter as if the question had been put to the vote among apostles and elders, and that then a synodical decree was passed in form, which was afterwards assented to by the brethren. Now this may be an *ingenious* supposition, but I must be allowed to say, that there is no truth in it, so far as the present narrative informs us. If you and your ingenious friend have any other more full and authentic accounts of this transaction than what are recorded in this chapter, you would do well to favour the world with the discovery. There was no formal separate sentence of the apostles and elders previous to that of the church. There was no voting. James decided the matter in the most absolute language, without supposing any room for difference in opinion. Nor does the narrative give room to suppose that his sentence needed to be strengthened even by the formal assent of the other apostles. It is not said that the apostles, or the apostles and elders, or the apostles, and elders, and brethren, unanimously adopted the opinion of James. This is taken for granted; and in consequence of this decision of James, the apostles, and elders, and brethren, did not proceed to a formal decision, but to act upon the decision already unalterably pronounced by James. "Then pleased it the apostles, and elders, with the whole church, to send chosen men of their own company to Antioch," &c. But how will this ingenious hypothesis agree with your still more ingenious discovery, that these brethren, or the whole church, were other ministers? If it appears from this narrative, that those called *the brethren*, and the *whole church*, were not allowed to signify their assent to this decision, until the sentence was fully passed and settled, and if these were prophets, evangelists, and foreign ministers, does not this establish an invidious distinction between the clergy of the city, and those of the country? Would not this make the foreign ministers inferior in power, even to the city lay-elders? for if there were any lay-elders at all in the assembly, they must be included in the elders that are mentioned. If then the apostles and elders settled the whole matter, before they allowed the brethren to express their approbation; then upon the supposition that those brethren were ministers, the clergy and lay-elders of Edinburgh alone should settle every matter in the General Assembly, without allowing the foreign ministers either to speak or vote in any matter. After the vote should pass, and the sentence be fixed, the foreign ministers might be allowed humbly to express their assent to the metropolitan decrees. Now, Sir, you exert all your ingenuity to support each of these hypotheses. I am confident, if you had not allowed your zeal to drown your reflection, you must have seen that it is altogether impossible for the same author to adopt both; that you were pulling down with the one hand what you were building with the other; that every argument that could give an accession of strength to the one, takes as much from the other. You wantonly triumph when you suppose you have discovered a difference of sentiment between Mr. Innes and Mr. Ewing, though there is not the slightest inconsistency when the different views of the passage are fairly considered; but this is Brown against Brown. There is no possibility of reconciling these two theories. A disinterested reader, totally unacquainted with the subject, could not but discover from your perplexity, and variety of inconsistent solutions of difficulties, that it cannot be the truth you are defending. Your arguments have no resemblance to those of a man strongly impressed with a distinct conception of a divine model. On that supposition, you would not be racking your invention to show in how many ways your antagonist might be answered, or how such and such arguments may be evaded. When a man really understands a passage, and wishes to give the just view of it, he is no way solicitous to persuade people that there are several ways of understanding it almost equally evident. Whenever I hear a preacher expounding a text in different ways, giving several meanings, without discovering a preference to one, I immediately conclude that he has yet no clear conceptions of the subject; that his own mind is not fully made up. For although he should give twenty views of the same passage, if his mind is fully convinced of the truth of one, as but one can be true, he will decidedly adopt that, and labour to discredit all the others. Now, Sir, it appears to me that you have really no correct, decided views on this subject at all. You appear almost at a loss, which of many theories upon the different parts of your subject you should adopt. Between these theories, you are writing like a man in convulsions. If you were completely confident of the truth of one, you would have laboured not to establish, but overthrow every other. As those who wish to pass bad money, sometimes instead of giving a shilling, will give a handful, hoping that some of them may be taken; so you, justly suspicious of the validity of your principle theory, give us others, with the hopes that some of them may serve your purpose. This, with superficial observers, may serve to impress ideas of the richness of your cause, from your variety of resources; but with those who will take the trouble to consider the matter a little more attentively, it will only excite suspicions of poverty.

"The church, moreover, he adds," (Mr. Muir), "if we choose rather to retain this translation of the word, and intend by it the members, might well be pleased with the measure, and to express their acquiescence, though they were not allowed in any view *judicially* to signify their mind respecting it." What is meant by this refinement? Neither the rest of the apostles, nor the elders and brethren, were called upon judicially to express their approbation of the sentence given by James. The 22nd verse does not represent the confirmation of this sentence by the whole assembly, or by any part of it, but relates to what took place pursuant to the sentence. The truth of James' sentence is taken for granted, and the assembly does not proceed to confirm it, but to act upon it. It was the sentence of the Holy Spirit, and therefore needed no confirmation. In the transmission of the sentence of the Holy Spirit, the apostles, elders, and brethren, united in a joint letter, and sent it by the hands of chosen messengers. It is not said that the church was pleased with the measure, and expressed their acquiescence in it, as this gloss supposes; but that it pleased them, with the apostles and elders, to send chosen men to Antioch, transmitting through them the sentence of the Holy Spirit, recognized by the whole assembly. The sentence was the sentence of the Holy Ghost, pronounced by an apostle of Jesus, and agreed to be transmitted in the name of the whole assembly to Antioch.

"The apostles and elders might determine, that two of the brethren should go up to Antioch with Paul and Barnabas, to testify the acquiescence of the whole in the decision, and might call upon the multitude, as at the election of the deacons, to look out among themselves two men for this purpose." Sir, how are you warranted to interpose your *might be's* in direct contradiction to what the passage itself asserts? It is not said, that the apostles and elders determined to send men to Antioch, and commanded the church to choose them; but that, "It pleased the apostles and elders, with the whole church, to send chosen men," &c. These chosen men, *i.e.*, the men chosen by the apostles, elders and brethren, were Judas and Silas. There is here no such thing as one thing asserted with respect to the apostles and elders, and another with respect to the church. The church is as much joined with the former in determining to send, as they are in the choice of those sent.

"But the letters, it may be said, which were written to Antioch, were written in the name of the brethren as well as of the apostles and elders; and the whole of them are represented as saying to the church at Antioch (ver. 28), that it seemed good to them as well as to the Holy Ghost, to lay upon them no greater burden than necessary things. It seems plain, however, that it might be represented as pleasing the members, if they be referred to only so far as *acquiescing* in the decision which was made by the apostles and elders, and not as themselves joining judicially in the deliberation and determination; and that it is in this view that their names are inserted in the letters."—p. 125.

Sir, if conjecture would prove anything, there could be no end to this, or any other dispute. There is here not the smallest intimation of what you suppose. The apostles, and elders, and brethren, are all represented as united in the same things, in the same manner. The obligation of their joint decrees certainly depends upon the inspiration of the whole, or of one part of them. If there was one inspired man among them, this is completely secured. But it is not said, that it pleased the one to acquiesce in the decision of the others; but, "It seemeth good to the Holy Ghost, and to us"—*to us*, the apostles, elders, and brethren. That the decrees of the church and of the elders, if uninspired, were obligatory, arises from their being also the decrees of the apostles. Why any uninspired men, whether elders or brethren, were allowed to join the apostles, it is not incumbent upon me to account.

"The reference was not made to them, and would they ever have presumed to have judged in a cause in which they were not appealed to?" Fact surpasses reasoning *a priori*. We see that they have been actually admitted to join in this letter with the apostles in transmitting the judgment of the Holy Spirit. What was most fitting, was better known to the Spirit of God than to you or me. For my part, it is sufficient to me to know that the apostles, who were the accredited transmitters of the oracles of God, thought this the most eligible manner. I will take the account as it stands, without adding anything to make it more full, or defalcating the account, to make it square with a system. I will never presume either to dictate to God how he should proceed, or presumptuously demand from him a reason of his conduct. I am satisfied that the records of Scripture are both sufficiently plain, and sufficiently full, for every necessary information to Christians. I therefore take their accounts just as they stand, in their most obvious and consistent sense. The Spirit of God here tells me, that the brethren were joined with the apostles in laying on those burdens, as plainly as ever any proposition was contained in language. Instead, then, of denying that this could have been the case, from arguments *a priori*, as previously established opinions, I think it proper rather to inquire what instruction the Spirit of God means to convey by this fact. Pray, Sir, does it not take a long time for you to read a passage of Scripture, if you are accustomed to take the meaning of it with you? According to your interpretation of this, and every other passage of Scripture which comes under your review, there is so much to be supposed, so much to be added, so many distinctions, so many passages seemingly mean one thing, yet really mean another, that I think you must be a long time labouring through a chapter. If this is the just method of interpretation, it is absolute absurdity to put the Bible into a man's hand, before he is well acquainted with the system, and has been accustomed to view the Scripture language through the interpretations of the rabbies. This method, I believe, has been practised by the recommendation of some of the spiritual guides.

"They are never named among those who are said to come together to consider the matter." They did meet, and it seemed good (verse 25) to them as well as to the others, *being assembled with one accord*, to send chosen men, &c.

"Besides, when the sacred historian speaks of the decision which was contained in these letters, and of the persons who passed it as ecclesiastical judges, he affirms, as has been said repeatedly, that it was pronounced only by the apostles and elders; chap. xvi., ver. 4. To make the historian therefore consistent with himself, it is necessary to consider him here as telling us, that the brethren merely acquiesced in what was done by the apostles and elders."—p. 125.

A sufficient answer has already been made to this, as far as the representation is founded in fact. But it is a falsification of the language of Scripture. The historian indeed calls them, the decrees of the apostles and elders; but that they were also the decrees of the whole church, is as clear from the letter, as that they were the decrees of the apostles and elders is clear from this. The reason of being thus called in Acts xvi. 4, I have assigned; but without positively assigning any, I might insist upon their being the decrees of the church, as well as of the apostles and elders, from the phraseology of the letter. If the reason assigned does not please you, look for a better. The historian's language in the different places is altogether reconcileable in my view, according to principles every day recognized by the best use. Your supposition would not reconcile the two passages. For it is absolutely, fully, and unequivocally stated in the letter, that the brethren were joined with the apostles, just in the same manner as the elders. Now, any supposition that contradicts this, will not reconcile the two passages, but destroy the testimony of one of them. Why do you say that the decision was pronounced only by the apostles and elders? The passage does not say so. It was pronounced by the apostle James, and neither the elders, nor even the rest of the apostles, are represented as giving their votes as ecclesiastical judges, more than the brethren. They are then the decrees of the apostles, and elders, and brethren, according to the undeniable tenor of the letter in which they are transmitted. They are obligatory decrees, because there was inspiration in the assembly, and are therefore in reality, and are called, the decrees of the Holy Ghost. But if the decrees were pronounced only by the apostles and elders as ecclesiastical judges, and if this is so evident, that all other parts of the narrative must be explained to tally with this, how will you contrive to bring *the brethren* from the back ground, upon the supposition that they were ministers? It cannot be because they will then be contained in the elders mentioned; for this would make the sacred historian speak nonsense, which is full as bad as to contradict himself. Whoever the brethren might be, they must be different from those previously mentioned.

"How could the brethren (p. 126) of one congregation *lay judicially* any necessary burdens upon the brethren of another congregation?" I will answer this question by another. How can the uninspired elders of one congregation *lay judicially* any necessary burdens upon the brethren of another congregation, or upon their own? I will answer both: certainly upon no other consideration than that they joined with the inspired apostles. The apostles were the representatives of Jesus; the Church of Jerusalem, like every other church of Christ, was the body of Christ; the whole body therefore were joined with those who represented their head. Had not the apostles been at their head, their decrees would have been entitled to the same respect with the Dictata of Hildebrand. This to me seems a clear and sufficient solution of the question; if it does not seem so to you, search for a better. But without giving myself the trouble to satisfy you on this head, I will peremptorily insist that *the brethren* did so, let the reason be what it may. To account for this, is no more incumbent upon me than it is upon you; and the matter is no more strange with respect to uninspired brethren, than with respect to uninspired elders. The apostles, guided by the Spirit of God, joined to themselves in this affair whom they pleased. If the elders were uninspired, they were equally with the brethren unfit for this business; and if, as you allege, the apostles themselves were uninspired, they were altogether unfit for it, and are worthy of no regard. Without inspiration, no burdens can be laid on the disciples of Jesus, either by themselves or by others. But if this should be allowed to sanction the propriety of ecclesiastical assemblies still laying burdens on the disciples of Christ, the brethren, even in that view, can never be excluded from their full share in it. Indeed, the supposition that this was an uninspired obligatory decision, would establish the right of every church member equally with their rulers. If they were all uninspired, as they are all in the same way represented as joining in the sentence, there is no reason why the brethren should not always be admitted to the same privilege. If the question had been to be determined by votes, the apostles would have had little share in the decision.

I come now to review your 17th letter. "But though this assembly at Jerusalem cannot be allowed to be the meeting of a particular congregation only, did it resemble a Presbyterian Synod in every respect, and include representatives from the churches of Antioch, Syria, and Cilicia, as well as of Jerusalem? Such was the opinion of the Presbyterian divines in the Westminster Assembly—of the London ministers—of Wood, Ayton, Hall, and Muir; but this, whether the case or not, is by no means necessary for our present argument in support of Presbytery. The appointment of the ministers of the different churches *next* to any congregation to constitute a Presbytery, for reviewing the deeds of the overseers of that congregation, and the appointment of the ministers of various Presbyteries *next* to a Presbytery to form a Synod, for reviewing the conduct of that particular Presbytery, are matters altogether circumstantial, not essential to the first principles of Presbytery, and adopted merely from convenience. It is not of fundamental importance in Presbytery, whether its courts of review are composed of the ministers whose local situation is nearest each other, or of ministers who are placed at a considerable distance; or whether a Synod be made up of a particular number of separate Presbyteries, or of an assemblage of ministers from different and more remote places, but superior in number to those who constitute the Presbytery from which a reference is made to them. These circumstances must be determined from the particular pleasure and situation of those churches which agree in government, and can be more easily arranged in modern times than among ancient believers. Though then it could not be proved that there was a Synod at Jerusalem corresponding in all respects to a modern Synod, it will by no means, as Independents have often asserted, enervate the argument. The grand point to be ascertained is simply this: Were the ministers and Church of Antioch subordinate, in this reference to the authoritative review of a number of other ministers convened at Jerusalem as ministers of Christ, though the assembly should have resembled strictly neither a Presbytery, nor Synod, nor any such association? If this can be established, all the other arrangements will necessarily follow, and nothing more is requisite to demonstrate their propriety."—pp. 291, 292.

If you pretend to have a divine model, you must produce it from the Scriptures in every part. I will not indeed expect it to be exhibited in one place, under one view. This would be unanalogous to the manner of conveying every other Scripture truth. But without doubt, every wheel, and every pin of a divine machine, must be divine. Whatever is left to be added by the ingenuity of man, according to circumstances, is not divine but human. The complete machine would not then be divine, but partly divine and partly human. It would come far short of proving Presbytery, to prove that there ought to be courts of review. There might have been such courts instituted, yet upon a model essentially different from the Presbyterian. Supposing then that it is proved, or taken for granted, that this passage warrants such courts, the next question will be what is the constitution and form of those warranted by it? The copy must correspond to the original. Every part of the model must be exhibited in the copy, and nothing must be admitted, which has not a corresponding part in the original. If this meeting in Jerusalem establishes subordination to a superior court, such superior court must be of the same construction with that represented in this passage. It must be composed of the apostles, and elders, and brethren of one church.

If Christ appointed courts of review, and left the constitution of these courts to the wisdom of men, we have then no divine model at all. You here give up the defence of Presbytery, as constituted after a divine model. Everything is left to be modelled by man. There is nothing determined, but that there should be reference to higher authority. Now, if this is the case, you cannot vindicate the *divine right* of the Presbyterian *form* of church government. You do not contend that you have a true copy of a divine pattern, but rather that you have a *divine right* to form a model for yourselves, and to add to or take from even the model which you pretend to have discovered in this chapter. This reasoning entirely proceeds upon the supposition that there is no divine model; for a model that may be altered by addition or defalcation, is not an obligatory model. Instead of showing that the Scriptures give a model, you attempt only to show that they give authority to make up a complete model, only stipulating that the court shall consist of church rulers. It seems Jesus is not at all concerned about the exact plan of the ecclesiastical court, provided that it consists of ministers. He has determined that there should be such courts, composed of such persons; but as to the series of subordination, and the plan of the constitution of each, he has left this to the discretion of the Presbyterian clergy, to be regulated by circumstances, and has given them letters patent to sanction the particular form they should adopt, and to preclude every other denomination from the same privilege. Nothing can be more absurd, than for those who pretend to have here a divine model, to contend that they are not to be guided by that model. Your reasoning amounts to this: Christ has not indeed given a complete model, but he has given some *hints towards a model*, with a patent to establish it, when it is completed by the clergy.

It requires little penetration to discover from this paragraph, that you are convinced of being on bad ground, and that you are anxious to escape from it. You are afraid to speak, lest you should not speak sufficiently guarded; you are afraid to be silent on this point, lest your cause should appear desperate. You hint at the opinion of others, wishing it to be adopted, yet afraid positively to sanction it, and conscious of its total want of proof, wish to appear to do independently of it. What caution! What circumspection! Yet in the greatest danger, safety sometimes depends upon assuming apparent unconcern. The sage distinction between *fundamental importance*, and things *altogether circumstantial*, adopted *merely from convenience*, pronounced with an air of confidence, as if the matter could not be doubted, or for a moment disputed, brings you safely, and even triumphantly out of this most critical situation. You artfully confound the question as to the propriety of reference, with the question as to the authorized referees, and take for granted, that if the former is proved, Presbytery will follow of course. Now, Sir, there can be nothing more fallacious than this. These two questions are entirely distinct; and though we deny both, yet the former might have been the case, without sanctioning the latter. These questions then should be handled separately, and independently of each other. I will for a moment grant the propriety of reference, and superior authority among the churches, to be established from this chapter, and upon this ground will oppose classical Presbytery. The persons who composed this model, were the apostles, elders, and brethren, as a single church. I will even go farther, and grant, for argument's sake, that in this assembly there were none but ministers; even then it would be but the ministers of one church. I will go farther still. I will grant that there were ministers in this assembly from other places besides Jerusalem, and will undertake to prove that this will not establish Presbytery. This would only be a common ground for the Church of Rome, the Church of England, the Church of Scotland, and all others who might choose to embrace it. To show that it was a Presbyterian assembly, it is necessary, not only to prove that they were ministers who composed it, and some of them foreign ministers, but that there were ministers and lay-elders in it from every congregation bound by the decision; in short, that its construction was exactly similar to whatever Presbyterian assembly it is pretended to correspond. Instead then of huddling these two questions together, and passing them for true almost by taking their truth for granted; by telling us what is fundamental and what is circumstantial in the Presbyterian constitution; there is no part of the subject required to be more largely handled, and more clearly ascertained from Scripture. Yet you have not a single proof from Scripture, nor a single reference to it. You give us nothing but some general observations, founded on the nature of your ecclesiastical constitution, not on the constitution of the assembly which you pretend to adopt as a model. You have wasted whole letters upon nothing; and have fatigued yourself in beating the air, while matters of vital importance in the debate are entirely evaded.

Suppose then that there is a power lodged somewhere, of settling disputes, and of authoritatively declaring what is to be believed and practised, there cannot be a question of greater importance, than who has this power? What is the construction of that assembly appointed by Christ to determine things of such infinite consequence? Does this authority belong to the Pope alone, or to the Pope and his council; to a convocation of bishops; to a general assembly of Presbyters; to some single church definitely, with its elders and brethren, or indefinitely to any church to whom the parties may agree to refer their cause; or to any kind of assembly at the option of the disputants? I insist, Sir, that this is no more a defence of Presbytery than it is of Popery, Prelacy, or any other modification of courts of reference, appeal, or review, that actually exists, or may be hereafter invented. All that you attempt to fix by divine authority, is the propriety of reference to a superior court. Now, there might be a thousand different modifications of assemblies, which may all equally claim the protection of this theory. If there is no divine model given of the assembly legally constituted for this purpose, it is absurd to give any one of them the exclusive title of a divine right. I ask you, Sir, do you yourself believe the divine right of the *Presbyterian model?* Do you believe that the constitution and forms of your assemblies are exhibited in this assembly at Jerusalem? Answer the question without equivocation or shuffling. If you cannot sanction the particular construction of your highest assembly by the model pretended to be here exhibited, with the number, conformation, constitution, gradation of rank, manner of process, &c., of all the subordinate courts between this and the congregation in which the dispute happened, I call upon you as an upright reasoner to abandon *the divine right*, and ingenuously acknowledge the principles upon which you defend the Church of Scotland. You have here virtually given it up, but you do not candidly confess this. You wish to retain the divine right in name, while you disengage yourself from the obligation of its particular forms. In other words, though this meeting at Jerusalem, even after all the refinements, defalcations, distortions and additions you could make, cannot afford anything like a model, for the Gothic fabric erected at Geneva, yet the latter must nevertheless be divine, because the former was an appeal to clergymen. The minds of some of the good people of the kirk would have been startled, had you directly abandoned the divine right of that form of ecclesiastical government for which their ancestors *fought* and bled. To vindicate the kirk upon the principal of apostolical practise not being binding, and the form of government and order of churches in particular countries being left to be regulated by circumstances, at the discretion of ecclesiastical and civil rulers, might have been acceptable to a certain class of readers, but would have been far from serving the cause with the bulk of the people.

The arcana of your art consists in amusing the serious part of those attached to the establishment with the fullest claims of a divine right, while at the same time you defend the particular construction, number, and subordination of your courts, as being optional, and of trifling importance. Your great aim accordingly seems to be to entangle and perplex the question, render everything uncertain, unhinge the whole principles of reasoning, and throw sand into the eyes of those who were beginning to use them for themselves. Your confidence surely arises from supposing that you have so involved the question in uncertainty and darkness, that it would be impossible to develope it, rather than from the conviction that you have succeeded in proving Presbytery. For I cannot think that you have so far imposed upon your own understanding, as to believe that you have defended successfully the Presbyterian constitution. This is seen through the whole tenor of your book. You do not depend so much upon being able to show your model, as in showing that the arguments of Independents may be evaded; and that their model cannot with unanswerable certainty be proved from the passages of Scripture on which they found it. If you could succeed in this, it would serve your purpose almost as effectually as if you could prove Presbytery. In your circumstances, a drawn battle would be as good as a victory. An established church can never be effectually injured, so long as it could be shown that its plan of government was equally divine with any other. If the balance is even beam, there are so many prejudices, so many temptations that will turn the scale in its favour, in opposition to all practical errors and corruptions that may have been incorporated with the system.

I am not astonished then that you touched this part of your subject but lightly, and wished to lead your readers so quickly over the ground, that they might not have time to discern the fallacy. You pass this point almost without attempting proof, lest people might be provoked to think that proof was necessary. But we cannot agree to let the matter pass in this manner. We cannot allow it to be taken for granted, that, if the propriety of reference is proved, the right belongs to Presbytery. Were the propriety of reference fully proved, the divine right of Presbytery would still remain to be proved. This would be only a step in your favour, in common with innumerable other actual or possible sects. This is only the foundation or platform upon which the model is to be erected and exhibited. From this we can see neither the length, nor breadth, nor height, nor form, nor materials, nor number, and dimensions, and relative proportions of apartments of the building. What do we mean, Sir, when we speak of a model? Should you ask a projector for a model of a house, would you think that he gave you sufficient information, when he barely pointed to the situation of the house, and fixed the spot on which the building should be erected? Would you not expect a plan of every part of the work, and the various proportions that each part should bear to every other? Yet, when Jesus gives a model, you think it sufficient to point to the hill upon which the edifice is to be raised. Is this like the instructions given for the construction of the tabernacle, or of the temple? Was there anything here left to the wisdom of man? Were even the outlines given to be filled up at discretion? Shall Jesus then appoint the clergy to decide what his people are to believe and practise, and leave it to the clergy to plan the construction, constitution, &c., of their own assemblies? Then, Sir, if you have a divine model, produce it in all its parts. I will admit not a single apartment in the house, that cannot be shown to be in the model. No form can be called divine, which has not a corresponding part to every part of the divine model, of which it pretends to be the copy, and which has nothing more.

But let us examine the above extract a little more particularly. You ask, "Did this assembly at Jerusalem resemble a Presbyterian Synod in every respect, and include representatives from the churches of Antioch, Syria, and Cilicia, as well as of Jerusalem?" You answer, "Such was the opinion of the Presbyterian divines in the Westminster Assembly—of the London ministers—of Wood, Ayton, Hall, and Muir."

For what possible purpose do you state the different bodies and individuals who held the affirmative of this question, without giving us the grounds of their opinion? Do you mean that we should argue against the mere authority of names? If you believed this opinion yourself, you ought, without respect to those who adopted or those who rejected it, to have confirmed your opinion by producing your evidence of the fact. If you did not believe it, it was only a waste of paper to advertise us of the opinion of these men. It appears evidently that you yourself do not believe it, and I am afraid there is still less probability of its gaining credit with us. But it is not difficult to see your object. You are aware that there are many with whom these names will weigh full as much as argument. You state the opinion then with its *venerable authors*, that those *may* who *can* believe it; and while you seemingly lay no stress on it, you do not renounce it, lest your antagonist should take advantage of the concession. You pretend to be able to do sufficiently well without it, while, from the authority you produce, you insinuate that the opinion is defensable, were it necessary to your argument. Should you fail in your way of defending Presbytery, you have still a retreat in this. I have made it a rule in my observations, to attack no views of Presbytery but those you adopt or suggest. As you must have stated this opinion for some purpose, I will ask you upon what grounds is it alleged that there were representatives present in this assembly from Antioch, Syria, and Cilicia? Does the narrative declare or suggest anything that can possibly give the smallest foundation for this opinion? Is this fact asserted in any other passage of Scripture? If not, I ask if there can be an instance of more shameless effrontery, than to assert what the Word of God nowhere affirms? Would it be more unwarrantable, if an enthusiast were to assert that there were also present a deputation from all the hosts of the angels of heaven? Were a man in the City of London to run over the bills of mortality, and point out how many of the deceased were in heaven, and how many in the abodes of misery, we would rather ascribe his conduct to derangement than presumption and impiety. Yet he has an equal warrant to do this, as any have to allege that there were representatives from distant countries at Jerusalem, when the Scriptures nowhere give such information. To what height of absurdity and presumption will even grave and temperate men be carried, when they give themselves over to prejudice and system!

Besides, as it was an accidental assembly, there could not have been representatives present from all those churches. In this case, we would have heard of the summoning of representatives from those churches; and, if a General Council, from all the churches of the world. Do we read in church history of any General Council, in which we are not informed of the summoning of those who were to constitute it, and of the person by whom it was called? But of the summoning of members, we have here no account from any single church on earth, far less from all the churches in the world. Would not the summoning and meeting of the members have taken up a considerable time? Yet there is nothing that leads to this conclusion. On the contrary, that there was no such concourse is clear from the narrative. The brethren at Antioch are said to send up to Jerusalem *to the apostles and elders.* If this had been a General Council, would it have been said that they sent up to Jerusalem to the apostles and elders? It is here plainly implied that there were no foreigners there.

But this supposition is as much opposed to your new hypothesis, as it is to us. The defence of your theory requires you not to strengthen, but to discredit the opinion which we are now considering. If there were representatives from Syria, Cilicia and Antioch, it was an astonishing breach of the Presbyterian constitution for the uninspired apostles and elders of Jerusalem to determine the business themselves, and allow the representatives from those countries to signify their assent only after the matter was settled.

After all, what shall it serve those gentlemen whose opinion you state, could they even prove that there were representatives from Antioch, Syria and Cilicia? If it was a General Council, representatives were as necessary from all other churches in the world, as from these churches; and if it was only a subordinate Synod those churches who had no representatives in it, were not bound by its decrees, unless it is also established that one Synod combined the churches belonging to another. And if it was only a subordinate Synod, why did not the judaizing teachers appeal to a General Council? If it is said, because they submitted to the decision of this; I answer, this is not true with respect to all. Many continued in after-times to teach the same doctrines.

Again, the Presbytery founded upon the supposition that there were present representatives from those churches, stands upon a different foundation from that which your arguments defend. Were this a truth the former would have a divine model. But yours is upon a human construction, and might be modelled in various ways.

Once more, I ask what could tempt those writers to suppose that such representatives were present, without having any evidence upon which they could found their judgment? I ask you why you have laboured so hard to bring foreign ministers into this assembly? I ask you why you appear so willing that this opinion of the Westminster divines, &c., should be believed, while yet you do not pledge yourself for it? Is it not because it is the sober judgment of these writers and yourself, that your system requires this supposition? You may affect an air of unconcern about the truth of this opinion, and pretend that it is a matter of little importance; yet this anxiety to have it believed, proves the judgment of your consciences better than the most direct words. Had it not been considered to have been necessary for making this a model for Presbytery, that there should have been representatives from these places, such an absurd, totally unfounded assertion never would have been made. I appeal to your own conscience, would it not be an infinite triumph to you to be able to prove satisfactorily this opinion which you affect to treat, not as of fundamental importance, but merely circumstantial? Whatever you may pretend, whatever sophistry may devise, this assembly can never be made a model for Presbyterian courts upon any other supposition, than that representatives were present from every church bound by the decision. No wonder then that those writers have laboured so hard to prove this point. Nothing can prove more clearly than this unfounded supposition, that Presbyterians have at first gone to Acts xv. with a system, not for a system. Some errors have taken their rise from a superficial view of detached parts of Scripture, which, considered in themselves, and without reference to the connection and design of the passage, may have suggested views to the careless which they do not contain. But this cannot plead this apology. There is nothing in the chapter at all calculated to suggest to the most inattentive reader the idea of classical Presbytery. This has been first invented, and then the 15th of Acts has been thought of as a sanction. Human schemes in religion would not pass so well in the world under human names. The laws of Numa must be sanctioned by the goddess Egeria.

"This, whether the case or not," you think, "is by no means necessary to your present argument in support of Presbytery." Why is it not necessary? "The appointment of the ministers of the different churches next to any congregation to constitute a Presbytery, for reviewing the deeds of the overseers of that congregation, and the appointment of the ministers of various Presbyteries next to a Presbytery to form a Synod, for reviewing the conduct of that particular Presbytery, are matters altogether circumstantial, not essential to the first principles of Presbytery, and adopted merely from convenience." By this you must surely mean that it is a matter indifferent whether any particular congregation be subjected to the nearest or most remote Presbytery; and whether any particular Presbytery be immediately subjected to the nearest or most remote Synod. I beg you will be so kind as to show me how you wish this to bear upon the point. Do you mean this as a reason why it is of no importance whether or not there were representatives from Syria and Cilicia, although they are bound by the decision? If I understand your meaning, this is not to the purpose at all. If this was a Presbyterian assembly, we argue that there must have been representatives from Syria and Cilicia, and every other place which was bound by the decrees. You answer, this is not necessary, because whether a congregation is subjected to the nearest or most remote Presbytery, is a matter not of fundamental importance. You might as well have said, this is not necessary, because Shem, Ham and Japheth were the sons of Noah. If this were a general council, it would be absurd to object to the distance of Syria, Cilicia and Antioch, from Jerusalem. Upon this supposition, our objection is not to the distance of the places, but to their having no representatives in the assembly in which they were bound. If they had not, they were not Presbyterians.

"It is not of fundamental importance," you say, "whether a Synod be made up of a particular number of separate Presbyteries, or of an assemblage of ministers from different and more remote places, but superior in number to those who constitute the Presbytery from which a reference is made to them." If this is the case, you have no model for a Synod. If the constitution of it is left to the particular churches that agree in government, the model is then human. This may be the case with Presbytery, but it would not have been the case had it been a divine institution. Christ would have constructed this as well as every other part of the machine. But what is all this to the purpose? Does this tell us why there should not have been representatives from Syria, &c. ?

"Though *then* it could not be proved that there was a Synod at Jerusalem, corresponding in all respects to a modern Synod, it will by no means, as Independents have often asserted, enervate the argument?" Not at all; why should it? No matter of what construction this meeting of Jerusalem was; it will be the most perfect model for Presbytery. This sentence is a consequence drawn from your preceding reasoning. Now what is the sum of that reasoning? Does it not altogether respect local arrangements? Do you even attempt to give any reasons why there were not representatives from Syria, &c. ? Yet you draw a consequence, as if you had sufficiently proved the point with which you set out; to wit, that it is not necessary to your argument that representatives should have been in this assembly from Syria, &c. Did you really think, Sir, to impose this upon us for argument? Did you believe that you were speaking to any purpose? Did you imagine that your reasoning warranted your conclusion?

"The grand point to be ascertained is simply this. Were the ministers and Church of Antioch subordinate in this reference, to the authoritative review of a number of other ministers convened at Jerusalem as ministers of Christ, though the assembly should have resembled strictly neither a Presbytery, nor Synod, nor any such association?" What do you mean here by *convened?* Do you mean any others than the apostles and elders who were previously at Jerusalem? If you do not, your expression is improper; for it gives us the idea of the persons alluded to assembling at Jerusalem for that particular purpose, at that particular time, and not as being already at Jerusalem. Do you intend by it the convening of other foreign ministers. I beg you to remember, that though you have supposed this, you have not proved it. You cannot then argue from it. If you wish to reason, you should then have said, 'the apostles and elders at,' instead of "a number of other ministers convened at Jerusalem." What do you mean by *review?* Do you mean the settling of a dispute primarily referred to them? If you mean anything more, you mistake the fact. If you mean this, your language is incorrect; for a review of any affair by a court, implies that a decision had previously been made, of the propriety of which such court was to judge. Instead then of saying, 'authoritative review,' you should have said, 'authoritative determination or decision.' What do you mean by 'ministers and church?' Do you mean by this distinction, that in this business the ministers acted as a distinct body, or that the reference had gone from them? This is not fact. In the reference, there is no distinct point of view in which the rulers can be distinguished from the brethren. If then you mean to suggest anything more by this phraseology than that the church, as consisting of ministers or elders, and brethren, were subordinate, &c., you have no ground in the history. What do you mean by *subordinate?* Do you mean to hint at a series of subordinate courts? Do you mean anything by it more than *subject?* If you do, it is unwarrantable. Is this then the sum of this paragraph? "Was the church at Antioch subject in this reference to the authoritative decision of the apostles and elders at Jerusalem?" Now, Sir, if this is not the substance of your language, it is not founded upon anything that you have proved, or that can be proved from the narrative. If it is, instead of being the grand point to be ascertained, it is a point taken for granted on all hands. Not only the ministers and church at Antioch, but all the ministers and churches of the world, were subject to this decision. So far from this settling the dispute, it does not advance one step towards it.

But I will go farther with you: I will grant you for a moment, that this transaction affords us a proof that there ought to be, in difficult cases, a reference to some superior court. Still I will contend, that it can sanction only one particular assembly modelled after itself. The question still remains, of what constitution and form is the model here exhibited? The grand point will be, to determine which of all the churches in the world is sanctioned by this; or whether, even upon this supposition, it will favour any of all who have ever laid claim to it? If this is to be a model, must not the model be exactly copied? I will grant, that if the propriety of reference could be proved from this, our present views of it are false. But in this case, we would not yield the palm to Presbytery, as it would establish the propriety of reference to the pastors, or the pastors and brethren of some single church. How can it be the grand point to be proved, which does not determine, whether the right belongs to the Church of Rome, the Church of England, the Church of Scotland, or any other? Shall that be called a model which may or may not be copied? Granting you then that there ought to be courts of reference, what is their construction? What are the constituent parts of the model? The apostles, elders, and brethren. Granting that it is obligatory without the apostles, elders, and brethren of one church. Elders or pastors, no lay-elders: elders of one church, the elders at Jerusalem alone. You say indeed, that "the members of this court appear to have been officers alone, and even the brethren seem to have been of this description." Counting nothing on what I have said to disprove this, a *seem to be*, will prove nothing. If you cannot prove it, you cannot reason from it.

This then, and a similar passage in your 18th letter, p. 324, I will not take for reasoning. "It must certainly be of little importance to object that this court at Jerusalem did not resemble a Presbytery or Synod, since it was unquestionably composed of ministers of Christ acting in an ordinary and common capacity, and different from those from whom the reference was presented. This, I presume, is the grand point in dispute; and since it is established, it authorizes, I apprehend, courts of review to any extent that the circumstances of the church may be found to require." Similar reasoning would equally establish any form of associated church government, from this passage. The Pope might say, 'It must certainly be of little importance to object, that this court at Jerusalem did not in all respects resemble a meeting of the sacred college, since it was unquestionably composed of ministers of Christ. This I presume is the grand point in dispute, and since it is established, it warrants the authority of the Pope and his council over the whole world.' Indeed those conversant in the disputes after the Reformation, will easily see, that the adherents of the Pontiff have used this chapter to support his claims, with much more plausibility, and colour of argument, than the Presbyterians can do. The Church of England may next step in upon this ground. 'It must certainly be of little importance to object that this court at Jerusalem did not resemble a convocation of bishops, since it was unquestionably composed of ministers of Christ.' The ancient Independents might also put in their claim. 'Notwithstanding that congregations are completely independent of each other as to their government and discipline, yet, in matters of doubt, it is proper to have an association to determine these things, which determination must be received as far as agreeable to Scripture.' You cannot hold these sentiments and really believe that there is a divine model. You do not defend Presbytery more than you defend any other worldly system. You make it a matter of indifference upon what model superior courts are constructed. And as you have begun to *reform backwards*, I see no security in your views, that you would not embrace the communion of the Church of Rome, should it ever become established in Scotland. Divest Popery of the absurdities which are not essential to the system, as far as respects the form of government, and it will be much easier defended than Presbytery. The machine is much more simple, and its motions much more equable and regular. The infallibility which it needs and claims, is equally necessary to your courts, for their decrees must as positively be obeyed. If you do not pretend to be infallible, the absurdity is only the greater. Though infallibility is disclaimed in words, it is acted upon in spirit by all who enact human laws, or use a discretionary power in the affairs of Christ's kingdom. Why might you not then go back to some of the purest General Councils as your standards; and, agreeably to your convenient distinction between principles and practise, could you not imagine and defend a very fine theory? You might show in the abstract, the many possible advantages of such a system when rightly administered, and that it is not just to take into the account its possible abuses. Should you be pressed by the infallibility, you would have nothing to do, but to distinguish between the Pontiff of Rome and the court of Rome. Nay, if you have found out a plan to make the apostles themselves fallible, even in the things of Christ, it could not be a great affront to his Holiness, if now and then he should become only an ordinary teacher. Indeed, Sir, I should be glad to know upon what consistent principles you could oppose the Church of Rome, or refuse her communion, were she established in Scotland, reformed of those abuses which do not resspect the form of her government. Your reasoning against Independency is exactly analogous, to that used against the Reformers. Why is Erasmus condemned for acting upon such principles? "Erasmus! that much injured name, the glory of the priesthood, and *its* shame." It was the plan, not the administration, which he defended. There is not an argument you state upon this point, that would not have tenfold force in the hands of Roman Catholics. Let them defend a universal Episcopacy without taking into the account its possible or actual abuses, how will you overturn them? If the corruptions of a church are no cause for deserting her communion; and if it is of no consequence upon what construction superior courts are formed, I request to know why you are a Protestant?

But there is another thing in the above quotation to which I call the reader's attention, and the same thing is often exemplified in your book. You often set out with the guarded profession of making a thing probable or plausible; but afterwards in your reasoning assume this probable or plausible thing, as an unquestionable fact. Such disingenuity in your mode of reasoning is unworthy of a good cause. In assigning your reasons for your opinion as to the persons intended by the words *the brethren*, a *seemed to be* was all you claimed. *Now*, that they were ministers, is a fact unquestionable. When you set out to show that the apostles were uninspired in this assembly, you were contented with saying, that, p. 298, "*it seems probable, from a number of circumstances*, that, in the whole of this business, they acted only as common ministers." *Now*, that they acted in an ordinary and common capacity is a fact *unquestionable*. When you are directly giving us your proof, you assume little, that we may with less scrupulosity examine and weigh your arguments, as you appear to put but little stress on them yourself. But as soon as your pretended proof is out of our view, you assume an air of demonstration. You would persuade us that it would be unreasonable to doubt it, after what you had said. Your conclusions are not only true, but unquestionably true, though founded only on *probable circumstances*, and *it appears* or *it seemeth*. Ah! Sir, defend your cause with the whole force of your genius, but let us have no artifice.

Upon this critical part of your subject, in which it is dangerous to speak, and dangerous to be silent, you bring, in a note, another of your ingenious friends to your support. He does indeed appear to be an ingenious gentleman, and the case requires all his ingenuity: *Dignus vindici nodus.*

"The positive precepts of Scripture," said a very distinguished character, when speaking on the subject of church government, "are so expressed as to comprehend every possible case which can occur in the subject to which they relate; and, in referring to them, there can never be a deficiency either of direction or authority. But when we refer to scriptural examples for the authority of modern practise, we must not forget that an example could not go beyond the circumstances of the particular case in which it occurred, although by fair inference or analogy it may authorize many things which that case did not require or admit of. The application of the church at Antioch to what has been called the council of Jerusalem, is an example and authority for a *reference*, from an inferior to a superior court. The example could in this point go no farther from the nature of the case. But its *authority* goes far beyond it. It is quite sufficient to authorize an appeal, or a complaint (as well as a reference) from an inferior court to a superior, and every other jurisdiction of the superior which the circumstances require. It authorizes not merely the subordination of one inferior to one superior court, which is all that the example mentions, but such a gradation of court-jurisdiction as the circumstances of the church of Christ, in different situations, render expedient. This is but one illustration—but the idea may be illustrated by a multitude of similar cases, and shows the absurdity of the conduct of Independents, who, while they neglect or explain away a great part of the *practise* which is clearly found in the Bible, affect to fix down the practise of modern times to the precise *letter* of the *examples* they choose to refer to, though ever so contrary to *their true spirit* and *design*. Every pin of Presbytery could not possibly be found in any Scripture example, although the general system is not only explicitly but clearly authorized by the practise of the primitive church *as far* as the cases occurred."—pp. 292, 293.

The writer strains hard to extend the authority of this example to sanction Presbyterian assemblies, but his conclusion is founded on a fallacy, and gratuitous assertion. Instead of illustrating his meaning, and corroborating his argument, by an example upon a different subject; he takes the very point under debate, and stretches it to the standard height by mere arbitrary supposition. The fallacy lies in considering an example as extending its authority, not merely to all similar cases, but to things of a quite different species. A single example will indeed extend its authority to an infinite number of similar cases, but can never effect things that are no way related. When we speak of the different extent of example and its authority, we mean, if we reason justly, its extent as to different cases coming under the same head, not as to different kinds. An example has indeed authority beyond the particular case exhibited, and not only may, but must, include every other similar case. If the incestuous person was put away from the Church of Corinth, so must every other incorrigible transgressor be put away. If the 15th of Acts exhibits a model of reference as to the particular case of the doctrine of circumcision, it establishes reference in general. One case being referred to any particular assembly, will prove, that any other case may be referred to the same assembly; and could it be proved that this was designed as a model to fallible assemblies, it will give the authority of arbitration to that assembly which is formed upon the model here exhibited. One case of reference given as an example to the churches of Christ, will prove that every doctrine, precept and institution of the Gospel may be equally referred. If this is the meaning of the writer, I perfectly agree with him. But upon what principles of reasoning does the writer find himself justifiable in asserting, that an example of reference, will authorize, not merely reference in general, but appeal from the decision of reference? If this matter was referred, and settled by this reference, how does it give authority to appeal from the reference? Does it not even forbid such appeal? If this was a final decision, and you yourself declare that we are expressly told that the Church of Antioch referred the matter for final decision to the assembly convened at Jerusalem; if the decision was final, how is there room for appeal? Appeal then, so far from being warranted by the example of reference, is cut off by this example, except that there can be shown another example of appeals which will prove that this reference was not final. Courts of reference, and courts of appeal, are quite different: though one example of reference to uninspired authority will prove reference in general, and one instance of appeal will prove appeal in general, yet the example of reference cannot by any means extend to appeal. A court to settle controversies when referred, is quite another thing from a court to receive appeals from the decision of other courts. They must stand either upon different precepts, or different examples. Having thus taken the foundation from this reasoning, I might allow it to tumble in a piece. But as it is an exceedingly important part of this debate, and as you evidently wish to steal out of our hands, I will be a little more particular.

This very distinguished character observes, that "the application of the church at Antioch to what has been called the council of Jerusalem, is an example and authority for a reference from an *inferior to a superior court.*" Now, taking it for granted at present, that this is authority for reference, is it accurate to say, that this reference was from an inferior to a superior court? Was it referred to Jerusalem by a court at Antioch? Was it referred by the congregation at Antioch, or any individual among them, from the decision of a court of Antioch? If neither of these can be shown to have been the case, is it consistent with truth or candour, to represent this as authority of reference from one court to another? It is not the reference of the church rulers at Antioch, unable to settle the dispute themselves. It is not an appeal from any part of these from the judgment and decision of the majority. It is not an appeal from the church members of Antioch from the decision of their church rulers. It is the reference of the whole brethren at Antioch to a source of infallible direction. There was no decision at Antioch. The matter is referred to Jerusalem in the first instance. It is not one court reviewing the deeds of another; or judging after decision had been made by an inferior court; it is the first and the last court (if you must have this name) to which reference was made in the matter.

"The example," he continues, "could go no farther, from the nature of the case." Why then does he add, "But its authority goes much farther?" Can an example have authority in cases to which it cannot be extended? Had he said, that from the nature of the case we have only one example, and therefore it is absurd to look for a particular example for every case to be referred, he would have reasoned incontrovertibly. But when he alleges that the authority of an example will reach far beyond the boundaries of that kind of jurisdiction of which it is an example, and that a case being referred will warrant a case being appealed from reference, it is not reasoning, but rant. Might I not as well reason in this manner: 'The meetings of the primitive churches on the day on which Christ rose from the dead, prove the change of the Sabbath from the seventh to the first day of the week. The example could go no farther, from the nature of the case. But its authority goes far beyond it. It is quite sufficient to prove, that we should keep every day in the week as a Sabbath, as well as the first. For we must not forget, that an example could not go beyond the circumstances of the particular case in which it occurred, although by fair inference or analogy it may authorize many things which that case did not require, or admit of.' In the same manner we might prove, that church courts not only should decide matters of religion, but assume civil jurisdiction, and judge in cases of life and death. 'This case at Jerusalem, from its nature, only extends to religious disputes, but its authority goes much farther. It is quite sufficient to show, that church courts should exercise the power of dispensing life or death.' Nothing can be more gratuitous than this reasoning. It is mere assertion. There is nothing to which we might not extend any example upon the same principles.

He observes farther, "It authorizes not merely the

subordination of one inferior to one superior court, which is all that the example mentions, but such a gradation of court-jurisdiction as the circumstances of the church of Christ, in different situations, render expedient." Truly this is a very fruitful passage. Was there ever such a huge multifarious system, built upon such a slender foundation? There is here a divine model, yet the construction of every part of it is left to the church rulers, and in different situations and circumstances the model may be altered. But so far from warranting a gradation of church-jurisdiction to an indefinite length, it does not afford an example of one inferior court applying to one superior. Allowing then the propriety of reference in cases of dispute, will this prove that there is an appeal from the first decision, to an indefinite number of superior courts? Will the proving that this was a court exhibiting a model of decision by reference, prove that we may not abide by this reference, but appeal to other courts? The establishing then of a court of reference from this passage, will not establish, but destroy every gradation of court jurisdiction. If the matter was here finally decided by the first court applied to, there is no room left for either inferior or superior courts. If this assembly was a Presbytery, it cuts off Synods and all superior councils, on the one hand; and kirk-sessions on the other. If it was a General Council, nothing can be determined by any court below a General Council, even in the first instance. Had this been a General Council, and Presbytery of divine institution, the example here given would have exhibited the whole series of subordinate courts. We would first have heard of the decision of the kirk-session at Antioch; then of the appeal of the church, or some part of them, to the Presbytery to which they were subject; then, if this did not satisfy them, to the Synod &c., until finally they bring the matter to this General Council; of the summoning, and meeting, and transactions of which, we would have been informed. I contend then that the example here exhibited, even allowing it to establish the propriety of courts to settle disputes referred, so far from necessarily implying other superior and inferior courts, gives us a complete refutation of that opinion. An example of reference cannot in itself prove the existence of courts of appeal. If they exist, they must be shown from other passages of Scripture. But this example of reference is of such a nature as to show that they are not appointed in any other place. Had this been the case, the example not only might, but must have embraced them. The case could not have come to the highest, without passing through all the subordinate courts. The example, so far from necessarily giving an imperfect model, from the nature of the case, was calculated to unfold every part of the machine, from the first reference to the kirk-session at Antioch, through all the subordination of courts to this General Council. I ask then, where do you found the subordination of one court to another? I ask you, where do you found an optional, unlimited gradation of courts? This, so far from being sanctioned by the example, is absolutely disproved by it. If there is to be reference, it must go no further than the first assembly, because that assembly is a General Council, and in this case immediately applied to.

"Independents," this writer asserts, "while they neglect or explain away a great part of the practise which is clearly found in the Bible, affect to fix down the practise of modern times to the *precise letter* of the examples they choose to refer to, though ever so contrary to *their true spirit* and *design*." I ask you, Sir, as you have adopted this writer's language, and therefore must make good his charge, what is that great part of the practise which is clearly founded in the Bible, which Independents neglect or explain away? If you can show us this, we will be your debtors. We have no standards, like you, to prevent us from receiving any part of truth when discovered. We do not profess to have attained to a perfection of knowledge in the Scriptures, but agreeable to what we have attained, we profess to walk. He then who will show us the way of the Lord more perfectly, will do us a more essential service than were he to enrich us with the treasures of the Indies. But what sort of a spirit appears in this? One should be led to think from this language, that it is offering violence to a person to attempt to acquaint him with any part of his duty hitherto unknown. He takes it for granted that Independents would look upon this attempt as an injury, rather than a favour. Surely this must proceed from what Presbyterians are conscious of in their own situation. If they were in earnest inquiring after truth; if they had their ears open to hear, and were ready to be guided by the Word of God, they would not consider those who call their attention to their duty as the disturbers of their repose. They are like men who hold an estate with a bad title; conscious of being unable to keep possession if their title should be examined, they are beyond measure incensed against those who wish to bring the matter to a fair trial. Being thus affected themselves, they fancy that all others must feel in a similar manner. How strange is the contrast between men's conduct in temporal and in spiritual concerns! Had our neighbour discovered a rich mine of gold, he would take it for granted that he could do nothing more acceptable to us, than to invite us to come and partake of the treasure. He would not make the discovery in language that would intimate our reluctance to part with our poverty to partake of his riches. Yet, strange! when men call our attention to some hitherto unknown truth of Scripture, they take it for granted that it will be as unwelcome as the robber to a miser.

But is this practice, which Independents neglect or explain away, yet is clearly found in the Bible, such as is practised by Presbyterians? If it is answered in the affirmative, I ask what part of the practice of the apostolical churches is observed by Presbyterians and omitted by Independents? If it is neglected both by Presbyterians and Independents, though clearly found in the Word of God, how do those Presbyterians who think so, excuse their contempt of this part of Scripture? Do they plead that practice may be clearly found in the Bible, yet notwithstanding be not obligatory? Do they think that it is left to their discretion what part of Scripture practice to observe, and what to neglect? If any practice is clearly found in the Word of God, let them first follow it, and then we shall believe that they are in earnest. But they act like the people of the world, when they are reproved for sin. These recriminate against their advisers, and allege that the latter are guilty of other sins, not to induce them to abandon them, but to excuse themselves by their example. As if they should say, 'Though I am guilty of this, yet, you are guilty of that; therefore you should be silent, and let me enjoy my sins without disturbance.' Just in the same manner, Presbyterians allege that Independents neglect some part of apostolical practice, not to induce them to comply with it, but to excuse themselves for the neglect of apostolical institutions.

What does this writer mean by the opposition which he seems to suppose as existing between the *letter* of an example, and the *true spirit and meaning* of the example? Does he mean that the language in which an example is contained, says one thing, and that the true spirit and meaning of the example says another? I have been in the habit of thinking that the Bible *speaks* just what it *intends*, and that its language is in itself the fittest of all others to convey its meaning. I apprehend that a distinction between the *meaning* of any passage, and the language in which that meaning is conveyed is most absurd, and must be a fruitful source of enthusiasm. It must lead people to disregard the language of Scripture as unfit to discover its true meaning, and induce them to give scope to the imagination to find out the meaning of particular passages, not from the words, but from enthusiastic impulses. Now, as to the point in hand, I know of no lawful way to find out the meaning of this example, but from *the letter* or the language in which it is conveyed. If anything more than is contained in the words of this chapter has been revealed to Presbyterians, I do not envy them the discovery. I will endeavour to find out the meaning of the Holy Spirit by his language. I know indeed he leads Christ's people into the knowledge of the word; but it is not by giving them any discovery in opposition to, distinct from, or not contained in his words, but by opening their minds to perceive the true and legitimate import of these words. I contend then that the meaning and spirit of an example can never go beyond its letter, or the language that contains it, for that is what I understand by it in such a connection. There is no way of knowing its true spirit and meaning but by its letter.

But perhaps the writer means by *the letter of an example*, the single case exhibited in that example. If this however is his meaning, his language is improper to convey his meaning, and his assertion would be unfounded. The letter of an example does not signify the single case contained in that example, and Independents do not confine the authority of an example to the single case exhibited, but extend it to all similar cases. If our Lord cured a withered hand on the Sabbath, we may do any necessary work of mercy on the Sabbath. But his example of curing the afflicted on the Sabbath, will not warrant our following our temporal business on the Sabbath, because this does not come under the same denomination with the case exhibited in the example. But upon this writer's principles, this example of our Lord might be made to sanction common labour on the Lord's day. 'This example,' it might be said, 'establishes the propriety of doing works of mercy on the Sabbath. The example could in this point go no farther, from the nature of the case. But its authority goes far beyond it. It is quite sufficient to authorize our following our worldly business on the Sabbath.' This reasoning is every whit as legitimate and conclusive, as that which from an example of reference would prove a court of appeal or review.

"Every pin of Presbytery," adds the writer, "could not possibly be found in any Scripture example." We do not look for every pin in every, or in any single example. But we expect, that if the machine be divine, the different examples recorded in Scripture, when brought together, will exhibit a complete view of the whole. Though we do not expect to see every part in every example, we lawfully expect that every part and every pin will be somewhere contained in Scripture, in precept, example, or undeniable inference. That part, that pin which is not contained in the model pretended to be divine, is not divine. That which is no where exhibited in Scripture, we justly deny to be any part of the will of Jesus, and any part, even the most minute pin, of the model which he has given for his churches. If this assembly was a Presbytery, I do not expect that it will give me a model for a kirk-session, but a kirk-session must be shown me in some other place of Scripture. If it was a Synod, I do not expect that it will give me a model for a Presbytery, but a Presbytery must be shown me in some other part of the Word of God. If it was a General Council, I do not expect that it will afford also a model for a Synod, but a Synod I must see from some other example or precept before I admit it to be divine. I will expect that this can be only one of all the series of Presbyterian courts. I will not look for a model for any other from the example itself, but an example or precept for each of them I will have in some part of Scripture, before I am authorized to admit them as divine institutions. Prove one of your assemblies from this, and the rest from different examples, or a distinct precept. Whichever of your assemblies you choose to pitch upon as a copy of this model, you must prove to resemble the model in every part, without either deficiency or redundancy. If it was a Presbytery, why should it not give us every constituent part of a Presbytery? A Presbytery cannot be justly expected to give at the same time a model for any other of your assemblies, but why should it not give a model of itself? If it was a Presbytery, is it unreasonable to demand how it resembled a Presbytery? If it was designed as a model for Presbytery, how can it afford a pattern, without exhibiting all its essential parts? I do not then expect in it every pin of the system; but I must find every pin of the system in the Scriptures some where. If any where, I care not how scattered. And if it was a Presbytery, I will expect to find in it every pin of a Presbytery. This is not expecting too much; this is not demanding what the example, from the nature of the case, could not be supposed to give, but what the example, from the very nature of the case, would certainly have given. How absurd is it to allege, that this example exhibits a model for Presbytery, while it does not give a model for any one of its courts, from the highest to the lowest! How absurdly do they act, who with you contend for a divine and exclusive model, yet allege that it does not affect the argument, though the assembly which you take for your model "should have resembled strictly neither a Presbytery, nor Synod, nor any such association!" What effrontery must the man have, who can talk (for I cannot say reason) in this manner! If you vindicate Presbytery as a good human device, upon the principle that the particular form of church government has been left by Christ to be particularly moulded by the rulers of the church and state, agreeably to the prejudices, prepossessions and customs of different countries; then abandon at once all respect to the practice of the churches planted by the apostles. We shall then be obliged to prove to you that the approved practice of the apostolical churches is a part of that Scripture which cannot be broken; but it is altogether inconsistent to vindicate Presbytery as divine, yet that she may be modelled by the fancies of men, and that it is a matter indifferent whether or not she be formed resembling the construction of the model of which you profess that she is a copy. You hold this to have been a General Council; a General Council then you must prove it to have been. The model must exhibit all its parts, springs, wheels, pivots and pins. When you do so, I will take it for a General Council. After this, you will be so kind as to show me that part of your model which corresponds to each of all your subordinate courts in their proper rank and gradation, from this General Council to the kirk-session. I require no more from you in behalf of Presbytery, than I will engage to do in behalf of Independency. The part of the system to which I cannot produce corresponding parts in the model, I promise to renounce. The parts of the model which you can show are not yet taken into the copy, we will receive when you discover them, and thankfully adopt them in practice.

But though every part of the divine model of Presbytery cannot be expected from every example, yet if this was a General Council, the example here recorded, from the very nature of the case, would have afforded room for an exhibition of the number, rank and gradation of courts. I do not expect that this meeting should afford a model for any but one corresponding assembly, but the whole narration containing various examples, must have given us the process of the business through the different courts, had any such courts existed. We are informed of the origin of the dispute, and the proceedings of the disciples at Antioch about it, and of every material circumstance respecting it, till the messengers came to Jerusalem. Here then, though the assembly at Jerusalem could not be supposed to give a model for the subordinate assemblies, if the case had been handled after the Presbyterian manner, we would have had in this chapter a full view of the whole series of courts in their due order, and the constituent parts of each of them. The matter could not have gone to a General Council, till it had passed through each of all the subordinate courts in their order. The messengers would have been sent from kirk-session to Presbytery, from Presbytery to Synod, from Synod to National Assembly, &c., till at last they arrived at this famous General Council. The example then here recorded, is such that, from the very nature of the case, the narrative would have given us the most complete view of the whole Presbyterian system. How absurd then is it for this writer to assert, that " the general system of Presbytery is not only explicitly but clearly authorized by the practice of the Primitive church, *as far as the cases occurred!*" A case here occurred, which might have exemplified, nay, if it was a General Council, must have exemplified them all. This might have some plausibility, if the affair here recorded had been settled by a kirk-session. It might then be alleged that a case did not occur to give an example of any of the superior courts. But even in this case, if cases did not occur to give an example in model, they must be given in precept; for if neither cases occurred to exhibit each of the assemblies, nor a precept was given to provide for such cases when they should occur, how have we a divine model? What are we to do with those cases for which we have no direction in Scripture, either from precept or example? If sufficient cases did not occur, and if sufficient precepts are not given, we have then no sufficient model. Had it even happened, which we see it has not, that a case had not occurred to give an example of the gradation of church power from the lowest to the highest court, it would have been incumbent on the apostles to have supplied the defect by a precept. A verse or two additional in precept would have supplied the want of example. But the apostles omitted this forsooth to give some scope to the prerogatives of the clergy. To save the trouble of a few verses, they must leave ground for a foundation to the antichristian edifice. The Pontiff may defend his usurpation in the same language. Every pin of the Roman hierarchy could not possibly be found in any scriptural example, although "the general system is not only explicitly but clearly authorized, by the practice of the Primitive church, *as far as the cases occurred.*" In this way, we might make as many additions to the Scriptures as we please. To justify them, we would have nothing to do but allege that the cases did not occur during the time recorded in Scripture history.

Were we then to allow that this chapter establishes the divine right of some superior assembly to settle disputes, and command what is to be believed and practised, the constitution and construction of such an assembly must be the same with that exhibited here as a model. It must consist of the apostles, elders and brethren of one church only. It would not prove any subordination of courts, or a right of appeal from the first decision. Even had it been an appeal from a Presbyterian congregation, or any part of it, in Antioch, it will not warrant an optional gradation of courts. It would sanction one superior court of appeal only. The first appeal and the last must be to a General Council. Had there been a Presbyterian series of courts, the matter would have been first tried by the Session at Antioch; the appellants would have brought it to the Presbytery, from Presbytery to Synod, from Synod to National Assembly, &c., until it came at last to this General Council. And upon Presbyterian principles, it can be only on the supposition that it passed through all these that it came to a General Council. Could it have been settled by any of the inferior courts to the satisfaction of all parties, it never would have come to this assembly. Would one of your kirk-sessions be allowed to appeal to the General Assembly, without previously having brought the matter through all the subordinate courts? How does it consist with Presbyterian principles, that reference was made in the first instance to a General Council? Whether this assembly was a court of primary reference or appeal, it cuts off every other. If a General Council, all subordinate courts are cut off; if a Presbytery, all superior courts are cut off, for this decided for the whole world. A superior court being granted, Presbytery has no just pretentions to the sanction of the model here exhibited. Before you can succeed, you must prove that this assembly to which you refer as a model, is exactly represented in your corresponding assembly; and likewise prove each of your other courts from different examples or precept. You must show that these elders were officers of different congregations in Jerusalem, and not of one church; that the half of them were lay, and the other half clerical elders. You must tell us whether all the elders at Jerusalem, both lay and clerical, were present; and if not, how many of each kind, that we may know how to constitute a similar assembly. Were they present in their own right, as the representatives of their distinct orders, or was one or both orders of them the representatives of their respective congregations? If all the clerical, and only some of the lay-elders were present, you must prove this, or show why they should not. If they were all present of both kinds, whatever assembly pretends to be formed on this model must be similarly constituted. You must also show that there were representatives present from all the churches in the world; and if all the elders of all the congregations in Jerusalem were present, so must all the elders of all the congregations in the world. By what right did all the elders of all the congregations in Jerusalem sit in an assembly representative of the whole Christian world? To make the representation equal, there must have been no more of the elders of the congregations at Jerusalem in this assembly, than of every other congregation. When you have done all this, and have arranged this assembly in complete Presbyterian order, a single dissenting voice in your assemblies will destroy the obligation of their decrees. If there be one member in a General Council to object to the measures adopted, it cannot shelter its decisions by this model.

But how do you make this assembly, though, in your estimation, uninspired, rise to the dignity of a General Council? Will not the reader be at a loss to guess how such a position can be established from this passage? Yet it does not give you the smallest trouble. You have not even the trouble to make out this point by the usual method of appealing to the testimony of Scripture, and by reasonings and deductions from this. This is effected in a moment, in a single sentence, by the help of one of those subtile distinctions, which so much abound in this work. The apostles were present, who, though nothing but *uninspired, ordinary, common ministers*, were nevertheless *universal pastors, and ministers to all the churches in the world*. *Uninspired, ordinary, common ministers*, yet *universal bishops!!!* Monstrous absurdity! Then all uninspired, ordinary, common ministers, are universal pastors. *A universal bishop* is nothing but *an ordinary minister!* Can it be necessary to give a particular answer to such quibbling? It sufficiently refutes itself, for it is a contradiction in terms. It makes the apostles ordinary ministers, yet, as ordinary ministers, universal bishops, who are certainly extraordinary ministers; for there are no such ministers now, except you choose to make the Roman pontiff an exception.

The apostles were indeed universal bishops, but, as such, they were not *uninspired ordinary, common* ministers. They were universal bishops in no other sense than as they were apostles. If, in any instance, they did not act as apostles, they could not be considered as universal bishops. As uninspired men, they had no authority over all the churches in the world. As uninspired men, they could indeed have acted as elders in any church in which they might be called to the pastoral office; but, as uninspired men, they could have no authority in any church, in which they did not labour as stated pastors. If, in discharging the office of elder in a church, they could lay aside their apostolical character, they would have had then, even in that church, no more authority, or more extensive jurisdiction than the other elders. If they were ordinary ministers, and uninspired teachers, what entitled them to distinction? If, in this assembly, you divest them of their apostolical character, and make them ordinary ministers, they must fill the place, not of all the churches of the world, but of so many common ministers, and their presence will never give the character of universality to any council which was not in itself universal. Nay, if you divest them of their apostolical character, and make this a representative assembly, you must prove that each of them was a pastor and representative of a particular church, or they will have no right even to the seat of a common minister in this Presbyterian court. But the apostles never laid aside their apostolical character. Though they were subject to the sins and infirmities of other men, yet, in declaring the will of Christ upon any subject, upon all occasions, they were as infallible as Christ himself. Nay, they were in Christ's stead. They were ambassadors for Christ. It was not they who spoke, but the Holy Spirit by them.

I ask you, Sir, upon what portion of Scripture do you found this distinction between the apostles as apostles, and the apostles as universal bishops? Do you find the apostles so called, and so acting in any situation in which they are said not to be apostles? Was there ever an order of officers in the church of Christ of this description? Where have you found these officers? If there never existed such a separate order, and if the apostles are never represented in this character, distinguished from their apostolical office, why have you made the distinction? Is this a distinction previously established, or have you invented it, without any authority, merely to serve a turn? I could have wished to have preserved a good opinion of the uprightness of the intentions of my antagonist; but really it is almost beyond my power to think, that a man can reason thus upon the Word of God to the satisfaction of his own conscience. Beware of handling the Word of God deceitfully, and of shutting your eyes against the light. In justice God may give up the man to his own blindness who comes to his Word, not to learn what it speaks, but to teach it what to speak. Is this like receiving, like a little child, the will of the heavenly Father? "Speak Lord, for thy servant heareth," should express the disposition of every one who inquires after the mind of God in his Word. Could this idea ever have suggested itself to a man desirous above all things to know the will of Jesus that he might obey it? I beseech you, Sir, to ask your own conscience whether you are defending the Church of Christ or the Church of Scotland. I beseech you to consider whether the glory of God is the great aim of such reasoning. Do you expect the reward of this work in the approbation of Jesus, or in the smiles of the world and in church preferment? Did you commence and carry on your work with a mind open to conviction, and willing to be solely guided in your conclusions and subsequent conduct by the Word of God? or was it your determination to see what might be said to evade the conclusions of your antagonists? Was the conviction of the divine right of the Presbyterian form of church government which you now profess, obtained after much earnest prayer for direction, impartial examination, with the glory of God principally in view, and a readiness to give up your present situation, had the evidence preponderated on the other side? or has your investigation of the subject originated from your desire of vindicating your church, as far as the Scriptures could be made to bend to your system, and of distinguishing yourself as one of her champions? I leave these important questions with your conscience. Though your motives and mine are nothing to our arguments, yet they are of great importance to ourselves. I do not mean to insinuate that our arguments are the stronger from the uprightness of our intentions. But what an awful thing will it be for that one of us, who shall be found to have perverted the Word of God to sanction rebellion against Jesus, by overturning and changing the laws and constitution of his kingdom! If those who attempt to subvert the constitution of earthly kingdoms are the abhorrence of civil rulers and of the peaceable community, how dreadful is it to attempt to overturn the plan of government instituted by Jesus, and to substitute another in its stead. Remember that this King sits in heaven, and that it is vain to oppose him, for he will bring to nought the understanding of the prudent. Remember that Jesus will judge the world; and that those very apostles whose decision you refuse to admit as infallible, shall sit on twelve thrones judging the twelve tribes of Israel. Think of the awful threatening against those who stumble any of the weak children of God. "Whosoever shall offend one of these little ones that believe in me, it were better for him that a mill-stone were hanged about his neck, and that he were drowned in the midst of the sea."

I cannot recognise in such advocates of Presbytery, the successors of Knox, and the other illustrious reformers. They were the reformers of their day; and as they acted according to their light then at every hazard, no doubt, did they still exist, they would be the foremost in reformation. But those who pretend to be their successors, instead of advancing, take a fixed station at the point where their ancestors left off, as if they had been infallible.

But what will this distinction serve you, were we to indulge you with it a little, for the sake of argument. If the apostles were present in that assembly, of whatever description it may be supposed to have been, as universal bishops, and if this assembly is exhibited as a model for the settling of all future controversies, then the court formed upon this model, must always have universal bishops among them, or the copy will want the most distinguishing part of the original. Instead of being a model for a universal council, it would be a model only for one church judging for the whole world, having a few universal bishops among them. And as these universal bishops, it seems, are ordinary ministers, so they will easily be found. What a charming model for the court of Rome! If your reasoning stands good, the decrees of the Vatican, with their universal bishop at their head, are much more worthy of respect than those of any Presbyterian assembly.

Again, if the apostles, acting as universal bishops, could serve instead of the presence of representatives from the churches of Syria, Cilicia, &c., there was no need for the presence of the elders of Jerusalem, or of any foreign ministers. Why could not the apostles, as universal bishops, have represented the different congregations supposed to be in Jerusalem, &c., as well as those of Syria, &c.? Upon this principle, the apostles alone, even as *uninspired, common, ordinary ministers,* could have formed a universal council. Nay, if being universal bishops gave the apostles a right to represent and bind the whole Christian world, then as each of the apostles was a universal bishop, so each of them could have represented the whole visible church. Paul then, though degraded from his apostolical character, as an *uninspired, common, ordinary* minister, by virtue of being some way unaccountably at the same time a universal bishop, might have settled this matter at Antioch, as the representative of the whole Christian church. You affect to think that it is an argument against the supposition of Paul's inspiration, that the matter was brought up to the council of Jerusalem. But if there is anything in this, it militates with equal force against his universal episcopacy. Was Paul a universal bishop, and in virtue of being so, could represent and bind the whole Christian world; and could he not, in virtue of these high prerogatives, have silenced a few false teachers, and have commanded the obedience of a single church?

But the proving of the apostles to be universal bishops, as ordinary uninspired ministers, would not prove this to have been a General Council. If all the Christian world was bound by these decrees, because there were present in this assembly universal bishops, then the obligation of the decrees results from the power supposed to be lodged in the universality of this episcopacy, not in the universality of the council as to the number of its members. If the apostles bound all Christians by virtue of their universal episcopacy, the obligation of the decrees depends upon the authority supposed to be in this office, and not from this council being composed of representatives of all the churches in the world. This would not make the assembly a universal council, but a council of universal bishops. A universal council is understood to be a council composed of the representatives of all the churches in the world. Now the apostles, as universal bishops, were not universal representatives. As universal bishops, they could do anything, to which the prerogatives of that office may be supposed to extend. If it is one of the prerogatives of a universal bishop, that he can bind decrees upon churches, not being present in themselves or in their representatives, this is but another name for an apostle. It will make nothing for your system, were we even to grant that the apostles were universal bishops independent of their apostolical office, except you could prove that they were appointed by all the churches in the world as their representatives. And upon this supposition, nothing would depend upon their universal episcopacy; for any other ordinary ministers might have been equally chosen as representatives. If then they acted as universal bishops, and had authority to make decrees for all the churches in virtue of that office, they did not act as representatives; and if they acted as representatives, their authority was not derived from being universal bishops, but from representing all the churches in the world.

Again, if a universal bishop, in virtue of his office, can bind the universal church, then a particular bishop can bind a particular church. The same authority that the former has over the universal church, the latter must have over his particular church. If then a universal bishop could make decrees for the universal church, without being nominated to represent them, a particular bishop can do the same in his congregation. Every pastor then is an absolute lord in his congregation; he may decree according to his pleasure, without any interference from the people. This will entirely cut off the kirk-session. If a council of universal bishops can give law to the Christian world, a council of particular bishops can give law to their particular congregations; and a General Council of the clergy may bind the church universal, the latter having not a single representative in the assembly. This will exclude all laymen from church courts. It will cut off all representation. Recollect then, Sir, that a council of universal bishops, and a universal council, are two very different things. The apostles might have been the former without being the latter, and they might have been the latter without being the former.

But why do I spend time in disproving a mere fancy? Why do I pick down by piece-meal an edifice that is raised upon the sand? Why shall I trouble myself to show, that the constituent parts of this assembly do not resemble any of the Presbyterian courts, seeing each of these courts is erected upon a supposition that has not the smallest countenance from Scripture? The whole system is founded upon the idea of representation. If this foundation is not in any part of the Scriptures, the building being baseless falls at once. Why do we spend time in arguing whether church rulers as representatives may not be called a church, when there is not in all the Word of God the shadow of evidence that there is any such representation? I ask you then, Sir, where do you find that one man may represent another in religious matters? Where do you find any church assembly composed of representatives? Can you produce any example, or any precept? Is there anything like it in this fifteenth chapter of Acts? I care not then what you call the apostles: still this assembly is not a representative assembly. No matter as to this argument whether they were particular bishops, or universal bishops, or apostles. Neither they, nor any one present, is a representative. The very soul and essence of the Presbyterian system has not even an appearance of foundation in the Word of God. Were your whole reasoning upon this point allowed to be conclusive, it establishes a system quite different and opposite from Presbytery. It would exclude laymen from all share of church power. The ministers, and the ministers without being chosen as representatives, would then in their own right determine all controversies, and enact all decrees. If no such thing as representation is taught in the New Testament, why have Presbyterians argued upon this, as if it were granted? Why shall we be called upon to show that a church ruler cannot be a church representative, when there is no such thing as representation? Here then, Sir, is a previous question to be settled: till you prove this as a foundation, it is vain to attempt to raise a superstructure. Were I even then to allow you, that this assembly was an uninspired assembly, composed of ministers alone, and that in that capacity they had a right to bind the Christian world, and to leave a model for future ages, it makes nothing for your system.

Again, granting you that this was a representative council, and that the apostles had been nominated by all the churches in the world as their representatives; why had some of these churches other representatives besides the apostles, and others none? Had not the apostles as good a right to represent the congregations of Jerusalem, &c., as all others in the world? or if the apostles were only the representatives of those churches which had no others present, was this a fair and equal representation? All the congregations in the world had only a few common representatives, while the single church at Jerusalem, or if you will all the congregations of Jerusalem, had all their elders present. If the apostles had not a vote for every congregation they represented, of what service was the universality of their episcopacy? Where is the use of giving them a great name, if the meanest member of the council had a vote that would go as far to influence the determination as any of the apostles? Their universal episcopacy could in no way fit them for such an extensive representation. If Scotland and Ireland could only send one member to Parliament between them, who should be called a universal representative, of what use would this name be to his constituents, if every county and borough member in England had as good a vote as he had. Notwithstanding you dignify these uninspired men with the pompous title of universal bishop, you in reality make them only cyphers. Instead of directing, according to your scheme, they must have been directed by this assembly. But the idea of representation never occurred to any man from this narrative itself; it has been taken from the systems of civil governments, and transferred to religion. Like every other distinguishing part of your system, it is a child of human wisdom.

Once more, if the churches in Syria, Cilicia, &c., were bound by these decrees, because the apostles were present as universal bishops, then, upon your own principles, the ordinary elders at Jerusalem could no more be said to bind those churches, than the church members. The church members, you allege, could not have been in this assembly, because they could not bind other churches; now, if this were conclusive reasoning, it would also prove, that the ordinary elders could not have been in this assembly, because they could not bind Syria, Cilicia, &c. Whether you call the apostles by their own title, or by that of universal bishops, it comes to the same thing. Syria and Cilicia, &c., were bound by *them*, not by the ordinary elders. I cannot yet see then, Sir, how it will ever be possible for you to escape from the horns of Mr. Innes' dilemma, which you thought this distinction would enable you easily to avoid. The apostles as uninspired men, had no authority over the church of Christ. Neither their doctrines nor their decrees had any power of obligation, but as his infallible ambassadors. If it had been possible that Jesus would have allowed them to teach in his name without infallibility, they deserved no attention nor obedience, farther than they could produce Scripture to support what they delivered; *i.e.*, just the same authority that is possessed by the meanest saint on earth. As uninspired men, they had no authority to settle any controversy, or impose any burden.

But whatever was the model of this assembly, if the apostles were infallible in their decision, an infallible council can be no precedent to a fallible one. Infallible decrees are made to be obeyed, not to be imitated by other decrees of fallible men. Justly supposing, that you could never establish the propriety of reference from this chapter, if the apostles acted in their proper character, you have ventured to suggest the most daring hypothesis, and have attempted to divest them, in this instance, of their inspiration and apostolical authority. Were you to succeed in your attempt, without proving your point, you would leave no basis whereon to rest the inspiration of the Scriptures. If the interpretation of the passage of Amos, quoted by James in this assembly, is not infallibly true, what better security have we for the infallible interpretation of the Old Testament, in the various sermons and letters of the apostles? If a letter written by one apostle has the authority of infallibility, shall a letter written by all the apostles jointly have less weight? You require that it should be proved by positive declaration, as to this instance, that they were infallible. The proof of the contrary lies upon you. As apostles, they were infallible in every thing which they taught, either by preaching or writing. It remains for you to show, that in this, or any other instance, they were not infallible in their interpretation of Scripture, or in their commands to the churches. It must be proved, that on this occasion they were divested of their apostolical character. Whether they were directed in every instance by immediate afflatus from the Holy Spirit suggesting a new discovery of his will, or infallibly secured from error in their manner of relating what they knew without such new revelation, makes no matter. As the ambassadors of Jesus, they must, upon all occasions, upon all subjects relating to the kingdom, have been in the room of Jesus himself. Those who are fallible will sometimes err, and if they are fallible in one case, why may they not be fallible in another? Once establish the position which you here lay down, and every man may object to any part of Scripture that may displease him. The Lord Jesus Christ left his apostles in his own place, and gave them full authority as to every thing to be believed and practised. Whatever they did, was done by himself, in all that they taught the churches. "I will give unto thee the keys of the kingdom of heaven, and whatsoever thou shalt bind on earth shall be bound in heaven, and whatsoever thou shalt loose on earth shall be loosed in heaven." Here incontrovertibly is given unto Peter, authority infallibly to declare whatever was necessary to be believed and practised by those who should enter into the kingdom of God. If he had the keys of the kingdom, when he opened that kingdom to any one without insisting on circumcision, he was infallible in doing so. Had he insisted on circumcision, it would have infallibly shown that this was the mind of his Lord. When he abolished it, the same thing is as evidently seen. "Whosoever sins ye remit, they are remitted unto them, and whosoever sins ye retain, they are retained." They have here infallible authority to declare how sinners were to be pardoned, and to describe the characters of those who give evidence that their sins are pardoned, and of those who give evidence that they are yet in their sins. Now, the question, whether circumcision was necessary to salvation, came within this commission. They had authority to declare the mind of Jesus as to this matter. Indeed, if they had not, they were not ambassadors of Christ. Upon a question, whether such a thing was or was not necessary to salvation, that the apostles of Jesus Christ had not infallible information! Suppose that the apostle Paul was not infallible when teaching at Antioch, and yet strenuously contended against the necessity of circumcision, he might notwithstanding have been wrong. For if he was a fallible teacher, he might have been in an error. Had it then turned out to have been the will of Jesus, that circumcision should be preached as necessary to salvation; that he did not know this till after his going to Jerusalem, and that many whom he had taught at Antioch died before his return without circumcision, hath not the apostle of Jesus deceived them? Upon whom should the Lord Jesus have charged their blood? What would then have come of his promise? Matt. xvi. 19; John xx. 23, &c. Would not the Lord Jesus himself have been to blame for deceiving them? for they were deceived by one who had his commission, infallibly to declare his will and promise to be with them. Nay, if the matter was not infallibly determined at Jerusalem, there is still a possibility that they were all mistaken. The sentence might have been reversed by a succeeding revelation. It is no answer to this, that this was not the case; it might have been the case, unless the sentence was infallible. But what is of still greater importance, if the determination of this question at Jerusalem was not infallible, how are we infallibly sure that circumcision is not still necessary, and that we are not yet in our sins? It is no answer to this, that Paul writes against the necessity of circumcision in his epistles; if he was fallible at Antioch, he may be fallible in his Epistle to the Galatians, &c. What better reason have we to consider him inspired in the one case than in the other? If all the apostles at Jerusalem were fallible, and a letter, written jointly in the name of the whole, is to be looked upon as an uninspired letter, shall we consider any one of them singly to be inspired in their individual letters? Paul was bound by this Synod to teach what they had determined, and if he, and the other apostles, were uninspired at that time, upon this subject, there is no probability that ever after they should be inspired. His letters and preaching then afterwards may only be considered as inculcating the decisions of this Synod, just as Presbyterian ministers preach and write to inculcate and defend the articles of the Westminster Assembly. Nay, it would be altogether absurd to suppose, if inspiration was unnecessary in the determination of this question, in a General Council, that afterwards it was necessary to individuals to inculcate the decision. Inspiration was unnecessary in those who exercised the power of framing articles of belief and practice to be received by the whole world, yet it was necessary for those who individually published the result of the deliberation! Unparalled absurdity! If the question was not infallibly determined at Jerusalem, it is not infallibly determined yet. We should then, without depending on this Council, or the writings of the apostles afterwards, inquire for ourselves in the Old Testament—nay, rather we should reject the whole as a fable. If ever inspiration was necessary, it was before the question was decided: if ever it had been given, it would have been previous to this decision. To decide the matter by human wisdom, and afterwards teach the decision by divine revelation, would be as if a judge should order the criminal to be hanged, and then examine into the evidence of his guilt. I call upon you, Sir, to show me upon what consistent grounds you believe the plenary inspiration of the New Testament? If all the apostles at Jerusalem might have erred, may not any one of them have erred in his writings and preaching? Was it not as necessary to be infallible in writing a joint letter to all the churches and Christians in the world, as in writing an individual letter to one church? There is not an argument in favour of the inspiration of the epistles, if at any time you suppose the apostles to be fallible in their directions to the churches, either verbal or written. If upon any part of the will of their Lord they were uninstructed, they could not pronounce their decisions, or issue their commands, until they were illuminated and infallibly directed. To suppose that they would enjoin one thing as fallible, and another as infallible, especially without telling us of it, would render everything suspicious. We have no means of knowing that this decision was certainly right, but from the infallibility of those by whom it was made. If the apostles acted as uninspired ministers in this assembly, their decisions might have been overturned by a subsequent General Council. To say that they are right, yet not infallibly right, is foolish. For if they are not infallible, how do we know that they are right? Every man must then be guided by his own judgment, according to the evidence they produce. When you rob the apostles of the infallible direction of the Spirit, it makes no compensation to them or to us that you allow them the *common aids* which all faithful ministers enjoy. This teaching of the Spirit is common to all Christians with the ministers of the Gospel. Had this been sufficient to have determined the question, the brethren at Antioch had no need to send to Jerusalem. Besides, this direction of the Spirit is not the standard of the word; the word is the standard by which we are to know that it is the Spirit's teaching. We cannot distinguish the teaching of the Spirit from the suggestions of enthusiasm, but by the agreeableness of the former to the word. How do we know that they enjoyed this

common aid? We have no greater certainty that they possessed this than infallible direction. Do ministers at all times, upon all questions relating to the kingdom of Christ, enjoy these common aids? Are these common aids sufficient to lead them at all times into the truth? Then this amounts to inspiration and infallibility. If they do not at all times enjoy these, or if they are insufficient to lead them into the truth, then how do we know, either that they were favoured with such aids in this case, or that if they were, they were sufficient to direct them. If all Presbyterian assemblies have these common aids of the Spirit, how does it happen that there is such a difference between their decisions at different times? The people of God do indeed enjoy the teaching of his Spirit, but he teaches by his Word only, and their opinions derive no additional weight, not the smallest, from being supposed to be influenced by the Spirit. This is a thing which cannot be subjected to evidence. If you wish me to believe Presbytery, you must show me that the Scriptures contain Presbytery. It will not have the smallest weight with me, were you to tell me that you have written with the common aids of the Spirit. I will judge of this by the correspondence of your doctrine with the words of the Spirit. Yet it is plain that you place some importance upon the common aids, as to our satisfaction with the propriety of the decision. Indeed, though you here rob the apostles of inspiration, you are willing to have it thought, that these common aids, *which all Presbyterian assemblies have ever enjoyed*, sufficiently directed them in the determination. I have frequently heard persons who in words disclaim all idea of direct inspiration for the Westminster Assembly, lay a very great stress upon *common aids*. Many speak of this matter in such a manner as plainly to intimate, that this assembly enjoyed something equivalent to inspiration. "They were not indeed inspired, but if ever any body of men enjoyed an uncommon portion of the common aids——"
In some great difficulty, one of that assembly sat for some time writing on a slip of paper, "Lord give light; Lord give light." All was darkness before, but now he arises, and all is light; he astonishes the

ON PRESBYTERY. 519

assembly with his discoveries. Is not this something like inspiration? Yet the apostles were not inspired in the determination of the question at Jerusalem?

But that the apostles were infallible in this assembly, is clear from the history of the transaction.

1. Their decisions are called decrees or dogmas. Now, if these decrees were the commandments of men, we are forbidden to teach or submit to them. " In vain do ye worship me, teaching for doctrines the commandments of men." If then *the necessary burdens* were bound by uninspired men, it would have been rebellion against Christ to have received them. This also would be contrary to the precept, " Call no man, Father." If they are obeyed as uninspired men, issuing decrees according to their private judgment, our obedience is not to God, but to man. I can avail myself of your whole reasoning upon the word *dogma*, and bring every example which you quote to bear upon this point, to show that they are the decrees of the Spirit. It denotes decrees or decisions that are not to be disputed, or submitted to the discretion of those who are called to obey them. They are made to be obeyed, not to be submitted to examination, and to be received or rejected according to the judgment of those for whom they are made. This, Sir, you clearly prove so as to convince me, that if you had a good cause you could defend it. But what is the reason that upon points in which consists the very essence of the debate, you pass on so hastily, either by taking the foundation of your argument for granted, or giving us a mere assertion: while upon points which cannot be disputed by your antagonist, nay, in which his argument requires that he, rather than you, should produce proof, you are so diffuse and particular? Does not this show, that your cause cannot afford you a sufficiency of just arguments? Could you have proved that these dogmas might be changed or disobeyed, according to the conviction of the individual, it would have made much more for your system. Because, as you put this assembly upon a level with any other Synod, you must either prove that the decrees of every Synod are absolutely binding, independent of the conviction of the individual; or that these decrees

enacted at Jerusalem, are binding only as far as we see them to be just.

2. These decrees are laid as a burden upon all the churches, without any intimation that they are after all to judge for themselves, and compare them with the Scriptures, obeying them no farther than they should see them to be agreeable to that standard. Had the decision been fallible, this certainly would have been necessary.

3. The brethren at Antioch are said (verse 31), to have rejoiced for the consolation contained in the epistle. If this was the opinion of fallible men only, their rejoicing was groundless. They were rejoicing in the testimony of men, and not in the testimony of Jesus Christ. What gave them consolation? Was it this decision being the mind of Jesus their Lord? This indeed was good ground of consolation. But was the judgment of fallible men the source of this consolation? How then could it be said to them that they "received this decision not as the word of men, but as it was indeed the Word of God?" The apostle, in writing to them again, might have reversed this sentence, and expressed his joyfulness that they 'received it not as the Word of God, but as it was indeed the word of men.' They rejoiced in the opinion of men as to the way of salvation. They had nothing but the testimony of fallible men as the ground of their hope. The epistle indeed declares, that this seemed good to the Holy Ghost; but that it was infallibly so they had no evidence. They had no proof but the assertion of uninspired men. Nay, they had not even the portions of Scripture pointed out to them upon which this judgment was founded. Therefore,

4. The decision could not have been merely the opinion of uninspired men, because it claimed obedience without producing the grounds on which it was founded. Had the apostles acted as uninspired men, they would have, along with their decision, exhibited the portions of Scripture upon which it was grounded, and the fact related by Peter. They would have wrested the duty of obedience of the brethren at Antioch, &c., upon the agreement of this decision with these standards. How

did the brethren at Antioch know that the decrees were agreeable to the Holy Ghost? They had nothing for it but the testimony of this epistle. The fact related by Peter, the quotation from Amos with respect to the reception of the Gentiles into the church of Christ without circumcision, and the reason of the necessary burdens, are not brought forward in the letter as the ground of conviction to the brethren at Antioch, &c. They must then have considered their judgment as infallible, or would they have imposed it in this manner upon others? And the joy of the brethren at Antioch must have arisen from implicitly believing the decrees to be the will of the Holy Spirit. If, in reality, they were the decrees of uninspired men, their joy was false and unscriptural. It was nothing better than the joy of those deluded children of superstition, who rejoice when their absolution is pronounced by their clergy. Nay, if this letter was not inspired, I would have no hesitation in pronouncing the conduct of the apostles to have been entirely unscriptural and antichristian. They claimed faith to themselves, and not to the Word of God. Had they been fallible, they should have stated the Scriptures upon this point to the brethren at Antioch, and have confessed that they were not infallible in the interpretation of them. They should not have presumed to decide in such an absolute manner, upon a point on which they had no infallible guidance. Should any person write to you, that he is at a loss to know whether good works may not be partly the ground of justification, would you think it sufficient to answer in the negative, without producing those passages of Scripture which declare a free and full salvation through the atonement? Would you answer after this manner? 'It seems good to the Holy Ghost, and to me, that sinners shall be saved through faith.' Such language would be suitable to none but those who had infallibly the mind of the Spirit. Even the apostles themselves, with Christ their Master, produce frequently the passages of Scripture from which the doctrine they inculcate is deduced. This was their usual practice. From the manner therefore of instructing the churches in this letter by the authority of their judgment, without referring to the Old Testament Scriptures, every pretext is taken away for considering it as merely the judgment of men. Had this then been a fallible decision, the Scriptures would have been stated as the means of convincing; and from this source alone could their joy have justly arisen. Had the apostles been fallible, they never would have made their opinion the ground of the consolation of believers. The same thing is still more evident, from the necessary burdens which they lay upon them. They do not report in the letter, the reason of this necessity alleged by James in the meeting. They do not refer them to any portion of Scripture as their authority. They allege as motives of obedience, that this seemed good to the Holy Ghost, and to them. Their own word as to the mind of the Holy Ghost, is the ground of the obedience which they challenge. Now, if they were uninspired, they act in a much more arbitrary and lordly manner than you pretend that Presbyterian Synods use in the exercise of their similar authority. The authority for which you contend, " is not intended to supersede, but to promote inquiry; to present to them more commanding incitements to examine, and more powerful, though secondary enforcements and obligations to obey the truth"—page 321. But this decision enjoins obedience, without having the grounds of it submitted to examination, and is implicitly received. It was given, not to assist them in their inquiries, but to be obeyed as the mind of the Holy Spirit. Therefore,

5. The manner of receiving this decision shows that it was infallible. They received and submitted to the decrees instantly, rejoicing for the consolation which they afforded, although they had nothing but the testimony of the writers of the letter, that this was the will of Jesus. They did not remain in suspence till they had searched the Scriptures more fully to see whether they agreed with this letter. As soon as they read the letter, they were convinced; the result of which was, exceeding joyfulness. And indeed, what ground of conviction did they enjoy now, which they did not enjoy previously, but the judgment of those who wrote

the letter? They had the Old Testament Scriptures previously; the letter did not refer to them, or give an exposition of any part of them, which might enlighten them in the knowledge of some things of which they might have been previously ignorant. When then they instantly received the sentence, and rejoiced in it as the mind of the Holy Ghost, it is very plain that they looked upon those who gave the decision as infallibly directed. There was no other reason why they should rejoice. Whether this assembly was fallible or infallible, they acted as if they were infallible, and the brethren of Antioch received their decision as if it were infallible. They gave the letter a reception becoming the Word of God alone. The authority of the epistle itself was the ground both of their obedience and joy. Now, on a question that affected the way of salvation, had they not had implicit belief in the infallibility of those who decided it, they could not have received the decision until they had compared it with the Scriptures, and had seen its foundation there; nor would they have rejoiced, until they had considered maturely the testimony of the Scriptures. But this letter afforded them no more means of doing this than they enjoyed before, which plainly proves that it is Scripture itself. Never was an epistle received by the churches of the saints from any of the apostles with greater or more instantaneous submission and gladness.

6. James, having quoted a passage from the Old Testament, speaks not as a fallible man delivering an opinion upon a point, which might be notwithstanding otherwise determined. He pronounces his sentence in the most authoritative manner, as an apostle of the Lord Jesus Christ. He did not say, 'I move that the assembly shall adopt such a resolution,' but 'I pronounce sentence.' None but an inspired person could speak in this manner. In a representative assembly, such language from a fallible man would have been arrogant in the highest degree, and must have subjected him to censure. But we find that after he pronounced sentence, there was not a single objection, or even additional observation. There was not even a formal acquiescence in his sentence; the word of Jesus in person

could not have been more cordially assented to. Had not his decision been infallible, if there had not been farther discussion and a formal vote, there would at least have been a formal assent of the house to this opinion. The greatest leader in the General Assembly, or in the British Parliament, must have his opinion sanctioned by the formal assent of the house, before it is considered as their decision. You are even at pains to show, that the word which James uses to signify his judgment, "imports the most decided exercise of authority." But if James was only an uninspired man, why did he assume such an air of authority in an assembly, in which the most ignorant lay-elder has as good a vote as he had himself. He could not authoritatively pronounce sentence by himself, if the decision must be carried by a majority of voices. But if he was guided by the Spirit of God, he might in the most absolute manner make the decision; for the same would be the mind of all in the assembly who had the Spirit of God. What should you think of the member who should rise up in the General Assembly after much discussion, saying, 'I pronounce sentence in this matter; it shall be so or so?'

7. Their decision is expressly said to have been the decrees of the Holy Ghost. It affects not the argument, that this should be supposed to relate to the words of the Holy Ghost, *i.e.*, the Scriptures quoted by James. It is no matter to me how they came to know this, whether by immediate afflatus, or infallible direction in the interpretation of Scripture. It is enough for me to know the fact, that it was the mind of the Holy Spirit; and that it was so is witnessed, not by one only, but by all the apostles of Jesus Christ. I have as good evidence of this, as I have of Christ's resurrection. If I am deceived as to this point, the apostles of the Lord Jesus have deceived me. Those persons whom Jesus promised to fit, by the gifts of his Spirit, to declare all the truth, tell me that this decision was the decree of the Holy Spirit. I beg to know any fact better authenticated in all the Scriptures. When Paul says, 1 Tim. iv. 1—"Now the Spirit speaketh expressly, that in the latter times some shall depart from the faith," whether he is supposed to

refer to the Old Testament prophecies, or to the immediate communications of the Spirit to himself, no man thinks that it should have less weight upon the one supposition than upon the other. Paul's interpretation of Scripture is itself Scripture. But if it is not infallibly certain that the sentence passed at Jerusalem was the mind of the Spirit, neither is it infallibly certain that this is the mind of the Spirit which Paul declares. If what all the apostles declare to be the mind of the Spirit, might notwithstanding be otherwise, much more may that be otherwise which is asserted only by one apostle, and that very apostle who you affirm was not inspired when he was preaching the Gospel at Antioch. Though then it should be found that by "it seemeth good unto the Holy Ghost," nothing more is referred to than the words of Amos, it maketh no difference. The interpretation is an apostolical interpretation. When an uninspired man tells me that such a thing is the mind of the Holy Spirit, I wait for his proof that it is so, and my conviction rests upon the Scriptures which he produces. But when an apostle tells me that such a thing is the mind of the Spirit, I look for no other proof but his word. Here then that this letter was the mind of the Spirit, we are assured by all the apostles. But,

8. The words, "It seemeth good to the Holy Ghost," cannot be confined to the quotation from Amos; they must also extend to the testimony of the Holy Ghost to the preaching of Peter, in giving the Gentiles to believe, and to have their hearts purified by faith, without circumcision. Nor can they be confined to both of these things; for the necessary burdens which are also said to be the mind of the Holy Ghost, are not inferences either from the fact related by Peter, or the Scripture quoted by James. The Holy Spirit then must have made this known to them in some other way. If it seemed good to the Holy Spirit to lay upon the brethren at Antioch, &c., certain necessary burdens, which necessary burdens were not contained in the passage quoted by James, the Holy Ghost must have made this known to them by immediate suggestion. The reason for laying on these burdens is not

said to be deduced from any text of the Old Testament, but from this circumstance, that "Moses of old time hath in every city them that preach him, being read in the synagogue every Sabbath-day." Now, how did they know that it seemed good to the Holy Ghost to lay these necessary things as a burden upon the Gentile believers? In this part of his sentence, James must have had his instructions immediately from the Holy Spirit. That this was the mind of the Spirit, for the reason assigned, he could have known no other way. He must have had the most direct revelation. Not that I think an apostolical interpretation of the Old Testament to be in any manner of inferior credit to the most immediate revelation. But this is sufficient to cut off every pretext for quibbling in those who prefer the credit of a sect to the integrity of Scripture. The whole decision was the judgment of the Holy Ghost, as testified by the fact related by Peter, an apostle who could infallibly understand the import of the fact; by the passage quoted by James, an apostle who could infallibly interpret the Scripture which he alleged; and by the immediate communication from the Holy Spirit suggesting to him certain necessary things to be enjoined as a burden. There is in this letter then, an example of almost every different kind of inspiration: immediate and independent revelation, infallible interpretation of prophecy, infallible superintendency in the relation of a fact, and infallible exposition of the intention and import of this fact.

9. If they were not infallible in the laying on of this burden, and if this assembly is designed to exhibit a model for other uninspired assemblies to impose burdens which they may judge necessary, then such assemblies as resemble this, have a discretionary power that any part of the ceremonial law they please may become obligatory. Nay, I see no reason why they may not enjoin abstinence from flesh, pilgrimages, penances, and every other thing their wisdom may judge necessary. If this was an uninspired assembly, which hath imposed upon the disciples some things as a burden, for which they did not quote Scripture authority, if it

is a model, it will warrant all the superstitious observances of Antichrist.

10. Knowing the infallibility of the interpreter, we are assured of the legitimacy of the inference from the passage of Amos; but it is evident that it required infallible interpretation to make the inference. It is not an obvious inference. It required the most intimate knowledge of the Scriptures, and the illumination of the same Spirit that dictated the prophecy, to enable the interpreter to make this inference with complete certainty. Nay, it requires full confidence in the infallibility of the interpreter, to be thoroughly convinced that it is not strained. Those who do not consider the apostle as infallible, may doubt whether this text from Amos is completely decisive and clear; especially as the inference from it is so immensely important, affecting the very essence of the Gospel, and the plan of salvation. We should think it a very audacious thing, if any writer were to undertake to canvass and disprove the interpretation here given to this passage by James; yet, upon your theory, there would be nothing improper in it, nay, it would be a very lawful and useful inquiry to examine into the legitimacy of this inference with the utmost jealousy, and re-examine the whole subject with respect to the obligation of the ceremonial law. Even were we, upon the whole, to be satisfied with the decision, we might reject some of the particular proofs alleged in this assembly; and the man who should say that the passage from Amos quoted by James, fails to prove that for which he alleges it, you could not condemn upon your own principles. If you cannot show him that the inference is so clear and obvious, that it presents its own evidence, you fail to convince him. This interpretation by James, if he were uninspired, may as lawfully be questioned, as the interpretation of any other passage of Scripture in the sermons or writings of ordinary ministers. But how great is the power of attachment to ancient systems! Presbyterians in general, without a murmur, can bear you to divest the apostles of Jesus Christ of their apostolical character, and to represent them as ordinary uninspired ministers; yet they cannot, without the

utmost indignation, bear to hear the decisions of the Westminster divines called in question. In this country at least, the bulk of them, I mean of those who are attached to the old school, are accustomed to reverence the writings of Boston, the Erskines, Willison, &c., as the Word of God; they never think of questioning any interpretation of Scripture by them. Though they were not inspired, yet they had such an uncommon share of *the common aids*, as sufficiently served the same purpose. If at any time we should call in question any of the dogmas, or even forms of expression, of the Shorter Catechism, there is a cry of sacrilege, as if we had attempted to invalidate the authority of the Scriptures. Yet these very persons have taken no offence against your book, in which, without scruple, you attempt to disprove the inspiration of the apostles, represent the letter written by all the apostles as worthy of the same reception with that of Claudius Lysias, and endeavour to establish principles totally and necessarily subversive of the inspiration of the New Testament. Can that system be from God, that leads its votaries so far from himself? Can that be of divine appointment, which transfers to men the respect and confidence due only to the Word of God? Yet this is the visible tendency of the system which you endeavour to uphold. This is the inevitable tendency of every system that allows human interference in the things of God. If church-rulers have any power distinct from the word which they inculcate; if anything is left to be supplied by their discretion, it is impossible, in the very nature of things, but an undue weight will be attached to their opinions and decisions. It is impossible for the very best men, in such circumstances, always to keep within just limits, when the limits are not distinctly marked.

But you allege that ordinary ministers might have made the decision. I answer, that ordinary ministers might as well have made the whole New Testament. There is nothing in it (if the book of Revelation is not an exception, and perhaps even this is not an exception) which is not contained in, and inferred from the Old Testament. The most important doctrines of the New, are deduced from the Old, both by our Lord and his apostles. This indeed was their usual mode of preaching. If then there is no need of inspiration, with respect to every point that can be deduced from the Old Testament, there is not an inspired book in the New Testament. According to you, the Gospels, being a history of matters of fact, needed no inspiration; the Epistles, containing doctrines founded upon the Old Testament, needed no inspiration. There is not in all the New Testament any doctrine that cannot be as easily deduced from the Old as this. We have seen such a specimen of the kind of inferences, that the ecclesiastical assemblies of different denominations have drawn from the Scriptures, even after the New Testament has been completed, as should make us beware of easily assenting to such fallible deductions. If all the passages of the New Testament, which are even direct deductions from the Old, are to be considered as uninspired, what have we left? If ordinary ministers had been sufficient to infer all the doctrines of the New Testament from the Old, why was there instituted such an order as apostles, or why were these furnished with the effusion of the Holy Ghost? If ordinary ministers had been sufficiently qualified to expound with complete certainty the Old Testament Scriptures, why were there secondarily an order of prophets for this very purpose, to supply the lack of the apostles' presence, and of the writings of the New Testament, before they were delivered to the churches? God does nothing in vain; he gives no gift or office that is not necessary. What then is the use of the gift of interpretation of prophecy, according to your system? If fallible uninspired men could have suited this purpose, why such a waste of divine extraordinary communications? Ordinary ministers may indeed make inferences from the Old Testament, and expound its prophecies; but they have now the New Testament key to unlock the treasures of the Old. They have now the sermons of our Lord and his apostles. They have now the Gospels, the Acts and Epistles of the apostles, in which these prophecies are expounded. These afford a clue to conduct us into every labyrinth, which the first churches had not immediately in writing. But there is still a greater difference between the exposition of prophecy by those who are inspired, and by those who are only ordinary teachers. The exposition of the former is infallible, that of the latter is fallible, and must be judged of, and approved by the Scriptures themselves, before it is received. The apostle James had need of inspiration in this interpretation, because we are to be implicitly guided by his determination. But in our controversy, you and I have no need of inspiration, because there is no credit to be given to our interpretation of Scripture, farther than every one is persuaded from his own examination that we handle the Word of God fairly. If any man is led astray by the apostle James, the Lord Jesus Christ is answerable for his error. But if any man is led astray by either you or me, he is inexcusable. He has the Word; by that he is to prove all things, and hold fast only that which is good. The Lord Jesus Christ has not told him that he has commissioned either of us to declare His will with infallible certainty. The truth of our respective systems must be judged of by the Scriptures. From this therefore it follows, that in the very plainest case, in the most obvious inference, the apostles needed infallible superintendence, both in ideas and words, because if they had either misconceived or ill-expressed any sentiment, the mischief was irremediable. The fault must lie upon Jesus, because the apostles were in his place. But in the most difficult cases, ordinary teachers have no need of inspiration, nor infallible superintendence, because nothing depends upon their judgment. The conviction of the hearers should arise solely from the Word, and the evidence from other passages of Scripture which they may produce to illustrate and confirm their doctrine. If then this is the case as to the plainest inference, much more is it the case with the less obvious. And the inference in question is one of these. For my part, such an inference would never have occurred to me, had I been an uninspired member of that assembly.

11. The apostles are referred to in their apostolical character, and the answer returned in the same. They are addressed, not as universal uninspired bishops, but

as the apostles of Jesus Christ. They are addressed also as an order distinct from the elders; " To the apostles and elders :" and in the letter, they have their own place, as a distinct order, which is not that of universal uninspired bishops, but of apostles. " The apostles, the elders, and brethren." They are then referred to in their official character, and they answer in their official character. Besides, even according to your fanciful distinction, they acted in *an* official character, why then should it not be in their proper distinguishing official character? Why is an office that never existed, distinct from their apostolical office, devised for them on this occasion? They are referred to as apostles, they answer as apostles; apostles then they must be considered. When Paul elsewhere wishes to prove his inspiration and infallible authority, he says, " Am I not an apostle?" He supposes the establishing of his character as an apostle, to be the same thing as establishing his divine warrant and infallible authority. For this very purpose, he introduces most of his epistles by styling himself an apostle, and is often very particular in asserting that he was called to be such by God the Father, and by our Lord Jesus Christ. This could not be out of clerical parade, as the clergymen style themselves *Reverend*, because all religious titles were forbidden by his Master. It must then be to gain the unlimited confidence and obedience of those to whom he wrote, as an infallible teacher commissioned and furnished by God. " Whereunto I am ordained a preacher and an apostle (I speak the truth in Christ, and lie not), a teacher of the Gentiles in faith and verity"—1 Tim. ii. 7. To what purpose is this solemn asseveration as to the truth of his being an apostle, if, as such, he was not inspired, and had infallible knowledge of the will of God? Why does he so often, in such a solemn manner, assert his apostolical character, if it is not that those to whom he speaks may have complete confidence in his doctrine, as the Word of God? If it is not, this is a useless and impertinent preface to his declarations. What should we think of the minister, who, while he was delivering some important part of his discourse, should gravely assert his ministerial character, and assure his hearers that he was a minister of the Gospel? Would it not be as if he should say, 'I am a minister of the Gospel; therefore you may believe me, and receive my doctrines.' This would not suit an uninspired man, for it was not by his ministerial authority, but by the Scriptures which he should produce, that his hearers were to be convinced. When then Paul thus solemnly asserts his apostolical character, it must be that as such his words may be received, not as the word of man, but as the Word of God. His declaring himself to be an apostle, he considers to be the same as declaring his infallibility. Accordingly, immediately after this assertion, he proceeds to give his commands as if Jesus spoke in person. "I will therefore," &c. "I am an apostle, I lie not." But of what importance is it here that he was an apostle, if an apostle was not infallible? "I am an apostle," said he, before he gave the command as to men's praying, and women's dress. 'But what suppose you are an apostle,' might the females answer, if they would be taught by Mr. Brown; 'an apostle is sometimes inspired, and sometimes not inspired? You must work a miracle, or we will not obey you.' The idea of inspiration, and the idea of an apostle, are, in my mind, inseparable. The latter never presents itself without the former. I have no other idea of the distinction between an apostle, and those other ministers who also witnessed the resurrection of our Lord Jesus Christ, but that the former were appointed infallibly to report that fact with its true import. Many others were witnesses of the death and resurrection of our Lord; and understood also the import of these facts. But the apostles were qualified to explain perfectly, without being subject to the smallest misapprehension, the whole plan of salvation, with all its connections and bearings.

12. These decrees were delivered to the churches *to keep*, (φυλοσσειν) not to be canvassed. Had they been the decrees of uninspired men, the churches would have been commanded to prove them by the Word of God. More could not have been said for any other part of Scripture.

13. "And so were the churches established in the faith"—Acts xvi. 5. Established in the faith by human decrees!! They were then nourished up in the words of men, not in the words of faith. Christians may be nourished by the teaching of ordinary ministers from the Word of God; but there is no possibility that they could be nourished by a human decision, without the grounds of that decision.

Such are some of the internal evidences of the inspiration of this portion of Scripture. But there are many other arguments that peremptorily demand our assent to this truth.

1st. The very insertion of this epistle in the New Testament Scriptures, and the detail of the whole transaction being embodied with the other epistles of the apostles, shows that it is infallibly agreeable to the Holy Spirit. Were it not so, it could not be exhibited either as the divine decision of a particular point, or as a model. Had not the decision as to the question about circumcision, and the necessary burdens, been infallibly agreeable to the will of our Lord, it would not have been recorded with approbation for our instruction. When Luke inserts it in his history, he stamps it with the broad seal of heaven. The speeches, letters, and reasonings of uninspired men, are not recorded in Scripture, either as models for imitation in religious assemblies, or as divine decisions. The letter of Claudius Lysias is not inspired, but who looks upon it as a model? If this epistle of all the apostles is equally uninspired with that of Cladius Lysias, I will pay them equal deference. I will no more be bound by fallible apostles than fallible military officers. If the apostles were not inspired, for what purpose is this whole transaction recorded? If they were uninspired, the model which they exhibited is uninspired, and instead of having the authority of obligatory example, it must itself be sanctioned by either a divine model, or divine instructions in direct commandment.

2nd. Those that could not infallibly decide this question, could not infallibly preach the Gospel. Nay, of such importance was it in the estimation of the apostles, that the making of circumcision necessary is called another Gospel. If then they could not infallibly declare whether it was necessary, they did not infallibly know the Gospel method of salvation. Peter shows it to be connected with the very essence of the Gospel; and to make circumcision necessary, is opposed to the free salvation of Jews and Gentiles through the grace of Christ. "But we believe that through the grace of the Lord Jesus Christ we shall be saved, even as they." This could not have been the case, if circumcision, which would have made us debtors to do the whole law for justification, had been necessary. No man then was qualified to preach the Gospel of Christ, as his ambassador, who was not infallibly instructed on this point. The commission received by the apostles was, "Go ye, therefore, and proselyte all nations, teaching them all things *whatever I have commanded you, and, lo! I am with you alway.*" Here they are supposed to have in command everything that they are to teach. If ever they taught anything for which they had no command, it is not sanctioned in this commission. Was this matter any part of the mind of the Lord? Was it any point about which his people needed instruction? If it was, the apostles have it in command to resolve the question. Have they not Christ's promise, that he would be with them, that he would be with them *alway?* Dare any one say that he was not with them on this occasion? There is no subject in which they needed his presence more than in this. Infallibility in no case could be more necessary. If this decision was not infallible, the Gospel was not yet infallibly preached, nor at any time till it was infallibly determined; and, as we have no better authority for the inspiration of the apostles at any other time, have we yet infallible authority upon which to rest our faith.

3rd. Nothing can show that the apostles were fallible in anything regarding the kingdom of Christ, but an absolute assertion of Scripture. And in whatever instance they are fallible, or not completely instructed, we must have some other more infallible director. If not, there will be points upon which we have no divine instructions, which are notwithstanding a part of

Christ's will with regard to his people's conduct, which supposes a defective revelation. If on any matter the apostles spoke without divine illumination, their opinion cannot be obligatory, and the point cannot be of any importance. If the apostles should declare some things as inspired, and others as uninspired, without advertising us of it on every particular occasion, there would be an end to all confidence in them as the oracles of God. How should we separate the chaff from the wheat? So far however from this, the apostles on no occasion speak, in giving directions to the churches, without infallibly knowing the mind of their Lord. Some things they taught by permission, and not by commandment; but this respects the commandment which they gave, and not what they received.

4th. If the apostles were not here infallible, there might have been a contrary determination, and the apostles of our Lord Jesus Christ were so forsaken by their Master, that they might have deceived the world with respect to the very nature of the Gospel, which, as ambassadors, they were appointed to preach. But if they were infallibly saved from this, it is the same as inspiration. The reason, and the only reason that ordinary preachers do not need infallible guidance, is that there is nothing which depends upon their opinion of the Scriptures which they illustrate and enforce. They are not ambassadors, and have no testimony of their own to give. Christ's honour is not pledged for their veracity, judgment or accuracy. Their business is to call men's attention to the testimony of the apostles. If, in any instance, they lead men into error, Jesus is not to blame for this; for he has given the Scriptures as a standard, and has not given the world reason to suppose that anything depends on the authority of preachers. But if the apostles were at any time left to themselves to teach what they might possibly misunderstand, Jesus is not clear of deceiving the world. Blasphemous thought! How desperate is the cause that must be supported at the expense of the inspiration of the ambassadors of our Lord Jesus Christ!

5th. If this was an authoritative, yet uninspired assembly, then the apostles of Jesus might have been outvoted, and consequently been obliged to teach what was contrary to their opinion of the will of Jesus, or have been condemned and excommunicated by this General Council. The apostles of Jesus would then have been directed in what they were to preach over all the world by an uninspired assembly. Those commissioned to teach, might have been obliged to submit to be taught by those whom they ought to have taught, and if they had not submitted to the council, have been obliged to go into the world excommunicated from the universal visible church of the Lord Jesus Christ, to teach under all these disadvantages.

6th. Infallibility is implied in the very notion of a decree of a religious nature. If those who command or decree are fallible, they may decree and command contrary to the will of Christ. The authority of an uninspired church ruler must rest on the divine command which he produces. He has no authority distinct from this. The law which he enforces receives no additional weight from his office. Therefore obedience to him must arise from the conviction of those upon whom the law is enforced. Yea, although it should appear to him the most evident law of Christ, he is to enforce it upon them only as understanding it; for if they do not obey out of faith, their submission is sin; and to possess authority to command compliance without conviction, would involve a power to command them to sin. A church ruler then, though he has no discretionary power, has all the authority of the law which he enforces: still, however, obedience is only due to the law, upon conviction that it is a law of the kingdom. If an individual does not understand it, he is not to submit to it. His sin is not in disobeying the authority of the ruler, but in being slow of heart to understand the Scriptures. The church ruler is to call upon him to understand and submit to the law of Christ, never to his authority or superior judgment. If they cannot agree, and the matter is of such a nature as to prevent the exersise of mutual forbearance, they are to turn away from each other.

7th. If the decision was not infallible it was useless, nay sinful. Those who had doubts upon this subject, must either have rested implicitly upon the wisdom of men to remove them, or they might have retained them, even after this decision. If the former was the case, then they acted not in faith: their conduct was sinful, although the judgment of the assembly had been just. They obeyed not God, but man. And a fallible decree commanding obedience is guilty of tempting to that sin, by usurping the place of God's Word. It can be of no use to decree upon doubtful or dark passages of Scripture, except those who assume the authority of issuing decrees, have infallible guidance to direct them to form a true judgment. They cannot otherwise challenge obedience. But if the decrees were not to be received implicitly, they were useless, and instead of effecting complete concord, they would have excited a keener discussion. The judaizing teachers, who were so warmly and zealously attached to circumcision, would not have been likely to submit implicitly to men as liable to error as themselves. Nor would it have been their duty to have yielded the point upon such grounds. The reception of their decrees would then have depended upon the conviction of each individual who was to obey them; and as we before showed, there was no grounds of evidence submitted to them in the letter which contains the decrees. Every individual must, after all, judge for himself of their conformity to the Scriptures, without any assistance from the decrees themselves to search for and weigh the evidence of this conformity. They must then have met with a very different reception in the different churches over the world, yea even in the same church. If this question was not divinely determined, the Lord Jesus has given just grounds for a separation of his disciples into two sects. There would in this case have been no advantage resulting from the decision. The idea of an assembly invested with a power of settling controversies and imposing necessary burdens, whose decisions may be canvassed, and received or rejected according to the judgment of those for whom decision is made, is an absurdity.

They are then not decrees, but advice, judgment, or exhortation.

8th. There can be no divine authority to command, in any instance in which it is not the duty of those commanded, to obey. The authority of the one, and the allegiance of the other, must have the same extent. A divine authority in an assembly to command, and yet a divine authority in those commanded to disobey! what an absurdity!

9th. The apostles never claim authority as fallible men. On the contrary, if any one had received the Gospel from them as uninspired men, Paul supposes that it was useless. "For this cause also thank we God, without ceasing, because when ye received the Word of God, which ye heard of us, ye received it not as the word of man, but as it is in truth the Word of God." Now, had this assembly been fallible, and this decision the word of man only, although it were agreeable to the Word of God, the reception of it upon this ground would have been matter of grief, not of glorying to an apostle. The reception even of a divine truth upon anything but divine testimony, is not pleasing to God. In such a case it is not divine truth to us.

In all human references, the parties who make the reference are supposed to be determined to settle the matter of dispute by the judgment of the referees, whether they themselves should be convinced or not. If they must both be convinced, reference is useless. It is then not a reference for decision, but a reference for opinion. But in matters of religous opinion, which cannot be received or given up, but with full conviction, there is no room for reference to any but infallible referees. The decision of fallible men cannot change the mind of either party, any further than they convince the judgement by argument. Nay, even about civil matters, parties referring a case, and engaging to abide by the decision of the arbitrators, do not oblige themselves to change their opinions; for this they could not do. If my neighbour and I have a dispute about property, we may leave it to a reference, and doing so we ought to be finally decided by their opinion, though it is very possible that the arbitration may not be strictly pleasing to either of us. But we cannot do so with respect to religious matters; if we are not convinced by the arbitration, it is sinful to obey it. I may give away my civil property agreeable to the decision of men, although I may be convinced that there is no just claim to demand it. "If any man will sue thee at the law, and take away thy coat, let him have thy cloak also," *i.e.*, as I take it, when any man brings a legal process against us, and carries his point by the laws of the land, we are to give up to that authority, although we are convinced that the judges have been partial or mistaken. We are not to suppose, that because we are convinced that the decision has been unjust, we are therefore warranted to resist the civil powers, and refuse compliance. Nay, if our adversary brings another process as unjust as the former, and carries it by the opinion of the legal judges of the land, we are to submit to that also. Here then is not only a warrant, but a divine command, to submit to the judgment of those legally authorized, although we are not convinced of its justice. But can you produce any such command as to religious matters? Does the Lord Jesus tell his disciples to submit in the same manner to the judgment of uninspired church rulers? And if there was any such assembly of uninspired men commissioned by Jesus to settle religious controversies, would he not give us some instructions with respect to the extent of their authority and of our obedience? Would he be so particular in showing us our duty to the laws of the land in which we live, and say nothing about our duty to the laws of these assemblies? Though in civil matters Jesus commands us to be amenable to the decision of the lawful judges of the land, yet he does not command us to believe that their judgment is always equitable. How absurd it is then to suppose, that parties having a difference in religious sentiments should leave it to the determination of fallible men, and engage to act accordingly! The very engagement to do so would be perjury; for they may not be convinced, and it is a first principle in the law of Christ, that no one is to act contrary to his convictions.

Having now stated some reasons to establish the

infallibility of the apostles of our Lord Jesus Christ, I shall briefly advert to your objections. I have the less need to be tedious, as most of them have been already answered in substance, in the preceding part of this letter. You set out with a principle, which, were it proved, would shake our confidence in the apostolical character. "That the apostles were not uniformly directed by a miraculous influence I think you must grant, if you reflect for a moment on what is recorded in the Gospel history. Many of their actions, as was formerly noticed, such as the ordination of deacons, the dispensation of the sacraments, the preaching of the Word, and, in many instances, the government of the church, did not require such a preternatural influence, for they were performed by men who were not inspired, and are still performed by men who have no miraculous influence, either of suggestion or of superintendence."—pp. 297, 298.

Indeed, Sir, I will not grant that the apostles were fallible in any one of those instances to which you refer. In some of these things, they must have had a direct communication from the Spirit, and in others an infallible superintendance. Were not the apostles infallibly directed by the Spirit, in what manner to ordain the deacons? If they were not, I deny the obligation of their example. To prove the propriety and the manner of ordination, you might as well quote the ceremonies of dubbing a knight-errant from the annals of chivalry, as the example of the apostles in ordaining deacons, if they were not inspired. As to dispensation of sacraments, I have never heard of the apostles dispensing any sacraments either civil or religious. If you mean the Lord's supper and baptism, I will also affirm, that in these they must have had infallibility. In the preaching of the Word also, they must ever have been guided by the unerring Spirit. The apostle Paul commands Timothy to "hold fast the form of sound words, which he had *heard* of him, *in faith* and love." The words of the apostle were to be received *in faith;* but the words of uninspired men are not to be received in faith. They are to be tried by the word of inspiration, and when found agreeable to that unerring standard, then it is to the Scriptures that faith is given. You seem to think, because these things are still performed by ordinary teachers, that therefore the apostles, in doing the same things, were no more inspired than the latter. I have already shown you the reason why inspiration, or infallible guidance, is necessary to apostles, and not to ordinary teachers. Christ is answerable for every error of the apostles; but as he has given us the New Testament revelation in addition to the Old, as a form and standard of sound words, there is no occasion for inspiration in ordinary teachers. If they go into error, Jesus is not accountable for it; for he never gave us reason to suppose that he would make them infallible. If others are led astray by them, they are inexcusable; for they have the form of sound words in the Scriptures. But the apostles of our Lord Jesus Christ, as his ambassadors, in every instance, must have been infallibly secured from error in their teaching and presiding in the churches. These things are indeed still performed by men, who have no miraculous influence either of suggestion or of superintendence; but they are not standards in performing them. Their conduct in them is to be tried by the apostolical precepts and example. These things, you say, did not require a *preternatural* influence. To perform them infallibly right, they did require supernatural guidance. If not, why are there such differences upon each of the points to which you have referred? Infallible superintendence was necessary on all points to the apostles, for it is by their words that Christ shall judge the world. According to your reasoning, the apostles and sacred penmen had no need of infallible superintendence, in anything of which they could have information from others. If infallible guidance was not necessary to the apostles in preaching, &c., neither is infallible guidance necessary in the writers of the Gospels, and the Acts of the Apostles, nor indeed of the Epistles; for if the apostles could preach without infallible guidance, why could they not write without it? For what reason should the apostles be inspired in writing their epistles to the churches, and uninspired in preaching to the churches or to sinners? The evangelists might have had personal knowledge, or particular information with respect to the facts recorded by them, yet they needed infallible superintendence in relating the very things of which they were eye-witnesses. I really cannot see upon what consistent principles you can pretend to hold the inspiration of the New Testament. If, in the doctrines and institutions of the Gospel, the apostles were not under infallible guidance, I cannot see any foundation left on which to rest the divinity of the Scriptures. There are indeed many things recorded in the Scriptures of which the penmen might have personal knowledge; but in these very things, infallible superintendence is necessary to entitle them to full credit. Had they not been infallibly directed, they might in many things have been mistaken. But why do you think that in the instances to which you refer, the apostles were not inspired? Is it not because, in your estimation, they needed no inspiration? But the point about which this meeting was held, was not one of these. Inspiration, direct inspiration, was necessary. It was not merely like a fact which required nothing but infallible superintendence; it was a case of dispute among the disciples of Christ, and therefore was not one of those things which needed no direct inspiration. But how absurdly do you contend that this case did not need inspiration, when you affirm that the apostles themselves were of different opinions upon the subject, and had a long and warm debate! Indeed, Sir, I am often shocked at the sentiments which you discover in this treatise. You appear to me to have no proper reverence for the Word of God. According to you, the Scriptures are not the Word of God. The greater part of them, at least, **are** the words of men.

Your first objection against the inspiration of the apostles in this assembly is as follows: "In the first place, Paul and Barnabas, at the original discussion at Antioch, acted not in the high character of apostles, but only of ordinary ministers. Had not this been the case, they could never have submitted to the $\tau\alpha\xi\iota\varsigma$ or appointment of the Church at Antioch to go up to Jerusalem (Acts xv. 2), for, as an apostle, Paul was far superior to them all, as Barnabas was to many of them, and could never have been authoritatively appointed by them."—p. 298.

Strange indeed, if the apostle must lay aside his apostolic office before he can bear a message. It was not necessary indeed that the messenger should have been an apostle, but it was not necessary for him to lay aside this office, before he could carry a message from his inferiors. Must the Lord Lieutenant of Ireland lay aside his vice-royalty, before he can present a petition to the King? The apostles were totally unacquainted with the etiquette of Presbyterian church-courts. But, my good Sir, you forget where this position will lead you. Paul must also lay aside his office as an ordinary minister, for he was deputed by the brethren, who were his inferiors, even considered in that office. But to suppose that a man must lay aside a superior office, before he can exercise an inferior, is an idea too absurd to need refutation. Why do you represent the choice of Paul and Barnabas as an authoritative appointment? They were chosen for this service, not constrained by authority. The great apostle of the Gentiles authoritatively commanded by a kirk-session at Antioch!!

"Secondly, If this question was to be determined by inspiration, it was unnecessary to have gone to Jerusalem for the decision. Paul certainly, as well as the other inspired ministers, was as able to have delivered such a decision as the apostles at Jerusalem; and unquestionably if evidence had been presented to the ministers of the Church of Antioch, that the Holy Ghost, in a supernatural manner, had settled the matter, by communicating to them his will through a single minister, it must have been as decisive as if he had spoken to them by twelve."—p. 299.

As to the reason why it seemed good to God to have the question thus publicly determined, it does not lie upon us to justify him. It is sufficient for us to know that the question was settled by the apostles. This assures us of the infallibility of the decision, and whether we can discover them or not, we know that he had good reasons for the manner of the determination. Sufficient reasons may be, and have been assigned for it; but if you do not like them, we are not bound to please you in this matter. The apostle Paul was at Antioch; he opposed the Jewish teachers; there was no doubt upon his mind; he taught this as he taught every other doctrine. If he was not infallible in teaching it, the commission which he received from Jesus was void. He could not preach the Gospel as an ambassador. Was infallibility less necessary now than when he wrote his Epistle to the Galatians on the same subject?

You suppose, that he might have settled the matter by a miracle. But, Sir, the apostles were not obliged to resort to miracles to prove every sermon, or every doctrine which they delivered, nor did they so. They established their character as apostles in general by the working of miracles, and this implied their infallibility in all that they taught in the name of Jesus Christ. If they should have resorted to miracles whenever any should oppose them, they might have done nothing else than work miracles. Paul did not work a miracle when he wrote his letter to the Galatians, more than he did at Antioch. If at one time the apostles were fallible, and at another infallible, what confidence could we repose in them? We must have a miracle for every word they speak. I desire you to show that at any period of their lives, from the effusion of the Spirit on the day of Pentecost, till their death, they were not infallible in what they taught. What an absurdity to suppose that the apostle Paul was teaching at Antioch, and that he could not infallibly declare the Gospel! for if he could not decide this question infallibly, he could not preach infallibly. The moment the apostles ceased to be infallible, they ceased to be ambassadors for Christ. No longer was it a truth which was spoken to them by Jesus, "Lo! I am with you alway."

"In the third place," you say, "the persons to whom this reference was made, were not only apostles, but ordinary elders." As ordinary elders, it was proper to refer to them, to ascertain the matter of fact whether this was the doctrine taught in the church at Jerusalem. If it is said, that, as uninspired men, they also joined in laying on the necessary burden, I answer, so also did the whole church, and if the apostles had joined the whole Christian world with them, it could not in the least invalidate their infallibility, any more than Paul's joining the brethren with himself invalidates the Epistle to the Galatians. If there was one inspired man in the assembly, the infallibility of the decision is completely secured. But if there was a real difficulty in reconciling the inspiration of the apostles, with the co-operation of uninspired elders, there is a necessity rather to suppose the inspiration of the latter, than fallibility in the former. The apostles at no time were fallible in delivering the doctrines, laws and ordinances of the churches of Christ; anything must be supposed rather than this.

"Lastly," you say, "the manner of procedure in this court does not indicate that they acted as extraordinary ministers," &c. It is sufficient to answer to this that they were always extraordinary ministers, and executed not even any inferior office, but as it was contained in their superior. A general may submit to the duty of a drill-sergeant, but he is still a general, and, even in that, has all the authority of the general as well as of the sergeant.

As to the disputing in that assembly, it is enough to show that it is not necessary to suppose that it was among the apostles. The bare possibility of this is sufficient for my purpose, although it is very evident. And although it should have been among the apostles, it is not necessary to suppose that anything is meant by the word but discussion. Much might be said to prove these points, but positive proof does not lie upon us; the contrary must be positively proved by you. If you cannot positively show that the disputation was among the apostles; and if so, that it was such as to imply that they had different opinions, it will avail you nothing. At all events they could finally say, that it " seemed good to the Holy Ghost." At what particular time, or in what particular manner God communicated his mind to the apostles on this point, is not at all material. We know that it actually seemed good to the Holy Ghost, for this is unitedly attested by those who were commissioned to declare his mind. Had all the apostles been uninformed by the Spirit on this point, till the moment that James spoke, it would not affect the inspiration of the epistle. Before they gave decision, they were informed. It is not only absurd, but impious to fix precise rules of etiquette, which the Holy Spirit must scrupulously observe in communicating his will. Were we to indulge ourselves in the liberty of questioning the inspiration of the sacred penmen on every occasion in which their writings might contradict our opinions, interests, and prejudices, there are innumerable instances in which we might reason with all the plausibility you can employ upon this point. But as long as these decrees are prefaced with "it seemeth good unto the Holy Ghost," attested by the accredited ambassadors of Jesus Christ, I will look upon them to contain infallibly the mind of Christ. I have nothing but the testimony of the same witnesses for his resurrection.

But under what obligation are we to prove the infallibility of the apostles in this matter? None, certainly. Give you all you ask; there is nothing more effectually rids us of all difficulties, if there were any, than your own hypothesis. If the apostles did not here act as apostles, we have then no apostolical authority for this assembly. You may as well sanction such assemblies now, by a General Council of the fourth century, and determine the form of them by the model of a former General Assembly. If the apostles were uninspired here, I refuse to submit my faith and practice to their decision. I have therefore discussed this subject rather to vindicate the authority of the apostles in general, than to support the views with respect to church order, which I judge agreeable to the Scriptures. You have struck at the foundation of the authority of the Word of God. Your hypothesis can only rise on its ruins. I am indeed sorry that any who make a profession of Christianity should entertain such sentiments. But it must be to us a most convincing evidence of the truth of our views of church order, to find our antagonists driven to such a desperate mode of defence. In this view, I did rejoice to find such an hypothesis suggested. If our views of this passage must stand good as long as the apostles maintain their own character, they will remain for ever. I have no desire that our members should be increased by the addition of any who strip the apostles of their commission and infallibility. Such persons I should consider as unfit for membership in apostolical churches. Did I need anything to convince me of the unscripturalness of the Presbyterian form of church government, no external circumstance could more effectually contribute to this than your defence of it. You are labouring from first to last; and have recourse to so many evasions, as, in the estimation of any impartial reader, though not deeply acquainted with the subject, must make it apparent that the cause which needs such a defence, cannot be the cause of Christ. I am much mistaken if your book will not make more Independents from among those who tremble at the Word of God, than even a direct defence of Independency. You have indeed furnished with arguments those who love darkness rather than light; but there is not in all your book anything calculated to satisfy an enquiring Christian. The glory and prosperity of the Church of Scotland, rather than the glory of God, appears to have been your great aim.

But, my good Sir, had you succeeded in establishing the divine right of Presbytery, what have you done for the Church of Scotland, or any other of the Presbyterian denominations? Were I convinced as fully of the divine right of the Presbyterian form of church government, as I am of the divinity of the Bible, I would not acknowledge as a church of Christ any Presbyterian body that I know. In all of them, the kingdom of Christ, and the kingdoms of this world, are confounded; nor are they formed of the same kind of materials that composed the churches planted by the apostles.

The question respecting the form of church government, however important in itself, is quite a subordinate one. The first, the great question is, what is a church of Christ? Of whom is it composed? Of those who give evidence of knowing and obeying the Gospel, or of the whole inhabitants of a parish, except such as are grossly ignorant and immoral? Is it a number of Christians united in fellowship, and separated from the world, or is it a few Christians mixed with a multitude of visible unbelievers? The Church of Scotland is not a church of Christ, although its form of government corresponded exactly to the divine model, and although one half of those who compose it were real believers. Believers alone, as far as they can be distinguished, compose a church of Christ. You may as well, upon this ground, defend the Church of Rome as the Church of Scotland, as being a church of Christ. There are, no doubt, Christians in both. It cannot certainly be the similarity of the form of government, and all other ordinances, to those of the apostolical churches, that constitutes any body a church of Christ. There might be the most exact resemblance in each of these points, yet not a feature of a church of saints or holy persons.

Suppose, for instance, the devils were to mimic a church. Let them adopt your form of Presbytery, with all its courts of review, from a kirk-session to a General Council, with a rigidity of discipline exceeding the severity of John Knox, and with all the Presbyterian sacraments and ordinances—would you call this a church of Christ? If not, it is not the form of government and ordinances of worship that constitute a church. Suppose again that a number of those devils were to become incarnate, and that they were known to be such. Let them form a church upon your model, with an ample establishment for the clergy, do you think that the servants of Jesus might lawfully join them, because they lived in the same parish?* or if they did, could such a union be called a church of Christ? Yet there is no difference between the devils, and the devil's children, as to their fitness to be members of that body which is the emblem of the body of Christ, and the habitation of his Spirit. Until men believe the

---

* I have heard it said of a member of the Church of Scotland, that he could sit down to the Lord's supper with the devil on his right hand. It appears to be almost an universal declaration by those of the Established Church, that they have no concern with those who join in the same acts of worship with themselves.

Gospel, they have fellowship not with Christ, but with devils. They have no place in the kingdom of Christ. Let us then, Sir, discuss *this subject* before we enter upon the form of government. They are entirely distinct, and the former is certainly the previous question. Until we agree about the materials of the house, we need not contend about the plan of it. After you have settled the one point, we will cheerfully hear what you have to say upon the other. If you could *then* convince us that the Presbyterian form of church-government is divine, there is nothing in our situation or circumstances that can for a moment prevent us from adopting it. We should not lose a parish-stipend by our change of sentiments and conduct. On the contrary, we would thereby avoid much popular reproach, and vastly increase our numbers. But, Sir, could you succeed in this, it would be the most deadly wound that ever the Church of Scotland received. Those godly persons who are detained with you only by the prejudices of education, would then come out of the corrupt mass to enjoy their favourite system free of its corruptions; whereas now they remain in their situation, because they see no greater purity with any other body of Presbyterians.

Remember then, you have not only to defend Presbytery in the abstract, but the Church of Scotland with all its corruptions. Upon what foundation rests the right of patronage? By what process of reasoning does the orthodox brother satisfy his conscience in complying with the imperious injunctions of a higher court, to lay hands upon one whom he cannot consider as a minister or a servant of Christ? How do you defend the mixing of the kingdom of Christ, with the kingdoms of this world, when Christ says, " My kingdom is not of this world?" Do you believe that the magistrate, as such, has power in the church of Christ? Do you not subscribe the 23rd chapter, with the rest of the Westminster Confession? Do all the ministers of the Church of Scotland, from their sermons and conversation, appear to believe all the doctrines which they have subscribed, and to have taken the oath in judgement, in truth, and in righteousness? Is it possible for any man who is not infallible, conscientiously to subscribe a formula, in which he vows never to change his opinions? What is the casuistry that gives ease to the conscience of a godly minister in the Church of Scotland, when he is obliged by a higher court to administer ordinances to unworthy characters?

A member of the Church of Scotland must defend her conduct, as well as her constitution. There is therefore more art than Christian simplicity and uprightness in the plan of your defence. The Presbytery you defend is the best you can conceive; the Presbytery you practice is the very worst. Nay, the Presbytery you defend is so good, that it exists as yet only in theory. You are a nominalist, not a realist. Show me one like it in all the world, in all the ages of the world. The Presbytery you defend, and the Presbytery you have adopted, are as different as any two systems. If you would act up to the principles upon which you reason, you could not remain in the Church of Scotland, nor in any of its ramifications. If it is the divine form of Presbytery you have defended, that of the Church of Scotland is not divine. Nay, you virtually give up the Church of Scotland, when you profess to defend her standards only. If the church had been defensible, there would have been no occasion to abandon everything but her original constitution.

We therefore, Sir, wait with impatience for that part of your work, in which you propose to "examine the argument for separation from the Church of Scotland, drawn from what have been called her corruptions." We wish to know what you call them; for we think, that if the Presbytery you have imagined is the divine form, those deviations from it in the Church of Scotland *must be* corruptions, even in your own account; and to overthrow you, if you attempt to defend the present state of things, we shall have nothing to do but to bring one part of your performance to bear upon the other. Lose no time then; such a defence is much needed, and I am sure if you can effect it, your brethren will not allow you to be called from it by parochial avocations. Indeed, it requires little time to state and defend truth. The pen that is guided by a good conscience, and a strong impression of the importance of the subject, will move swiftly. Truth requires only to be fairly exhibited, and she will defend herself. The most illiterate men can comprehend our arguments and defend our cause. There is nothing to do on our part, but to refer to the different portions of Scripture, and leave them with the consciences of those whom we address. If we are obliged to go into abstract reasoning, it is only to answer the perversions and evasive explanations of Scripture employed by our antagonists. To satisfy those who wish to know the mind of the Spirit, we might content ourselves with transcribing the different Scriptures that refer to the subject, without giving any explanation. It is only to silence sophistry, that we have occasion to employ tedious deductions.

Now, Sir, if I may hope to be indulged with the honour of your future correspondence, I request that you will give me a volume to myself. Do not address a book to me, as you have done to Mr. Innes, in which, instead of replying to my arguments, you shall state and canvass the sentiments of almost every person who has written on the subject. I care not with whom I agree, or with whom I differ, if I agree with the Word of God. Your book is a professed answer to Mr. Innes' Reasons for Separating from the Church of Scotland; yet Mr. Innes is very seldom in your view. You are mostly engaged in wrestling with the ancient Independents. You artfully evade Mr. Innes, by exposing theories long exploded, or by bringing ancient Independents to disagree with him. Mr. Innes' book is still unanswered; and what is most astonishing in a work professing to be an answer, you never consider the very argument which lies at the bottom of his reasoning, and which first led him to suspect the foundation of the Presbyterian system. Let us then, my good Sir, bring the matter to a fair trial at the bar of the Scriptures. If I have misinterpreted any part of the sacred volume, I shall be ready upon conviction to abandon it. I am extremly glad that you have brought the contest to the public. It can never be dismissed until the triumph of truth takes place. Many who never considered the question will be roused to inquiry, and a good cause will never suffer by investigation. There is an observation which I have frequently made, and which I believe will hold good upon every subject, that truth comes forward to every reiterated attack with fresh vigour and new arguments; on the other hand, that a false hypothesis will always be weakened by every succeeding charge, and that it is exhausted almost as much by its own attempts to defend itself, as by the assault of the antagonist. The reason is obvious; all that can be said for the latter, lies in difficulties and forced explanations, which can never be reiterated with success. With respect to the former, the deeper the subject is investigated, the greater number of proofs will occur. Evidence will arise even out of objections. Truth is an inexhaustible mine; and if it was to be worked by a thousand successive generations, there will still be as much left as will recompense the labours of posterity.

All divine truth is connected and interwoven, and a deeper acquaintance with any one part will enlarge our knowledge of the whole. Many treat the question of church government as quite insignificant. I am persuaded that it is of very great importance. For until it be fully understood, there cannot be any cordial and enlightened union and co-operation among Christians; and the world will be stumbled by the multitude of sects and denominations. Division among Christians certainly must be sinful. It is then surely no useless inquiry to seek where this sin lies. Let us then discuss this subject as largely as the subject demands.

I have not considered your views of the government of the churches in the ages succeeding the apostolic, because it does not come into the immediate subject of investigation. I take it for granted, that whatever form of government was instituted by the apostles, will have its traces for a considerable time after. But before any of us can be allowed to make this appeal, we must fully prove our hypothesis from the New Testament. That subject never has been set in so clear and impartial a light as by Dr. Campbell; but after your freedom with the apostles, I was not at all astonished that you forced the Fathers to speak the language of Presbyterians.

One other thing I would call to your remembrance. We are writing for eternity. Recollect that the literary reviews of our friends and of our enemies are not final. Our works shall be reviewed at the dread tribunal of the God of truth, whose Word we are handling. How awful will it be to be found at that day to have perverted his directions, and to have contributed to make his children mistake his commands! We cannot allege that the Scriptures were dark upon the subject, and that we were necessarily led astray; for that would be to arraign the Judge himself. Besides, we both seem to think that the Scriptures are very clear upon the subject. Whichever of us is wrong, is inexcusably wrong; for Jesus has given a plain revelation.

Consider also how many may be influenced by our reasoning, and that that one of us who is wrong may be found to have led thousands into his error, or to keep them in it. Consider, that in a short time we shall be far beyond the reach of praise or blame, but that the influence of our labours may affect many generations. Can you then look forward to the smiles of the Lord Jesus on a judgment seat, for your reward in this undertaking?

I have now concluded my observations on your book. I have spoken very plainly, but with the most perfect good will. I do indeed consider that your defence of the Presbyterian form of church government indicates a very bad state of mind, and I should not act kindly by you did I not tell you so. "Your *arguments* I have endeavoured to refute by *argument*. Mere *declamation* I know no way of refuting, but by *analysing* it; nor do I conceive how *inconsistencies* can be answered, otherwise than by *exposing* them. In such *analysis* and *exposition*, which I own I have attempted without ceremony or reserve, an air of ridicule is unavoidable; but this *ridicule*, I am well aware, if founded on *misrepresentation*, will at last rebound upon *myself*."*

I am, &c.

* Dr. Campbell.

INDEX.

	PAGE
ADDRESS, the AUTHOR'S, to MR. BROWN, on his defence of Presbytery	549–551
On his motives for writing it	506
On his mode of reasoning	415, 448
On the reverence due to the Word of God	247
His using so much freedom with it	385
And attempting to prove, that the assembly at Jerusalem was a model for Presbytery	483
On denying the inspiration and infallibility of the apostles	546
On appearing at last before the judgment-seat of Christ	553
Antichrist, could not have arisen had Christians acted faithfully	264
Rules given by the apostles to prevent his rise in after ages	311
Apostles, the power of opening and shutting the kingdom of heaven given to them exclusively	171
Commission of preaching the Gospel infallibly, confined to them	171
Their office paramount to every other office in the church of Christ	182
What they did as apostles no rule for elders	182
Were ambassadors for Christ	183
They decided the question referred to the assembly at Jerusalem	459
Were universal bishops, but in no other sense than as they were apostles	505
In declaring the will of God, they were as infallible as Christ himself, and acted in his stead	506
As uninspired men, they had no authority over the church of Christ	513
Were infallible in everything which they taught	514
Whatever they did, was done by Christ himself	514
Mr. B. attempts to divest them of inspiration	514
If they are obeyed as uninspired, our obedience is not to God, but to man	519
As fallible men, they never claim authority	538
Mr. B.'s objections to their inspiration answered	542, 545
Arbitration, none in matters of religion	538

	PAGE
Assembly at Jerusalem, of whom composed	449
Nothing done in it by votes	459
This could have had no effect on the consciences of those who referred to it	462
It was not a model for Presbytery	474
Does not afford a model for any of its courts, from the highest to the lowest	500
If it had, would be a better model for the Church of Rome	508
Acted as infallible	522
Assembly at Westminster, spoken of by some as enjoying something equivalent to inspiration	518
How one of its members acted in a case of difficulty	518
Associations of ministers, for giving counsel and advice to the churches, unscriptural	456
Pernicious consequences of them	456
BAPTISM does not constitute church membership	193
Does not exclusively belong to a church, as such, but is the privilege of individuals, as believers	193
Binding and loosing, the meaning of in Scripture	173
Bishops, city and country, by whom this distinction was made	394
Brethren, meaning of the word in Scripture	388
Is never appropriated to ministers, as such	390
Whether those who are mentioned as being present at the assembly at Jerusalem were ministers, or the body of the church members	398, 459
If their approbation and consent were necessary or useful in the decision of the apostles and elders in that assembly, they are much more so in matters decided by fallible men	451, 452
Though they *acquiesced* in the decision, it is not argued that they were equally concerned in *determining* the will of God, and why	463
Their improper conduct, when at a distance from their own church, should be noticed by other churches, and reported	461
CAMPBELL, Dr., quoted on the meaning of words	419
The clear and impartial manner in which he has given the history of the government of the churches in the ages succeeding the apostolic	552
Church, meaning of the word in Scripture	403, 448
Uncommon and mysterious acceptation of the term	146
The literal and appropriated name of each congregation in the church at Jerusalem, supposing it to have consisted of more than one	332
As used by Presbyterians, it practically disproves their own theory	333

	PAGE
When applied in its religious use, has an appropriated meaning, and cannot be otherwise applied on that subject	406
Never used by our Lord in reference to the Jewish judicatories	205
The disciples so called in contradistinction to the apostles and elders	407
Signifies a single congregation	409
Includes all rulers and ruled, when not applied in contradistinction to its rulers	413
Why the members may be called so, in contradistinction to their rulers	201
Church of Christ, what	547
Different from all worldly churches as to authority	156
Its authority extends only to the judging of the application and execution of the laws enacted by Christ himself	156
Is not formed by the majority, but by those who are obedient to the laws of Christ	158
In judging of offences, is freed from the entanglements to which worldly churches are subject	159
Does not admit into, or retain any in its fellowship, but with the consent of all its members	192
Complete unanimity necessary in all its procedure	157
Does not consist in a mere similarity in government and ordinances to the churches planted by the apostles	548
Church at Jerusalem, consisted of only one congregation	197
The matter considered in it by the apostles and elders was done in the hearing, with the approbation, co-operation, and concurrence of the whole church	244
If it consisted of more than one congregation, it could not be called *a church*, either literally or figuratively	331
Shown from Scripture to have been but one body	337
Cannot mean the ministers alone of that city	348
Dispersion of, remarks on	351
Assembled all in one place	366
Church at Corinth, in what they were to blame concerning the incestuous person	233
Why bound to act as a body in cutting him off	236
Church, the Jewish, is entirely different in its constitution from the Christian church	207
And in what respects	207, 320
Church of Scotland, constitution of, different from that defended by Mr. B.	187
Reception of members by the congregation, no part of its constitution	186
Is of no use though it were	186

558 INDEX.

	PAGE
Character of the majority of its members	193
Is a worldly society, governed and regulated upon worldly principles	158
Not a man in her of literary eminence, who would undertake to show that the New Testament contains a complete and unalterable model for church government	443
Is not a church of Christ	548
Dreadful saying of one of its members	548
What it is that detains any godly persons in that communion	549

Churches, see Independents, see Presbyterian .

Church-courts, whether they are useful for the exclusion of corrupt members	191
A Christian has no security of obtaining an impartial hearing in them	191
The characters which compose them	191
Mr. B.'s attempt to cover their practice	243
Neither mentioned nor exemplified in all the Word of God	292
Are unnecessary—see Assembly at Jerusalem	226
Church-government, the most Scriptural plan of	310
The idea of a complete and unchangeable model of, opposed by all the learning of both the British religious establishments	444
And why	444
The great importance of understanding it	552
Church, visible and invisible, the contrast supposed by this distinction altogether fanciful	292
Has no foundation in the writings of the apostles	296
Commentators illiterate, the danger of	355
Cyrus, anecdote of	288

Deacons, their office belongs to one congregation exclusively	338
By whom they should be chosen	380
Decrees, the obligation to obey those delivered by the apostles, arose from the infallibility of the determination	459
Meaning of the term	519
Infallible, made to be obeyed, not to be imitated by those of fallible men	513
Deputation, the very possibility of acting by it in matters of discipline cut off	246
Devil, no difference between him and his children as to their fitness to be members of the church of Christ	548
Discipline, the apostolic command to judge of, and execute, not given to the rulers only, but to the whole church	246,
Effects of, among Presbyterians	308

INDEX. 559

	PAGE
Disputing, in the assembly at Jerusalem, what	545
Was not by the apostles	545

Elders alone rulers in the church 167
   Are not the successors of the apostles, and cannot
      claim an authority like theirs 180
   How the limits of their office are to be ascertained 180
   Are all pastors invested with the full character . 272, 280
   Cannot plead the right of succession to the office
      of *evangelist* 316
   No example in the Word of God, of the elders of
      one church ordaining those of another . . 316
   When admitted to judge, the individual members
      are also admitted 450, 453
Elders, lay, Mr. B.'s doctrine of, considered . . 261
   Do nothing in the churches where they are that
      entitles them to maintenance 279
   The only expenses necessarily incurred by them . 279
   No such office mentioned in Scripture . . . 280
Eldership of a church, why it must be obeyed . . 211
   Distinct provinces in it, though there is no distinction in office 266
   Ought to be composed of persons possessing a
      variety of talents 266
   The great advantages arising from this . . 267
Erasmus, the character given him by some . . 490
Evangelists needed infallibility in relating the things
   of which they were eye-witnesses . . . 542

Fear, meaning of the word in Scripture . . . 373
   Difference between the fear of God, by which
      Christians are influenced, and the fear of wicked
      men 373
   Different effects of these on both 373

Gifts, miraculous, not possessed by the church at
   Corinth only 295

Haldane, Mr. quoted on the believers in Jerusalem
   meeting together in one place 338
Hoornbeek, quoted on church power . . . 291
Hume, Mr. his observation on the different effects
   of extended and confined civil government, as it
   respects literature 314

Jesus has given in his Word sufficient directions as
   to the government of his churches . . . 142
Left his apostles in his own place 514

	PAGE
Gave them full authority as to every thing to be believed and practised	515
His usual method of preaching	521, 529
Independency, eminently adapted to promote union among all the disciples of Christ	299
Possesses every advantage that Presbytery hath to prevent the spreading of corruption	306
Must be from heaven	311
Mr. B.'s reasoning against it exactly analogous to that used against the Reformers	489
Independents, ancient, their mistake as to associations of ministers for advice, being sanctioned by the Word of God	455
Independents have no barriers in their way to prevent them from receiving the truth when discovered	549
Independent churches, their superior liberty to worldly ones	276
Those lately formed owe much of their superior conformity to Scripture, compared with that of the ancient Independents to the objections of their opposers	290
Infallibility, though disclaimed in words, is acted upon in spirit, by all who enact human laws, or use a discretionary power in the kingdom of Christ	489
Was necessary for the apostles in dispensing the ordinances of the Gospel. See *Apostles*	540
Inspiration, an example of almost every kind of, given in the decrees made by the apostles at Jerusalem	526
Interpretation, the great liberties taken with it by Mr. B.	255, 270
Consequences of	256, 386
Josephus quoted on the meaning of the word *church*	205
Judging and ruling, different things—See *Rulers*	167
Keys given to Peter	170
For what purpose	170
Not carried by any but the apostles	171
Are an emblem not of church, but of apostolical power	171
Do not signify the power of admitting to, or excluding from church communion	176
Kingdom of Christ, not of this world	320
Is entirely spiritual in its constitution	320
Confounded by Presbyterians with the kingdoms of this world	547
Kingdom of heaven, does not signify the visible church	176
Consists of Christ and his people	176

	PAGE
No where in Scripture distinguished into the kingdom of grace, and the kingdom of glory	176
The evil of making this distinction	176
The impossibility of a hypocrite ever being a member of it	176

LAWS of Christ, sufficiency of, and insufficiency of human	142
A first principle in, that no one is to act contrary to conviction	140
Legislation, in a church of Christ what	140
Right of it inherent in the Presbyterian constitution	140
Carried to the most extravagant length	141
Its progress	145
Entirely disclaimed by the Independent Churches lately formed	144
Louvet, anecdote of	144
Love, what meant by confirming it	253
Brotherly, what	389

MEMBERS of a church, are to judge in every thing concerning that church	168
Capable of judging of the application of the laws of Christ. See *Brethren*	169
Ministers ordinary, not qualified to act the part of apostles	528
Have no need of inspiration	535
And why	532
Distinction between them and the apostles	532
Muir, Mr. quoted by Mr. B. the fallacy of his reasoning respecting the assembly at Jerusalem	465
Multitude, meaning of the word in Scripture	425
Does not signify tumult, as argued by Mr. B.	429

NATION, the Jewish, why called a church . . 297

OFFENCES, the mode of trying them in the church of Christ different from what it was among the Jews	207
Offenders, no appeal to a higher court from the sentence passed on them by Christ—Matt. xviii. 17	220
Ordination, nature of	316
Manner of conducting it	316
Is entirely executive	194
No where in Scripture represented as conveying an office	316
Origen, a sentiment of, concerning the Scriptures	200

2 o

	PAGE
PASTORS, if negligent or faulty, to be judged and admonished by the brethren	260
Not at all entitled to the same support from the churches	262
Not necessary that they should all possess the same abilities	263
Why churches in general are not able to support a sufficient number of them	263
Have no private decisions	264
Pastoral office, a distinction of departments in it	271
Paul the *Apostle*, how he was first admitted into the church	183
Why he introduces his epistles by styling himself an apostle	531
His teaching by permission, and not by commandment, what	535
Pentecost, whether on the day of, Peter addressed the whole multitude in the same language	365
Presbytery, even when acted upon, is insufficient to attain the great ends of government	137
That which is defended by Mr. B. *ideal—note*	185
Mr. B.'s views of it opposite to what is universally practised	289
Mr. B. unwilling to rest it on a divine institution	323
The defence of, as constituted after a divine model given up by him	475
Presbyterians, authority of, legislative	139
Differ from the Roman Pontiff, not in the power of legislation, but in the degree of that power	151
Disclaim infallibility, yet act as if infallible	151
Enforce their laws, though contrary to conviction	163
Their authority supersedes enquiry	163
An instance of their inconsistency	245
In pleading for the right of legislation, claim more than was enjoyed by the Jewish hierarchy	322
How they act when their faults are pointed out to them	497
Presbyterian Churches, their office-bearers both receive their commission from the superior courts, and are completely dependent upon them for the exercise of it	290
Not formed of the same kind of materials that composed those planted by the apostles	547
Principles, without practice, indefensible	134
Contrary to Scripture	136
Prophecy, the gift of, enjoyed by many of the individual brethren in the first churches, and even by some females	422
Exposition of, difference between that of those who are inspired, and those who are not	529

	PAGE
Punishment corporal, none to be inflicted on the fallen brother after his exclusion from the church	250
QUESTION under debate, importance of	134
REFORMERS, acted according to the light they had	508
Did they still exist, would be the foremost in Reformation	508
How those act who pretend to be their successors	508
Representation, in matters of religion, origin of	171, 513
Is a child of human wisdom	513
Representatives, none sent from the churches to the assembly at Jerusalem	481
This could not be the case, and why	482
Robertson, Mr. his distinction between the meaning and use of certain Greek words unfounded, childish and unnatural	352
Consequences of his criticisms	354, 355
His account of the persecution raised by Saul completely contradicts the Word of God.	358
Rulers in the church of Christ have no right to make decisions among themselves	151
They call the attention of the brethren to the laws of Christ	151
Authority of their office nothing	152
The commandments of Christ have no need of ministerial authority	164
They do act with authority, but in what respect	165, 166
As such, are not the representatives of the church in which they act	211
Enforce the laws of Christ, not in the name of the church, but in the name of Christ	211
Absolute submission to them, the consequence of acting on Mr. B.'s principles	231
Rulers in Presbyterian Churches, their authority, such as Christ never gave to any body of uninspired men on earth	156
The awful length to which it extends	157
The great body of them appear never to have been appointed by the Lord, and why	157
SENTENCE of a church of Christ, nothing in it corresponding to the infliction of a penal sentence of the civil law	250
Separation, means employed by the clergy to prevent it	149
Socinian Churches, of whom principally composed—*Note*	137

	PAGE
Spirit, common aids of, what	517
His teaching common to all Christians	517
How his teaching may be distinguished from the suggestions of enthusiasm	518
Teaches only by his word	518
Stillingfleet, Dr. absurdity of his interpretation of the word *church*	424
Systems, ancient, of religion, the power of attachment to, discovered by Presbyterians	527
Are much dearer to Presbyterians than the authority of Scripture	528
Tendency of those that allow human interference in the things of God	528
TARES and wheat, the parable of, considered	177, 299
Teaching and ruling, though distinct things, belong to the same office	272
Official, in what the difference between public and private consists	282, 287
Toleration, not allowed by the standards of the Church of Scotland—*Note*	149
UNION with Christ, by what it is represented	299
Among the members of the Church of Scotland, specimen of	304
Universal visible church, has no existence in the Word of God	295
Universal church government, Mr. B.'s plan of absurd	300
Consequences of	302
WELCHMAN, anecdote of a	334
Word of God, a serious thing to explain it	387
Best method of doing it	429
World, the people of, how they act when reproved for sin	497

INDEX OF TEXTS

OCCASIONALLY ILLUSTRATED.

	PAGE
Numbers xxxv. 24	216
Deuteronomy xvi. 18	219
,, ,, 19	241
,, xix. 11, 12	218
,, xxxiii. 8, 10	283
Joshua xx. 4, 5	219
2 Samuel ii. 13	368
Psalm ii. 2	368
,, xxxiv. 3	368
,, xlix. 2	368
Jeremiah v. 28	241
Matthew v. 40	539
,, xiii. 24	177
,, xxiii. 1, 2, 3	321
,, xxviii. 19, 20	172, 173
John xv. 1, 11	293
,, xx. 23	171
Acts i. 14	372
,, ii. 9	344
,, ii. 14	365
,, iv. 4	345
,, v. 12	370
,, vi. 5	380
,, viii. 1	203
,, xi. 19	357
,, xxi. 20	359
Romans xi. 17	292
,, xii. 6	273, 275
1 Corinthians v. 1	242
,, vi. 1	169
,, xii. 28	273
Colossians iv. 10	258
Galatians vi. 1	259
1 Timothy iv. 1	524
,, ii. 7	531

For an illustration of many others, see meaning of the word church.

A Biographical Sketch of Alexander Carson (1776-1844)

by

John Franklin Jones

A Biographical Sketch of Alexander Carson (1776-1844)

Alexander Carson—Irish Presbyterian-turned-Baptist, pastor, expositor, author—was born at Artrae, ("BS" 24) not far from Cookstown, Tyrone Country, Ireland in 1776 of a family of Scotch origin, who probably came to North Ireland during the reign of James 1. Converted at an early age, he graduated with first honors at Glasgow University and received the LL.D. from Bacon College, Kentucky (Cathcart).

He settled as a government-paid Presbyterian pastor at Tubbermore in 1798, (Armitage, 571). Tubbermore was a town of 500 surrounded by a large population of Scotch-Irish farmers (Cathcart).

Early in his ministry, he came to three Baptist principles which set him in opposition to the Presbyterians: that congregationalism was the Scriptural form of church government; that immersion was the New Testament mode of baptism; and that only believers should be baptized (Cathcart). Concerning the presbytery, he said: "Scripture presbytery is the eldership, or plurality of elders in a particular congregation" (*Answer to Ewing*, 382; Chapter 10, n. 8; cited by Armitage, 130).

Thereafter, he gave up his living, (Armitage, 571) and departed his congregation upon the testimony of his favorite hymn:

And must I part with all I have,
My dearest Lord, for thee?
It is but right, since thou has done
Much more than that for me.

Yes, let it go, one look from thee
Will more than make amends
For all the losses I sustain
Of Wealth, of credit, friends (Cathcart).

The Baptist church he started grew to 500 members in his lifetime. His reputation spread and among his lasting friends were the Haldanes—Robert and James—of Edinburgh (Cathcart).

Carson was a Greek scholar, a clear reasoner, a logician, and a philosopher, and possessed a piercing intelligence. His Presbyterian friends called him the "Jonathan Edwards of the nineteenth century" (Cathcart).

He was an expository preacher. Cathcart said: "Few ever heard him take a little text and suspend some weighty subject upon it by a slender connecting link" (Cathcart).

His earlier writings included a work on figures of speech, developing the self-evident principles on figures of speech which was regarded as a standard on the subject matter ("BS", 25).

Carson's intensive pastoral desire to promote holy living among his worldly and wayward parishioners. His initial warnings to his congregants about their dangers developed into a failed attempt at church discipline, then an appeal to the ecclesiastical courts of the Synod. He came to the conclusion that his only appeal lay in that spiritual appeal to the teachings and simple order of Scripture. Thereupon, he left the Synod of Ulster ("BS," 26-28).

His *Reasons for Leaving the Synod of Ulster* maintained via strong reasoning the independence of the primitive churches of the New Testament. That volume declared his insistence that his participation in the Synod was a surrender of his conscience to one other than Christ. He systematically argued that the form of church government most likely to be divine was (1) the one capable of the least abuse–independence; (2) the one most able to preserve purity of doctrine without human expedients; and (3) the one which most leads to, and compels church members to, Scripture itself ("BS," 28-29).

From his firm commitment to the Bible as the only law-book, he first adopted congregational order, then regenerate church membership, and finally, believer's baptism ("BS," 31,33). His *Baptism: Its Mode and Subject* was first published in London and later republished by the Baptist Publication Society, Philadelphia. Cathcart said of this work:

> His octavio volume on baptism is a masterpiece of learning and logic; it overthrows quibbles about the Abrahamic covenant, giving authority to baptize children, as old as Augustine of Hippo, and as wide-spread as Pedobaptist Christendom, and allegations that baptism might mean sprinkling or pouring, with as much ease as a horse, unaccustomed to a rider, hurls to the ground the little boy who has ventured to mount him (Cathcart, 187).

Regarding his dogmatic writing style, Cathcart continued:

> Truth coming forth like a defiant giant is more attractive than when it appears making simpering apologies for venturing to show its face, and to disturb the equanimity of error and wrong, though sturdy truth, carrying a sharp and needful sword in a sheath of love, pleases us most (Cathcart, 188).

While returning from delivering addresses to the Baptist Missionary Society, he fell into the dock at Liverpool in 1844. Though rescued, and continuing upon his journey to Belfast, he became ill during the night and died the next day after landing, August 24, 1844. Carson spent nearly fifty years in ministry

(Cathcart). Armitage called him "most illustrious of the Irish Baptists."

At his untimely death, Carson had completed all the necessary work for a treatise on the atonement. Among his stated, but unfulfilled, intentions was a book on the best mode of teaching the churches and the characteristic style of Scripture. He also left unpublished commentaries to the Galatians, Hebrews, and several smaller articles ("BS", 44-45).

His wife--the mother of his thirteen children–and some of his children, preceded him in death. One son died of brain fever simultaneously with his ordination to the pastoral office ("BS", 47-47)

BIBLIOGRAPHY

Armitage, Thomas. *A History of the Baptists; Traced by their Vital Principles and Practices, from the Time of Our Lord and Saviour Jesus Christ to the Year 1886.* With an introduction by J. L. M. Curry. New York: Bryan, Taylor, & Co. 1887.

"Biographical Sketch of Alexander Carson," in *Baptism in its Mode and Subjects*, by Alexander Carson, 13-47. London: Houlston & Stoneman, 1844.

Cathcart, William, ed. *The Baptist Encyclopaedia: A Dictionary of the Doctrines, Ordinances, Usages, Confessions of Faith, Sufferings, Labors, and Successes, and of the General History of the Baptist Denomination in All Lands, with Numerous Biographical Sketches of Distinguished American and Foreign Baptist, and a Supplement.* Philadelphia, Louis H. Everts, 1881; reprint, Paris, AR: Baptist Standard Bearer, 1988. S.v. "Carson, Alex., LL.D."

BY JOHN FRANKLIN JONES
CORDOVA, TENNESSEE
JULY 2004

THE BAPTIST STANDARD BEARER, INC.

a non-profit, tax-exempt corporation
committed to the Publication & Preservation
of the Baptist Heritage.

CURRENT TITLES AVAILABLE IN
THE BAPTIST *DISTINCTIVES* SERIES

KIFFIN, WILLIAM   A Sober Discourse of Right to Church-Communion. Wherein is proved by Scripture, the Example of the Primitive Times, and the Practice of All that have Professed the Christian Religion: That no Unbaptized person may be Regularly admitted to the Lord's Supper. (London: George Larkin, 1681).

KINGHORN, JOSEPH   Baptism, A Term of Communion. (Norwich: Bacon, Kinnebrook, and Co., 1816)

KINGHORN, JOSEPH   A Defense of "Baptism, A Term of Communion". In Answer To Robert Hall's Reply. (Norwich: Wilkin and Youngman, 1820).

GILL, JOHN   Gospel Baptism. A Collection of Sermons, Tracts, etc., on Scriptural Authority, the Nature of the New Testament Church and the Ordinance of Baptism by John Gill. (Paris, AR: The Baptist Standard Bearer, Inc., 2006).

CARSON, ALEXANDER	Ecclesiastical Polity of the New Testament. (Dublin: William Carson, 1856).
BOOTH, ABRAHAM	A Defense of the Baptists. A Declaration and Vindication of Three Historically Distinctive Baptist Principles. Compiled and Set Forth in the Republication of Three Books. Revised edition. (Paris, AR: The Baptist Standard Bearer, Inc., 2006).
BOOTH, ABRAHAM	Paedobaptism Examined on the Principles, Concessions, and Reasonings of the Most Learned Paedobaptists. With Replies to the Arguments and Objections of Dr. Williams and Mr. Peter Edwards. 3 volumes. (London: Ebenezer Palmer, 1829).
CARROLL, B. H.	*Ecclesia* - The Church. With an Appendix. (Louisville: Baptist Book Concern, 1903).
CHRISTIAN, JOHN T.	Immersion, The Act of Christian Baptism. (Louisville: Baptist Book Concern, 1891).
FROST, J. M.	Pedobaptism: Is It From Heaven Or Of Men? (Philadelphia: American Baptist Publication Society, 1875).
FULLER, RICHARD	Baptism, and the Terms of Communion; An Argument. (Charleston, SC: Southern Baptist Publication Society, 1854).
GRAVES, J. R.	Tri-Lemma: or, Death By Three Horns. The Presbyterian General Assembly Not Able To Decide This Question: "Is Baptism In The Romish Church Valid?" 1st Edition.

	(Nashville: Southwestern Publishing House, 1861).
MELL, P.H.	Baptism In Its Mode and Subjects. (Charleston, SC: Southern Baptist Publications Society, 1853).
JETER, JEREMIAH B.	Baptist Principles Reset. Consisting of Articles on Distinctive Baptist Principles by Various Authors. With an Appendix. (Richmond: The Religious Herald Co., 1902).
PENDLETON, J.M.	Distinctive Principles of Baptists. (Philadelphia: American Baptist Publication Society, 1882).
THOMAS, JESSE B.	The Church and the Kingdom. A New Testament Study. (Louisville: Baptist Book Concern, 1914).
WALLER, JOHN L.	Open Communion Shown to be Unscriptural & Deleterious. With an introductory essay by Dr. D. R. Campbell and an Appendix. (Louisville: Baptist Book Concern, 1859).

For a complete list of current authors/titles, visit our internet site at:
www.standardbearer.org
or write us at:

he Baptist Standard Bearer, Inc.

NUMBER ONE IRON OAKS DRIVE • PARIS, ARKANSAS 72855
TEL # 479-963-3831   FAX # 479-963-8083
EMAIL: Baptist@centurytel.net   http://www.standardbearer.org

Thou hast given a standard to them that fear thee; that it may be displayed because of the truth. — Psalm 60:4

www.ingramcontent.com/pod-product-compliance
Lightning Source LLC
Chambersburg PA
CBHW020259010526

44108CB00037B/159